ARBITRATION AND MEDIATION IN SEVENTEENTH-CENTURY ENGLAND

ARBITRATION AND MEDIATION IN SEVENTEENTH-CENTURY ENGLAND

DEREK ROEBUCK

HOLO BOOKS
THE ARBITRATION PRESS
OXFORD
2017

First published 2017 by
HOLO Books: The Arbitration Press
Clarendon House
52 Cornmarket
Oxford OX1 3HJ

email: holobooks@yahoo.co.uk
www.holobooks.co.uk
and www.centralbooks.com

British Library Cataloguing in Publication Data
A catalogue record for this book is available from the British Library

ISBN 978–0–9572153–1–3

This book is printed on paper suitable for recycling and made from
fully managed and sustained forest sources. Logging, pulping and
manufacturing processes are expected to conform to the
environmental regulations of the country of origin.

10   9   8   7   6   5   4   3   2   1

Produced and typeset for HOLO Books by
Stanford DTP Services, Northampton, England
Printed in the European Union

Dedicated with affection
to the memories of
Ray Addicott and Arthur Marriott
who in their different ways contributed
so much to previous volumes

CONTENTS

Preface   xiii

Part One: Background

1. BACKGROUND   3
   1 Introduction   3
   2 Government   3
   3 The Economy   7
   4 Dispute Resolution   10
   5 Conclusions   12

2. SOURCES   14
   1 Introduction   14
   2 Primary Sources   17
   3 Law Reports   19
   4 Abridgments and Entries   21
   5 Texts   23
   6 Readings and Moots   26
   7 Conclusions   27

3. THE MEANING OF ARBITREMENT   28
   1 Introduction   28
   2 Private and Public   30
   3 Mediation and Arbitration   30
   4 Inspection and View   36
   5 Merits or Expediency?   38
   6 Arbitration Clauses   41
   7 Conclusions   42

4. PUBLIC ARBITRATION   43
   1 Introduction   43
   2 The King   45
   3 Privy Council   48
   4 Star Chamber   58
   5 House of Lords   60

6 Chancery   62
7 King's Bench, Common Pleas and Exchequer   65
8 *Nisi Prius* and Assizes   67
9 Justices of the Peace and Quarter Sessions   71
10 Masters of Requests   75
11 Referrals from Other Courts   75
12 Conclusions   76

Part Two: Substance

5. LAND   81
1 Introduction   81
2 Dower, Settlements, Jointures and Portions   87
3 Commons and Enclosures   88
4 Copyhold   90
5 Way, Water and Other Rights   91
6 Boundaries and Building Disputes   92
7 Public Works   95
8 Conclusions   98

6. FAMILY AND INHERITANCE   99
1 Introduction   99
2 Inheritance   102
3 Father and Son   103
4 Mother and Son   106
5 Siblings   107
6 Husband and Wife   108
7 Marriage Settlements   110
8 Conclusions   111

7. COMMERCE   114
1 Introduction   114
2 Trade   115
3 Debt   119
4 Compositions with Creditors, Protections and Postponements   121
5 Commercial Transactions   125
6 Accounts   126
7 Maritime   131
8 Insurance   132
9 Agency and Partnership   134
10 Competition   135
11 Guilds and Companies   143
12 Employment and Apprenticeship   148
13 Conclusions   149

8. THE CHURCH, UNIVERSITIES, SCHOOLS AND
   CHARITIES   151
   1 Introduction   151
   2 Pews   153
   3 Tithes   155
   4 Differences Within the Parish   157
   5 Oliver Heywood   160
   6 Ralph Josselin   161
   7 Universities   170
   8 Schools   172
   9 Charities   172
   10 Conclusions   173

Part Three: People

9. PARTIES   177
   1 Introduction   177
   2 The Poor   178
   3 Royal Servants and Public Officers   179
   4 Local Authorities   183
   5 Foreigners   183
   6 Immigrants   185
   7 Jews   189
   8 International Relations   189
   9 Conclusions   191

10. ARBITRATORS   192
    1 Introduction   192
    2 Qualifications and Choice   193
    3 Number   195
    4 Examples   196
    5 Judges   201
    6 Justices of the Peace   202
    7 Law Officers   203
    8 Committees of the Council   203
    9 Umpires   204
    10 Fees   208
    11 Conclusions   208

11. NATHANIEL BACON   210
    1 Introduction   210
    2 The King   214
    3 Parliament   215
    4 Privy Council   223
    5 Chancery and the Chancellor   224

   6 King's Bench   228
   7 Common Pleas and Assizes   229
   8 Court of Requests   230
   9 Lord High Treasurer   230
  10 Commissioners for Prisoners   231
  11 High Steward   231
  12 Edward Coke   232
  13 Francis Bacon   242
  14 Private Mediations   244
  15 Private Arbitrations   246
  16 Nathaniel's Appointments   250
  17 Compositions with Creditors   251
  18 Nathaniel as a Party   252
  19 Women   254
  20 Conclusions   256

12. EDWARD COKE   259
   1 Introduction   259
   2 Coke the Man   261
   3 Coke and Lady Hatton   262
   4 The Early Career   263
   5 Coke the Historian?   265
   6 Chief Justice Coke   267
   7 The First Fall   269
   8 Amending the Reports   270
   9 Coke as a Party   271
  10 Coke as Arbitrator   274
  11 Conclusions   275

13. FRANCIS BACON   277
   1 Introduction   277
   2 Bacon the Man   278
   3 Rise to Power   279
   4 Arbitrator for the Council   280
   5 The Downfall   281
   6 The Crooked Arbitrator   286
   7 The End   287
   8 Conclusions   288

14. GERARD MALYNES   289
   1 Introduction   289
   2 Malynes: the Man and the Merchant 290
   3 *Consuetudo, vel, Lex Mercatoria*   291
   4 *Gibson v Ferrers*   295
   5 Conclusions   299

15. THE DIARISTS 300
    1 Introduction 300
    2 Richard Cholmeley 300
    3 Walter Powell 307
    4 Adam Eyre 308
    5 Samuel Pepys 313
    6 Robert Hooke 328
    7 Conclusions 338

16. WOMEN 339
    1 Introduction 339
    2 Margaret Hoby 340
    3 Anne Clifford 344
    4 Women as Parties 359
    5 Women as Mediators and Arbitrators 365
    6 Conclusions 367

Part Four: Arbitration and the Law

17. THE LAW: THE SUBMISSION 371
    1 Introduction 371
    2 Law Reports and Abridgments 374
    3 Validity of Submission and Arbitrability 376
    4 The Requirement of a Specialty 387
    5 Bonds 387
    6 Capacity of Parties 390
    7 Arbitrators 394
    8 Conclusions 396

18. THE LAW: THE AWARD 397
    1 Introduction 397
    2 Scope 398
    3 Certainty 401
    4 Mutuality 402
    5 Validity 404
    6 Pleadings and Quibbles 405
    7 Performance and Enforcement 409
    8 Stay and Bar 410
    9 Rule of Court 412
    10 Conclusions 416

19. VYNIOR'S CASE   418
    1 Introduction   418
    2 The Facts   419
    3 Coke's Report   420
    4 The Arguments   422
    5 Other Reports   422
    6 The Extensions of *Vynior*   425
    7 Coke After *Vynior*   426
    8 Conclusions   426

20. LAW REFORM AND THE ARBITRATION ACT 1698   428
    1 Introduction   428
    2 Law Reform in the Interregnum   428
    3 William Sheppard   429
    4 John Locke   432
    5 The 1698 Act   435
    6 The Effects of the Act   436
    7 Conclusions   437

Part Five: Conclusions

21. CONCLUSIONS   441
    1 Introduction   442
    2 The Economy   442
    3 The Law   443
    4 The Professional Arbitrator   445
    5 The End?   446

Appendix 1 Arbitrium Redivivum 1694   449
Appendix 2 Arbitration in Sheppard's *Abridgment* 1675   470
Glossary   488
Chronology   491
Bibliography   495
Index   513

PREFACE

Go but apart,
Make choice of whom your choicest friends you will
And they shall hear and judge it all 'twixt you and me.
William Shakespeare *Hamlet* Act 4 Scene 4

1. BACKGROUND

Claudius was suggesting to Laertes that he should arrange for his own friends to mediate no paltry difference. Laertes believed that Claudius had killed his father, Polonius, and was out to avenge him. Shakespeare did not set out to shock; he could rely on his audiences' familiarity with mediation as a routine process for resolving disputes of all kinds then.

I did not start work on this book with an agenda, other than to describe the development of mediation and arbitration in England in the 17th century. I confess, though, that I expected to find, if not a moment, at least a period of what has been called 'legalisation', when the lawyers took over, not only as the predominant arbitrators but as those who fixed the rules, imposing a whole new scheme – a new Common Law of arbitration.

That is not what the sources show. The people of England overcame perils of all kinds: civil war, lethal religious strife, plague, piracy and in London fire. For many the economic relations changed, from communal to capitalist. Yet, even at the end of the century, lawyers did not dominate the practice of arbitration.

The period covered is 1603–1703, from the death of Elizabeth I to the accession of Anne. Exceptions have been made when, as in the chapter on Nathaniel Bacon, the story starts earlier; and where something in the early years of Anne's reign needs to be comprehended. The place is England, with rare sallies into Wales and the Channel Islands. Scotland and Ireland have different histories.

2. PRESENTATION

There are five parts: Part One describes the background; Part Two the subject matter: land, family, commerce, the church; Part Three the people: the parties and the arbitrators; Part Four the law and Part Five draws conclusions.

The law of arbitration was embryonic in the 17th century; the practice was what mattered; and, to understand the practice, the lives and characters of some of the outstanding figures of the century must be investigated: Edward Coke and Francis Bacon, Lady Anne Clifford and Samuel Pepys. Women appear nearly as often as men in many of the primary sources. They demand a chapter to themselves, not so much to rectify their usual exclusion but because their roles and functions were so important, both routinely as parties and occasionally as mediators and arbitrators.

The bibliography and index are as full as possible. The glossary explains difficult, technical or unusual terms, especially legal jargon, for which an explanation in the text would hold up the narrative. There is a chronology to help readers who, like me, cannot keep dates in their head.

3. CONVENTIONS

Calendar years start from 1 January, even though they then began on Lady Day, 25 March. In most quoted passages, spelling had been modernised and the text redacted slightly to remove verbiage such as 'the said' and 'aforesaid'.

Citations give enough information about each work the first time it is mentioned in each chapter, usually just the author and title, with an abbreviation for further citations, leaving full details for the Bibliography. My own relevant earlier books: *Background of the Common Law*; *Ancient Greek Arbitration*; *Roman Arbitration* (with Bruno de Loynes de Fumichon); *Charitable Arbitrator*; *Early English Arbitration*; *Mediation and Arbitration in the Middle Ages*; *The Golden Age of Arbitration*; *Disputes and Differences* and *Miscellany of Disputes*, are similarly abbreviated. Standard Oxford University Press reference works are: *OED* (*Oxford English Dictionary*), HTOED (Historical Thesaurus of the OED), *ODNB* (*Oxford Dictionary of National Biography*) and *OHLE* (*Oxford History of the Laws of England*).

4. ACKNOWLEDGMENTS

A continuing source of pleasure is the generosity of friends, old and new. Neil Kaplan has continued to transform friendship into support of every kind. He carries the full responsibility for directing me to the study of arbitration history. Two other friends, Doug Jones and Gary Born, have joined him, as they did for *Golden Age*. They have done much more than deal with the costs of publication. My need for the *imprimatur* of three leading practitioners ensures that I constantly heed the realities of practice. I am proud, too, to know I have David Neuberger's friendly eye on me. I have needed their support all the more since I can no longer count on Michael

Mustill's. Arthur Marriott's death has robbed me of one of my oldest, firmest and most generous friends. This volume is dedicated to his memory.

So many scholars have supported this work with comments and suggestions. I have tried to acknowledge their help in the right place. Francis Boorman, now my colleague at the Institute of Advanced Legal Studies, once again found me the archival material which is the foundation of much of this book. I treasure his collaboration. Chapter 11 is founded on the papers of Nathaniel Bacon. Without the meticulous scholarship and generosity of Alan Metters and his editorial colleagues no such chapter could have been written. Horwitz and Oldham's article on Locke is a masterpiece. It is where anyone with an interest in 18th-century arbitration should look not only for knowledge but standards of workmanship. I am lucky to be able to call on James Oldham for advice whenever I ask him.

I have known Susan Faircloth as an editor for more than thirty years. I have relied on her professional skills in this book more than any other. Knowing that my manuscript would be subjected to her scrutiny has kept up my standards; knowing she has approved it brings reassurance and relief.

Ray Addicott, the master craftsman who produced the earlier volumes, died in June 2016. He had done me the last great favour of handing me over to Dave Stanford, whose professional and friendly care has ensured the continuation of quality. The dedication to Ray is only a formal attempt to express my feelings of loss and thanks.

The librarians of the British Library and the staff of the archives departments listed, and all the staff of the Athenaeum have been specially helpful. I am proud to be associated with the Institute of Advanced Legal Studies, University of London, whose Director Jules Winterton is always there to encourage me. All the library staff are invariably knowledgeable and friendly, but Hester Swift deserves special thanks. Not only has she found me everything I have asked for, and much more of her own initiative, but she has patiently taught me the simple computer skills I should have known and too often forgot. I wonder whether most scholars, let alone readers, realise the contributions to research made by librarians. Someone should devote a thesis to how it works in practice, with concentration on work generously done with no thought of job descriptions.

It is impossible to give proper credit for what my wife, Susanna Hoe, has contributed. She has read it all several times, making sure that the reader will take in what I have tried to transmit. More than that, she brings new ideas of her own. I had barely heard of Robert Hooke and would never have known he was an arbitrator, if Susanna had not picked up a slight reference from Melvyn Bragg's radio programme. She found the cover picture. Her knowledge of women's writings and willingness to read more, like Margaret Hoby's diaries, for anything of relevance, have done much more than save me work. I look forward now to working with her on our next joint effort, Susanna Hoe and Derek Roebuck *Women in Disputes*, a study of women as parties and resolvers through the ages, which we hope will be published by the end of 2018.

Oxford
July 2016

PART ONE

BACKGROUND

1 BACKGROUND

Me seemes the world is runne quite out of square
From the first point of his appointed sourse;
And being once amisse growes daily wourse and wourse.

Spenser The Fairie Queene (1590, 1596)

Arbitrement is much esteemed and greatly favoured in our Common Law; the end thereof being privately to compose differences between parties by the judgment of honest men; and to prevent the great trouble and frequent expense of lawsuits.

Arbitrium Redivivum[1]

1. INTRODUCTION

This book attempts to show how disputes were resolved in England (and Wales, the Channel Islands and the Isle of Man, but not Scotland or Ireland) between the death of Elizabeth I in 1603 and the accession of Anne in 1702.[2] Most people with a difference, then as now, either resolved it between themselves or let it lie. Some took it to court but only a tiny portion of disputes ended in a judgment. People of all kinds, with disputes of all kinds, made use of a process which at the start of the 17th century they called arbitrement, but by its end had its modern name: arbitration.

If the reign of Elizabeth was the Golden Age of arbitration in England, its halcyon days were the 17th century, despite plague, fire, political upheaval and religious strife. The great names of that century have left ample documentary evidence of their involvement as parties and arbitrators: Francis Bacon, Edward Coke, Samuel Pepys, Robert Hooke, James I himself. They all took the ever-present process they called arbitration for granted as the best way of resolving disputes they could not manage themselves. But arbitration could be abused, and a powerful woman like Lady Anne Clifford might prefer to insist on her Common Law rights as landowner, withstanding the insistent demands of James I to arbitrate in her land dispute with her husband and family.

2. GOVERNMENT

James I and Elizabeth I may have had one thing in common. Their first childhood memories may have been of someone telling them that one of

---

1. Anon *Arbitrium Redivivum: or the Law of Arbitration* [*Arbitrium Redivivum*].
2. Good examples of the rich material on Ireland are *APC* 33.15 and 33.167.

their parents had killed the other. There is no question that Henry VIII had Anne Boleyn's head chopped off. Whatever the truth, few had any doubt that Mary, Queen of Scots, got rid of Darnley.

James's childhood was as difficult as Elizabeth's. King of Scotland when he was just a year old, he had no natural family about him. He was always a piece in a game played very seriously by adults. By the time he became King of England at 37, he had been married 14 years to Anne of Denmark. He never met his mother. He was crafty. He needed to be.

It may be unwise to accept that there was then any opinion held generally in England. Before mass media, attitudes must have been fragmented. But Elizabeth I seems to have died popular with those who thought about such things. James I was not so much welcomed as accepted. The English called him the Scotchman and treated with suspicion what they considered his uncouth manners, his scarcely comprehensible speech, his preference for male lovers and his still to be discovered political and religious proclivities. The saying went the rounds: '*Rex fuit Elizabeth, nunc est Regina Jacobus*', which many with no acquaintance of Latin hexameters could tell meant: 'Elizabeth was King, now we have James for Queen'. James's homosexuality is relevant because he gave such political power to his lovers and such ammunition to those who would demean him. He became obsessed with personal kingly rights.

From the start of his reign, James I had to face attempts to murder him, the closest to success being the Gunpowder Plot in 1605. His reign was largely peaceful, though, with an end to the war with Spain in 1604. His quarrels with Parliament, later often represented as a battle between the divine right of kings and parliamentary democracy, arose from his need for revenue, which only Parliament could supply. Under him and his Stuart successors, Parliament met only when the King summoned it and sat only until he dismissed it. Since 1694 it has met every year and – at least in political theory – has held political power.

Religious differences, too, were excuses for taking sides. Though James I's mother had died for her Catholic faith and her claim to Elizabeth's throne, James proved himself an unequivocal Protestant, as his concern for the new English translation of the Bible in 1611 showed. But that did not satisfy the many MPs whose Puritan beliefs and personal ambitions set them against him.

James I died in 1625 at the age of 58 and was succeeded by his son, Charles I, who forthwith married the French Catholic princess Henrietta Maria. He always needed money, waging wars against France and Spain which Parliament paid for unwillingly. Even more egotistical than his father, he believed he ruled by divine right. In 1628 he summoned a Parliament to find him the money for his wars, which responded by drawing up the Petition of Right, by which any new tax needed its approval. Such a tax was 'ship money', a tax to raise money to build ships, which in 1635 the King tried to levy for the first time on inland landowners.

Charles supported Archbishop of Canterbury Laud's attempts to impose his High Church forms, first on England, then Scotland. In 1639 the Scots took up arms and withstood Charles's forces. They invaded England and occupied much of the north. The King asked Parliament for money to fight them. Unsuccessful, he was forced to capitulate to their rejection of the English prayer book. James I's lover Buckingham continued to exert influence until he was assassinated in 1628. Charles I had to dissolve Parliament three times between 1625 and 1629. The direct taxes he levied without Parliament and the measures against Puritans drove many to emigrate to North America. His differences with Parliament resulted in armed conflict; the civil war is usually dated from 1642. The Royalist forces were no match for the Parliamentarians, allied with the strongest Scottish forces.

If only the differences between Charles I and Parliament had been resolved by mediation! There was no shortage of suggestions and offers to help, even from well-wishers abroad. The Parliamentary Archives preserve a letter dated 7 November 1644 from the ambassadors of the States General, as the Netherlands then called itself, asking for a reply to their offer to mediate between King and Parliament; and on 7 December a message to the Commons desiring their concurrence in the answer to be returned. Four days later Parliament's answer was negative.[3]

In June 1647, separate petitions from the 'peaceable and well-affected inhabitants' of Norfolk and Suffolk, and of Buckingham, asked Lord Fairfax to mediate with Parliament 'for the settling of their liberties'.[4] And in August the Assembly of Divines wrote to Parliament, expressing their desire to mediate between Parliament and the army.[5] They were a group of theologians and MPs, established by the Long Parliament to reform the Church of England, against the policies of Charles I and Archbishop Laud. All those initiatives came to nothing.

The Long Parliament, first called in 1640, passed the Triennial Act, requiring Parliament to be called every three years. The Dissolution Act required Parliament's consent for its dissolution. The Grand Remonstrance 1641 was a list of parliamentary grievances, which passed by a slim majority. In January 1642 Charles tried to take advantage of the split by arresting five MPs for treason. He was rebuffed and left London. Both sides began to raise armies. After four years of intermittent fighting, in May 1646 Charles I surrendered to the Scots. In December 1647 the Scots

3. Parliamentary Archives [Parl Arch] HL/PO/JO/10/1/176 and 177.
4. Parl Arch HL/PO/JO/10/1/235.
5. Parl Arch HL/PO/JO/10/1/237.

agreed to support the King. They invaded England but Cromwell defeated them at Preston. Parliamentary forces then ruled England. On 17 March 1649 they abolished the monarchy and the House of Lords. Cromwell became Lord Protector. What was left of a parliament under Cromwell had Charles I convicted of treason and executed on 30 January 1649.

Cromwell was a clever politician. He knew the importance of the distinction between talking and doing. He would listen patiently to anyone, and often talked so that they believed that something would come of it. He would listen just as keenly to opposing arguments and give the same impression. He knew he could get away with prevarication because he had power. He also knew that, if he acted, he must make one side an enemy, while securing the support of the other side only until the next time he refused it something.

Cromwell died on 3 September 1658. In February 1660 General Monck, who commanded the English army stationed in Scotland, marched south. He entered London in February 1660. He recalled the surviving members of the Long Parliament, which had first met in 1640. They agreed to invite Charles I's son Charles to return as king. He accepted and from then he acted as if he were.

It would be easy to expect that such revolutionary changes would have overturned the old ways of resolving disputes. The evidence of the primary sources supports no such conclusion. Even the formal evidence of what was going on in the courts shows no upheaval. As Stephen Sedley has summed it up:[6]

> The few law reports which span the Commonwealth and Protectorate (principally Hardres' Exchequer Reports, Style's KB/Upper Bench Reports, and Nelson's chancery reports) show no obvious change in the kinds of issue and the kinds of litigant coming before those courts, or in the outcomes.

In April 1660 Charles II issued a declaration from the Dutch town of Breda. He promised a general pardon (except for the regicides who were responsible for the death of his father) and freedom of religion. In 1662 he married a Catholic Portuguese Princess, Catherine of Braganza. In 1670 he made a secret treaty with Louis XIV of France, the Treaty of Dover. By it Louis promised to give Charles money (so that he would no longer be dependent on Parliament). Charles agreed to join with Louis in another war with Holland and to announce he was a Roman Catholic (Louis promised to send 6,000 men if the people rebelled when he did so). In 1672 he issued the Royal Declaration of Indulgence suspending the laws against non-conformists. In 1673, however, Parliament passed the Test Act, which banned non-conformists and Catholics from holding public office. Charles II died

---

6. Stephen Sedley *Lions Under the Throne* 101 fn72.

in 1685. He was 54. He had no legitimate children. His Catholic brother James was next in line.

Charles II did have an illegitimate son, the Duke of Monmouth. He landed in Dorset and tried to raise rebellion in the south-west of England but was defeated at the battle of Sedgemoor. Then in June 1688 James II had a son, whom everyone assumed would be brought up a Catholic and succeed his father. There is no evidence that James II ever showed interest in dispute resolution, though that of his subjects continued as before.

In 1688 Parliament declared that the throne was vacant and invited William of Orange to accept it with James II's daughter Mary. Mary died in 1694. Though official documents provide little evidence, private papers, particularly diaries, show the regular preferences for mediation and arbitration were undiminished.

3. THE ECONOMY

RH Tawney wisely advised caution against easy anachronism:[7]

> Capitalism is clothed today with the unquestioned respectability of the triumphant fact. But in its youth it was a pretender, and it was only after centuries of struggle that its title was established. For it involved a code of economic conduct and a system of human relations which were sharply at variance with venerable conventions, with the accepted scheme of social ethics, and with the law.

When the 17th century began, optimists did not look forward to reform but hoped for a return to the good old days. No one in England had developed a capitalist or even a progressive agenda. England's economies were 'socially embedded' locally,[8] with no external over-arching power pulling the strings. That was obvious in the manors, detectable in the boroughs, already less so in the handful of cities.

In 1657, just before Cromwell died, two events of an importance not recognised then, or commonly since, were the establishment of the General Post Office and of the East India Company as the first permanent joint stock company. England had by then the makings of a capitalist economy. The creation of the Royal Exchange in 1671 and finally the Bank of England in 1694 established capitalism in power.

At the start of the 17th century there were few shops. Retail trade was largely from market stalls, with regular visits to villages by itinerant peddlers. By its end shops were everywhere, with concentrations in the bigger towns, to which a greater part of the slightly declining population was moving. By the middle of the century, London had a population of

---

7. RH Tawney, Foreword to Max Weber *The Protestant Ethic and the Spirit of Capitalism* 1(c).

8. The insight is from Karl Polanyi *The Great Transformation* .

over 500,000 (Paris 350,000), 'more than the next fifty towns in England combined'.[9]

It would be a mistake to assume that life was in every way simpler then or that our forebears were less sophisticated or cosmopolitan. Of course there have been great advances in all forms of science and technology, most dramatically in medicine, since the Privy Council in November 1624 gave permission for Henry Atkinson to stay in London to look after his wife, who was 'labouring of a grievous infirmity, for cure whereof she had one of her breasts newly cut off and was still in the hands of physicians and surgeons for the perfecting of that cure'.[10] But two months later the Council wrote to the Lord Keeper, the Chancellor of the Duchy and the Justices of the Peace for the County of Middlesex, instructing them all to support an Italian living in London. He had opened a delicatessen where he sold imported Italian food and wine and provided meals:[11]

> Whereas Jeromio Sadley, an Italian, hath made humble suit unto us that he may be permitted to sell Parmesan cheese, Bologna sausages, Genoa anchovies, Genoa oils, olives and capers, Venice wax lights, Venice torches, and some other commodities that come from those parts and likewise to keep an ordinary and sell wine in his house…. yield him your aid and assistance as often as he shall need it… as far as shall be fitting.

The best translation of 'ordinary' into modern English would perhaps be 'bistro'. He could hardly have kept going if his only customers were his fellow countrymen. Is it too fanciful to imagine Privy Councillors and their families enjoying the same sort of Italian cuisine then as they do today, somewhere off the Strand?

There is no shortage of background information and scholarly argument about the history of the 17th century. Hundreds of books and articles describe and comment on everything from the rise and fall of population and the impact of new learning and practical inventions to the relations between monarchs and their lovers and how much lace was on the collar of Lady Fanshawe's husband and how little on Cromwell's wife's. Religious controversies fill libraries but need no attention here. A more telling insight comes from the story of the farmer working on Marston Moor in the summer of 1644. When told to clear off to allow the battle to commence, he is reported to have said: 'What, has them two fallen out then?'[12] Though tens of thousands of ordinary men took part in the battles of the Civil Wars and slaughtered one another for what they believed in, or others said they should, most must have wanted none of it and for them the struggle for a

9. John Morrill 'The Stuarts' in KO Morgan ed *The Oxford History of Britain* [Morrill] 335.
10. *APC* 39.383.
11. *APC* 39.449.
12. Quoted by Asa Briggs *A Social History of England* 141.

decent living was more immediate than any political or religious conflict:[13] 'Many, maybe most, followed the line of least resistance and did what they were told by those in a position immediately to compel obedience.'

Even the Levellers and Diggers, those who in the 1640s wanted the most radical changes to the constitution, looked not forward to a Utopia but back to the days of Good Queen Bess or even to the Anglo-Saxons. Cromwell himself always put property above liberty and had no time for democracy. However fundamental some of his reforms, including clearing away the remnants of feudal relations, he took care not to disturb copyholds, and broke all his promises to abolish tithes and advowsons, or to reform the legal system.

Yet the infancy of the ideology of capitalism is detectable. Stephen Sedley has generously allowed me this quotation, in which he pointed to:[14]

> a quite different example: the abandonment two centuries ago, for ideological reasons, of a set of criminal sanctions designed to protect the poor and to keep civil order without force. The sanctions were the old market crimes of engrossing, regrating and forestalling – creating scarcity and forcing up prices by cornering supplies before or after they reached market. These activities had been criminalised by statute since the reign of Edward VI – a time when, as Keith Thomas notes in *The Ends of Life* (p144), the view that the pursuit of self-interest was both ineluctable and socially beneficial first began to be articulated; and John Baker records prosecutions for regrating and engrossing, evidently at common law, even earlier than this.[15] Adam Smith, although he was alive to the dangers of monopoly, contended that such market crimes were comparable to 'the popular terrors and suspicions of witchcraft'[16]; but when in 1772 Parliament repealed the statutes which created them (12 Geo. III c71), the judges held that they were still crimes at common law. In more than one prosecution in the years that followed, Adam Smith's writings were cited to the court as arguments for acquittal. For a time the more conservative judges held out against this. Lord Kenyon CJ, trying a regrater named Rusby at the London Guildhall in 1800[17], said to his jury:
>
> > A very learned man, a good writer, has said you might as well fear witchcraft. I wish Dr Adam Smith had lived to hear the evidence today.... If he had been told that cattle and corn were brought to market and then bought by a man whose purse happened to be longer than his neighbours, so that the poor man who walks the street and earns his daily bread by his daily labour could get

---

13. Morrill 362, 361.
14. Stephen Sedley 'The Law as History', All Souls Neill Lecture March 2016.
15. JH Baker *The Oxford History of the Laws of England* VI 1483–1558 272.
16. Adam Smith *The Wealth of Nations* IV chapter 5.
17. *R v Rusby* (1800) Peake Add Cas 189; 170 ER 241: 'though in an evil hour all the statutes... were at one blow repealed, yet, thank God, the provisions of the common law were not destroyed'.

none but through his hands, and at the price he chose to demand,... would he have said that there was no danger from such an offence?

Kenyon went on to tell his jury:

> It has been said that in one county, I will not name it, a rich man has placed his emissaries to buy all the butter coming to the market: if such a fact does exist, and the poor of that neighbourhood cannot get the necessaries of life, the event of your verdict may be highly useful to the public.

With Erskine leading Garrow for the prosecution, and egged on by Kenyon's not entirely dispassionate summing-up, the jury convicted Rusby on the spot.

But by 1702 England had become accustomed to:[18]

> a free market, free from government interference and from government protection of the poor; Parliamentary government, the local supremacy of JPs, the union of England and Scotland; religious toleration, the nonconformist conscience, relative freedom of the press, an attitude favourable to science; a country of landlords, capitalist farmers and agricultural labourers, the only country in Europe with no peasantry.

With trade and manufacture booming, the practice of arbitration was beginning to reflect the new ways of thinking that sprang from the political, economic and social changes.

4. DISPUTE RESOLUTION

Throughout the century, old communities were dissolving as the state solidified. The assemblies of hundred and shire had already lost their general jurisdiction. The old customary law which had governed most people's way of life was being replaced by new economic relations and the state laws which went with them. Eventually it was reduced to an accessory to be pleaded as a matter of fact in the all-powerful courts of the new centralised state. But old attitudes to arbitration and mediation did not change. Even in the Civil Wars, most people of all kinds must have hoped for peaceful settlement. There were many attempts to limit the strife by agreement, sometimes applying skills learned from the prevailing cultures of alternative dispute resolution.

When the internal strife was over, great matters of state had no higher authority to which the parties could refer them for adjudication. They were therefore naturally subjects for mediation and sometimes arbitration. And English monarchs from time to time were asked to mediate and arbitrate disputes between the heads of other states. By the end of the century London

18. Christopher Hill *God's Englishman* 254.

newspapers were regularly reporting on foreign affairs; the *London Post* on 21 April 1700:[19]

> The Prince de Auvergne has obtained leave of the King to go solicit the King of England to be arbitrator between him and his father, upon a difference that has happened between them, about the Marquisate of Bergen op Boom.

It was no disqualification if the monarch was a woman:

> Hague July 19 [1707] The Minister of the Elector Palatine has acquainted some members of the Council of State that the Elector, his master, to put an end to the dispute which the King of Sweden has raised about the Duchy of Veldens, submits to the arbitration of Queen Anne and the Elector of Hanover.

The surviving evidence shows that methods of resolving disputes were no less ample and refined, whether over a private matter of inheritance or involving the most violent breaches of public order. The primary sources, preserved for the most part in national and county archives, in government records and in diaries and other private papers, reveal arbitration ending all kinds of disputes. The arbitrators were expected to bring about a settlement, if possible a reconciliation, even friendship restored. A king or a yeoman might be called on to give his services freely.

Earlier volumes in this series, relying on contemporary primary sources from the earliest times to the end of the reign of Elizabeth I, have shown that the parties to disputes preferred not to go to the courts.[20] Arbitrement was their preferred way of settling a dispute they could not end themselves. Each party chose one or more arbitrators and together that even number would try to mediate a settlement. If an adjudication could not be avoided, they would at least try to get the parties to agree on who should do it.

In the 17th century 'arbitrement' included all the processes and skills the arbitrators could command, used in no fixed sequence, at every stage once they took over the dispute. The preference for a settlement was so strong that mediation could follow arbitration. John Aldersey, perhaps the former Mayor of Chester or his son, agreed to lease tithes to George Spurstowe, on their own terms, after their arbitrators had, they thought, finally disposed of the matter.[21] Lady Mildmay had a complaint against William Bradshaw. The Solicitor General had 'heretofore made some arbitrament', but the Council then commissioned Sir Julius Caesar MR, who played so many important roles in the Government of Elizabeth I, described in *Golden Age*, and will in the chapters which follow. His instructions were, 'calling Mr

---

19. *London Post with Intelligence Foreign and Domestick* issue 136.
20. D Roebuck *Early English Arbitration, Mediation and Arbitration in the Middle Ages* [Roebuck *Middle Ages*] and *The Golden Age of Arbitration* [Roebuck *Golden Age*].
21. Cheshire CR 469/180.

Solicitor unto him', to 'draw the parties to some such mutual agreement as shall be most indifferent and agreeable to justice'.[22]

Because they did not allow any conceptual distinctions to inhibit their efficiency – though they were well aware of them – they could use 'arbitration' and 'mediation' more freely and loosely than would be allowed today. No attempt will be made in this book to impose on that reality the modern categories, now distinctly defined.

Arbitrations were usually arranged after the dispute had arisen. The use of standard contracts had barely begun and few contracts then included arbitration clauses, but enough evidence has survived of tailor-made arbitration clauses for disputes arising in the future to show that parties might incorporate them when they thought they would be useful.

Though the Council was concerned to keep the costs of a petition low, and charged no fees, attendance in London would have put its arbitrations outside the means of most parties. Private arbitration was commonplace, arranged by the parties themselves by consent and accepted by their chosen arbitrators. Privately arranged arbitrations may have had many perceived advantages over petitions to the Council. Though there was a risk of favouritism, local arbitrators had the advantages of knowing the place and often the parties. A good reputation did no harm and was often expressly mentioned as a factor in the search for a solution on the merits. All the advantages could be achieved if local government could be called on. That meant the appointment of JPs and others, who routinely accepted commissions to mediate and arbitrate, sometimes at the request of the Council, the Attorney General, a judge or a Master of Requests.

The efficacy of arbitration and mediation depended on the parties being part of a community concerned to restore order when a dispute arose. When there was no comprehensive state and no ubiquitous police force, it was up to victims to institute some procedure for redress. Parties chose arbitration not only for its speed or cheapness, or for decisions on merits rather than rights, but for the likelihood of an award being enforced, with a lasting end to the dispute.

5. CONCLUSIONS

Constructing reliable statistics on 17th-century litigation is tricky and their usefulness always overshadowed by the inescapable reality that there is no means of knowing the reasons why so few, probably never more than 10 per cent, of actions came to trial, let alone ended in a judgment.[23] Surely, one factor must have been the ready availability of arbitration as an alternative, whether publicly provided or privately arranged. In most

22. *APC* 37.327.
23. WA Champion 'Recourse to the Law' 179.

cases it is impossible to know whether the claimant started the action just to get the defendant to negotiate. There is no way of counting which would allow reliable conclusions about volume, let alone trends. There is nothing conceivably better than carefully chosen samples, which depend on fortuitous survival and to some extent, it must be confessed, ease of access. The next chapter describes the sources on which this study rests, and all those which follow attempt to show that they are sufficient for the conclusions drawn from them.

2 SOURCES

The sources remain in an appalling state of intellectual, if not physical, neglect, But some day a history of the law of Renaissance England will be written from the material which is now coming to our notice.

JH Baker[1]

See the inconveniences of these scambling reports! They will make us appear to posterity for a parcel of blockheads.

Holt CJ[2]

1.   INTRODUCTION

With some earlier books on the history of arbitration it was possible to be confident that all the relevant primary sources could be discovered and exploited. There are comprehensive online databases for the surviving literature of Ancient Greece, Rome and even Anglo-Saxon England. There is no hope of such reliance for the 17th century, but the loss of completeness is more than compensated for by the richness, variety and increasing accessibility of the surviving documents. At the start of the century they are predominantly official records, like the *Acts of the Privy Council* (*APC*); but as it progressed they are supplemented by personal papers and diaries, less regular but full of colour.

Archives throughout England have provided rich resources. They are so extensive that it would not only be beyond the scope of this book, it would take scores of scholarly lifetimes, to ensure that each original manuscript was read. There are certainly tens of thousands, and may well be hundreds of thousands, of documents surviving from the 17th century, which refer to the resolution of disputes.

The parties committed themselves to submit to the arbitration and carry out the award by entering into mutual bonds, of which hundreds survive. Far too many awards survive for them even to be noted here. A search of almost any archive would produce examples.[3] And among the documents associated with them may be found the documents which carry

1. JH Baker 'The Dark Age' [Baker *Dark Age*] 23.
2. *Slater v May* 2 Lord Raymond 1072. 'Scambling', an unused but potentially useful word, means there 'slipshod', or 'irregular'.
3. e.g. East Sussex GLY/1030f; SAS-M/1/506.

out their provisions, such as the indentures transferring the title to land, the acquittances which each side would give the other discharging them from all claims,[4] and the leases ordered by arbitrators, 'in consideration of arbitration had'.[5] The parties might formally ratify the award, 'to avoid further disputes', perhaps going into greater detail than the arbitrators had.[6] When the arbitrators had mediated a resolution, the parties would record their settlement.[7] In addition there is general correspondence which illuminates the practice, for example a letter among the Duchess of Norfolk's deeds saying that the writer will be willing to discuss a proposal to submit a dispute to arbitration, but later, when he is less pressed.[8]

Most of the mediations and arbitrations recorded in the archives were privately arranged, without the involvement of any public authority. So too were those recorded in the diaries which survive from the time. Any attempt to find and exploit every surviving diary is bound to fail, because more continue to be discovered, edited and published, but those which have been used provide ample material.[9] Chapter 15 relies on such legacies, left by those who preserved priceless information about their own experiences of dispute resolution, all the more valuable and reliable for never having been intended for the historian.

Choices have had to be made, in the hope that they are the best examples, sometimes on no better criterion than ease of access. There would otherwise have been no end to this book. Whatever criticism may be made of the examples and the criteria on which they were selected, they will at least be enough to reveal a new reality, upsetting some common assumptions. The best hope is that this preliminary background study will lighten the burden of future scholars by providing a context, even a foundation, rather than that its shortcomings should merely provoke rebuttals, though that would be better than nothing.

In any case, sampling is inevitable. For example, there are no long runs of carefully archived papers which would allow statistical analysis. A good example is the single cache of assize orders from the six counties of the Western Circuit, which just covers the twenty years 1629–1648, 'the value enhanced by the fact that they are the only such volumes to have survived'.[10] And even they have many omissions. What has survived

4. Leics 44'28/585.
5. Lancs DDL 563.
6. Sheffield SpSt/139/9.
7. Leics DE728/24 and DE728/248a (glebe and tithes).
8. Nat Arch C115/66.
9. I thank Craig Muldrew 'The Culture of Reconciliation' for most of the references to the diaries used in Chapter 15.
10. JS Cockburn *Western Circuit Assize Orders 1629–1648* [Cockburn *Western*].

has been calendared and that printed source, rather than the original manuscripts, has been relied on here. Fortunately, that reliance can be confident. TG Barnes has provided transcriptions of the manuscripts for just one of the counties, Somerset, for 1629–1640.[11] Comparison of Barnes's transcripts with Cockburn's calendar reveals not a single error of epitome, far less anything that might mislead.[12] Barnes's Introduction and Cockburn's monograph are essential background for any study of the assizes.[13] Barnes described what was in an order book (pxi):

> The assize order book was one of three main documents drawn up by the clerk of assize... One, the *postea* book, was a short-form entry book of the civil actions heard under *nisi prius*... the second was the gaol-book... the kalendar of prisoners accused of criminal offences.... The third, the assize order book, was the residual depository for the business of assizes, matters brought to the judge on the Crown side by directions from the Privy Council, letters from officials, petitions from private persons... it recorded the administrative activity of the judges as the overseers of local government.

What Cockburn's calendar reveals is crucial to understanding the prevalence, indeed the ordinary, routine use of mediation and arbitration. It records the business transacted at 179 sessions, for Cornwall, Devon, Dorset, Hampshire, Somerset and Wiltshire. It has 1,215 entries; almost all discharge administrative responsibilities, few relate to criminal trials, none to ordinary civil claims, unless they were dressed up to threaten a breach of the peace. Of those 1,215 entries no fewer than 200 are referrals, most of them to JPs, for mediation and arbitration, some in so many words. On average there are more than one a session. The referees are ordered sometimes to settle, sometimes to determine a dispute. While the words 'mediate' and 'arbitrate' are freely used, it is clear that all orders to determine a dispute, which empowered the JPs to make an award, assumed that they would first mediate. Sometimes their powers were limited to mediating and, if unsuccessful, reporting back, 'certifying', following Privy Council practice. If parties were recalcitrant, the JPs were ordered to bind them over to be dealt with at the next assizes.[14]

---

11. TG Barnes ed *Somerset Assize Orders 1629–1640* [Barnes *Assize I*] and *Somerset Assize Orders 1640–1649* 1971 [Barnes *Assize II*].
12. The entries in both are: Barnes *Assize I*=Cockburn *Western*: 6=23, 20=79, 28=87, 29=88, 30=89, 37=169, 43=196, 49=251, 55=257, 56=258, 58=260, 68=282, 71=285, 84=408, 85=409, 93=434, 102=477, 103=478, 106=510, 120=609, 131=658, 134=718, 135=719, 137=721, 139=723, 162=860. It has not been necessary to repeat the comparison of the calendar in Cockburn *Western* with Barnes *Assize II*.
13. TG Barnes 'Introduction to Coke's Commentary on Littletton' [Barnes *Coke*]; 'JS Cockburn *A History of English Assizes* [Cockburn *History*].
14. The entries are used where apposite throughout the chapters which follow, referred to as Cockburn *Western* with the number they have there.

2. PRIMARY SOURCES

Acts of the Privy Council[15]   The *APC* record, with some gaps, the work of the Council throughout Elizabeth I's reign. But from her death in 1603 to 1612 the relevant volumes are missing. They were destroyed by a fire at the Mansion House:[16]

> 12 January 1618 the great Banqueting House at Whitehall was by casualty of fire quite burnt to the ground, under which the Records of Council were kept, which being not possible to be all saved from so furious and sudden a conflagration, all the bundles, papers and also all the Registers and Books of Council from part of the year 1601 inclusive to May 1613 were quite consumed.... Those books of Council which yet remain safe are entered in a list in this Register at the latter end of this month of January.

That list of 28 items shows a few to have been saved but from the end of 1601 to 1613 'all burnt'.[17] The loss would have made it impossible to track the new king's personal intervention, but for the survival of another record, covering the work of the Council from 12 May 1603, two months after James I's accession, to June 1616,[18] by which time the *APC* have recommenced. The Masters of Requests recorded the Council's responses to petitions addressed to the King. In the first year 466 private matters are recorded; 416 were referred to arbitrators, of which 67 were attempts to mediate 'a charitable composition' with creditors. Many instructed the arbitrators to settle disputes over title to land.

Documents in the National Archives sometimes deal with disputes before the Privy Council.[19] They are evidence that it was referring petitions to arbitrators as usual during that period. In 1610 it commissioned arbitrators to settle a dispute between Sir Francis Cheyney and Robert Seabrooke in Tring.[20] The number of petitions tailed off later but still about 80 per cent were referred to arbitration, 'that His Majesty be no more troubled':[21]

> The chief reliance was on the country gentry.... However, all kinds of dignitaries were employed – nobility, eminent clergy, and officers of the towns – and the common law judges and practicing lawyers were very prominent. Francis Bacon served as a referee [Lansdowne fol 11b 1613], and Coke was frequently called upon [Lansdowne fols 8a 1603, 54b 1605, 80a 1607, 153a 1611 (2 cases), 211a 1612, 238a 1613, 252a 1614 and 271b 1615].

15. *APC* 38.383.
16. *APC* 36.342; 'casualty of fire' it may have been, but Richard Gore, labourer, was arrested and imprisoned in the Gatehouse on suspicion of arson.
17. *APC* 36.354.
18. Brit Mus Lansdowne MS 266; I have worked from a British Library microfilm [Lansdowne]; JP Dawson 'The Privy Council and Private Law in the Tudor and Stuart Periods: I and II' [Dawson *I* and *II*] 630ff.
19. Nat Arch WARD 2/54A/184/17 and 18; Nat Arch PL 6/1/31 29 March 1607.
20. Nat Arch E 178/238.
21. Dawson *II* 632 and 633 fns 134 and 135; and for Coke also 262b.

And Sir Walter Raleigh, 289b.

When the *APC* start again, with Volume 33 for 1613–1614, James I's Council was working somewhat differently. It appears to have received fewer petitions asking for private disputes to be resolved. It is possible that the record is faulty. Even in the reign of Elizabeth I, internal evidence shows that not all the Council's work was recorded. For James I there is similar evidence.[22] But the difference is too great to be explained by such omissions. Moreover, whereas Elizabeth I's Council received petitions from claimants of all classes, James I's and Charles I's are predominantly, though by no means exclusively, from the higher ranks.[23]

JR Dasent, the *APC*'s careful, skilful and devoted editor, made it clear in his first preface that the surviving records are not comprehensive. They were never intended to be.[24]

> It is not stated that all subjects of deliberation were to be entered, or that the duty of selection was left to the Clerk, who could only act under instructions given by the Council…. the minutes must sometimes have been dictated to him…. A record made under such limitations must naturally observe a most disappointing silence as to many topics of absorbing interest… the deliberations of a body which was practically the predecessor of the modern Cabinet of Ministers must often have been of too confidential a nature.

Intrinsic evidence from the Council's own reports includes intermittent references back to previous acts of which no trace can be found. For example, on New Year's Eve 1622, in setting up a mediation by two Somerset JPs, the report says that the case of the petitioner, Gobbons, a clothier with a wife and 12 children, had been previously referred. There is nothing in the *Acts*. Similarly, six months later, the record shows that the Council had 'lately heard and settled' a dispute about enclosures.[25] There is no record of that either. Perhaps one criterion for inclusion may have been whether a party would need to rely on the record to establish something of value.

Assize Orders   The records kept of the work of the assize judges as they went on their circuits were discussed above. Only those calendared and therefore most easily accessible have been taken as samples. Their significance is clear from their citation throughout the following chapters.

National Archives   The National Archives are the Public Record Office under its new name. They are by far the most copious collection

---

22. e.g. *APC* 33.158 'Whereas we did heretofore address our letters unto you', but no record.
23. Even the frequent orders protecting debtors from importunate creditors become restricted to debtors from the higher ranks, see below Chapter 7 under 'Compositions with Creditors, Protections and Postponements'.
24. *APC* vol 1 vii–viii.
25. *APC* 38.491.

of documents from the 17th century and include many collections. The records of the Palatinate Courts of Chester and Lancaster hold many relevant documents.[26] Documents relevant to arbitration are found in unlikely places, rarely neatly together, from the King's Remembrancer's to those of the Ministry of Agriculture.[27] Navy Board records contain letters of 18 and 20 December 1676 from Thomas Pope of Bristol, saying he will send the Board an award when the arbitrators get back to Bristol. Two days later, the record shows that Pope's opponent was Francis Baylie and names the arbitrators. Later the same day Pope sent in the award, which showed that 'Baylie's allegation was false'.[28]

County and Other Archives   Relevant documents have been found in forty or so local archives.[29] Submissions, bonds,[30] awards and related documents are often found in bundles with other papers coming from one family or estate, sometimes over centuries.[31] They are invaluable and ineluctable evidence of the prevalence of private arbitration, with occasional references to the intervention of public authorities. There may well be caches of relevant papers preserved without knowledge of their significance by lawyers, architects and others.

3. LAW REPORTS

A search for 'arbit!', 'mediat!' and 'award' in Westlaw's database of the *English Reports* from 1603 to 1703 produced just under 3,000 hits. Many of those from 'award' were irrelevant – 'an award of damages', or 'award of a writ of fieri facias'. But not all, and some cases would not have otherwise been discovered. None are totally without interest. Few make any attempt to lay down legal principles. Judges then were not so concerned to state a

26. Nat Arch CHES 11 and 13; PL11 and 21.
27. Nat Arch E 195; MAF Division 1.
28. Nat Arch ADM106/318/401; ADM106/318/399; ADM106/318/404; ADM106/318/402.
29. Bristol Record Office (RO); Cheshire RO; Cornwall RO; Coventry History Centre; Cumbria Archive and Local Study Centre; Derbyshire RO; North Devon RO; Plymouth and West Devon RO; Gloucestershire Archives; Hackney Archives Dept; Hampshire RO; Hertfordshire Archives and Local Studies Centre; Kent History and Library Centre; Lancashire Archives RO; Leicestershire, Leicester and Rutland RO; Lincolnshire Archives; London Metropolitan Archives; Corporation of London RO; Longleat RO; Norfolk RO; Northamptonshire RO; Northumberland Archives; Nottinghamshire Archives; Sheffield Archives; Shropshire Archives; Staffordshire and Stoke-on-Trent Archive Service; Suffolk RO; Surrey History Centre; East Sussex RO; West Sussex RO; Warwickshire County RO; Wigan Archives Service; Wiltshire and Swindon History Centre; Worcestershire Archive and Archaeology Service; East Riding of Yorkshire Archives and Local Studies Service; West Yorkshire Archive Service; Yorkshire Archaeological Society. Also Borthwick Institute for Archives and Shakespare Centre.
30. Lancs DDB 80/5; Lincoln NEL V/13/21.
31. Too many to list but e.g. Glos D340a/T103.

ratio decidendi. Even if they had been, those who reported their decisions did not think in that way; if they had, few had the skill to produce a reliable report.[32] As their most disparaging critic concluded, describing in detail the processes by which they came to be published:[33]

> As if to avenge the seclusion in which this knowledge had been held, the nation dragged to light every thing which bore so much as semblance to the aspect of law. 'Then came forth', says a historian of the time (5 Mod viii), 'a flying squadron of thin reports', and past doubt there must be meaning in the sudden and unexampled increase of this sort of publication at the epoch of which we speak....' Most of these reports are *posthumous, were printed from MSS not original; and that even the originals were not designed for the press.* Ignorance and interest and accident all combined to produce error.

The reason is simple: profit. Bad as many were, lawyers had to have them if they were not to be outwitted by their opponents' citation of unexpected authorities.

Only four sets of reports published in print in the 17th century are certain to have been prepared by the authors whose name they carry: Coke, Clayton, Bulstrode and Style.[34] Baker has described how most reports were prepared:[35]

> A majority, or at least a substantial minority, of the reporters in this period continued the tradition of taking what are better described as notes of cases than reports.... It would be incorrect to assume that such notes were necessarily scribbled down by someone sitting in court.... We ought not even to assume that the writer was an eye-witness. Often he was noting what a friend had told him, or what was going round the inns.... They show what ordinary lawyers felt to be the kernel of a case – what they regarded as worth using again.

A contemporary authority, Coke's son-in-law Sir Harbottle Grimstone, later Master of the Rolls, said in 1657, in an Address to the Students of the Common Laws of England:[36]

> A multitude of flying reports whose authors are as uncertain as the times when taken, have of late surreptitiously crept forth. We have been entertained with barren and unwanted products, *infelix lolium et steriles avenae* [unproductive weed and sterile grasses (Virgil *Eclogues* 5.37)], which not only tends to the depraving the first grounds and reason of the young practitioners, who by such false lights are misled, but also to the contempt of divers our former grave and learned justices, whose honoured and reverend names have, in some of the said

32. The printed reports of 17th-century cases are discussed in WH Bryson 'Law Reports in England from 1603 to 1660'; Michael Macnair 'The Nature and Function of the Early Chancery Reports'.
33. JW Wallace *The Reporters, Chronologically Arranged* [Wallace].
34. Baker *Dark Age* 7.
35. Baker *Dark Age* 15.
36. Wallace xv.

books, been abused and invocated to patronise the indigested crudities of those plagiaries.

Not all reports deserved such scorn. Rolle, Chief Justice of the Upper Bench, as it was called during the Protectorate, published reports for 1614 to 1625, which were of high quality, according to Sir Matthew Hale.[37] A reading of all three thousand reprinted in the *English Reports* from 1600 to 1703 consecutively over a week was sometimes tedious but provided the best evidence there is of what the law was then and it has been used to support its statement in Chapter 17. After all, whatever their shortcomngs, at least they show what lawyers were arguing then, and the artificial, clumsy and often irrelevant outcomes those who made use of arbitration managed to avoid.

And those reports are invaluable for their material on attitudes, practices and background which could not have been found elsewhere. For example, they say nothing of any law relating to mediation, but they provide plenty of evidence of the judges' willingness, eagerness even, to help the parties to settle. And there are the occasional apophthegms, like this on the burden of proof: 'he that is cold must blow the coal'.[38]

The last intemperate assessment must be left to Holt CJ in the epigraph to this chapter. He knew if anyone did.

4. ABRIDGMENTS AND ENTRIES[39]

Few lawyers, then as now, when first approached by a client, would go to primary sources: neither legislation, of which there was almost none relevant to arbitration; nor law reports, whether printed or in manuscript, of which there were no comprehensive collections in any library. Each Inn of Court had its own large library, restricted to its members. A few practising lawyers, like Coke, had magnificent libraries, of manuscripts as well as the printed books, of which there were few by modern standards.[40] Those at the top of the profession, the judges and counsel who used their own strange pidgin Law French, which they made up as they liked, would keep their notes in commonplace books and in the margins of manuscripts and printed texts. Some were later used, rarely with their permission, to produce commercially profitable printed collections. But most lawyers, whether in London or in the country, would be happier with a less elaborate text in English. Those were first available as abridgments, in which the case law was digested, and later as textbooks devoted to arbitration law.

---

37. Wallace 35.
38. *Herrick v Herrick* (1667) 2 Keb 431; 84 ER 271.
39. JD Cowley *A Bibliography of Abridgments* [Cowley].
40. Baker *Dark Age* 24 fn22; RJ Schoeck 'The Libraries of Common Lawyers in Renaissance England'.

The first collections of notes of cases relating to arbitration are in abridgments of reports from the Year Books. The earliest, known as *Statham's Abridgment* (*c*1490),[41] has 14 miscellaneous entries under 'Arbitrement' and a dozen or more scattered under other heads. The three volumes of Fitzherbert's *La Graunde Abridgement* were first published between 1514 and 1517. The third edition in 1577 had 27 entries under 'Arbitrement'. *Brooke* (eight editions between 1568 and 1597) had 53.[42] *Rolle's Abridgment*, the best of the 17th century, had no fewer than 218.

If lawyers' books consistently reiterate statements of the law, they may be relied on as the best evidence, better than the law reports themselves, of what rules were being followed by lawyers, and perhaps of what courts were likely to apply. To show how the law developed, six of the most popular authors have been chosen for particular consideration, one of the 16th and five of the 17th century: William Rastell *Colleccion of Entries* (1564) 1670, John Doddridge 1628, 1631, William Style *Regestrum Practicale* 1657, John March *Actions for Slander ... Arbitrements* 1674, William Sheppard *Grand Abridgment* 1675, and the anonymous *Arbitrium Redivivum* 1684, which has been used as a template and is reproduced complete as Appendix 1. Gerard Malynes *Consuetudo, vel, Lex Mercatoria* 1622 is quite different, the work of a merchant, not a lawyer, but more experienced in mercantile law and practice than any of the others. The part on arbitration is reproduced in Chapter 14.

William Rastell (1508–1565)   No remedy was available at Common Law without a writ. What we would now call precedents of pleading were then collected in books of entries. The first book to which a 17th-century attorney would turn might well be Rastell's. William Rastell was the nephew, disciple and publisher of Sir Thomas More. In 1558 he became a Queen's Bench judge. In 1564 he published his collection of precedents, comprehensive, up to date and based not only on the older books but the manuscripts used every day by the prothonotaries, the clerks who entered the pleadings which started litigation.[43] It was reprinted in 1574, 1596 and 1670 and even in the 18th century Roger North could write:[44] 'Certainly the most useful book of entries.... It contains a complete and very systematic arrangement of forms, and consequently possesses great facilities for consultation'. The entries relating to arbitration are in Latin and scattered under many headings. Where they have been referred to, they have been digested and translated. A lawyer looking for a precedent of a

41. MC Klingelsmith *Statham's Abridgment of the Law*.
42. Robert Brooke *La Graunde Abridgement*; Cowley xlix, 30; Roebuck *Golden Age* 305–306.
43. William Rastell *A Colleccion of Entries* 1670 [Rastell].
44. Roger North *Discourses* 86.

writ, to begin an action, would go first to *Rastell*; but counsel, looking for reliable authorities on the law, would have to look elsewhere.

William Sheppard (1595–1674)   Sheppard's *Grand Abridgment* (1656) is a ragbag, into which he stuffed higgledy-piggledy everything he had accumulated over his lifetime in practice or could take from others. Appendix 2 reproduces the relevant bits. Among much padding, no fewer than six times he states what is no more than a particular example of the obvious general policy, that the parties can make their own agreement and that the law will leave them to it. They could insist, then as now, that the award may be made in Hebrew or in Halifax. It is hardly, therefore, a rule of law, needing to be repeated as if each repetition were an accumulation of authority, that, if the submission is to four arbitrators, with the proviso that any four, three or two of them may make a valid award, then so be it. Sheppard's *Epitome* is a much better effort, neater and concise, presenting the same material, often in the same words, but without the padding and repetition.[45]

William Style   Style published his *Practical Register* in 1657.[46] Its section 'Awards' has entries similar to those in the abridgments – few, without order, and miscellaneous. Style's third edition of 1694 added only one substantial item, a later case of Sir Henry Hobart, appointed Chief Justice of the Common Pleas in 1613, in which he pronounced his opinion in no uncertain terms that something must be given to each side; but Style was careful to say that there was no decision to that effect, and the case was settled.[47]

Edmond Wingate   Wingate's *Maximes of Reason* is an abridgment with a dozen references to arbitration, with little the others do not have, though its report of *Vynior's Case* (see Chapter 19) is neat and accurate, unlike Coke's.

5. TEXTS

The 17th century is the first in which textbooks devoted to arbitration were published. They were preceded by extended treatments of dispute resolution in books of larger scope.

45. William Sheppard *An Epitome of all the Common & Statute Laws* [Sheppard *Epitome*].
46. William Style *Regestrum Practicale* [Style].
47. *Nichols v Grunnion* Hobart 49. The report ends: 'There was no judgment in this case, for though I was clear, and am clear of that opinion, and the rest concurred, yet there was some varying after; and so it hung, and I think was compounded, for I heard no more of it.' Chapter 18 deals with the controversy.

John Doddridge   I have James Oldham to thank for references to two works by Sir John Doddridge (1555–1628), unusually a Doctor of the Civil Law as well as first a Common Law serjeant then a King's Bench judge from 1612 until his death. His opinions on how to plead in matters relating to arbitration dominate King's Bench reports in his time. He is now credited with authorship of the manuscript which Thomas Edgar expanded into *The Lawes Resolutions of Womens Rights*,[48] more curious than convincing. His treatment of arbitration in *The Lawyers Light* was perhaps the first extended effort to express the law coherently. That was written for students and published shortly after his death, followed by an improved version for the legal profession in 1631, *The English Lawyer*.[49]

The English Lawyer is a curious work, comprehensible only as part of a grand attempt to state English law within the discipline of contemporary logic, in the tension between the new (16th century) ideas of Peter Ramus and the old of Aristotle. Fortunately, nobody then or since has taken any notice of it and it is in no sense a source of legal learning on arbitration. Its interest is in its early exposition of relevant case law and attempts to marry the law in the Year Books with Roman Law. Doddridge used arbitration to show off his logical method. He declared on pp91–92:

> An arbitriment, which is also called an award, is a judgment or determination which one or more do make at the request of two parties at the least, for or concerning debt, trespass, or other controversy had between the parties....
>
> But to the intent that the student may know how to collect definition or description of any legal part or title out of his books of report, I will leave him here a description of an award or arbitriment, whereof every part is drawn or deduced out of sundry law cases here and there scattered, which I have gathered as sundry dispersed stones into one building....
>
> What is done here concerning an arbitriment (of which hereafter I shall make a larger discourse) may be likewise performed in sundry other titles.

He was as good as his word and on p129:

> In an arbitrement the matter *in qua* are the parties in strife, *circa quam* the thing whereof the controversy riseth... the material cause *ex qua* is most eminent... that which is *loco generis in descriptione*, in which as there is *genus propinquam* and *genus remotum* so is there *materia remota* and *materia propinqua*.

And much more of the same, pp166–190, with short statements of the contents of reported cases and digressions into fanciful etymology and unhelpful apophthegms: *chacun accord resemble un arbitrement* p189.

48. [TE] ed *The Lawes Resolutions for Womens Rights*.
49. From James Oldham and Su Jin Kim 'Arbitration in America: The Early History' 245–246; [John Doddridge] *The Lawyers Light*; John Doddridge *The English Lawyer* [Doddridge *English Lawyer*].

John March   John March (*c*1611–1657) was a lawyer who from 1644 was working for the Commonwealth Government, towards the end of his life for the trustees for the sale of Crown lands. In 1648 he published the first English treatise devoted to the law of arbitration, though bound up with a text on slander.[50] In 1674 a new edition was published. Those years between the trial of Charles I and Charles II's Treaty of Westminster, which ended the Dutch War, were as full of incident as any one generation in English history, but March's editor William Brown saw no reason to make the slightest alteration to the text, to take account of whatever changes there might have been to the law of arbitration. All he did, when opportunity was provided by a completely new type setting, was to add at the end 100 pages of precedents relating to arbitration, and 150 more of *Quaeries*, 'doubtful cases collected out of our old and new books, put under their proper heads or titles, together with the books cited *pro* and *contra*, very useful and necessary for all students of the law'. The *Quaeries* are quite miscellaneous but there are two items under 'Arbitrement' which merely refer the student to 'my treatise of Arbitrements'. Apparently Brown detected no changes in the law at all.

March tried hard to be accurate and comprehensive and to communicate in an easy style, though he could not avoid technicalities and the pleadings are in Latin. He was not afraid to doubt the authority of Coke (p191):

> Yet I conceive the judgment of these learned men, *viz* Fairfax, Starkey, Yelverton and others, ought not to be so undervalued, especially upon no less than four several debates of the point, as to be called a sudden opinion, as it is in *Fraunces Case* in my lord Coke's 8 Book.

Arbitrium Redivivum   Throughout the period, the courts were deciding cases which arose out of arbitrations, a few laying down new principles of law. Fortunately, just before the legislation which in 1698 transformed the law and practice, a learned but practical treatise on the law of arbitration was published, the anonymous *Arbitrium Redivivum*.

Redivivus was a strange adjective to use. In classical Latin it meant 'secondhand' or 'used for a second time', as bricks sometimes were. Though the word is found in medical texts of the time, the great Ducange[51] could find only one reference, to cannabis which had sprouted but not seeded.[52] But in later Latin it acquired a different meaning to which it

50. John March *Actions for Slander* 1648; 2nd edition 1648 added *The Second Part of Actions for Slanders, with a Second Part of Arbitrements*; 3rd enlarged edn by WB [William Brown] 1674. All are accessible online. Unfortunately March offers no suggestions about arbitration in his *Amicus Reipublicae* 1651.
51. My edition is *Glossarium Manuale ad Scriptores Mediae et Infimae Latinitatis* 1772 [Ducange].
52. Ducange V 633: 'REDIVIVUS Glossae MSS ad Alexandrum Iatrosophistam: *Canapis*

became restricted: 'restored to life'. What did the anonymous author hope
his readers would understand from it in his title? Perhaps he was trying
to get over the message that what he was putting forward was nothing
new. Arbitration had always been there, waiting to be revived and used
again, in ways which he hoped his pioneering textbook would foster. But
where did he get the word from? A generation earlier, a book had been
published in London, *Theatrum Redivivum*. Its author had translated that
as *The Theatre Vindicated*.[53] So that may have been what our anonymous
author was up to.

Whatever its faults, *Redivivum* is the best evidence of what lawyers in
London were thinking the law was then. It does not purport to deal with all
the decided cases, nor even all the important ones (p80):

> There may be many other things said of arbitrement in later books, as in the
> three books of Keble's Reports; but these things being no more than what is
> already said, and especially belonging to pleading, I shall omit them.

Its importance justifies the recension of the whole of its text for ready
reference in Appendix 1. As it brought legal learning almost up to the date
of the Arbitration Act 1698, it has been the template against which the
other sources have been compared to find correspondences.

Gerard Malynes   Malynes's text is quite different from the others. He
was a practising arbitrator, whose work is described in Chapter 14, where
the chapter on arbitration in his *Consuetudo, vel, Lex Mercatoria* and the
case which resulted from one of his own awards, *Gibson v Ferrers*, are
reproduced in full. He was not a lawyer but a businessman, and all the
more important as the first of many non-lawyer arbitrators to add their
quite different insights to learned discussion of the law of arbitration. He
states clearly that the English courts follow his *lex mercatoria*, but it was
the Common Law authorities which the Court of Common Pleas chose
to follow in upholding his award – uphold but not enforce, because the
judges, having dealt with the law, preferred to adjourn to allow the parties
to come to a mediated settlement.

6. READINGS AND MOOTS

The Inns of Court provided some instruction in the form of readings,
lectures which senior members would deliver to junior members of their
own Inn exclusively. They would also arrange moots, in which points
of law would be argued. Hundreds have been preserved from the 17th

---

Rediviva, id est quae nascitur, et non seminatur'. Charles Du Fresne, Sieur Ducange
   (1610–1688) was a lawyer and philologist who became Treasurer of France.
53. Richard Baker *Theatrum Redivivum* 1662.

century, but, interesting as they are within their limits as historical sources, by their nature they could not form part of the body of authority to which ordinary lawyers could turn.[54]

7. CONCLUSIONS

Primary sources, official and private, have provided the information for this study but it would have been impossible to get at them without the leads given by earlier scholars. There is not yet a substantial corpus of learning about dispute resolution in the 17th century; just a few outstanding contributions to what Professor Baker was looking forward to in the epigraph to this chapter. JP Dawson's two-part article and Craig Muldrew's cornucopia of references stand out. They and the editors of the papers and diaries, and dozens of archivists from all parts of England, have made it possible. Many others have contributed references and insights; their names are among the more than two hundred entries in the Bibliography.

54. Baker *Dark Age* 10–11.

3 THE MEANING OF ARBITREMENT

The English have always been given more to peaceableness and industry than other people and, rather than go so far as London to be at so great charges with attorneys and lawyers, they will refer their difference to the arbitration of their parish priests, or the arbitration of honest neighbours.

Edward Chamberlain (1684)[1]

As they [the judges of the King's Bench] could not agree in opinion, they advised the parties to compound, and afterwards by their mediation the matter was finished by arbitrement.

Clerk and Andrew's Case (1624) Cro Jac 693; 79 ER 602

1. INTRODUCTION

The word most often used for the involvement of third parties in resolving a dispute was 'arbitrement', sometimes spelled 'arbitrament' or 'arbitriment'. It is first found in general use in our sense in the middle of the 16th century. It would have been pronounced in the modern English way by the start of the 17th. By its end 'arbitration' had supplanted it.

In the 17th century the parties and lawyers would talk to one another in English. Latin was used for pleadings, some law reports and deeds. It was not the language of Cicero. Those who used it were familiar with the stock phrases they needed, but stuck for everyday equivalents. The best one could manage for a shop was *shopa*. Occasionally a technical phrase of the Civil Law would creep into a Common Law document, as the *de alto et basso* which comprehensively submitted all possible existing differences to Wild J, one of the judges hearing the case in King's Bench, when he took over the case as arbitrator.[2]

Law French was already an oddity, a kind of pidgin with roots in the Anglo-French which followed the Norman Conquest, but transformed into a way of speech and writing used only by lawyers. There is no evidence that William the Conqueror imposed French.[3] By 1362 hostility to all things French led Parliament, responding to 'the outrageous grievances and oppression done to the people', to enact (in French):[4]

---

1. Edward Chamberlain *Angliae Notitia*.
2. *Hawkins v Hawkins* (1672) 3 Keb 264; 64 ER 712.
3. Derek Roebuck 'The Corporeity of a Cobweb'.
4. (1362) 36 Edward III cap XV.

28

Because the laws, customs and statutes of this realm are not commonly known ... because they are pleaded, shown and judged in French, which is much unknown in the said realm, so that the people ... have no knowledge or understanding of what is said for or against them by their serjeants and other pleaders; and that reasonably the said laws and customs shall rather be perceived and known and better understood in the tongue used in the said realm, and every man may govern himself better without offending the law and keep ... his heritage and possession, [and the king and nobles have seen that in other countries there is better government because it is in the vernacular] the king has ordained ... that all pleas ... in any courts ... shall be pleaded ... and judged in the English tongue and entered and enrolled in Latin.

There is dispute about the effect of that legislation. Some scholars hold that it made no difference at all,[5] others that it did all it set out to do.[6] Lawyers certainly continued to use their argot. In 1534, the last Roman Catholic Archbishop of Canterbury, Reginald Pole, appealed to Henry VIII to get rid of the barbarous law and language of the Normans and replace them with the sweet and rational Roman law in English, describing the imposition as 'the great infamy and rot'. In John Doddridge's hands Pole's 'infamy and rot' became 'the badge of slavery',[7] a powerful political symbol for revolutionaries like John Lilburne[8] and Bulstrode Whitelock, Cromwell's Lord Commissioner.[9]

In 1650 and 1651, the revolutionary Parliament enacted that English should be the language of the law[10] but at the Restoration those reforms, like most advances made under the Commonwealth, were abrogated. Many lawyers rejoiced[11] and kept Law French artificially alive for another seventy years. At last in 1733, against the judges' strong opposition, legislation was passed which insisted on law in English.[12] It was not entirely effectual. Two years later Roger North wrote: 'For really the law is scarcely expressible properly in English, and when it is done, it must be Francoise or very uncouth' and 'Counts, Bars, and such transactions as reach no farther than the Bench and Counsel, with the Officers, and not to the Country [that is, to the jury] ... are to be done in Law French'.[13] An example from 1625 is enough to show the absurdity:[14] '*Et est wittily observe, que touts parols... serront expound accordant al intent, come*

5. MD Legge 'Anglo-Norman and the Historian' 175; GE Woodbine 'The Language of English Law' 396.
6. KR Kiralfy *Potter's Historical Introduction to English Law* 4th edn 267 n27.
7. John Doddridge *The English Lawyer* 51.
8. John Lilburne *The Just Man's Justification* 1647.
9. Anon 'By an Impartial Hand' *The Lives of All the Lords Chancellors* II 135–145.
10. Statutes of the Commonwealth 1650 cap37; 1651 cap4; 1654 cap28; 1656 cap10.
11. e.g. Edward Bulstrode *The Reports of Edward Bulstrode* Pt II introduction.
12. (1733) 4 George II cap26 and (1735) 6 George II cap14.
13. RA North *Discourses on the Study of the Laws* 13, 17.
14. *Daniel v Uply* (1625) Latch 39; 82 ER 264.

Parliament, testament, arbitrament, &c. ergo l'intent doit estre observe'.
'Wittily' was perhaps not a word lawyers using Law French often needed.

Care has to be taken also to avoid the traps set by changing English usage. 'Business' then was a synonym, perhaps a euphemism, for dispute. 'Convenient' often meant just coming together, and 'by convention', by agreement.

2.   PRIVATE AND PUBLIC

To a modern mind arbitration is something arranged by the parties themselves and rests on their agreement. State intervention is thought of as exceptional. It is as well to retain that assumption, which also represents reality in the 17th century, despite the overwhelming preponderance of records of public arbitration. There is plenty of evidence of all kinds to illustrate private arbitration: awards, bonds, correspondence between the parties and with the arbitrators and, in the second half of the century, diaries. Yet, though it adds much colour, it does not match the public records in variety, comprehensiveness or consistency.

It was because private arbitration was so much a part of life in England then that the Government, in all its range of manifestations, was able to suggest to disputing parties that they accept an arranged arbitrement. That recommendation might be worded in the most minatory language but rarely went as far as compulsion. James I himself could not compel Lady Anne Clifford,who appears so boldly in Chapter 16.

3.   MEDIATION AND ARBITRATION

Arbitrators, usually one or two from each side, first sat together to mediate a settlement if they could. That was almost always their first objective.[15] But sometimes the record expressly uses the words 'mediate' and 'mediator' or otherwise makes it clear that no decision was expected; and sometimes it reveals that the mediators did nothing more than get the parties to agree that their dispute should be arbitrated, and perhaps who should be arbitrators.[16] References expressly to mediation are found in Elizabeth I's time, a dozen in the archives of that half century;[17] but they become more frequent as the 17th century progressed.

15. Shakespeare Centre Shakes DR12/63/22.
16. 'by mediation of friends have bound themselves to stand to the award', Shropshire 445/39 (1567); Nat Arch 1037/6/73 (1568).
17. Shakespeare Centre Shakes DR10/785 (1558, Saunders LCJ, lease); Nat Arch WARD 2/53/179/76 (1559, 2 mediators, land); Nat Arch C 78/24/19 (1561, Sir John Thynne, estate); Bristol AC/D/1/161 (1568, 2 mediators, land); Surrey LM/COR/3/94 (1569, Bacon LK to 2 mediators delegation from Chancery 'to bring about equitable settlement'); Surrey 6729/9/83 (1573, letter from Burghley, mediator, to William More, wreck); Nat Arch MS 2008 (1591, PC to Whitgift, bond); West Sussex LAVINGTON/459 (1593, 1

Documents in the National Archives refer to mediation by that name.[18] Some refer to the mediation of disputes between states.[19] Most dispose of differences relating to the ownership of land. The mediation could result in a settlement by creation of a trust,[20] and it was appropriate for the use of executors in distributing land under a will where the beneficiaries could not agree.[21]

It was not unusual for concerned relatives to offer their services as mediators. In 1608 Thomas Tyldesley wrote to Thomas Bowld about his unsuccessful attempts to mediate between him and his kinsman Eccleston, which threatened to bring their dispute before the next assizes if it were not settled.[22] In 1630 Sir Edward Trevor mediated between his cousin, Sir John Trevor, and John's mother, not only in their differences about the family collieries but in the equally divisive squabbles about pews in the parish church.[23]

Throughout the 17th century it was common for judges of all courts to take over the mediation of a dispute in litigation before them. The King's Bench in 1604 'mediated an agreement and so it was concluded';[24] and 'the cause was ended by the mediation of the judges and £300 given by order to Parry and general releases signed';[25] in 1612 'afterwards upon the mediation of the justices the parties agreed to try the case in the Guildhall before the Lord Chief Justice';[26] in 1621 'The Defendant therefore durst not insist upon his plea but paid (by direction and mediation of the Court) £100';[27] in 1624 the epigraph to this chapter is a good example: 'As they could not agree in opinion, they advised the parties to compound, and afterwards by their mediation the matter was finished by arbitrement'.[28] In 1670 'by mediation of the Court and by consent… a juror was withdrawn'.[29]

    mediator, land); Nat Arch MSS/3192–3206 Talbot (1594, Shrewsbury between Essex and Derby, land); Fulke Greville (between Shrewsbury and Countess of Warwick, land); Nat Arch C 115/101 (*c*1600, Earl of Pembroke, stewardship of Hereford); Wigan D/D La/5 (1601, 2 mediators, land).

18. Nat Arch SP 46/64/folio100; E 134/20JasI/East15; E 134/22JasI/Mich8 (claim by Spanish Ambassador); SP 46/73/folio120 (offer to mediate); E 134/22JasI/Mich1 (farming of customs duties on French and Rhine wines).
19. Nat Arch SP 75/8/463; SP 78/81/54; SP 75/10/266; SP 88/8/50; SP 88/9/46; SP 81/50/232; SP 80/10/138.
20. Glos D2455/T2/10/1 (1624).
21. Glos D2957/84/17 (1628, widow and son).
22. Wigan D/D Wr C4/1.
23. East Sussex GLY/560.
24. *Symonds v Cockeril* (1604) Noy 151; 74 ER 1113.
25. *Parry v Dale* (1604) Cro Jac 146; 79 ER 128 and (1606) Hob 119; 80 ER 268.
26. *Greenway v Baker's Case* (1612) Godb 193; 78 ER 117.
27. *Steward v Coles* (1621) Cro Jac 627; 79 ER 540.
28. *Clerk and Andrew's Case* (1624) Cro Jac 693; 79 ER 602.
29. *Ridley v Egglesfield* (1670) 2 Lev 25; 83 ER 436.

The Common Pleas worked similarly: in 1624: 'the Court did command the parties to come before them on the morrow in the Treasury, and as it seems this was for mediation to make an agreement'.[30] The Court of Exchequer, too, in 1672, arranged an arbitration by mediation: 'upon mediation of the Court, the parties submitted to Mr Attorney-General to end all differences';[31] and in 1674, in a tithes dispute, 'through the mediation of the Court the plaintiff accepted … £65 in satisfaction'.[32] In 1679: 'afterwards, by the mediation of the Court, the costs were mitigated, and the party submitted to pay them and to conform to the laws'.[33]

The parties did not have to agree to the Court's mediation. In 1650, in a matrimonial dispute 'of great consequence and between persons of quality, the defendant refusing to comply with the Court's mediation, [the Court of Chancery] decreed the defendant to pay to the plaintiff £300 per annum so long as they lived apart'.[34] That Court might dispose of a matter by referring it to a Chancery Master 'to the end that he might mediate and settle an indifferent deed between them, if he can'.[35] Or in 1666 'The Master of the Rolls said he would see to moderate and mediate this matter between the parties, in order to which he was several times attended by the plaintiff and the defendant'.[36] In 1670, even where the law was clear: 'Law being against the plaintiff (as it was admitted it was) Equity could not help the plaintiff. Yet they did mediate with the defendant to pay the plaintiff Martha £20 for her life'.[37] And in 1676, in another land dispute, the Master of the Rolls 'mediated an agreement, which produced a consent that the father should convey to the son, and the son should pay'.[38] In a family land dispute in 1682: 'the lands were incumbered; £2,000 of the portion being unpaid a suit was in Chancery; which by mediation of the Court was composed, the £2,000 paid. Lands of £1,200 per annum settled, and so all things quiet'.[39] That was what the judges wanted.

Or a court might terminate its own consideration of a dispute when it was satisfied that it would be settled elsewhere:[40] 'referred to Mr George

30. *The Residue of the Case of Gibson v Ferrers* (1624) Winch 120; 124 ER 101.
31. *The King's Attorney General and the Queen Dowager and her Trustees for her Jointure v Tarrington and Rainsborough* (1672) Hardres 219; 145 ER 461.
32. *Dashfield v Curnocke* (1674) Hardres 329; 145 ER 482.
33. *Browne v Sir Edward Lake* (1679) Hardres 503; 145 ER 569.
34. *Ashton v Ashton* (1650) Rep Ch 164; 21 ER 538.
35. *Tanfield v Davenport* (1638) 2 Cooper t Cottenham 244; 47 ER 1151.
36. *Underwood v Staney* (1666) 1 Ch Cas 177; 22 ER 703.
37. *Wilmer and his Wife v William Kendrick and Jo Vylet* (1670) 1 Ch Cas 159; 22 ER 741.
38. *Webb v Webb* (1676) 3 Swans 658; 36 ER 1011.
39. *Sir Charles Lee & Uxor v Sir John Boles, Administrator to his Deceased Wife* (1682) 2 Ch Cas 95; 22 ER 863.
40. *Holford's Case* (1620) 2 Rolle 205; 81 ER 752; *Sir William Chancey's Case* (1611) 2 Brownl 18; 123 ER 790 (CP); *Sir Francis Holles v Sir Robert Carr* (1676) 3 Swans 638; 36 ER 1004 (Ch); *The Earl of Athol v The Earl of Derby* (1672) 1 Ch Cas 220;

Crooke and Mr [Orlando] Bridgman'; 'and after, by the mediation of the Metropolitan, he was reconciled to his wife and this was the end of this business'; 'I recommended it to Mr Attorney and Sir John Churchill to mediate'; 'to certain Lords in Parliament'; '*sed adjornatur* to mediate'. Most commonly the report records that the matter was referred to the mediation of friends of the parties.[41] Sometimes the policy behind the referral was expressed, as it was by the House of Lords in 1695: 'Marriages ought to be procured and promoted by the mediation of friends and relations, and not of hirelings', where the word has a different range of connotations, not necessarily encompassing a dispute.[42] Whether the court referred the matter to others to mediate or to arbitrate seems to have been of little concern. It may well be that the reporters took no care to record the actual words used, for example when using Law French: '*submitter le matter al arbitrement*'.[43]

The Council used the word 'mediation' freely but not always in the same sense. It often preferred it, even when it was asking those it appointed to determine the dispute. It meant something different when it asked our ambassador to mediate with the Estates General on behalf of an Englishman.[44] And something different again when it sent him this petition on behalf of a London merchant:[45]

> In commiseration of his long trouble and loss in following a suit in that state twelve years together, without other fruit of his travail than that he is in hope to have an end by your mediation.... We have been moved to make this address to you... to mediate some arbitrable and summary end, such as may stand with justice and conscience, and clear the cause from this overlong circuit of law.

But almost always it is clear that the meaning was 'act as an intermediary in bringing about a settlement'.

The Council expected those it appointed to resolve the dispute. Its instructions varied. Sometimes it gave the arbitrators power to end it themselves. More usually it added some condition, such as 'if you can'.

---

22 ER 771; *Menlee v Guy and Lloyd* (1672) 3 Keble 181; 84 ER 664; and *Wale v Hill* (1610) 1 Bulst. 149; 80 ER 842 (KB); 'the administrators before Sir John Bennet, by his mediation and not judicially' *Tooker v Loane* (1617) Hob 191; 80 ER 338.

41. *Rawlinson v Greeves* (1616) 3 Bulst 237; 81 ER 200 (KB); *Bamfield v Bamfield* (1666) 1 Sid 336; 82 ER 1142 (KB); *Tall v Ryland* (1670) 1 Ch Cas 183; 22 ER 753; *Attorney General v Mayor &c de Coventry* (1700) 2 Vern 397; 23 ER 856 (Ch); (1702) Colles 280; 1 ER 286; *Brownlow Sherard Esq and Dame Mary Anderson his Wife v Simon Harcourt* (1702) Colles 233; 1 ER 264.

42. *Hall & al' Executors of Tho Thynne v Jane Potter Aministratrix of George Potter* (1695) Show Parl Cas 76; 1 ER 52; *Francis Scribblehill v Henry Brett* (1703) 4 Bro PC 144; 2 ER 97.

43. *Darcy v Jackson* (1621) Palm 224; 81 ER 1053.

44. *APC* 41.431.

45. *APC* 34.483.

If the condition, express or implied, was not satisfied, the instructions would continue: 'or *certify* your opinion', so that the Council could 'take an order'.[46]

The Council's most usual response to a petition was to appoint an even number of its members or officers to examine the parties and just to report. An odd number was not unknown and slowly became more frequent.[47] It occasionally commissioned London aldermen,[48] and might arrange for a dispute to be resolved by a panel of merchants, for example three (or any two) Bristol merchants 'to compromise... in equity and good conscience'.[49] It often asked the commissioners to mediate a settlement if they could, but still it would make an order and record it; then it was the order that did 'finally end and determine' the dispute.[50] The power of a mediated settlement comes from the binding nature of the contract in which it is expressed. That contract can only be enforced by litigation. But the Council did not leave it there. If it had initiated the mediation, it would make an order enforcing the settlement, which could be executed without resort to the courts.

Pasco Peperill had leased Lyme House from the Mayor and Commonalty of Plymouth. He complained that they were refusing to perform. The Council commissioned Sir Ferdinando Gorges, Governor of the fort of Plymouth and famous as an early coloniser in North America, and Sir Christopher Harris of Plympton, a town five miles from Plymouth:[51]

> Forasmuch as the poor man desireth some indifferent and arbitrable agreement rather than to run the circle of the law, we have therefore thought meet hereby to authorize and require you to call the petitioner together with the Mayor and such others of the town of Plymouth as you shall think fit before you, and to hear and examine the truth of this complaint, and thereupon to mediate some such final end between them as shall be agreeable to equity and good conscience, without further trouble to us.

As usual there was an even number of arbitrators. They were men of power and authority in the local community. They were to 'mediate' a final end to the dispute. Even the Mayor might be expected to find sufficiently persuasive whatever together they might propose for a settlement.

Other arms of government used mediation freely. The assize judges, discharging their administrative responsibilities, were usually happy that those to whom disputes were referred should use all appropriate means, without making a distinction between mediation and arbitration. But they

---

46. e.g. *APC* 39.279.
47. *APC* 34.270 (three).
48. *APC* 34.295 (six); 34.363 (six or any three).
49. *APC* 33.169.
50. *APC* 33.72; 33.168; 34.248.
51. *APC* 33.49.

followed no forms, and there are plenty of examples in the Western Circuit Assize Orders of express references specifically either to mediation or arbitration.[52] They could be to 'end' or 'determine' a dispute, or to perform an award;[53] but they could just as easily be to mediate a settlement:[54] 'to bring it to a peaceful conclusion',[55] 'negotiate a settlement',[56] 'resolve it if they can',[57] to 'reconcile the two men if they can',[58] or, twice in so many words, 'to mediate a settlement'.[59]

The reality cannot be understood without keeping in mind the consensual element. As often as not the record expressly says that the reference was 'by consent'. One or two records prove that that was no formality:[60]

> Order in the dispute between Rev Henry Byam, vicar of Luccombe, and widow Worth, who was bound over to this assizes on an attachment for contempt for disobeying an assize order made with the consent of the parties. After reading the order and the award of Dr Walter Raleigh made in accordance with it and hearing counsel for both sides, it appears that Worth never consented to the order. The court therefore discharges her and Alexander Worth, her son, from the contempt, the order and the referee's award.... Worth is to bring down the cause for trial at the next assizes.

The random survival of documents can give no true picture of how common and widespread private mediation was. The 17th century was blighted with violence, private and personal as well as institutional and general. The occasional diary entry can only allow a glimpse. Adam Eyre, the Yorkshire self-made man, kept a journal, in which he recorded an attempted mediation which turned to a fight.[61] It would appear that, somehow or other, the dispute was settled.

The essential element of all forms of dispute resolution at that time was flexibility. There were no forms. There was none of the bureaucracy of the courts of Common Law. A dispute which had been partly resolved by litigation could be looked at again and the result improved by arbitrators. Denham B at the Devon Assizes on 23 July 1632 had to deal with cross actions sent to him for trial at *nisi prius*.[62] One action had been heard and judgment would be entered. But, with the parties' consent, the records of

52. JS Cockburn *Western Circuit Assize Orders 1629–1648* [Cockburn *Western*].
53. e.g. Cockburn *Western* 79, 89, 163, 339, 425, 525, 609, 906, 1088, 1093, 1094.
54. e.g. Cockburn *Western* 2, 23, 206, 285, 287, 306, 309, 331, 352, 364, 365, 696, 779, 780, 825, 851, 885, 1018, 1073, 1110, 1120, 1128.
55. Cockburn *Western* 306.
56. Cockburn *Western* 309.
57. Cockburn *Western* 364.
58. Cockburn *Western* 1120, 1128.
59. Cockburn *Western* 696, 825.
60. Cockburn *Western* 892, Crawley J at Somerset Assizes 20 July 1640.
61. Craig Muldrew 'The Culture of Reconciliation' 931.
62. Cockburn *Western* 239.

the outstanding actions were withdrawn and arbitration referred to one JP, who would also determine costs and damages in the action already tried.

4. INSPECTION AND VIEW

One of the functions of arbitrators might be to inspect the place where the dispute had arisen and see for themselves, as well as taking the testimony of witnesses there. Or other experts might be asked to make the surveys and distributions, with arbitrators appointed to deal with any arising disputes.

Private Arbitrations   An award of 1609 records the outcome of a privately arranged inspection and view of escheat lands in Wales.[63] And on 6 October 1621 the 'lords, freeholders and inhabitants' of Fulbeck appointed seven named men 'with others', to 'plot, divide and set forth the land according to the quantity or quality of each person's lands and likewise the common and waste grounds according to each person's oxgangs'.[64] Four arbitrators were appointed to deal with any disputes. On 30 March 1622 they dealt with three disputed plots and confirmed the other distributions.

The Privy Council   Public arbitrations, too, might require a view. On Christmas Eve 1622 the Council wrote to six Warwickshire men, five of them JPs:[65]

> We have received your letters in answer to ours on the complaint of Matthew Collins and John Potter, citizens of Coventry, against John Buggs and others.... Because many things were diversely alleged and some things of importance affirmed and denied by direct contradiction, the truth whereof shall best appear upon view of the place, we commend the business again to your care and further examination, authorizing you, or any three of you, to repair in person to those grounds or coaldelphs [open cast mines] from whence these questions arise and, having taken view and made survey of the place, to proceed further by inquiry and examination... for further clearing or ending of the business in controversy and that the public be not prejudiced for either of their private gains. And, because the final decision is likely to be a work of some time, if you find any ancient watercourse stopped, or any lately made, which may breed any inconvenience to the general good of the parts adjacent, do what in your judgments shall seem best till further course may be taken for the perfect settlement of this work.

If necessary they were to certify who was at fault for the Council to make a final order 'as shall be agreeable to justice and equity and most for the public good'. Such government intervention was then commonplace.

63. Nat Arch E 134/7JasI/Mich5.
64. Lincoln 1 FANE 1/2/1.
65. *APC* 38.375.

A decision on the merits between the parties, certainly, but the priority was 'the public good', in this case the unimpeded supply of coal for local industry. It took the commissioners three months to report but then it was in great detail and the Council was happy to accept their opinion and make it an Act of the Board.[66] All the parties had agreed to 'freely submit the cause and differences to be composed and finally ended by us'. But one problem could not be resolved then and there:

> Because the citizens are desirous to have the water which they shall draw at their pits to run through a part of the farmer's mowing ground, although it be no usual watercourse from their pits and by the running of that coal water Griffe pool will be so floated that the yearly value will be much impaired... for the good of the country we hold it reasonable that the citizens shall yield to the farmers a yearly sum for the damages already done or which hereafter they shall yearly sustain as we, upon our view yearly taken, shall set down under our hands.

What a sensible conclusion! And the Council's order went further, extending the future jurisdiction of the arbitrators beyond fixing the compensation for the run-off to 'any controversies that should arise about this business hereafter'. Nearly seven years later, on 24 February 1630, the Council wrote again to six Warwickshire gentlemen, one of whom, Richard Chamberlain, had been a member of the earlier commission.[67] Buggs and Robinson were 'now about to get coal to serve divers counties'. Anthony Robinson was still obdurate:

> having only half an acre lying by the delph did of purpose to overthrow the work hinder the petitioners' proceedings and threateneth to bring actions of trespass against such as come upon his ground, though the petitioners have offered more and better land in the same field, or to leave him all his coals in the same field and pay him double damages for any trespass.... Besides the private interest of the petitioners, the encouraging and advancing of coal works much imports the Common Wealth in provision of fuel... we require you or any three of you... to examine well the petitioners' allegations as well as all other needful and material circumstances which may occur in this business. And thereupon to accommodate the difference between the parties if you can in such sort that the petitioners be not discouraged or hindered in the working and venting of their coals nor Anthony Robinson be in any sort damnified but that good and full recompense may be given upon view taken of the damage or, in case you cannot settle the same, you make certificate... to the end such further order may be taken as the case shall require.

When in 1616 Cyprian Gabrie's neighbours complained that he had stopped up a watercourse 'to their great annoyance', the Council

66. *APC* 39.197.
67. *APC* 45.288.

commissioned three JPs and a counsellor-at-law (or any three) 'to appoint some convenient time to repair thither, and to take particular notice of the pretended annoyance' and 'to order some such course as you shall find just and reasonable, without further trouble to this Board'.[68]

Enclosures were a ready source of conflict and often best resolved by a view. The Council had already made one order in respect of George Melsome's attempts to enclose common land in Garsington, by which he was blocking access to traditional footpaths and water for the parishioners' cattle. On 14 May 1622 it wrote to four Oxford JPs, asking them, or any three:

> who are neighbours to the place, to make repair to the grounds and take an exact view thereof and, if you find the partition to be unwarrantable, or any other which you find unjust or unreasonable, deal effectually by way of mediation... for the better settling and accommodating of the business.

If either side refused 'to conform to your arbitrament, make certificate to the Board'.[69]

Assizes   The assize judges made similar orders in discharging their administrative responsibilities. On 16 July 1638, at the Devon Assizes, Serjeant Heath ordered two JPs to inspect a bridge and an alleged obstruction and 'to order Pease to cut his banks, to whatever extent they think necessary. Their order is to be final'. Sometimes as many as six JPs were appointed to make an inspection before deciding whether the cost of repair was the responsibility of the county or a particular parish or individual.[70]

The Great Fire 1666   After the Great Fire of London the whole area of destruction had to be viewed and the City joined the Government in arranging for that to be done speedily and with great efficiency. The man who did most of the work of surveying and arbitrating was Robert Hooke, the inventor. His hundreds of views are the subject of his part of Chapter 15 below, on the Diarists.

5.   MERITS OR EXPEDIENCY?

In every surviving document which provides evidence of a private arbitration, it is either expressed or impliedly assumed that the award is to be on the merits, and that every settlement by mediation would meet this test. The phrase 'on the merits' is first found in English sources in

68. *APC* 34.492.
69. *APC* 38.491.
70. Cockburn *Western* 829; ordering a stay of proceedings 908.

1621.[71] The criterion which the Council applied, itself and through those it commissioned, was fairness: 'agreeable to equity and conscience' or 'equity and justice' or 'justice and reason' or some such. It did not demand the strict application of any rules.[72]

For example, on 24 November 1613 the Council wrote to four JPs in Somerset.[73] The letter's first words give an insight into its policy:

> Although it is not usual for this Board to interpose our authority in things which may otherwise be determined by course of justice, yet the equity of the cause is such, and of that consequence to the petitioner, as hath moved us to address these letters to you on his behalf.

The defendant was alleged to be guilty of a breach of trust, in withholding from the claimant bonds to the value of £120. The unnamed petitioner had served 'both the late Queen and his Majesty for forty years'. The JPs were required to: 'inform yourselves of the true state of the difference and thereupon to mediate such a course for the final ending thereof as shall be agreeable to equity and good conscience'.

'A final end' is what arbitrators are commonly asked to determine. Mediators now try to produce a compromise which the parties find mutually acceptable, without concern for what might objectively be 'agreeable to equity and good conscience'. But in all the records of the Council, too much significance should not be deduced from the Council's choice of verb. It used 'mediate' and 'arbitrate' almost interchangeably for the process which often included both, in any sequence.

The Council stuck to no rigid routine. Its purpose was to get to the merits and impose a resolution which would accord with them, as efficiently as possible, often expressly avoiding the costs and delays of litigation. And it did not give up easily. It had asked the Mayor of Bristol to examine a complaint by Joyce Cottrell, a widow, against her son-in-law Tristram Cottrell. The Mayor had sent in his opinion. The Council had considered it but, before it could summon the parties, they settled. But Tristram reneged and, since 'the poor woman remains hopeless of any relief', the Council instructed the Mayor to summon him and 'let him know that we did expect such conformity and readiness on his behalf as the equity and justice of the cause did require, and as in conscience ought to have been performed without our mediation'.

A letter to the Earl of Derby as 'Chamberlain of Chester' shows the Council's policy of preferring an efficient process to any jurisdictional quibble.[74] A plea had been 'first in the Court of Equity and after at the

71. The earliest reference in *OED* and *HTOED*, from House of Lords Debates.
72. Roebuck *Golden Age* 37–38.
73. *APC* 33.283.
74. *APC* 33.551.

Common Law and now likely to stand upon some points and questions, as well in law as equity'. So the Council suggested that Sir Richard Lewknor, 'who heard the matter for the common law, should be present at the further hearing' in the Court of Exchequer for Chester.

Just how little concern the Council expected its arbitrators to have for the niceties of the law was well exhibited in its referral of Dorothy Gervaise's petition to the arbitration of the Solicitor General and the Recorder of London.[75] She was presumably the widowed sister of Lord Stafford, the fourth baron, who was related to the Stanleys and Howards but, the gossip said, had 'been basely married to his mother's chambermaid'. She complained that her husband had mortgaged all his property to goldsmiths, that is moneylenders, who had sold it for much more than the loan secured, but would not account to her for the balance.

> Forasmuch as the case deserveth pity, and commiseration in the meanest, and much more in the person of the petitioner being descended from so great and noble a house, left a widow and charged with divers fatherless children that are like to perish

the arbitrators were instructed: 'if you find the complaint to consist upon any just and likely grounds, to order some such course for the satisfaction of the petitioner's demands as shall be agreeable to reason and good conscience'. Presumably reason would require privilege for 'someone descended from so noble a house', even if 'good conscience' might be blind to such favour.

This insistence that disputes submitted to arbitration should be resolved according to the merits rather than the strict rules of law was a reflection of the great battle being waged between the courts of Common Law and Equity, personified by the personal struggle between Bacon (and Ellesmere LC) and Coke. Bacon won when in July 1616 he persuaded the King to take the unprecedented step of presiding enthroned in Star Chamber, saying:[76]

> We do will and command that our Chancellor or Keeper... shall give unto our subjects upon their several complaints such relief in Equity (notwithstanding any former proceedings at the Common Law against them) as shall stand with the true merits and justice of their cases, and with the former ancient and continued practice and precedency of our Chancery.

It is hard to imagine a statement clearer than that.

Yet expediency was sometimes declared expressly to be the preferred touchstone, as when the assize judges for Bedford were commissioned to arbitrate a disputed enclosure 'for the ending thereof as shall be expedient'.[77] When it wrote to the Lord President of the Council of the

---

75. *APC* 35.409.
76. Bowen 376.
77. *APC* 36.39.

North in 1613, the Council required him to take another member of the Council and the two of them to 'make a final end consonant to justice and expedient for good and the future quiet' of the province.[78]

Perhaps a shift in the Council's criteria may be detected through the reigns of James I and Charles I. From the various formulae inherited from Elizabeth I – equity, good conscience and the other synonyms for fairness – there can be seen a growing preference for expediency. A typical and ordinary example of a reference to mediators is sufficient illustration, though many more will be found scattered in later chapters.[79] In 1623 the Council wrote to three Bedfordshire worthies with the complaint of Edward Sibley that his brother Nicholas and two others had kept him out of his land for eleven years:

> Now forasmuch as your residence is not far distant from the place where the lands in question lie and where the proofs concerning the premises are to be produced... use your best endeavours... to settle a good agreement (if you can) or report on whom the fault resteth that such final order may be taken as to us shall seem most requisite.

That final phrase is unambiguous. If it had to, the Council would decide the dispute as it thought 'most requisite'. Neither law nor fairness – expediency.

6. ARBITRATION CLAUSES[80]

Golden Age took pains to dispel the myth that agreements providing for the arbitration of disputes which may or may not arise in the future – arbitration clauses – were a modern phenomenon. From quite early times parties inserted them in their contracts, or sometimes created them specially as separate agreements, whenever they thought about it and deemed them useful. For example, it was thought wise to insert an arbitration clause into a marriage settlement, appointing those who had negotiated it to resolve any disputes that might arise.[81]

Bess of Hardwick's determination to hold on to and increase her landholdings figured in *Golden Age*, matched but never successfully overwhelmed by the intransigence of her husband, the Earl of Shrewsbury.[82] It is not surprising, then, that a generation later, her sons by a previous marriage, the Cavendishes, were at odds over her will. Bess kept land in the family by arranging the marriage of her son Henry Cavendish at 18 to Shrewsbury's daughter Grace, aged 8; and her daughter Mary, aged

78. *APC* 33.103.
79. *APC* 39.98.
80. Roebuck *Golden Age* 303–306.
81. Wigan D/D An/Bundle 26/102.
82. Roebuck *Golden Age* 165–180 and *passim*. Shrewsbury's will is Notts DD/4P/46/1. It contains an arbitration clause.

12, to Shrewsbury's eldest son, Gilbert, aged 16. Her fourth child by Cavendish was William, who became the 1st Earl of Devonshire, and her fifth was Charles, who had a son, William. In 1626 that William, then Earl of Devonshire, signed an agreement with William, then Viscount Maunsfield, soon to become 1st Duke of Newcastle.[83] The Earl would pay the Viscount 4,000 marks by instalments, to discharge legacies given by his mother's will to the Viscount's father, Sir Charles Cavendish. For £1,000 the Viscount would convey tithes of corn and hay. The Earl would pay the Viscount £2,000 he owed him, plus the £2,000 the Viscount owed Mrs Murray on a bond. The parties had grown up under the influence of Bess, who knew as much as anyone of dispute resolution from her own experience. As she said:[84] 'Arbitration is to be used in appeasing those troublesome suits by which I think in the end neither party will gain but the lawyers will be enriched.' Their stepfather, too, had a wealth of experience as party, mediator and arbitrator.[85] So into their agreement, for private arbitration of course, they inserted an arbitration clause: to accept the arbitration of Sir Thomas Crowe MP and William Noy, legal scholar and later Attorney General, in any dispute regarding the manor of Blackwall.

The Archbishop of York's Vicar General was also careful to provide for disputes to be resolved by arbitration, inserting a clause in his settlement of differences about the payment of canons and prebendaries for attending divine service.[86] He had inspected documents from as early as 1258 in the custody of William Turbatte, notary public, and he provided that any dispute should be arbitrated by the sacristan or his proctor.

7. CONCLUSIONS

The most striking feature of dispute resolution in the 17th century was its flexibility. Each process was tailor-made to suit the parties' needs, whether established by the state or privately. There were no forms until, at the end of the century, stationers began to sell forms for arbitration bonds, which in no way inhibited the procedures. That meant that arbitrators could accomplish all that any judge could and much more. Third parties could easily join in the submission, even after the process had begun. The range of remedies was limited only by the imaginations of the parties and arbitrators. Even private arbitrators could award damages against a party for delay in payment.[87] It is no wonder that arbitration was so commonplace, as the following chapters show.

83. Notts 157/DD/P/48/24.
84. Roebuck *Middle Ages* 69, citing Keele U Library Plas Newydd Papers Early Paget Correspondence series 1 box 7 folio 77.
85. Even into the 17th century: Nat Arch MSS/3192–3206 Talbot (1605 mediator).
86. Notts DD/SR/234/125.
87. Leics DG39/447.

4 PUBLIC ARBITRATION

It was impossible to define in advance the types of cases in which some interest of the administration might appear.... The explanation must be found in the persistence of medieval ideas as to the responsibilities of the Crown in dispensing justice.... that political authority implied a duty to ensure the realization of justice in the ordinary affairs of men.

JP Dawson[1]

Philosopher: And though a Judge should (as all Men may do) Erre in his Judgment, yet there is always such power in the Laws of *England*, as may content the Parties, either in the Chancery or by Commissioners of their own choosing, Authorized by the King; for every Man is bound to acquiesce in the Sentences of the Judges he chooseth....
Lawyer: You are very much deceived in that; for on the contrary the Contention between the Courts for Jurisdiction, is of who shall have most Causes brought before them.
Philosopher: I cry you Mercy, I smelt not that.

Thomas Hobbes[2]

1. INTRODUCTION

Arbitration is essentially a private arrangement. The parties agree to submit their dispute, whatever they decide it is, to a third party of their own choosing, to determine by whatever means they prefer, according to whatever rules they choose, or none at all. They can ask the third party to toss up if they like. But there is another category of dispute resolution, usually called arbitration by all concerned, which originates with the state, which may intervene, if it wishes, as it may in any other human affair. Or a party may call upon it, as will usually be necessary if the other party refuses to comply with the submission or the award. Moreover, a court may arrange an arbitration and appoint its own arbitrators and fix its own rules. But what no one can do, not even the King, is force an unwilling party to submit to arbitration. That is not to say that there are not many

1. JP Dawson 'The Privy Council and Private Law I and II' [Dawson *I* and *II*] 655; cf the fancies of AV Dicey *The Privy Council* 124: 'to an observer of a later age it seems manifest that from the time of James's accession the Council's struggles were the agonies of death'.
2. Thomas Hobbes *Dialogue Between a Philosopher and a Student of the Common Laws of England* 98.

examples of a reluctant party acquiescing when the Government made its wishes sufficiently compelling.

As Chapter 2 showed, for the earlier part of the 17th century the sources are predominantly official, particularly the *Acts of the Privy Council*, though there is plenty of evidence in local archives. Later there is much more colour in personal documents, especially diaries, but even they provide testimony to the state's regular use of arbitration. This chapter considers the whole range of that activity, starting with the monarch's personal involvement, then the Government through the Privy Council, and continuing through all the royal courts until it ends with the work of the JPs.

It must be kept in mind that James I was not English. There is no evidence that he knew or cared for English law. In 1603 Thomas Craig published *Ius Feudale*, which was intended to facilitate the merger of Scots and English law.[3] The English civil lawyer John Cowell wrote his *Institutiones Juris Anglicani* in 1605, proposing a fusion of English and Scottish law, with the Common Law fitting into a Civil Law scheme.[4] There was no lack of interest and some enthusiasm for such a merger as part of the new Britain, but none discernible among the Common Lawyers.

So James I inherited from Elizabeth I a government that had at its disposal a proliferation – it cannot be called a system – of courts of many kinds.[5] There were no substantial changes, though the Chancery courts began to produce and follow their own rules, and conflict grew between courts claiming competing jurisdiction. Many kinds of courts retained some local jurisdiction, of shire, hundred, borough and port. Landlords still held courts for their tenants. Merchants had their own courts. The City of London had its court and its customary law. The Court of Admiralty had jurisdiction over some maritime matters. Church courts became less important.

There were also the courts established by royal prerogative out of the Council, which undertook whatever tasks were delegated to them by the Government, then personified by the monarch. The Court of Requests, and the regional prerogative courts, the Council in the North and the Council in Wales, operated until they were all abolished when the monarchy fell. The Star Chamber was different, though usually included among the prerogative courts. It was where the King himself sat, exercising the judicial functions he insisted on retaining. As Francis Bacon put it:[6]

3. Best edn Thomas Craig *Ius Feudale* 1732.
4. John Cowell *Institutiones Juris Anglicani*.
5. They were described and their relations with the Privy Council examined in Chapter 4 of Roebuck *Golden Age*.
6. TG Barnes 'A Cheshire Seductress' [Barnes *Seductress*] 369, citing Folger Library ms V a 133 fol 33v.

The King himself has his seat prepared here always and many of his progenitors have sat in person, and the King is supreme judge and the Council are as assistants, as the King really judges in this court where in others he is judge but by fiction. [It] is not confined to ordinary principles as other courts are to which the common law or statute laws have assigned limits.

The Common Law courts of King's Bench and Common Pleas were already claiming precedence over all others, but Professor Barnes, who had ransacked the primary sources, was able to write with confidence in 1981 (p368): 'I have not been able to find a single common-law court process issued in denigration of or hindrance to Star Chamber's powers and jurisdiction'. By the end of the 17th century the claims of the Common Law were clear:[7] 'The Common Law is the overruling jurisdiction in this realm; and you ought to entitle yourselves well, to draw a thing out of the jurisdiction of it'. But that change was slow and uneven.

Throughout the period, volumes of reports contain decisions which illustrate the courts' involvement with arbitration. They give a partial but nevertheless revealing picture of the ordinary and widespread use of arbitration in practice, as Chapter 17 will show.

2. THE KING

Golden Age described Elizabeth I's preference for and personal involvement in mediation and arbitration.[8] Her reputation lived on into the 18th century in the popular press, when the *Country Journal or the Craftsman* declared:

Nay, it might, I believe, be proved (to the honour of this immortal Princess, and to her whole sex) that she was the first English monarch who understood that great secret of holding the balance of Europe... she delighted more in making herself the arbitrator of others' differences than in any quarrel contracted of her own.

Unlike Elizabeth I, who seems not to have attended Council meetings, James I's attendance is occasionally recorded,[9] and his direct involvement in its work is often evident, as on Saturday morning of 17 July 1613. He left the members to themselves, though, when they continued to sit the next day.[10] He arbitrated himself. On 3 October 1618 he made an award in favour of the Earl of Ormond in a dispute with the Earl of Desmond. It is preserved in the Lambeth Palace archives:[11]

7. Holt CJ in *Shermoulin v Sands* (1697) 1 Lord Raymond 272.
8. Roebuck *Golden Age* 156–180.
9. *APC* 34.595.
10. *APC* 33.141.
11. Lambeth MS 613 p31. The award is also set out in full in JS Brewer and W Bullen eds *Calendar of the Carew Manuscripts* V doc 199.

We, of our disposition to plant and settle peace and amity between the parties, the one being heir general and the other heir male of an ancient and noble family in Ireland, have at their suit, notwithstanding our other weighty affairs, been contented to take this burden upon us, to mediate a quiet arbitration of the controversies.... To have the true merits of the cause on both parts, as well for matter of fact as for matter of law.

Years later Charles I had to allow the Earl of Desmond time to pay the resulting debt and protect him from his debtors.[12]

From 1603 to 1616 James I heard petitions personally, in most cases arranging for them to go to arbitrators. The numbers are scarcely credible:[13]

In the first year alone, James appears to have handled some 466 private disputes.... In the vast majority of these cases the matter was referred to other courts or to outside arbitrators.... They rarely dropped below a level of 100 petitions per year.

Law reports occasionally tell the story:[14]

The matter was referred to the King: who by the advice of the Archbishop of Canterbury, and the Lord Keeper Coventry awarded that the £100 per annum should be distributed to the three parishes... the residue to Dr Frier and his heirs; this award was confirmed by several orders in the Court of Wards, but no formal decree was made, neither there nor in the Court of Chancery, where the King in his award ordered it should be settled by decree also. And the trustees, who were to convey the lands subject to these uses, made a decree, whereby they settled the whole estate to charitable uses, without regard to former proceedings, the King's award, or the former orders of the Court: and this decree of the commissioners was now quashed by the Lord Keeper....

Charles II showed a similar willingness. *Seal v Crowe* reports that, in 1683 in a matter in which an umpirage was disputed:[15]

The lord the now King, at Bromsgrove, took upon himself the burthen of the umpirage, and there did arbitrate, order and adjudge between the parties, of and upon the premises in the condition specified, to wit, that against John, because he saith that well and true it is that William Smith did arbitrate, order and adjudge that John Crowe, his executors, administrators or assigns should pay....

The King's award settled the dispute between the parties but to ensure that it bound the whole world it might be reinforced by an Act of Parliament.[16]

---

12. *APC* 44.223.
13. JS Hart *Justice Upon Petition* [Hart] 33, relying on BL Lansdowne MS 266 of 290 folios and 59 fn778 citing *APC* 1621–3 13, 145, 1623–5 78, 170, 433 and *Cal SP Dom* 1619–23 148, 179, 184.
14. *Attorney General v Matthews in Chancery* (1675) 2 Lev 167; 83 ER 501.
15. (1683) 3 Lev 161 and 164; 83 ER 629 and 631.
16. *R and Lord Hunsdon v Countess of Arundel and Lord William Howard* (1615) Hob 109;

the King made an award between them, which award because it could not state the lands accordingly, afterwards in March, 35 Henry 8 [1544]. [A]n Act of Parliament was made for ratification of the King's award, which was extant in the Rolls of Parliament, and now was certified under the Great Seal of England.

Chapter 16 relies on the diary of Lady Anne Clifford to show the keenness with which James I pursued her to submit to his arbitration, though quite without success, her determination to preserve her legal title to family land being stronger than his efforts to exercise royal authority. So much for the myth that no married woman could own land!

About noon on 27 March 1626 James I died. The plague raged in London. Members of the Council had their several duties to perform, and no doubt mourned him in their different ways, but by 31 March they were sitting again to deal with petitions, asking the Bishop of Ely and three others to settle a land dispute which the petitioner claimed his opponent was dragging out in lawsuits.[17]

Charles I attended the Privy Council even more frequently than James I, usually for matters of state which he dealt with himself.[18] Sometimes he appointed arbitrators, as he did in a letter of 17 May 1625, requiring them to settle a dispute – 'according to honour and agreements heretofore made' – between Edward Coke's wife Lady Hatton and the Duchess of Richmond and Lennox over a house in Holborn.[19] The Council wrote back to the King on 14 November: 'We are of opinion that Lady Elizabeth Hatton should in honour and equity make payment to the Lady Duchess the sum of £4,000, all which nevertheless we humbly submit to Your Majesty's deep and princely judgment'.

And on the morning of 20 February 1628:[20]

His Majesty was pleased to refer the consideration of the causes and actions depending between Lady Catherine Coningham and Sir John Buchanan unto the Lord President, Lord Steward, the Earl of Carlisle and the Earl of Lithgow, authorizing and requiring them to give such order therein as they should find just.

They remitted all the matters to 'the realm of Scotland... to abide the judgment as by the justice of that realm shall be made'. And among the private papers preserved in the Kent archives, which concern a dispute between the Earls of Middlesex and Desmond, there is Charles I's own reference of the matter to the Lord Keeper and the Attorney General.[21]

---

80 ER 258; *Murry v Eyton and Price, or the Earl of Derby's Case* (1690) 2 Show KB 104; 89 ER 823.

17. *APC* 40.16.
18. e.g. *APC* 45.177; 45.198; 45.255; 45.355; 45.378; 46.5.
19. *APC* 40.57; 40.82; 40.236.
20. *APC* 43.305.
21. Kent U269/L40.

Charles I deigned to act as arbitrator himself. On 3 July 1637 he wrote to the Earl of Derby.[22] A dispute had arisen between the Earl and Elizabeth, widow of Sir Robert Stanley, the Earl's second son, concerning the provision made for her and her sons. Charles I had agreed to arbitrate and this letter recorded that he had awarded her an annuity of £600 to be paid by Lord Strange, the Earl's eldest son, to whom the King awarded various pieces of land out of which he expected the annuity to be paid.

3. PRIVY COUNCIL

Under James I and Charles I the Privy Council was the Government's executive committee, as it had been under Elizabeth I. At her death, a state-sponsored dispute resolution scheme provided its services quickly and without charge to people of all stations in life, English and foreign, in all kinds of controversies but with special concern for the poor and women. Her Privy Council, in response to petitions, routinely commissioned arbitrators to end disputes on the merits. That continued soon after her death, to the Bishop of Carlisle and Sir Wilfrid Lawson 'to order some such course as shall be agreeable to equity and good conscience',[23] and to three arbitrators to 'procure (if you can) some favourable and charitable end'.[24] The work of the Stuart Council will be considered under the headings Jurisdiction, Volume, Procedure, and Policy.

Jurisdiction   James I's Council assumed without argument that it had jurisdiction superior to any other court. It could take to itself and delegate to arbitrators a matter which had been before the assizes and then Chancery, as it did to the Lord Chancellor and two Barons of the Exchequer a dispute between Lord William Howard and William Browne and other tenants of land in Cumberland.[25] The arbitrators were told to 'order such a course for the final ending thereof as shall be agreeable to justice'.

Appeals from the courts of the Channel Islands went to the Privy Council, which then as now sat as their highest court; but in June 1614 it substituted arbitrators to deal with an appeal from a decision of the Bailiff and Jurats of Guernsey.[26] The parties assented to the order of Sir Francis Bacon, then Solicitor General, and George Calvert, one of the Council Clerks. They dealt with title to land and the payment of rents, which was to be in wheat. 'Four indifferent arbitrators' were to be appointed to fix the rent and value the land to be transferred. When the arbitrators had

22. Lancs DDK/11/16.
23. *APC* 33.156.
24. *APC* 33.416.
25. *APC* 36.360.
26. *APC* 33.72.

made their award, the Council would confirm it and instruct the Bailiff and Jurats to enforce it.[27]

By 1629, however, the Council was insisting that petitioners follow the procedures provided by the court system of the islands, with appeal to the Council, even taking a disputed will back from arbitrators and sending it to the court.[28] And the next year arbitrators appointed directly by the King himself reported that 'finding the matter in question to be a trust… denied by the defendant, who for clearing himself preferred to answer to a bill preferred in Chancery', the Council ordered, with the parties' consent, that the plaintiffs (as it called the petitioners) 'forthwith exhibit their bill into the Court of Chancery'.[29]

Volume　　It is impossible to know from the records how many times the Council responded to petitions by setting up an arbitration. Those records do not purport to include all the activities of the Council. For example, a letter from July 1613 to Sir Julius Caesar, Sir Daniel Dunn and Sir Roger Wilbraham reminded them of previous letters appointing them arbitrators in a dispute between the captain of a ship and the consignors of goods, and told them to get on with it.[30] But there is no trace of the earlier correspondence.[31] The scholar whose researches led me first to the Council's records concluded:[32] 'In the eighty years for which the record is published, the number of cases referred to arbitration by the Council must have reached into the thousands'.

One explanation of the later dearth of records of commissions to arbitrators who were not members of the Council may be that it had set up a scheme of committees to handle its routine business. One committee had the responsibility of hearing petitions. No records of that committee's work have survived and there may have been few such references. The tone of the records suggests rather that the Council preferred to make its own plenary decisions. This reduction of the range of appointees continued under Charles I. By then there was none of Elizabeth's preference for Civil Lawyers, or regular referral to merchants, let alone foreigners resident in London. Even submissions to the Lord Mayor of London became infrequent and limited in scope. Yet the fact that some private disputes continued to be referred to arbitrators must mean that the Council still accepted that they could be useful and appropriate. We know only what the

27. *APC* 33.377.
28. *APC* 45.35; reference to arbitrators 44.183.
29. *APC* 46.20.
30. *APC* 33.158.
31. Or *APC* 38.383 in a letter to two Somerset JPs, 'we formerly referred'; or 40.300.
32. Dawson *I* 424.

records say and even that may be open to different interpretations. As far as possible, they will be allowed to tell their own stories.

Perhaps the tale of the waggoner and the stolen trunk is evidence of when the Council began to lose its appetite for arbitration and insist that ordinary disputes should be litigated.[33] On 12 June 1629 the Council wrote to the Mayor, Recorder and Aldermen of Chester enclosing the petition of Richard Stubbs who had been 'robbed of a portmantle delivered to him (being a waggonman) to carry from London to Chester'. He had been imprisoned in Chester for '£100, pretended to be the value of the goods, yet had no notice that they were of much worth, which might have caused him to provide for their safety'. So the Council,

> in commiseration of the Petitioner's distressed estate have thought good seriously to recommend it to your care, to mediate and proceed effectually with Walter Kennedy, owner of the goods, to deal charitably with the Petitioner and afford him all reasonable and fitting favour. Wherein, if you find them not well inclined, we hereby authorize and require you to take special care and give order accordingly, that all such lawful courses may be held for the Petitioner's relief as shall be agreeable to the equity of the Court of Exchequer of Chester. And so, not doubting of your forwardness in all charitable works and especially such as are recommended to you from this Board, we bid etc.

But just a year later a meeting of the full Council took the matter back and wrote to seven Buckingham JPs:[34]

> By the petition enclosed you may at large perceive the Petitioner's complaint touching a portmantle (in which were goods of great value) stolen from him at the house of Thomas Chaddock of Brickell, either with the knowledge or through the great negligence of Chaddock, his wife or some of his family. The Petitioner, being brought to that distress and poverty that he is not otherwise able to seek relief, hath made humble suit to us.... We authorize and and require you or any two or more of you, to call Chaddock, his wife and such of his family as you think fit, and strictly to examine them touching this business, also to make diligent enquiry of such of the inhabitants of the town or others to discover the truth and to inform yourselves of the quality and condition of the persons complained of and in what credit and repute they live amongst their neighbours and how far they are conceived to be at fault, and to take some such course for the Petitioner's relief as you shall find fittest.

But more often the Council preferred to send disputes to the appropriate court which would normally have had jurisdiction, for example the manor court in a land dispute.[35]

33. *APC* 45.46.
34. *APC* 46.21.
35. *APC* 46.125.

Procedure   There is no reason to suppose that the procedures adopted by those commissioned by the Council differed from those in private arbitrations. There are many examples of the same people acting in both public and private arbitrations and some evidence of them following the same processes. The Council could refer the petition for mediation or arbitration, or for inspection and view, or it could send the petitioner off to the court it considered appropriate, or dismiss the complaint as frivolous:[36] 'how weakly they found the complaint grounded on John Bargrave's part... ordered Bargrave should forbear troubling His Majesty or this Board further or else receive condign punishment'; and 'merely clamorous and deserves rather punishment than any commiseration and relief... cause him forthwith to be sent to the House of Correction, there to remain during their Lordships' pleasure'.

When the defendant was a judge, like Sir Henry Gaudie, and James I himself had referred the petition to it, the Council appointed Sir Nicholas Bacon [Francis's half-brother] and three other knights 'to compound the difference (if it were possible)... and either to mediate some good end or to certify to us your opinions... that such order may be given as shall agree with justice and equity'.[37] That panel had both status and authority, which was usually enough to bring the parties to a compromise. Usually but by no means always. There was none of the modern reluctance of mediators even to suggest, let alone impose a settlement. If attempts to mediate failed, the commission, sometimes called referees, were asked to report, usually 'certify', where the merits lay, so that the full Board of the Council could decide the dispute itself. Often it did not even ask the commission to mediate, but merely to inquire and report.[38]

In the course of the century, arbitrations were ordered more rarely. Even mediations, where the Council retained the power to decide if the parties failed to settle, became less frequent[39] than requests for expert opinions on which the Council would decide.[40] Two consecutive records illustrate the difference.[41] On 19 November 1619 Sir Robert Mansell complained that Clavill, Bigo and Bungard, glassmakers, were interfering with his royal patent. The Lord Chief Justice and the Lord Chief Baron were commissioned to arbitrate, 'to order such a course therein as shall be just

36. *APC* 38.396; 46.29.
37. *APC* 33.400.
38. *APC* 33.9.
39. But see e.g. 45.274 (to 4 to mediate on stopping up of path to church and market, or report); 46.10 (to 4 JPs to mediate failure to repair bridge over Mill Ditch, or certify).
40. *APC* 34.71 (Francis Bacon on buildings); 34.74 (Coke, Caesar and Dunn on whether Samuel Palache, a Jew, was a pirate or a servant of the King of Morocco); 34.216 (Caesar, Dunn and Parkins, admiralty); 37.393 (one a land dispute, the other on 'how silver might be brought more plentifully into the kingdom);
41. *APC* 37.68.

and expedient'. They were expected to make an award. The next record is of a letter to five Wiltshire gentlemen to consider the complaint of three sisters that they had been defrauded of land they had inherited jointly from their brother:

> For the discovery of which wrong, if any such there be, as also in commiseration of the petitioners, who are poor and not able to prosecute in course of law (as we are informed), we refer the matter to your examination, and pray and require you... having heard what can be said on both sides, to certify your opinions... that such course may be directed as shall be agreeable to justice and equity.

But that would be for the Council to decide. By 1630 the Council's preference for opinions was clear. In some referrals, the subject matter required the opinions of referees more expert than any members of the large Council but it kept the final decision to itself. Chapter 7 contains commercial examples.

At Whitehall on 20 February 1628, Charles I's Council had laid down rules for itself, and obliged historians by recording in detail how it expected its business to be run:

> Orders to be observed in assemblies of Council.
>
> 1. The Lords are to be warned to meet in Council either by order of the Lord President of the Council or one of the principal Secretaries of State.
> 2. When the Council is warned, every Councillor is to keep the hour of meeting, or if urgent occasion suffer him not to come, he is to send his excuse by that hour, that so the Lords may not stay for him.
> 3. In the Term times, the Councillors, of ordinary course, are to sit on Wednesdays and Fridays in the afternoon for the despatch of suitors, if the greater occasions of State do not hinder.
> 4. When any three of the Lords are assembled in the Council Chamber, all suitors, attendants and others are to avoid the room, and the Chamber to be kept private, both for dignity and that the Lords may with privacy confer together and prepare business before they sit, as occasion shall be.
> 5. When the Lords are set, if it be a day of ordinary business, all petitioners are to be admitted and every one to deliver his petition at the upper end of the table kneeling, and having there presented their petitions, they are without talking or troubling the Board to withdraw themselves and not to come in afterwards except they be called for.
> 6. When the Lords are set, then the Lord President or one of the Principal Secretaries are to acquaint the Council with the cause of that meeting; and if His Majesty send anything to be considered of, or that anything requires dispatch for the public, that is ever to be preferred before any private business.
> 7. And if either of the Principal Secretaries have anything to deliver from the King, or of other intelligence, this is to be done by the Principal Secretary, standing at the upper end of the Board, and when he hath put the business in a way, then he is to go back and take his own place.

8. In debate upon all businesses there is to be freedom and secrecy used; everyone is to speak with respect to the other and no offence to be taken for any free and fitting advice delivered, but as little discourse or repetition to be used as may be for saving of time. And when any Lord speaks at the Board to the Council he is to be uncovered; but if he speaks to any other man, he is to be covered.

9. When any causes are handled and parties heard speak on both sides, the Lords are by questions or otherwise to inform themselves of the truth of the matter of fact, but not to discover any opinions until all have been fully heard.

10. When any cause is fully heard the parties are then to retire, and the Lords to debate alone, and if any variety of opinions continue, which cannot be reconciled, then the Lords are to vote it severally, if it be demanded, and the Lord President, or one of the Principal Secretaries if the Lord President be absent, is to take the votes.

11. In voting of any cause the lowest Councillor in place is to begin and speak first, and so it is to be carried by most voices, because every Councillor hath equal vote there. And when the business is carried by the most voices, no publication is afterwards to be made by any man, how the particular voices and opinions went.

12. Upon the petitions of suitors, the Clerk of the Council who then waits shall set a note when the petitions were exhibited, that the Lords may thereby see how the suitors stand in seniority, and according to that and other necessity of occasion they may be dispatched, wherein respect is to be had to the poorest petitioners, that they be not wearied out with over long attendance.

13. There is to be but two of the clerks of the Council allowed in the Chamber when the Council sits, whereof the clerk of the Council whose month it is to wait always to be one, and that clerk that waited the month before to attend with him the first week at the least; and that clerk that is to wait the month following to come and give his attendance at least a week before his waiting month come in, that so he may acquaint himself with the business depending, against the time his turn comes to wait; and the clerks extraordinary not to come in but when they are called.

14. At every Council before the Lords rise from the Board the Lord President or one of the Principal Secretaries in his absence is to signify to the Lords what businesses of the day do remain, and to take their resolution with which to begin the next sitting, if greater occasions intervene not.

So the proceedings were intended to be quite formal, even when the Council was working in private. Efficiency was all. In allocating priority, 'respect is to be had to the poorest petitioners'. It would be a mistake to assume that those words were not meant to be taken seriously. What may be assumed is that these rules were expressing the existing reality rather than introducing reforms; so they may be read back, with care, to the time of James I.

Privy Councillors were kept busy. They met at least two or three times a week and on most Sundays. On Christmas Eve 1628 a full Board of Lord Keeper, Lord President, Lord Steward, Lord Chamberlain, Earls of Dorset, Holland, Morton, Danby and Totnes, Viscounts Wimbledon, Dorchester and Wilmot and Secretary Coke dealt with an impressive amount of diverse business. They began by sending letters to the Lords Lieutenants of five south coast counties and the Cinque Ports, warning them to secure their coasts from the danger of enemies, 'His Majesty having had advertizements of hostile preparations'. Then a further six letters were sent to the Lord Mayor of London and the Mayors of Yarmouth, Ipswich, Hull, Harwich and Newcastle, with copies of a petition from the Masters of Trinity House, declaring that the regular channel, the Spits, had become dangerous and requesting them to prepare a new one for ships 'trading to Newcastle for coal to Russia, Greenland, Norway, the East Land and Hamburg'. The greatest danger was the threat to Portsmouth. A letter to the Earl of Pembroke spoke of 'great and hostile preparations' and ordered him to see to the viewing, mustering and training of able-bodied men of Portsmouth and arms and provisions for war. Another letter warned Viscount Conway to make sure his trained bands were ready to respond to 'the first firing of the beacons'. Then the Council took a step back from the preparations for invasion to deal with a matrimonial dispute.

The previous February it had heard the petition of Lady Jones for maintenance against her husband, Sir Henry. Lord Vaughan had mediated a settlement and the Council had ordered Sir Henry to pay her £180 a year, quarterly. He had failed to honour his agreement and that order, despite his wife being 'a languishing sick woman, for want of necessary help by physic and relief brought to death's door'. He was told to pay up all he owed immediately and to give security for future payments.

The Council then returned to the problems of Portsmouth, sending to the Master of the Ordnance a list of required munitions, with details down to 'farmers' lanterns proportionate to the ordnance'. Next it issued a warrant for the arrest of Richard Smith, an Englishman but 'a Popish priest styling himself the Bishop of Calcedon', whose preaching and writings and 'continual intelligence with His Majesty's enemies' was no less than high treason. Next came a general warrant for the assistance of the Mineral and Battery Works in the exercise of their monopoly.

Ireland was a regular source of work and the Council often sought the help of arbitrators, usually from those who held high office. The next letter was to the Lord Chancellor of Ireland, asking him to make a final order relieving the petitioner 'as you shall find agreeable to justice and equity'. Next was an instruction to the Paymaster to pay 'Officers of the Army lately discharged at Portsmouth' their arrears of pay. Then came another payment instruction, relating to 200 soldiers in Jersey. Then an order allowing 200 lasts of barley and malt to be exported to Emden. Finally, another order for payment for soldiers in Jersey. But the strangest record came three from the end of those dated 24 December. The mystery is not so much in its content as its date. The intruder is dated Christmas Day, 25 December 1628. Is that an error, or did someone really attend the Council's office that day to send this?

> A letter to Sir Thomas Freake, Deputy Lieutenant of the County of Dorset.
>
> Whereas his Majesty is informed that his servant Mr Endymion Porter (who hath the honour to attend him in his bedchamber) hath lately suffered shipwreck on the coast of Dorsetshire coming from Spain in a ship of the King's; and that although it hath pleased God to save the lives both of him and all his company (to the number of above 100 persons) yet he complains of strange barbarism used to himself and the rest by the inhabitants of a small town called Burton, who have not only robbed the persons as they came on shore but cut in pieces the ship, also despoiling her of all the arms, munitions and other goods that were in her. His Majesty's pleasure, therefore, is that you shall take special care not only to protect the persons of all those who are so cast on shore with Mr Porter from any violence or injury, but that you provide also for their well usage until such time as provision may be made to embark them again for Spain, wherein you shall do an acceptable service unto his Majesty and more particularly by using all courtesy and respect unto those of the better sort amongst them, for that he is informed there are some of good quality.... Inquire what hath been taken from Mr Endymion Porter and procure him restitution, and give him all the respect due unto a person so near attending upon his Majesty. You shall also require the Bailiff of Beaufort to take notice of this his Majesty's pleasure, of whose incivility Mr Porter makes a particular complaint.

That is not the only example of the Council's Christmas spirit.[42] On Christmas Day 1626 the Lord President and Lord Conway had signed a warrant for the release of John Kettle from the Marshalsea. At least some of the members of the King's Privy Council led a busy and useful life.

Policy   When Privy Council records resume in 1614 they start to show the beginnings of a change: it was no longer as a matter of everyday routine commissioning outsiders to arbitrate petititioners' disputes; but it frequently asked committees of its own members to mediate or to advise it, so that it could make an order itself. That does not mean that the Government's preference for arbitration had weakened. There is no evidence that it ever resiled from the policy expressed in 1613 in a letter to the Earl of Derby:

42. In this it was following the example of Elizabeth I's Council, Roebuck *Golden Age* 24–26.

We send your Lordship a petition exhibited unto us by Sir George Beverley, whereby you may perceive his willingness to have the controversies between him and Richard Browne rather determined by arbitration of friends than by prosecution of suits, a course we so well approve, as we cannot but recommend the same to your Lordship... command Browne to repair unto you, and with Sir George Beverley's consent and his, appoint some indifferent gentlemen of the country to examine and compose their differences, whereunto if Browne refuse to yield, it will then appear that vexation is his principal end, whereof we desire to be informed.

The Council's overarching concern remained settlement and an end to strife. For example, on 2 December 1629 it approved the report of a committee of its members in a land dispute in Wales. The title of Sir Thomas Williams, baronet, had been challenged by John Williams, alias John ap William ap Richard ap David. It ordered Sir Thomas to pay John £3 a year for the terms of three lives, in return for him giving up all claims to the land and refraining from vexing His Majesty, the Council or anyone else with his false claims. And John, 'for his unjust accusing of Sir Thomas to his Majesty and the Board, shall acknowledge his fault in the parish church where he dwelleth and ask forgiveness'.

By then it was clear that the Council preferred disputes to go to the courts; but its recognition of their delays, costs and general inefficiency might move it to accept responsibility, particularly if those shortcomings threatened the administration. John Hill, a Yeoman of the Guard, had a claim against Ferdinando Huddleston. The Council had sent 'divers letters' to the assize judges and others without response; so it formed a committee of four Councillors (any two to act) 'to settle and end this business, if they can', or to report.

No one at the time supposed that the state courts offered a legal system which protected them and provided a remedy whenever they considered their rights had been infringed. Those who could get no help from any of the multifarious but not comprehensive range of courts might go direct to the fount of state justice, the monarch, usually represented by the Council, sometimes by Parliament in the House of Lords. But royal intervention was a discretionary supplement to the ordinary private ways of resolving disputes, not the other way round as it is so easy to assume, looking back with what we now take for granted. But then, so was Chancery's issue of a writ, giving access to a Common Law court.

The Council was always ready, in its concern for efficiency, to consolidate arbitrations. Sir Ralph Sidley complained of wrongs done to him and his wife by Lord and Lady Lambert. The sisters Sara and Mary Malbie complained of quite separate wrongs done to them by the Lamberts. The Council, 'not having leisure for other His Majesty's weighty affairs... for accommodating all differences by some friendly agreement', referred both petitions 'and every particular suggested therein' to Sir Julius Caesar MR 'to make some good atonement', with their consents, if possible, otherwise to state 'on whose side the equity doth incline'.[43] Sara married John Paulet, who joined in the fray.[44] The Council was advised that Sara's claim had been dealt with by the Lord Deputy and Council in Ireland and approved of that resolution, writing to the Lord Deputy telling him to make Lady Lambert pay up.[45] Then it added Lord Carew and Edward Coke to help Caesar MR with whatever still had to be done.[46] By 6 December 1619 it had had enough:[47]

> Forasmuch as the cause is *vexata quaestio* and has drawn many directions as well by orders as by letters from the Board without any effect, their Lordships have now thought fit to give an end thereto, and accordingly have ordered that Lord Carew, the Master of the Rolls, and Sir Edward Coke, or any two of them... to order present payment of the £3,000 out of the ward's estate as of what is justly due... as in justice or equity.... And withal to give a speedy end to the difference betwixt Lady Lambert and Sir Ralph Sydley, according to the tenor of an order of this Board dated in July 1618. Of both which differences their Lordships expect a final and speedy end to be made without further trouble to the Board.

On 7 April 1620 Lady Lambert had still not complied and was summoned to appear the next day with the money or go to gaol.[48] But that was by no means the end of it. On 10 June the record shows that Lady Lambert, mistress of the arts of delay, had asked to pay the £150 by instalments, '£50 here and the rest in Ireland'.[49] She was ordered to pay £100 forthwith in London and give security for payment of the balance. The whole £150 would 'be taken as Lady Sidley's dower money for this year'. The Council's apparently endless patience had been exhausted:

> It is further ordered that all suits, questions and complaints between the Lady Lambert, Sir Ralph Sidley and his lady, George Malbie, esquire, and John Paulet, gentleman, and his wife and Mary Malbie, or any of them, shall be clearly and absolutely dismissed from this Board, and be no longer retained here, but left to such legal trial as any of the parties shall be advised to prosecute in any of His Majesty's courts of justice, either here or in the kingdom of Ireland, without further trouble to this Table.

43. *APC* 36.211.
44. *APC* 36.250; 36.328.
45. *APC* 36.361.
46. *APC* 37.6.
47. *APC* 37.87.
48. *APC* 37.173.
49. *APC* 37.220.

On 21 July the Council still had to deal with John Paulet and his wife's claim against Lady Lambert. They sent it to the Chancery Court in Ireland.[50]

When the Council referred a matter to any other tribunal, it implied thereby that neither a party nor anyone else could start or continue proceedings elsewhere on the same cause. Sometimes the stay was express.[51]

The Council was concerned to ensure the awards of its arbitrators were enforced. It did this by confirming the award, making it an order of the Council,[52] and by following up any complaint from a successful party that the award had been ignored. Mr and Mrs Stebranke petitioned the Board for the payment of a debt they said Richard Phillips owed them.[53] He said there had already been an award. He was ordered to pay the sum awarded and they must give him a full discharge of all their claims.

An order of the Council applied to everyone, not just the parties. It was not unusual for it to say so expressly; conversely it could limit it to the parties. In an Irish land dispute, the Council had made an order against Captain Henry Skipwith in favour of the Irishman Florence McCarthy. When Lord Courcy claimed the land, it wrote to the Lord Deputy:[54] 'It was never our intention that the title of Lord Courcy (being a third person and not then spoken of) should receive any prejudice by the compounding a difference between Florence McCarthy and Henry Skipwith'. And it ordered that Lord Courcy 'be maintained in quiet possession of such lands as he now holdeth... until by due process of law he shall be evicted'. The Council might adopt a judgment, for example of the Admiralty Court, and make an order for its enforcement.[55] Surviving records show that the Privy Council continued to arrange arbitrations under the Stuart kings until it was abolished in 1641.

4. STAR CHAMBER

James I intervened in disputes partly through his Star Chamber, which not only acted itself as mediator and arbitrator but took responsibility for seeing that arbitrations commissioned by other courts worked.[56] The irresistible pressure it put on parties to arbitrate threatened one of the essential elements of any definition of arbitration – its voluntary nature –

50. *APC* 37.260.
51. *APC* 38.131. The law is discussed in Chapter 18.
52. *APC* 33.377.
53. *APC* 41.81.
54. *APC* 33.573.
55. *APC* 40.488.
56. Nat Arch STAC 8/80/15, STAC 8/70/8 (1606); STAC 8/39/12, STAC 8/145/26 (1609). The subject matter was all-inclusive and the allegations might even include perjury, Nat Arch STAC 8/85/5 (1618).

but did not reduce its utility. How the Court of Star Chamber worked then was meticulously described by William Hudson, who spent his working life there. His manual of the court's practice was first written in 1621. It circulated widely in manuscript and all those who practised in that court – and they were few – knew it well, but it was not published in print until 1729. He described how the court's referral to arbitrators worked:[57]

> The defendant giveth the plaintiff day to join in commission with him, and delivereth to his attorney six gentlemen of quality, all men without exception for indifferency, out of which the plaintiff chuseth any two to be commissioners; and then the plaintiff delivereth to his attorney six of equal condition, out of which the defendant chuseth two also: all these are mutually entered into either of the attornies books kept for the purpose, and the place of execution, and the time, which is mutually agreed upon (which is for the most part in equal distance), especially favouring the plaintiff and his commissioner's ease; unless the plaintiff be decrepit, and then they may have a clause in the commission, that the commissioners shall go home to their houses *si commodè laborare non queant* [if they cannot work conveniently]; and either of the parties may require a day certain to be expressed in the commission for the execution thereof, if they please; otherwise it goeth upon fourteen days warning to be given by the one side to the other; which warning is oftentimes expressed in the commission to be left at a certain place, and the commission is awarded to four, three, or two, so that less than two cannot execute it.
>
> If the plaintiff will not join with the defendant in the commission, he hath day given to him to join; and, if he do not, a second day is given him, that the defendant shall have it alone; and if by that time the plaintiff deliver not his commissioners names, and agree to the commission, the same is awarded to four justices of peace next adjoining to the defendant's place of habitation, who are presumed to be persons of integrity and indifferency. But the court or the Lord Keeper may, if he please, appoint all the commissioners himself, there being no means to abridge his antient power.

Hudson then explained in the most careful detail how the arbitration was set up by the issue of a writ of *dedimus potestatem*, 'we grant power', which read:

> James, by the grace of God &c, ... take note that we grant you, or three or two of you, full power and authority to accept the reply of JC and RT to the petition of WB... at H on 18 May from day to day until you have finished.

Hudson was careful, too, to stress that the commissioners' authority came from their royal appointment, not the agreement of the parties. That was why it did not matter that the two commissioners who made the award were originally put forward by one party:

---

57. William Hudson *A Treatise of the Court of Star Chamber* with an introduction by TG Barnes 182–183.

> And it hath been justly by the Lord Chancellor Ellesmere held, that any two of the commissioners should execute the same, and shall be held indifferent howsoever named by one party; for they are the King's commissioners, and not the parties. And the difference was taken between commissioners and arbitrators: the latter having authority from the parties are not intended indifferent, unless they be of both parts to make the award; but the commissioners being commanded by the King ought (and is intended that they will) to perform their duties; and therefore no exception can justly be taken unto them.

When we look back at the practice in Stuart England, and admire the ease with which parties and arbitrators moved between mediation and arbitration, unrestrained by theoretical categories, that passage from a man at the heart of it reminds us that there was no lack of a refined understanding then of the differences we now insist upon – just a better recognition of who is to be master: theory or usefulness.

5.   HOUSE OF LORDS

For the first half of the 17th century the House of Lords sat as a court of law.[58]

> Ancient custom and statute law had actually conferred on the upper house a much broader legal authority. It could be called upon, for instance, to correct errors in lower court proceedings, to decide suits long delayed in other venues and, more generally, to offer remedy in cases where no extant law applied, or where the law itself remained unclear…. In the 17th century on a scale that would surpass anything which had gone before…. almost entirely in response to the pressure of public discontent…. In the Parliaments of the 1620s, petitions were counted in dozens… nearly 200 for the decade… By the Long Parliament in 1640… over 200 cases in the first three months… by the close of 1641 nearly 650. Only the outbreak of civil war in 1642 stemmed the tide, and even that did not interrupt the flow completely.

The Commonwealth abolished the House of Lords in March 1649: 'finding by long experience that the House of Lords is useless and dangerous to the People'.[59] The Star Chamber and the judicial work of the Privy Council went, too. They never came back, but the Restoration brought back the House of Lords and the jurisdiction of Parliament over petitions. The Convention Parliament was faced with more than 850, whose subject matter was as multifarious as the parties.

Volume requires routine, which creates systems. Two lawyers acted as clerks with only a short break between them, for seventy years from 1621

---

58. Hart provides invaluable references. His perception of society at that time is different from mine and I have found nothing to support his democratic assumptions about support for the Restoration, 219: 'the general public had been canvassed on the nature of a future political settlement – in the form of elections to the Convention Parliament'.

59. *Acts and Ordinances of the Interregnum* I 18.

to 1691, Henry Elsyng and John Browne. They kept the petitions and the defendants' answers and their minute books and drafts are in the Braye manuscripts in the House of Lords Record Office. The final record was in the *House of Lords' Journal (LJ)*; which included the order and usually the petition and answer, providing ample evidence of the routine referral in their hundreds of all kinds of disputes to arbitration.

Elsyng knew that those with disputes were supposed to take them to the appropriate court and that Parliament was there only for exceptional cases and to correct abuses.[60]

> The answer is: let this petition be delivered into the Chancery; and the justices and the King's Serjeants being called, and the matter well examined, let that be done which right and reason demand. But in the following times most petitions have the same words: 'by authority of Parliament'.

In May 1621 the House appointed a standing Committee for Petitions. It had eight members, chaired by the Earl of Bridgwater, 'to consider all Petitions exhibited to the House and unanswered; and to report to the House what answers are fit to be made unto them'.[61] Whether the petition went first to the House or to the Privy Council, it might end up with arbitrators:[62]

> Most often these cases involved disputes over property or outstanding debts. A long-standing argument, for instance, between the widow Rogers and Sir Arthur Ingram, over boundaries and property rights belonging to two adjoining manors in Somerset, found its way into the house in 1624, and was conclusively settled after arbitration by the earl of Bridgwater and Lord Russell. A similar conflict between Sir John Savage and Thomas Taylor, over title and possession of the manor of Wooton in Hampshire, was brought to the house in 1624 and again in 1626 and was heard extensively by the Committee for Petitions.

When Parliament rose before the matter could be disposed of, Savage petitioned the Privy Council, which referred it to three to arbitrate. When they failed, the matter went back to the Lords, where the parties finally concluded a settlement. It was not unusual for the unavoidable delays to lead parties to ask the House to delegate to arbitrators.[63] However much the official line might be proclaimed, that 'Their House is not an extraordinary remedy, but an ordinary remedy in extraordinary causes',[64] for the many hundreds of petitioners, 'Generally, what they needed from the House of Lords was a forum for officially sanctioned arbitration'.[65]

60. Henry Elsynge *The Manner of Holding Parliaments* 133 (ms), 297 (tr).
61. Hart 35.
62. Hart 51 and 63 fnn178–181.
63. Hart 54.
64. Hart 106, quoting Denzil, Lord Hollis *The Grand Question* 91.
65. Hart 132.

By the end of the Long Parliament the House could not cope with the flood of petitioners who were unable to get redress anywhere else. Many asked permission to withdraw their petitions; many of them may have turned to private arbitration.[66] The House would have made use of London merchants to escape the turmoil but a party could easily frustrate their efforts, as in *Langham v Limbrey*, which occupied the House from 1643 to 1647.[67] The dispute was between London merchants over the hire of a ship which was lost at sea. The House left it unresolved, satisfying neither party.

When the House of Lords was recreated in 1649 it had to deal with the restoration of civil servants to their former offices, which were valuable and often transferable property. Henry and Thomas Jermyn had held the office of Chancery registrar in trust for their father, Sir Thomas Jermyn PC. Sir Thomas had directed that the proceeds of the office be settled on Henry's wife and children. But the Parliament in December 1643 had confiscated them and given them to its own Walter Long. In 1654 Cromwell took them from Long and gave them to Jasper Edwards and William Goldsborough. Long and Henry Jermyn's wife then petitioned Parliament in 1660 and their claims were submitted to the arbitration of Harbottle Grimstone and Denzil, Lord Hollis. Both were Parliamentarians turned Royalists. Grimstone was then Speaker. On 1 May 1660 Long petitioned the new House of Lords and on 2 May Lady Jermyn entered her similar petition. The House referred them both to the Committee for Petitions, which mediated a settlement by which Edwards and Goldsborough retained their offices as deputy registrars, but all profits were to go to Lady Jermyn and her children.[68]

6. CHANCERY

The applications of legal rules, though they could not be challenged in themselves, might produce an unfair result in the circumstances. However refined and worthy of obedience, they were not God's law. In *The Earl of Oxford's Case* (1615), Ellesmere LC said:[69]

> The cause why there is a Chancery is that men's actions are so divers and infinite that it is impossible to make any general law which may aptly meet with every particular and not fail in some circumstances. The office of the Chancellor is to correct men's consciences... and to soften and mollify the extremity of the law.

Even as late as 1765, Blackstone was able to write:[70]

> Equity   From this method of interpreting laws, by the reason of them, arises what we call *equity*; which is thus defined by Grotius (*De Aequitate* 3): 'the

---

66. Hart 198 and 214 fnn115 and 116.
67. Hart 201–203 tells the story in fascinating detail.
68. *House of Lords Record Office (HLRO)* Main Papers HL 1, 2, 4, 15 and 18 May 1660, *LJ* xi 9.
69. (1615) 1 Ch Rep 1; cf Aristotle *Art of Rhetoric* 1.13.13.
70. William Blackstone *Commentaries on the Laws of England* I para 62.

correction of that, wherein the law (by reason of its universality) is deficient'. For since in laws all cases cannot be foreseen or expressed, it is necessary, that when the general decrees of the law come to be applied to particular cases, there should be somewhere a power vested of defining those circumstances, which (had they been foreseen) the legislator himself would have expressed. And these are the cases, which according to Grotius, '*lex non exacte definit, sed arbitrio boni viri permittit*' (the law does not define exactly, but leaves something to the discretion of a just and wise judge).

Blackstone's free translation gives no hint that Grotius's Latin original uses as particular and technical a term as any in the vocabulary of Roman law: *arbitrium boni viri*.[71] The meaning of Grotius's Latin is: 'the law does not exactly define it, but leaves it to the judgment of a good man'. Specifically not a judge but a good lay arbitrator. It necessarily follows that there is little point in seeking precedents in the few 17th-century reports of Equity cases.

In James I's time, and generally in the 17th century as later, Chancery was grievously overloaded, or, put another way, incompetent to deal with its business. In 1617 Timothy Turner of Gray's Inn wrote:[72]

Note that this term I heard a Clerk of the Chancery affirm that there were 8,000 suits depending in court there, of which without doubt 7,900 are thrust into chambers and corners by reference to the Masters of the Court, and to merchants and others in the country to arbitrate them or make report of their opinions.

It is not surprising that many cases were referred to arbitrators.[73] The Court would accept a 'certificate' from the arbitrators setting out the terms of a mediated settlement. On 27 January 1607 it appointed Sir Lawrence Tanfield, then a King's Bench judge, to arbitrate; on 4 July it made a decree enforcing the settlement he had mediated. No one there could complain of delays in Chancery.[74] Tanfield had become Chief Baron on 25 June.

JP Dawson was the first scholar to make use of the surviving Chancery records to illuminate arbitration in the first half of the 17th century:[75]

The pervasiveness of arbitration in Tudor and early Stuart England was a symptom of a general condition. The remedies of the Chancery at this stage were a response to an immense and scattered range of particularized injustices produced by the common law.... Common sense, inspired by a morality that did not need to be highly refined, could dictate practical solutions.... The device of

71. Roebuck and de Fumichon *Roman Arbitration* Chapter 5 46–66.
72. *Liber Timothei Tourneur de Gr Inne appr in lege* BM Ms Add 35957, cited JH Baker 'The Common Lawyers and the Chancery' repr Boyer *Liberty* 274 fn124.
73. Nat Arch C6/388/72; JP Dawson *A History of Lay Judges* [Dawson *Lay*] 163; Donald Veall *The Popular Movement for Law Reform* 32–35.
74. Nat Arch C78/136/6.
75. Dawson *Lay* 169–170. No doubt an exhaustive search of Chancery records would produce much more valuable material, eg 'Awards and Agreements 1694–1844' C42.

arbitral commission brought powerful help to the Chancellors in effectuating their reforms. Common lawyers, judges, merchants, gentry – the whole network of social and political leadership in English communities – were enlisted in the effort to find specific solutions that were acceptable to the parties themselves and that conformed to the ethical standards prevailing in English society.

Documents preserved in county archives are further evidence of matters being transferred from Chancery to arbitrators,[76] sometimes to one of the Chancery Masters.[77] By 1630 it was called a mediation, even though the result was the same: the determination of ownership of land.[78]

In 1610 Richard Lee had prepared a deed of release.[79] Four arbitrators, one of them Sir William Fleetwood MP JP, had found against him in favour of Partridge, in a dispute over copyhold lands in Middlesex, referred to them by the Chancery Court. That deed was never executed but, on 20 February, Partridge wrote a letter confirming the release, relating how the award had gone against him but that the arbitrators had asked Lee to make him a gift of £10, on account of his poverty. The document was then signed and sealed by the parties and endorsed as delivered to Lee.

In 1614 four arbitrators, apparently non-lawyers, 'according to the commission from the Court of Chancery', ordered lawyer Anthony Ludford and his wife Elizabeth to convey the manor of Kyngswood to Henry Ferrers for the sum of 40 marks.[80]

Richard and Mary Old had an action before the Court of Chancery against Richard and Mary Manning.[81] They agreed that part of their claim should be referred to two arbitrators. On 19 February 1606 the Court commissioned them to summon and examine witnesses. They were to make their award in writing before 1 June, when it would bind the parties. They were not to interfere with a Chancery judgment in another matter between different parties. If the 'referees' could not agree, on the law or equity, the opinion of Thomas Burton, counsellor at law, would be conclusive.

A provincial Chancery court, like that of the Duchy of Lancaster, could commission four arbitrators to deal with a land dispute, and they in turn could delegate to other arbitrators the task of enclosing and allotting the commons and waste.[82]

Arbitrators in the course of their hearings might ask the Chancery for help. In the dispute between John Gregory and Simon Chamber in 1633,

76. Glos D1571/L6 (award); Glos D340a/L3 (debt).
77. West Yorks WYL100/L/5/3.
78. Glos D1677/GG/742.
79. Nat Arch WARD 2/54A/184/15.
80. Shakes DR 3/616.
81. Shropshire XD3614/1/4/74.
82. Lancs DDBL 50/68.

the arbitrators found that the date on a deed had been altered. It was ordered that the deed should be produced for the Court of Chancery to inspect.[83]

The successful party in a private arbitration might have the award confirmed by an order in Chancery.[84]

Once having referred a matter to arbitrators, the Court would not look into the merits of their award:[85]

> The matter was referred to Mr Ambrose Phillips by consent of all parties, and his Award to be conclusive. Mr Phillips made an Award, which was confirmed *nisi causa*. At the day appointed several reasons were offered against confirming it... But the Court declared, that the parties having bound themselves by consent, they would not look back into the Award, and thereupon it was confirmed by the Lord Chancellor.

Chancery would take note of Civil Law, as in *Warren v Warren*:[86]

> By the Civil Law, the Arbitrators can judge nothing but what is submitted to their Judgment, by the Compromise, and if they do not observe the Conditions therein prescribed, but judge otherwise, their Award is void. *Domat* I 226.

Chancery was ever concerned to leave parties to arrange their own arbitrations.[87]

> The Award was by the direction of the Plaintiff's friends, and ought not to be set aside... it would involve many Suits; it is in the nature of an agreement, and ought to be performed. This Court taking Notice that the Award was not made by the Order of this Court, but that it proceeded from the voluntary submission of the parties, two Judges being chosen by themselves, who declared their opinion, that they saw no Cause to decree the Award to be set aside.

7.   KING'S BENCH, COMMON PLEAS AND EXCHEQUER

Local archives and the law reports provide evidence that all the Common Law courts referred matters before them to arbitration.

King's Bench   The Court of King's Bench often referred litigation to arbitrators.[88] If the judges could not agree, an easy way out was to submit the matter to one of them as arbitrator, with the consent of the parties, as it did to Coke CJ in *Johnson v Lemmon*.[89] Sometimes the poverty of the

---

83. Shakes DR/10/1726a and b.
84. Shakes DR10/1628.
85. *Halford v Bradshaw* (1661) Nels 83; 21 ER 795.
86. *John Warren and Richard Warren v Thomas Gree et al* (1674) Rep t Finch 141; 23 ER 77.
87. *Eyre v Good* (1670) Ch Rep 34; 21 ER 608.
88. *Powell v Harris* (1615) 1 Rolle 263; 81 ER 447; *R v Burdett* (1697) 1 Ld Raym 148; 91 ER 996; *Lawrence v Dodwell* (1698) 1 Ld Raym 438; 91 ER 1190.
89. (1619) 2 Rolle 144; 81 ER 714; as *Johnson v Leman* (1619) Cro Jac 562; 79 ER 481.

plaintiff was given as the reason.[90] Robert Anderson, declaring himself to be a poor man, and 'a mark set up to shoot at', complained to Coke CJ that Christopher Davy was suing him because he refused to pay him bribes. Coke sent the petition to Nathaniel Bacon JP, whose work as an arbitrator is described in Chapter 11 below, endorsed: 'I desire Sir Nathaniel Bacon to inform himself of the true state of this case and to end it or certify'.[91] There is a further endorsement:

> Sir, I was retained in this cause and I spake to Mr Gibson to appear for Anderson by reason it was in the King's Bench and the cause was brought down and tried at the assizes without any knowledge given to either of us. Per me Jacobum Wilshore.

Common Pleas   Common Pleas made similar use of arbitration; in *Weeks v Wright*:[92] 'so that the matter might be put to arbitrement, and if the arbitrators could not determine the matter, the Court would'.

An example of a criminal case referred to arbitration by the Court of Common Pleas is William Atwood's action against a man who had thrown beer in his face, but with part of the glass as well, so that 'the glass did break off from the foot thereof, and so fell upon or near the said Atwood's eye'. The court sent the matter to the Gloucester Assizes and the assize judge 'did mediate an end... which this defendant and Atwood yielded unto'. The defendant was later brought before the Star Chamber for failure to perform the mediated agreement, where he pleaded payment of the £40 agreed upon.[93]

Exchequer   The report of the Exchequer case *William Preston v Thomas Mercer* is revealing:[94]

> The court seemed to be of opinion against the plaintiff; but advised the parties to agree it; and so it was referred to arbitrement. But the reference proving ineffectual; the court gave judgment at last for the plaintiff, after great wavering in opinion and arguings.

Arbitration may have provided an escape from the Court's own failings:[95] 'The cause was heard in the Exchequer, and, after a long hearing, it was referred to two gentlemen to arbitrate'.

In 1610 the Council commissioned arbitrators whose award settled the dispute between Sir Francis Cheyney and Robert Seabrooke 'relating

90. *Shawes Case* (1619) Palm 76; 81 ER 985.
91. Victor Morgan et al eds *Papers of Nathaniel Bacon* [Morgan et al *Nat Bacon*] V 43–44.
92. (1616) 1 Brownl 81; 123 ER 679.
93. Nat Arch Star Chamber ms 8/34/14.
94. (1656) Hardres 60; 145 ER 380.
95. *Sir Cornwall Bradshaw v William Sutton* (1698) Colles 25; 1 ER 162.

to common of pasture' in Tring, which had been before the Exchequer Court.[96]

8. *NISI PRIUS* AND ASSIZES

The records of the work of assize judges show that, in their administrative capacity, they also took responsibility, frequently and as a matter of routine, for arranging arbitrations of a wide range of disputes.[97]

Subject Matter   Those which most exercised them arose from the need to determine which parish should bear the burden of sustaining poor people, by far the most of whom were young unmarried women who had borne children, and those children, who sometimes had been left to fend for themselves. The Government was determined to ensure that all were cared for, after the fashion of the time, by the parish which they came from. JPs were instructed to decide those disputes. Sometimes what they did looks very like arbitration, but the hundreds of entries have been excluded from consideration here as not quite fitting any category of mediation or arbitration.

There are dozens of references to the suppression of unlicensed alehouses, to relations between apprentices (some female) and their masters (some female), and to appointments of constables and tithingmen. There are a few records of criminal matters, though they were properly assigned to the other judge as Crown cases.

Often the dispute was over land, its ownership or possession, trusts, rights of way, responsibility for repair of roads and bridges, and detailed provision for sequestration of rents or profits, and the harvest. Ecclesiastical disputes were settled, quarrels between clergy being sometimes referred to two clergymen who were not JPs, or the Bishop of Exeter.[98] Some related to the recovery of simple debts, though none to compositions with creditors.

The judges on assize in Southwark on 1 April 1650 had to decide which church, St Saviour's or St Olave's, should provide for a widow, Anne Eliott, and her four children. They appointed arbitrators.[99] At the Somerset Assizes in September 1648 two JPs were instructed to examine witnesses and Joan Garland, a single woman accused of murdering her newborn child.[100] The Council could refer a dispute to the assizes, as it did, to the Somerset Assizes in 1635, the complaint against Lady Skory and her new third husband.[101] If nothing else, these survivals show that the Council,

96. Nat Arch E 178/238.
97. JS Cockburn *Western Circuit Assize Orders* [Cockburn *Western*].
98. Cockburn *Western* 11, 49, 68, 248, 518, 575.
99. Met P92/SAV/1431.
100. Cockburn *Western* 1215.
101. Cockburn *Western* 251 citing PRO PC 2/44 608.

during that period 1603 to 1614 when the *APC* were lost, was referring petitions to arbitrators as usual. Other references support that inference.[102]

Policy   The arbitrators were expected to produce a fair determination, on the merits, not one which mimicked that of a Common Law court. The order would usually take that as read, but occasionally it makes it express, instructing the arbitrators 'to make an equitable order'.[103] 'As Tudor monarchs had fashioned the Privy Council into the premier executive organ, so they had made of the JPs the chief administrators of royal policy in domestic affairs' and the assize judges 'the voices, the ears, the eyes and the arms of the Council in the counties':[104]

> The judges were still only the senior partners in administration. The extent to which they relied on their junior partners, the JPs, for the fulfilment of their administrative functions is illustrated by the great majority of these orders referring investigation and even determination of matters to the justices. The mutual respect and deference exhibited in the assize orders was a measure of the soundness of the judges' and the justices' relationship and a firm basis for their effective co-operation in local government.

James I could hardly have expressed his Government's policy more clearly than in this order to the assize judges:[105]

> Remember that, when you go to your circuits, you go not only to punish and prevent offences but you are to take care for the good government in general of the parts where you travel... you have charges to give to JPs, that they do their duties when you are absent as well as present: take an account of them and report their service to me at your return... I know not whether misunderstanding or slackness bred this, that I had no account but in general of that I gave you in particular in charge the last year: therefore now I charge you again that at your next return you repair to my Chancellor, and bring your accounts to him in writing of those things which in particular I have given you in charge: and then, when I have seen your accounts, as occasion shall serve it may be I will call for some of you, to be informed of the state of that part of the country where your circuit lay.

After the execution of Charles I, the assizes were essential means of persuasion and enforcement. For example:[106]

> In March [1649] Thorpe B persuaded the grand jury at York to frame a petition acknowledging the wisdom and justice of executing the king and promising to support Parliament in future.... A year later Rolle and Nicholas, the Western

102. Nat Arch PL 6/1/31 29 March 1607.
103. Cockburn *Western* 1136, 1158, 1214.
104. Barnes xx and xxx–xxxi.
105. *His Majesty's Speech in Star Chamber 20 June 1616* from Cockburn *Western* 10.
106. Cockburn *Western* 244.

Circuit judges, were commended for settling 'the people's minds as to the present government'.

That was not an easy task and some judges were not happy to accept it. 'Before the summer assizes of 1659 all the judges were required to take the oath prescribed by the Rump Parliament before having their patents renewed'.[107] Some judges were sacked. The circuits were etiolated. The Winter Circuit of 1660 was cancelled. But then came the Restoration.

Procedure   Actions begun in King's Bench, Common Pleas or Exchequer would be heard there, 'at bar', unless before (*nisi prius*) the set date of hearing they had been heard in another court: the assize sittings in London or Middlesex or on circuit. Two judges were delegated for each assize and *nisi prius* cases usually occupied the whole time of one of them. Parties were represented by counsel. The judgment of the assize judge was recorded in a *postea*, lodged with the court from which the case arose. The oldest surviving order book for a circuit court is that for the Western Circuit 1629–1648.[108] It records many orders delegating disputes to arbitrators:[109]

> By the consent of the parties that the last juror be withdrawn and that the matter in controversy be put to the arbitrement of [two names] to hear and determine... and to give damages and costs on any side as they shall see cause.

Horwitz and Oldham provide an illustration of how those final determinations of the arbitrators were enforced:[110]

> Should a losing party refuse to comply with the terms of an award, motions for enforcement might be heard in Westminster Hall. So, for example, the Remembrance Rolls of the Court of Common Pleas for the late 1650s contain a series of entries in connection with a reference made at the Lent 1658 sitting for Suffolk culminating in an order to the non-complying defendant to pay the £30 awarded to the plaintiff within one week or face attachment for contempt.

The *nisi prius* judges made orders for good behaviour, they bound people over, they initiated inquiries; but of the 1,215 orders in the Western Circuit order books, made at 179 sessions for the counties of Cornwall, Devon, Dorset, Hampshire, Somerset and Wiltshire, 200 are references, almost always to two or four local JPs, to mediate and arbitrate.[111] They appear

---

107. Cockburn *Western* 244.
108. Henry Horwitz and James Oldham 'John Locke, Lord Mansfield and Arbitration' [Horwitz and Oldham] 140; Cockburn *Western* and Cockburn *Assizes* 136.
109. Horwitz and Oldham 140 citing PRO Assizes 22/1 folio 1. There are other records from 1672 in Nat Arch ASSI 34.
110. Horwitz and Oldham 140 citing PRO Common Pleas 45/416 *Lamb v Hudson* 6 and 16 May 1659.
111. Cockburn *Assizes* 137 estimates 'the delegation to arbitration of perhaps one-half of all cases'; and points out that judges and other staff received fees for each matter they handled, were over-burdened, and had every incentive to delegate, 135–136.

in the appropriate place in the following chapters.[112] All but 19 of the 200 references were to JPs. The 19 others included the Bishop of Exeter (4), a judge or counsel, constables, or gentlemen of the county. Serjeant Nathaniel Finch (to be distinguished from his contemporary relative Sir John Finch CJCP, later Lord Keeper) was busy at that time on the Western Circuit, often arranging arbitrations in matters in which he was briefed.[113]

The judges rarely made a clear distinction between mediation and arbitration. They instructed the referees to resolve or settle the dispute, if they could, and if not to certify their conclusions and send it back. Sometimes the referees were merely instructed to examine the dispute, yet it is later expressed that a party shall 'be bound in 100 marks to perform their order and award'.[114] Many of the orders calendared could not be simpler:[115] 'Examination of the difference between John Davis and Thomas Bracy is referred to John Farwell JP. He is to hear and determine the dispute, and the parties are to perform his order and award'.

Sir Thomas Richardson CJKB, recently promoted from Common Pleas, presided in Winchester Castle on 23 February 1632. He showed how practical the Assizes could be:[116]

> Order in the dispute between Richard Purse and Richard Browninge. If Purse will stay the Common Law proceedings against Browninge upon the bond of £20 until the cause can be heard in the Court of Requests, or if he will refer settlement of the issue to Sir Richard Norton and Sir William Lewis JPs, or any two gentlemen of the county, and will perform their order, then he is to be discharged of the bond binding him to good behaviour. If he will not, he is to be bound to good behaviour and appearance at the next assizes.

The JPs were expected to resolve the dispute by any means at their disposal, almost always making an attempt to mediate. If all their efforts failed, they might refer it to a single umpire:[117] the arbitrators and the umpire were to settle the matter before 24 August and, if the parties had not performed the award by that date, the matter was to be tried at Common Law. Awards made by JPs commissioned at the assizes were as vulnerable as any others to the machinations of disappointed parties but the assize judges had the means of enforcing them; usually the threat of gaol or binding over to the

---

112. Cockburn *Assizes* declares: 'civil matters – actions involving title to land, the equitable arrangement of an orphan's estate, or separation and desertion settlements – lay wholly outside the justices' competence and were referred automatically to assizes'; but then they were, as likely as not, referred to the arbitration of JPs, as later chapters will show.
113. Cockburn *Western* 575.
114. Cockburn *Western* 79.
115. Cockburn *Western* 169.
116. Cockburn *Western* 174.
117. Cockburn *Western* 887, 893.

next assizes was enough.[118] The defaulter might be required to apologise, or to pay 'the expenses and charges in obtaining an attachment'.[119]

Without appearing to wish to disparage their jurisdiction, the Council wrote to the assize judges for Devon with a petition:[120]

> Which carries such a show of equity and reason as we have been moved to pray Your Lordships to move Arthur Hatch to refer the cause to some meet and indifferent persons for an arbitrable end, rather than to leave them to the extremity of the law, by a trial before you this next Assizes... take notice with as much favour as the equity of the cause shall require.

The assize judges themselves assumed that those they appointed would act swiftly and sometimes gave them what seems now little time to complete their work. On 1 August 1631 Denham B gave two JPs only until 29 September; and on 11 March 1635 Finch CJKB gave until 1 May.[121]

The assize judges sometimes considered it necessary to stay all other proceedings expressly when they arranged arbitrations.[122] At the Devon Assizes on 16 July 1638, Serjeant Heath ordered:[123]

> In the presence of counsel for both sides, the court orders Berry to pay Hooper and Forteskue the £6 mentioned in the order made by Sir Lewis Pollard JP and 40s costs and damages. He is to enter a bond to pay the £8 within one month. Counsel for Berry has requested permission for him to proceed in his suits in the courts of equity, whereupon the court desires Sir Lewis Pollard to certify next term whether or not he ordered or intended to order that those suits should terminate. If this was his intention, Berry is forbidden to proceed further; otherwise he may continue with the actions. With reference to the ground called Splatine, Pollard is again required to certify whether or not he included it in his award; if not, Berry is at liberty to proceed further.

The last assizes before the civil war were in the summer of 1642.

9. JUSTICES OF THE PEACE AND QUARTER SESSIONS

The first person to whom someone who needed help with a dispute would turn was often the local Justice of the Peace, if he was one of those who took his responsibilities seriously and was prepared to offer that important

118. Cockburn *Western* 43 (the recalcitrant widow Edith Moore), 153 (Simon and Edith Taylor and their daughter Elizabeth).
119. Cockburn *Western* 227, 463.
120. *APC* 33.349.
121. Cockburn *Western* 159, 357.
122. Cockburn *Western* 2 'All suits between the parties are to stay until 1 November'; 87 'all suits about the tenement are to cease'; 88 'all suits in Star Chamber are to cease' (to await a commission from Chancery); 228 'the two actions in the hundred court are to stay'; 230; 669.
123. Cockburn *Western* 678.

service.[124] There were no fees or other charges and often his was the best hope of an objective and experienced intervention. Almost all JPs were men of note in their own community and nearly every man of sufficient substance, land worth at least £20 a year, aspired to appointment. They included holders of the highest public offices: every Lord Chancellor and Lord Keeper was a JP – except Francis Bacon. Half of the Members of Parliament were JPs. In all there were no fewer than 15,000 appointed in the eighty or so years between 1558 and 1640.[125]

JPs were the only organs of central government of which most people would be aware. The law-abiding would meet them only if they were unlucky enough to be victims of crime or needed as witnesses; and those who required a licence to trade would call on them to perform one of their many administrative functions. JPs did most of their work, administrative and even judicial, sitting either on their own or in petty sessions of two. Only a minority of more serious matters were referred to quarter sessions and assizes. From 1363 to 1972, JPs met at least once every quarter to try certain indictable offences and appeals from petty sessions.[126] Writing a manual for JPs in 1619, William Lambarde expressed his preference for a JP to 'occupy himself in pacifying the suits and controversies that do arise amongst his neighbours; yea, rather I wish him to be a compounder as a commissioner of the peace'.[127]

Urien Leigh, a Cheshire JP, will have to stand as an example of how one approached his task:[128]

> There had been a quarrel in his district between two of his acquaintances whom he bound over to appear at quarter sessions.... However, 'afterwards myself with other gentlemen that wished well to both parties did pacify the parties and

124. There are a number of general studies of this period and some of particular jurisdictions. Norma Landau *Justices of the Peace 1679–1760* provides background but little on mediation and arbitration. Her attempts to extrapolate from limited statistics are not always convincing, e.g. 197, that rural women settled their own differences and urban women did not; and she declares, 193–194, against all the evidence, that 'mediation produced no legal document'. JH Gleason *The Justices of the Peace* [Gleason] gives many helpful lists and much information on individual JPs but little on arbitration. Some of his conclusions are disproved by Morgan et al *Nat Bacon* VI 6 December 1609, e.g. he omits arbitration from 'the whole activity of JPs' 104, and states: 'there cannot have been many weeks in which even a diligent JP devoted to his labours more than one day'.
125. Gleason 2, 4, 119; 120 John Donne was a JP for Kent in 1621. Gleason Appendix B 145–163 gives annotated lists of Norfolk JPs for 1562, 1584, 1608, 1626 and 1636.
126. It has been feasible to exploit only a small and easily accessible sample of the records of quarter sessions: EH Bates-Harbin ed *Somerset Quarter Sessions Records 1625–1639* and *Somerset Quarter Sessions Records 1646–1660* [Bates-Harbin *Somerset QS*]. There are references in Cockburn *Western*, e.g. 9, 11.
127. William Lambarde *Eirenarcha* 10.
128. TC Curtis 'Quarter Sessions' 135–154 [Curtis].

made them friends, and thereupon released them'.... On occasion, therefore, the authorities could regard a case as having been resolved to the greater good of the commonwealth.

TC Curtis, who focussed his study on Cheshire, found plenty of evidence of arbitration, indeed of a system, though:[129] 'One of the problems of using quarter sessions as a principal source is that, virtually by definition, only failed attempts to arbitrate come to notice. Even so, there is sufficient evidence'.

Craig Muldrew provides two further examples. The Cheshire JP Sir Richard Grosvenor advised his colleagues to do their best to reconcile those who appeared before them, 'too apt to fall into contentions', rather than deal with them judicially as magistrates.[130] And from Essex:

Paul Bowes of Great Bromley in Essex claimed that when his father was a JP he prevailed with his neighbours 'by Councells, perswations and his owne example to live peaceably, forgive injuries and compose differences whereby he became signalized for a great peace maker and doth enjoy the blessed fruites thereof'.

In a speech delivered on 29 November 1610, Ellesmere LC addressed the JPs on the need for them to help to staunch the flood of litigation going to the higher courts:[131]

I have noted one thing, that your ancestors though they had no authority, were so painful and careful as soon as they heard of any differences or suits between any of their neighbours, that they would interpose themselves and mediate an end, by which the expense of time and much money saved, and the courts at Westminster nothing near so filled and pestered with causes as they now are.

For as long as there have been JPs, up to the present day, they have been able to enforce their authority by a process known as binding over. On satisfying themselves of the validity of anyone's complaint that another person represented a threat to the peace, or merely was likely to behave sufficiently badly, they could order that other to keep the peace, or to be of good behaviour. There was no need for evidence of any criminal act. The order, which was neither a conviction nor a punishment, required a person to make a promise, called a recognisance, to pay a sum of money if

129. Curtis 153.
130. Craig Muldrew 'The Culture of Reconciliation' 930 fn61 citing Cheshire Record Office Grosvenor MS 2/20 fo53; Richard Cust and PG Lake 'Sir Richard Grosvenor' 40: 'In Grosvenor we are confronted with a personification of the clichés of the period' and 41 and fn4: 'he was a senior JP and therefore called upon to arbitrate their disputes'; East Suffolk RO, Paul Bowes Diary of Great Bromley 1659–1683 (typescript) HA93/10/4 8. The riches of the Grosvenor archive demand the attention of a scholar able to spend the weeks with them they deserve.
131. LA Knafla *Law and Politics* 108 citing Hastings Mss IV 229.

they did not behave for a fixed period. The promise was supported by an oath and sureties. The power to bind the parties over was a handy tool for magistrates trying to mediate.[132]

In the early 17th century, many of the hundreds of JPs remaining from Elizabeth I's reign were disaffected, lazy or otherwise engaged, so the central government delegated responsibility for making the system work to the more active and efficient. One of them was Nathaniel Bacon (1547–1622), son of Sir Nicholas Bacon, Lord Keeper, and older half-brother of Francis. Among his voluminous surviving papers, which provide the resources on which Chapter 11 is based, is a letter from the Privy Council dated 6 December 1609 and endorsed: '1609 direction from the lords to select some Justices for peculiar services'.[133] It began by stressing 'how great a portion of power and government is left to your care... in the execution of the laws... in the commission of the peace... and proclamations, letters and commissions' but:

> Although there be many in the Commission of the Peace in that county of great integrity and discretion... yet we find... the rule seldom faileth... that those duties which concern all men are neglected of every man, we think it high time.... To move you with these our letters to make it one of your first consultations at your next meeting to select by mutual consent among yourselves some three or four or more of your number... to whose peculiar care you may at the beginning of every year commend the execution and despatch of such directions as you received.... That the ship of this commonwealth which hath so judicial and so royal a master to steer it may be carefully sailed by those that have the charge under him of all sorts.

So that singled out Nathaniel Bacon as one of those responsible for seeing that the Council's instructions were implemented. One of its major concerns was to control and reduce the number of petitions to it; and one way was by sending them to be mediated and arbitrated. His papers provide evidence of his work as arbitrator.[134]

A matter which had already been before the justices might be referred to arbitration. After the 'Great Sessions at Chester' had tried the case of Welshman against Coddington on 4 May 1655, it was agreed by the parties 'and the Earl of Shrewsbury and the agents of the City of Chester that the dispute should be referred to the ordering of Thomas Mainwaring and Thomas Croxton, arbitrators, and of Thomas Brereton, umpire'.[135]

---

132. Steve Hindle 'The Keeping of the Public Peace' 223–232. There may well be much more to be discovered by someone able to search the Grosvenor mss which Hindle cites 228ff, Chester RO MS 2/2, 2/19, 2/22 fols 49 and 53, 2/52 fol 2v–3.
133. Morgan et al *Nat Bacon VI* 6 December 1609.
134. Morgan et al *Nat Bacon IV* LXIV 2000.
135. Cheshire ZA/B/2/108.

10. MASTERS OF REQUESTS

The lucky survival of a manuscript now in the British Library is evidence
of perhaps the busiest of royal offices.[136] From 12 May 1603 until June
1616 it records the work of the Masters of Requests, both in dealing with
petitions themselves and referring them to arbitrators. Hundreds of such
referrals are recorded, few with any detail. Many manage land disputes,
particularly arising from enclosures. The Masters made use of many
different arbitrators, including the Law Officers, Francis Bacon once and
Edward Coke many times, as discussed in Chapter 12. They adopted the
formula the Privy Council used, instructing those they commissioned
'to order or certify' and for the process of mediation: 'for toleration... a
charitable composition'.

They were busy. Dawson has attempted various counts, for example
416 referrals in the first year alone. Many ask the arbitrators to supervise
a composition with creditors:[137] 'of 416 cases of all types referred to
arbitrators, 67 involved arbitrations with creditors'. For 1612–1614, of 282
references to arbitrators, 129 were for compositions with creditors.

11. REFERRALS FROM OTHER COURTS

It was common for one court to refer a matter to another.

Courts Leet and Baron   The Lambeth Palace Library, among the
Shrewsbury papers, holds a letter from Anthony Dyot to the Earl of
Shrewsbury, dated 9 January 1608, asking him as steward of the honour
of Tutbury to order an action relating to land held in copyhold to be heard
in the Court Baron rather than in Chancery, as both parties were poor and
Dyot's attempts to arbitrate had failed.[138] On 8 October 1640 Sir Richard
Wilbraham and John Crewe, arbitrators in a dispute between Cotton and
Cudworth, ordered Cudworth 'to yield his appearance at the Court Leet
of the manor of Newhall and to submit to the customs and orders of that
court', and also to reform his encroachment.[139]

Borough Courts   A document dated 13 March 1603 removed a cause
relating to an arbitration from the town court of Clitheroe to the Chancery
Court of the County Palatine of Lancaster and an action in the Rye Court,
between some Romney men and some of Rye, was referred to a single
arbitrator, whose award is preserved in the Kent archives.[140]

136. B Mus Lansdowne ms [Lansdowne] 266/1; Dawson *I* 419, Dawson *II* 632.
137. Dawson *II* 631 fn128.
138. MS.702.
139. Cheshire CR72/AppendixA/2.
140. NR/JZ/6.

12. CONCLUSIONS

James I's Council regularly repeated that the ordinary course was litigation.[141] Sometimes it would refuse its help, sending the matter for trial elsewhere; for example, in a dispute it thought better resolved by the ecclesiastical authorities, to the Archbishop of Canterbury and his High Commission.[142] Or it would accept a report from its referees disposing of the immediate dispute and send the successful petitioner's other grievances 'for his remedy in the course of law'.[143] By 1627 and Volume XLII of the *APC*, there are fewer references to mediation and arbitration, and thereafter most were to members of the Council, judges or law officers. One reference asked the Lord Keeper to take back into the Court of Chancery the suit of Margaret Massy, 'an aged poor widow', whose claim had been heard there by the previous Lord Keeper.[144] 'In regard of her years and great poverty', he was asked to 'give a speedy end consonant to equity and justice', but presumably as Chancery judge, not arbitrator.

Yet the primary sources show that, from beginning to end of the 17th century, every arm of the Government was making regular, if not routine, use of alternative methods of dispute resolution. Though it became commonplace to declare that government policy favoured the use of the courts, there is no sign of a diminution of references in practice.

The Privy Council was much maligned by Edward Coke, who had his own reasons. Some historians have accepted his ideology. Dicey could say: 'James's whole reign was a series of encroachments which were checked, and acts of tyranny, even more useless than oppressive', and 'The most conspicuous acts of Charles's Council are too notorious to need more than a passing allusion', which saved him the bother of looking at the evidence, which is not all one way, as the many examples in the following chapters show.

The Long Parliament met in November 1640 and soon it had not only abolished the Court of Star Chamber but stripped the Council of almost all its jurisdiction. That government arbitration scheme was no more. But that was by no means the end of public arbitration. The courts of the Commonwealth had no less positive opinions of the qualities of arbitrators:[145]

> Why, certainly the courts according to their discretion must be umpire, the judges being indifferent arbitrators between the commonwealth and the subject;

141. *APC* 34.264.
142. *APC* 34.267.
143. *APC* 46.348.
144. *APC* 42.110.
145. *Anonymous v Chillender* (1657) Hardres 97; 145 ER 399.

and being intrusted with the declaratory power of the law *secundum bonam & sanam discretionem* [according to good and fair discretion].

The chapters which follow show that there were many other ways in which later governments made use of arbitration. If there were no other evidence, the City of London's cooperation with Charles II after the Great Fire of London, in which Robert Hooke played such an important part (Chapter 15) would be enough.

PART TWO

SUBSTANCE

5 LAND

> I being desirous not only of quietness between ourselves… but also between our posterities afterwards, and that suits (that commonly are mothers of unkindness) might stay, desired you (as likewise my cousin Paston did) to inform yourselves of the true state of the matter in variance; and by your good mediation to end the same…. wherein as you shall do a charitable and friendly work, so shall you make us much both beholden to you for your pains and indifferency herein. And so I commit you to the blessed protection of the Almighty.
>
> Letter from Sir Edward Coke to Nathaniel Bacon
> and Sir Miles Corbett (1604)[1]

> But a freehold is not arbitrable.
>
> William Sheppard *Abridgment* (1656)[2]

1. INTRODUCTION

The 17th-century legal authorities would have us believe that serious crimes, particularly public order offences, were not arbitrable; similarly some kinds of matrimonial dispute. They may reflect ecclesiastical law and an unrefined grasp of later Roman law. The evidence is against them. The most important misunderstanding relates to land disputes. It has been allowed to lead astray scholars who have believed what some judges said: that title to land was the preserve of the Common Law courts. Those who had differences over the ownership of land knew better. If they were aware of those authorities, and no doubt their legal counsel were, they ignored them and looked to arbitration – or in Edward Coke's own case mediation – whatever the title, freehold, copyhold or leasehold. The award or settlement ordered the parties to execute the conveyances necessary to establish ownership according to the directions of the arbitrators or the settlement. Those indentures established a Common Law title with as good, and in some cases better, protection than a judgment or a transfer with livery of seisin, as the surviving documents relied on in this chapter will show.[3]

1. Morgan et al edd *Papers of Nathaniel Bacon* [Morgan *Nat Bacon*] *V* 128–129 1 September 1604 in a dispute between Coke and Edward Paston over the ownership of freehold land in Flitcham.
2. William Sheppard *Grand Abridgment* [Sheppard *Abridgment*] under Arbitrement and Arbitrators.
3. The riches of the National Archives prohibit any attempt to cite them all but examples

Moreover, arbitration allowed flexibility. The courts could rarely do more than find simply for the plaintiff or defendant. Arbitrators could arrange for swaps, and for money payments or even marriages to make up the difference. And they could leave the parties reconciled, at least publicly, by mediating a settlement, with a right of way granted for the cost of a stile.

A good example is the award, preserved in fine detail in the Shropshire Archives, in a dispute over the freehold title of just half an acre of Welsh land, 'in a field called Tir Myngoch in Llanvechan'.[4] There were, however, 'divers other variances like to accrue', so the parties submitted all to Robert ap David Lloyd and Evan ap Robert ap Mores, gentlemen. They ordered money payments, the right to use a footpath avoiding damage to growing corn, an exchange of the half acre for another piece of land, plus 'so much of the lands adjoining thereto as shall make the parcel in variance of the like value as the piece given in exchange'. The necessary indentures would be executed, with bonds taken to observe their covenants. While they were allocating title, arbitrators could deal with the paying-off of any mortgages.[5]

Sir Henry Spelman MP, antiquary, member of the New England council and treasurer of the Guiana Company, was High Sheriff of Norfolk when he submitted his dispute over land to Sir Nathaniel Bacon (half-brother of Francis), Sir Miles Corbett (later executed as a regicide) and Owen Shepherd, general receiver to Henry Howard, Earl of Northampton, and executed the necessary conveyances to carry out the award.[6]

Mediation was sometimes expressly stated to have been the means whereby disputes over the title to land were settled.[7] In 1622 successful mediations were recorded in three land disputes. In the first, the mediators were Sir Edward Verney, who was close to Charles I and killed at the battle of Edgehill, and Sir Oliver Cromwell, the Lord Protector's Royalist uncle; in the second Egerton LC and three others; and in the third Sir John Lenthal and Mr Crippes, where the subject matter included an advowson and tithes.[8] Sir William Tate is recorded as having successfully mediated

---

are: Nat Arch WARD 2/54A/184/13 and 15 (1604); WARD 2/59/221/15; C 2JasI/
B24/9; E 134/7JasI/Mich5; C 7/585/55; E 134/3and4WandM/Hil18 (measurement);
E 134/10Chas1/East18 (title to capital messuage); E 134Jas1/Hil10; C 6/387/64; E
134/21Jas1/Mich13; C 6/385/35; C 6/413/43; E 134/34Chas2/East22 (waste); and
many awards in C147. There are relevant documents to be found in unlikely places,
e.g. the records kept by the Ministry of Agriculture, Fisheries and Food Nat Arch MAF
Division 1.
4. Shropshire 3890/2/3/8–9.
5. Sheffield OD/845.
6. Norfolk How 123 341x5.
7. Nat Arch SP 46/64/folio100 (1617 two mediators 'rectory and lands adjacent'); Shropshire
1514/288 (1630 swaps, agreement to share costs, Sir Andrew Corbett mediator).
8. Nat Arch E 134/20 JasI/East15.

an agreement 'for the ending of all suits' between Lord Harrowden and Godfrey Chybnale and his wife Elizabeth about their adjoining properties in Orlingbury.[9] It required detailed redistribution of land, chief rents, and commons of pasture, and the agreement of a third party in possession of a sheepwalk. A dispute over the title to land in Wales, 'depending in law', was 'composed by the mediation of friends'.[10]

Women were parties, often acting on their own, as the widow Elizabeth Ward did in 1678 in the dispute over the title to the manor of Overlands in Ash and the rectory of Yalding.[11] Widows and married women were parties in the 1630s and 1640s to bonds and awards preserved in the Cornwall Record Office, where the subject matter was land.[12] The victory which Lady Anne Clifford eventually won over her uncle Cumberland, and indeed James I, described in Chapter 16, should be more than enough evidence to dispel the popular assumption that married women could not hold land in their own right.

Private Arbitration   Many private arbitrations were of land disputes.[13] Some were for land of modest value. William Harris and Ralph Grubb, customary tenants of the manor of Shenley Bury, 'in consideration of 12d paid to them by John Fletcher of London, barber', had entered into a bond 'to stand to and perform the award and arbitration' of John Bristoe and Joseph Bryan concerning 'the moiety of Bell's Croft and Haynefields'. Fletcher entered into a reciprocal bond on the same terms. They were to perform what the award ordered before the lord of the manor.[14]

In January 1608 four Dorset worthies arbitrated a dispute between Hugh Chichester and Christopher Bramble over the ownership of Turner's Puddle farm, which they awarded to Bramble.[15] A year later Christopher Bramble and John Bramble reached a settlement whereby they agreed to pay Matthew Chubb £50 and release Hugh Chichester from the bonds by

9. Northants YO 564 (1614).
10. Shropshire 3890/2/15 (1607).
11. C 6/298/154.
12. Cornwall RD/1251; CN/1134; CN/1135; AR/3/161; AR/3/163PP/654; R/4482.
13. Cumbria PR 105/26 (four arbitrators, common rights); Cumbria D ING 1 (two arbitrators, hedge and watercourse); Cumbria PR 122/391 (four arbitrators, graving the Moss); Cumbria D AY 1/305 (after lawsuit); Derby D3580/T22 (four arbitrators, umpire Rt Hon William Cavendish, rentcharge); Derby D239 M/T 1737 (three arbitrators, rentcharge); Derby D5336/1/38/1 and D156 M/E 1/12; Glos D2071/L7; Lancs RCHY 2/3/3 (one lay arbitrator); Lancs DDHK 3/8/7 (two arbitrators); Lancs QSB/1/209, QSB/1/248/12, QSB/1/272/13, DDX 369/16; Leics 26D53/48 (exchange of plots); Norfolk MC 92/21, 536x8; Notts DD/SR/10.75 (four lay arbitrators); Shropshire 11/339 (two lay arbitrators), 445/215 (one lay daysman, with bond to execute conveyances); York Archae DD99/B2/79.
14. Nat Arch E 134/10ChasI/East 18 (Durham).
15. Nat Arch WARD 2/59/221/17, 15 and 24.

which he was bound to Chubb; Chichester would pay the Brambles out of rents from the farm. There were other matters in dispute and they would have to go to arbitration. In October the Brambles entered into a bond to Chichester for £500 to follow the arbitration 'over Turner's Puddle'.

Sir Robert Cholmondley and his brother petitioned the Earl of Derby to appoint Sir George Calverley and Sir Richard Grosvenor to arbitrate their disputes over land in Chorley in 1613. They delegated to a surveyor, Randulph Wylson, the task of measuring the land, which he found to be of 25 acres, according to the large customary Cheshire acre of '8 yards in length and breadth to every rood or perch'.[16]

Though the number of arbitrators was usually even, two or four, title to land could be the subject of an award by a single arbitrator.[17] The parties chose their own arbitrators, but they might by agreement leave the appointment to another, as Robert Miller and Thomas Dyke did in Kent in 1607.[18] They asked John Cheeseman, and he appointed Simon Payne and Thomas Maye 'to decide what the land lacked in enclosures, dykes, gates and rails'. They fixed their value at 25s.

An award was often taken as the root of title. Deeds in the Norfolk Record Office are evidence enough.[19] In 1606 the title deeds of Combersplace in Norwich were inspected. Ownership rested on an award made in 1459.[20] An 'inquisition' of 1627 confirmed the title of the inhabitants of Swaffham by reference to an award of 1551.[21] A dispute about the ownership of Corpus Christi Hall, Norwich, was first submitted to Edmund Beaupre and John Blennerhasset in 1563 and a little later a new submission added the Duke of Norfolk. The college had become private property on the dissolution of the monasteries. The mayor and others examined all the deeds in 1606 and accepted the authority of the award.[22] In 1658 an award of the Bishop of Winchester in 1377 was extracted from vestry minutes as evidence of the composition of a dispute about the chapel of Chiltington.[23]

All kinds of rights in and obligations arising from land ownership were submitted to private arbitrators, even the liability to pay lays (rates) and assessments.[24]

---

16. Cheshire DCH/A/579; DCH/B/87.
17. Glos D2153/147 (land in Wales); and occasionally three Norfolk PD 295/41 and 42.
18. Kent DYK/579.
19. Norfolk PD 295/40.
20. Norfolk KL/C50/224.
21. Norfolk PD 52/284-291.
22. Norfolk KL/C50/101–104.
23. East Sussex PAR293/12/1.
24. West Yorks WYL639/310.

The Privy Council   The Council regularly commissioned arbitrators to dispose of disputes relating to land,[25] freehold, copyhold or leasehold, with no signs that they felt in any way inhibited by a concern that such questions of title were the preserve of the Common Law courts. It usually appointed judges or law officers, for example Altham B to determine 'according to equity and justice';[26] or Fulke Greville, Chancellor of the Exchequer, when Greenwich Hospital complained that Sir Nicholas Stoddard would not pay his rent but treated the land as if he owned it, rooting up hedges and levelling ditches.[27] But sometimes non-lawyers only were commissioned, especially if they were of high rank, or JPs.[28] Sir Richard Bowle was in dispute with Florence McCarthy over a great part of McCarthy's estate.[29] In November 1613 they submitted to the arbitration of the Earl of Thomond and Sir Richard Vavasour, Marshal. But McCarthy was a prisoner in the Tower, so the Council wrote to the Lieutenant of the Tower, instructing him to allow McCarthy freedom to attend the hearing, 'which we think very reasonable and meet... as occasion shall require for the hearing... under such custody as he may be sure from escape'. In a different dispute, the Council had made an order against Captain Henry Skipwith in favour of McCarthy. When Lord Courcy claimed the land in 1615, the Council wrote to the Lord Deputy:[30] 'It was never our intention that the title of Lord Courcy (being a third person and not then spoken of) should receive any prejudice by the compounding a difference between Florence McCarthy and Henry Skipwith'. And it ordered that Lord Courcy 'be maintained in quiet possession of such lands as he now holdeth... until by due process of law he shall be evicted'. The Council had to return to this dispute in 1616, sending it to the Earl of Thomond and the Chief Justice of Munster for an order 'agreeable to equity and good conscience'.[31]

Staveley 'mortgaged the greater part of his estate' to Greenwood.[32] Greenwood took possession 'cunningly and fraudulently... contrary to all right or equity'. Staveley showed that he had 'fallen into great want and poverty, unable to right himself by the ordinary course of law'. The Council required the Earl of Bath and four others, or any three, to 'mediate

25. *APC* 33.264. These examples exhibit various stages, from mediation to drafting the necessary conveyances or perfecting a faulty assurance, 33.275. Though records are missing from 1604 to 1612, there is evidence in local archives of the continuing work of the Council, e.g. Norfolk KL/C4/17, an award of Attorney General Hobart and the Recorder of Newcastle upon Tyne in 1609.
26. *APC* 33.136.
27. *APC* 36.182.
28. *APC* 34.521 (for a very poor man, not able to prosecute his right); *APC* 39.311 (for a petitioner in prison, three laymen, a civil lawyer and a serjeant, 'or any 3 or 2').
29. *APC* 33.264.
30. *APC* 33.573.
31. *APC* 34.513.
32. *APC* 34.58.

some final end between them', or to report so that the Council could make an order 'as shall best agree with justice and equity, for the relief of the distressed state of this poor man'. So even a legal mortgage was not safe from the Council's determination to relieve a 'distressed' mortgagor.

Chancery   The Court of Chancery recognised an award as a good root of title:[33]

> An ancient Award performed by one Party. The Plaintiff had land descended to him from his brother who had bought it; but the Defendant brought an Ejectment upon a lease for 500 Years, and an Award being made concerning the title under which the Plaintiff claimed... a perpetual Injunction against the Lease.

Nothing could be plainer than the report in *Scott v Wray*:[34]

> Award defective made good. The parties in this cause did refer the differences between them to Arbitrators, who made their Award, by which Award it was awarded that Roger Whittey should have such and such Lands; and it was provided that if any doubts arose, the Arbitrators to interpret and expound the same. That the Defendant Wray found a defect in the Award, *viz* that Roger Whittey should have the lands, and not Roger Whittey and his heirs... so it was insisted that Roger had but an estate for life; whereupon three of the four Arbitrators only living, by a writing under their hands and seals, did declare they meant the lands in fee simple... considering that the Award was long since made and executed on both parts; and his Lordship calling to his assistance Crook and Crawley JJ, two reverend judges, took their opinion touching the point in question for decreeing the said Award and explanation thereupon; the Arbitrament being voluntary and without the direction of this Court, but executed on both sides, are all clear of opinion, that... Scott and his heirs do enjoy the lands against the defendants, and all claiming, &c. according to the Award and explanation as aforesaid.

The Assizes   The assize judges regularly commissioned JPs and occasionally others to arbitrate disputes involving possession or ownership of interests in land,[35] sometimes directly telling them to decide who had title to it.[36] JPs could be asked to value an ecclesiastical living.[37] Other arbitrations concerned leases[38] and mortgages.[39] The assize judge could direct the parties to obtain a commission from Chancery to arbitrators to resolve ownership.[40] Meanwhile, the commissioned JPs could be told

33. *Poole v Pipe* (1666) Rep Ch 20; 21 ER 716.
34. (1635) Rep Ch 84; 21 ER 514.
35. JS Cockburn *Western Circuit* [Cockburn *Western*] 3.
36. Cockburn *Western* 43; or to mediate an end to a title dispute 104.
37. Cockburn *Western* 235
38. Cockburn *Western* 73, 115, 162, 193, 775, 779, 902.
39. Cockburn *Western* 775.
40. Cockburn *Western* 87, 88, 89.

to make appropriate arrangement for harvesting corn and sequestering profits.[41] In Somerset in 1630 they had to deal with crafty Dame Sylvester, who, during a short period between marriages, had secretly conveyed property to trustees to her own use: 'This the court thinks incredible'.[42] Conversely, two JPs might be instructed to deal with a vexatious litigant, and, if they found his suits baseless, to bind him over, but 'not to meddle with any title to land or any issue arising therefrom'.[43]

For anyone who finds it hard to credit that title to land could be effectively and finally determined by arbitration, the following excerpt from the books of the Devon Assizes of 16 March 1640 may be sufficient evidence of how it was done. These are the very words of the transcript of Crawley J's order, made with the consent of the parties:[44]

> The devision of the houses and lands in Chulmley towne made by Christofer Baitson, clarke, and Roger Skynner shalbe profitted by the advise of Mr Hutchings, counsellor att lawe, and that a *dedimus potestatem* shalbe sued out to take the fyne from Francis Chant and his wife, Phillipp Lane and his wife, and Dorothy Wade for the better profitting thereof according to the said counsells direccion; and, if Jane Lane, widowe, will not acknowledge this fyne, with the rest accordinge to the said direccions, then the said Francis Chant shall covenant with the said Dorothy Wade or with such as she shall intrust in her conveyance that she, the said Dorothie, and her heyres shall quietly enjoy her parte of the said landes and tenements by the foresaid devision allotted her.... And that the said Francis Chant shall pay all the charges of suinge out the said fyne ... and half the charges of the writtings... and that the said Dorothy shall goe before Sir Lewes Pollard or some other knight upon request to make her acknowledgment with the rest of the cognisors of the said fyne.

Quarter Sessions   Quarter Sessions' records contain many examples of land disputes, including quarrels between neighbours. In Devon, at the midsummer Quarter Sessions in 1627, Richard Starr, gent, was ordered to make his peace with Mrs Walrond and live peaceably as her neighbour, on pain of being bound over to good behaviour.[45]

2. DOWER, SETTLEMENTS, JOINTURES AND PORTIONS

Landowners of any substance were rarely happy for their land on their death to descend according to the rules on intestacy. There were problems, too, on devising land by will. In any case, families of bride and groom

41. Cockburn *Western* 87, 88, 89; 221 (where both parties were single women).
42. Cockburn *Western* 89.
43. Cockburn *Western* 670.
44. Cockburn *Western* 851; tellingly, an earlier order setting up the arbitration does not reveal that the dispute is about land 622.
45. Cockburn *Western* 402, citing Devon RO QS Min Bk 6 (1625–1633) 105; further proceedings at the assizes found in Starr's favour, 436, 437.

on marriage were not shy of expressing their expectations about the land which each spouse might bring to their future together and the value they could take out.

Dower   The Common Law provided that husband and wife could not make a valid conveyance of land to the other, but continued the age-old practice of dower, by which the husband, at their wedding, would make his wife a gift of up to one-third of his land, called dower, which would pass to her on his death if she survived him and last for her life. The husband might describe the particular land or leave it until his death for the third to be specified.

Settlements[46]   By the end of the reign of Elizabeth I it was well established that land could be conveyed to trustees, who would have legal ownership but were bound to exercise it for the benefit not of themselves but others whom the grantor would specify. The trustees were at first called in Law French the feoffees to uses, and the beneficiaries the cestuys que use. The use, which became the trust, gave greater flexibility to those who were settling land on the new couple, and conveyancers were ingenious in devising schemes and the documents to protect them. A primary purpose was the equivalent of what is now called 'tax avoidance', getting round the traditional levies which were payable to the Crown on a change of legal ownership.

Jointures   Instead of dower, the families would settle specified land on the couple jointly for life, so that, if the wife survived the husband, she would have the benefit of the land – though not the legal ownership – for the rest of her life. That was her jointure.

Portions   Such a settlement of land on trustees allowed the settlor to make provision for descendants other than the heir by creating portions. It would give the benefit of the land to the trustees – but not the legal ownership – to hold for the husband for life, then for the eldest son of the marriage for life and so on – an estate in tail – but provide sums of money to the other children, to be paid at the age of 21 to males, to females on marriage. Those were their portions.

3.   COMMONS AND ENCLOSURES[47]

Disputes about commons and enclosures were routinely submitted to arbitrations arranged by the parties themselves.[48] The arbitrators would

---

46. The clearest exposition of the strict settlement is in JH Baker *An Introduction to English Legal History*.
47. DE Mingay *Enclosure and the Small Farmer* is a neat introduction to the economic history.
48. Lancs DDCL 762; Norfolk EVL 184, 454x7.

have to visit the land and give directions, for example where the dividing ditches should be dug.[49] The advantages which local arbitrators had over any central court were substantial. They knew the terrain. The detail of rabbit warrens and gorse bushes would send a judge to sleep but were of the liveliest interest to neighbours. As the applicable law was customary, it would have to be established by oral testimony. Local arbitrators could judge better not so much the veracity of the witnesses as their likely reliability as repositories of local law.[50] And the parties and witnesses would not have so far to travel. None of the proceedings would be confidential and the whole community might know every detail.

An account of how enclosures worked has been preserved in the Lincolnshire Archives, in an agreement between Sir Daniel Deligne and all the freeholders, landholders and inhabitants of Harlaxton.[51] Deligne was a recently knighted Flemish refugee who had just bought the manor, a prime example of a 'socially embedded' local economy on the cusp of capitalist development. The agreement declares:

> The fields of Harlaxton lie in common and undivided and every one's particular and known grounds lie in several parcels intermingled with the lands of others. The parties are determined to make a division and improvement of the lands and yet to avoid all depopulation and decay of farms; and sufficiently to provide for the poor inhabitants and landholders. All agree that in any case they cannot agree among themselves between this and St Thomas Day next concerning their intended division and enclosure of their lands, meadow and pasture in the fields of Harlaxton, then [six named arbitrators] or any four or three of them, together with one or more surveyors, shall be plotters and arbitrators, and shall have full authority to survey and measure every one's several lands, arable, meadow and pasture, and all grounds lying in the common fields of Harlaxton not enclosed and kept in severalty, and to set up and appoint what parts of the fields every one shall have his proportionable part of grounds allotted to him to have and to hold to him and his heirs for ever in severalty and enclosed, in lieu of all his lands and grounds lying in common and unenclosed and not kept in severalty.
>
> Every freeholder, landholder and inhabitant to have a part allotted to him equal in quantity and quality to that he held before the division and enclosure, to be held in severalty.
>
> The parties all agree to be content with such plots as shall be allotted to them by the plotters and arbitrators, and to make such conveyance, exchange and assurance thereof each to other as by counsel agreed upon by the parties shall be advised. Every one to fence, enclose and maintain for ever such fences, hedges and enclosures of the grounds and plots allotted to them as by the plotters and arbitrators shall be appointed.

49. Nat Arch E 134/21JasI/Mich 13.
50. Adam Fox 'Custom' 102–103.
51. Lincoln 1 PG/2/1/2/1.

It is agreed that the commons, wastes and waste grounds shall be used in common as heretofore, and that every one of the parties shall abate out of the stint and number of cattle which they now keep on the commonable grounds such a number and proportion as the plotters and arbitrators shall determine, in order to provide sufficient common for the cottagers and the poor.

It is agreed that, if any question or controversy arises among the parties concerning the division and enclosure, it shall be determined by the plotters and arbitrators or by counsel nominated by the parties.

It is agreed that all chief rents and services shall remain as heretofore, and that Mr Barksdale, now parson of Harlaxton, and his successors shall have their parsonage and rectory made fully as good and better than it is now.

Then follow 23 signatures, mostly by a mark, one of a woman, Alice Exton. The date is 7 December 1623. The agreement bears an endorsement: 'Memorandum of agreement that, if any controversy shall arise which the plotters and arbitrators cannot compose, the parties shall submit themselves to the final order of Sir Thomas Ellis and Anthony Thorold'. The arbitrators moved quite quickly. They declared a partial order on 14 October 1624, which may have concluded the process.[52]

In 1610 the Council commissioned arbitrators whose award settled the dispute between Sir Francis Cheyney and Robert Seabrooke 'relating to common of pasture' in Tring, which had been before the Exchequer Court.[53] In 1615, two men of lower status, Peter Middleton and William Paver, as mediators brought about an agreement between two great Yorkshire landowners, Sir Thomas Fairfax (son of 'Black Tom', later the leader of the New Model Army), and William Vavasour, in their dispute about an encroachment on an enclosure, and 'the cutting of turves and pulling of ling'.[54]

Twice assize judges had ordered William Combe of Stratford-on-Avon to desist from his attempts to enclose and turn into pasture 400 acres, to which claims had been made for charitable uses.[55] In 1619 Coke CJKB and Sir Julius Caesar MR were told to 'order such a course as is agreeable to justice', inviting the assize judges to assist them if they wished.

4. COPYHOLD

Copyhold tenure was the relationship between lord and villein by which the villein possessed land according to customary law in exchange for work done on the land. By the 17th century villein status had long gone and all

---

52. Lincoln 1 PG/2/1/2/2.
53. Nat Arch E 178/238.
54. West Yorks WYL639/70.
55. *APC* 36.370; and in Garsington *APC* 38.491, to view, mediate and if necessary make an arbitrament.

copyhold tenants were free, but their hold on the land was no stronger than their ability to prove the necessary customary law.

Cartwright was lord of two Nottinghamshire manors, North Wheatley and Gringley, which he had bought from the city of Nottingham. His tenants petitioned the Council, which referred them to the Chancellor of the Exchequer.[56] They complained that he had sold off their lands, though they had been tenants 'time out of mind at a certain rent'. Cartwright offered a settlement: the copyholders of North Wheatley could buy their properties at the price he paid the city for them, with detailed provisions for the resolution of the other claims. If the petitioners were not satisfied, 'all the tenants should be left to take their course in the Exchequer Chamber'.

5. WAY, WATER AND OTHER RIGHTS

Rights of way still rouse heated strife and no doubt did so then.[57] Two arbitrators were called on to resolve such a dispute and ordered John Pigott to allow the tenants of Sir William Brereton a right of way across his land.[58] Even a disputed gate was not too trivial for the attention of two arbitrators.[59] Four were considered appropriate to order one party to build a stile on the footpath between the other's house and the church.[60] And two arbitrators might provide, just to be sure, that a party and his servants exercising the right of way were not to leave any gates open.[61]

Rights to water and responsibility for containing it were ready sources of conflict.[62] Sir Roger Owen, a Shropshire landowner – Shrewsbury School, Christ Church, Oxford, Lincoln's Inn, JP, Member of the Council of the Marches, MP – disposed of a dispute over two weirs.[63] On 18 October 1612 the parties submitted to his arbitration, the award to be delivered before 1 November. But it took him only a day. On 19 October he awarded that, first, the parties shall be 'lovers and friends'. By 1 November they must execute mutual releases of all prior actions.

Disputes over other property rights – marshes and warrens in Kent and peat and water in East Anglia – were sent to private arbitration.[64] Then, as now, the right to lop trees was contentious and considered suitable for arbitration.[65]

56. *APC* 45.29.
57. York Archae MD335/1/1/14/3 (four arbitrators, four separate rights of way).
58. Cheshire D 181/52.
59. Cheshire DLE/74.
60. Met ACC/0566/013.
61. Notts 157 DD/P/104/4.
62. Cumbria Ca/3/5/3/48 and Ca/2/129.
63. Shropshire 2028/1/2/91.
64. Kent U274/L5; NR/CPI/24/4; U442/L3/1.
65. Shakes DR5/1269.

6.   BOUNDARIES AND BUILDING DISPUTES[66]

Arbitration was much the most efficient way of dealing with boundary disputes.[67] So thought the Mayor of Doncaster and Thomas Mounteney, in their dispute over boundaries on the moors between Doncaster and Wheatley. They appointed Sir John Jackson, of the Inner Temple, MP, JP and Richard Hutton, serjeant at law, then Recorder of Doncaster, later a judge of the Common Pleas who defied the King over ship money.[68]

Henry Robinson in Austin Friars   Henry Robinson was a London builder.[69] He wanted to erect a new stone building alongside the Dutch congregation's church in Austin Friars in the City. The Dutch church complained to the Council that he was intending to break down a party wall, which would have threatened their structure. The first relevant entry is a letter of 7 June 1613:[70]

> To Henry Robinson of London, merchant.
>
> We greet you well; forasmuch as we have this day received information that in your proceeding to pull down the Dutch Steeple and the rest of the buildings purchased from the Marquis of Winchester, you do so far endanger the rest of the church, by breaking down a partition wall with the buttresses and arches which support the church, which we are informed you threaten to do, as, if it be permitted, a great part of the body of the church must needs fall down, by the opinion and report of divers honest persons that have viewed and certified the same; we are therefore in His Majesty's name to will and command you to forbear the demolishing and pulling down of any part of that building... until you have made your appearance here to make answer... whereof fail you not as you will answer the contrary at your peril.

Two days later the Council wrote to Robinson again, an 'open placard', telling him not to erect any building near to the church of St Peter the Poor, next door to the Dutch Church, at his 'utmost peril'.[71] St Peter the Poor is close to where the monastery of the Augustinians once was, in Old Broad Street in the City, and belonged to St Paul's Cathedral. The Dutch Church is still there, also off Old Broad Street in Austin Friars. The parishioners of St Peter the Poor had complained that Robinson's new building would affect their light. So, the following week on 13 June, Robinson appeared before the Council:[72]

66. MC McGaw 'Travels in Alsatia' 131–187.
67. WYL500/815; York Archae DD154/98 (fence).
68. Sheffield CWM/43.
69. *APC* 33.82 13 June 1613.
70. *APC* 33.67.
71. *APC* 33.71.
72. *APC* 33.82-84.

Henry Robinson made answer to both those complaints and said that it is true he had a difference with them both, which he always was and is now content to refer to arbitrament; that concerning the Dutch Church to four men Commoners, indifferently chosen, to set down what is fit to be allowed to Robinson by the Dutch congregation for suffering either the arches, buttresses or walls, which now are his, to stand for the upholding of their church, being a great hindrance to his own building, as he affirmeth; and, for the complaint of the parishioners of St Peter's the Poor, he offers that for the wall in question he is content to refer himself likewise to two counsellors-at-law indifferently chosen by himself and the parish, and for the lights said to be stopped, to make satisfaction in lights... as by Sir Thomas Smyth and Sir Thomas Lowe, having regard to the benefit of the increase of light happening by the pulling down of the high wall, shall be thought fit.

Lastly, whereas on 12 June an offer was made by the parish of St Peter's the Poor to Robinson in their vestry, to buy off him the ground and stone which he purchased of the Lord Marquis [of Winchester], with the intent to enlarge their church and churchyard, he is also well content to accept thereof, and to sell the same unto them, provided that, before the last day of July next, he be paid so much money as the purchase cost him of the Lord Marquis, together with all his charges and losses in and about the same, and before the 28 of this month receive assurance thereof; provided also that the parish employ the same to that purpose pretended and not to private uses. And in testimony of his own readiness to further them in so good an action, he hath promised freely to give them £20, otherwise he desireth he may be no longer stayed, but suffered to proceed in his building as he hath begun.

All which offers being held reasonable, their Lordships approve the same, and order that Henry Robinson perform every part thereof accordingly with expedition, requiring both the Dutch congregation and the Parish of St Peter the Poor to take notice thereof, and to proceed with the like diligence, so far as this order concern them, or either of them, and in the meantime he is permitted to go forward with his building as before without interruption.

That Sir Thomas Smyth (?1558–1625) was, like his father, a successful haberdasher. He became an MP, Governor of the East India Company and special ambassador to the Czar, sailing to Russia in 1603 and acting for the Muscovy Company. He financed many trade initiatives and voyages of discovery, and in 1609 obtained the charter for the Virginia Company. James I trusted his advice. Sir Thomas Lowe MP (d1623) was also a London haberdasher, Lord Mayor in 1604 and a governor of the Levant Company. On 8 July the Council took a further step.[73] It issued a warrant for its messenger to go to Austin Friars and apprehend Robinson, to stop him building, and to bring him before it. On 19 July Robinson appeared and was 'enjoined to attend until by order he be dismissed'.[74] Sitting on

73. *APC* 33.124.
74. *APC* 33.141.

Sunday afternoon, 25 July, the Council received this report from Smyth and Lowe:[75]

> ... we find that the building already begun of one of the houses will darken one window and obscure one other light, for the preservation of which lights the parishioners have offered to Robinson to pull down that building which is offensive and to new erect the same in some other convenient place on the said ground, where Robinson shall appoint, at their own costs and charges, or to give Robinson so much money for the pulling down thereof, and the new erecting of the like, as workmen shall judge it will cost, by our appointment and consents, so as no buildings may hereafter be set there. Their offer (in our opinions) seems very reasonable and fit for all parties.

The Council 'thought meet to confirm the certificate as an order of the Board', and Robinson

> ... willingly submitted himself, with this proviso, that if any doubt or ambiguity fall out in the execution of this order, Sir Thomas Smyth and Sir Thomas Lowe shall explain their meaning therein, as shall be reasonable and indifferent between the parties.

The entries so far show that the Council did not condone delay. It was concerned that this matter be terminated not just on paper but by the completion of the buildings. Two months later the record shows:[76]

> Whereas, upon a new complaint of the Dutch congregation, Henry Robinson of London, merchant, was this day convented before the Lords to answer in the building which he is about to erect near to the Dutch Church, and that, upon hearing, it was found that he had not done anything contrary to a former order but was and always is ready humbly to submit himself thereto; forasmuch as by the order it was provided and appointed that certain indifferent persons should be nominated by either party, to set down what recompense and consideration the Dutch congregation should allow to Robinson for suffering certain arches and buttresses of their church to stand undemolished, which otherwise they did pretend might prove dangerous to their church, and yet was part of Robinson's purchase from the Marquis of Winchester and appertained to him as it then appeared; since the said indifferent persons are not yet agreed upon, and nothing hath yet been done in accomplishment of the order, their Lordships now nominate the arbitrators... Sir Thomas Smyth, Sir Lionel Cranfield [later Lord High Treasurer] and Mr Baldwyn, Controller of His Majesty's Works, to view the building, buttresses and arches, and rate some such reasonable recompense to be given by the Dutch congregation to Robinson, as they in their judgments and discretion shall think meet, as also to compound, if they can, any other difference that may arise betwixt them concerning the said building, or, if they cannot, to certify their opinions to this Board.

75. *APC* 33.153.
76. *APC* 33.186 18 August 1613.

It is uncommon for the primary sources ever to tell the story of an arbitration complete from start to finish. Other evidence suggests that this dispute was settled, perhaps according to Robinson's apparently reasonable offers, by transferring the land to St Peter the Poor, because it shows that that church was enlarged in 1615. But, by a stroke of luck, the Council's own records reveal incontrovertible evidence:

> Whereas Henry Robinson [and three other citizens of London] were called before the Board for refusing to pay such money as they had been compounded for with His Majesty's Commissioners for new buildings... their lordships... order that if any... neglect to make payment by the 27th of this month, being Tuesday next, the Attorney General do proceed against them in the High Court of Star Chamber.

Lincoln's Inn Fields   The Council had received petitions from both sides of a dispute about new buildings in Lincoln's Inn Fields.[77] Lincoln's Inn wanted to stop Sir Charles Cornwallis from building; he wanted to get on. In 1614 it ordered Sir Edward Phelips MR, Sir Francis Bacon, then Attorney General, Sir Henry Yelverton, Solicitor General, and Sir Henry Montague, serjeant-at-law, or any three (the Master of the Rolls to be one):

> Calling both parties before them, they shall take view and consideration of the place, where this building is intended, also of the allegations and reasons of either party, and thereupon either to mediate some reasonable and indifferent end between them, or otherwise to certify... that such further order may be taken as shall be meet.

Cornwallis had been ambassador to Spain, treasurer of Prince Henry's household and in this year a member of the commission to investigate troubles in Ireland, finding the Irish 'naked barbarians' who must be made to follow English ways and speak English. In that year 1614 he was imprisoned in the Tower, allegedly suspected of plotting but probably for no more than ranting against Papists and Scots, which displeased the King. After a cringing apology he was released under house arrest in June 1615 to see to his many lawsuits, then completely freed in October. But the Council records reveal no more of his ambitions to build in Lincoln's Inn Fields.

The Council's instruction 'to take view' is an early example of the technical use of 'view'. Robert Hooke, the inventor and surveyor, took hundreds of such views after the Great Fire, in his capacity of City Surveyor, some resulting in arbitrations, described in Chapter 15.

7. PUBLIC WORKS

Lighthouses   A dispute had arisen between 'divers coastmen' and Sir William Erskine and John Meldrum about who should pay for the erection

77. *APC* 33.350.

of a new lighthouse at Wintertonness and who should receive the charges. The Council, 'not willing that a work so necessary should be stayed upon uncertainties', referred it to a committee of Lord Zouche, the Treasurer, the Comptroller and the Master of the Rolls, 'to mediate a friendly composition by mutual consent of all parties', so that the 'light be maintained as it ought to be for the safety of His Majesty's subjects and others that shall pass along that coast'.[78]

Drains and Sewers   The Council took responsibility for the construction and maintenance of drains and sewers, if public interests were threatened, as they were when differences arose among the Commissioners for Sewers in the Isle of Ely and 'parts of Holland' about a drain called Clowes Cross and the outfalls of the Rivers Neene and Welland.[79] It commissioned the Lord High Treasurer, the Earl of Exeter and the Bishop of Ely, 'to whom the state of those countries is best known in respect of their Lordships' great estates and authorities there', to take over from the full Board the hearing of disputes about whether the Clowes Cross drain was necessary and who should pay for it, and for diking and sluicing, which they were to mediate: 'to accommodate and settle, if they may, by mutual consent of the parties'.

Cornelius Vermuyden (1595–1677) was a Dutch engineer who specialised in land reclamation. Charles I commissioned him to drain his land at Hatfield Chase in Lincolnshire, intending to enclose a third of the common land, leaving only one-third for those who had customary rights of common, in particular turbary, to take peat for fuel. Vermuyden managed to get rid of the water but, as the land dried, the peat shrank. This led to litigation, even rioting. Vermuyden was knighted in 1629 and became an English citizen in 1633. On 23 June 1630 the Council took these differences into consideration and:[80]

> conceiving that the truth of the allegations, especially the points of fact, might best be discerned and discovered by enquiry and information taken upon the place, having thought fit to refer the same to [Viscount Wentworth and either Lord Darcy or Hutton J]... to call Vermuyden and such of the inhabitants as they think fit, and on due consideration of the true intent of the former agreements and the complaints on either side, to accommodate and settle the differences between them (if they can) so that his Majesty and this Board be no further troubled, or otherwise make certificate in writing of the true state of the differences and in whom the default rests for their non-performance, and in particular how far and in what degree the work (complained of to be imperfect) is proceeded in or perfected.

78. *APC* 36.341.
79. *APC* 35.125.
80. *APC* 46.25.

The King, if not a party, certainly had an interest in the outcome of 'these differences'. He, at least, was content that an attempt should be made to resolve them by mediators who would know the facts better from an 'enquiry and inspection taken upon the place'.

Two days later Vermuyden faced another petition, from the inhabitants of Misterton, Nottinghamshire, who complained of the great damage his drainage schemes had done by drowning their meadows, pastures and arable lands.[81] But:

> The points principally in question concerning the perfecting of the work by him undertaken as the securing of the grounds of the Petitioners from future damage or drowning by reason of stopping up of rivers... and conceiving that the truth... especially the points of fact, might best be discerned and discovered by enquiry and information taken upon the place, have referred the same to any two of the Earls of Clare and Newcastle and Sir Gervis Clifton... to call Vermuyden and the inhabitants and... to accommodate and settle the differences between them (if they can), so that his Majesty [etc as above].

The Vermuyden story in the *APC* ends with a full report on 25 May 1631.[82] The tenants and inhabitants of five villages in the West Riding:

> set forth that, on a reference from his Majesty to the Board and another from the Board to Lord Wentworth [Lord President of the Council of the North], Lord Darcy and Hutton J, by virtue whereof they met at Hatfield and there took a view of the works made by Sir Cornelius Vermuyden, as the said lords, with his Majesty's Attorney General and Sir Thomas Fanshaw, Surveyor General, did 16 August last meet a second time in the said place, and again viewed the works; and then and there they by their order or award (with the privity of Hutton J) composed all the differences betwixt the parties to both their contents, and with the consent of Sir Cornelius and his partners, and the Attorney and Surveyor, which order or award was thought fit by their Lordships to be decreed by the Court of Exchequer Chamber and before the Lord President and Council at York, with the consent of Sir Cornelius and his partners.... Whereas the petitioners have exhibited their bill of complaint in the Court of Exchequer Chamber against Sir Cornelius and his partners, desiring the order to be decreed, whereunto Sir Cornelius only hath answered, and refused to give way for the passing of a decree, the Board, having called both parties before them, seen the order, heard at large the arguments and having well weighed and considered the importance of this business, did unanimously order that Sir Cornelius and his partners shall suffer the order to be decreed in the Exchequer Chamber and before the Lord President and Council at York.... The bill now depending in the Exchequer Chamber may be answered by Sir Cornelius and his partners before the fifth day of next term, so that a decree may be had by consent without any further suit or delay. And, if Sir Cornelius shall make default in performance of

81. *APC* 46.29.
82. *APC* 46.348.

their Lordships' order, the Board will take notice thereof and direct such further course as shall be fit.

There is so much evidence there, not only of the Council's purposes but of its methods of achieving them.

8. CONCLUSIONS

The sources cited in this chapter have shown that mediation and arbitration were not 'alternative' but primary means of resolving land disputes of all kinds and values, great and small, readily and routinely availed of by all kinds of parties, including women. Though awards were sometimes looked to as roots of title, they did not usually make such a claim. They were more efficient than that. They ordered and supervised the execution of the deeds which would carry out the provisions of the award or settlement, tailor-made to produce a fair result for the parties and to maintain order to the satisfaction of the community.

Arbitration of land disputes was not only the preferred choice of many parties, it was Government policy. Later chapters will include much more, and more detailed, evidence.

6 FAMILY AND INHERITANCE

And a man's foes shall be they of his own household.

Matthew 10.36

In the overwhelming majority of cases the solution adopted by the Council was not the entry of a final or conditional order addressed to one of the litigants, but the arrangement of arbitration. The advantages of this solution were obvious.

JP Dawson[1]

1. INTRODUCTION

There was a general revulsion against litigation within a family. Many surviving documents relate to privately arranged mediations and arbitrations to avoid it, often relating to disputed inheritance.[2] Among the riches of the Cumbria Archive Centre is an award of 20 June 1642:

> To set John Aglionby and Thomas Brougham being uncle and nephew at peace, unity and concord, and to prevent suits and unkindnesses between them concerning their various claims to the house and land at Skelton Scales and to the tithes of Plimpton... and to the lands at Wharton and Kirkby Thure.

The King himself might take steps to end discord between husband and wife and, if that attempt failed, to see that she was given adequate maintenance. On 12 October 1612 George Abbott, Archbishop of Canterbury, wrote to Ellesmere LC:[3]

> By reference from the King's Majesty... having heard the cause between Thomas Staples, gentleman, and Dorothy his wife, I do find there is little hope of reconciliation between them; or that they are likely to live quietly together as becometh man and wife... from the forwardness and unsociable disposition of him.

The money then in Chancery, which represented the balance of Dorothy's portion, should be paid out to Thomas, but he must pay her £70 a year maintenance:

1. JP Dawson 'The Privy Council and Private Law' [Dawson *I* and *II*] 423.
2. Cumbria D AT 1/301; Cumbria PR 122/428; Cumbria D NT/37; and Lancs DDX 1094/8 (two brothers and two sisters over legacies); Nat Arch E214/1001; E134/35Chas2/Mich34.
3. *Acta Cancellariae* CXXIV 173–174.

and that sufficient bond with sureties should be entered into for the true and quiet payment thereof. And this so to remain, till it shall appear to the Lord Chancellor, or to the Lord Archbishop of Canterbury, and the Bishops of London and Gloucester, or any two of them, that there is like to be such concord and agreement between Thomas and Dorothy as that peaceably and contentedly they may live together. All which I humbly refer to the judgment and determination of that honourable Court of Chancery.

James I did all he could to persuade Lady Anne Clifford to accept his arbitration of her dispute with her male relatives but she stoutly withstood him, as described in Chapter 16.

The Council, too, made its displeasure plain.[4] It regularly appointed arbitrators to resolve family differences, particularly relating to land, inheritance, and wife's maintenance, sometimes making it clear that they were to mediate a settlement if they could. There are too many examples for all to be quoted extensively but the problems are so complex, the means of resolution so refined, and the outcome so reasonable in one that it may stand for all.[5]

The Solicitor General, Sir Thomas Coventry, reported first that he had 'composed a difference between Sir Michael Greene and Edmund Gregory... touching a farm called Ives Ground, Oxford, of the yearly value of £90'. Gregory owned it but it 'was left to the disposition of' Greene. The settlement provided that the farm should be conveyed from Gregory to trustees nominated by Lady Greene, 'for the payment of her alimony of £60 per annum', with the profits of the farm until the alimony arrears had been paid off. The Council ordered Sir Michael Greene, his father Sir William, Edmund Gregory and 'such others as are now interested in the farm' to convey Ives Ground and its rents and profits to the trust for Lady Greene's life. She should also have the rents due on Lady Day. Sir Michael had a portion worth £4,000 from Lady Greene. He had taken £800 and the manor house at Milton with £140, part of her jointure. He had settled lands worth £1,000 per annum on their marriage but then mortgaged them so that their son William, now 13 years old, was likely to be unprovided for. So Lady Greene was awarded the rest of the profits of the farm for her maintenance for life, being £30 or thereabouts, in addition to her alimony of £60, 'as recompense for the £800, of which she had been defeated'. Arrears of alimony of about £75 would be satisfied out of her husband's other lands. After her death the farm would go to their son William in tail male. Just to be sure, Gregory and all others whom it might concern were forbidden to cut wood on the farm. If he failed to comply with any of this,

---

4. Not always; as in *APC* 33.156, submission of the Musgrave brothers' dispute to the arbitration of the Bishop of Carlisle and Sir Wilfrid Lawson.
5. *APC* 36.391; Dawson *I* 423.

'their Lordships think fit that their favour extended to Sir Michael shall be withdrawn'.

Assize judges were concerned to have family disputes resolved, to ensure that husbands paid their wives proper maintenance, and to see that trustees discharged their duties to family beneficiaries.[6] The stages of one such dispute at the Devon Assizes tell a sorry story, first on 16 July 1638:[7]

> John Bussacott, junior, whose wife Sarepta brought him a good marriage portion, has, after much cruel usage, deserted her and their three small children, leaving them without any means of support.... His father promised to allow Sarepta a house, garden, grazing land and certain household goods which belonged to her before the marriage, a promise which he repeats in open court.

The court ordered that Sarepta should enjoy them during Bussacott senior's lifetime, unless they reached a different agreement. Two JPs were ordered to see that the children were maintained by their grandfather. The husband is not heard of again. A year later, on 5 August 1639, Sarepta's counsel told the court that Bussacott senior had failed to perform the order. He was told to pay £10 'to such friends as Sarepta shall appoint, so that her husband will not be able to dispose of it, and to remain in prison until he pays the money and enters into a bond'. At the following session, on 16 March 1640, a further order was needed, to make Bussacott senior pay the £10 to John Garland, to the use of Sarepta and her children, and allow her 'the hall house with the garden and cowlease'. Sarepta was to keep the children and Bussacott was to stay in gaol. But Sarepta refused to keep the children, so a further order was necessary, cutting the payment to £5, with the other £5, the house and pasture to go to grandfather Bussacott. Sarepta had until the next assizes to make a decision. That order was confirmed again on 22 March 1641. Nobody comes out well from this sad tale. From the order made on 6 September 1641 it is clear that one of the children must have died. The court had been told that the surviving two children were likely to starve in their grandfather's care, which would be understandable if he had been in prison:

> The churchwardens and overseers of East Down are therefore ordered to visit John's house and to take measures for the appropriate relief and upkeep of the children. If John refuses to give the children adequate care, the parish officers are to inform the two nearest JPs, so that they may take legal action.

There the records end, but they have given enough detail to show the care with which assize judges attended to family problems. They must

---

6. e.g. JS Cockburn *Western Circuit* [Cockburn *Western*] 257, 324, 352, 408, 696, 721, 759, 1012, 1038.
7. Cockburn *Western* 679, 788, 56, 857, 926, 995.

have failed, because as late as 1658 there were proceedings in Chancery between Sarepta and a John Bussacott over East Down.[8]

Mediated settlements often provided for annuities, and disputes arose when they were unpaid.[9]

2. INHERITANCE

Administration   Arbitrators were often privately appointed to manage the administration of estates. In 1629 four arbitrators dealt with the estate of Hugh Newenden. His Common Law heirs were his nephews and nieces. The award provided that they should have his lands in the Isle of Sheppey and the Isle of Oxney and £160, giving up their rights to the rest of his real and personal property. His gavelkind heirs were to have his land in Headcorn, with 'Marler's money due upon mortgage of his lands in Smarden'.

The Council might take a hand. Captain Parker had died, leaving debts including arrears of wages.[10] His sister, Oliva Reyly, took out letters of administration. William Mabbs claimed he should handle the matter. The army paymasters recommended that the arrears 'with more safety and justice' be paid to Oliva, and Mabbs should be left 'for his remedy to the ordinary course of law'.

Sometimes the problems were considered more appropriate for what was expressly called mediation. Robert Gray died intestate, with neither wife nor children. In 1643 the claimants, who presumably did not want their differing claims to become disputes, petitioned the House of Lords to refer the administration of his estate 'to some persons to mediate'.[11]

Wills   The Church was supposed to have exclusive jurisdiction over disputes about wills, except insofar as they involved real property. Coke tried to extend the grasp of the Common Law courts by insisting that, if a will dealt with real property at all, a Common Law court could dispose of the chattels as well.[12] It is hardly surprising then that a well advised executor would strive to have any differences resolved by private arbitration.

Colonel John Booth and the Reverend Charles Herle mediated a settlement between the Bold family claimants under their father's will and a previous settlement.[13]

8. Index of Chancery Proceedings Bridge Division 1613–1714 PRO p175 no53; and Nat Arch C5/400/53.
9. York Archae MD335/3/5/6.
10. *APC* 46.55.
11. Parl Arch HL/PO/JO/10/1/152.
12. *The Case of Powlett, Marquess of Winchester* (1599) 3 Co Rep 303; LA Knafla *Law and Politics* 142.
13. Greater Manchester E7/16/2/1 (1645).

Among collections of documents preserved as evidence of the due administration of an estate, and therefore of later ownership of land, there are not only wills and probates but arbitration documents. A bundle in the Gloucester Archives contains documents from 1623 to 1840, including the petition to Charles I of William Ducie for the appointment of arbitrators to resolve a difference with his brother Sir Richard. They were joint executors of the estate of their mother, Lady Elizabeth Ducie.[14]

John Herault's brother disputed a will purported to be made by John in favour of strangers in whose house he had died. The Council commissioned four Isle of Man worthies:[15]

> we require you, or any three of you, together with four or three indifferent men, nominated by the contrary party, by such means as you and they shall think fit, and are usual for the finding out of the truth, end all differences or else by consent of the parties choose an umpire, to whose judgment and resolution both parties may submit themselves; or certify... that thereupon such further course shall be taken as shall be fit.

The parties might arrange for a private arbitration, as John and William Turner did in Canterbury in 1637, to resolve differences about their father's will.[16]

The National Archives preserve evidence of the settlement of disputes arising in the work of the executors, including the expert settlement of accounts. Women were often parties, sometimes as executrix.[17]

3. FATHER AND SON

Members of a family often preferred to have their differences mediated privately. In 1605, Thomas Wrenford mediated the settlement of a dispute of father George Mathew and his son George with his other son Goodier.[18] It allocated many separate properties, freehold, leasehold and copyhold, creating life interests and annuities.

The Common Law was clear. Owners of land in fee simple had by the 17th century the right to transfer it during their lifetime to whomever they liked. Their heirs had no legal right to object. That was not socially acceptable, however, nor how the Council saw it. On 20 May 1623 it wrote to Denham B enclosing a copy of the petition of John Rodes complaining that his father, Sir John Rodes, a wealthy landowner in Derbyshire and

---

14. Glos D340a/F1.
15. *APC* 44.183.
16. Kent U442/L3/2.
17. Nat Arch E 134/22Jas1/Mic22; C 6/413/81; E 134/8Jas1/Hil3; E 134/1657/Mich24; E 134/30 and 31Chas2/Hil6.
18. Warwick CR2440/1/2–5.

Yorkshire and High Sheriff of Derbyshire, had unconscionably disinherited him:[19]

> In a case of such tenderness as between father and son, being desirous that matters be ended rather by composing than compelling... we require you to... deal as effectually as you can by way of persuasion and mediation and to reconcile and accommodate all differences between them.

On 20 June it wrote again to Denham B.[20] He had reported that, on the marriage of the petitioner's mother to his father, his grandfather Rodes J, his father Sir John Rodes and two uncles had granted land to the value of £300 per annum to his mother for life, remainder to the heirs male of the marriage. The petitioner was her only son. But after her death her husband had a son by a second wife and sold his dead wife's land. Denham B had suggested he make appropriate provision for the petitioner out of his other land, but he said he had transferred it all to a son of his second marriage. The Council was not satisfied:

> We, finding these courses very rigid from a father to a son without any just exception, and very full of compassion in regard of the petitioner and of the evil example in regard of others... on your next circuit for the County of York... treat with Sir John Rodes to allow a reasonable maintenance to his son. And whereas you make mention of an allegation made by the father that he had trusted his son as a servant with a stock of cattle and corn and profits of lands, and managing of ironworks and coalmines to a great value and to have departed without giving an account, which by his son's answer we conceive to be rather a pretence and colourable exception, examine the truth and take such course as you shall think fit.

On 13 October the Board ordered Sir John to pay the petitioner £30 per annum for life, backdated to 20 February 1623.[21] Still he refused to pay and had to be brought before the Council to explain his contempt.[22] It accepted his humble apology and submission to perform its order, spared him imprisonment, but required him to provide sufficient security before he left town. And it knew how to turn the screw. Sir John had married for a third time:

> We further think fit and order that the eldest son of Sir John by his third wife (upon whom a great estate hath been settled by the father to the great disinheritance of the complainant) shall the first day of next term attend the Board to show cause why he should not join in conveyance with his father to settle some further competent means by way of inheritance on the complainant, unless he, together

19. *APC* 38.499.
20. *APC* 39.22.
21. *APC* 39.338.
22. *APC* 39.480.

with his father, in the meantime condescend to do the same, or that all parties shall otherwise make agreement without further trouble to this Board.

The matter was finally settled by an order of the Board sitting in the Star Chamber on 13 May 1625:[23]

> Francis Rodes this day presenting himself alleged that the estate to descend upon him on the death of his father was settled by a solemn conveyance upon intermarriage of his father and mother; and he had divers brothers and sisters, whose portions were to be raised out of that estate, and that he himself was a married man with five or six children to provide for, but that he was contented nevertheless at the motion and request of their Lordships (which they took very well at his hands) to condescend to join with his father for the settling of the £30 per annum upon John Rodes for the term of his natural life, but not his assigns, to prevent him from passing it away and falling into like want again. Their Lordships have thereupon thought fit and ordered that the same be settled by conveyance to be indifferently drawn and agreed on by counsel learned on both sides; and that John Rodes be satisfied therewith without further trouble to Francis Rodes or this Board.

No doubt a satisfactory conclusion. But how many hours of the Government's time had been spent on a family row, caused no doubt by a surfeit of marriages of one man and his many competing offspring?

Edward Rich's petition explained to the Council that William Rich, his great-grandfather who had brought him up, had settled all his lands on him and given the deeds to the trustees in a chest. His father, mother and younger brother had broken open the chest and burned the deeds. That brother had confessed to it on his deathbed. The parents were now trying to settle the lands on a younger brother. Edward was 'most unwilling to begin a suit against his father'. The Council declared itself 'ready and willing by all good ways and means to prevent unnatural suits betwixt father and son'.[24] It appointed Viscount Wentworth and the royalist MP Sir Francis Wortley 'to mediate and by pressing persuasions and all good means to settle and end the difference, if it may be', or certify 'that such further order and direction may be given as shall be fit and requisite'.

The Council might make use of the assize judges as mediators, as it did of those in Southampton in 1631.[25] It asked them to mediate and settle, agreeable to justice and equity, Henry Ludlow's claim that his father had disinherited him and stopped his allowance, resulting in his imprisonment for debt. They ordered the father to make regular payments and, when he failed, the Council 'for his unnatural dealings and contempts', threatened him with imprisonment in the Fleet.

23. *APC* 40.51.
24. *APC* 46.144.
25. *APC* 46.33; 46.404.

A father might protest about the way his son was treating him. Humphrey Sydenham had years before transferred his estate to his eldest son, John, reserving only small annuities for his younger sons.[26] He accused John of harsh and unkind proceedings, in refusing to provide adequately for him and the other sons. The Council asked four Somerset JPs (or any three):

> for avoiding such unnatural suits in law, to the scandal of their family and to avoid future disagreements, to use your best endeavours for accommodating and reconciling the present differences and putting the business into a due and settled course for the future.

Such disputes might lead to a petition to the House of Lords, which would routinely refer them to arbitration.[27]

At the Somerset Assizes in August 1646 Rolle J referred a dispute between Richard Browne and his sons John and Richard 'to the two nearest JPs to Ilchester' to settle.[28]

4. MOTHER AND SON

The Lord President of York had his own court there but the Council sent to him and his Council as arbitrators the petition of a widow, Beatrice Stanton, against her son, Robert Brown Lilley.[29] She complained that he had dispossessed her of house and lands inherited from her father, 'an offence much more heinous considering the relationship between the parties, mother and son'. The Lord President and Council were required to settle the possession and recover the rents and any damages for selling the mother's property, with 'restitution or satisfaction according to justice and equity'.

Jane, the widow of Andrew Harris, complained that her son Peter was trying to get payment of a debt which his kinsman Peter Beauvoir had already paid.[30] Peter Harris had already got a judgment in King's Bench, 'because the acts and receipts produced by Beauvoir were found insufficient by the strict rules of the common law'. Jane had stood surety for Beauvoir, and so would have to pay, to her ruin, if the judgment were to be satisfied. The Council delegated to three of its members to call the petitioner and defendant or their attorneys, 'to mediate and make a full end between them, if they can', or to 'certify what they think fit to be done in course of equity for the final determining of the controversy'. Meanwhile all suits were stayed.

---

26. *APC* 38.368.
27. JS Hart *Justice Upon Petition* [Hart] 62 fn144.
28. Cockburn *Western* 1038.
29. *APC* 36.95.
30. *APC* 39.343.

At the Dorset Assizes in 1642, a dispute between Elizabeth Williams, widow, and her son John was referred with their consent to two JPs.

5. SIBLINGS

It has never been unusual for brothers to quarrel over family property.[31] Instructions to the Bailiff of Guernsey, 20 March 1614, show the Council's continuing preference for arbitration.[32] Thomas Marchant complained of wrongs done to him by his younger brother:

> between whom and him many differences, as well for matters of account as for titles of land, have long depended, notwithstanding the several sentences there given by the ordinary course of law, and the approbation of those sentences here, signified by our letters. And forasmuch as the desire of the petitioner is chiefly that some good course may be prescribed for the ending of all differences, suits and accounts, between his brother and him, having found by experience that the course of law (besides the length and charge thereof) do rather increase than extinguish their enmity: these shall be to will and require you, having called both parties before you, to cause them to make choice of three indifferent persons on each side, who may summarily arbitrate and end all their suits and questions; wherein, if those six so chosen shall not agree, yourself then, taking notice of the difference or difficulty, may become an umpire and make some final end between them, having first taken good security from them both, to stand to your awards.

That one example almost says it all: the Council did not like family discord; litigation was no answer; title to land could be arbitrated; equal numbers of arbitrators from each side; an umpire of higher status if required; take bonds from both sides first. As will be explained in Chapter 10, where each side chose arbitrators, the result would be an even number. That need not apply when they were appointed by some Government authority. The next year an almost identical reference was made to the Earls of Pembroke and Worcester, umpire the Archbishop of Canterbury, of a dispute between the Earl of Lincoln and his brother, Sir Henry Fynes.[33]

Sir John Stradling, 1st baronet (1563–1637), is remembered as a poet and scholar. He was Sheriff of Glamorgan in 1608 and 1620 and in 1625–1626 MP for Glamorgan. In June 1626 the Council appointed him sole arbitrator in a dispute between Mary Williams, 'a poor woman', spinster, and her brother John Williams over land:[34] 'forasmuch as the matter cannot but be known unto you and the woman (as it seemeth) hath been long troubled with suits'. It instructed Stradling: 'upon examination of such proofs as can

31. Nat Arch C 6/394/25.
32. *APC* 33.387.
33. *APC* 34.348.
34. *APC* 41.23.

be produced to end and determine the controversy, if you can, or certify…
that such further course may be taken as shall be fit'. The Council would
be happy to pronounce on the ownership of land, not according to law but
'as shall be fit'.

Of course, the Council's response was even more solicitous if the
petitioners were orphans. It wrote asking the help of four Lincoln JPs (or
any two) on behalf of three orphan (though adult) sisters, whose younger
brother refused to allow them their portions and would not hand over the
deeds they needed to establish their rights:[35]

> We have therefore thought fit in favour of justice and commiseration to
> recommend their case unto you, that you may take some such course to assist
> them towards the recovery of that which is their own from so unnatural a brother
> and to prevent that mischief which these courses of his seem to threaten as in
> equity and conscience you shall see cause.

On 22 June 1613 the Council wrote to the Lord Mayor of London and
Sir Julius Caesar, then Chancellor of the Exchequer, appointing them to
dispose of a petition on behalf of four orphans.[36] Their father had left them
leases and money to be divided between them, appointing another son by
a previous marriage, Thomas Whittie, as executor. Some of the lands lay
within the City, some outside. So:

> We have thought fit to require you to meet together and to call Thomas Whittie
> before you, and such others interested in this cause as you shall think fit, and to
> take order herein for the relief of the poor orphans, so as there may be no further
> occasion of complaint unto this Board.

That was a dispute between step-siblings.

Assize judges sometimes appointed JPs to arbitrate family disputes.
Finch CJCP at the Somerset Assizes in March 1639 referred to three JPs
(or any two) an unspecified dispute between Anne Kittowe and her brother
James.[37]

6.   HUSBAND AND WIFE

Both the Privy Council and the House of Lords heard petitions from wives
for orders in matrimonial disputes; and assize judges were often called
on. The Council would take time in a busy meeting to order a defaulting
husband to pay his wife arrears of maintenance.[38] Even when a maintenance

---

35. *APC* 35.370.
36. *APC* 33.94.
37. Cockburn *Western* 721; other relationships: cousins Derby D258/17/31/15; husband and
     wife against husband's brother and nephew Shropshire 5586/13/15.
38. e.g. *APC* 33.460; 34.204 (on Sunday morning 18 June 1615); *APC* 38.288 ('reasonable
     and just'); *APC* 39.383 (husband 'in the open street had beaten her with his sword').

dispute had been settled amicably by private arbitration, the parties might ask the Council to 'have this agreement to be allowed of and ratified by this Board', as it did the settlement agreed by Sir Henry and Lady Jones.[39]

Lady Hawksworth had left Sir Richard and gone back to her parents, taking their son with her. Hawksworth had started an action against his father-in-law for custody of his son.[40] On 14 December 1628 the Council wrote to the Archbishop of York:

> Because differences of this kind are more proper for a friendly composition than a legal prosecution, and that good and charitable work lieth most fit for your Grace, being their Diocesan, to receive a mediation and agreement by your Grace's hand and interposition... endeavour a reconciliation between them (if it may be) and order the disposition of the son, and in whose custody he is to remain.

Otherwise the Archbishop was to report 'what course is most reasonable and just'. Nearly a year later, on 21 November 1629, the Council wrote to Hawksworth.[41] The Archbishop had reported 'what pains his Grace hath taken, although in vain, in seeking to settle and compose matters in such sort as were to be wished between persons so nearly joined both by divine and human laws', and the Council had approved his opinion. Lady Hawksworth and her parents would bring up the child, to whom Hawksworth would make an allowance of £30 a year. He must drop the action he had commenced against the grandfather. The Archbishop and the Lord President of the Council of the North would see that the order was enforced.

Denham B at the Dorset Assizes in 1634 had to deal with a criminal husband and made use of an arbitrator who was not a JP:[42]

> John Paty, now in custody for attempting to murder his wife, refuses to allow her any maintenance. The court orders, with Paty's consent, that the assessment of her medical expenses and a yearly amount for her maintenance, both payable by her husband, shall be referred to Lewston Fitzjames.

At the Hampshire Assizes on 28 February 1639 Trevor B referred to three mediators (or any two) the petition of Agnes Whitehart against her husband George: 'to mediate a settlement for maintaining Agnes out of her estate'. On 18 July a further order was made by Finch CJCP with the parties' consent:[43]

> He is to allow her £10 arrears of maintenance and £10 for the coming year, payable in instalments.... He is also to enter into a bond of £40 with some friend,

39. *APC* 43.283.
40. *APC* 44.263; 44.334.
41. *APC* 45.185.
42. Cockburn *Western* 324.
43. Cockburn *Western* 696, 759.

in trust for the use of Agnes, to make these payments. If the couple remain unreconciled for a further twelve months, the court will make a further order.

It was not always the wife who had cause for complaint. William Goare complained to the Dorset Assizes in 1635 that his wife Elizabeth had put him 'to great trouble and vexation'.[44] John Finch CJCP asked two JPs:

> to settle the matter and to decide how much Goare shall pay to his wife annually for her maintenance. If Elizabeth fails to perform their order or to accept the agreed sum, Goare may allow her whatever amount he pleases.

In May 1641, Elizabeth Walter petitioned the House of Lords for maintenance, complaining that her husband had driven her out.[45] In June they attempted a reconciliation, instructing her to return and him not to wrong or abuse her, but providing that, if that failed, he was to pay her £60 a year. A week later she told them that when she returned her husband was not there. He had said he was going to sell up and escape to France. The Lords ordered that all Walter's property be sequestered, that land to the value of £60 a year be settled on trustees of Mrs Walter's choosing for her use, and that, should Walter's estate increase in value, the trustees were to have half of the increase. That order was made not by arbitrators but by the House itself, acting more like a court exercising a broad equitable jurisdiction.

7.   MARRIAGE SETTLEMENTS

It often took the efforts of mediators to fix the details of marriage settlements, where the distribution of property was the particular concern of the parents and, indeed, of the more extended family. In 1633 Roger Bradshawe and Robert Hope, mediators, worked out an agreement between the families of Cecily Ince and Peter Winstanley, the spouses.[46] It was made between Peter and Cecily and her brother Thomas. First it expressed the desire of all for amity; then it provided that Thomas should make various payments to Myles Winstanley in trust for Cecily; that Thomas should receive certain payments due to Cecily until he could transfer them to four trustees to hold for Cecily and her children; lastly it provided that any dispute should be decided by the mediators. Then Cecily and Peter entered into a bond of £300 to Thomas to keep the agreements so mediated, which Cecily and Peter both signed and sealed.

By an agreement of 16 November 1638, Sir John Monson and the Earl of Lincoln agreed that Sir John should arrange the wardship and marriage of George Booth, 'if a liking should be taken' between George and either

44. *Cockburn Western* 352.
45. Hart 134, 141 fn121.
46. Wigan D/D An/Bundle 26/102 and Bundle 19/49.

of the Earl's elder daughters.[47] George was then 16. His father George was a baronet and great landowner in Cheshire. His mother was Sir Thomas Egerton's daughter. He did indeed marry Catherine, the Earl's daughter, and became the 1st Lord Delamer. Perhaps there was no need, then, for the settlement's arbitration clause, which provided that the Earl of Kingston was to settle any disputes.

In 1652 Sir Orlando Bridgman, Royalist MP, was Solicitor-General to the Prince of Wales. Later he became CB, CJCP and then Lord Keeper (1667 to 1672) and a member of the New England Company. By then he was known for his part in the trial of the regicides, and also for his skill in devising conveyancing documents, the equivalent of modern tax avoidance schemes. The marriage settlement of Anne Sneyde and Rowland Nichols of 23 January 1652 provided for Anne to have a portion of £1,000 plus a further 1,000 marks.[48] Rowland promised, when these sums had been paid or security given for them, to convey specified property to trustees. But, if only part of the portion were paid, then only part of the property would be transferred, as Sir Orlando Bridgman, 'the indifferently chosen arbitrator, should appoint'.

8. CONCLUSIONS

The sources show that few families and fewer communities in which they lived considered litigation and insistence on Common Law rights to be the appropriate way of managing family disputes. If no private arbitration could be arranged, the Government might help. *APC* provide ample evidence of the Council's determined preference for mediation, for example on 13 June 1631, when the Council sent to a panel of five the complaint of Edmond Yeo that he, his wife and five children were victims of a breach of trust. They were to 'mediate and settle such an end (if you can) most agreeable to equity and good conscience', or certify.[49]

One last example demands inclusion for its comprehensiveness. On 12 June 1621 the Council commissioned Caesar MR and Attorney General Thomas Coventry to mediate the settlement of a family dispute.[50] Sir Thomas Mildmay had been a wastrel. His widow and children, Walter, Thomas and Joan, sought the Council's help. He had mortgaged the last of their lands to William Bradshaw, a Welsh MP (1604–1611) and JP, known more for his litigiousness than his Parliamentary activities.[51] Mildmay sold the land and paid off Bradshaw, handing over to him what was left:

47. Lincoln MON 28/A/3.
48. Shropshire 2028/1/2/131.
49. *APC* 46.17.
50. *APC* 37.398–340.
51. *History of Parliament 1604–1629*.

'content to commit it to Mr Bradshaw, answering interest for the same and securing both principal and interest by such a pawn of land as should be competent'. But Bradshaw included so little of the residue of the land in the mortgage that it did not suffice to secure his obligation to pay the interest. In any case he failed to pay anything: 'whereby Sir Thomas, his wife and children were exposed to great extremity'. Bradshaw's son Edmund had married Mildmay's daughter and had joined with his father in some Exchequer litigation which resulted. It rested on a bond which they had entered into to a Mr Turner in the sum of £3,000 to secure performance of the Bradshaws' mortgage obligations. They had no defence to Turner's claim on the bond but persuaded the Chief Baron to submit the matter to arbitration: 'a juror was drawn and the matter by order of the Court' referred to the then Solicitor General, now the Attorney General Overton:

> After several hearings, by an award in writing, the debt was reduced to £1,486, being much less than on a strict account the same would have amounted to, but that Sir Thomas Mildmay and Mr Turner (by mediation) were drawn to consent thereto, for payment of which with some allowance of interest from that time, Sir Thomas and his family having no other means of livelihood.

Bradshaw was given plenty of time but made only the first payment. Sir Thomas died and his widow and children had nothing but their claim on Mr Turner to live on. Bradshaw's only answer was that he was hard up too. The arbitrator was sympathetic, 'we were inclined to have eased him in lengthening the time and abridging the interest', but there was not enough to go round and, finding that 'the fault lieth altogether on Mr Bradshaw and that he is much better able to bear the burden... there being a good estate of land remaining between him and his son' (who was not a party to the arbitration), Bradshaw must pay the balance of the debt already awarded, £1,400 with interest at 10% from the time of the award, 'whereof £100 in hand for the relief of the poor lady's necessities'. The earlier award had required Bradshaw to get his son join in the mortgage. If he could not persuade him, '*bona fide* doing his best endeavour', then the bond which bound young Bradshaw should be 'presently put in suit against them... at the next Court of Great Sessions... of Pembroke'.

Whereupon their Lordships, in commiseration of the miserable and distressed state of the lady and her children, thought fit to establish 'as much as in them lieth the said report and do order that Mr Bradshaw without delay pay the £100... and before his enlargement enter into the assurance'.

So Bradshaw would be kept in custody until he had done as he was told. His son, though never a party, had better comply too. There was not enough to go round but Bradshaw should be the one to suffer, because it was all his fault for taking unfair advantage of profligate old Mildmay and not doing right by his family. Would any procedure offered by any Government since then have worked as well as the Council did in resolving the Mildmay family's legal and practical problems? Could any have had less regard for the law?

7   COMMERCE

Aid to merchants could be explained through the interests of the Crown in the promotion of trade, and especially through the large influence that economic factors had already acquired in foreign policy. Aid to debtors served in some degree the interests of merchants and the orderly conduct of trade.

JP Dawson[1]

And, (which we wish to be the principal fruits of your labour, as it is the principal end and scope of our reference), that you would so accommodate all differences and questions between them, as they may both depart from you satisfied.

Privy Council commission to eight merchants (1617)[2]

Until he understood the difference between the Law of Merchants and the Common Law of England, he did not a little marvel what should be the cause that in the books of the Common Law there should be found so few cases concerning merchants and ships, but now the reason was apparent, for that the Common Law did leave these cases to be ruled by another law, the Law Merchant, which is a branch of the Law of Nations.

Richard Zouch quoting Sir John Davies (1686)[3]

1.   INTRODUCTION

Plenty of 17th-century records survive to show that, when disputes arose out of business transactions, parties were wont to arrange for their arbitration. Many awards survive in the National Archives, like that of London Alderman George Whitmore, as single arbitrator in 1622.[4] They arose from agencies and partnerships,[5] and the widest imaginable range of commodities, whether jewels or bacon or red wood.[6] Women were often parties, as was Dame Mary Edmonds, who had her accounts settled by arbitration in 1624.[7]

1. JP Dawson 'The Privy Council and Private Law' [Dawson *I* and *II*] 655.
2. Over disputed accounts 13 March 1617 *APC* 35.189.
3. Richard Zouch *The Jurisdiction of the Admiralty* 89 cited by JH Cohen *Commercial Arbitration and the Law* 72. Davies (1569–1626) is better remembered as a poet than a lawyer.
4. Nat Arch E214/1180.
5. Nat Arch E134/18JasI/Trin10 (agency).
6. Nat Arch E178/4137 (1624); E134/5WandM/East30 (1693); E214/1180; Nat Arch E 178/4317.
7. Nat Arch E134/22Jas1/Mich59.

2. TRADE

Foreign Trade   The Government then gave high priority to the encouragement of commerce and the highest to international trade. In 1606 James I concluded a treaty of mutual defence with Henri IV of France.[8] Together they would support the Netherlands against Spain. It provided that in London and certain French cities all controversies between English and French merchants should be referred to the arbitration of a tribunal of two English and two French merchants, called Conservators of Commerce. But Henri IV was assassinated in 1610 and his son, Louis XIII, was then only nine years old. His mother, Marie de Medici, became Queen Regent. She had few good qualities and no interest in commerce. It would seem that the English Government was more assiduous in its support for trade than the French, because on 30 July 1614 the Council wrote to Sir Thomas Edmonds, the Ambassador to the French King:[9]

> It is provided by a late treaty betwixt His Majesty and the French King, in respect of many difficulties that may arise in point of commerce between the subjects of both nations, as also for divers other good considerations mentioned in the 7th article of the Treaty, that there should be named and appointed, by His Majesty and the French King and their ambassadors, merchants of both nations being of good reputation and credit, to be resident in some principal cities and towns of trade in each kingdom, who shall jointly receive and hear and, according to equity and right, compose the complaints and controversies there arising in matters of traffic betwixt the subjects of both nations, to be called Conservators of Commerce... That has not been put into practice as it ought to be, whereby His Majesty's subjects trading into that kingdom find themselves much prejudiced for want of speedy redress, which they might expect if the Conservators were established, and have therefore been humble suitors here to His Majesty and this Board... to appoint Conservators of the nation in the cities of Rouen, Bordeaux and La Rochelle.
>
> For that purpose we recommend to you the persons named at the foot of this letter as meetest for their quality and reputation to undertake that charge, and further pray and require you instantly and effectually to move the King and Queen Regent to name the like of the French nation to join with the English in those places; to whom, French and English named and appointed in every town, His Majesty there is to give joint commissions... and the like is to be done by the King here.... It would have been effected long since but that the French Ambassador, notwithstanding many instances from this Board to appoint Conservators for the City of London, is so full of excuses and delays that nothing is yet performed. Therefore we pray you to procure thence some effectual commandment to him to name some of his own nation to be Conservators here together with the English, to whom His Majesty will give joint commission, and

8. Rymer *Foedera* XVI 644.
9. *APC* 33.523–52.

so shall that Article of the Treaty be performed, which was so carefully and well conceived for the benefit of both nations.

For Rouen	*For Bordeaux*	*For La Rochelle*
Richard Buggon	John Boulton	John Stroude
Roger Gyfford	William Gostling	Edward Welbye

On 16 June 1621 the Council heard the petition of the East India Company 'complaining of the many and insufferable wrongs done unto them by the Dutch nation', in particular by taking their goods and dealing violently with their factors in the East Indies.[10] Such claims should have been submitted to the commission of arbitrators for which the treaty provided. The Council summoned the ambassador, Sir Noel Caron:

> It had been oftentimes promised that commissioners sufficiently authorised should be sent hither by Whitsuntide last past for the accommodation of those differences which, according to a peculiar article of the treaty, were to be determined between the King and the States, when the merchants could not compound them between themselves....
>
> The ambassador... made answer that these complaints were not new to him, so had he often represented them to his superiors, pressing as much as in him lay the coming over of such commissioners as were promised.... By midsummer they should be here with sufficient instructions and authority to give His Majesty full satisfaction.

Charles I shared that concern for trade. The *APC* records, in full and in French, his reply to the concerns of M Joachim, Ambassador of the States General.[11] He was concerned to ensure free trade between France and the Low Countries. He gave licence for the *Renard* and the *St André*, restrained in Bristol and the Isle of Wight loaded with contraband, to be released. If English merchants took the risk of trading to Dunkirk, against the law, Dutch ships should be allowed to take them. 'As for the goods of Fernando Diaz seized at Dover', they belonged to Portuguese subjects of the Dutch, who had the same obligations and privileges as the native Dutch. And:

> As for complaints made in general, which the Admiralty Court has not dealt with at all, to deal with this problem His Majesty will grant a commission to some of his Privy Council and some Doctors of the Civil Law, to whom the offended parties may bring their complaints, without costs or delay.

So another standing arbitration tribunal was set up specifically to deal with disputes involving subjects of the States General.

Domestic Trade   Charles I's Council was similarly concerned with the regulation of domestic trade. In 1629 it commissioned a panel of eight JPs,

10. *APC* 37.397.
11. *APC* 43.326.

two each from Essex, Suffolk, Cambridge and Norfolk (any one from each county to act) to 'accommodate and settle the differences (if you can)' between cloth merchants and the local authorities of Norwich and Norfolk who had 'taken away their goods upon pretence they are falsified';[12] and the next year took particular care to prevent abuses in the dyeing of silk in 1630:[13]

> the merchants trading in raw and thrown silks petitioned showing that in former times the trade of silks in this kingdom consisted almost wholly of thrown silks and other sorts of dyed and wrought silk brought from parts beyond the seas, having first received their full manufacture.

But the trade had doubled in the last twenty years. Silk workers had immigrated. England could now supply those countries from which it used to import.[14] But the dyers were adulterating the colour and weight. 'Many thousands of his Majesty's poorest subjects' were employed. There were factors which 'so much import this kingdom, as well in regard of his Majesty's Customs and the setting of his subjects on work as the maintenance of mariners, ships and navigation'. The adulterations were 'to the great prejudice of the Common Weal and dishonour of the English Nation'. So the Council referred the matter to the Lord Mayor and Aldermen of London, requiring them to call before them the petitioning merchants and 'silkmen, shopkeepers, dyers, workmen of all sorts as they think fit', to find out how to rectify the abuses in dyeing and working of silk. The referees were to report in writing 'for the settling and establishing of this business for the time to come' and the Council would take such further course as in its wisdom it thought expedient.

At the end of September that year, the Council had to deal with a different problem.[15] It wrote to the Lord Mayor and Aldermen:

> It is not unknown to your Lordship and the whole City how careful both his Majesty and ourselves have been to have this notorious abuse in the false dyeing of silk to be reformed.... whereupon a just and legal course hath been taken in the Court of Star Chamber... some of the greatest delinquents were there censured... and divers others shall be proceeded against... yet some persons do assume unto themselves the liberty to give out that this so good a work is already disposed of.... Use the best means you can to find out those who boldly take upon themselves to disperse those false rumours... and cause them to be apprehended and put into safe custody... so the offenders may receive punishment to the example of others, according to their deserts.

There was still much to be done and the King and Council were determined to see it through.

12. *APC* 45.65.
13. *APC* 45.252.
14. *APC* 45.252.
15. *APC* 46.85.

The very next entry records a straightforward commission to six leading London merchants 'finally to end all controversies between' William Bagwell and Thomas, John and Raph Blackhall for soap and other goods.[16] Their 'fraudulent combinations' had drawn Bagwell with his sureties into bonds of great value. Now he was 'disabled to contest with them by tedious and chargeable suits in law'. He had therefore asked the King to set up an arbitration and the King had referred it to 'his Privy Council'. If the referees could not end it, they were to certify the true state of the cause 'that such further course shall be taken agreeable to equity and good conscience'. And indeed they failed.[17] All six of the referees reported on 14 May 1630 that they had tried four times to compose the differences but could not, and so they were returning their certificate. Thomas Blackhall had refused to appear. John and Raph Blackhall did attend but were:

> so refractory and peremptory that they said they neither could nor would show us the particulars how their debts grew from Bagwell to them. Neither would they yield to stand to any award or arbitrament to be made by us, albeit we divers times propounded the same unto them in very friendly manner.

Bagwell had produced affidavits proving the Blackhalls' 'frauds, deceits and misdemeanours' and even cruelty against Bagwell's wife, and that the Blackhalls had 'taken out the Statute of Bankrupt against Bagwell nine months since but never prosecuted the same'. They had produced no evidence, 'which gives us cause to believe the Blackhalls have very much wronged Bagwell to a great value and abused him to his loss and disgrace'. He was now too weak to go to law. The evidence of two arbitrators, chosen with the consent of both parties, was that 'the cause was very foul and ill on the Blackhalls' behalf and found them very averse and obstinate'. They had forced their way into Bagwell's home and stolen his wife's money and other things. Moreover, Bagwell had a receipt signed by the Blackhalls for goods worth £214, £190 of which they had admitted under oath in Chancery should go to relieve a surety, Benjamin Hyde. Bagwell, his wife and children, and his surety Hyde, were 'like to perish, having no hopes of relief from the Blackhalls more than by law they shall be compelled unto, which we conceive he is in no way able to prosecute against so powerful and wilful adversaries'. The Council considered the certificate and asked the Lord Keeper to call all the parties before him and, after consideration of their allegations and the report and 'any other thing that may conduce to the clearing of the truth', to make 'such a conclusion between the parties as to equity shall appertain for the present relief of Bagwell and his surety Hyde'. Arbitration and opinions lived side by side.

16. *APC* 45.253.
17. *APC* 45.391.

3. DEBT

Disputes relating to simple debts, for example for money lent, were regularly referred to mediation and sometimes to arbitration,[18] both private and public, both by the Privy Council and the House of Lords. Assizes also dealt with simple debt enforcement.[19] The Court of Chancery would send a debt claim to arbitrators and then enforce their award, requiring the debtor to execute a bond.[20]

This was despite the attempts of the Common Law courts to lay down a law against such arbitrations. A report of *Farrer v Bates* declares:[21]

> debt and other controversies lie in arbitrement though debt solely does not. In an *indebitatus assumpsit*, the defendant pleaded a submission of all actions and controversies to arbitrement, and that the arbitrators awarded that the defendant should pay the plaintiff £4 in satisfaction of all accounts, and... it was found for the defendant, and upon motion in arrest of judgment it was agreed, that though debt itself doth not lie in arbitrament, yet that and other controversies doth.

But *Godfrey v Godfrey* shows that the Court would readily fabricate a means to avoid that rule:[22]

> On a submission to arbitration respecting £72 due for rent, an award that the party shall pay £50 in full satisfaction is good.... But it did not appear that any other matter was in controversy between the parties, though the submission was general; and arbitrators may reduce uncertain things to a certainty, but they cannot make a debt certain to be less... the award was good, for that the arbitrators might consider other matters between the parties.

A creditor might have to resort to drastic measures to encourage a debtor to submit. Thomas Somerscales, chapman of Settle, had got three of his debtors outlawed. The sheriff of Yorkshire was instructed to arrest them and bring them before the justices at Westminster, but they all submitted to arbitration instead.[23]

The Common Law courts claimed jurisdiction over actions to recover debts, but what they had to offer was unacceptable:[24]

> Whatever the debtor's status, the system itself produced ruin out of all proportion to the default. The chain of forfeitures, once begun, brought bonds and counterbonds into suit, brought sale of assets at knock-down prices, brought arrest of the debtor and disaster to his sureties. Any body of responsible men who conceived their duties to society in the widest sense and had the power to act must

---

18. Rastell *Entries*; West Yorks WYL100/L/7.
19. Cockburn *Western* 403.
20. Nat Arch C6/419/31.
21. (1646) Al 4; 82 ER 884.
22. (1678) 2 Mod 303; 86 ER 1086.
23. York Archae MD335/1/10/2/3.
24. Dawson *I* 411.

have wished to avert results so contradictory to good sense and so harmful to the interests of the creditors themselves. The chief means of rehabilitating debtors was simply through extension of time. The method used was characteristic, a system of arbitration which enlisted the aid of influential laymen.

That suggestion of a system is supported by ample evidence from the primary sources.[25]

> Generally, what they needed from the House of Lords was a forum for offi-cially-sanctioned arbitration.... More often, the cases involved complicated commercial transactions, with multi-layered credit relationships (secured by a variety of interlocking penal bonds) which made straightforward litigation enormously complicated.

In May 1641 John Beaumont petitioned the Lords with the other creditors of the London merchant, Sir Edward Abbott, for £30,000 for goods supplied for Abbott's overseas trade.[26] Abbott's debts totalled £120,000. He tried to defraud his creditors by transferring all he had to his father and brothers. The Lords found him bankrupt and, under the statute 13 Eliz I c7, referred the matter to Lord Keeper Littleton, who had just replaced Finch, who had been impeached and fled into exile in Holland. He was to appoint 'some judicious and honest men' to do a full account and apportion payments. First they sequestered all Abbott's assets. Then they found that the King was owed £12,000 and made sure that debt was paid first. The residue was eventually paid out proportionately.

The Lord President of the North had his own court and could have been asked to act judicially, but the Privy Council preferred him to mediate, 'to call both parties before you and mediate such a reasonable end betwixt them as to you shall seem fit', when the claim was for 'great sums of money lent many years since'.[27] It was enough that the petitioner claimed to be 'not able to prosecute in a chargeable course of law'. Similarly, the Council asked the Earl of Derby, Lord President of the County Palatine of Chester, to arrange for an action of debt pending in the court there to be ended and determined 'by both their consents by some friendly arbitrament'.[28] The Earl did nothing and a party insisted on his legal right. So the Council 'thought good to forbear any further imposition and to leave the matters in question to a legal trial in the Courts of Justice there, where your Lordship may be pleased to give it the best expedition you may'. Assize judges were considered appropriate arbitrators in debt cases: 'to order and set

25. Hart 132, with examples 140 fn112; Israel Treiman 'Majority Control in Compositions'.
26. Hart 133.
27. *APC* 33.424.
28. *APC* 33.501.

down some course for petitioner's relief, agreeable to equity and good conscience, so as we may not be further troubled'.[29]

The Council regularly appointed local men of standing, JPs, MPs and such, for example to help the Dutchman, Ruteghert Barnavelt, to recover a debt of £440 from Matthew Came of Totnes;[30] and to relieve the baker George Beeton, in prison for a debt he claimed he had paid but was too poor to prove in litigation: 'upon due information of the state of accounts between them, mediate such an end and agreement as shall be most reasonable and indifferent'.[31]

The Council might arrange the mediation of a simple debt claim. Either Preston owed Anderton £1,000 or he did not. Preston's daughter had married Anderton and they had a daughter. Preston promised Anderton £1,000 'towards the preferment of the grandchild'.[32] But the Council asked the Bishop of Chester and either Serjeant Davenport or another barrister 'to mediate a friendly end between them, if you can, wherein you will do a work of charity to free them from suits in law and this Board from further trouble'.

Henry Rutter lent Gilbert Reresby £120.[33] In payment Reresby assigned that amount out of £300 Lady Reresby (his mother?) was holding 'proceeding from an annuity of £42 per annum'. 'She refuseth to satisfy him, on the pretence that Mr Reresby is dead'. The Council commissioned Lord Darcy and William West[34] to 'call both parties before you and, if the petitioner can prove the assignment and that Reresby is yet living, to mediate such an end for his relief as shall be agreeable to equity', or to certify for the Council to make an order for the poor man's relief 'as shall be thought expedient'.

4. COMPOSITIONS WITH CREDITORS, PROTECTIONS AND POSTPONEMENTS [35]

In the 17th century, neither debtors nor creditors assumed that debts would be paid in full and on time. Good proof of that apparently strange contention is the life of such a compulsive bad debtor as Francis Bacon, detailed in Chapter 13. Whatever the community in which they lived, creditors were expected to allow some leeway. It was their Christian duty:[36]

29. *APC* 34.259.
30. *APC* 35.5.
31. *APC* 37.222.
32. *APC* 41.23.
33. *APC* 45.400.
34. Perhaps the young barrister who later wrote *Symboleography,* including the best two stories about arbitrators, Roebuck *Miscellany* 15–17.
35. Westminster O xvii 116 H vii piii 80 p n440.
36. Muldrew 'The Culture of Reconciliation' [Muldrew] 915–942, 930 citing Henry Wilkinson *The Debt Book* 103.

The first direction for coming out of debt, is that which Solomon gives for getting out of suretyship, *Proverbs* 6.3,4,5. Submit thyself and entreat thy neighbour, solicit the creditor, *ut diem ampliet* [to extend the date], to have patience with thee and to grant some respite: solicit the debtor for which thou art engaged [i.e. as surety] *ut fidem liberet*, to clear his fidelity by keeping promise: solicit thy friends to interpose themselves, to mediate for thee, to put to their helping hand… till thou be delivered as a roe from the hand of the hunter.

Government policy followed popular sentiment:[37]

In the reigns of the first two Stuarts… the program of relief to debtors followed two quite divergent lines. Pure arbitration, through *ad hoc* committees empowered only to mediate, remained extremely popular…. The other main alternative was the royal protection, operating as a rule quite independently of any organized system of mediation.

Under James I and Charles I, as under Elizabeth I,[38] one of the Council's most regular items of business was arranging compositions with creditors. It dealt at least once a month with requests from embarrassed debtors, sometimes of the highest rank, sometimes county gentry, to arrange for repayment to be postponed and to be by instalments.[39] The process often included verification of the debts' validity, requiring a commission of arbitrators to hear the creditors' claims. The policy was express:[40] 'the general rule of charity, to do unto others as you would be done unto yourself'; and, to a creditor who did not oblige, 'we shall hold you very unworthy of our good opinions'. The Council was moved by all kinds of ill fortune, from the debtor having simply relied unwisely on his own debtors paying on time to dramatic events like piracy and shipwreck.[41] No trace yet of 'sanctity of contracts'. On the other hand, it was aware of the dangers of abuse:[42] 'Their Lordships are very tender in cases of this nature'.

A good example of the procedure is the commission to the Mayor, two sheriffs and a merchant of Bristol of John Brindon's petition.[43] Brindon was

37. Dawson *II* 650.
38. Roebuck *Golden Age* 186–190 and *passim*.
39. *APC* 33.102; 33.472; 33.522; 34.55; 34.72; 34.704 (goods abroad); 35.5; 35.120; 35.190; 35.283; 36.109; 36.124 (widow, to merchants); 36.184; 37.126; 38.176; 38.234; 38.246 (infancy); 38.346 (merchants, tobacco); 38.381 (41 of 49 creditors agreed); 38.386; 38.451; 39.32; 39.43 (Council letter to all creditors); 39.52; 39.65; 39.6; 39.130; 39.165; 39.166; 39.355; 39.361 (recalcitrant barrister, first to Archbishop of Canterbury, ill, then to MR); 39.400; 39.431; 39.432 (three in one day inc. Mary Wroth again, renewed 44.371 and 46.318 in 1631); 39.445; 39.478; 39.488 (widow); 39.501. There were at least 20 in vol 40, inc 40.204 in favour of the Earl of Londonderry and 40.222 for the Governor of Virginia. These had usually become protections rather than compositions and in favour of the nobility or gentry, eg 44.398; 45.1; 45.371; 45.373; 45.376; 45.396; 46.81; 46.270.
40. *APC* 33.185; Dawson *I* 420.
41. *APC* 33.378.
42. Dawson *II* 651 fn210.
43. *APC* 33.204.

'a merchant heretofore of good trade and credit' but now fallen into debt as a result of 'great oppression'. They were to 'call such persons as he shall name... and deal with them in such sort as the books and papers... detained from him' would reveal, 'for the better clearing of the difference depending amongst them'. They were first to establish the validity and amounts of the creditors' claims, then to assess the debts owed to Brindon, then 'to mediate with his creditors to accept of such an agreement as may stand with their reasonable satisfaction'. They were then to report to the Council.

On 14 May 1613, the Council wrote to Sir Henry Townsend (?1537–1621), judge and member of the Council of the Marches, and Sir Richard Wilbraham (1579–1643), first baronet and squire of Woodhey in Cheshire, asking them to arrange a composition between Ellen Smyth, probably of Stopford, Cheshire, and her creditors:[44] 'You shall understand by this enclosed petition the poor and lamentable estate of a distressed widow, Ellen Smyth'. She deserved special commiseration because she was willing to hand over all she had to 'all who could justly claim any debt or bargain from her... to relieve her poor aged parents and children'. The debts were those of her father and late husband. The creditors were to be asked to allow her time and to be satisfied with repayment of the debts without interest and, if any should be 'obdurate and obstinate', the Council wanted their names, so that they could be dealt with according to equity and justice.

Those examples will have to stand for the hundreds of entries, some full, some scant, in the *APC*.[45] In the 17th century most dealt with the debts of nobility, gentry and merchants. During that time, the Council's technique changed. Instead of asking arbitrators first to ensure what debts were just and then to arrange some allowance of time and perhaps apportionment, it allowed a royal 'protection' from enforcement, usually for six or twelve months, often repeated, sometimes over and again. The Council routinely ordered not only the creditors of royal officials but the judges to postpone actions against them.[46] The debts were enforceable at Common Law. The relief of the debtors was under the royal prerogative. Coke CJ might be the champion of the Common Law, but he was regularly the instrument by which the Government forced reluctant creditors to forgo their Common Law rights.[47]

On 29 February 1617 the Council instructed four London merchants 'forasmuch as both parties have made choice of you for ending and compounding of their differences... to mediate some reasonable and

---

44. *APC* 33.31.
45. The *APC* indexes are inadequate; but e.g. 39.117; 39.200; 39.217; 39.240; 39.297; 39.309; 39.337.
46. Dawson *I* 405.
47. Dawson *II* 652 fn210 tells the story, with the supporting citations.

indifferent end and agreement as is desired', of differences about 'certain accounts and disbursements in the business of farthing tokens' arising between Gerard Malynes senior, former Master of the Mint, and his two sons, and the heirs of Lord Harrington.[48] One of those sons has Chapter 14 to himself. Like his father, he knew the realities of imprisonment for debt from personal experience and argued for reform.[49] In his great text on commercial law and practice is a comparative study of how debts were recovered in Germany, France, Italy, Spain, the Low Countries and Russia. He showed how imprisonment for debt was against the law of God (no example in the Bible); the Common Law (*Magna Carta*, *habeas corpus*); justice and the law of nature (*Plutarch's Life of Solon*). Then, most telling:

> But it will be said, that imprisonment is no punishment, for prisoners live at ease and pleasure etc, according to the received opinion: but the miseries and afflictions of imprisonment are inexplicable and cannot be conceived by any that have not felt or had proof thereof…. For imprisonment is a corporal punishment, a grief and torture of the mind, a long and lingering dying, and sometimes a short killing by the plague.

The prisoner's family suffer, too, and he the more for knowing that. There spoke the voice of personal experience, more eloquently than today's slogan 'Prison Works!' The debtor might not have been in any way at fault. The debt might have arisen from helping out friends and family with loans or guarantees, or from fire, shipwreck or any other natural disaster. Penalties on bonds were unfair, wrote Malynes (who no doubt had as often been the beneficiary as the giver of bonds) and it was no use replying that Chancery gave relief: 'the remedy is worse than the disease, for all courses of relief by law in Chancery are hard, tedious, uncertain, long and extreme chargeable'. Malynes dealt with the objection that debtors must take the risks they have assumed, what we would now call *pacta sunt servanda* but he, for want of that phrase then, called it *volenti non fit injuria*, 'no wrong may be committed against one who is willing'. His solution was to restrict recovery to the debtor's property. If that meant that lenders would be less willing to lend, so that commerce would suffer, so be it. The commonwealth would be the healthier for it.

As protections increased, Government-mediated compositions dwindled but did not disappear.[50] For example, on 27 July 1621 the Council allowed a postponement of one year in favour of two London merchants who owed a total of £13,000 to no fewer than 57 creditors. It was all the fault of troubles in France. Any two of Lord Brooke, Secretary Calvert and

---

48. *APC* 35.171; Roebuck *Golden Age* 18–19, 132–3, 193, 215, 242, 301, 313–14.
49. Malynes *Consuetudo* [Malynes] Chapter XII 285–292.
50. On 5 November 1628 Charles I extended a protection for the Earl of Desmond for a second six months, so that he could pay a debt to the Earl of Ormond, awarded by James I himself, *APC* 44.223; later 46.29.

Caesar MR were to mediate.[51] By the end of the century royal protections
and postponements had disappeared. According to Blackstone, the last
recorded protection was granted in 1692 to Lord Cutts, so that he would
not be outlawed for debts to his tailor.[52]

At the very end of the *APC* there is a full record of the appointment of
Lord Matrevers, 'if his Lordship will be pleased to take so much pains',
and the Mayor of Norfolk and six aldermen (presumably whether they
liked it or not) to mediate a friendly end between 12 imprisoned debtors,
one of them a woman, and their creditors.[53] Any four, three or two of them
were to consider the situation of each of the prisoners separately and 'what
they are able to pay, either presently or by their endeavours when they shall
be set at liberty'. If any of the creditors proved 'obstinate or refractory',
in 'accepting payment or giving days', the Board would take 'such further
course as shall be thought fit'.

In 1643 Morgan Davies, in prison for debt, petitioned for his release.
He imputed his inability to pay to his estate being in Barbados.[54] The
Commissioners for the Relief of Distressed Prisoners 'mediated an end for
his enlargement', even though one creditor refused to abide by their order.

The Act for the Relief of Creditors 1697[55]   At the end of the century
legislation provided that if two-thirds in number and value of the
creditors agreed, then all a debtor's creditors should be bound to accept
the composition. It began: 'Whereas many debtors, disabled by losses
and misfortunes to pay their whole debts, are often willing to make what
satisfaction they can for the same, so as they can enjoy their liberty...'.
It seems to have worked well enough.[56] Certainly there were no more
Government orders for protection or postponement.

5. COMMERCIAL TRANSACTIONS

Perhaps not so often as under Elizabeth I, but not infrequently, the Council
referred commercial disputes to a panel of London merchants, often
including the Lord Mayor and aldermen, for example authorising five such
'to order and compound as in conscience and equity shall be found meet'.[57]

---

51. *APC* 38.27. Also *APC* 38.117 (where the King was a creditor, 'he hath done the King
    very good service in the alum works); *APC* 38.118 20 out of 144 creditors stand out;
    APC 38.288 ('deadness of trade' of mercer); *APC* 38.431 (Lady Mary Wroth, repeated
    many times).
52. Dawson *II* 652 fn219 citing Blackstone *Commentaries* III 365 citing 3 Levinz 332 and
    652 fn210.
53. *APC* 46.211.
54. Parl Arch HL/PO/JO/10/1/152 and 169.
55. (1696–7) 8 Will III 4.2.
56. William Holdsworth *A History of English Law* VIII 233–245 [Holdsworth *HEL*].
57. *APC* 34.424.

Richard Gore complained that the Council had provided William Russell with letters to the Senate at Hamburg, which had allowed him to perpetrate a fraud on Gore.[58] On Sunday 14 January 1615 the Council deputed the Chancellor of the Exchequer and the Master of the Rolls 'to make a final determination of the matter in controversy by consent of the parties, if it may be, or to report... touching the equity of the complaint'.

The Council would interfere to encourage entrepreneurial innovation. In 1614 it wrote to the Mayor of Lymington and three other local gentlemen, sending them the petition of Thomas Mosley, who had set up a trial salt works on land he had contracted to buy from John Dore.[59] The purchase was conditional on the success of the trial; but the price was fixed. But Dore refused to complete the conveyance unless he was paid more. The Council would have none of that:

> Forasmuch as the endeavours in this new work, which tendeth to the public good and benefit of His Majesty's service, are to be seconded by all lawful and just favour, and that the petitioner is not able to run the circuit of the law without great prejudice to his new work, we have therefore been moved to authorize and require you, calling both parties before you, to hear and examine the state of this business, and thereupon to mediate some such course between them as shall be agreeable to equity and good conscience.

That must have meant that the way was open for the mediators to persuade the successful saltmaker to give a bit more. So much for sanctity of contracts! *Pacta sunt servanda* but only up to a point.

Increasingly, though, the Council would delegate to a committee of itself the mediation of matters which formerly would have gone to a tribunal of merchants, perceiving perhaps an element of public policy requiring Government intervention. In March 1620 it set up such a committee of the Chief Justices and Law Officers to 'accommodate the differences and settle an orderly course' between the owners of shut-down alehouses and the gentlemen who had taken over their 'forfeited recognizances'.[60]

6. ACCOUNTS

Arbitration, both private and public, was commonly used when accounting skills were needed. There are private examples from 1605 'over accounts for lead sold'; from 1624 'for settlement of accounts under arbitration'; and from January 1669 a reference from Queen Catherine's Council concerning accounting problems in relation to her jointure.[61] The arbitrators do not

---

58. *APC* 34.373.
59. *APC* 33.636.
60. *APC* 37.166.
61. Nat Arch C78/127/7; E134/22/JasI/Hil2; DL41/369/5. The reference could arise from the distribution of an estate Nat Arch E134/30 and 31Chas2/Hil6.

always seem to have been accounting experts, for example a yeoman and a clothworker.[62]

The Council could not itself, nor even by a committee of its members, unravel the difficulties presented by merchants' accounts. For that purpose it would commission a panel of merchants themselves. In March 1617 it wrote to eight merchants, explaining that John Bate, 'a poor person and decayed in his means, having been a merchant of good credit... but not able now to prosecute his demand in a legal course', had complained that Robert Bowyer was 'detaining certain books of account belonging to him'.[63] It asked them (or any six or four):

> being men of experience and understanding in these matters of trade and accounts... by authority of the Board to cause them to produce the books of accounts... and diligently to peruse them and... consider what portion belongs to each of them.... And, (which we wish to be the principal fruits of your labour, as it is the principal end and scope of our reference), that you would so accommodate all differences and questions between them, as they may both depart from you satisfied.

Not all barristers were presumed innumerate. Finding that 'the full clearing' of accounts in the business of soap boiling in Ireland required further time, the Council commissioned two, one from Gray's Inn, the other from the Inner Temple, 'to mediate and use their best endeavours for the composing and ending the controversies between them'.[64]

Sir Ferdinando Gorges, Governor of Plymouth, had appointed Andrew Batten master of the *Great Neptune*.[65] They had a disagreement about the payment of the French seamen's wages. The Council referred it to Caesar MR, who 'for his better information, because the difference consisted in matter of account, did think fit that the account should be cast up by four men indifferently chosen'. So Gorges chose Slayny and Moyer, and Batten chose Pierce and Bromefield, 'who met oftentimes about it'. They asked Trinity House for help in fixing the amount due to the French sailors. But Pierce and Bromefield must have backed off. It was an award of Slayny and Moyer only which found that Batten owed Gorges the three months' wages he had paid out, plus another debt of £7. Batten objected that this was the award of Gorge's arbitrators, and was given time to bring his two to testify. Meanwhile the money was deposited in the Office of the Ordinance. He did nothing for six weeks. The Council had ordered him to show cause forthwith why Gorges should not have the money. Now, 'it being almost a year past', it ordered payment and wrote to Gorges, requesting him to

62. E214/1110.
63. *APC* 35.189.
64. *APC* 39.350.
65. *APC* 43.334.

say just how much he needed 'of men and means to repair the wants and defects of that place whereof you have the charge'.

The next report tells how the Council dealt with an appeal, in the normal course, from a decision of the court in Jersey, 'as in like case is usual and accustomed'.[66] Because it involved 'accounts which have not been so well examined as in this case they ought to have been', it was referred to five Channel Island worthies, including the regular Philip de Carteret, 'to have those accounts re-examined... and to accommodate the difference between them, if you can'.

In 1629 the Council reversed this practice. Gardner and Blatchford were in dispute over Customs duties. The Council referred it to the Chancellor of the Exchequer.[67] He reported on 15 July that:

> The differences between them consisted of matters of account fittest to be examined by men of their own quality. I referred the same (by their own desire and agreement) to two chosen by themselves in the country to arbitrate the differences and to examine whether Blatchford had satisfied His Majesty's Customs... they made choice of two merchants who certified me they found the matter difficult to determine, the rather for that Gardner refused to give them any power at all to end any one of the differences but that Blatchford was very ready.

The parties then asked the Chancellor of the Exchequer to refer the dispute to two London merchants. They too found 'the accounts to be so difficult and intricate, consisting upon producing witnesses far in the country', that they too could not 'make any end between them'. The report advised the Council 'to refer them to the ordinary course of Justice, where each of them may prove his allegation by a legal way and so receive a decree or judgment', that is from Chancery or a Common Law court. The Council agreed.

The long tale of another dispute illustrates again many of the problems of accounts.[68] Thomas Thornton, 'a poor decayed merchant', petitioned the Council against William Audley, London grocer, whose factor he had been, for 'withholding of a certain sum of money due to him upon account by reason of intercourse of merchandise in Ireland'. The Council referred the dispute to its own Commissioners for Irish Affairs. On 25 April 1626 it received their report. They had 'thought it expedient, being ourselves unacquainted with merchants' accounts, to refer the auditing thereof to four expert gentlemen of the city mutually chosen by the parties'. But they had got nowhere, mainly because they lacked authority to administer oaths. They recommended the matter be referred to three aldermen, with

66. *APC* 43.335.
67. *APC* 45.86.
68. *APC* 40.458; 41.159; 45.237.

power to administer oaths. Audley had agreed to pay Thornton 5s a week until the matter was determined; but not only had he failed to do so, he had 'cast the poor man into prison for a pretended debt'. So the Commissioners had ordered his release and Audley to pay him the 5s a week and 20s for arrears. The Council accepted the report and ordered Audley to continue to pay the 5s a week so long as Thornton 'doth prosecute the commission with effect'. Thornton did not do as he was told. Therefore the parties were summoned before the Council on 1 August 1626. Audley said he owed nothing to Thornton. On the contrary Thornton owed him £533, as he could prove 'if he might proceed in legal course', as the Commissioners for Irish Affairs had advised 'by a commission granted by the Lord Keeper to the aldermen of London... to hear and examine upon oath'. The Council ordered Thornton to 'sue forth this commission' by the first week of the next Michaelmas term, otherwise he would lose the weekly 5s. Nearly four years passed. On 15 January 1630 Thornton petitioned the Council again:

> Audley, pretending a suit against him in the Christmas holidays last past, had caused him to be committed to a dark vault or cellar in St Martin's le Grand, being a prison belonging to the liberty of the Dean of Westminster, whereafter he had been close divers days; in the end he set him at liberty of his own accord, he having endured much misery, being a poor, poor impotent man aged 76 years and having nothing to relieve him, his poor wife and family but the moneys unjustly denied from him by Audley.

The Council commissioned two London aldermen, who had 'formerly taken some pains' in these differences, to examine the complaint and certify their opinions. 'After ten several sittings and much labour', they found that Thornton could prove nothing against Audley.

> Yet they so prevailed with Audley by persuasions that they procured him to give Thornton £50 to be rid of his clamours and both parties to seal a general release each to other as by a certificate under the hands of the aldermen following *in haec verba*.

The certificate was comprehensive and formal and witnessed by a notary's clerks. The aldermen had first worked under a reference from the Council but Thornton refused to cooperate. So they sought and were granted a commission from the Lord Keeper out of his Chancery. Their report is in great detail.

> Thornton then perceiving we had power to certify our proceedings did submit himself unto us, and Audley and Thornton did condescend to refer themselves unto us and with much labour we prevailed with and persuaded Audley to forgive Thornton what he owed him, because he was poor and in no way able to pay him, and to give him £50 to send him for his country [to go home], and that each party should release the other and so that there might be a final conclusion.

The Council accepted that report and ordered that Audley be released from further attendance in respect of all matters up to the previous Christmas. But Thornton's claim for false arrest at Christmas was referred to Aldermen Freeman and Moulson. This unhappy tale shows that arbitration did not always produce a speedy resolution, but it might well ignore all legal rights in favour of a settlement that would embody Christian charity. Or it may be that all then recognised that the burden of a time-wasting claim, however ill-founded, was a cost that might be taken into account.

The parties often made private arrangements for their accounting disputes to be submitted to arbitrators. It is not always easy to be sure that the Council was not involved. Four documents from 1624 relate to an arbitration settling accounts between Thomas Weston, London merchant, and his factor in Amsterdam, Edward Pickering, and on Pickering's death his executors.[69] The Attorney General sat with four merchants and dealt not only with the intricacies of the accounts but with allegations of fraud and forgery. And four arbitrators made an award in a dispute about the partnership accounts of Urie Babington and Robert Bromley, relating to 'the appareling of soldiers in the Low Countries'. On Urie's death, the Council enforced the award on the petition of his widow, Anne.[70]

Another widow's accounts were referred to arbitration at the very end of our period.[71] The record of the Mayor of London's Court of 19 March 1703 declares that it had made an order on 29 January sending to arbitrators a dispute with Mary Mount, widow of Jeremy Mount, late clerk of the hospitals. Sir Gabriel Roberts, Auditor General of the hospitals, reported that he and the committee appointed for that purpose had had several meetings with her to settle the accounts, but had failed because she refused to produce her husband's books and papers, insisting that: 'it was not advisable for her to produce them unless the hospital would be concluded thereby'. Alderman Sir Gilbert Heathcote, on Mary's behalf, told the court that she was willing to account for the period after her husband's death in 1696 and produce all the relevant books and papers:

> And she is willing to refer the same: and all matters in difference to the determination of arbitrators to be appointed for doing as this Court shall direct. Whereupon and upon long debate of the matter and hearing what could be insisted on on all sides This Court doth think, sit and order: That all matters in difference between Mary Mount and this Hospital be referred to Sir Gabriel Roberts and Sir Gilbert Heathcote to Examine State and Settle all accounts and differences between the parties since 1696. And in case they cannot agree then Sir Gabriel Roberts and Sir Gilbert Heathcote to choose an umpire. Which settlement and award either by the arbitrators or by the Umpire is to be made on

69. Nat Arch E 134/22JasI/Hil 2 and 8, Mich 22, Mich 59.
70. Nat Arch E 134/8JasI/Hil10.
71. Nat Arch BHMC 19 March 1703.

or before Midsomer day next ensuing and is to be conclusive to all parties, Mary Mount being now present in Court and consenting thereto.

That is clear evidence that a woman might exercise the duties of clerk to the hospitals and be held responsible for their exercise herself, submitting her accounts to arbitration.

7. MARITIME

The Government protected English shipowners by forbidding the importing of a wide range of articles in other than English ships, including hemp, flax, pitch, tar, soap-ashes, masts, oars and similar. Merchants tried to get round these prohibitions. Those of the Eastland Company, trading to Scandinavia and the Baltic, complained that 'the shipping of this kingdom are not so conveniently built for such kind of loading as the Flemish or Holland shipping are'.[72] Moreover, foreign merchants were importing such goods more cheaply. 'Some of the Trinity House', however, had told the Council that they were ready to supply 'sufficient shipping and at reasonable and easy rates'. So the Council commissioned three shipowners and three merchants, requiring them:

> to call such merchants, officers of Trinity House, and masters of shipping... and settle some such course for the freight and importation of the commodities as the trade of those Eastern [i.e. North Sea] countries may entirely be continued unto the merchants and the shipping of this kingdom wholly employed therein, to the general good of all His Majesty's subjects.

Chancery referred maritime matters to arbitrators, for example a dispute over a vessel lost through unseaworthiness.[73]

Navy Board records note arbitrations. An entry of 7 March 1676 records that Sir Thomas Lynch, Governor of Jamaica, had received freight from Mayor Beckford and Alderman Beckford and paid for unloading the goods, Customs charges and the 'cost of arbitration'.[74] Thomas Pope of Bristol was in dispute with his father-in-law Francis Baylie. On 10 December 1676 he wrote to the Board disputing Baylie's debt claim and consenting to arbitration. On 17 January 1677 it noted a letter from Pope 'about some difference between him and Mr Baylie and will put it to arbitration'.[75] On 17 January 1677 the excuse is recorded that arbitrators in a dispute between the purser of the *Stavereen* and his deputy would not be able to

72. *APC* 34.142.
73. Nat Arch C2/JasI/M5/13 (1603–1625).
74. Nat Arch ADM106/317/284.
75. Nat Arch ADM106/318/401; ADM106/318/399; ADM106/318/404; ADM106/318/402; ADM106/327/90.

send their award that day.[76] One of hundreds of bonds is that of mariner George Chambers 'to obey and abide by' an arbitration.[77]

Prize   The National Archives hold the records of the Prize Court from 1592 onwards.[78] The Council had appointed Sir Henry Martin, Judge of the Admiralty, to hear and determine a controversy over prize. On 28 November 1628 his report was recorded verbatim, with the sad news: 'I have in vain laboured to reconcile all sides'.[79] He had already awarded the goods to Russell, Gardiner and Blatchford in equal shares. Russell and Gardiner pleaded that Blatchford had assigned his share to them to sell. Blatchford said he had countermanded that assignment before they sold. Martin J said he could not deal with that difference, 'the matter being not of my cognizance but appertaining to the common law' – just the kind of procedural obstacle that the Council's referees had brushed aside in earlier years. In any case Blatchford claimed that that issue had already been the subject of an award by arbitrators, who Martin J said had been 'indifferently chosen in the country... two whereof seemed willing to justify the same in my presence'. He concluded: 'Since I could not draw them by mediation to an end, and the examination thereof would require a longer time than I suppose your Lordships did expect or the parties were willing to endure, I humbly return the same'. The Council made the obvious order. Russell and Gardner would deliver the goods they had sold and the buyers would pay them the price. They would then give Blatchford one-third. Blatchford's claim of malpractice would be sent to the Court of Chancery. Neither the Council's attempt at mediation nor the arbitration in the country had done more than prolong delay and increase expense. On 11 March 1629, recognising that 'the parties have since fallen into new disputes, their Lordships were pleased to give them another hearing and do hereby confirm the aforesaid order of 28 November'.[80]

8. INSURANCE

Chapter 12 of Roebuck *Golden Age* describes the efforts of Elizabeth I's Government to provide a scheme for the resolution of differences arising from insurance. She herself wrote to the Lord Mayor of London telling him not to meddle, as he was prone to do by means of fictions. She had no use for the Common Law courts and their technicalities and delays. She wanted to promote trade, not fee lawyers. So she got Francis Bacon

76. ADM106/327/5.
77. Nat Arch HCA30/840/111.
78. Nat Arch HHCA32.
79. *APC* 44.243.
80. *APC* 44.360.

to introduce legislation which in 1601 provided a permanent arbitration commission to hear 'every such cause concerning policies of assurance in a brief and summary course, as to their discretion shall seem meet, without formalities of pleadings or proceedings'.[81] All insurance, not just marine, was encompassed, though marine policies predominated. The commissioners were the Admiralty Judge, the Recorder of London, two Doctors of Civil Law, two Common Lawyers and 'eight grave and discreet merchants'.

That general provision did not inhibit the Council from setting up its own arbitrations. In 1616 it commissioned seven merchants (or any four or three) to hear the complaint of Richard Whidborne of Exmouth 'concerning the refusal of some adventurers with him in a ship of his to Newfoundland to undergo such fortune and adventure as befell unto him'.[82] Because 'divers of the adventurers are willing to come to some reasonable agreement', the tribunal were required 'to mediate with them for some friendly and conscionable end as in equity shall be found'. And 'whatever shall be recovered from the French rovers now living in La Rochelle by the instance of His Majesty's ambassador there shall be ratably divided amongst them towards the repair of their losses'.

It took half a century for the lawyers and judges to demolish the statutory scheme. Oliver Cromwell appointed John Glynne Chief Justice of the Upper Bench (as King's Bench was then called) in 1655. Even among the many such of his time, his side-switching was notorious. He was reappointed by Richard Cromwell but wisely resigned when he foresaw Charles II's restoration. His horse fell on him in the coronation procession, with general approval, but he lived on, in various offices adding to his enormous fortune. In 1658 there came before him *Came v Moye*.[83] The Commissioners appointed under Elizabeth's statute had dismissed a claim on a marine policy. Thanks to the ideological excesses which followed the Restoration, the report is in a sort of Law French, though the whole proceedings had been in English. The outcome was so devastating that it deserves translation here:

> An action on the case was brought on a matter pending on the policy of insurance (which court is of the nature of a court of Equity according to the statute 43 Eliz cap 12) but the suit was dismissed. And the question was whether the party could have an action at Common Law for the same thing for which he had sued.
>
> Twisden for the Defendant: It seems that no action will lie and that the plaintiff will not recover, for the preamble to the statute recites a general mischief, but I do not argue that that has taken away the Common Law remedy, because I say that it has a concurrent jurisdiction with the Admiralty in recognising several

81. (1601) 43 Eliz 12; Roebuck *Golden Age* 238.
82. *APC* 35.293.
83. *Came v Moye* (1658) 2 Siderfin 121.

things which the Common Law also recognises. Yet, if an action should be brought here on something which there had been adjudged in the Admiralty, I would plead that judgment. Also the plaintiff had made his election by suing before the Commissioners of Assurance and their judgment will be a bar to this action, for *interest reipublicae ut fit finis litium* [it is in the public interest that there should be an end of litigation].

Glynne CJ, and the whole Court, that an action lay because the policy of insurance, being a court established by statute, did not give jurisdiction *in rem*, but *in personam*, all courts of Equity may not act *in rem* and on the equity of this case there is a certain rule that a decree of a court of Equity will not be a bar to an action brought at Common Law, so that, if Chancery makes a decree on a covenant on which an action lies at Common Law, the party notwithstanding this decree may have his action, or if a bill should be exhibited in Chancery – for a legacy or a marriage portion (as is the usual course) – which is dismissed, that will not take away the remedy which the party had at Common Law.

Judgment that the plaintiff could have his action at Common Law.

How could the Chief Justice have got away with such a claim, that no decree of any court of Equity could bar an action at Common Law? Or that the arbitrators appointed under legislation could be transmuted, by some hocus-pocus about actions *in rem* and *in personam*, into a court of Equity? The answer is simple: because there was no one who could challenge his authority – and what he said suited the lawyers and judges of the time. Oliver Cromwell had just died and Richard Cromwell's Government had more on its mind. After *Came v Moye* it became routine to obtain from Common Law judges prohibitions against claims before the Commissioners of Assurance, who slumbered in desuetude.

9. AGENCY AND PARTNERSHIP

Arbitration was often chosen by the parties when their disputes were manifold. For example, in Worcester in 1620, a dispute between an agent and his principals involved their accusation that they had hired him to go to London to make payment for the herbage they were buying but that he had committed a breach of trust by telling a rival of their purchase and trying to get it set aside.[84]

Partnership disputes, often requiring examination of accounts, were best sent to a tribunal of those who knew the business. In October 1616 four London merchants were asked:[85]

as these grievances depend on accounts of merchandise, wherewith you are so well acquainted, you may easily certify the same, without putting the petitioners

---

84. Nat Arch E 134/18JasI/Trin10.
85. *APC* 35.43.

to troublesome suits of law, we require you to confound [*sic*] the differences by such equal mediation as the cause shall require.

The dispute was between partners who fell out about a voyage to Bayonne, some alleging that another, Handcorne, had not 'discharged the trust reposed in him as he ought, but concealed a great part of the profit of that voyage, converted much of the goods to his own use, and put to account greater costs than were disbursed'.

Many documents survive recording different aspects of arbitration between partners, not only awards[86] but bonds and arbitration clauses in partnership agreements. Just one collection in the National Archives, starting in 1694, contains 'awards and agreements. Records of actions which were ended by arbitration or agreement, relating mainly to disputes arising from partnerships and the administration of estates'.[87]

10. COMPETITION

In 17th-century England monopolies were an important source of revenue for the King and offered him opportunities for patronage. They fomented quarrels between Crown and Parliament. The Government took careful responsibility for overseeing how they worked. Customary law reinforced by legislation required apprenticeship of all those, female as well as male, who aspired to the privileges of membership of a trade or profession. There were clear demarcation lines between trades, traditionally accepted to control competition. New ideas about free trade did not fit with the traditions. There were bound to be disputes.

In disputes between individuals, the parties might prefer private arbitration. In 1619 Henry Goodwin claimed that Roger Dromant had caused him loss by drawing the customers of his mill in Great Torrington away to his newly built Frithelstock mill. They agreed to put their dispute to arbitration.[88] But nearly all the relevant evidence is of Government intervention, through the Privy Council. Under James I and Charles I it was vigilant and active in its supervision, using arbitration as its preferred process for managing the differences which inevitably arose from increasing competition.

Members of different trades and professions clashed over the sale of similar products and services. On Sunday 29 May 1614 the Council commissioned Coke CJ and Sir Thomas Lake, a great favourite of James I and soon to be one of his Secretaries of State, to deal with such a dispute

---

86. Between distillers Nat Arch C 103/189.
87. Nat Arch C 42, 'held by the National Archives: Chancery, Wardrobe, Royal Household, Exchequer and various commissions'.
88. Nat Arch E 13416JasI/Mich 21.

among apothecaries, physicians and grocers in London.[89] Differences
often arose between retailers and wholesalers, particularly in the London
wine trade, and between importers and local suppliers. The Council
commissioned the Lord Mayor and Aldermen of London as arbitrators to
set prices between the wine merchants and the vintners, fixing 'a course
therein as the merchants be not discouraged'.[90]

Pins   In 1616 the Council had to deal with a dispute between the
retailers of pins and the pinmakers, represented by the Pinners' Company.[91]
On Sunday morning, 21 April at Whitehall, it renewed an earlier order
with the parties' consent. It provided first that the pinmakers should stop
confiscating imported pins. Secondly, because public policy required a
ready market for all pins made in England: 'the traders shall weekly take
from the pinmakers such quantity of pins as they shall have in readiness...
brought on Saturday every week to the Pinmakers Hall, to be seen, viewed
and received by the traders'. The traders would pay cash unless credit had
been agreed. Thirdly, the pinmakers would make and bring whatever pins
the traders wanted made according to the foreign patterns they supplied,
of the same quality and at the market price. Then provision was made
for disputes:

> Two of the Company of Haberdashers of small wares to be chosen yearly by
> the traders, and two of the Company of Girdlers, to be chosen yearly by the
> Pinners, shall be present and view the pins sold, and judge... goodness and
> prices allowable for the service of the realm... and to arbitrate and agree any
> difference.

If they disagreed, the Masters of the Companies of Haberdashers and
Girdlers would decide. But on 16 June 1616 the Pinmakers' Company
complained that the Haberdashers had failed to observe that agreement,
which had been made an order, upon a report of the Lord Chief Justice and
with the consent of both parties. The Council ordered that 'the petitioners
may be admitted to relieve themselves by the course and benefit of the
laws of the realm, without further trouble to their Lordships'; that is, they
could execute the order as if it were a judgment.[92]

But even that did not resolve the matter. On 14 October 1618, sitting
in the Star Chamber, the Council ordered Coke CJKB, the Law Officers
and Serjeant Carew to consider the patent again and 'such clauses as are
considered to be prejudicial' and to order and settle the same as shall be

89. *APC* 33.450.
90. *APC* 34.503.
91. *APC* 34.499.
92. *APC* 34.590.

requisite'. Their report was considered the following week.[93] Coke said that he had 'accommodated the material differences by way of consent of parties'. The Council adopted his report 'and an act entered in the Register of Council Causes', but asked Coke, 'for the preventing of any further difference and for the perpetual settling of that manufacture', to look at the clauses in the patent which referred to imported pins and 'accommodate' any remaining matters of contention.

Then 'the Deputies of the States General of the United Provinces residing here complained of the interruption to free commerce by the restraint upon foreign pins'; and they were supported 'by the Haberdashers and some of the Pinners themselves'.[94] The Council heard both sides' counsel and then told the Haberdashers to set down their complaints in writing and submit them to the Pinners, for them to answer in writing, and then Sir Julius Caesar MR and Coke CJKB would consider them and hear them further. Proceedings brought by 'certain traders in pins' before the Court of Exchequer would meanwhile be stayed. 'The question betwixt them was, whether a mere merchant, such as Thomas Aldersey is, may retail any wares within that city'. That was Chester, and Aldersey had married an ironmonger's widow and was selling the stock she had inherited. Other retailers had broken his shop windows, spoiled his goods and ejected his customers.[95] Both sides appeared with their counsel, Aldersey pleading an Order in Council of Elizabeth I, his opponents relying on custom. The Council commissioned the Lord Chancellor, Sir Julius Caesar MR and Sir Thomas Lake, with the 'assistance of Sir Peter Warburton, Justice of the Common Pleas, in respect of his experience in the state and governance of that city... to impart their opinions to the Board... to be finally determined according to justice'. Until then, Aldersey was to 'have free liberty... to retail those wares in his house or open shop', there being 'no reason to restrain him but rather equity on his part, having by marriage goods of great value'.

On 26 June 1616, after dealing with Coke's debasement, the Council heard the commissioners' report, signed by Ellesmere LC and Sir Thomas Lake, recorded it in full, and ratified and confirmed it, ordering that it be 'entered in the Register of Council Causes as an Act of this Board, to be hereafter duly observed by the parties in every point and respect according to the true intent and meaning'. The dispute had been based partly on a misunderstanding of an old charter which was intended to help Chester out of a slump by fostering the trade in calfskins. Wholesalers had been licensed to trade retail and vice versa. The Government now saw

93. *APC* 36.272; 36.279.
94. *APC* 37.6.
95. *APC* 34.93.

no reason to put limits on trade. Times were bad enough in Chester and anything to encourage trade should be welcome to all. So the relaxation of the monopolies was continued. If either side 'shall be found refractory', a new licence would be granted 'for the benefit and relief of the city'.

Textiles   There are some records of private arbitrations from the early years of the textile industry, for example the award of Sir Edward Trafford about mills in Bollin,[96] but most relate to the work of the Council. On Sunday 2 June 1616 it had to deal with petitions from woolgrowers, including 'persons of quality' from all parts of England, complaining of the inconveniences which would arise if the statute of 5 & 6 Edward VI were enforced.[97] It had already asked Coke and other judges to report. It asked them to hear what the clothiers had to say and report by the following Friday. On that day it postponed the hearing to the following Wednesday, pointing out that it had often heard the matter debated by counsel and insisting 'that no learned counsel for either party or any of the staplers be there present'. There is no record of any such hearing or later proceedings.

In a dispute between the drapers and mercers of Shrewsbury in 1619 the Council appointed the Lord President of the Council of Wales and Sir Thomas Chamberlain, Chief Justice of Chester, as mediators to 'accommodate and settle such order as may suit with the general good of those parts'.[98] Each side claimed a monopoly of buying 'Welsh cloths and cottons at Oswestry market'. They reported in person.[99] Their efforts to mediate had failed. Arbitration would be necessary and they did not feel up to that without further authority from the Board and the strengthening of the panel. So the Board agreed to add Sir Peter Warburton and Sir John Croke, JPs for Shropshire, 'formerly employed by the Board in settling that trade of cloth in Shrewsbury and Oswestry'; Sir Edward Bromley, Baron of the Exchequer and Recorder of Shrewsbury; and three assize judges of the North Wales circuit 'as persons of great experience in the state of those countries'. That mighty panel was 'to order such a course for the final settling of that difference as shall be expedient and may best serve for the maintenance and support of the trade to the general benefit of the country and the good of that town'.

That was on 27 October 1619. On 10 November they reported their award.[100] They had first considered:

> the question of law being first propounded by the Lord President to the rest of us, we upon consideration had of the laws and statutes in this case, and custom

96. Nat Arch WARD2/58/218/1/30.
97. *APC* 34.564.
98. *APC* 36.487. TC Mendenhall *The Shrewsbury Drapers*.
99. *APC* 37.49.
100. *APC* 37.56.

of the town of Shrewsbury, are of opinion that a mercer of Shrewsbury ought not by law to use and exercise the trade and mistery of a draper, for that trade is within the statute of *anno* 5 Elizabeth... and requireth men of experience and skill which cannot be attained by those that be strangers to the trade and have not served as apprentices... by their unskilfulness the ruin of this trade may follow... the mercers ought not to meddle.

The drapers brought in no less than £2,000 to every monthly market, loss of which would impoverish all the shearmen and other workers and all the sellers of Welsh cloth. 'For which causes and many others which we forbear to mention, the mercers should content themselves with that trade wherein they have been brought up.' This award did not apply to any complaints of the shearmen and others employed in the dressing and working of cloth, or to outsiders in Wales who sent their cloth to be sold in Oswestry. The panel was prepared to hear any complaints from them separately, 'in some convenient time'.

The Council sent to legal experts disputes about the quality of cloth, for example to Sir Julius Caesar MR and Coke CJKB on the buyer's refusal to pay for 'false cloth', which had been inspected and passed, 'to give such indifferent and equal order as the cause shall require'.[101]

The Alnager was the royal official who, until 1699 when the functions were abolished, tested cloth and collected the duty on it. In 1613 he was in dispute with some clothiers in Shropshire and Wales. The Council wrote to the Chief Baron and the other Barons of the Exchequer, 'forasmuch as those differences concern His Majesty in his revenue, and are properly to be determined by you and the clothiers pretend disability to prosecute in any legal course', instructing them as arbitrators, not as the Exchequer Court:[102]

Call before you as well some sufficiently authorized by the Alnager, as by the clothiers... and, upon hearing of counsel on both sides, order some such course for the avoiding of any further trouble between them as to justice shall appertain.

In 1614 John Brownlow had 'been employed in a joint stock in the trade of cloth in Antwerp' working for George Lowe and Company for seven years.[103] He had a credit against the company of £1,500, and that was all he had; so 'he is utterly disabled to right himself by ordinary course of law'. Therefore the Council instructed four London merchants: 'to call the parties before you and, upon a full hearing of the cause, to mediate some conscionable and indifferent end'.

Four judges were considered appropriate for a commission to mediate between the 'poor weavers and shearers' in Suffolk and the clothiers

101. *APC* 36.42.
102. *APC* 33.32.
103. *APC* 33.643.

they alleged were preventing them from making cloth, 'taking some time, as soon as you may, to settle the difference, if you can, to both their contentments'.[104]

When the clothmakers of Totnes complained that His Majesty's Customs were levying unjustified dues on them,[105] the Council referred the dispute to the Chancellor of the Exchequer, the Master of the Rolls and Coke CJKB to 'reconcile the differences between them'.

In 1618 the Council wrote to no fewer than ten Norfolk knights:[106]

> It is not unknown to you… what care this Board has taken for the settling of the differences between the Wardens of the Worsted Weavers of Norwich and the Sellers of Worsted Yarn of Norfolk, Suffolk, Essex and Cambridge concerning a privilege claimed by the city of Norwich of seizing all worsted yarn brought into the city wanting length or number of threads.

The first five named knights had reported to the Council, which had accepted their report and made an order. Now the worsted weavers of Norwich and Norfolk complained that that order had been made 'for want of due information'. Two of the referees, the ones for Norwich and Norfolk, had been absent. They asked for a new reference. The Council 'conceiving it fit rather sharply to reprove the neglect of those referees who were absent', granted a new hearing with substitutes and additional referees. The original order would stay in force until the Council replaced it. 'To the end that in a work of this nature, so much importing the orderly governing and settling of a trade upon which so many persons and families depend, no unnecessary delays may be used', it instructed the ten knights, every one of them, to meet at Bury St Edmunds before 10 December, seven weeks later, and to 'do your best endeavours to settle and accommodate such course between them as you shall find just and reasonable', or certify.

Mining and Minerals   Accounts of disputes between miners and landowners which attempt to put them into their social and legal context do not mention informal methods of resolving them. In a thorough study of free miners, Andy Wood has shown that:[107]

> Nowhere is the ambiguous place of customary law within the early modern English legal system more clearly revealed than in the contests fought in ancient mining areas between independent miners and those who sought the abolition of the miners' rights.

104. *APC* 35.126.
105. *APC* 36.212.
106. *APC* 45.155.
107. Andy Wood 'Custom, Identity and Resistance' and RR Pennington *Stannary Law*.

He gives a comprehensive account of the miners' own courts and of the customary law which they insisted should establish and govern their mining rights; but it would be a mistake to assume that they had only the courts to go to or that they always preferred litigation to other processes. Sometimes they asked the Government to provide arbitration. Sometimes they arranged their own.

When disputes arose among lead miners in Somerset in 1614, the Privy Council accepted that they were too poor to go to law.[108] It commissioned five local gentlemen (or any two or three) 'to mediate some such course agreeable to equity and good conscience'. And when local landowners tried to get a tenth of the profits of the 'poor miners in the High Peak... whereon there hath not anciently been paid any tithe at all', the Council:[109]

> Forasmuch as the petitioners inform that they are ten thousand in number and, if they should pay a full tenth part, they should be forced to leave the mine, to the prejudice of His Majesty in his revenue, and the utter overthrow of themselves, their wives and children.... Take special notice of this complaint and, on your coming into that county this next circuit... order some such course for the final determining as to justice shall appertain, without further trouble to the petitioners or other vexation by unnecessary suit.

The West Yorkshire archives provide plenty of evidence of private arbitration and mediation. Sir Arthur Ingram was a working-class Leeds boy who became one of Yorkshire's largest landowners, an MP and perhaps the most successful financial expert of his time. The Yorkshire alum mine was not one of his successes. He first bought a share in it when it went bankrupt in 1608 and later took further advantage of its financial difficulties, despite being found guilty of corruption with the Earl of Suffolk. He took over the works in 1621 but even he could not make it profitable. He was at first promoted at court, knighted in 1613 and made Cofferer of the Household. His shady business dealings might have been ignored but never his humble origins, and he was snubbed at court. So he went back to Yorkshire and devoted himself to profitable and ostentatious property development. The West Yorkshire archives reveal his involvement in arbitration. In 1618, after mediation by John Mayle, he signed an agreement with George Lowe by which he would first account with Mayle and then receive 10s a ton from Lowe; pay £1,400 to the King, taking 15s of the 40s for each ton carried; take Henry Wood's share of the profits, which he had just bought for £1,500; and observe other ancillary provisions. An arbitration clause provided for John Mayle to decide any resulting disputes.[110]

108. *APC* 33.367.
109. *APC* 34.224.
110. West Yorks WYL100/PO/8/1/24.

In 1625 three arbitrators awarded that three men would release all claims on the disputed alum works to Ingram, who would pay one of them £105 in return. The following year William Turner wrote to him asking him to agree to arbitration of their dispute about the alum works and about an annuity. The next year Christopher Brooke of Lincoln's Inn made an award in Ingram's dispute about the Sussex manor of Stanner. In 1630 Ingram signed articles which provided for a final end to all his differences with the lawyer Sir Thomas Bludder MP; the arbitrators would study all accounts between them and finally resolve the dispute. In 1634 an award recorded that the Earl of Suffolk would pay him £550 in lieu of debts of £1,380. In the same year John Mitchell's deposition declared that, fifteen years before, as arbitrator he had received from Ingram all he had awarded to be owing to George Lowe and paid it to him. Then there is an award of 1636, relating to some commons; and a bond of 1638 to submit his dispute with Lowe, with power to the arbitrators to appoint an umpire if they could not agree, so terminating the matter as rapidly as possible.[111] He corresponded with Wentworth, Earl of Strafford, in 1630, about a dispute between them, suggesting Sir Thomas Tildesley, the Royalist soldier, as arbitrator.[112] A letter survives from 1638 to Ingram from Dr Thomas Comber, asking him to confirm a settlement between them, which had been achieved 'by the mediation of divers knights of quality'.[113]

It is hardly surprising, then, that Ingram's experience was called on to help in the resolution of disputes. In 1614 he had already, as sole arbitrator, mediated a settlement between 'the farmers of the Great Customs' and those who collected the customs duties on silk.[114] And he is named as one of the successful mediators, with the Earl of Suffolk and the Duke of Somerset, in a 1625 document recording the composition of the questioning of a lease and sequestration of profits on wines.[115] He was appointed a JP in 1626 and again in 1636 and may have had opportunities for exercising his mediation skills more often than we know.

Those who had traditional mining rights, like those who had rights of common, could claim that their property predated their feudal lords': 'When Adam delved and Eve span, who was then the gentleman?' At best the landowner was some Johnny-come-lately from Normandy. The sturdy black-eyed miners, as they saw themselves, were proud of an older family and of a law founded in custom – which, of course, allowed it to change without formality as need required.

111. West Yorks WYL100/PO/8/I/58; WYL100/PO/8/VII/41; WYL100/DZ/49; WYL100/PO/8/I/73; WYL100/L/15; WYL100/PO/8/III/49; WYL100/L8; WYL100/PO/8/14.
112. West Yorks WYL100/PO/7/II/29; WYL100/PO/7/IV.
113. West Yorks WYL100/NO/C/7.
114. West Yorks WYL100/PO/6/IV/4.
115. Nat Arch E 134/22JasI/Mich1.

The Mint   Sir Richard Martin was a goldsmith, Lord Mayor of London, and Master of the Mint. When he died in 1617 his successor wanted to take over the tools used there. Martin's widow made a claim for them, some gold, and 'iron works for the strengthening of the furnaces, set up at her husband's charge'. Fulke Greville, Chancellor of the Exchequer, was commissioned 'to give order for such satisfaction to the suppliant as in conscience and equity shall be found reasonable'.[116]

11. GUILDS AND COMPANIES[117]

It was usual for the merchant guilds of London and the other cities to provide in their charters for disputes among members to be arbitrated by their officers. For example, clause V of the charter issued to the Drapers' Company in 1610 provided that one member aggrieved by another must ask the Master to arrange an arbitration and must not sue.[118]

Sometimes a disappointed party brought an appeal against an award made by a company's own procedures. In *Dr Steward v East-India Co*,[119] the Court of Chancery had to deal with a 'Bill to be relieved against an award made by some of the members of the East India Company touching the quantum of freight due to the plaintiff'.

The guild's own procedures may have sufficed for most internal disputes but not for major factional strife. The Privy Council met nearly every Sunday. On 31 October 1613 there was a full attendance: the Archbishop of Canterbury, Lord Chancellor, Lord Privy Seal, Duke of Lennox, Lord Admiral, Lord Chamberlain, Earls of Worcester and Pembroke, Lords Zouche, Knollys, Wotton, Stanhope, and Sir Julius Caesar, then Chancellor of the Exchequer.[120] Their main concern that morning was the behaviour of the recently incorporated Company of Merchants of London Trading into France. The merchants of the west coast had complained that the new London company threatened to 'utterly overthrow their whole trade, to the undoing of themselves and many thousand handicraftsmen and others who depend on them'. They had produced to the Council evidence of 'the danger like to fall on the whole country, unless some speedy course be taken'. The Council had heard the evidence and the arguments of counsel for both sides. It commissioned Sir Thomas Parry, Chancellor of the Duchy of Lancaster, with the two Chief Justices, Coke and Hobart, and a Master of Requests, Sir Daniel Dunn, to hear the parties and 'order some such

---

116. *APC* 35.345.
117. Steve Rappaport *Worlds Within Worlds* and IW Archer *The Pursuit of Stability* have information about London guilds but of the 16th century. Roebuck *Golden Age* 194–200.
118. Coventry History Centre PA 99/1; *APC* 45.312 records the Council's request to the Attorney General for an opinion in a dispute between the Shipwrights and a member.
119. (1700) 2 Vern 380; 23 ER 842.
120. *APC* 33.247.

indifferent course between them, as may serve to keep the trade under a settled and meet government.' The Council would then make the formal order. Meanwhile, it instructed the Treasury to write to the western ports, giving them liberty of free trade until 'the matter be fully settled between the parties'.

In October 1617 the Merchants of the Staple complained that the East India Company had taken over their premises in Leadenhall and changed the locks, 'pretending to have got a lease from the city'.[121] That needed a powerful committee: Caesar MR, Coke (now back in favour), both Chief Justices, and the Law Officers. They were to call not only the parties – the Staplers and the East India Company – but also the 'committees for the leasing of the city's lands', and then to 'order such a course as shall be just and expedient'. That was an express injunction to the tribunal to look to the legal rights but only so far as that would produce an award consonant with 'expediency'.

Sir Henry Yelverton took over, with the office of Attorney General, the burden of enquiring into disputes and advising the Board which Sir Francis Bacon had discharged for many years. The Masters of Trinity House in Newcastle claimed primage, a levy of threepence on every last (commonly two tons) of corn imported by the merchants of that city.[122] They claimed that the merchants had been refusing to pay primage for three years. Both sides agreed to submit the dispute to Yelverton. He reported his opinion. The merchants should be required to pay primage, but only three halfpence a last, and arrears for only a year and a half, 'because they may not be discouraged to bring in so great a commodity for the good of the kingdom'. But threepence as before for all commodities other than corn. Any importer other than a 'free merchant' of Newcastle should pay the full threepence, even on corn. That would, he hoped, 'breed a perpetual peace between the Masters and merchants'.

The Council commissioned four of its own members to deal with a dispute between the new and old Company of Merchant Adventurers, because they were already 'well acquainted with the state of this business... to reconcile the difference, if you may, according to your best discretions'.[123]

The merchants of the Eastland Company had become divided in their interests between those who resided in London and the rest 'on the coast', who complained that the Governors of the Company were imposing 'unjust exactions and taxes' on them.[124] The Council first referred their petition to the Attorney General, Sir Francis Bacon. He heard the testimony of rep-

121. *APC* 35.345.
122. *APC* 35.367; 35.372.
123. *APC* 35.116.
124. *APC* 34.553.

resentatives of both sides and the arguments of their counsel and made
a report:

> which was read at the Board in presence of the merchants of both sides. But
> those of the coast towns not finding themselves satisfied or likely to be relieved
> by that report in such sort as they desired, we did direct them to set down their
> principal exceptions in writing and their brethren in London... were to make
> reply.... The questions now reduced to a narrower point, taking unto you for
> your assistance Altham B and the Attorney General, or either of them, set down
> some order for reconciling the differences... with as much indifferency as may
> be, that the trade may continue and prosper to the general contentment of them
> all.... In case there shall need further authority for confirmation thereof, we may
> supply it.

Again, efficiency was preferred to legal niceties. That was on 26 May
1616. On 30 May the tribunal reported and on 5 June their certificate
was recorded in great detail; and 'their Lordships ratified and allowed of
the same; and did order for the final concluding of these controversies
the certificate... should be put in execution as an Act of this Board'. The
by-laws which restricted the imports of the merchants of the coastal towns
were annulled. No new by-laws would have effect unless they had been
approved at an annual meeting attended by representatives of the coastal
towns, except in emergencies, and they were subject to ratification by the
Lord Chancellor, Lord Treasurer and the two Chief Justices. Apprentices
from the coastal towns would no longer have to go up to London to be made
free, and henceforth would be charged only ten shillings to the Company
and twelve pence to the registrar of the coastal town. Other sections dealt
with seizure of ships abroad, impositions on the Company arising from 'the
late disturbance of the Government of Poland (of which the coastal towns
had not paid their shares), evaluation of cloth, equal relief for 'decayed
traders', and the fair distribution of funds between London and the coast,
the coastal towns to have the right to inspect the Company's accounts.
The allowances made by the Company to the officers of the coastal towns
should be raised in line with inflation, 'comparing the difference betwixt
these times and the former'.

When Richard Lewis, a member of the Eastland Company, was reported
to have disobeyed an award of the Company at Elbing, 'and afterwards
refusing to come to any reasonable agreement fled into Poland', causing
trouble for the Company there, the Council ordered that he should be
'committed to the custody of a messenger' and called, with the Company,
before Caesar MR, Sir Christopher Perkins, Master of Requests, and
Serjeant Finch, who would 'hear and end the difference'.[125]

125. *APC* 35.34.

The debts of the Muscovy Company had to be discharged by a levy on its members. John Bedell, merchant, complained that he had paid his share but, 'by default of the accountant who had drawn the leviation', he had not been credited with it.[126] The Council asked five other members (or any three) to examine the difference between the Company and Bedell 'by search of the books of the Company and otherwise, and end and determine the same (if they can)', or certify their opinions.

As early as 1616 the Council dealt with the Turkey Company, as the Levant Merchants were known.[127] On 13 July 1627 it ordered it to 'present the names of some fit and indifferent persons to be commissioners' in a dispute between the Company and Nicholas Leate, a London merchant, about his contribution to the cost of 'settling the peace at Algiers'.[128] Leate objected to the Company's choice. He said they were all subscribers and therefore not disinterested. He 'humbly prayed that the Board should nominate 4 or 5 indifferent persons, or any 3, that have no relation to this business'. The Council responded by appointing nine 'referees', of whom any five should examine and make a final end, or 'report the true state of the cause' for it to make an order for the petitioner's relief 'as shall be agreeable to justice and equity'. The Company prevaricated. On 31 March 1628 it claimed it had 'just exceptions, as well against the proceedings of the referees as against the matters by them reported'.[129] The Council allowed an adjournment but insisted the Company put its objections, procedural and of substance, in writing without delay. Still the Company played for time. On 31 May 1628 Leate complained that it 'had been five several times required by the Board and often solicited by him to bring in their answers'.[130] Now it put up the spurious excuse that it could not answer because its counsel was absent. The Council told it to supply its answer forthwith and thereupon a date would be fixed for a hearing.

Elizabeth I's Council would never have allowed such blatant contempt. But by 1628 the Council's interest in private disputes was perhaps waning. On 8 July it received a petition from the Company 'wherein they remonstrate that Leate hath for the space of three years kept them in suit before the Board'.[131] They said that they had at all times been ready to answer 'but because the business dependeth upon accounts, articles and instructions, which hitherto have received no due trial, and as the cause is of so great consequence', they humbly sued that it be sent to 'some of

126. *APC* 39.154. The story of the failures of the old and new Muscovy Companies is told in Hart 51–54.
127. *APC* 35.356.
128. *APC* 43.19.
129. *APC* 43.366.
130. *APC* 43.474.
131. *APC* 44.18.

His Majesty's Courts of Justice either in law or equity'. And the Council
agreed. The Company's audacity seemed to have paid off, but on 7 August
Leate showed the Council that he was 'a lone man and through age grown
weak and infirm, while the Company are many and potent, and that the
cause hath depended before the Board near on four years'.[132] The Council
appeared to rouse itself:

> This cause hath dependance upon the State, wherein the Company engaged
> themselves for performance, and therefore necessarily to be heard and
> determined by this Board. The Commissioners' cause is not a matter of fact, but
> depends upon Commissions and Instructions given both by his late Majesty, this
> Table and the Company.

And Neate had asked again that the Council should make the Company do
what it had many times been required to do, to make its case to the Council
in writing, so that the Council might make a final end.

> Their Lordships, well approving of the reasons and cause shown, have thought
> fit and ordered that the parties attend on Wednesday next in the afternoon for the
> further hearing and determining of this business and the Company bring with
> them the Report with their answer in writing, according to former Orders.

But it was not until 3 October that the parties came before the Council
again, and then it was only for the Company to prevaricate further.[133] It
claimed it had 'divers material exceptions to make to the former Report,
wherewith they came not so fully prepared'. Leate could make no answer
without seeing them, so the Council ordered the Company – yet again – to
produce them in writing. Leate would have to reply in writing and give the
Company time to respond. The hearing was adjourned until the last Friday
of the month and 'in the interim the Exceptions, Answers and Reply should
with convenient time be set down by either party in writing and delivered
to each other respectively'.

The Company's lawyers had managed to transform the Council's
expeditious procedures into no better than those of a court of law. After
further delays, on 17 December 1628, the record simply states:[134]

> This day the differences between the Levant Company and Nicholas Leate,
> merchant, were heard at the Board and were debated by counsel on both sides
> in the presence of the parties. On consideration of the debate their Lordships
> did think fit and order that the differences should be dismissed to be determined
> legally by suit in Chancery before the Lord Keeper of the Great Seal of England.

132. *APC* 44.76.
133. *APC* 44.186.
134. *APC* 44.266.

A triumph for the 'rule of law'? The power of wealth and influence had prevailed over the merits after five years of expert procrastination and the beggary of the individual merchant faced with a corporate monopoly.

Perhaps that moment marks the end of the Council's scheme of arbitration. But on 31 March 1630 the King himself commissioned a panel of the Lord Keeper, Lord President, Earl of Bridgwater and Vice Chamberlain, or any two or more, the Lord Keeper being one, in a dispute between the Goldsmiths Company and John Reynolds, a member of the Company and formerly its Deputy Assayor.[135] Reynolds was seeking to be restored; the Company did not want him but, 'at their Lordships' mediation they are willing to give him £100, besides that which is due to him £24, provided he shall deliver to them quiet possession of their house' and the assay stamps. Reynolds had also published a book defaming his predecessors and former wardens. It must be suppressed and he was 'admonished and strictly required to carry himself respectfully towards the Company in general and in all peaceable and quiet manner towards the particular members as becometh a Brother of the society'.

Rival Towns   The competition could be between towns. Totnes and Dartmouth were in dispute about their respective shares of the 'sum required for the suppressing of pirates'.[136] Secretary Calvert and the Chancellor of the Exchequer were on 18 May 1619 delegated to 'settle such a rate as shall be most reasonable and indifferent'. Five days later letters went to the Mayors of the two towns with detailed instructions.[137]

12.   EMPLOYMENT AND APPRENTICESHIP

Assize judges sometimes had to resolve disputes between employer and employee. The Reverend Nicholas Honey was a scoundrel who had been convicted of extortion, upon which he had 'delivered very idle and scandalous words of the justices'. When Jenken Jones complained that Honey had not paid his wages, Davenport B called on three JPs (or any two of them) to deal with the dispute and 'to bind Honey to the next assizes if he refuses to perform their order'.[138]

From 1601, the Elizabethan Poor Law had provided for two JPs to create parish apprenticeships, by which they could require farmers and tradesmen and women to take poor, illegitimate or orphaned boys and girls, providing for their sustenance and training, whether they liked it or not. The assize judges had to deal with many disputes which arose from such compulsory

135. *APC* 45.330.
136. *APC* 36.453.
137. *APC* 36.456.
138. Cockburn *Western* 300.

apprenticeships. Some would go to great lengths to avoid that statutory burden. A record from the Somerset Assizes in 1648 shows:[139]

> Joseph Griffen was indicted and acquitted at this assizes of stealing 12d from Richard Hunt.... Griffen is a small boy apprenticed to Hunt, and thus his offence was not a felony. Nevertheless Hunt wishes to be freed from his apprentice but refuses to return the £5 and three pecks of wheat paid to him by Griffen's father under the apprenticeship indenture. Consideration of the matter is referred to the four nearest JPs, who are to make an equitable order settling the dispute.

But the records of the following Somerset Quarter Sessions show that Hunt was ordered to keep Griffen as his apprentice unless he could show good cause.

The statutory obligation fell on women, as on men. What a story must lie behind this record from 1642![140]

> Elizabeth Clarke of Trent, widow, was bound to this assizes for refusing to take Edith Durnford as an apprentice. Her counsel, Richard King, has informed the court that Clarke is worth only £15 a year, although her sons have estates of their own, and has no work for Durnford, who is not more than nine years old and 'of mean capacity to do service'. Consideration of the matter is referred to the two nearest JPs to Trent, who, if they find the information to be correct, are to release Clarke from the apprentice.

But that was not the end of Edith's troubles:

> The suggestion made by counsel at the assize hearing was adopted, Durnford being bound out in 1643 as a parish apprentice to John Clarke of Trent. About three years later she was taken ill, and was still unfit for work in April 1647 when John Clarke petitioned Quarter Sessions for permission to exchange her for a male apprentice. Sessions unwillingly allowed his request on proof that her lameness was not the result of ill treatment.

13. CONCLUSIONS

All kinds of commerce changed in the 17th century until, with the Promissory Notes Act 1704, England was prepared for a credit economy. Yet as early as 1606 the Government tried to provide by treaty a system of international commercial arbitration with France. It even named the forerunners of those modern-day arbitrators, more experienced, more skilled and some more scholarly than most commercial judges, who do the work today. In every form of domestic business, too, mediation and arbitration were usually preferred by those who became successful. And they were prepared to serve in resolving the difficulties of others. Where

---

139. Cockburn *Western* 1214; *Som QS Recs* iii 73, Cockburn *Western* 290.
140. Cockburn *Western* 1003; *Som QS Recs* iii 35.

practicable, it was thought best to postpone unpayable debts and arrange for their payment by instalments.

By the end of the century the Government was no longer offering to set up arbitrations in response to petitions in any routine or systematic way. But those involved in commerce had efficient means at hand for the private resolution of most disputes, and in most cases took full advantage of them. They still assumed without argument that fairness should prevail over legal rights unless otherwise advised. Only when state interests were at risk would the Government, again without debate, insist on expediency as the criterion.

8 THE CHURCH, UNIVERSITIES, SCHOOLS AND CHARITIES

Many times, things which otherwise can have no speedy end by law, are compounded by arbitrement.

Archbishop Thomas Ridley (1662)[1]

On the evidence of the York archives, we may safely conclude that the system of ecclesiastical justice in Tudor and Stuart England allowed every chance for a more or less amicable settlement.

JA Sharpe[2]

The Merry Wives of Windsor opens with Justice Shallow complaining of Falstaff's affront to him, which he insists was a riot and worthy of the attention of the Court of Star Chamber. Sir Hugh Evans, stage Welshman, tries to calm him down and offers his service as mediator: 'I am of the Church and will be glad to do my benevolence, to make atonements and compremises between you'. And, when Page and Falstaff appear, Evans says: 'Peace, I pray you. Now let us understand. There is three umpires in this matter'. Page: 'We three to hear it and end it between them'.

Roebuck *Miscellany* 100

1. INTRODUCTION[3]

In the culture of the time, it was usual to seek the intervention of the clergy in disputes among parishioners, and 'manuals of godly conduct and the biographies of pious clergy stressed the duty of the Christian minister to reconcile differences and prevent recourse to law'.[4] The poet George Herbert, himself a parish priest, was one of the most popular authors in England in 1652 when his *Country Parson* was published and sold for a shilling. He knew he would be well understood when he wrote of an ordinary parson:[5]

1. Thomas Ridley *A View of the Civile and Ecclesiasticall Law* 105.
2. JA Sharpe 'Such Disagreement Betwyx Neighbours' 178.
3. James Behrens 'The History of Mediation of Probate Disputes' 141: 'There is no published research as to the use of mediation in Church disputes over this period'; but see RH Helmholz *Marriage Litigation in Medieval England*.
4. MJ Ingram 'Communities and Courts' [Ingram] 110 and similar references in his *Church Courts*.
5. Keith Thomas *Religion and Magic* 182–183, citing George Herbert *A Priest to the Temple* Chapter xxiii.

151

He endures not that any of his flock should go to law; but in any controversy that
they should resort to him as their judge… he never decides it alone, but sends
for three or four of the ablest of the parish to hear the cause with him, whom he
makes to deliver their opinion first.

There are primary sources, too, 'act book references indicating that certain
suits were *sub spe concordie*, *in tractatu pacis* or *concordata* [in the hope
of a settlement, working towards peace, or settled]', including actions for
debt and trespass, which were in theory outside ecclesiastical jurisdiction.[6]
One example will illustrate the continuity. A document from the first
year of James I's reign is preserved in the Derbyshire Record Office.[7] A
rentcharge had been imposed on lands 'in the town and fields of Great
Longsdon' since 1356. After 250 years it was still intended to fund repairs
to the church, mending of highways and relief of the poor. Litigation
to recover arrears in the Consistory Court at Lichfield had resulted in a
sentence which was now being appealed. But then:

to save expense and preserve amity among neighbours and to the end that the
rent should not be extinguished, the parties with mutual consent and freewill,
and with the good liking of most and the best sort of inhabitants of the chapelry,
have submitted to the arbitration of Raphe Whyte, George Harries, Robert Wood
and Richard James, with the umpiring of the Rt Hon William Cavendish.

And that William Cavendish (1552–1626), who if necessary would have
unquestioned authority to decide as umpire, was later to become the 1st
Earl of Devonshire. In 1604 he had just become a JP. Perhaps more to the
point, he was the second son of Bess of Hardwick's first marriage, and so
came from a family with much experience of dispute resolution.[8]
Assize judges regularly referred to arbitrators disputes with an
ecclesiastical element.[9] At the Devon Assizes on 16 March 1635,
Finch CJKB referred a dispute between the Rev William Lange and his
parishioners to three JPs to settle.[10] If they failed, the Bishop of Exeter was
to decide, 'however, those matters which have already been decided in the
consistory court or otherwise determined are to be varied only by order of
the bishop.' It was clear that the assize judge was in charge, but equally
that he was sensitive to ecclesiastical authority.
The award of a privately arranged arbitration was successfully pleaded
as a bar, where a prioress and a bishop had submitted their dispute to the
Chief Justice of the King's Bench.[11]

6. Ingram 326 fnn99–101; Roebuck *Middle Ages* 290.
7. Derby D3580/T22.
8. Roebuck *Golden Age* 165–180.
9. Cockburn *Western* 9, 11, 49, 68, 366, 892, 1085, 1110, 1127, 1131, including property
    matters like presentments 562, profits of a parsonage 1110 and tithes 892, 1127.
10. Cockburn *Western* 366.
11. Rastell *Entries* under 'Barres en Quare Impedit'.

Two country parsons, Oliver Heywood the royalist and Ralph Josselin the parliamentarian, kept diaries which provide detailed evidence of their efforts to resolve disputes during the most troubled times of the century, noting the impact of the civil strife but showing that the work of dispute resolution went on as usual.

The Church of England might even use its experience and good offices to attempt to bring concord between denominations abroad. A large bundle of documents (1631–1640) in the Parliamentary Archives records the mission of John Durye, appointed by Archbishop Laud expressly to mediate the differences which beset the Lutherans and Calvinists in Germany.[12]

2. PEWS

The Church could create new kinds of property rights. One which has required the attention of arbitrators over the ages is the right to occupy a designated pew. Where one sat in church was a matter of rank and nothing could be less trivial in a parish community. The best pews belonged to the local gentry. The lower orders, while required by law to attend, had to find space for themselves at the back. After all: 'God made them high and lowly and ordered their estate', as the hymn has it, and such squabbles are not unknown now. They were best resolved by private arbitration without outside or formal intervention.[13] They were for the squire and the vicar and 'a chief parishioner' to handle.[14]

William Purefoy was able to end the differences between Sibilla Holbech, widow, and William Priest, yeoman, over pews in the parish church of Fyllingley. Sibilla's ancestors had built the pews in question, so she must have them; but she had to find another pew for William elsewhere in the church.[15] A simple practical problem of audibility was not beneath the attention of the Government. In 1612 the Privy Council instructed churchwardens to give an old deaf woman a seat nearer the pulpit, if that could be done without too much prejudice to other members of the congregation.[16] And the assize judge might be called on:[17]

> Settlement of the dispute between the churchwardens and inhabitants of South Molton and Mr Molford about seats in the aisle of South Molton church, about which an order was made at the last quarter sessions, is referred on the motion of Mr Barton, to [three JPs or any two].

12. Parl Papers HL/PO/JO/10/1/41.
13. Lancs DDHK 5/2/43 (1608 four arbitrators and umpire).
14. Ingram *Church Courts* 125ff.
15. Lincoln JARVIS I.C.35.
16. Dawson *II* 632 fn132 Lansdowne MS fol 217a (1612).
17. Cockburn *Western* 1085.

But private initiative must have been the most prevalent means of settling such differences. An action had begun in the Consistory Court of the Bishop of Salisbury between William Beale and Elizabeth Sherer over a pew in Brinkworth church.[18]

> But before any sentence passed, John Ayliffe esquire... taking notice of their differences and controversies, and endeavouring to make a peace between them, called Beale and Sherer before him in the church there and, among other speeches tending to a settlement of a peace twixt them, spoke to them: 'I know not whether either of you have any right in this seat for which you strive, but this I know, that I have a right to a place, for a tenement called Jordens, and I will rather forgo my right than you shall go on with such unnecessary suits.' Mr Ayliffe, using further means for a peace twixt them, called Mr Hutchins, the minister there, and Mr John Richman, a chief parishioner, and by their assistance prevailed with them so far as that they were contented to draw lots which of them should sit in the uppermost seat, and then and there presently lots being made and put into the church book, they drew them forth, by which lot the uppermost seat fell to William Beale.

In 1630 Sir Edward Trevor was trying to mediate in the quarrel between his cousin, Sir John Trevor, and his mother about the Trevor collieries. The family were wealthy Welsh landowners, who found it hard to contain their differences, not only between the Brynkinalt and Trevalyn branches but even about pews in the parish church.[19]

Why any sensible claimant would prefer to have the matter settled is clear from just one example of litigation. For once there is no need to translate the Latin to get the point. In *Bridges v Bedingfield*,[20]

> Exceptions to debt upon an arbitration bond. Debt was brought upon a bond of award, and the breach assigned was for not delivering of quiet possession to the plaintiff of seats in a church. The defendant craves oyer of the bond and condition, which was for performance of an award to be made *de praemissis vel aliquâ parte inde*; and if there should be no award made, then for the performance of an umpirage: and pleads, that the arbitrators made no award *de præmissis*, but the umpire awarded that the plaintiff should *abinde* upon all occasions hold two seats quietly and peaceably in such a church.... The plaintiff demurred. Jones, Serjeant, maintained the demurrer; and said, that the pleading of *nullum fecerunt arbitrium* is not good; for it is said, *de præmissis* only, whereas it should have been *nec de aliquâ parte inde*: for if a bond be to perform an award of two persons, or either of them, it will not be sufficient to plead that those two persons made no award, without adding *nec eorum aliquis*....
>
> Seys, Serjeant, for the defendant. As to the first exception, *nullum fecerunt arbitrium de præmissis* is well enough; for that implies *nec de aliquâ inde parte*,

18. Ingram *Church Courts* 126.
19. East Sussex GLY/560.
20. (1675) 2 Mod 27; 86 ER 921.

especially if the contrary is not shewn in the replication; and therefore it shall never be intended that an award was made of some part....

3. TITHES

Church courts shared with lay courts jurisdiction over tithe disputes.[21] Ellesmere LC propounded the official line in 1611:[22]

> The right of tithes is properly to be tried and determined in the ecclesiastical courts and therefore, when the right of tithes appears to be in question, the temporal judges ought to surcease *ex officio*, although the party do not plead against their jurisdiction.... When a suit touching the right of tithes is well commenced in the ecclesiastical court every circumstance or matter incident, which may bar or exclude the plaintiff from that benefit which the common right gives him, may and ought to be tried in the same court by the Judges Ecclesiastical.... And so *via versa*, if a suit be well commenced in the temporal court in many cases, matters which are properly triable by the ecclesiastical law shall be tried by the Common Law, where the suit began.

But Coke insisted on the right of Common Law courts to issue writs of prohibition to halt processes begun in the church courts in a wide range of subjects. As was his wont, he passed off his own opinions as law when it suited him and he thought he could get away with it. He reported that the King's Bench had decided in 1596 that ecclesiastical courts could not judge a plea on a discharge of tithes.[23] That was what he said as Attorney General, appearing for the plaintiff, not a finding by the court – but enough for Coke.

In the King's Bench in 1614:[24]

> A man sued in the Spiritual Court for tithes of apples, the defendant pleaded an arbitrement and asked for a prohibition because the arbitration is a matter triable at Common Law, but that was denied by the Court... Coke said that, if the Spiritual Court had judged otherwise on such an award than it ought according to Common Law, then a prohibition would have been granted, which was conceded by Doddridge J.

And five years later,[25] in a dispute between a parson and parishioner for tithes, which they had submitted to arbitration, the arbitrator had awarded that the parson should make a lease of the tithes to the parishioner. A

21. Roebuck *Golden Age* 254–256; Norma Adams 'The Judicial Conflict over Tithes'; Cockburn *Western* 892, 1127.
22. In 'Some Notes, and Remembrances' in LA Knafla *Law and Politics* [Knafla] 282.
23. *Bishop of Winchester's Case* (1596) 2 Co Rep 38r–45v; similarly in *The Case of Powlett, Marquess of Winchester* (1599) 3 Co Rep 303; Knafla 142.
24. *Anonymous* (1614) 1 Rolle 12; 81 ER 291.
25. *Aldered v Wray* (1619) 2 Rolle 121; 81 ER 698. Common Pleas would also enforce an award of tithes, *Meridith Mady v Henry Osnan* (1627) Het 4; 124 ER 296.

prohibition was sought in the Church court, which denied it 'because he had his remedy on the award'.

Ellesmere LC had Coke's measure:[26]

> *Boswell's Case*. In which the Court gave no resolution at all, but *pendet huiusque indiscussum*, and was ended by arbitrement. Yet does the Chief Justice say it was resolved that the plaintiff should have his writ to the bishop generally. And for all the rest reported in that case, it is merely his own discourse, for neither did the matter bear any such argument, neither was there ever any such point argued either at the Bar or at the Bench.

Coke debated the jurisdiction issue with Archbishop Bancroft before the Privy Council on 23 May 1611,[27] insisting that, because only Common Law courts were allowed to interpret statutes, they had a monopoly in cases where rights were created by statute. Ellesmere LC played the mediator and James I himself made the necessary compromise, limiting the jurisdiction of the Court of High Commission.

Parties to tithe disputes would usually prefer not to finance the resolution of such politically charged controversies, as many surviving documents attest.[28] The process usually began with an attempt at mediation.[29] The tenants of the Dean and Chapter of Hereford Cathedral referred to arbitration their tithes dispute with All Souls, Oxford,[30] as did Winchester College.[31] Those were private arbitrations, but the Council might step in, usually making sure to appoint at least one churchman. It delegated a tithes dispute in the Consistory Court at York to two arbitrators; and Sir Richard Hutton, judge of the Common Pleas and a favourite single arbitrator in Yorkshire, disposed of another in 1635.[32]

The Council did not set out to usurp the jurisdiction of the ecclesiastical authorities or override the civil law. Its concern was efficiency. One example from the last volume of the *APC* has sufficient detail to illustrate this.[33] On 25 May 1631 the Council heard the petition of Yeo and Gradden, two churchwardens of the parish church of Shebber in Devon. They had spent £20 on roof repairs twelve years before, 'for payment whereof they had a sequestration of the sheafe', the Devon term for a tithe of grain. After long suits in the Arches and elsewhere, they had obtained a monition

---

26. 'The Lord Chancellor Egerton's Observacions on the Lord Coke's Reports' in Knafla 296–318, esp 311.
27. Knafla discusses this fully 138–144.
28. Nat Arch C2/JasI/E2/15 (Somerset); Norfolk PD 239/66; Shropshire 11/763; West Yorks WYL230/2746. Ingram 125–127 describes how mediation and arbitration worked in all kinds of disputes, with many citations to church court deposition books 326 fnn 98–103.
29. Greater Manchester E7/12/2/1 and Northants Th 488 (1634 two mediators).
30. Shropshire 1123/7; and in 1688 Nat Arch C110/182.
31. Nat Arch E214/1180.
32. WYL230/2751 and 2752.
33. *APC* 46.343.

against Sir Thomas Hele and others, the proprietors of the tithe, for £44 5s 'upon remission from the Court of Arches to the Consistory of Exeter'. The defendants had been excommunicated when they failed to pay. They had appealed against the orders of the Archbishop of Canterbury and were threatening the petitioners 'with Star Chamber suits and other vexatious courses'. The Council decided that the Archbishop should be asked to 'hear and examine all allegations on either side and to use the best ways and means he can to make a final end of the difference'. If the defendants refused to stand to the Archbishop's order, he should grant a sequestration of the sheafe 'for the satisfaction of the petitioners according to equity'.

4. DIFFERENCES WITHIN THE PARISH

Private Submissions   Private mediation was often the first choice of parishioners with differences they could not handle themselves, and they might prefer a lay to an ecclesiastical mediator. Among the papers of Sir Nathaniel Bacon JP is a petition signed by 24 parishioners and endorsed: 'To the Right Worshipful Sir Roger Townesend Knight and Baronet'.[34]

> Whereas our Parish of Wevenhoe for these two years... hath been distracted with pernicious contentions... we the inhabitants, many of us tenants of your Worship for our copyholds, having much desired but in vain to see them come to an end of their own accord, have now brought into your hands these drops of grief... to interpose your greatness and virtue to the curing of these desperate distempers.... This our first and joint supplication that you will not let slip the opportunity of doing a deed so full of piety, charity, honour and happy reward.

Some of the parish of East Harling in 1611 submitted their differences with the widow Ruddock to the rector, with Mr Rowse and Mr Dickerson.[35] Church land was the subject of an award recorded in 1608. Robert Swaffield was the tenant of a mill in Maiden Newport and Thomas Cliffe the 'farmer of the parsonage' there. The dispute concerned the taking of turf to repair the bank of a watercourse running by the glebe.[36] And private arbitration was the method chosen in a dispute between the owner of the living and the lord of the manor over a foldcourse.[37]

Of course, attempts to settle disputes often failed. Craig Muldrew tells of William Wright, parson of the Cheshire parish of Waverton and Chancellor of the diocese, writing to the Cheshire JPs in 1597 that he and his neighbours had fruitlessly endeavoured to settle through a 'Christian reconciliation'

34. HW Saunders ed *The Official Papers of Sir Nathaniel Bacon* 197–198 [Saunders *Nat Bacon*].
35. Norfolk PD 219/167.
36. Nat Arch WARD 2/62/241/148.
37. Norfolk WLS/XXX/1–3/416 and 417; foldcourse or faldage is the lord of the manor's right to insist that his tenant graze his sheep on the lord's land, to manure it.

the 'variance and dissension' which had long existed between two of his parishioners.[38] John Faulkner and his wife were 'persons of evil fame and behaviour' and their children were no better. The neighbours 'had never heard children use such bad language'.[39] They persuaded the parish priest to speak to Faulkner but that did no good, so he was brought before the quarter sessions.

Reasons for failure are as instructive as those for success. In a meticulous study of one parish, Sileby, Bernard Capp related the testimony of sexual shenanigans which led to a dispute coming before the ecclesiastical court. Attempts to mediate failed because the parties were obdurate and there was no authority powerful enough to force them to see reason:[40]

> The primary goal of ecclesiastical justice was to restore Christian charity and harmony within the community. In disciplinary ('office') causes this was achieved by offenders submitting to 'correction', which in serious cases meant public penance. In instance causes a citation often served as a warning shot, prompting the other party to seek a private accommodation, or triggering mediation by neighbours. A cause that proceeded all the way to a sentence and public penance was in many ways a failure.... The answers lie in the status as well as the personalities of the principal actors, and in the political and ecclesiastical circumstances of the parish... lengthy proceedings were clearly divisive, and humiliating for witnesses and protagonists alike. Vexatious litigation was... all the more destructive when the usual mechanisms of conciliation and arbitration failed. The failure of accommodation and compromise at Sileby underlines the crucial importance of mediators and figures of authority within a local community.

Government Intervention   The Government was not shy of interfering in parish disputes and preferred to have them arbitrated. The Rev Meredith Madey was a bad lot. When 'divers poor men to the number of 30 or more' complained to the Privy Council of the 'multiplicity of suits prosecuted against them (even to the undoing of them, their wives and poor families) by Meredith Madey, clerk, sometime parson of the parish' of Blaydon, the Council was ready for him.[41] 'Madey was known to some of their Lordships to have been deprived as a person scandalous to the ministry'. So it asked the Bishop of Bath and Wells, plus any two of six other local worthies, to enquire and send their opinion, 'an exact certificate, whereupon this Board will give such further order as the cause shall require'. All suits were stayed, in courts spiritual or temporal. The Council made an order on 22 February 1622 but the matter was back before it on 25 March 1625.[42]

---

38. Muldrew 930.
39. Curtis 142.
40. Bernard Capp 'Life, Love and Litigation'.
41. *APC* 38.416.
42. *APC* 39.507.

The inhabitants 'were still complaining of Madey's multiplying causeless suits and troubles'. He had agreed to a reconciliation meeting, chosen the date, and then failed to turn up. The Council decided:

> before they proceed to give any final order in this business (to the end Madey be left without all excuse or colour of complaint and clamour) once more to refer the examination of these complaints and differences to the Bishop of Bath and Wells, the Bishop of Bristol [and four others, or any three or more, of which Bath and Wells to be one], to accommodate and end the differences (if they can), or otherwise to certify.

All suits were to be stayed. The judges of the several courts were required to take notice. 'Madey and all others whom it may concern are required to conform themselves as they will answer the contrary at their perils'.

The Council in June 1628 had referred a dispute between Thomas Mellis and Edward Parris about the Norfolk parsonage of Rockheath to the Archbishop of York and the Bishop of Norwich. In the following May it noted that those referees had certified that 'Parris had for many years been possessed of the fruits of the benefice... and Mellis is a very poor and aged man', and recommended that Parris should allow him 20 nobles a year until the matter was decided 'in the country'.[43] The Council so ordered.

In 1623 Alexander Lumsden, pastor of Braybourne in Kent, had complained against Henry Impet, his parishioner.[44] Both appeared before the Council, which resolved the matter itself, ordering Impet to pay Lumsden twenty marks 'for the hurt done to his person', to remain in custody till he paid, and to apologise in church on the Sabbath.

Durham is a long way from London. In 1630 the Council received a complaint from Robert Dodsworth, holder of no less an office than 'one of the Sewers of his Majesty's Chamber in ordinary', against one of the prebendaries of Durham Cathedral.[45] 'In regard to the remoteness of the place, this present long vacation and the authority of your Lordships in those parts', the Council appointed the Archbishop of York and the Lord President of the Council of the North 'to settle such an order as you in your wisdoms shall find consonant to justice and equity, so as neither the Church be in any way wronged, nor the Petitioner (especially being his Majesty's servant) unjustly overborne'.

During the Long Parliament the House of Lords sent parishioners' petitions against clergy to the Committee for Petitions to be arbitrated. In May 1641 the vicars of Kensington and of Abbotisham, Devon,

---

43. *APC* 45.12.
44. *APC* 39.58.
45. *APC* 46.55; a sewer attended at table, not to serve dishes but to arrange seating and to taste the food.

were accused of being drunken and absent; and the vicar of Cropredy, Oxfordshire, of non-residence and underpaying his curates.[46]

Government might seek the answer to local disputes in the authority of a JP:[47]

> On three consecutive Sundays Simon Quick has locked the doors of Calverleigh church and prevented Mr Birch, the minister, and his congregation from entering; he has also barred Mrs Elizabeth Southcott from her aisle in the church during this period. Examination of the matter is referred to the nearest JP, who is to examine witnesses and, if he finds the complaint to be justified, to bind Quick over.

5. OLIVER HEYWOOD

Oliver Heywood (1630–1702) was an active evangelical Presbyterian and royalist parson in Lancashire and Yorkshire.[48] His own fortunes went up and down with the times, sometime excommunicated, usually without a living, but settled and accepted before he died. He kept a diary, chronicling his devotions and – often with relish – the many deaths he encountered in his work. Tempers did not necessarily cool when the parties agreed to bring their dispute to their minister and Heywood was not always immediately successful:[49]

> It troubles me much and I am afraid it is a presage of evil that there is such desparate and implacable contentions among many. Mr Thomas Wakefield and Sam Pollard came to my house on Monday 12 December 1681 and I must make them friends, but such bitter spite appeared, grievous words uttered, that I am afraid they parted more enraged and will sue about a trifle.

But later he wrote that they were reconciled. And he got better with experience. In his old age he recounted:[50]

> This last year viz 1697 I have but travelled about 500 miles being hindered by old age. A severe cold I have had, yet I have preached 82 sermons on weekdays, kept 40 fasts, 15 days of thanksgiving, baptized 12 children, writ above 100 letters, writ some treatises, but printed none. There have been 2 remarkable occurrences this year, of composing differences, which had much exercised my thoughts. One was an old controversy of 10 years standing betwixt old JP and me about a field he should have bought for me and bought it for himself: I was silent but JS told him of it, saying he dealt basely with me. The controversy being thus unadvisedly started, grew high, several meetings in vain, sharp letters, censures past. He forsook us, both at sacrament and also fast-days. I

46. Hart 161 and 173 fnn86–88.
47. Cockburn *Western* 1131.
48. JH Turner ed *The Rev Oliver Heywood* [Turner *Heywood*].
49. Turner *Heywood II* 286.
50. Turner *Heywood I* 274.

tried all means for accommodation, but all in vain. At last I bethought myself of this expedient, upon Lord's Day night I called about 12 of our Christian friends Oct 31 1697, told them JP had done me no wrong about the field. I was sorry if I had given him any just occasion of offence. They acquainted him with what I said, he was well satisfed, sat down with us at the Lord's Supper, comes to our private fasts, and hath been at my house several times, and shews himself very friendly. Blessed be God for this sweet return of prayer, I must say, as Jacob, Genesis 33 10.[51] The other was Mr Timothy Ellison, curate at Coley, taught our school, let it go to naught. I took my 6 lads away, he locked the school-door, took the key with him which when we demanded. He sent me 2 or 3 angry letters challenging an interest in our school... I writ him a peaceable letter, desired him to meet me and let us lovingly debate things. We did meet. He was very high, threatened to enter me into the spiritual court, which I dreaded. He demanded a great sum of money, which he said I owed him for teaching. I gave JP junior the purse with all the money I had in it, which I had of J Wharton's Executors, and bade him please himself out of it, upon condition he would resign up the title he pretended to in the school. Accordingly JP gave him £3 12s, Mr Ellison gave his resignation [witnesses John Priestley, John Priestley, junior] under his hand and seal, and discharge which we have, and set another master to teach the day after, viz Mr John Paul, after the school had been vacant near half a year, by which means we had so much money in Bank, and he was the more willing, because he was for going from Coley to Sowerby. Another happy accommodation God made me an instrument of was betwixt old Joseph Wright and his son Joshua. It had been long in sharp debate about a piece of land at Shipden head. I persuaded Joshua to give his sister Bently 50s (though by law it fell to him). He yielded. They were not contented with that. We got him up to 60s. Accordingly on Jan 12 1694 we met at his house, sealed writings betwixt them, at least 4 writings, and parted friends. Blessed be God.

Perhaps his most successful intervention in conciliation was in 1691 in the London agreement between Presbyterians and Congregationalists, known as the 'happy union'. On 2 September 1691 he preached in Mrs Kirby's house at Wakefield to twenty ordained and four licensed preachers of the two denominations and heads of agreement were adopted.

Heywood may have learned from his mother. He acknowledged her skills:[52] 'She was very useful in reconciling differences and making up breaches, taking much pains, yet great delight in that work'.

6. RALPH JOSSELIN

Even fuller and more revelatory is the diary kept by Ralph Josselin, vicar of Earls Colne in Essex, in which he recorded his activities as arbitrator, and his satisfaction when he had accomplished what he saw as part of his

51. 'And Jacob said, Nay, I pray thee, if now I have found grace in thy sight, then receive my present at my hand'.
52. Turner *I* 50 quoted by Muldrew 932.

duties:[53] 'above all I know 'tis an acceptable service unto God to continue peace and concord among brethren'. The diary is full of references to disputes and well illustrates the role of a country parson in their resolution.

Josselin (1617–1683) was the son of a farmer who was not wealthy and struggled to keep his son at Jesus College, Cambridge, where he graduated in 1637. He was ordained in the Church of England in 1640, and the next year appointed vicar of Earls Colne, Essex, where he remained for the rest of his life.[54] He was conscientious in his work and diary-keeping. Like many diarists he was a hypochondriac, but in his case to the point of paranoia. He recorded every sniffle and twinge, and the more serious illnesses of his wife and family, not only for himself but for his idiosyncratic god, who, Josselin was convinced, took a constant and meticulous interest in his health. When Ralph, his newborn son, died on 21 February 1648, Josselin thought one of the reasons for divine disfavour was that: 'I have given my mind to unreasonable playing at chess'.[55] And the next day's entry gets back to his obsession: 'Somewhat sensible of my cold' and the next: 'Somewhat worse with my cold. I sneezed'. To that was added a new fixation, a morbid concern with his navel, recorded daily, which seems to have been healthy when he left it alone but angry when he applied various medications. He kept his wife breeding, as he put it, pretty well every year until she was no longer able. She had miscarriages and at least ten births, though most of their children died in his lifetime. Like so many of his status, he was always worried about money, though his wealth grew as he acquired land and became a successful farmer; and he could always rely on his patrons, the Harlakendens at the Priory, his lords of the manor, to help him out.

Many entries tell of political events, at home and abroad, from the return of the Jews, noted on 5 April 1645, welcome because of the opportunities for their conversion, to the events of the civil wars and execution of the King. Josselin was a man of his religious times, constantly concerned with the struggle of ideas, discussing with those of his 'society' the contending views of the various protestant sects and sometimes the physical intrusions into his services of the Quakers. It was not easy to stay out of trouble with the authorities, even in disputes like that over the wearing of a surplice, but he rode the troubled ecclesiastical waters as he did the political. Though employed as chaplain by Fairfax and making no secret of his support for the parliamentarians, he approved of neither the Levellers nor the killing of the King. On 12 June 1648 royalists overran Earls Colne and

53. Alan Macfarlane ed *The Diary of Ralph Josselin* [Macfarlane *Josselin*] 69.
54. Alan Macfarlane *The Family Life of Ralph Josselin*.
55. Macfarlane *Josselin* 23 February 1648.

plundered Josselin's house, 'of all that was portable except brass, pewter and bedding'.

Josselin was not a hypocrite. Certainly, when it came to dispute resolution, he practised what he preached, both in his mediation of the differences of others and when a party himself. The references in his diary to dispute resolution are slight, as brief as his medical observations are full, but they span the whole of its forty years, from 1644 till his death in 1683. A chronological presentation has been chosen as most illuminating of the work of one country parson of the time, though there is no evidence that he was in any way representative of others. Quoted passages are identified by their dates.

Josselin knew his vocation early, as a boy hiding in a corner and pretending to preach. Resolving disputes, too (1635):

> Toward my sisters god gave me a heart to seek their good in some measure, my father living and dead, and especially my sister Anna in hindering her from marrying a widower, when my father had cast her off, and in reconciling her unto him again; and this I did before I was 17 years old.

The first reference to an arbitration is on 7 October 1644, when Josselin was still only 27 and had been at Edens Colne for four years:

> I went up to Goodman Bridges and bought his hops at an easy rate. I was used there kindly. When I came home, Stisted men were with me about their reference to Mr Burroughs and myself, whether Mr Archer or Mr Templar had the clearer call to their town.

That is, which of two clergymen had the better claim to the living at Stisted. The two arbitrators must have found for Burroughs, because the diary on 23 July 1644 reads:

> Mr Archer and I met about his accusing me, Lord learn me patience and wisdom by this dealing and help me to watch my heart that I may be kept from every evil way and the good god be praised for his mercy in damping my accusers in some measure.

On 6 and 7 August: 'employed in composing matters betwixt Mr Harlakenden and the Nevills, which I praise god I effected to their contents, and I hope it was a work of charity and love'. But on 21 October the Archer matter was still a problem, 'business' always meaning 'dispute':

> Rode to Chelmsford, motioned my business with Mr Archer to Colonel Cooke, pressed him to nominate place and time to end the same; he answered that he knew not it was reserved to him.... we discoursed about our business.... [22 October] we made a fair progress in our business.... [23 October] finished our business.... [29 October] a meeting at Goodman Mathews to declare to our christians and others what we had done in the church business. I hope it will be our healing. The good Lord command it to be so.... 13 March 1646: Mr Archer

preached as if the Presbyterians were all of them proud conceited persons, upon which I asking him whether he meant so, he said he would not answer me, but gave me very unkind words.

Colonel Cooke was involved in the failure to resolve a dispute which ended in one party being jailed, despite it being Christmas Day 1645, when Josselin was called to sit with JPs:

At Colonel Cooke's: Paflin cleared in the matter of the widow Ward. He accused Potter about the death of his maid Alice, and children by her, upon which Edward Potter took out a warrant to examine the matter; we sat all 25 day about the business and in conclusion the justices had so much against him as to send him to jail, the chamber where he had his mittimus [the warrant committing him to prison] was the room where he was born, at Mother Abbott's. The Lord's finger was in this business.

His attempts to resolve disputes could be as formal as that, with JPs and imprisonment, or as informal as the paternity suit brought by a maid against a fellow servant on 24 August 1646, where Josselin 'prayed with them and laboured in all solemness of spirit that could be to discover the truth... he denied... she continued constant.... She died within two years'.

Not all attempts had unhappy endings. Those that succeeded gave Josselin great satisfaction, particularly when they contented the Harlakendens, for whom he had a strong personal affection, not just because of their patronage. On 16 September 1646:

Rode to Chappell with Mr Harlakenden and Mr Nevill to settle businesses betwixt them and the sisters. I bless god I brought them to a fair end and gave them all content. Mr Nevill promised to allow to his sister Mrs Mary £1 quarterly to help maintain his sisters. We came home safe, praise to god, my endeavours acceptable to all, and above all I know 'tis an acceptable service unto god to continue peace and concord among brethren.

Then just one line on 24 September 1646: 'Drove through a bargain betwixt Goodman Death and an orphan of the Nevills for her land, more to her advantage than she expected, etc.' What could that 'etc' have meant? And on 28 September just a mention of another arbitration: 'Wrote to my uncles to meet at Chelmsford October 8, with either of us a friend, to make a final end and conclusion in our business if possible'; and on 8 October: 'my uncles met, not only Simon, we resolved to go over to Joseph's executors. Mr Grimston kind in giving me advice in my case'. Then on 14 and 15: 'Rode to my uncle Hudson's.... My uncle Simon met not. My other uncles are very confident they shall enjoy the estate, which if they justly do I am content. We agreed that our Counsel should discourse in the business'. Litigation followed, 12 November: 'I was subpoenaed into the Chancery by my uncle Hudson and Richard Josselin... let not strifes always continue, it was in the business of of Joseph's land'.

On 27 January 1647:

> Preached about payment of debts, and restitution; some are stirred, the Lord make his word thoroughly effectual. Mr Thomas Harlakenden and Wm Kendall, at suit, we drew them both to arbitration, they entered into bonds to perform it, but providence through the death of Mrs King's daughter so crossed us that we could not perfect our hopes of peace.

On 29 January back to the uncles:

> I am now preparing for London to answer the suits of my uncles about Joseph's land. My resolution is this (by god's grace) to repair to learned Counsel and, if they say the right is mine, to endeavour an arbitration, and make an end of the controversy peaceably if possible, and to stand to the end of the arbitrators whatsoever.

Who could say fairer than that? On 11 March he was in London again:

> Rode to London safe, met my uncle Simon. Went down to Serjeant Turner's. He could not attend to end our business... I met my uncle Richard and Hudson. We went together, lay together, and that night and next morning we concluded our business, I to enjoy the land and to pay them £100....
> 13. Came safe praise be god to Colne... the Lord be praised for this comfortable, contentful end, the Lord bless them and theirs with the money, and me and mine with the lands.

On 30 April the settlement was put into effect:

> This day rode to Bollinghatch. All my uncles met and gave me free and peaceable possession of those parcels of land given to Joseph. I paid the executors of Joseph £20, gave them bond for £80, received £7 16s of my uncle Simon for rent due; god good in his providences for us outwards and homewards; this land part of our ancient inheritance.

The occasional passing references continue: 16 September 1647 'In the afternoon we rode to Fordham Street and made an end we hope in the matter betwixt Mr Faulconer and Taller'; 21 September 'Went up with Mr H[arlakenden] to Wm Cowell: made up that difference betwixt his landlord and him'. So Josselin was acting with the squire in mediation. But he also helped to manage his 'business': 'Mr Harlakenden paid my cousin Josselin his wife's Mrs Ellen's portion. They agreed very well in the business'. A brief entry on 28 October 1647 shows that mediating was not without risk of involvement: 'Mr Harlakenden subpoenaed into the Exchequer at Mr Faulconer's suit, wherein both sides rely on me as their witness. I hope in god I shall discharge my conscience uprightly'. But it also had its satisfactions, 10 November 1647: 'Made an end after many journeys and much trouble of a suit between Mr Thos Harlakenden and Sir J Jacob, Wm Kendall. Sir J Jacob and Mr Jacob'.

On 19 June 1650 Josselin helped in a Harlakenden business:

Had some discourse with Mr Harlakenden about Mrs Mary's business; we agreed very lovingly in the value of the land, Mrs Mary's part £6 per annum, the other at £10 per annum, the free at £5 per annum. He set both the fines at £20. He acknowledged they were too hard. I hope in god we shall do all our businesses with quietness; god leads me into it lovingly.

Sometimes a reconciliation was no more than a sorting out of accounts, 14 May 1641: 'Made up the reckonings between Mr Nevill and the widow Browne; and quieted their minds in their dealings with one another'. Sometimes Josselin eased the settlement from his own pocket, 29 April 1652: 'This day I made an end of a difference between Catt and Pease. I lent 21s out of my purse to do it. Catt and Wm Adams were by. He and his wife promise me payment very careful before Michaelmas next'. It might be worth borrowing money to achieve a settlement, 27 July 1654: 'ended a great business between Robert Potter and his kinsman, much to my content, with much justice and moderation. I laid down £20, 50s whereof I borrowed of G Burton'.

There is no means of knowing whether Josselin noted all his attempts to reconcile, but there is a little clutch of notes in the spring of 1655; 12 April: 'rode to Messing; advised with cousin Josselin in the Sams business. He wishes me to make the best end with them that I can'; on 30 April: 'This morning I ended a great difference between landlord and tenant, which could not any ways agree formerly'; and 3 May: 'busy this day in composing young Butcher's business between his father and Mr Harlakenden'.

When Josselin himself was one of the protagonists, he was sure that his god was as keen as he was to avoid litigation; on 30 December 1653: 'It is a great mercy of god that I am not forced to sue Hedge at law'; and on 14 January 1655:

I had sought the god of my mercies, on whom I leave myself to make provision for me to facilitate my matters for me; where I was apprehensive of hard dealing, and I had no present answer, my spirit went on in seeking him; then I met with a temptation that I must use means, I had done that in my power, loth was I to go to law, my journeys in vain. While this was a trouble, on the 15th, the worst business was ended to my content beyond my expectations by the persons coming unto me, and on 16th another business was dispatched that was in my mind. This is thy goodness.

When the Sams business resurfaced, on 5, 23 and 27 October 1655:

Met at Chelmsford about Sams business. I thank god who framed my heart, waiting to end my business comfortably and for them as for myself. I found no such matter in them, no way desiring to end it, hoping the law would be their advantage, lord pardon them.... Sought unto god to give a blessing to me in Mr Sams business, and that it might be ended peaceably, the lord remember me in this also, according to the greatness of his mercy.... I bless god I was not now engaged in law, the lord end my business peaceably and for his own glory *fiet*, *fiet* [so be it].

But his god had other ideas. On 4 November 1655:

> God good to us in many outward mercies, though he answered not prayer in Sams' and Shaw's business, yet I trust he will.... An arbitration between sisters was submitted to me, the lord in mercy help me to walk in wisdom uprightly. I desire to deliver a poor shiftless one from the hand of another that would oppress. 19 November: I was sole arbitrator in the Nevills business with hope to end it.

God relented the next year. On 28 January 1656: 'employed with others in making peace between father Appleton and his son, which was done contentedly through mercy from god on us'. About this time Josselin began to believe that he could read divine intentions in his dreams, 16 February 1656: 'a dream of mine in Mr RH's [Richard Harlakenden?] law suit accomplished; we were in great trouble for his business, he came home, it ended very well, *deo laus et gloria* [praise and glory to God]. On 18 March: 'almost ended a business between Mr Cress and Mr Harlakenden, which he feared might have bred a quarrel, but I hope and trust will not, though the man is heady'. Josselin's attempts to end the Nevills business ended badly, 3 June 1656:

> A court was kept about the Nevills business. I agreed with Mr Butcher for his part and bid fair for Mr Weales. My back turned, Mr Butcher endeavoured to buy Mr Weales and did, Mr Harlakenden helping it on very earnestly. I was troubled to see men's spirits but not disquieted in myself, discerning God's hand in it, for my good, or some hidden providence to them they are not aware of. I did them the best service in all their affairs that I possibly could. None can imagine the distempered workings of our spirits but those that have experience.

Josselin had made an award of land as sole arbitrator. He then unwisely tried to buy the land himself. He should have known better. On 7 July 1656 the dispute was unresolved.

Josselin was busy again in the autumn of 1657, 28 October, 1 and 2 November: 'I ended Crows and Days difference, a son suing the mother of his wife for a promise of the father in marriage. I found a strange spirit in persons, but the widow treated us very friendly and freely' then dealing with 'discontent in some unkind passages of neighbours' and 'ended a difference between poor Layer and a soldier who wounded him. The soldier gave him 18s. A warning to take heed of quarreling'. And an example of mediation of a felony. The dispute could be quite homely, though the mediation just as necessary, 17 November: 'Mrs Margaret Harlakenden having laid out £120 at London about wedding clothes, her father being exceeding angry, I appeased him so that, though he chid her for her vanity, yet he paid the scores'. And just hints, 16 June 1658: 'I gave a great stroke to a purpose of parting families at the Priory, and I hope I shall compose that business quietly'. On 17 July: 'I was helpful to end my cousin Blundell's and Johnson's business'; 26 August: 'Helped to make up the widow Clarke's marriage with Mr Wheely, which was agreed on all particulars by my interposing'; 9 October 'did my help between parties to joint their business'. He had noted, 3 September: 'Cromwell died. People not much minding it'. Then 17 December: 'put another difference in the family of the Nevill sisters into a fair way of composing the same'. As usual, there was no mention of Christmas. On 23 December: 'ended the bargain between Mr Butcher and Morley and made peace' but the Butcher business was not yet ended. On 12 March 1659:

> A sad day at my house with myself, Morley and Butcher. Our passions were up and hot. The good lord pity and pardon us in christ Jesus and do all our business well. I bless god who purged it out of my heart and made it very grievous to me.

But all ended well, 17 May: 'I rode to Hedingham and put an end to Mr Butcher's and Morley's troublesome business; god's hand was towards me'.

There was more trouble at the Priory. Margaret's profligacy had not been limited to her trousseau; 12 May, after noting 'Cromwell's family under much odium for tyranny etc':

> Made an end of Mr Harlakenden's business with his daughter to my good content. She oweth him £2,400. He upon my serious proposal forgave her about £60, for which I was very glad, promised her her board and man and maids and one horse for £45 yearly, a great kindness, and to give her the diet of a friend.
> 14: Mrs H having a desire to receive a farther kindness from her father, wrote her mind and sent it by her daughter, he doth it. The good lord make a sweet compliance between them in the family. Ended a great and difficult business between persons because they were cross and untoward.

On 31 May more Priory business was settled: 'Ended Mr RH's great business with Mrs Elizabeth Harlakenden, with whose estate he was entrusted, very quietly and comfortably, god keep all hearts in calmness and in holy uprightness'.

Towards the end of 1659 there are the first two bits of evidence of Josselin being paid for his services, 29 November:

> Rode with Mr Harlakenden to Stortford where I managed his business, the lord helped me, that an account of about £12,000 wherein there was about £2,900 remainder, was given up and the money divided, with much love and peace... and the Dennies gave me 4 pieces for my pains and care for them....
> 7 December: finished the Dennies business, paid their moneys... Mr Harlakenden gave me £5 for my pains in that difficult affair....
> 31 December: Mr RH and I had close discourse of his private affairs, wherein I think we agree and fix. I see his great confidence in me.

The new year brought more business, 20 January 1660: 'Made an end of divers quarrels between Robert Crow and other persons to my good content... lord remember the peacemakers'. And more Priory work, 2 February: 'God good to me in my dear friend young Mrs Harlakenden's business with her father, wherein god hath helped me to steer them both, I hope to a final loving friendly end'. 5 February: 'I find Mrs H business crowding much into my thoughts'. 5 February: 'I rode to Dedham, where I found my best of friends Mrs H very well and somewhat cheerful, glad of the news I carried her from her father in giving her the £100 and abating her £15 in the interest'.

Josselin's odd religious views did not make him an unfeeling zealot. He could use his emollient skills even in an accusation of witchcraft, in this case a man accused, 30 September 1656:

> one J Biford was clamoured on as a witch, and Mr Cressener thought his child ill by it. I could no way apprehend it. I took the fellow alone into the field and dealt with him solemnly, and I conceive the poor wretch is innocent as to that evil.

There is no sign that Josselin's preference for the peaceful resolution of disputes ever abated; though, as he grew older, fewer parties sought his intervention and he sometimes felt he was not given proper respect. As early as 30 September 1656: 'made an end of all differences between Mole and Iserson. Oh how I rejoice to do good to a person that gives me no respect, lord for thy sake, I shall deny myself through grace'. But references to disputes became rarer. There were none from the next three years, until a general one on 14 January 1663: 'spent in making peace, giving good advice, a good employment of time'. Then a gap of two years to 7 March 1665: 'made a good end in Cousin Hurril's business'; then to 28 January 1666, a bad year for the plague: 'I was employed in ending a difference between one Bull and Sir Thomas Honywood, rescuing that poor man from the bailiffs'. The diary itself thins out and the next relevant reference is not until 24 September 1668: 'going out in the morning to end a tedious difference between the Lady Tryon's husband and Mr Woolhouse, which I effected, blessed be god'; and the next 1 and 3 April 1672: 'employed in ending differences among neighbours'. Then nothing for three years.

A sad entry on 1 April 1675 may provide some explanation for the dearth: 'I am involved in troubles for other men's business. If the lord please to bring me clear of these, as I trust he will, I will not engage while I live but in my own and childrens' concerns'. What had happened to the peacemaker's partnership with his god? The retirement did not extend, however, to matchmaking, 25 and 26 May 1675: 'Very instrumental to bring on the match between Mr Marryon, son of Braintree, and Rose Abutt of Colne. Their fathers seemed satisfied with me on both sides, god prosper it'. By 13 November 1676 any reluctance seems to have passed:

'The Lady Honywood sent for me. The businesses she intended came not to me but I ended matters between her and Mr Livermore'. By the autumn of 1677 he was back at work for the Harlakendens, 19 September: 'I was engaged by all to assist in their business. Mr Abbut gave me 5 guineas, lord thy name be praised'; 31 October: 'ended the great business at the priory to all contents'; 2 November: 'I hope I put the marriage at Pateswicke into a hopeful conclusion... the terms are all agreed but one and I hope that shall never break', but concluding sadly: 'but for my own children to some I am even useless, my counsel noways regarded'.

The last few scrappy entries are of successful settlements; 20 March 1678, 'struck a good stroke in Mr Androws' business to settle it with all goods therein, and I observed how hard Mr Eldred and Bowes yielded'; 4 April, 'farther discourse with Mr Eldred... of the progress in the affair of Mr Androws and his grandmother Harlakenden. Blessed be god I ended the law suits between Ravens, Newton and Appleton'. On 12 November 1679 Josselin records an arbitration: 'Ended Clare Hall business wherein I was a commissioner with Mr Potter to all contents etc'. On 29 January 1680 a mediation: 'at Colchester I endeavoured to compose the difference between Mr Wheeler and Mr Harrison'; and 10 June 1680: 'ended the difference between Mr Newton and Mrs Seymour about dilapidations'. And so Josselin's story ends. He died in 1683, still convinced of the importance of resolving disputes without litigation, if only because, as he recorded after perhaps his last trip to London on 16 May 1682: 'the Judges much pervert justice'.

7. UNIVERSITIES

The Stuarts did not make as much use of the Civilians as Elizabeth I had done; but they appointed them in the most appropriate cases. The Council wrote in December 1628 to three Doctors of Civil Law and one other whom it had previously appointed, to dispose of a dispute between the Students (that is Fellows) of Christ Church College, Oxford, and the Dean and Canons of the Cathedral.[56] It had decided that the best way to ensure that 'the business may be carried with the better moderation on both sides' would be to order a 'documents only' arbitration. Therefore the instruction was: 'do not admit any personal disputes which may occasion heat on either side; but receive in writing and peruse all such allegations as the Students shall present, and the answers also in writing on behalf of the Dean and Canons'. They were then to report back, 'with as little delay as may be'. Any two of the four could act, so long as 'such as have been named for either party one'.

56. *APC* 44.266.

On 30 January 1630 Charles I sat in Council to dispose of the dispute.[57] The 'documents only' arbitration had failed. The Students were still protesting. The King heard learned counsel on both sides and decided that there was no substance in their complaints. They asked for 'some wholesome statute and laws for the government of that church'. He said he would 'take order for that in due time'. Meanwhile they should 'return back to their studies and submit themselves to the Dean and Canons... and obey such decrees and ordinances (until his Majesty did otherwise provide) as the Dean and Canons should from time to time think fit'. He commended 'the sincere and charitable dealing of the Dean and Canons towards the Students'.

Charles I had sat with his Council on 2 December 1629 to deal with a quarrel at the other university and:[58]

did hear at large the controversy between the University of Cambridge and certain Burgers of the town concerning the rating and setting of the price of *Victualia* and particularly of candles and other necessaries comprised under the term of *Focalia*.... His Majesty finally ordered by advice of the Board that the late Mayor [and six others] shall acknowledge and submit themselves to the jurisdiction of the University, as well for the rating... as for the correcting and punishing of all inhabitants as shall exceed the said rates.

Offenders were not only to pay their fines to the Vice-Chancellor but make public confession in his court. And:

Touching the discommoning of any persons in this order mentioned, peace and agreement shall be settled between both parties according to performance of that respect and submission which is due from the inhabitants of the town to the University.

The King was not arbitrating there but laying down the law as he applied it.

The charter founding Queen's College, Cambridge, provided that disputes among the fellows should be submitted to the Chancellor of the University (or in his absence the Vice-Chancellor) 'and the greater part of the *Praepositi* [i.e. heads] of the colleges'.[59] Simon Patrick brought an action against Richard Bryan, senior fellow of the college, requiring him to confirm Patrick as President. The defendant raised a preliminary point: the college was a religious institution and therefore within the Bishop of Ely's jurisdiction. The judges of King's Bench split: Norton and Keiling JJ for the plaintiff; Twisden and Wyndam against. The arbitration clause was ignored.

57. *APC* 45.255.
58. *APC* 45.198.
59. *Patrick's Case* (1663) Raymond 101; 83 ER 54.

8. SCHOOLS

In 1610 an arbitration about tithes is recorded in a matter involving Winchester College.[60] The Council took pains to protect the provision of education. On 16 February 1629 the Master and Scholars of Etwall and Repton School, the forebear of the modern Repton, complained that a Lancashire landowner, Sir Thomas Gerrard, had wrongfully taken possession of their land.[61] The Council referred the dispute to the Lord Keeper, who reported that Gerrard was holding over on a lease from the school which had expired two years before, paying no rent. Being a governor of the school and descended from the founder, he considered that he should not have to pay the fine on renewal, which the constitution of the school required, or pay rent at a new valuation. So the school had let the land to John Henshawe. The Lord Keeper had found that Gerrard had no right to remain in occupation, but tried to get Henshawe to give up his lease. Henshawe wanted more than Gerrard would pay. So the Lord Keeper gave up:

> knowing no way without the parties' consents to draw it to any conclusion by bargain or agreement, I have thought fit to certify the true state of the case as I find it, conceiving it to be just and fit that Sir Thomas Gerrard should deliver up the possession and give satisfaction for the rent arrears.

The Council ratified that report and ordered Gerrard to give up possession and pay the arrears, or appear before the Board 'to show cause to the contrary'. But Gerrard did not give up. On 1 April he complained that the lease to Henshawe was conditional: it was on trust on condition that Henshawe would give it up if Gerrard was prepared to accept a lease on the terms the school's charter required.[62] The Council asked the Lord Keeper to find out whether that was true. On 24 April he reported that his enquiries had shown there was no truth in Gerrard's claim and that it was made just to delay repossession. He was ordered to get out and pay the arrears forthwith.[63] Gerrard needed bigger guns, so on 1 May he had Sir John Finch, the Queen's Attorney, plead successfully for a delay until the end of Trinity term next for him to produce evidence of the trusts and condition.[64]

9. CHARITIES

When charitable funds were in issue, neither side wanted to fritter them away in legal costs, and usually the issue was not heated. Arbitration

60. Nat Arch E 178/4493.
61. *APC* 44.338.
62. *APC* 44.385.
63. *APC* 44.412.
64. *APC* 45.2.

was preferable.[65] A 1638 bond in the East Sussex archives evidences the use by private parties of arbitration to protect the income of charitable foundations.[66] Six gentlemen, five of them local Jurats, bound themselves to stand to the award of two arbitrators 'to determine all matters concerning the arrears of an annuity of £4 issuing from the Mermaid Inn'.

Sir William Sutton as single arbitrator declared that a house and land in Southwell belonged to the inhabitants of Caunton in Nottinghamshire for charitable uses and would revert to them on payment of £14; and he granted a 21 year lease.[67] He appears to have been one arbitrator who was loved by all, if the inscription on his tomb in the parish church may be believed:

> Sir William Sutton's corpse here tombed sleeps,
> Whose happy soul in better mansion keeps.
> Thrice nine years lived he with his Lady fair,
> A lovely, noble and like virtuous pair.
> Their generous offspring (parents' joy of heart),
> Eight of each sex: of each an equal part
> Ushered to heaven their father; and the other
> Remained behind him to attend their mother.

10. CONCLUSIONS

One of the reasons for parties to arrange a private arbitration was that they could choose arbitrators of integrity, whose reputation in the community, if nothing else, would deter them from corruption. The venal dishonesty of the ecclesiastical authorities of that time was notorious. It did not always go unpunished. In 1622 Sir John Bennet, Judge of the Prerogative Court of Canterbury, was convicted of distributing the assets of intestates' estates to the highest bidders, 'as corrupt a judge as any in England, for he would not only take bribes of both parties... but many times shamefully begged them'.[68] He even stole from the estate of Thomas Bodley, whose executor he was, who had sought his help in raising funds for the Bodleian Library. His villainy was said to be such as to make even Francis Bacon look an honest man.

The Council usually respected the Church's authority. It did not so much usurp its jurisdiction as use its wide-ranging powers to get round the artificial obstacles of ecclesiastical litigation, in the same way that it bypassed the delays, costs and chicanery of the lay courts.[69]

65. West Yorks WYL639/362 and 500/2 'in respect of £100 left to charitable uses'.
66. East Sussex RYE/112/10.
67. Notts DD/BB/118/1 and 2.
68. Donald Veall *The Popular Movement for Law Reform* 43, citing Howell *State Trials* 2 1145–1154.
69. *APC* 46.343.

The prevailing ideology was that all Christians were equal in the eyes of God and therefore should be in the eyes of the law, but the hierarchy of social standing in every parish was relied on in the resolution of disputes of all kinds. It has to be remembered:[70]

> Yet rank and hierarchy were there for all to see, even at holy communion – a celebration of Christian community among neighbours, who by definition had to be 'in charity', at which it was not unknown for two qualities of wine to be served, malmsey or muscadine for the 'better sort', cheap claret for the rest.

70. Keith Wrightson 'The Politics of the Parish' 19.

PART THREE

PEOPLE

9 PARTIES

The best law, the most excellent custom, the most useful that I have ever seen, is in Holland. When two people want to sue one another, they are first obliged to go before a tribunal of *juges-conciliateurs*, called peacemakers. The peacemakers say to the parties: 'You are very foolish to want to consume all your money in making one another unhappy. We are going to make a settlement for you and it is going to cost you nothing.' If the frenzy of chicanery is too strong.... They are allowed to litigate, as gangrenous limbs are abandoned to the surgeon's steel.

Voltaire in a banned letter[1]

1. INTRODUCTION

Parties of every station in life submitted their disputes to arbitrators they chose for themselves, from the labourer John Boulton[2] and John Sharples, the servant of Cuthbert Clifton, in his dispute with Richard Cowborne,[3] to the Earl of Derby in his with the widow of his second son, who together asked the King to arbitrate.[4] James I tried hard to mediate in Lady Clifford's dispute with her male relatives. Women have such a pronounced place that they demand Chapter 16 to themselves. Foreign nobles, too; 'the Prince of Auvergne and his father' asked William III to arbitrate, according to the *London Post* of 17 April 1700. There were parties of all ages, from infants[5] to George Armstrong, who was 102 when in 1645 he petitioned for an award to be enforced.[6] Parties from every rank were happy to submit, including the most influential landowners in the shires, the Edgecombes in Cornwall and the Cholmondleys in Cheshire.[7] People of every avocation submitted their disputes of all kinds to arbitration. It does not follow, when they are described as mercer or miller, that the dispute is a mercantile matter.[8]

Though the records of the Privy Council's work in the 17th century show it commissioning arbitrators much more frequently in the disputes of

---

1. Roebuck *Charitable Arbitrator* 62 translating Louis Moland *Oeuvres Complètes de Voltaire* Paris, Garnier 1877–1885 XXIII 127–128.
2. Lancs QSB/1/203/55.
3. Lancs DDKE 9/1/12.
4. Lancs DDK/11/16.
5. In fact if not in law, Chapter 17 below, under 'Capacity of Parties'.
6. Met WJ/SP/1645/6.
7. Cornwall 30 April 1613 and Cheshire DCH/A/579.
8. Nat Arch WARD259/221/17 (1608); WARD262/241/148 (1608).

those in the higher ranks of society, the claims of ordinary men and women were not unheard. For example, Robert Monday was a Southampton husbandman. His complaint of 'many unjust wrongs and oppressions' against Andrew Reade, esquire, had been submitted to two local knights, 'to take such order as shall be agreeable to justice'. They did nothing. The Council expressed its concern: 'which seemeth very strange to us... forthwith call both parties before you and take some present order ... agreeable to equity... that His Majesty nor this Board be no further troubled'.[9]

2. THE POOR

The Stuart Privy Councils continued Elizabeth I's special concern for the poor. James I's Council commissioned the Archbishop of York and the Lord President of the North to arbitrate, 'to set down some final order for the petitioner's satisfaction, whereto, if the other side shall not condescend', to inform the Council so that it could take such further course for the petitioner's relief as it thought fit:[10]

> Although the courses of justice are and ought to be equally open to everyone for the recovery of their right, for that the petitioner pretends his estate to be overweak to run the length and circle of the law, especially against his adversaries, being many and men of power and wealth.

The Government had no illusions that the chances of success in litigation were equal for rich and poor. In 1616 it appointed Lord Sheffield to deal with George Robinson's complaint against Sir Francis Boynton. Robinson alleged that Boynton had bought up all the land about Robinson's house and was harassing him with lawsuits to make him sell his modest ancestral home, so that 'his whole estate is like to be overthrown and ruined'.[11] The Council knew what its duty was in such a case:

> Forasmuch as amongst many other blessings we enjoy, it is not the least that we live under the protection of a gracious sovereign, that hath his ears open to the just complaints of the meanest of his subjects; and that it is meet some course be taken for the relief of the petitioner... call Sir Francis Boynton and the petitioner before you and... order some course for a final end and agreement between them.

Otherwise the Council would make 'such an order for the petitioner's relief and quiet as shall be just and reasonable'.

A letter to the Lord President and Council of York asked that judicial body to deal with the complaint of Thomas Parslow, who had been in prison

9. *APC* 34.527.
10. *APC* 34.264.
11. *APC* 34.400.

in York for two years, for debts he could not pay because John Rushworth and others had taken away his ancestral lands and were fraudulently keeping from him rents due to him from the Court of Wards 'to the utter impoverishing of the poor man'.[12] The instructions were:

> to call both parties before you and to examine the truth of this complaint and order some course for the poor man's relief, and the final ending and determining of these differences between them as shall be agreeable to equity and good conscience.

The Council was specially alert to any complaint that charitable provision for the poor was being subverted for private gain. It asked the Earl of Bath and four others to mediate an end agreeable to equity and good conscience on a petition on behalf of the poor of South Molton in Devon, 'forasmuch as the complaint carrieth an apparent show of oppression'. The poor claimed that Robert Sherland, trustee of lands granted by the King for their benefit, had taken the rents himself when he was mayor.[13]

The assize orders give a flavour of the reality. William Richman has the name of the villain in a parable. On 8 August 1631 Sir Thomas Richardson CJKB bound him over to appear at the next assizes for refusing to pay his poor rates 'and other abuses'.[14] One of those abuses was the subject of an order at the next assizes, not against Richman but his accuser:[15]

> Whereas George Vauham hath informed this court concerning William Richman of Staunton Prior that thirteen of his maidservants have been begotten with child in the house of William Richman within these fourteen years, which is a great scandal to Richman and worthy of punishment if it be true, it is ordered that the examination of the matter be referred to Sir Francis Popham and Mr Harrington [JPs].... If Vauham shall not prove that seven of the thirteen maidservants have been begotten with child during the time of their service, then Vauham is to be bound over to the next assizes.

The 'great scandal' that was 'worthy of punishment' was the defamation of Richman, not the seduction of the young women. It was up to Vauham to prove not that all the thirteen had been made pregnant by Richman, any seven would do to justify the allegation. The Chief Justice would not easily have found any Common Law to support his arbitrary solution.

3. ROYAL SERVANTS AND PUBLIC OFFICERS

Royal Servants   The costs, delays and uncertainties of litigation were ever in the minds of members of the Council. They were specially sensitive

---

12. *APC* 34.203.
13. *APC* 34.506.
14. JS Cockburn *Western Circuit Assize* [Cockburn *Western*] 200; TG Barnes *Somerset Assize Orders* [Barnes *Assize*] 47.
15. Barnes *Assize* 56; Cockburn *Western* 258.

to the effects litigation could have on the efficient performance of any royal servant, civil or military, or of any other public official.

The Council asked the Earl of Derby to appoint 'some indifferent gentlemen of the country to examine and compose' differences between Sir George Beverley, in government service, and Richard Browne, preferring 'the arbitration of friends to prosecution of suits'.[16] Submission to arbitration had to be consensual, but the Council could make it hard to resist: 'if Browne refuse to yield, it will then appear that vexation is his principal end'.

'Whereas there hath of late years many questions and controversies arisen betwixt the Lieutenant of the Tower and the city of London concerning each other's jurisdiction', the Council in 1615 decided 'for the perpetual settling' to appoint a commission of 'some persons of quality and judgment... whereof the questions may either finally be determined, or at least some speedy course prescribed by the Commissioners for determination thereof'.[17] It commissioned Sir Francis Bacon, then Attorney General, and the Recorder of London to confer and prepare a draft of such a commission for the Council's consideration.

When fighting broke out between royal servants and the inhabitants over rights of common in Lewisham, the Council instructed the local JPs to 'use their best endeavours to preserve His Majesty's peace' and punish the disturbers; but wrote to Tanfield CB and Bromley B 'to mediate some indifferent end between them'.[18] It explained that the King's right to the land had already been 'by a due and legal course declared':

> and a verdict or judgment passed; yet, to avoid the clamour of so great a multitude, and the prevention of future inconveniences, it is thought fitting some indifferent course be taken for the ending of the question, by way of compromise or otherwise... except both parties shall be contented to refer themselves to a second trial, which has already been offered them as the most even and upright course. As your Lordship is best acquainted with the causes, having judicially heard the proofs and evidences on both sides... use your best endeavours for the mediating between them some final end and agreement, either by giving satisfaction to the patentees or by procuring the parties to refer themselves to another indifferent and speedy trial, or by any other way or means of agreement, which in your wisdoms you shall find fitting and convenient [i.e. agreeable to the parties].

That does not seem to have given undue favour to the King or his servants. The Council's concern seems rather to have been to produce an amicable and therefore a lasting peaceful outcome. Then as now, a judgment or

16. *APC* 33.109.
17. *APC* 34.81.
18. *APC* 34.118.

award may not end a dispute. Arbitrators today occasionally hear that their awards have been renegotiated by the parties.

Three Suffolk JPs were required to 'use their best endeavours for the mediating some good end' on the petition of John White, Yeoman of the Guard, against Thomas Golding of that county for wrongs which meant that White was 'impedimented' in his royal duties by having to deal with litigation.[19]

Sir William Becher was a Clerk of the Privy Council, which helped him to recover a debt of £550, secured – if that is the right word – by a complicated series of assignments of bonds, of which Becher had been unable to enforce payment because 'he was absent on His Majesty's service'.[20] It delegated his petition to four of its members, or any three, for final determination.

While Abraham Tooke was away, employed in His Majesty's service, his wife and her father took over his house and made off with a charterparty worth £42 and a bond for £50.[21] Abraham was 'unable by reason of his poverty to right himself by an ordinary course of law'. The Mayor and two Jurats of Dover were appointed 'to accommodate and end this difference', or certify.

Military Matters   Billeting of troops must often have caused friction. In 1628 a dispute between Captain Butler, 'billeted with his company in the city of Norwich, against the magistrates and one of the sheriffs' was referred to the Bishop of Norwich and four other local gentlemen, or any three; and then three deputy lieutenants were added.[22]

Captain Powell, too, whose troops had been billeted at Wellingbourne, had a complaint against officials there.[23] He could not be spared to attend the Council, so the Earl of Dorset was commissioned to dispose of the matter where it had arisen. These good intentions were thwarted when Powell was transferred to Portsmouth. The Council had to make an order that his inability to attend at the Wellingborough hearing would not prejudice him.[24]

Public Offices   The Lancashire Archives Record Office has a bundle of documents from 1621 to 1648 relating to a dispute about the office of Clerk of the Peace for Wigan.[25] Alexander Rigby of Gray's Inn (1594–1650),

19. *APC* 34.135.
20. *APC* 39.272.
21. *APC* 45.123.
22. *APC* 43.367.
23. *APC* 44.64.
24. *APC* 44.75.
25. Lancs DDKE 1/26.

who held the office in 1621, wanted to assign it to his younger brother Joseph. Rigby had been an Esquire of the Body to James I but became a radical MP and successful military commander on the side of Parliament. As a newly elected MP in 1640 he sat on the committee to look into the abuses of the Star Chamber and other courts, famously declaring:

> Shall we be so weak men, that, when we have been injured and abused, will be gained again with fair words and compliments? Or like little children, that when we have been beaten and whipt, be pleased again with sweet meats? Oh no, there be some birds that in the summer of a parliament will sing sweetly, who in the winter of persecution will, for their prey, ravenously fly at all, upon our goods, nay seize upon our persons ... and now shall not some of them be hanged, that have robbed us of all our property? ... foolish pity, foolish pity.

Parliament appointed him a Baron of the Exchequer in 1649 but he and his fellow assize judge died 'of a virulent disease' in Croydon the next year. He had interests in North America, at Sagadahock in New England and in Maine.

The documents in the Wigan bundle include an agreement to assign the office of Clerk of the Peace to his brother Joseph, dated 17 April 1621; an assignment by another brother George to Joseph of 15 June 1630; and an assignment, dated 6 June 1648, by Alexander to Joseph on trust for the profits of the office to be divided between Joseph and the daughters of George, according to the terms of an award.

On the complaint of the Recorder of Canterbury against the Mayor and Aldermen, who, he alleged, had removed him from office without cause,[26] the Council formed a committee of the Archbishop of Canterbury and Lord Zouch to 'mediate and treat for such an amicable agreement between them as may give satisfaction and reparation of any prejudice that has happened to either party by occasion of this difference'. Zouch himself was a party to a dispute with Aquila Weekes about a lease of the Westminster Gatehouse, of which Weekes was Keeper.[27] Both parties agreed that it would be better heard in Chancery, so the Lord Keeper was 'entreated to give it a speedy hearing'.

On 1 July 1628 Charles I sat with his Council when it ordered that the transfer of the post of Receiver of royal rents for Yorkshire should be suspended until the Lord Keeper and the Earl of Marlborough had determined the differences between Richard Oliver and Edmond Lassells, who were to have surrendered Oliver's patent, and John Bland and Robert Edwards, who said Lassells owed them money.[28] On 2 August those deputed heard all the parties and made a consent order on who should have

26. *APC* 37.61.
27. *APC* 45.241.
28. *APC* 44.78.

the patent, with detailed provisions for their further awards and bonds to ensure performance.

When the keeper of the gaol at Ilchester complained that the Deputy Lieutenant's clerk was interfering with his fees, the Council sent his petition to six local worthies, for any two of them 'to end the difference and controversy between them 'in the best and most convenient manner it may be effected by you' or certify for an order to be made according to justice and equity.[29] These initiatives were meant to deal with administrative problems rather than just the private disputes which gave rise to them.

4. LOCAL AUTHORITIES

The Council sometimes arranged the arbitration of disputes between boroughs or other local authorities, but they might make their own arrangements, as Winchelsea and Romney did in 1637, over who had jurisdiction over that part of Broomhill which lay in Sussex,[30] and as did the Sheriffs and Town Clerk of Chester, about who should collect the fees for executing writs.[31]

On 23 November 1613, the Council dealt with a petition from the master pilots and seamen of Trinity House, Newcastle, who complained that they had to pay 'buoyage and beaconage', 'whereas the Mayor and Aldermen of that town receive the profit and benefit thereof'.[32] The Council sent that to four arbitrators, including Sir Daniel Dunn, Master of Requests, 'to order some such course between them as shall be agreeable to equity and good conscience'.

When in 1619 the towns of Totnes and Dartmouth were in dispute over how much each should pay towards the suppression of pirates, the Council appointed two of its members, Secretary Calvert and the Chancellor of the Exchequer, to fix their shares.[33]

5. FOREIGNERS

The Privy Council regularly heard the petitions of foreigners, 'strangers' as they were usually called then. For example, in 1616 it commissioned four Devon dignitaries to help the Dutchman, Ruteghert Barnavelt, to recover a debt of £440 from Matthew Came of Totnes.[34] And 'divers merchants of Amsterdam' complained that their ship, with its goods, had been wrecked

29. *APC* 45.74.
30. Kent NR/CPIb/142.
31. Cheshire ZCHB/3.
32. *APC* 33.282.
33. *APC* 36.456.
34. *APC* 35.5.

on the east coast.[35] The master had then sold it to Wallis, a King's Lynn merchant, for £310. The Dutch merchants claimed it was worth £3,000. Their ambassador was making a fuss. So the Council deputed Mr Secretary Lake and Caesar MR to 'order such a course for the final ending of this difference as shall be agreeable to equity and good conscience'.

The Council did not shrink from disposing of disputes where both parties were foreigners, even if the subject matter had no connection with England. On 12 May 1613 it sent this 'letter of assistance with general direction':

> Whereas a certain vessel called a carvell, belonging to divers Frenchmen, being laden with sugars and other merchandise, did of late arrive in Guernsey, whereupon question arose between the two ambassadors of France and Spain to whom the property of the same should belong; for deciding whereof it pleased His Majesty to refer the hearing and determining of that difference unto four commissioners, who, upon due examination of the same, found the said carvell and goods properly to appertain to John Terrier and other Frenchmen; these are therefore in His Majesty's name to will and command you and every of you to whom it may appertain, to be aiding and assisting unto the bearers hereof for restitution of the said carvell and merchandise, whereof you may not fail, etc.

On Sunday morning, 20 March 1614, at Whitehall, ten members of the Council, the Archbishop of Canterbury presiding, heard the petition of Harman Holtsho, a German, acting as procurator for some merchants of Lübeck. Pirates had taken their ship and goods to Ireland, where Captain Henry Skipwith, Vice-Admiral of Munster, was detaining some.[36] Skipwith appears elsewhere in the *APC*, usually in a bad light.[37] The Council referred the complaint to Sir Daniel Dunn, Master of Requests, and two others with business experience, whose report to the Board is recorded in full. They had tried 'to make an agreement between them, to the satisfaction of all parties'. They had made a full inventory of the goods Skipwith was holding. But Skipwith did not answer the arbitrators' summons and nobody knew where he was. So they humbly submitted the matter back 'to their Lordships' grave wisdom'. The Council knew Skipwith and knew what to do: in his absence they ordered him to pay Holtsho £16 17s.

Holtsho appears again in February 1616, representing Lübeck merchants in their claim for restitution of their ship, wrongfully taken by Captain Mainwaring and held in Dover. Lord Zouch, Warden of the Cinque Ports, was asked:[38]

35. *APC* 34.507.
36. *APC* 33.384–387.
37. *APC* 33.452 in a letter to the Lord Deputy of Ireland to enforce an award of the Earl of Ormond and Lord Vavasor; and *APC* 34.513.
38. *APC* 34.414.

> Forasmuch as the particulars of this difference are not unknown to your Lordship, and that both parties seem very willing to come to some reasonable agreement... order some such course for the disposing of the ship and her tackling, as in your wisdom you shall find fit and reasonable, without further trouble to this Board.

A resolution 'fit and reasonable' was preferable to any disposition according to legal rights.

The habits of foreigners could cause offence to the locals. The foreigner Cyprian Gabrie had a house in Stoke Newington. He had stopped up a watercourse 'to the great annoyance of the petitioner' and other neighbours.[39] The United Provinces' ambassador had intervened to speak for him. The Council commissioned three JPs and a counsellor-at-law (or any three) 'to appoint some convenient time to repair thither, and to take particular notice of the pretended annoyance' and 'to order some such course as you shall find just and reasonable, without further trouble to this Board'.

6. IMMIGRANTS

Disputes arose between immigrant communities and the local tradesmen whose business they affected. The immigrants were often religious refugees from Catholic persecution in the Netherlands. Many families had been made welcome in Elizabeth I's time. James I's Government, too, dealt with them as religious congregations and his Council continued to dispose of their problems by appointing arbitrators, showing clear evidence of sentiment and policy – Christian charity and for the skills they brought.

The only surviving document known to be in Shakespeare's own hand is a fragment of his emendations to the play *Sir Thomas More*, which we know was performed in 1613 when the Globe Theatre was burned down.[40] It contains lines as apt today as then. Thomas More, as Sheriff of London, was trying to calm a mob of apprentices intent on attacking immigrants.

> Imagine that you see the wretched strangers,
> Their babies at their backs, with their poor luggage
> Plodding to the ports and coasts for transportation.

They should think how they would feel in the immigrants' place, as they well could be, banished for insurrection. What then?

> Whither would you go?
> What country by the nature of your error
> Should give you harbour? Go you to France or Flanders,
> To any German province, Spain or Portugal –
> Nay, anywhere that not adheres to England –
> Why *you* must needs be strangers. Would *you* be pleased
> To find a nation of such barbarous temper?

39. *APC* 34.492.
40. Jonathan Bate and Eric Rasmussen eds *The RSC Shakespeare* 2464–2470.

Shakespeare was in charge of the King's own theatre company, the King's Men, and James I knew his plays. He echoed Shakespeare's sentiments on 9 April 1617 at Greenwich:[41]

> A petition was this day exhibited to the Board in the name of the French and Dutch congregations in the city of London, showing that whereas it pleased the late queen of famous memory to permit and suffer strangers (fled hither for their consciences in times of persecution) peaceably to use their trades and handicrafts for their maintenance and relief, which liberty has likewise been continued unto them by the gracious and princely favour of His Majesty, until of late, upon information of their great increase above the proportion of former times, the strangers are by informers arrested and sued... though their Lordships have divers times declared themselves, as well for the maintenance of the privileges and liberties of the city to the benefit of His Majesty's natural and liege subjects as the avoiding of any unjust vexation to such strangers as of ancient continuance and have repaired hither in the time of the late queen for their consciences and the profession of the gospel.
>
> Yet, forasmuch as there appeareth cause of grievance on both sides, it is ordered that Lord Carew, Sir Ralph Winwood [Principal Secretary of State], Sir Fulke Greville [Chancellor of the Exchequer], Sir Julius Caesar MR or any three of them, calling before them four or five such as the Lord Mayor shall appoint... together with as many of the elders of the outlandish churches, on Wednesday next in the morning, shall inform themselves of the true state thereof, as well concerning the number of foreign handicraftsmen as their continuance and abode in or about that city, together also with the prejudice and inconvenience which thereby arriveth to the home-born subject; and either to order it as shall be convenient for the public or otherwise to prepare it that further direction may be given as shall be meet.... In the meantime all suits commenced against such strangers be stayed until their Lordships shall signify their further pleasure.

That commission was to a committee of members of the Council. They were to produce a solution 'as shall be meet'. That would now be thought of as an administrative, rather than a judicial, solution.

There was trouble, too, in Norwich. Faced with complaints from the Mayor and the immigrant Walloons against the Dutch congregations there, the Council had referred them to the Chief Justices and Haughton J.[42] They had reported that the trouble arose out of a recent royal patent. On 23 November 1613 the Council asked the commission to produce that patent, for it to make 'such further order as the cause shall require'.

In 1616 the Mayor and Aldermen of Norwich wrote to the Council with the petition of 'divers bakers, strangers of the Dutch and Walloon congregations in that city'.[43] The Council asked Sir Henry Hobart CJCP and Haughton J 'calling to your assistance such of the Barons of the

41. *APC* 35.223; the date can only be 1617, though the heading clearly states 1619.
42. *APC* 33.281.
43. *APC* 34.481.

Exchequer as you shall think meet... to order and settle such a course as shall be most expedient for the benefit of the city, and the quiet and relief of the poor strangers'. There again the judges were asked to make administrative rather than judicial decisions.

The most intransigent problems seem to have beset Colchester, whose Bailiffs and commonalty had petitioned:[44]

complaining that whereas 200 strangers of the Low Countries were permitted to exercise in Her Late Majesty's time in that town the making of new draperies and other manufactures not then used in this kingdom, they are now increased to the number of 1,300 and upwards, and do (under colour of letters patents surreptitiously obtained from His Majesty), exercise all manner of trading there without limitation, confront the government of the town, and impose heavy fines and taxes upon His Majesty's subjects there, to their intolerable grievance and oppression, and to the ruin of that town.

The Council's response was to ask two serjeants-at-law 'to compose the differences between them', and later it added Sir Francis Bacon to their number. On Sunday 15 December they reported:

... we have received certificates from some principal gentlemen of Essex and Suffolk... hearing both parties several times, we think fit for a peace and concord that these orders be observed. First, that the orders now written in Dutch concerning baymaking and saymaking [baize and fine cloth] be translated and published in the English tongue. Secondly... one or two [Englishmen] be admitted at the viewing, measuring and sealing of the bays and says. Thirdly, a schedule of the names of persons admitted to the Dutch congregation be given to the bailiffs, that they may know who enjoy that privilege... and the admission of strangers be by the consent of the bailiffs... Fourthly, whereas there be two kinds of thickening of bays and says, one with the mill, the other with the foot, [the foot costing a third of the mill], the Dutch have restrained the thickening with the mill, to set their own poor people on work, which is nothing to the English, the English be free from the order, which is prejudicial to them in their charges and to the buyer in his price. Lastly, the Dutch congregation who meddle with trades prohibited by law... as the making of joined stools and the like, be warned to forbear....

Their Lordships ratified this, 'for the final concluding of these controversies', as an act of the Board. But there was more trouble with the immigrants in Colchester, some now of the second generation. They were preferring their Dutch countrymen's ships, 'transporting goods in foreign bottoms, contrary to statute'. That was not only to the detriment of the local shipowners but contrary to public policy, which required a strong English fleet. Francis Bacon and two others reported and a letter went on Sunday morning of 22 December with the necessary instructions to the

44. *APC* 34.590.

Bailiffs. Even that was not an end of the matters. On 20 February 1617 the Council wrote to the two Bailiffs, six Essex JPs, one Suffolk JP, and four current and three past Colchester aldermen, 'or to any eight or more of them, whereof the two bailiffs and two JPs adjoining to the town to be always four'.[45] It reminded them of the order of the previous 15 December and constituted them a permanent panel to deal with any further disputes, present or future:

> Forasmuch as, notwithstanding that order, complaint hath since been made unto us of some unjust vexation, to the disturbance of that quiet and agreement intended by the foresaid orders, we have thought meet, for remedy of such grievances as either party shall hereafter have cause to complain of, to make choice of you, hereby authorizing and requiring you, or any eight or more of you (whereof the bailiffs for the time being and two JPs adjoining to the town to be always four), that upon any question or controversy that is, or shall hereafter grow amongst them, you presently call the parties before you and... hear and compound the same, according to the rules and directions of former orders, particularly that of 15 December. And, if any person shall obstinately refuse to conform themselves to such arbitrament, you shall forthwith certify their names unto us, together with the cause of their refusal, and your opinion.

What could have been more conducive to a peaceful, satisfactory and lasting settlement? Some hopes! The parties were not in the mood for reconciliation. Within three months they were back.[46] The record recites the order by which the Council thought it had put an end to the disputes and provided for arbitrators to deal with any which might arise in future. The Colchester Bailiffs grumbled that 'the drawing in of gentlemen out of the counties adjacent' to participate as arbitrators on matters 'within their corporation is against their charter'. The Dutch immigrants, for their part, 'still complain of many unjust troubles'. So the Law Officers were told to consider the charter and advise whether the proposed arbitration scheme contravened it. They were also required to consider the Dutch congregation's grievances which had arisen since the last order, together with a new petition from the Colchester weavers, and to certify their opinion.

On 15 July Yelverton and Coventry reported.[47] They had heard the parties and perused the charters. The Bailiffs had jurisdiction 'to end and determine all causes and matters' arising in Colchester, to the exclusion of the local JPs. The Council's appointment of the JPs as arbitrators without the Bailiffs' agreement 'would be prejudicial to their charter'. The Dutch congregation's complaints 'arising since the last order of 15 December

---

45. *APC* 35.144.
46. *APC* 35.245.
47. *APC* 35.303.

had no good ground'. They were that the Bailiffs had wrongly prohibited one of the Dutch congregation from weaving without having served his apprenticeship, 'pretending that the trade of weaving is a trade annexed to theirs of bay and say making'. It would be bad for the English if all the Dutch could weave, but 'we think it convenient for the peace of the town and the Dutch congregation... they who have anciently used the trade of weaving with their bay and say making be still permitted'. When the English weavers understood this provision correctly, they would be more likely to accept that the Bailiffs had acted in their best interests. The Council confirmed that and ordered that it should be entered into the Register as an act of the Board.

7. JEWS

Though Jews had not been allowed to live in England since 1290 and were not formally readmitted until Cromwell's time, they are occasionally mentioned.[48] The official butchery of Dr Roderigo Lopez is well documented.

The Council wrote on 7 November to the Vice-Chancellor of the University of Oxford, instructing him to send an unnamed Jew 'under safe custody, to be disposed of as shall be thought meet'; an entry of 16 November makes it clear that that was Jacobus Bernatus. The Council sent him to Dover to be expelled.[49]

A Jew called Samuel Palache caused problems. At first he was treated as a pirate but then he claimed to be working for the King of Morocco and gained the backing of the Spanish Ambassador.[50]

8. INTERNATIONAL RELATIONS

Nations which became parties to international differences had no higher authority to which they could refer disputes for adjudication. They were therefore naturally subjects for mediation and sometimes arbitration. English monarchs from time to time were asked to mediate and arbitrate disputes between the heads of other states, as shown in Chapter 4. By the end of the century London newspapers were regularly reporting on foreign affairs. The *London Post* related that on 21 April 1700:[51]

> The Prince de Auvergne has obtained leave of the King to go solicit the King of England to be arbitrator between him and his father, upon a difference that has happened between them, about the Marquisate of Bergen op Boom.

48. The horrors of the treatment of Rodrigo Lopez, regretted but condoned by Elizabeth I in 1569, must still have been in public consciousness.
49. *APC* 33.25; 33.272.
50. *APC* 34.308.
51. *London Post with Intelligence Foreign and Domestick* issue 136.

It was no disqualification if the monarch whose help was sought was a woman. Later, Queen Anne would do nicely:

> Hague July 19 [1707]   The Minister of the Elector Palatine has acquainted some members of the Council of State that the Elector, his master, to put an end to the dispute which the King of Sweden has raised about the Duchy of Veldens, submits to the arbitration of Queen Anne and the Elector of Hanover.

Other newspapers of the time and a little later made greater boasts, that 'United Great Britain will become the arbitrator of Europe'.[52]

Like Queen Anne, inter-state arbitration is outside the scope of this book, but it occasionally serves to illustrate popular attitudes to arbitration. The National Archives hold many relevant sets of documents. For example, in the Foreign Office archives are documents describing the arbitration of a boundary dispute between Brazil, Venezuela and British Guiana (1640–1788).[53] The Dutch ambassador wrote in March 1662 objecting to the appointment of arbitrators in the negotiations about the Anglo-Dutch treaty.[54] Sometimes there is evidence of a foreign government's interest in a private dispute, as in 'the matter of the *Bonadventure* and the *Bona Esperanza*'.[55] Papers dated 27 September 1662 deal with the arbitration of claims by Holland and Friesland against other provinces.[56] On 27 February 1666 the Senate of Hamburg wrote to Charles II that it was happy with the treaties then in force but, if any doubt should arise, it was willing to refer the dispute to arbitration.[57]

Sir George Stepney, Fellow of the Royal Society, poet and diplomat, from 1692 envoy to Brandenburg and other German courts and Vienna, kept a letter book.[58] In agreeing to the treaty with Sweden, Charles II foresaw disputes and provided that they should be submitted to commissioners, if necessary to arbitration by the Republic of Venice. He also insisted on arbitration of any disputes which might arise from an agreement with the Dutch ambassadors to the Greffier of the States General.[59] Lambeth Palace Miscellaneous Papers preserve a letter from Villiers, Duke of Buckingham, to the Spanish Ambassador Gondomar from 1619, expressing the offer of James I to mediate between the parties in the Bohemia dispute;[60] and a letter to James I asking him to mediate on the Protestants' behalf and

---

52. *London Gazette* 17–21 April 1707.
53. Nat Arch FO881/8326X; with maps CO700/British Guiana 51; FO881/7037.
54. Nat Arch FO881/7132X.
55. Nat Arch SP84/166/53.
56. Nat Arch SP84/166/61; SP84/165/25.
57. Nat Arch SP82/11/11.
58. Nat Arch SP105/59; other letters are in the papers of Sir John Ellis BM Add MSS 28875–28947.
59. Nat Arch SP84/165/97 7 to 17 April 1662.
60. Lisa Jardine and Alan Stewart *Hostage to Fortune* 428.

attacking the Jesuits.[61] Documents in the National Archives include a manifest for Danish ambassadors on mediation with France; the French reply to Savoy about a mediation; the answer of Christian IV to a proposed mediation; and Charles I's commission to Sir Henry Vane in 1631 to 'mediate' between Poland and Sweden.[62] Perhaps most intriguing of all is the entry in Rymer's *Foedera* for 18 June 1614, a commission to Sir John Meyrick with Michael Feodorevich 'lord and great duke of all Russia' to mediate between him and the King of Sweden.[63] All these examples show how positive the British Government was towards arbitration. Other scholars may be tempted to do the research which would fill the gaps here.

9. CONCLUSIONS

Throughout the 17th century parties of every station in life preferred arbitration to litigation. Women appear as claimants and defendants with no sign of discrimination, though married women usually acted with their husbands, more often from a social convention than a legal requirement perhaps. The highest in the land as well as the humblest submitted themselves and, as the next chapter will show, there was similarly no bar to any ordinary person acting as mediator or arbitrator, though it was thought to help if those appointed were of higher rank than the parties.

---

61. Lambeth MS930.
62. Nat Arch SP 75/8/463; SP 78/81/54; SP 75/10/266; SP 88/8/50; SP 88/9/46; SP 81/50/232; SP 80/10/138. Also Surrey G85/5/2/25 'King's concern at King of Denmark's offer of private mediation to resolve the question of the Palatinate and the demands of the Duke of Bavaria' (1643).
63. TD Hardy *Syllabus of Rymer's Foedera*.

10 ARBITRATORS

Some people will say: 'So shouldn't he do what is practical or expedient?' Absolutely not! He must realise that nothing is expedient or practical which is not just. If he cannot say that, he cannot be a *bonus vir*.... Is it not appalling that philosophers should ponder over things which no farmer would question? That age-old well-worn proverb is what country folk say when they praise someone's honesty and goodness: 'with him you can play dominoes in the dark'.

Cicero *On Duties* 3.19[1]

An arbitrator hath herein absolute power, yet ought his judgment or censure to be sincere and incorrupt, according to right and equity.

William West *Symboleography* II (1647) p146

Optime Phoenix,	Best of all, Phoenix,
Arbiter aequi,	Arbitrator of fairness,
Pacis amator,	Lover of peace
Litis et osor	And hater of lawsuits.

Michael Maier *Jocus Severus* (1617)[2]

1. INTRODUCTION

The process which people in the 17th century usually called arbitration was pervasive throughout all kinds of communities and the last chapter illustrated how people and organisations of all kinds, particularly the Government, made use of it. This chapter is about the arbitrators themselves. It will show that parties chose arbitrators from all walks of life and that the Government appointed whomever it considered appropriate to mediate and arbitrate, whether it called them arbitrators, commissioners, or referees.

1. Not dominoes then but the game where you have to guess how many fingers your opponent is holding out, a bit like 'stone, paper, scissors'. Romans called it *mices*, 'flash'.
2. Michael Maier *Jocus Severus, hoc est, Tribunal Aequum, quo Noctua Regina Avium, Phoenice Arbitro, post Varios Disceptationes et Querelas Volucrum eam Infestantium Pronunciatur et ob Sapientem Singularem, Palladi Sacrata, Agnoscitur* [The Serious Joke: i.e. the Fair Tribunal by which, with the Phoenix as Arbitrator, the Little Owl is acknowledged Queen of the Birds and sacred to Athene, after various arguments and complaints of the birds bothering her and as a result of her special wisdom], see Roebuck *Miscellany* 93–95.

2. QUALIFICATIONS AND CHOICE

The parties could appoint whomever they wanted to be their mediators and arbitrators and give them whatever powers they chose. The law is explained in Chapter 17. In private arbitrations it was usually considered advisable to appoint those whose status placed them above the parties in their community. That, it was hoped, not only made it more likely that the parties would agree to their mediation, and that peace would be restored, but also that they would be less open to improper influences.

If their appointed arbitrators failed to make an award within the specified time, the parties might just appoint new ones.[3] Sir Rowland Cotton and Sir Andrew Corbett took over an inheritance dispute from the defaulting Arthur Chamber and William Hassall, who had failed to make an award in time, and ordered payment of £75 by instalments, guaranteed by bonds. No doubt the parties had more faith in their new and more distinguished arbitrators. Both Cotton (St John's Cambridge, Lincoln's Inn) and Corbett (Queen's Oxford, Lincoln's Inn) were MPs, JPs and Members of the Council of the Marches and commissioners of assize. They could be trusted to do a proper and timely job.

Whereas Elizabeth I's Council had regularly appointed arbitrators from all parts of the country and with whatever qualifications it thought sufficient, James I's and Charles I's preferred to delegate to members of the Council or other officials, including judges and law officers. They were no doubt chosen for their qualities but also for their availability.[4] It was usual to appoint an even number of arbitrators or mediators, though odd numbers became more frequent.[5] The Privy Council lost its judicial powers in 1641. Even after the Restoration it did not retrieve its old functions as the executive committee of the Government or resume to its former extent the old practices of appointing arbitrators.

The Stuart Council appointed those it was confident deserved the respect of the parties, not that the parties always complied with the arbitration or the award. It liked to appoint experts. Where some legal knowledge was desirable it chose judges (including assize judges), the law officers, serjeants and other experienced barristers, or JPs. It took advantage of local expertise, expecting those it appointed to take into account not only the evidence of witnesses but also their own knowledge of such things as the reputation of the parties in their own communities, as well as the lie of the land. It often chose those who had authority where the dispute arose, for example the Warden of the Cinque Ports in a land dispute to 'mediate and settle as most agreeable to equity and good conscience'. In 1605 the

---

3. Shropshire 103/1/4/123/2.
4. e.g. *APC* 33.631 (Admiralty judge, MR and Secretary of State).
5. Just a small selection are *APC* 33.643; Glos D333/F23 (1633 personal property).

inhabitants of Romney asked Henry Howard, 1st Earl of Northampton, Warden of the Cinque Ports, to take the hearing of a dispute himself or refer it to arbitrators.[6] Lord Zouche, Warden in 1622, wrote to the Bailiff of Pevensey, asking him to call the parties to nominate one arbitrator to join the Bailiff in arbitrating their dispute, using the Council's formula 'to terminate or certify in whom the fault is'.[7]

A dispute between Mrs Jane Lamplugh and Captain Bullock, who had competing interests in the Dungeness lighthouse, having begun before the Warden 'in whom it properly belongeth', had been moved into Chancery. The Council sent it back to the Warden to 'use his best endeavours to make a friendly end'.[8] The story should have had a happy ending. Captain Bullock reported to the Council – a full Board of 19 members on 22 April 1631 – that 'the matter with joint consent was drawn to heads, and would have received a final end, had not Jane at the very instant deceased'. Her successors would not submit to the compromise, claiming they lived outside the Warden's jurisdiction, 'so that the order is now of no force for the ending of the controversy'. The Council was having none of that. It had all the jurisdiction it needed. The Warden had been acting by its appointment as arbitrator not on his own authority. The parties must comply with the ordered settlement or 'answer to the contrary at their perils'.

Local authorities often acted as arbitrators. The Mayor of Chester and an alderman together arbitrated a controversy over land.[9] In a Plymouth dispute, between James Bagg, 'being one of the ancient magistrates of that town, whom we know hath deserved well', and the Mayor, who was maligning him, the Council appointed the Governor of the Fort of Plymouth, Sir Ferdinando Gorges, and six other local notables, 'being their neighbours and indifferently affected unto them... to use your best endeavours for the mediating a friendly end between them'.

The Council might take advantage of someone with suitable authority passing through. It asked Lord Digby, Governor of King's County, Ireland, in Plymouth on his way home, to deal with a dispute recommended by the French ambassador, 'to call the parties before you and examine the business and the particulars of the complaint and take such order as shall be reasonable and just'.[10] While he was there he might as well hear a dispute between that troublesome James Bagg and Thomas Harding. It sent him the warrant summoning them to be heard by the Council, but he would not need to deliver it if he could dispose of the matter by

6. Kent NR/CPIb/45.
7. East Sussex AMS6600/1.
8. *APC* 46.95; 46.211; 46.302.
9. Cheshire ZM/B/28b.
10. *APC* 38.167.

compounding their difference. Expediency and efficiency were foremost in the Council's priorities.

The parties did not always want the process to start with each side making a nomination. Gerard Malynes described methods relying on chance:[11]

> wherefore the maner to elect arbitrators is worthy the observation. Some are contented to name foure or six persons on either side in writing, and refer the naming or electing of foure out of them by reciprocal proceeding, when one named the first person, another the second, and then again the third, and the other the fourth person. Others putting severall names in a paper, are contented that a meere stranger shall upon the back side of the paper pricke their names with a pin, or that (as they are numbered) the dice shall be cast upon them, accordingly by the number. Others put their names in severall papers, and cause them to be mingled & drawne by way of lot, by an indifferent person.... Others will do the same by nomination of them, and drawing the longest and shortest straw, or by any other extraordinarie means of pointing, numbring, or describing, al tending to one end, to have indifferencie, and that partialitie may by al means be avoided.

That this was no aberration of a cosmopolitan civilian merchant is shown by evidence of the practice in a rural Gloucestershire property dispute:[12]

> In avoidance of suits and expenses, and the unkindness that accompanieth suits in law, they offer that let all the names of the serjeants-at-law or readers in court, or any one house be (after the lottery fashion) written in several papers. Draw you out of the hat any one to be sole arbitrator; and they will be bound in £1,000 bond or more to stand to his end, you doing the like.

Women   Women were rarely appointed arbitrators, though there was nothing in English law to prevent it.[13] So deep are the mistaken assumptions about their lives, in particular their landowning and commercial transactions, that they demand Chapter 16 to themselves.

3. NUMBER

There was no law which determined the number of arbitrators for any dispute. Practice varied. Forms came late in the century. Perceived efficiency rather than availability seems to have been the criterion. The parties usually chose an even number and the authorities followed suit. The way in which arbitrators worked provided assumptions about the appropriate number. The common perception was that each side would suggest one or two who would put their case to the other side, with give

11. See Chapter 14.
12. Gloucester Public Library ms 16,533 115 and v, cited by Willcox 'Lawyers and Litigants' 542 fn32 [Willcox].
13. Roebuck *Golden Age* 153–154.

and take producing an agreeable settlement or, in default, agreement at least on the scope of the dispute, who should decide it and how it should be run. That meant there was a preference for an even number. Where the arbitrators were not the direct choice of the parties, for example where the Council delegated a matter to a committee of its own members, there was no such preference.

The Western Circuit Assize Orders 1629–1648 record the assize judges referring a dispute to JPs 174 times. They chose just one 60 times. More often than not they chose an even number: two (74 times), four (17 times) and six when they wanted them to make a view (3 times). Even when they appointed three (17 times) or five (3 times), they usually said that any two could act.

4. EXAMPLES

The greatest arbitrators deserve chapters to themselves: Edward Coke, Francis Bacon, Gerard Malynes and, for the wealth of his archives, Nathaniel Bacon. Much, too, is to be found in diaries and Chapter 15 describes the activities of Samuel Pepys and Robert Hooke as well as others less well known. It will be enough here just to give one or two examples of a more ordinary kind and one uniquely negative.

The More Family   In *Golden Age* the story was told of the career as an arbitrator of the Sussex worthy Sir William More.[14] He died in 1600 but the family tradition of disputes and their resolution was carried on by his son Sir George, and documents in the Surrey History Centre illustrate the family's involvement.[15] George, who had sometimes sat with his father,[16] took over his father's responsibilities until his death in 1632.[17] Already in 1595 Lord Howard had written 'from the Court in Whitehall', appointing George and three others, in what would now be called a 'documents only' arbitration, to receive statements of the case in writing, 'so as the parties themselves shall not need to come together'.[18]

In 1604 he sat with three other knights to dispose of a dispute between Magdalen Herbert, widow, and Sir Edward, her son, ordering him to provide £900 for her, dowries for his sisters and annuities for his brothers. In 1608 she married Sir John Danvers, later MP for Oxford University and much involved in the affairs of the Virginia Company. Charles I made him

14. Roebuck *Golden Age* 90–95 and *passim*.
15. Surrey LM 348/272, 349/7.
16. Surrey History Centre 6729/1/45/1.
17. Surrey History Centre LM 348/272.
18. Surrey History Centre 6729/3/46; also LM/348/272 (advowson); LM 349/7 (dowries and annuities). George submitted himself to the Lord Chancellor's arbitration over a disputed inheritance, LM 349/78/1.

a gentleman of his privy chamber, but he took up arms against him and signed his death warrant. She died in 1627.

Sir Francis Woolley lived only from 1583 to 1609 but his short life was full of incident. Elizabeth I's godson, he was married at 17, and had an illegitimate daughter. By then his widowed mother had married Ellesmere LC. Francis became an MP at 18, nominated by his uncle, Sir George More. He was one of the recipients of the second Virginia Charter. In his will he made his cousin, Sir Arthur Mainwaring, his heir, with generous provision, the manor of Burgham, for his illegitimate daughter and legacies to his servants, and no less than £4,000 for a tomb in St Paul's. Ellesmere LC was called on to arbitrate a dispute arising from the distribution of the estate.[19] As a result, Sir Arthur Mainwaring covenanted to pay Sir George More £2,500 and Sir George to surrender to him any claim to a lease of Stoneham, the advowson of Wonersh and various other items of real and personal property. A document in the Surrey History Centre of 3 June 1610 records an agreement noting Sir George's debt of £261 6s 8d to Woolley's estate but his intention to retain that sum if the intended mediation of the Lord Chancellor between him and Sir Arthur Mainwaring did not take effect.[20]

In 1623 Sir George assigned to Robert Parkhurst, clothworker of London, a bond for £4,000 which Robert Garton had entered into to submit his dispute with Sir George to arbitration. Parkhurst was also given Sir George's power of attorney to collect the £60 awarded and to release the bond.[21] The last document relevant to arbitration in the More bundle is Lady Elizabeth More's agreement to submit to arbitration her dispute with Daniel Harding, yeoman, over the lease of the manor of Westbury.[22]

The Gregory Family   The Gregory papers in the Shakespeare Archives provide further evidence of how one family dealt with disputes. Among them is a letter from Simon Chamber to John Gregory of 29 August 1633.[23] They were the parties to a dispute. Chamber apologised for having forgotten to bring with him the original lease and asked Gregory to let him see his counterpart, 'so that thereby I might set down the state of the case truly'. He also said that he would try to find an arbitrator of equal rank to the one Gregory had chosen, John Wicksteed. The letter was endorsed with a note from Wicksteed, saying he could see nothing against Gregory showing

19. Surrey LM 349/78/1; Nat Arch PROB 11/119/212 and 11/115/169; LM/349/135/1 is an arbitration bond to Sir Robert More and LM/349/135/2 5 drafts of an award in that matter; LM/349/135/3 a quitclaim in performance of that award.
20. Surrey LM/COR/4/11.
21. Surrey LM/349/52/10–11.
22. Surrey LM/351/10.
23. Shakes DR10/1723.

Chamber the counterpart and other documents, provided he did not part
with them. Then he stated firmly that he would not accept appointment
unless his fellow arbitrator was 'one who is determined to put an end to the
matter, for I would have him no wrangler'.

Shrewsbury   When parties were arranging a private arbitration, one
might approach the intended arbitrator and confirm first that he was willing
to act. If he was, then it might be considered wiser for him to approach
the other party for his agreement to his acting as sole arbitrator. The
Talbot papers in the Lambeth Palace library contain two examples of such
letters asking the Earl of Shrewsbury to act.[24] Gilbert Talbot, 7th Earl of
Shrewsbury, had a disputatious father and stepmother, Bess of Hardwick.
He married her formidable daughter, Mary Cavendish. He carried on the
families' quarrelling tradition but his position appears to have made him
an attractive sole arbitrator. In 1605 Sir William Bowes wrote to him. He
claimed mining rights in the land of Thomas Foljambe. If the Earl would
agree to arbitrate, it would avoid the need 'to trouble judges and juries'.[25]
In 1609 Sir Roger Owen, who had been appointed arbitrator in a dispute
between the Earl and Humphrey Briggs, wrote to him to ask whether 'it
was the Earl's pleasure that he should so act'. Edmund Molyneux wrote
an undated letter to him, asking him to mediate on behalf of Richard
Clakwall, who was prevented by the Lord Chancellor's injunction from
suing to recover his cattle.

Titus Oates   It is rare to have to write about a man of whom nothing
good can be said. Titus Oates (1649–1705) commands attention because
his public life ended in an arbitration of such egregious depravity as would
have made Francis Bacon blush. Oates was a brute, all his life on the run
from prosecution for perjury (which secured the execution of 35 innocent
men), theft (including of consecrated wafers), various heresies and the
homosexual practices on which he relied for much of his patronage.
Nothing about him was genuine, not his academic qualifications, his
religious protestations nor his vaunted patriotism.[26]

After inventing and exploiting his 'Popish Plot', he got his comeuppance
in 1685 from Jeffreys J, a man as hard as he. Convicted of perjury, he was
sentenced to life imprisonment, pilloried and whipped. He was in and out
of prison until 1689, when William III ordered his release and employed
him as a spy at £40 a month. He got himself appointed minister of a Baptist

24. Lambeth MS3203.
25. Lambeth Shrewsbury Papers MSS/694–710 folio159 and Talbot Papers MSS3192–3206
    folio302.
26. Alan Marshall's *Oxford Dictionary of National Biography* entry is full, though it does
    not mention the arbitration.

church in London's Virginia Street, where he soon quarrelled with Hester Parker, a rich widow. He hit her with his stick and was fined £6. When she died 'of a spotted fever', Oates was not invited to the funeral. Enraged, he persuaded her estranged husband to contest her will. If there had been a gold medal then for lying, Oates would have won it. He knew the secret. It was certainly not charm; it was telling dupes what they wanted to hear.

The search of the English Reports to 1703 just managed to reveal *Anthony Parker v Humphry Burroughs and George Reynolds.*[27] This was an appeal to the House of Lords by Anthony Parker, who had married Hester in 1688. They had agreed to live apart because of their religious differences, stoked he said by the respondent Burroughs who, like Hester, was an Anabaptist. Then:

> by mediation of friends, they came to a second agreement... to live and cohabit together or separately at their pleasures and that she might dispose of her estate as she thought fit.; and that in her last illness, a spotted fever, when she was *non compos mentis*, a will was pretended to be made by her.... Respondents upon her death possessed themselves of her estate.

When Parker heard of his wife's death he challenged the probate and the Consistory Court granted him administration.

> Respondents appealed from that sentence and proposed a reference, and artfully persuaded appellant to name Dr *Titus Oates* for a referee... and bonds of £4,000 penalty were executed next day, conditioned to perform the award: And that Dr Oates, after several days hearing the parties and their witnesses, on 26 December 1700, made his award, and confirmed the sentence against the pretended will, and awarded appellant the leasehold estate, and £1,500 in lieu of the residue of his wife's estate, and mutual releases to be executed: And that respondents exhibited their bill in Chancery, to set aside the award, which appellant and Dr Oates answered; and witnesses were examined on both sides, and the cause heard 17 November 1702 before the Lord Keeper; who decreed that the award should be set aside, as unfairly made and obtained; but appellant insisted that respondents had not shewn any indirect practices... but appellant had, on the contrary, fully proved that respondents, their friends and relations, had, by evil practices, laboured to obtain an award in their favour, and had offered the Doctor great rewards, and solicited him 'for the honour of God, for the sake of the Gospel and for the sake and interest of the Anabaptists'; and though it was said the Doctor had expressed some resentment against respondents, appellant insisted he ought not to suffer by any misunderstanding between respondents and the Doctor, who was an arbitrator of their own choosing; and the rather so, because it was proved that Doctor Oates had fully heard all respondents' witnesses for several days, and respondents, at the conclusion of each day, thanked the Doctor, and declared he had behaved himself fairly and impartially, and made no complaint of partiality until the award was made: And though it

27. (1702) Colles 257; 1 ER 275.

were objected, that the money awarded exceeded the estate, appellant contended respondents might have much more in their hands than what was awarded;

The respondents replied that Hester had made her will when of sound mind. It had been prepared by a respectable attorney and signed before three witnesses. Oates had conceived a prejudice against Hester, having been turned out by the Anabaptists and 'by his management a sentence was obtained against the will'. The respondents appealed to the Court of Arches. Oates was able to persuade the respondents to submit to his arbitration by telling them he was on their side. He had only just seen the clause in the agreement giving Hester power to dispose of her property by will. He was satisfied of the will's validity. He 'pressed respondents' friends to persuade them to refer the matter to him', otherwise 'that damned crew of rogues in the [Doctors] Commons would get all'. He accepted the reference on express condition that no lawyers attend. The respondents entered into a bond of £4,000 to submit.

> And that several attendances were had at Dr Oates's house, where, contrary to the condition of the arbitration, [the lawyers] Porter, Lovell, and Jeffreys were all present; and that the Doctor abetted them in rude behaviour to respondents and their witnesses, whom the Doctor himself not only refused to hear but palliated manifest contradictions of appellants' witnesses, and at length, in vengeance to respondent, and from malice of mind, freely and indecently avowed, published his award under his hand and seal, whereby he not only confirmed the sentence against the will, but awarded respondents to pay £1,500 to appellant at his, Dr Oates's, own house, though no part of Hester's estate had ever come to the hands of the respondent Reynolds and very little to respondent Burroughs, to the utter ruin of respondents and their families: And that to be relieved against this award, respondents exhibited their bill, and appellant a cross bill, which were both answered: And to justify this extravagant award, the Doctor had sworn in his answer in Chancery, that the testatrix, a fortnight before she died, acquainted him that she had above £2,000 in Burrough's hands.

Oates ranted on about the 'cursed Babylonish Court of Doctors Commons… relic of Popery'. But the Lord Keeper:

> upon reading the several deeds and proofs, and the conviction of perjury of Doctor Oates, declared that neither the reference or award were fairly or indifferently obtained; and that the award appeared to be made revengefully and partially, and therefore decreed the award be set aside, and the award bond to be cancelled, and appellant to acknowledge satisfaction on the record of the judgment obtained thereupon… rather, because appellant had the sentence with him, if it could be supported, in the Ecclesiastical Court; whereas if the award should stand, respondents had no remedy at law or elsewhere.

On 28 January 1702 The House of Lords dismissed the appeal with costs. The editor of the report then adds his own curious postscript:

The editor hath been more circumstantial in the foregoing report than usual, because this being a private case, long after all the plot businesses were cool and laughed at, shows the true mind of the famous Titus Oates, about which some historians seem to entertain doubts.

5. JUDGES

The Council often asked the judges for help, sometimes appointing them as members of a panel when legal expertise was required. They were often the preferred choice in private arbitrations, too, as Sir Richard Hutton JCP was of the parties in a land and dower dispute in 1629.[28]

In 1615 the Council wrote to Sir Henry Hobart CJCP and the other judges of Common Pleas with the petition of Joan Fuljam, widow, against Serjeant Harris.[29] The matter had already been before Coke CJKB when he was Chief Justice of the Common Pleas. He had made orders 'compounding that difference'. Since then he had 'delivered as his opinion that the hearing and determining of this cause properly belonged to' Common Pleas; but he was always alert to the advantages of arbitration:

> But for that the poor gentlewoman in respect of her poverty desireth to avoid the charge and expense of time incident to the ordinary course of law, we have hereby thought fit to require you to examine what former orders have been already set down by that Court, and to command the execution of them, or else (if no order shall now appear) to call Serjeant Harris and Mrs Fuljam before you and to order and settle some such end and agreement between them as may free both His Majesty and this Board from further clamour.

Poverty is always relative in the eyes of the privileged and one may wonder what evidence the Council required of Mrs Fuljam's means. There is at least a suspicion that the Council was not hard to convince that anyone who had been through the costs and trouble of litigation, as Mrs Fuljam had, deserved its help to a speedy resolution.

Though the Council seems to have had a policy of sending legal issues to those with the necessary professional experience, that did not mean that a judicial resolution was expected. In 1617 Montagu CJKB was commissioned to resolve a dispute about 'letters patents lately granted... touching brokers'.[30] His would be an administrative decision. 'Upon due consideration of the letters patents and Acts of Common Council and full hearing of the allegations of all parties', he was told to 'order such a course as in his wisdom shall be found expedient for the benefit of the public'.

---

28. West Yorks WYL500/625.
29. *APC* 34.169.
30. *APC* 35.220.

The assize judges were often called on, as the best possible legal experts and on the spot.[31] It is not always easy to determine whether the Council was appointing them arbitrators or merely passing to them a matter to handle on their assize. The distinction never seems to have troubled the Council. It wrote to those for Hertfordshire recommending the poor petitioner, 'requiring you to take notice of his cause at the next assizes and to give some speedy end as in justice you shall see cause'. And the Star Chamber explained to those of Durham that 'in respect of their other weighty affairs' they were too busy; and of Gloucester, asking them to 'order some speedy and effectual course agreeable to good reason and justice, without further trouble'.[32]

There is no hope of calculating how many private arbitrations went to the judges, but a bond from 1651 in the Derbyshire Record Office is unlikely to be unique. It required Robert Houlden to submit to the privately arranged arbitration of Matthew Hale, Cromwell's Chief Justice, and William Allestrey, concerning the title of the manor of Weston and other lands.[33]

6.   JUSTICES OF THE PEACE

JPs were favourites for appointment. A thorough search of all those arbitrators whose names are found in the sources might well show that most of them were JPs. Though many were not lawyers by profession, but rather local landowners, they regularly sat in judgment locally, and were expected to know how to act judicially. They had authority to act against breaches of the peace.[34] But when, having been appointed arbitrators, they could not bring about a settlement and had to make an award, a party might challenge their authority.

Like assize judges, local JPs had the advantage of being on or near the spot. For example, in a dispute about a lease, the Council asked two Kent JPs, 'in respect of the nearness of your habitations to the place the truth of these complaints may best appear', to 'accommodate and end the differences'.[35] George More JP's arbitration work has been mentioned; Nathaniel Bacon's will have the next chapter to itself. Urien Leigh, a Cheshire JP, is another example of how one then approached his task:[36]

> There had been a quarrel in his district between two of his acquaintances whom he bound over to appear at quarter sessions…. However, 'afterwards myself

---

31. *APC* 34.259 (Worcester for debt).
32. *APC* 34.91; 35.378; 35.404.
33. Derby D3155/7918.
34. *APC* 34.118.
35. *APC* 39.470.
36. TC Curtis 'Quarter Sessions Appearances' 153.

with other gentlemen that wished well to both parties did pacify the parties and made them friends, and thereupon released them'.... On occasion, therefore, the authorities could regard a case as having been resolved to the greater good of the commonwealth.

TC Curtis, who focussed his study on Cheshire, found plenty of evidence of arbitration, indeed of a system, though: 'One of the problems of using quarter sessions as a principal source is that, virtually by definition, only failed attempts to arbitrate come to notice. Even so, there is sufficient evidence'.

A matter which had already been before the justices might be referred to arbitration. After the 'Great Sessions at Chester' had tried the case of Welshman against Coddington on 4 May 1655, it was agreed by the parties 'and the Earl of Shrewsbury and the agents of the City of Chester that the dispute should be referred to the ordering of Thomas Mainwaring and Thomas Croxton, arbitrators, and of Thomas Brereton, umpire'.[37]

The office of Deputy Lieutenant (DL) of a county gave status and authority. Often they were appointed from those who were already JPs and MPs.[38] The Shropshire landowner Sir Francis Newport is a good example: Shrewsbury School, Magdalen College Oxford, Inner Temple, JP, Sheriff, DL, Member of the Council of the Marches, knighted 1603. A bond in the Shropshire Archives dated 9 October 1610 provides that two arbitrators are to determine who had the right of possession of the Isle Pool, but that the award would be made by Sir Francis.[39]

Charles I's Council called on the services of DLs, seeking to exploit their local knowledge and authority; not to arbitrate, though, but merely to investigate and report back.[40]

7. LAW OFFICERS

The Attorney General and the Solicitor General are together called the Law Officers. They were on hand for the Council to call on to perform any tasks the Council wished to delegate to them. They were routinely asked to mediate and arbitrate. Two of them rose to greater fame, Francis Bacon and Edward Coke. Sometimes the two of them sat together on the same panel.[41]

8. COMMITTEES OF THE COUNCIL

It is not surprising that the Council made an effort to reduce its workload by distributing it to committees of its own members, attempting to impose

37. Cheshire ZA/B/2/108.
38. Willcox 543.
39. Shropshire 465/427.
40. *APC* 44.8.
41. *APC* 33.563 on Sunday 25 September 1614.

a scheme for the distribution of the work. On 31 March 1617, under
the heading 'Committees', there is a list of the six committees to which
matters would be allocated:[42] Ireland, Household, Navy, Wardrobe, Works,
'for putting the laws into execution' (Lord Chancellor and Lord Chief
Justice), and finally a catch-all: 'Grievances in general (the King's learned
counsel)', that is the Law Officers. The Commissioners were 'to call to
assist these services whomsoever they think fit'. From the frequency of the
records of the Council first receiving a petition and then sending it, not to
the Law Officers but to a bespoke commission, and from the lack of other
evidence, it would seem that that attempt at efficiency was not successful.

A record of ten years later may be evidence of a further attempt. It is
headed:[43]

At Whitehall the 4th of July 1627
   Present: Lord Keeper ⎫
        Lord President ⎬ Lords Committees
        Lord Steward ⎭

Sir John Savage, from a long line of landowners in Cheshire, had had
a difference with Thomas Taylor, which the King had referred to three
members of the Council, 'the Lords Committees', who had made an order
staying all suits in all courts except Chancery. But that stay was omitted
when the order was drawn up. The Lords Committees then stayed all suits
'whatsoever in Star Chamber or any other Courts of Judicature' until
Taylor showed good cause. The referees, Sir Julius Caesar and Humphrey
May, were asked to resolve the various disputes; but they returned a report,
not an award, and it was left to the Council to make an order ratifying it.

By 1628 the Council's usual practice was to refer disputes to an ad hoc
committee of its own members. A typical example is:[44]

17 December 1628   Whereas the ending of the differences betwixt the Sheriffs
of London, Sir John Langworth and one Snooke, a tailor, were referred by the
Board to the Master of the Rolls and Mr Chancellor of the Duchy, who have
made report *in haec verba*…. Their Lordships having read well and considered
of the Report in the presence of all parties do hereby for a final end of all the said
differences ratify and confirm the same in all parts thereof.

9. UMPIRES

The role of the umpire nowadays is to take over from arbitrators who
cannot agree. It is distinguished from an extra arbitrator added to produce
an uneven number to break an impasse. As in so many other aspects, the

---

42. *APC* 35.215. Apparently Bacon LC tried again in 1620, James Spedding *The Works* VII.
43. *APC* 42.399. But a dispute within a trading company would still be sent to merchant
    arbitrators, *APC* 43.19, above Chapter 7.
44. *APC* 44.266.

17th-century understanding was the same but the practice was more flexible. The matter arose directly in King's Bench in 1612 in *R v Hastings*:[45]

> An award, where the submission was of all actions, suits and quarrels unto four persons, and the umperage of another, and... to stand unto and perform the order of them five. The four persons, and the fifth as umpire, did make the award, and the party submitting did refuse to perform this order and award so by them made; the question propounded was, whether this award was made according to the submission or not. Williams J: the award was well made, and pursuing the submission; but otherwise it had been, if in the submission they had been divided; as if it had been in this manner: that if the four could not agree in their award, that then the submission to be to the umperage of a fifth man, then these five could not all of them joyn in the making of this award; but the submission being here to four, and to the umperage of a fifth, they all five may well joyn in their award; and so the award here made by them all five is clearly good and well made, according to the submission, and the same award ought to be performed. The whole Court agreed with him herein.

Not surprisingly, the King's Bench supported umpires, holding that words of a submission to arbitrators applied equally to an umpire appointed under it.[46] And in *Travers v Twistleton*,[47]

> Debt on an obligation conditioned to perform an award, and upon demurrer, the case was, that they submitted to the award of A and B so that they made their award before the first of May; and if they did not agree, to the umpirage of such a one as they should elect... The arbitrators chose an umpire and afterwards themselves make the award in question before the first of May, and whether this was good, was the question... they had determined their power, and put all matters in the power of the umpire... here the umpire is elected by the arbitrators, by which act they themselves have dismissed themselves from their authority.

But there were limits. The Court would not allow the arbitrators to resolve some of the issues and the umpire the residue.[48]

If the reports in *Reynolds v Gray* may be relied on, Holt CJ could argue himself into unnecessary difficulties.[49] From Salkeld's report:

---

45. (1612) 1 Bulst 183; 80 ER 872.
46. *Bean v Newbury* (1663) 1 Lev 139; 83 ER 337; *Bean v Newberry* 1 Keb 790, 832, 857; 83 ER 1245, 1269, 1284;
47. (1664) 1 Lev 174; 83 ER 356; 1 Keb 935; 83 ER 1329; 1 Lev 174; 83 ER 356; *Ward v Twistleton* (1665) 2 Keb 6; 84 ER 4; *Twistleton v Travers* (1665) 2 Keb 15; 84 ER 10. Also *Copping v Hernalt* (1668) 2 Keb 562; 84 ER 353; 1 Sid 428; 82 ER 1198; (1669) 1 Mod 15; 86 ER 694; (1669) 2 Saund 127, 129; 85 ER 849, 851; (1669) 2 Keb 619; 84 ER 389; *Copping v Harriard* (1669) 1 Lev 285; 83 ER 409; *Copping v Hurrier* (1669) T Raym 187; 83 ER 98. Also *Donovan v Maschall* (1670) 1 Mod 274; 86 ER 877; as *Dellovan v Marshall* (1669) 2 Keb 714; 84 ER 450; *Denovan v Mascal* (1669) T Raym 205; 83 ER 109.
48. *R v Leonard* (1623) 2 Rolle 348; 81 ER 844; Palm 369; 81 ER 1128.
49. (1697) 1 Ld Raym 222; 91 ER 1045; 1 Salk 70; 91 ER 64.

Motion for an attachment for not performing an umpirage of H chosen by arbitrators who were appointed by rule of Court. And it was held by Holt CJ that, if arbitrators choose an umpire before the time allowed for their award be expired, it is *ipso facto* void, though they absolutely resolve to make no award themselves: and that when their time is expired, if the arbitrators choose one, their authority is executed, and they cannot revoke or choose again, though the person elect refuse to accept.... When the power of the arbitrators and umpire is limited to the same time, if the arbitrators do in fact make an award within the time, that shall be considered as the real award, and if they make none, then the umpirage shall take place.... It is now finally determined, that arbitrators may nominate an umpire before they proceed to consider the subject referred to them.... It is not unusual to insert a condition that the umpire shall be chosen before any other act.

And from Lord Raymond's:

Per Holt CJ, if arbitrators have authority to chuse an umpire, and they chuse A accordingly, they have executed their authority and cannot make another... *ex relatione* Master Jacob. In the same case it was said also by Holt CJ that, if the arbitrators chuse an umpire, before the time for them to make their award be expired, it is void, though they are resolved to make no award themselves.

That cannot have been what the parties wanted, whatever the experienced Master might have suggested. The practice must have been for arbitrators to *choose* an umpire while they still had power to do so. They could leave the *appointment* until the last minute, but it would still have to be made before they became *functus officio*. And it was Holt CJ who warned against the 'scambling reports'; the reporters in fn 47 could not even be bothered to check the names of the parties.

Some good examples of umpires' work come from the Channel Islands. On 17 October 1621 the Council wrote to two Jersey knights: 'we do authorise you or either of you as umpires for the final ending and determining... agreeable to justice and equity'.[50] The dispute was about the guardianship of the orphans of Edward le Porc, which had been submitted to arbitration with the Bailly of Jersey as umpire. 'By reason of the absence of the Bailly the arbitrament has been protracted now for more than a year to the great prejudice of the orphans.' So the umpires were ordered to cause the parties to 'nominate some indifferent persons, not being of their kindred or allies or interested in this business, to arbitrate some final end', and to stand by to act as umpires if necessary. The two umpires were Sir John Peyton, Governor of Jersey, and Sir Philip de Carteret, Seigneur of Sark. They were appointed twice more that month.[51]

50. *APC* 38.63.
51. *APC* 38.70.

The Privy Council might transfer appeals from the courts of the Channel Islands to arbitrators, as it did when Jasper Chapman, Porter of the Castle Elizabeth on Jersey, appealed on the ground that not enough Jurats had sat at the trial of his case. The umpires were asked:

> to call both parties before you and cause them to nominate some indifferent persons of that isle such as are not allied to the parties to arbitrate some good agreement between them and, in case the arbitrators so chosen cannot fully compound their differences, we authorise you as umpires in this business to set down a final determination.

And two days later they were asked to act, not as umpires themselves, but to arrange the appointment of an umpire:

> Forasmuch as we are informed that the difference is a matter of so small value that the charge of prosecution of the appeal would amount to more than the thing controverted is worth... call both parties and cause them to nominate some indifferent persons not being of their kindred or allies for arbitrators, and to make choice of some fit person for umpire, who together with the arbitrators... set down such order for the final ending and determining of this business as shall be agreeable to justice and equity.

The Council found Carteret useful. His duties as Seigneur of Sark must have left him time to respond efficiently, because on 9 June 1623 he was asked to dispose of the many long-running differences in the De La Rocque family. Hester, widow of Peter De La Rocque, was now married to Dumaresq.

> By order from the Board Sir Philip Carteret hath determined what the defendant should pay for the great part of the differences and reduced it to a certain sum of £172 19s 2d which the defendant should pay, but there is yet no execution thereof.... Take present order that that sum be levied. And for the other differences which yet depend undetermined... the parties have already nominated arbitrators in the Isle for partition of their land... those arbitrators determine the other differences also... Carteret to be umpire... put that in execution which the arbitrators, or the umpire in their default, shall determine, that so this long and tedious suit, which hath so often troubled this Board, may receive a final end.

It referred back an earlier Guernsey dispute, for which it had authorised arbitrators 'to hear and order a difference depending between two brothers', both called Thomas Marchant.[52] They had ordered the elder to pay the younger £45 and the younger to restore certain lands to the elder. Both brothers had appealed to the Bailiff and Jurats. The younger now told the Council that he had restored the land but that the elder had paid him neither the £45 nor another £200 he owed him. He claimed that all this was the fault of some of the arbitrators, who favoured his brother. The Council had foreseen problems and had appointed the Bailiff and Jurats to be umpires. Now it ordered them directly to summon the brothers and 'make such a final end as shall be agreeable to the laws and customs of the said isle, and as to equity and good conscience shall appertain, that we be not further troubled.'

Assize judges often appointed umpires, in case the arbitrators failed in their determinations.[53] The umpire was usually another JP but could be someone with special qualifications or authority – a barrister for his skill,[54] or the Bishop of Exeter in a dispute between vicar and parishioners.[55] There might even be two JPs appointed to do the job.[56] The court could order the parties to choose two arbitrators each, but itself name the umpire to determine the dispute if they could not.[57]

10. FEES

Prest's researches suggest that a normal part of some barristers' earnings in the 17th century came from acting as arbitrator.[58] Two quotations from the records of the Founders Company provide not entirely unambiguous evidence:[59]

> 1617   given unto Mr Jarret when we met the Brashers at the Recorder's, being Counsel on both sides   £3 6. 0.
> 1619   given to Mr Jarrett at two several times for his counsel concerning the Brashers   £2 4. 0.

Chapter 8 showed Ralph Josselin being paid for his services as arbitrator in 1659. Further evidence will appear in Chapter 15, when the career is examined of the self-trained surveyor and architect Robert Hooke. After the Great Fire of 1666 he took modest fees for making surveys, called views, and for mediating and arbitrating in the disputes that sometimes followed. But his appointment as City Surveyor was peculiar to its time and place and payments to arbitrators do not appear to have become common until well into the 18th century.

11. CONCLUSIONS

The Stuarts continued the Government policy of commissioning arbitrators according to their skills, position and availability. They did not make as

53. Cockburn *Western* 23, 234, 357, 366, 792, 887.
54. Cockburn *Western* 23.
55. Cockburn *Western* 366.
56. Cockburn *Western* 234.
57. Cockburn *Western* 792.
58. WR Prest 'Counsellors' Fees' [Prest] 166.
59. Prest 179–180.

much use of the Civilians as Elizabeth I had done but they appointed them in appropriate cases.

In private arbitration, the longstanding routine appointment by the parties of third parties they chose to help them resolve their disputes is evidenced in the very language they used. Though it was usual to call them arbiters or arbitrators, there could be a dialect alternative. For example, on the Welsh–English border in 1615, Rearid Thomas was appointed sole arbitrator or daysman.[60] The word has Biblical authority: 'Neither is there any daysman betwixt us, that might lay his hand upon us both' *Job* 9.33, where Job recognises that there can be no third party who could intervene in his differences with Jehovah.

60. Shropshire 445/215. This digression could not be resisted, from John Cowell *A Law Dictionary*: 'Days-man. In some Northern parts of England, any arbitrator, umpire, or elected judge is commonly called a deies-man or days-man, which reminds me of what Dr Hammond well observes, in his annotations on *Hebrews* 10.25, that the word "day", in all idioms, doth signify judgment. And, on this occasion, it may not be improper to observe, (because no notice has yet been taken of so small a matter), that the addition of "Dey" or "Day" to the Doom-book or *Liber Judicialu*, the General Survey, in the time of Will. Conq., was not meant with any allusion to the Final Day of Judgment, as most persons have conceited. For "day" does not augment the sense of the word, but only doubles and confirms the same meaning... *Doomsday Book* is but more emphatically the judicial decisive record, the Book of Dooming Judgment, and decreeing justice.'

11   NATHANIEL BACON

The considerable labour involved in reconstituting the Bacon archive and preparing it for publication will be recompensed by other scholars finding within the edition as a whole grist for their particular mills.

Papers of Nathaniel Bacon V Editors' Introduction pxxxi[1]

Yet, knowing that it hath been agreeable with your good disposition not to think that time lost which is spent in so good a work as ending of controversies and dissentions, and making of peace and amity between gentlemen and your neighbours, pardon me if I seem troublesome, that am so wrongfully troubled (as I suppose).

Submission of William Cobbe to Nathaniel Bacon[2]

1.   INTRODUCTION

The first ten chapters have been in their different ways introductory to this and the next five, which look in greater depth at the work of individuals. The predominant sources change, too, from official records and local archives to collections of personal papers and diaries. Most of them were never meant to be seen by future generations seeking to understand the persons and the times. They are all the more dependable for that.

If no other documents had survived, Nathaniel Bacon's papers would have made it possible to construct a detailed model of 17th-century dispute resolution. His determination to preserve – and his secretary Martin Man's careful copying and filing – created a unique archive. Good luck and

---

1. All of this chapter is based on *The Papers of Nathaniel Bacon of Stiffkey* Norwich, Norfolk Record Society, of which five volumes have so far appeared: I 1556–1577 ed A Hassell Smith, GM Baker and RW Kenny (XLVI 1978/1979), cited as Hassell Smith et al *Nat Bacon I*; II 1578–1585 ed A Hassell Smith and GM Baker (XLIX 1983) [Hassell Smith et al *Nat Bacon II*]; III 1586–1595 ed A Hassell Smith and GM Baker (LIII 1990) [Hassell Smith et al *Nat Bacon III*]; IV 1596–1602 ed Victor Morgan, Jane Key and Barry Taylor (LXIV 2000) [Morgan et al *Nat Bacon IV*]; V 1603–1607 ed Victor Morgan, Elizabeth Rutledge and Barry Taylor (LXXIV 2010) [Morgan et al *Nat Bacon V*]. G Alan Metters, Victor Morgan, Elizabeth Rutledge and Barry Taylor, editors of *Nat Bacon VI* (1608– 1613) and *VII* (1614–1622) have generously allowed me to cite unpublished drafts. Two earlier selections were useful: HW Saunders ed *The Official Papers* and FW Brooks ed *Supplementary Stiffkey Papers* [Saunders *Nat Bacon*] .
2. Submission of William Cobbe to Nathaniel Bacon [Morgan et al *Nat Bacon IV*] 284 8 September 1602 set out in full below.

determination were needed to reassemble it. The extraordinary care and learning of the editors of the Norfolk Record Society, now represented by G Alan Metters, Victor Morgan, Elizabeth Rutledge and Barry Taylor, have produced volumes of the highest scholarship. Their generosity in giving me copies of their work in progress and commenting on drafts of this chapter cannot be adequately recognised. I have quoted many passages, unusual in number and length but justified by their detail and comprehensive range. Their appositeness has sometimes made me wonder whether I was making them up, so well do they suit my purposes. I have redacted them a bit, for consistency of spelling – which did not bother writers then – and to trim to size. Scholars, particularly of language, will no doubt examine the originals.

Early in the 17th century the Government delegated responsibility for making local government work to JPs. One was Nathaniel Bacon (1546?–1622), son of Sir Nicholas Bacon, Lord Keeper, and older half-brother of Francis, the future Lord Chancellor, and Anthony the spy. To avoid confusion with them, he is called just Nathaniel in this chapter.[3] After Trinity College Cambridge he entered Gray's Inn. At 23 he married his cousin Anne, daughter of Sir Thomas Gresham, and their fathers settled land on them, including Sir Nicholas's manor of Stiffkey. Sir Nicholas died in 1579 when Nathaniel was 32. Until then he had looked after his father's property under his tight control; but long before then he had chosen a future for himself. Not for him the fickle life at Court. He wrote to Sir Thomas Gresham in October 1572 (Hassell Smith et al *Nat Bacon I* 35):

> If I were not to dwell here in the country, I know to receive my living as an annuitant were the less matter. But now I am here to remain, it were to be wished by me to have tenants, which I may by well using so order as perhaps I may in time command and use in many necessary services I shall have to do.

He fulfilled his duties as a Member of Parliament but rejoiced in the life of the squire, performing with great assiduity the obligations, religious and civil, he considered essential if he were to create an orderly and godly community within his jurisdiction. The concern for order began at home and his huge collection of manuscripts provides the primary sources for a history of dispute resolution in his 'country' at that time. Most of the documents refer to his work as a JP, many of them commissions to mediate from a great range of authorities: from the King, Parliament and Privy Council, and the various Courts, to individual authorities. But there is also plenty of evidence of his popularity as a private arbitrator, where with no official interference both parties were content for him to sit alone; and he persuaded other local gentry to act as mediators and arbitrators.

---

3. Nor must he be confused with the Nathaniel Bacons who helped to found Virginia.

The records of disputes in which Nathaniel was himself a party show his determined preference for mediation.[4]

Nathaniel's papers were overlooked in *Golden Age* but they provide such rich evidence that the story of his life as a mediator, arbitrator and party demands full scholarly treatment. This chapter covers a period beginning towards the end of Elizabeth I's reign and ending with Nathaniel's death in 1622. The gap in the *APC* from 1603 to 1612 means that there is no way of checking the primary sources of the Council's work against the *Papers* for that period. But there is plenty there to show how mediation and arbitration were routinely available as a function of local government. Between 1600 and 1622, the *Papers* contain hundreds of documents relating to Nathaniel's activities as resolver of disputes.

Nathaniel was MP for King's Lynn, High Sheriff of Norfolk, Deputy Lieutenant and Steward of the Duchy of Lancaster's lands in the county. The office of JP required him to perform many other tasks of local government, yet he always seems to have made time for dispute settlement, whether commissioned in response to petitions to various authorities or privately arranged. The examples have been chosen to show the range, weight and regularity of Nathaniel's work, with preference for documents which contain the most detail.

Social class expected privilege. Obligations were the more readily accepted on the understanding they would generate reciprocity.[5] Nathaniel was expected to take responsibility for law and order. There was no effective police force. On 12 May 1614 George Leeds wrote to him as Deputy Lieutenant:

> Sir, yesternight very late I heard of a quarrel begun between my cousin John Cooke and another young gentleman at Walsingham last Friday which, as it was not then compounded so since (as it is said) some further purpose is intended, which to both howsoever may prove very fatal and dangerous. It is not only in

4. At the beginning of the century Nathaniel was engaged in a dispute with the local Admiralty judge, Dr Burham, who seems to have delighted in exceeding his jurisdiction, particularly in regard to a grampus, probably a killer whale, whose valuable carcase was washed up on Nathaniel's land. The weight of the story, like its subject, would sink any general treatment of disputes and must be left to be read throughout [Morgan et al *Nat Bacon IV*]. The gossip got as far as North Yorkshire, where Margaret Hoby (see Chapter 16) noted in her diary for 4 February 1602: 'I heard of a fish that was taken up at Yarmouth 53 foot long and 23 broad', Joanna Moody ed *The Private Life of an Elizabethan Lady* 177. How big might it have been by the time the story reached London?

5. In a footnote to the Introduction to Morgan et al *Nat Bacon V*, lxi fn163, Victor Morgan thanks his research student Peter Smith. Dr Smith has put online his PhD thesis 'Petitionary Negotiation in a Community in Conflict: King's Lynn and West Norfolk c1575 to 1662'. It sets Nathaniel in his milieu and arbitration in the wider context of petitions. I thank him not only for his substantial contribution to this work but for another example of scholarly generosity.

your power as an ordinary justice or conservator of the King's peace, but imposed upon you by imperial authority and special command, to hear and determine this cause according to his Majesty's edict and direction. Wherefore... I hope you will take some present course therein...

Postscript: I pray you lend me your treatise of Moulin, the minister of the French church in Paris written in Latin, *De Origine Pape*, as I do remember.

George Ledes

As the editors of volume IV of the *Papers* wrote (Morgan et al *Nat Bacon IV* xlii): 'Nathaniel Bacon's brother-in-law was injured in a duel and his son-in-law and later his step-son were to be killed in duels':

Resolution of minor local disputes may have been tiresome and time-consuming but the seeking out of a local gentleman such as Bacon as an arbiter by individuals in the locality or the referral to him of disputes that had reached the centre did two things. First, it reflected his existing standing in both local society and in the estimation of those at the centre.... Second, every act of mediation or arbitration helped to spin out yet further filaments of obligation.

There are hundreds of relevant documents. Many are drafts or copies of letters to and from Nathaniel, usually in the hand of his trusted clerk, Martin Man. Others range from formal records of every word of an award to scraps of paper with scribbled notes, taken by Nathaniel during his examination of parties and witnesses. They were working papers. A document from about July 1608, in Man's hand, is a memorandum – 'remembrance' he called it – of the questions Nathaniel intended to ask the claimant when he next sat as arbitrator, including:

A remembrance of part of the state of the cause between Mr Brend and Mr Branthwaite. To ask Mr Brend if upon first lending money to Musket it was not the meaning of the parties that interest after £10 the £100 should be answered and, if that be so, what he saith to Mr Branthwaite's offer to Mr Grimston to have accepted £8 the £100 with his charges.

The documents have been allowed to speak for themselves as much as practicable. They can be divided into three categories: official commissions to Nathaniel; private arbitrations appointing Nathaniel; and disputes in which Nathaniel himself was a party. The first category is presented here according to the many different authorities and persons who made the appointment. Various manifestations of the Government routinely took advantage of arbitration to delegate matters of dispute which had come to them on petitions. Sometimes the King's own hand is obvious, sometimes the initiative came from Parliament. It is not always clear from the *Papers* whether, for example, Popham CJKB was sending out a matter from his own court or acting on behalf of the Privy Council. In June 1602 John Atkin of King's Lynn wrote to Lord Keeper Egerton, on behalf of himself and his neighbours, complaining of the 'unjust malefactions' of Alderman

Thomas Baker, and asking him for permission to petition the Council for 'letters to be directed to 3 or 4 knights or gents in the county to call all the parties grieved before them... whereby some good order may be had for reformation according to their godly wisdoms agreeing with equity.' On 16 July Popham commissioned 'the right worshipful my very loving friends Sir Miles Corbett and Nathaniel Bacon Esq... to mediate matters between them and if you may finally to accord them' (Morgan et al *Nat Bacon IV* 273):[6]

> Where there are certain controversies and suits depending between Mr Baker and Mr Gurlyn, two of the aldermen of the town of Lynn, which occasioneth some division in the town to the hindrance of the good governance, I have thought good thereby to pray you to take the pains at this my entreaty to mediate matters between them and if you may finally to accord them wherein in mine opinion you shall do a very good office not only in making peace between these two in particular but in furthering thereby the continuance of the good government of that town.

2.   THE KING

The endorsement at the foot of a commission might reveal the King's own hand. Martin Hambleton had mortgaged his land for one year to John Mingay and his son Henry, for £60 at 10 per cent. The land was leased to Edward Murton. Murton and the Mingays took possession of the house and turned out the Hambleton family, even though Hambleton had offered to pay them all he owed. He specifically asked for Nathaniel and four others, or any two or three, to examine his petition. The petition dated 16 May 1604 is endorsed (Morgan et al *Nat Bacon V* 108–109) with an order from James I that, if the case was not being dealt with judicially, the arbitrators, or some of them, with two or more chosen by the other parties, should settle it equitably.

James I himself might take control of a matter which Popham CJKB had first referred to Nathaniel and Sir Christopher Heydon, often his co-arbitrator, on behalf of the Privy Council (Morgan et al *Nat Bacon V* 131, 135). They had examined Ralph Jermyn's petition about a breach of trust by Thomas Moore and reported back when Moore refused to accept their settlement. Jermyn then asked the King to refer it back to Heydon and Nathaniel to determine. The King did just that, provided it had not already been heard in any court, 'so that His Majesty be troubled no further', Moore being allowed to nominate two arbitrators of his own.

6. G Alan Metters 'The Rulers and Merchants of King's Lynn' 42–46 gives sufficient details of Baker's attempts to abuse every available part of the legal system, to say nothing of his depravity and other outrageous behaviour, to show why mediation was not likely to succeed.

Dr Julius Caesar, one of the two Masters of Requests, who had been so active under Elizabeth I, has already been shown to be one conduit through which James I channelled instructions. On 24 June 1603 he wrote to Nathaniel and Sir Christopher Heydon, referring to them the petition of Nicholas Ringold to the new King, who had asked that it be sent to 'some indifferent gentlemen' of Norfolk (Morgan et al *Nat Bacon V* 37–43):

> His Highness' good pleasure is that you should call both him and his adverse parties before you and examine the differences between them, and thereupon mediate such good end and order between them as you shall find to be agreeable to good conscience and dignity, that His Highness be no further troubled.

Expressly to mediate an outcome, not according to law, but conscience and dignity; but further documents as late as 28 July 1603 show that the matter dragged on.

On 17 February 1605 Caesar wrote to Nathaniel, telling him that the King had referred a petition to him, with Christopher Heydon and Henry Sidney, the other party being invited to name an equal number of arbitrators, to call the parties before them and to mediate an equitable settlement (Morgan et al *Nat Bacon V* 153).

Not all Nathaniel's efforts to mediate were successful. A matter referred to him and others on a petition to James I 'concerning a messuage and 103 acres in Briston' was returned on 1 May 1604 when they were unable to persuade the parties to a settlement (Morgan et al *Nat Bacon V* 107); but in such a case the committees' certificate would contain findings of fact and advice upon which the commissioning body would make its determination.

3. PARLIAMENT

Parliament, too, might send a matter to arbitration, even when it was the subject of a bill before it. Arthur Penning of Kettleburgh, Suffolk, had died in 1594. His heir and executor was his elder son Anthony. The will provided for his younger brother Edmund to receive £4,000 from the estate. The intention was that Edmund should have a substantial share of the family lands. As it would be impossible to convey land of exactly £4,000 in value, there would be a balance to be paid in cash. While a difference as to valuation might be expected, it might have been thought it would have been a simple matter to resolve.

On 6 June 1604 a bill was introduced in the Commons 'for the frustration of a release unduly procured by Anthony Penning from Edmund Penning his brother'. It was sent to a committee including Sir John Hobart, Sir Henry Hobart, Sir Francis Bacon and Thomas Oxborough (Morgan et al *Nat Bacon V* 134 fn 400 citing *Commons Journal* I 233–234). They recommended arbitration. Nathaniel and Sir Charles Cornwallis were appointed for Edmund; Anthony named Sir John Heigham and Robert

Kempe and the four of them chose Sir Robert Jermyn to be umpire. A letter in the *Papers* shows what happened next (Morgan et al *Nat Bacon V* 134–135). The first part was from a stranger to the dispute, Edmund Withypoll, whose only apparent interest was to see the matter peaceably resolved. He wrote to Nathaniel on 20 October 1604 in unusual English, probably influenced by his dialect. He offered his house for the hearing:

> I came hither with full purpose to have seen you myself and entreated your friendly travail unto my house at Ipswich for the determining and finishing of that business for poor Penning and his wife, which so charitably and kindly you travailed in at London. But my uncle Sir Charles Cornwallis assuring me that my letter would prevail sufficiently with you to that purpose, I have adventured the same, earnestly entreating you so far to favour me as to take the pain to be at my house the xvii of this month next, where I doubt not but your friendly pains and my uncle's shall sawlter[7] to the desired effect in making peace between the brethren. The poor man and his wife for so charitable a work shall have cause to pray for you, and myself will rest beholden to you for your kindness, and ready to requite you in the like kindness....

Following on at the foot of this letter is a note from Cornwallis:

> Sir, I must needs put to some lines in favour of the distressed and pray you also on my part not to fail at that day of meeting and withal to direct your letters wherein I will join with you to Mr Anthony Penning desiring him to be prepared with his arbitrators against the time, to the end we may upon the Monday following attend the cause and bring it to an end by agreement. Write it in both our names and send it by this bearer that I may also subscribe it and let me know by him how you determine your journeys....

In the margin William Sanders had written: 'A promise by letter in answer to avow the labour of the younger brother's behalf, and no labour in behalf of the elder for the meeting'. So Cornwallis had already declared a sympathy with Edmund, the thirteenth and last child of Katherine, née Brook, born when she was over forty. He was sixteen years younger than his brother Anthony, the fourth child but oldest surviving son and his father's heir. Edmund's marriage to Anne Middleton may have displeased his older brother, a man of position, JP and High Sheriff of Essex in 1607. He may have thought that Edmund had married beneath him. Cornwallis wrote of Anne in a letter set out below: 'The gentlewoman I know hath served my daughter 10 years in good and honest fashion and in my opinion deserves as good a man as this Penning, though he had his father's £4,000, given him by will, fully performed in ready money'. A good and honest woman, yes, but some sort of servant. The arbitrators met and their attempt

---

7. One cannot be confident in suggesting a meaning. My best guess is sawlter=psaltery; so that 'you and my uncle would play a sweet tune that might make your mediation more likely to succeed'.

to bring about a mediated settlement failed. They made an award but that did not end the dispute, which became the subject of Chancery litigation.

Heigham (sometimes Higham) and Jermyn were contemporaries, staunch Protestants and life-long friends. Heigham, of Lincoln's Inn, was called to the bar in 1565. He succeeded to the family estate at Barrow in Suffolk in 1571, Jermyn to Rushbrooke, Norfolk, in 1577. Between them they controlled Bury St Edmunds. Both were knighted when they entertained Elizabeth I in 1578. Both became MPs and JPs but their religious zeal got them into trouble and they lost their positions as JPs in 1583. Both were restored ten years later. Jermyn worked on until his death in 1614. He left a gold ring to Heigham and another to Sir Nicholas Bacon, his fellow magistrates, in remembrance of 'the unity by which they had much furthered the peace and profit of our country in the administration of justice and other public duties', with a request that they 'maintain the same to the uttermost of their power'.

Elected knight of the shire for the second time in 1604, Heigham was a busy MP, involving himself in debates on religion, the better execution of justice, alehouses, labourers' wages and apprenticeships, the plague and the drainage of the Fens. When in 1609 a bill to execute a Chancery decree obtained by William Le Gris of Norwich was sent to a committee, Heigham was appointed but had to report that its attempt to mediate had failed. He was named to consider a bill to confirm a judgment in Common Pleas that one of John Holditch's predecessors had made an error in conveying property in Suffolk to his tenants, as a result of which Holditch hoped to force the former tenants to pay him £1,000 between them. On 9 June the Speaker appointed five local knights, including Heigham, to arbitrate between the parties and reach a composition 'out of the equity of the cause and the poverty of the petitioner'. He was still active in county affairs up to his death in 1626. As Anthony's choice of arbitrators, Heigham and Jermyn were unlikely to disagree about anything.

A document now in the Folger Shakespeare Library in Washington DC (Morgan et al *Nat Bacon V* 222 citing Folger Ld464) is a Chancery order of 11 February 1606 reciting that Anthony Penning had said that certain lands plus £560 would be sufficient to satisfy the claim. Edmund and Anne said not. The dispute had been arbitrated and the arbitrators had agreed with Edmund and Anne and ordered Anthony to convey more land or pay more, though they 'cleared the defendant of any imputation laid to his charge'. It is not clear from any of the documents what gave Anne a role to play in the dispute but her influence, which at first can only be inferred, becomes manifest later.

The Court of Chancery considered the award to be just to both parties; but there was further dispute resolution to be done. Because Cornwallis was on His Majesty's service in Spain, the Court referred the matter, with the consent of both sides' counsel, to Jermyn, Heigham and Nathaniel 'to consider in town'. So Jermyn's role had changed from umpire to arbitrator. If he was not in town, the other two to end it before the end of term, otherwise all three to determine it 'in the country'. And: 'What they decide should be done is to be put into the hands of friends to preserve the interest of the plaintiff, his wife and children', that is, the land and money should be put in trust. There were then three arbitrators, Nathaniel appointed by Edmund, Heigham by Anthony, and Jermyn the former umpire.

So this difference between brothers had been to Parliament, arbitration, Chancery, arbitration, and was meant to end up in the hands of friends. But belatedly it was realised that that was not the right way to deal with what might only be a straightforward matter of valuation of property in a deceased's estate. The next month Nathaniel and Heigham appointed surveyors to value the land (Morgan et al *Nat Bacon V* 225–226), explaining to them that, as arbitrators appointed by the Lord Chancellor, they needed expert help:

> We have thought good for our help to make choice of you, praying you to take a perfect view and survey… to set down and certify us of the true state of them, their number of acres with their nature and tenure and your estimate of their values…. Your charge and travel shall be satisfied by the parties to your contentment.

On 12 April 1606 the surveyors, John Osborne, Clement Paman and John Darby put in their report (Morgan et al *Nat Bacon V* 227):

> May it please you to understand that whereas you have desired us to take the view of the lands and tenements that Mr Anthony Penning hath laid out and assured to his brother Edmund and his wife, as part of the portion of £4,000 given him by his father… as also to consider the several tenures, values and natures of the lands and tenements… we did meet at Bawdessey 7 April being Monday and hoping there that both parties would have met…. The plaintiffs failed either to come or send, and the defendant who met there could not deliver any certain measure of the lands, notwithstanding we spent three whole days there and two at Parham in perusing, viewing and enquiring… not being truly informed of the quantity of the several kinds done by a true measure we cannot set down anything to any good purpose for an end.

They suggested that the arbitrators write to the parties telling them to let John Darby know when it would be convenient for him to do the measuring. So Nathaniel wrote to the parties (Morgan et al *Nat Bacon V* 228) informing them that Heigham was not in town but he wanted a speedy end: 'I require you both to cause it to be measured forthwith' and to tell Darby when to attend. On 11 June Jermyn and Heigham wrote to Nathaniel. They were getting fed up (Morgan et al *Nat Bacon V* 236):

Though we could never had with less contentment employed our travail than now, being oppressed with multitude of business and the same of no small weight, yet for satisfying of our duties to the Lord Chancellor and the cutting of an unkind suit between two brethren, and that in a cause nearly concerning either of them, we have appointed to meet with you at Norwich next Tuesday night and so to spend that evening and the two next days doing our best endeavours to determine the cause if it may be, or otherwise to pray from the Lord Chancellor a longer respite, or else to certify our opinions in whose default the end could not be effected.

PS   We think it were more convenient for yourself and for us to have appointed Swaffham for the place of meeting being both nearer to you and us, which if you agree to and can so appoint the parties we pray you may stand.

Memorandum endorsed   14 June answer returned for meeting at the George in Tombland in Norwich at the date above mentioned.

On the morning of 17 June Nathaniel's first job was to deal with the paternity suit of a servant girl Katherine Todd whose master, the shepherd Richard Riplingham, had tried to disguise his responsibility by getting her to accuse another man falsely. Then, returning to his main concern, Nathaniel made this note in his own hand (Morgan et al *Nat Bacon V* 239):

Remembrance
A letter to my Lord Chancellor for certifying what our proceeding hath been and the cause of no full conclusion.
A protection for jointure both present and hereafter, if his wife die.
A setting down the entail with a remainder in Mr Anthony Penning.
A direction for the evidence or copies.
To agree of a time for the survey, by Mr Frogmorton and Mr Agar with Mr Darby.
For the present maintenance and the satisfying of arrears.
To agree upon lawyers to draw the conveyance.

The next day the arbitrators wrote this letter to Ellesmere LC (Morgan et al *Nat Bacon V* 239–240):

… we have met about the cause and heard the allegations of both sides… and have drawn the cause to a conclusion with their consents, saving for the conveyances and assurances making by the defendant of certain lands unto the plaintiffs in part of recompense for the said legacy, which is referred to be done by learned counsel, named by us indifferently with the parties' allowance.

The arbitrators had mediated a settlement and the terms were set out in full (taken here with permission and thanks to the editors' calendar in Morgan et al *Nat Bacon V* 240–241):

Anthony to convey land in Bawdsley and Alderton to 6 trustees to the use of Edmund and Anne for their lives, 'free of all encumbrances created by Anthony or Thomas Denney', with power to convey whatever of it they see fit to any second wife of Edmund up to £100 a year in value, the rest in tail to Edmund's heirs, reversion to Anthony. After the deaths of Edmund and any second wife, to his heirs in tail, all to revert to Anthony. Anthony to buy the reversions of land leased from the King in Bawdsey Butley and convey all to the trustees; also his land in Parham and Framlingham until they get the leased land. 'For speed' the arbitrators had accepted Anthony's valuation but Anthony must warrant they are worth £180 a year. The mansion house at Bawdsley was unfit for habitation, so Anthony must rough cast, glaze, floor and furnish it with doors and stairs, to be habitable by All Saints next. All copyhold land to be surrendered to the trustees and the parties to share the fine equally. If Edmund die in Anne's lifetime, she must allow his children £40 a year. Conveyance to be made with the advice of Sir Harry Hobart, Serjeant Hawton and Richard Godfrey. Anthony had already paid Edmund £460 and must pay a further £300 plus £360 rent arrears: £100 within 10 days, £200 on 16 October, £160 within 20 days after Christmas, £200 within 20 days of Our Lady, at the sign of the Greyhound in Ipswich. Bonds to Edmund for payment.

[At this point a marginal note shows that Nathaniel had attempted to add further sums but Heigham and Jermyn objected.]

Arbitration clause for any ambiguities or omissions.

[Endorsed] Added upon a meeting of Sir Robert Jermyn and Sir John Heigham since the former articles were agreed upon.

Memorandum that of the sum of £660, £200 shall go to the payment of Edmund's debt, £200 to the stocking of his grounds, and the residue to Anthony at 8 per cent until land may be purchased to the use of Edmund.

And the whole was subscribed by Jermyn, Heigham and Nathaniel. Not quite the simple matter of valuation which was all that at first seemed to be needed. The arbitrators had, of course, the assistance of learned counsel, but needed quite a knowledge of the law and its technical vocabulary themselves to comprehend the details of the settlement they mediated. Apparently they were not reluctant to dispose of the encumbrances of Thomas Denney, even though he was not a party to the arbitration. What relief they must have felt at this conclusion! But it was shortlived. Anne Penning's determination to preserve her own interests became clear from her undated letter to Nathaniel (Morgan et al *Nat Bacon V* 242–243). It must be kept in mind that he was her husband's choice of arbitrator and that Heigham was Anthony's.

> Sir, whereas by your order my husband's brother should have put us in bond for payment of the money at the days therein mentioned, he since refuseth and will pay the money but to Sir John Heigham and Sir Robert Jermyn and tells us that except they think it fit he will not pay it to us.

She complained that Anthony was using every means to delay payment, knowing that she and her husband had made commitments to buy land with the money, and that Heigham was conniving, allowing Anthony to make leases of the land which he had said was clear of any such incumbrance. She said she could not afford £100 a day for lawsuits, 'as you heard Anthony say he did'. 'If you cannot compel him to perform this order, I beseech you leave us at liberty to appeal to my lord, who honourably promised that, if you ended it not, he would be pleased to hear our cause and end it himself'. And she adds in a PS: 'Good sir, let me have your letter to the other knights of what you think fit, that the order may certainly be agreed upon, for Mr Penning says there is nothing agreed by it as it is now, as this messenger can inform you truly of'.

Then Cornwallis returned to the fray on Anne's behalf, writing to Nathaniel on 12 August 1606 (Morgan et al *Nat Bacon V* 250–251):

Sir, the gentlewoman whose prayers you have bound unto you for your pains taken in hers and her husband's business, the wife of the younger brother of the Pennings, perceiving the perswatitions [*sic*] of the elder brother likely to work more to their prejudice than what was agreed on and set down under your hands, with some other the commissioners, writes a lamentable letter to me, desiring mine to you, that you will not suffer any part of the order already set down and signed by your own hand to be altered or diminished in the good to her and her husband, whereto, I am easily persuaded, you will assent. So these do most earnestly entreat you not to be entreated otherwise which I do assure you sir I will attempt, as a just and gentle point of friendship from you to me, who you shall never find strange in any occasion of yours wherein I may show requital. The gentlewoman I know hath served my daughter 10 years in good and honest fashion and in my opinion deserves as good a man as this Penning, though he had his father's £4,000, given him by will, fully performed in ready money.

Sir, I dare presume my Lord Chancellor before whom this cause hath been shall think well of your indifferent ending of it, for the good of the younger brother and his wife who can make no such friends haply as the elder hath, and can make. And so with my very kind commendations unto you I commit you sir unto God and this to the Chancery of your own conscience, and curtesy for my sake...
William Cornwallis

It was clear that the arbitrators were divided. Heigham and Jermyn, 'such friends as the elder hath', were taking Anthony's side: Cornwallis Anne's. Nathaniel was not prepared to be swayed by extraneous factors and determined to continue to act judiciously, as two more letters show (Morgan et al *Nat Bacon V* 255). Anthony wrote to Nathaniel on 8 September that he had received a draft conveyance from Edmund and that he had taken exception to it. He had had his own draft prepared by counsel and submitted both to Nathaniel and whatever was acceptable to him, Heigham and Jermyn he would willingly perform. Heigham got in first. He wrote to Nathaniel on 9 September to say he had perused both drafts and preferred Anthony's: 'I hold it not reasonable that the woman, if she survive her husband, should hold the land without impeachment of waste'. Nor should Edmund have a life estate which he could dispose of, 'for then he may, through his want of experience, be brought to pass away that interest and live full meanly all his life after'. Better he should have only the profits from the land. Was he worried that 'the woman' would manipulate her husband? Had old Arthur's will authorised such interference in the legacy? Had what started as a commission to evaluate land, and fix what money it would take to make up a difference, become a concern to ensure that a strong-minded woman did not risk the welfare of a younger brother whom they thought could not look after himself? Did 'equity and conscience' require such intrusion? To show how fair-minded he was, however, Heigham pointed out that the clause in Anthony's draft which provided for the conveyancing charges to be shared equally did not represent the award, which said that Anthony should bear them.

A letter from Heigham and Jermyn to Nathaniel dated 30 October 1606 is preserved in the Folger Library (Morgan et al *Nat Bacon V* 261–262, Folger Ld378). Anne had been to see them at Bury St Edmunds. They had not enjoyed her visit. She had shown 'great mislike' of their preference for the land to remain in trust, with a discretion in the trustees as to where the profits should go in Edmund's lifetime:

> Her importunity was so great as we sent for Mr Anthony Penning to come to us at Bury, where we laboured him to yield so to assure the lands as his brother might have the very land itself during his life... a counsellor-at-law (whom the gentlewoman entertained) did affirm that it might be safely done.... Mr Anthony Penning desired to be advised by his own counsel, who fully resolved us that, if the land were assured for life as to the husband as it should be to the wife, with remainder to the issue etc, that the husband and wife might then by recovery cut off the entail, and so in a short time the husband's estate would quickly be overthrown. The gentlewoman misliked of this and urged us to a certificate, and we, perceiving her disposition and that nothing will content her but the sale of the land, have in a letter set down the whole truth and ascertained my Lord Chancellor thereof, whereof if you like we pray you to subscribe, to prevent the malicious purpose of the woman.

Nothing in all the seven volumes of *Papers* shows Nathaniel's qualities as an arbitrator so well as his reply of 1 November (Morgan et al *Nat Bacon V* 262–263):

> Sirs, I have perused the certificate sent unto me under your hands... and have considered also of your letter... yet I must entreat you to excuse me though I forbear now to join in the certificate. You have had your judgments satisfied by hearing the parties on both sides to speak before you, and it may be I shall be of your judgment when I hear the like. But I am doubtful at this present how to judge this point, *viz* how far forth Edmund Penning shall be barred during his life. I allow well that he be barred to do no act to overthrow the inheritance, and this seemed on our first meeting to be agreed upon between us, and the other point was left doubtful. Therefore I think it best that a cause of this importance

be at London determined upon, where the best counsel in law may be had, and where you, Sir John Heigham, and I are like shortly to meet, and then upon more advice we may certify Sir Robert Jermyn what there falleth out best to be allowed upon and in the meantime the causes may rest as they be.

Nothing further remains to reveal how the matter ended, but that ample evidence has shown how arbitration could be misused to frustrate the clear intentions of a testator simply to grant land to his son.

4. PRIVY COUNCIL

Elizabeth I's Council made use of Nathaniel's skills as a mediator. On 29 June 1600 it commissioned Nathaniel with five local worthies, mostly merchants, to examine the petition of William Seele, who had complained of 'most unconscionable dealing' by Henry Congham in the sale of barley. On 25 August a settlement was mediated, which Seele and Congham signed: 'Congham is content to remit the whole, and to accept at Christmas next £5 and at Christmas 1601 the other £5' (Morgan et al *Nat Bacon IV* 140). On the same day another settlement was mediated, on a similar Privy Council commission, between Henry Congham and Edmond Newby (Morgan et al *Nat Bacon IV* 140 and *APC* 30.398–399):

Newby oweth by bond £9, which hangeth in suit in the King's Bench, that in case Newby do pay £5 thereof at Hallowmas next and then put in bond with surety for other £5 such day twelvemonth, then Henry Congham to discharge the said debt, Newby paying the costs of suit.... If John Yates will affirm that by a former agreement the £10 was accepted for debt and costs of suit, then Congham is to bear his own costs of suit.

James I's Council used arbitration to deal with petitions just as Elizabeth I's had done. In giving instructions to those it commissioned, it rarely made a distinction between mediation and arbitration, or even between an order to resolve a dispute or just to report back, for example a commission of 12 November 1604 to Nathaniel with Sir Miles Corbett, Thomas Cromwell and Owen Sheppard (or any three or two). They took extensive evidence of the rights of warren over Castle Rising, which were disputed by the Earl of Northampton's tenant and, among others, Sir Henry Spelman, the antiquary's father (Morgan et al *Nat Bacon V* 137–141). The arbitrators were instructed: 'upon examination and perusal of such proofs and matters of evidence as they shall have severally... to end the controversy if you can, or otherwise certify us of your whole proceedings'. The *Papers* preserve copious and detailed though fragmentary notes of the evidence, some in Latin. The problem was that too many people were keeping too many rabbits. That meant there was not enough grass for the Earl's deer to eat, so that they strayed and fewer were available for the chase. On 10 January 1605 the arbitrators reported, not to the Council but to the Earl of Northampton. They told him:

Soon after our receipt of the letters from the Privy Council... we did meet at Lynn near unto Rising and did examine the state of the cause... Though we were not so prescribed in their Lordships' letters, yet we thought it more fit, and agreeing to our duties, to signify unto your Lordship and not unto their Honours in our answer... how our judgments be guided.... We have thought it our duties... not to resolve upon any thing before your Lordship be made therewith acquainted, that your Lordship may, as it shall seem good unto you, hereafter give direction.

But they were happy to report that they had successfully mediated a settlement of the dispute between Sir Henry Spelman and Richard Howell: 'ending their contention to both their contentments'. That agreement, expressly by mediation, is preserved in full in the *Papers* (Morgan et al *Nat Bacon V* 143). It required exchanges of land and money payments: 'the conveyances on either part to be referred to counsel for the drawing of them *viz* Thomas Athow'. And 'all trespasses remitted on either parts'. Nothing could be better evidence of the arbitrators' concern to bring about, by whatever means, as efficiently as they could, a satisfactory resolution of the differences. The earl's honour and dignity would be in no way compromised. No niceties of procedure or jurisdiction, let alone conceptual, ever entered their minds.

On 6 December 1609 the Council wrote Nathaniel a letter endorsed: '1609 direction from the lords to select some Justices for peculiar services'. It began by stressing 'how great a portion of power and government is left to your care... in the execution of the laws... in the commission of the peace... and proclamations, letters and commissions' but:

Although there be many in the Commission of the Peace in that county of great integrity and discretion... yet we find... the rule seldom faileth... that those duties which concern all men are neglected of every man, we think it high time.... to move you with these our letters to make it one of your first consultations at your next meeting to select by mutual consent among yourselves some three or four or more of your number... to whose peculiar care you may at the beginning of every year commend the execution and despatch of such directions as you received.... That the ship of this commonwealth which hath so judicial and so royal a master to steer it may be carefully sailed by those that have the charge under him of all sorts.

After 37 years of service, the Government had singled out Nathaniel as one of those with responsibility for seeing that its instructions were implemented.

5.   CHANCERY AND THE CHANCELLOR

Many of Nathaniel's appointments resulted from petitions, like the one from Thomas Pearce to Lord Keeper Egerton, which he passed to Nathaniel to deal with alone in June 1600 (Morgan et al *Nat Bacon IV* 126):

> I pray you take the pains, calling both him and his mother before you to examine the matter and by some quiet order agreeable to equity and justice, to prevent and stop these farther suits which were unfit to be between parties so nearly bound to one another in love and duty, and which the petitioner seems to desire to have by this course prevented.

When he became Ellesmere LC, Egerton continued his habit of commissioning Nathaniel to mediate an end to matters before the Court of Chancery. Thomas Fairfax, the soldier, was plaintiff in a Chancery suit against John Rust. On 15 February 1605 Rust petitioned the Chancellor expressly to appoint Nathaniel and by a letter of 18 February he was asked 'to make some quiet and friendly end between them according to equity and good conscience'. But meanwhile Edward Coke, then Attorney General, had stepped in and sent Rust to Nathaniel with a letter dated 17 February (Morgan et al *Nat Bacon V* 153), asking him:

> to hear and understand the controversy, and thereupon to do your friendly endeavour to end and determine the same between them... if by your good persuasion and means you cannot bring them to accept of such order and agreement as you in your wisdom and conscience shall think fit for them, then I pray you to certify to me the true state of the controversy and in whom you find the default to rest, that such order may be taken as is according to justice and equity.

A memorandum of 5 March (Morgan et al *Nat Bacon V* 156) explained that the dispute was about mutual bonds and that the parties were brought to a settlement, except that Fairfax would not agree to Nathaniel's finding that he should bear the costs of the Chancery suit. So Nathaniel had to certify and return the commission, which he did by a letter of 8 April not to Coke but to Ellesmere LC (Morgan et al *Nat Bacon V* 169–170). He explained that the bonds had arisen out of liability for customs duties on barley exported to the Low Countries. Fairfax had had no cause to start proceedings in Chancery, so he should bear the costs of them, £3 or £4. Fairfax could not be persuaded. And so he was certifying, as instructed, 'submitting my judgment to your Lordship's wisdom and grave consideration'. On 22 April Nathaniel wrote to Coke (Morgan et al *Nat Bacon V* 173–174) enclosing a copy of the certificate he had sent to Ellesmere LC on 8 April, and 'referring the poor man [Rust] to your further favour for his relief'.

Another failed attempt to mediate produced a certificate back from Nathaniel to Ellesmere LC (Morgan et al *Nat Bacon V* 213–214) in a land dispute in which both sides were represented by counsel.

On 28 June 1613, Ellesmere LC appointed Nathaniel, Sir Anthony Browne, Sir Augustine Palgrave and John Richers Esq (or any three or two), not to resolve a dispute but to enquire and report:

Whereas in a cause depending in the Chauncery between Sir John Windham Knt plaintiff and Thomas Blofeld defendant the court on 12 June was moved by the defendant's counsel, amongst other things, for some competent recompense to be given by the plaintiff unto the defendant in consideration of his travail and pains when employed by the plaintiff as his steward or surveyor of his lands. But hearing then also that which was alleged by counsel on the other side, and it not appearing certainly either what travail... or what profit the plaintiff had gained... I did then forbear to set down what recompense the plaintiff should give... but yet thought it fit... to refer the same to the consideration of some indifferent gentlemen that dwell near unto the place.... And for this purpose having now made choice of yourselves I... address these my letters unto you and for your better direction send you a copy of the order... proceed and make certificate into this court... that thereupon such further order may be taken as shall be meet.

Your very loving friend.

[*Signed*] T Ellesmere *Canc*

The commissioners wrote on 13 August to four local stewards, asking them to meet them at 8am on 24 August 'to inform us in such points as we shall have occasion to take instruction from you touching the matter in question'. On that day a detailed memorandum was prepared of their responses, listing the tenancies and their rentals and concluding: 'Mr Thomas Kinges judgeth the labour worth £100 upon the finishing. Mr Symondes thinketh 6s 8d per diem for 3 quarters of a year. Mr Eve esteemeth the labour hitherto at 100 marks & for finishing £26 13s 4d.' The same day an agreement was drafted between Thomas Wyndham, on behalf of his father Sir John, and Thomas Blofeld, to submit to the four arbitrators 'concerning the recompense to be made to Blofeld for engrossing the rolls of such courts as he kept in any of Sir John Wyndham's manors and his pains in surveying them' and to enter bonds in £100 to each other. But: 'Memorandum this submission being drawn by the direction of Mr Wyndham [Sir John's son] and the bond also, he broke off and would proceed no further.' Then the arbitrators wrote their report on the same day back to Ellesmere LC:

> We received your Lordship's letters together with an order in the honourable Court of Chancery, dated 12 June last, referring unto us to consider what travail Thomas Blofeld had been put unto for Sir John Wyndham, as steward or surveyor for him, & what profit Sir John Wyndham had gained by his travail, and what recompense should be given to Blofeld in respect thereof. Accordingly we met thereabout, and heard the allegations on both parts, as well by Blofeld as by Mr Thomas Wyndham in the behalf of his father. And having caused to come unto us 3 gentlemen experienced in surveys & courts keeping, and hearing their opinions of the labours of Blofeld for our better instruction, we enterd into considerations to judge between ourselves for the recompense to be given Blofeld. And touching his pains in surveying & new rentals making of 5 several manors we find his labour to have been great, and undertaken at the request &

motion of Sir John Wyndham, and much for his profit & behoof, and think him worthy of £50 for his travail hitherto, notwithstanding there resteth much to be perfected thereof. And for the rolls, (whereof divers were shewed us ready engrossed), we hold it fit to allow him 4s for every roll if he finish them as he hath begun.

A further fair copy was made and sent on 2 September to Sir Anthony Browne:

Sir I send you herein a draught of a certificate touching the cause of Sir John Wyndham & Mr Blofeld, praying you to peruse and correct it, as you shall see cause, and to send the same to Sir Austin Palgrave to be by him & Mr Richers also viewed. And having agreed thereof, I desire it may be fair written and subscribed by yourself and them and returned unto me, that I may join therein with you, and I will take order for the conveying it up.
Signed Na Bacon.

The next day Browne wrote to Palgrave:

I received this letter late at night this 3 September, and for my part do exceedingly allow of it, with desire it may pass from each to other and be fair written by Mr Riches' clerk unto whom it last cometh, and so be sent to each of us for our hands. Only I judge it not amiss, (if thought fit) that there be added with Mr Thomas Wyndham's meeting also his now steward that also was there with him. And (in the end) for the rolls shewed engrossed in no ordinary but good hand comprehending much which I refer notwithstanding to your considerations, and howsoever will subscribe.
Signed: Antho Browne.
Addressed: To the right worshipful Sir Austin Palgrave haste these speedily and safely.

When the non-lawyer John Williams became Lord Keeper, he continued the practice of commissioning Nathaniel. On 11 May 1622 he wrote to him:

This enclosed petition being exhibited unto me by Ezechiell Newton against Richard Newton, his brother's son, I have thought fit (in compassion of the petitioner's extreme age & poverty) to commend the same unto your consideration, praying you (upon calling both parties before you) to regulate R Newton according to reason & equity, or else to certefy me of his default with your proceeding therein, that I may take some course to compel thereunto.

Memoranda written down later on 28 May and 10 June record in detail the evidence Nathaniel had taken before his reply of 16 May 1622:

It pleased you to direct me by your letters that I should... calling both parties before me, regulate them according to reason & equity, or otherwise to certify in whom I found the default. Accordingly I have had them before me, and at two several days heard the proofs on both sides, and I find R Newton very obstinate and not conformable to that which I think in all equity he is tied to perform. For by sundry witnesses, men of credit & not to be excepted against, it was proved before me, and the same appeared also by the conveyances, that John Newton had from his father Ezechiell all his houses & lands and his goods, and should pay yearly 20 marks & his father's debts, and after his father's death £75 as Ezechiell should by his will appoint. And this was set down by indenture and... that the land should revert to Ezechiell Newton & his heirs, if there were default of payment... After this my hearing of both their proofs, I sought to persuade R Newton, that he should continue the payment of the annuity, and pay the arrearages and pay also the debts of Ezechiell Newton and make himself subject to the payment of £70 according to the just agreement between Ezechiell and John, and which John, when he died, charged him to perform.... But Richard Newton refused to give any ear to this... desiring to have your Lordship decree therein upon a legal proceeding, which Ezechiell, being exceeding poor & very aged, is unable to undergo.

It is not surprising there is no further record. Nathaniel was ill by then, the surviving papers end that year and he died on 22 November 1622.

6. KING'S BENCH

At some time in 1601 Sir John Popham (CJKB 1592–1607) directed Nathaniel, Henry Spelman and Thomas Layer, or any two, to arrange a settlement between Katherine Barr, widow, and the executors of a foreign merchant, Adam Kindt, whom she accused of cheating her of her trading goods. Kindt had died and his executors would not pay his debt (Morgan et al *Nat Bacon IV* 206).

Popham appointed Nathaniel sole arbitrator to determine all the disputes between the Reverend Edward Slynne and Robert Younger, gent, except for a matter between them in the Star Chamber. The parties entered into bonds to abide by his award, which survives (Morgan et al *Nat Bacon IV* 209). On 3 October 1601 he awarded that Slynne should allow Younger to enter the disputed land, of which some was copyhold in the manor of South Burlingham, and to release all actions other than that in the Star Chamber, to hand over the deeds and pay compensation. Younger must allow Slynne to enter land in South Burlingham and release actions and deliver assurances on request. But there was more to it than that. A memorandum of the same date, signed by Nathaniel, accompanies the award and is a fair example of how Nathaniel worked:

It was upon the sealing of the award agreed that Slynne should 'take the furze and some thorns growing on the lands which he was to forsake and yield to Mr Younger at Hallowmas.... Mr Slynne should be suffered after Hallowmas until the end of November to feed with his cattle the grass of the closes which he did leave and I promised Mr Slynne that it would be performed. Mr Slynne had by the award £50 to be paid at two days, and the lands lying in Beyton, 14 acres or thereabouts, besides the 6 acres of wheat sown by Mr Younger, which he reaped after he was bound and had submitted himself to my judgment and had been warned by myself not to meddle with the corn. It was doubtful on the hearing of the cause whether the title of Mr Younger or Tomson were the better. But Tomson being dead and Yardley having the right of Tomson's lands given unto him, did make two releases to Younger, the one with the exception of Coultons, and the other the next day without the exception of Coultons and Younger proved by witness his entry into Coultons lands before the release made and all this was done before Slynne had any interest of the land. The two bonds of £100 to be left in my hands to be delivered as I shall think good upon the breach of the award.

Commissions from Popham CJ in this period included one about trespasses to land and a stolen boar 'to end if he may' (Morgan et al *Nat Bacon IV* 234, and a petition from 'the poor inhabitants of Wiveton' against John King, 'a man of great wealth', who had got his hands on funds intended for the poor 'now ready to starve', which Popham had himself endorsed to Nathaniel and Henry Spelman to 'examine this cause and, if you may, take some course that the poor may have their due, otherwise to certify me the true state of the matter at the next assizes' (Morgan et al *Nat Bacon IV* 269–270). Such commissions continued until the end of Nathaniel's life. On 1 October 1617 he reported to Doddridge J that he had had only partial success in the matter of Gregory Plane, 'a poor man', and Richard Stileman. They had agreed a settlement of the debt but Nathaniel thought Stileman, who could well afford it, should pay Plane's charges. He refused, so Nathaniel certified.

7.   COMMON PLEAS AND ASSIZES

Judges holding assizes in Norfolk regularly referred matters to Nathaniel and other JPs. On 5 November 1609 Nathaniel wrote to Daniel JCP reporting failure. A simple debt claim for £18 had been referred to him with the consent of the plaintiff, Thomas Fairfax. Nathaniel found that the whole debt had been repaid by instalments, though some were late. Fairfax had accepted those payments in writing but insisted on proceeding, against Nathaniel's urging to settle. So Nathaniel had to send it back to Daniel J.

The referrals were not all one way. On 25 July 1622 Nathaniel and other Norfolk JPs wrote to Sir James Ley CJCP, sitting as assize judge:

upon the sight of your order touching one Edward Webster, we caused him and divers of his neighbours that complain against him to come before us, intending to have persuaded peace between them, which, for want of proof, we... did move the parties to submit themselves to the order of 2 of their neighbours, who dwelling in the town might with ease of travel have the witnesses & proof to be made; and hereunto both parties assented. But... Webster being required to meet several days by the arbiters, never came to them. The arbiters notwithstanding, having the other parties & witnesses present, took their informations touching the matters whereof they complained to your Lordship against Webster, and did also certify us that it appeared sufficiently to them that Webster had much wronged them and dealt unjustly with them all. After this, we gave order to have Webster served with your Lordship's warrant for his appearance before you at these Assizes. And he could not be taken in the country but at length was attached thereby in Norwich and now bound over to appear before your Lordship…. And thus commending the redress of his misdemeanours to your Lorship's resolution we humbly take our leave.

A letter of 27 February 1618 asked Nathaniel to favour the writer's son in a matter referred to him from Common Pleas 'as far as to justice and equity it appertain'.

8.   COURT OF REQUESTS

Some commissions came to Nathaniel to mediate through the Court of Requests[8] there, after a detailed memorandum of disputes relating to corn, oats, straw, malt, peas and a horse, the settlement is recorded:

It is agreed 6 August 1604 between Robert Barnard gent and Thomas Clarke as followeth *viz* Robert Barnard doth accept in full discharge of a debt of £250 due to him from Thomas Clarke the £239 14s 6d demanded by Thomas Clarke, and in discharge thereof, as also of all other demands, agreeth to seal him a special acquittance. And Thomas Clarke agreeth to seal the like acquittance unto Robert Barnard.

9.   LORD HIGH TREASURER

In the spring of 1600, the tenants of the royal manor of Pulham petitioned Lord Buckhurst, Lord High Treasurer, against Ralph Agas, surveyor and famous cartographer, who had, on the strength of a commission from the Court of Exchequer, forced them to pay for renewal of their copyholds and rights of common (Morgan et al *Nat Bacon IV* 121–125). On 10 April Buckhurst commissioned Nathaniel and three other Norfolk JPs, or any two, 'to hear and examine the several suggestions' and 'certify me of your proceedings and opinions of the truth of this complaint'. Just a fortnight later Nathaniel approved a draft response. He had already recorded the evidence of Robert Browne, a 95-year-old tenant, 'who affirmeth and will be sworn if called that he never did hear or know but that all the tenants did take and enjoy their timber… or that there was taken above 6d an acre for the fine'. So on 25 April the JPs replied to Buckhurst. Agas could not be found. They had nevertheless heard the tenants' complaints of his extortion and reported, 'praying your Lordship's favour towards them,

8. e.g. Morgan et al *Nat Bacon V* 121–124.

whom we know to be honest and dutiful in the service of Her Majesty and their country'.

10.   COMMISSIONERS FOR PRISONERS

On 2 July 1600 the Commissioners for prisoners in the King's Bench wrote appointing Sir Christopher Heydon, Sir John Townsend, John Hunt DCL and Nathaniel, or any two or more, to examine on oath the parties and witnesses in a complicated debt dispute between Elizabeth Santy, who as a widow had recently married John Santy, now in prison for debt, and Nicholas Browne and his sons (Morgan et al *Nat Bacon IV* 130–132). They were 'thereupon either finally to determine... or return to us the testimonies so taken with your proceeding and opinion', so that they could make a 'determinate order as we shall find the equity of the cause to require ... assuring ourselves your best endeavour and persuasions shall not be wanting, it being so charitable a work'. On 23 July Dr Hunt and Nathaniel replied (Morgan et al *Nat Bacon IV* 136). They had considered the evidence of mutual indebtedness and found against Mrs Santy but needed to refer the matter back for an order, as presumably their mediation had not been accepted.

11.   HIGH STEWARD

A petition might come to Nathaniel in his capacity as High Steward of the Crown and Duchy of Lancaster. In November 1604 Thomas Edwards of Wisbech complained to him that the brothers Griggs had wrongly taken his copyhold land by a suit in the manor court of Walpole. On 14 November Ellesmere LC made an order referring the case to Nathaniel as High Steward 'to decide in law and conscience', 'as the fittest person to decide this controversy' but 'to make a quiet and friendly end between them according to law and conscience' (Morgan et al *Nat Bacon V* 136, 141, 142). A nice little conundrum for the conceptual purist: mediation, arbitration or adjudication?

Nathaniel's Deputy Steward of the manor was Matthew Clarke, a merchant of King's Lynn. He wrote to Nathaniel on 22 April 1605 (Morgan et al *Nat Bacon V* 174) that he had dealt with this matter and: 'Howsoever I have been traduced and unjustly charged with corruption and indirect dealing were all honest and just and such as will maintain to be agreeable to law, for I did nothing but by good advice and counsel'. Both sides were represented by counsel, Thomas Athow for the Griggs and Robert Gawsell for Edwards. Edwards had refused 'an equal and indifferent trial by the tenants of the manor... so as they have no cause to complain but of their own obstinacy and folly':

And for the title it is so clear in law against Edwards, that I think Griggs will be contented (so as Edwards bear the charges) to come to a trial with him at the common law, and to take no advantage of the former judgment, but to continue the possession until the matter be tried, which if they will not accept, it may easily appear to your Worship what little cause they had to complain in Chancery against the steward, when they distrust their own case, and know, if it come to trial of law, it will go against them.

I would have attended upon your Worship but my ship is lately come home and I have very much business in getting her fitted for Iceland.

The next day Nathaniel heard the matter as High Steward and wrote forthwith to both counsel (Morgan et al *Nat Bacon* V 175) that he had considered the legal title and what could be alleged in equity for Edwards and had asked each of the parties whether they would be prepared to renounce the land to the other and for what price. Edwards was willing but the Griggs were not, insisting on their title. Nathaniel told counsel that he would therefore certify to the Lord Chancellor that a trial be held at the next assizes. Edwards assented but the Griggs said they needed further advice. So Nathaniel asked counsel to give him their opinions as soon as possible. But even at this stage he made his preference clear: 'I incline rather to have the cause mediated than referred to the law if the Griggs would be ruled by me'.

Nathaniel settled another dispute, referred to him by the Duchy Chamber with the parties' consent. Musket surrendered his rights in a tenement and orchard to Bretland, who agreed to pay him two instalments of £3 6s 8d 'in full satisfaction of money due under any cause now depending in the Chamber' (Morgan et al *Nat Bacon* V 268).

12. EDWARD COKE

Edward Coke is the subject of the next chapter and in some ways the dominant character in the legal scene of his time. The *Papers* preserve many records of Coke's interchanges with Nathaniel. They were friends as well as trusted colleagues. Coke held the higher offices: Solicitor General 1592, Attorney General 1594, CJCP 1606, CJKB October 1613 to November 1616. But Nathaniel was the outstanding figure of authority in the local government of his own 'country' and the *Papers* show that they treated one another with more than respect. They had already served together as MPs for Norfolk in 1593 and Nathaniel sat with Coke as a Commissioner for Sewers in 1605 (Morgan et al *Nat Bacon* V 187). Their collaborations in resolving disputes can be divided into three categories: formal commissions, private arbitrations of the disputes of others and disputes to which Coke was a party.

Commissions As Attorney General or Chief Justice, and also on assize, Coke commissioned Nathaniel many times to help him dispose of disputes. In the summer of 1606 he referred to Nathaniel 'to end or certify' a petition he had received as CJCP about a dispute over money deposited with Thomas Thetford in trust for the two brothers and five sisters of John Moretoft. It asked for 'some course to come by their money, being very poor and unable to sue for their rights' (Morgan et al *Nat Bacon V* 243–244, 249–250). Four sisters were married, one a widow. Nathaniel's own notes show that he addressed the problem, comparatively trivial in financial terms, with as much care as the Pennings' £4,000, discussed above, with the result that: 'Mr Thetford agreed to disburse presently 20s apiece' to three of the husbands and the widow, and the rest 'their portions out of the remainder' on Thursday at the house of Nathaniel. A memorandum dated 21 August sets out the final settlement in detail (Morgan et al *Nat Bacon V* 253).

Coke as CJCP similarly referred a petition for wrongful possession of a house and another – a grandiloquent effort with many Biblical references, some apposite – from 'your poor orator... whose cry ascends to God' (Morgan et al *Nat Bacon V* 244–245). On 13 August 1606 Nathaniel's reply to another Coke commission related that he had tried to mediate settlement of a claim against the heir of the debtor, who was answering that he had administered the estate and the claim was too late. Nathaniel wrote (Morgan et al *Nat Bacon V* 251):

> In conscience (in my judgment) he ought to pay, both in respect of the poverty of the man, who lent the money to old Lambart, and also of the portion of land which was left to the young man by his father being of the value of £40 by year being copyhold. I would have had him repair unto your Lordship with the bearer but he refused to do it without warrant. I have thought fit to certify thus much unto your Lordship referring the poor man to your considerations.

On 5 November 1606 Nathaniel reported failure to Coke on a matter Coke had referred to him from the Norfolk Assizes (Morgan et al *Nat Bacon V* 263):

> Bullen, notwithstanding his consent given to abide my arbitrement, refuseth to enter into a bond to perform my arbitrement as touching the matter passed by verdict for him before you.... Thus leaving the cause to your Lordship's further consideration, I take my leave.

A year later, on 2 November 1607, Nathaniel's letter to Coke revealed the work he was prepared to undertake to resolve a dispute, and the limitations he laboured under, even with Coke's authority as Chief Justice behind him (Morgan et al *Nat Bacon V* 300):

> ... by force of an order set down in the Court of Common Pleas between Bullen and Laseby I have had the parties sundry times before me and have heard their

contentions at large debated between themselves together with their proofs by witnesses and otherwise and had also the help of two other men of good understanding for the more thorough examining of the differences between them. And both in their opinions and mine own it was holden fit that each of the parties should set down with their losses and charges, and when I had made manifest by my speech to them both that this should be my order between them, then Bullen refused and withdrew himself in a froward and obstinate sort. And Laseby did condescend to that which I moved, and yet if I should have given any consideration from the one party to the other, I think it were rather due from Bullen to Laseby than otherwise. The causes between them were many and all of small moment, and yet their charges on both sides in suit of law were grown great. I found that the greatest ground of their contention grew by Bullen's keeping 120 or 140 sheep, and herein I moved Bullen to a most reasonable course (as I thought) for end. But his wilfulness was such as he would not be conformable in any sort, which will breed him great trouble from others of his neighbours as well as Laseby. Moreover, at one time this summer past when they came before me about their causes, I pressed them to be bound to abide my order, for so seemed the direction of the Court, and Bullen directly refused, and yet gave his promise to abide it, which now he hath refused. Thus, being sorry that my labour hath brought forth so little fruit, I yet hope that the wisdom and consideration of your Lordship and the rest will bridle this Bullen, who spareth not to hazard his own undoing for the trial to have his will.

Coke wrote fairly often and informally to Nathaniel (e.g. Morgan et al *Nat Bacon V* 143–144) and often simply referred petitions to him, like that from the widow Agnes Harper, probably from March 1608 in a land dispute, 'to end or certify'. When Coke sat in the summer of 1608 as an assize judge at Norwich, he sought to speed up the disposal of his list by sending matters to Nathaniel 'to end or certify', like Roger Townshend's action on a forged bond against Nicholas Holmes, and two actions against David Roote. At the next assizes on 24 January 1609 Coke endorsed a petition: 'It is referred to Sir Nathaniel Bacon and Sir Henry Sidney to end or certify, and if they find Chapman perverse, to bind him over to the assizes'. On 6 August 1610 a note in Coke's own hand referred John Jervis's petition: 'Referred to Sir Nath. Bacon to end or certify'. That was endorsed with Nathaniel's award.

And as assize judge at Norwich he referred a small debt claim of 20s to Nathaniel, Sir Augustine Palgrave and Sir Henry Gawdy JPs when it became complicated. Nathaniel wrote on 8 October 1608 telling Palgrave that the defendant Dawes had an excuse for not turning up: he had been arrested the day before and outlawed – he claimed just to stop him appearing. Dawes claimed he had paid the plaintiff Vincent 40s and been discharged, and Dawes's son was willing to stand surety for him in a bond of £40. Nathaniel was clear where the merits lay:

> We shall do well to help the poor man, if we may do it without wronging Mr Vincent. Therefore I pray you to persuade Mr Vincent to do Dawes right and, if he refuse, I will join with you.... If Mr Vincent will not be tractable, then Dawes must complain anew unless we agree to make a certificate.

Vincent must have been obdurate. Palgrave and Nathaniel were commissioned arbitrators, apparently for Dawes, and Sir Henry Gawdy and Sir Philip Woodhouse for Vincent. In August 1609 Palgrave wrote to Nathaniel three times, first approving his draft certificate with a few improvements, then suggesting the intervention of yet another, 'praying Sir John Tyndal's advice', and lastly:

> Dawes hath importuned me to write ex tempore what I remembered or conceived the day of our meeting. I was the rather encouraged for that he told me that Sir Henry Gawdy told him he would subscribe to what you and I did herein, you also wished my notes of remembrances.... Seeing I mean well, I commend them as misshapen to your ordering and, when you have corrected and added both form and substance, I will desire to see and approve it.

On 3 September Nathaniel wrote to Gawdy:

> Brother, it were fit that we the commissioners in the cause between Dawes and Vincent could agree in our opinions, whereby an end might be made of their contention, the rather seeing Dawes is so poor a man as he is, and to this purpose I have seen fit to set down the reasons which move my judgment, and pray you to consider upon them, if haply any of them may move yours.

And he set out a detailed draft award, with reasons. Gawdy replied on 6 September:

> Good brother, I do wish with all my heart that the poor man Dawes had an end of this business, and as you have set down your opinion in the reckoning, so now I do hereby set down what I observed and as much as I could against Mr Vincent [there followed the details of payments and positive assessments of the veracity of Vincent and his witnesses]. If we may meet at some convenient time, I make no doubt but we shall reconcile these differences.... So commending myself to you most heartily and to your good lady my sister... your very loving brother-in-law.
> Henrye Gaudy

As there is nothing more in the *Papers*, we can but hope there was a happy ending.

If criminal sanctions were appropriate, Coke took advantage of Nathaniel's appointment as High Sheriff of Norfolk; he referred the petition of William Bull, who complained of an assault by an attorney: 'Let the petitioner attend upon Sir Nathaniel Bacon and he will take such order therein as shall be fit'. When a petitioner asked for four named arbitrators, of whom Nathaniel was one, Coke wrote on it, probably in October 1611:

'It is referred to Sir Nathaniel Bacon to end or certify'. As late as 1618, an undated petition bears Coke's own note: 'It is referred to Sir Nathaniel Bacon by his good means to end or certify'. That was Coke's way to get his court's business done. There is no way of knowing how many other arbitrators he commissioned; but he knew he could rely on a speedy and useful response from Nathaniel, even when a party was obdurate, such as this on 5 March 1609:

> I, hearing them both speak together, do find that Mr Hamond hath no part of the land… Mr Hamond sheweth that Harlewyn complained hereof in Chancery and my Lord Chancellor himself dismissed him…. Harlewyn hath no colour of complaint against Mr Hamond, and yet will not be satisfied…. I thought fit to signify thus much unto your Lordship lest you be further troubled with this importunate clamour.

Private Arbitrations   The arbitrations discussed so far arose from official commissions, but Coke also encouraged arbitration informally. He was related to the Paston family, through his first wife, Bridget. On 8 September 1602 (Morgan et al *Nat Bacon IV* 284–288) William Cobbe, whose land adjoined Edward Paston's, wrote to Nathaniel seeking a private arbitration:

> Sir, I must confess my presumption to be far greater than my deserts, so as I cannot challenge that interest in your love I so greatly desire. Yet, knowing that it hath been agreeable with your good disposition not to think that time lost which is spent in so good a work as ending of controversies and dissentions, and making of peace and amity between gentlemen and your neighbours, pardon me if I seem troublesome, that am so wrongfully troubled (as I suppose) being not led thereto with self will, yet willing to defend my poor patrimony to my power, being resolved of my right by them of judgment and learning, as also by divers trials lately passed at the common law to my great trouble, charge and hindrance; which by your good means I hope shall now receive a friendly and quiet end (and the rather for that it hath pleased Mr Attorney General [Edward Coke] so earnestly to move the same).
>
> Sir, the sincerity of my cause is to be censured out of your wisdom to which I do appeal, desiring our cause may be weighed in equal balance. I covet not that which I never had, but what my ancestors time out of mind have quietly enjoyed without interruption of them that had the right Mr Paston now hath. Neither build I upon bare presumptions (as shall plainly appear unto you) but upon divers depositions which will be verified by ancient evidence.
>
> I wish the state of my body were such as I might safely adventure to attend you myself, but my cousin Athow [Thomas Athow serjeant at law 1614] and my wife will be ready at all times to attend your leisure for the same, and what you and they shall agree I will most willingly perform, and acknowledge myself bound to you in bonds of perpetual friendship.
> William Cobbe

Mary Cobbe took over. She wrote to Nathaniel on 21 September, referring to a visit she had made to him with a Mr Mingey, a relative of Coke's, with Coke's 'request that you should take pains to hear and end (if it may be) certain causes betwixt Mr Paston and Mr Cobbe, my husband'. If they could not mediate a settlement, the matter would go back to Coke, 'that he by his wisdom and better persuasions may effect that which you cannot'. She suggested possible dates. She had spoken to Paston and got his agreement to submit to Nathaniel and Henry Wyndham, 'to perform without delay what shall be then ordered by you and Mr Wyndham, and consented to by him, my cousin Athow and myself'. So William Cobbe had authorised his wife, with the lawyer Athow, to consent to a binding settlement: 'Mr Cobbe has assured you by his letter... so do I likewise assure you by mine'. 'The ground in question (whereof it is necessary you take the view) lieth in Babingley Common, your right way to Lynn', so Nathaniel could inspect it on his way to the hearing. Mary wrote to Nathaniel four days later. She had received his answering letter (which has not survived) and letters from Coke which she had not read but presumed were attempts to fix a date. She pressed for a date before the start of the legal term.

Shortly thereafter Nathaniel and Wyndham wrote to Coke, responding to his request for them to 'work for a peace between' Cobbe and Paston 'touching certain land' (Morgan et al *Nat Bacon IV* 287–288). They reported that they had 'had a meeting at Appleton, Mr Paston's house, with the allowance of Mrs Cobbe in the absence of her husband, and there we saw the ground in question and did after see their evidence and hear the depositions read'. Both sides had deeds, which conflicted as to whether rights of common were attached to Babingley manor or Newton manor, 'and this we left undetermined, with a consent that the same should be used for the graving of flags and such like as hath of late years been most accustomed'.

Differences as to who should have rights to feed sheep and rabbits were 'of no great moment' but the arbitrators had to listen to all the complaints of both sides' tenants. And that may have been the scarcely concealed collusive object: to get rid of the bickering between their tenants over rights of common and pasture, then a general source of more contention even than pews. They wrote a similar letter to William Cobbe, to tell him of their 'judgment', adding though that Athow, 'your counsellor in the cause' was at the hearing. Was that a private mediation, or arbitration, or did Coke's intervention make it Government-ordered? However classified, it seems to have worked. The Cobbes were recusants, as were the Pastons. Their grandson, also William Cobbe, was a colonel in the army of Charles I. Religious differences did not inhibit wealthy neighbours from seeking

Protestant Nathaniel's intervention, or affect his willingness to provide them his skilled and experienced services.

The parties could ask a public tribunal to take over a private arbitration. The same Thomas Thetford who had acted as trustee for the Moretoft children was himself a party to a dispute with no less than Sir Christopher Heydon, Nathaniel's partner in so many arbitrations. Nathaniel and the other arbitrators wrote on 29 December 1607 to Ellesmere LC (Morgan et al *Nat Bacon V* 306):

> It may please your Lordship to be advertized that, upon differences falling out between Sir Chr Heydon and Thomas Thetford in causes of great weight, they referred themselves to our arbitrement and became bound each to other in the sum of £10,000 to abide our order. And thereupon we bestowed our travail therein three several days and yet could not bring their causes to such end as we wished, partly because some witnesses were desired to be examined by oath, which we had no power to do. Therefore we did move them to yield their consents that upon bill to be exhibited before your Lordships this next term they might after join in commission for the examination of witnesses which they have condescended unto.

Coke as a Party   The evidence in the *Papers* of Edward Coke's involvement as a party shows his constant preference for mediation. A letter dated 2 March 1603 from Henry Warner, a friend of both sides, asked Sir Miles Corbett to arbitrate in a land dispute between Coke, Attorney General, and the same Edward Paston (Morgan et al *Nat Bacon V* 11–12). The disputed land in Flitcham may have adjoined both their properties. Nathaniel had agreed to be the other arbitrator and had suggested dates for the hearing. On 5 March Corbett wrote to Paston agreeing to Nathaniel's suggested date, 14 April. Paston was as tetchy as he was litigious. He wrote to Nathaniel on 23 March. Nathaniel had told Paston's steward he needed Coke to confirm his appointment. Paston told Nathaniel to write to Warner and he would do the same. He ended curtly: 'Thus having no other thing to write I commit you to the Almighty. Appleton this 23 March. Your ever loving friend.' Friend, yes, but Paston was as strong a recusant as Nathaniel was a protestant. The relevant records begin again with a letter of 1 September 1604 from Coke to Nathaniel and Sir Miles Corbett (Morgan et al *Nat Bacon V* 128–129), which included:

> I being desirous not only of quietness between ourselves (whereof I made no doubt) but also between our posterities afterwards, and that suits (that commonly are mothers of unkindness) might stay, desired you (as likewise my cousin Paston did) to inform yourselves of the true state of the matter in variance; and by your good mediation to end the same. Whereupon (as I am informed) you have taken the pains to view the ground, and to hear the allegations and proof of either party. These are to desire you to proceed in so good a work, and to the

> end your labours already taken may not be lost, and that either party may receive the better satisfaction, that you would be pleased to meet again at Flitcham some time this next week, and to set down the proof and matters tending to the maintenance of the claims by either party, and to the manifestation of the right touching these matters in variance, wherein as you shall do a charitable and friendly work, so shall you make us much both beholden to you for your pains and indifferency herein. And so I commit you to the blessed protection of the Almighty.

That letter was enclosed with the following, dated the next day.

> Sir, you shall perceive by these enclosed what a desire I have of quietness, and how bold I am to require your further travails. Sir Miles sent me word by the messenger that any day after tomorrow he would give meeting about the finishing of your former travails. Whereof I am the more desirous, because I would have it driven to an issue before I depart. What day it please you to appoint, this bearer shall give notice thereof to Sir Miles. It was my cousin Paston's resolute request that the reasons and proofs of either side should be set down or else he would no further proceed. And so with my very hearty commendations to you and your good lady I commit you to the blessed protection of the Almighty and ever rest, your assured friend.
> Godwike 2 September 1604   Edw Coke

Sadly, the *Papers* tell us nothing more of how this matter was resolved, so research must continue elsewhere.

Coke might come in at a late stage to encourage a successful mediation, where someone connected to him was involved. Jerome Alexander[9] was a King's Bench attorney, employed by the Earl of Arundel. Nathaniel seems to have tried to mediate an end to his dispute with his brother-in-law Robert Plandon over copyhold lands in Thorpland and elsewhere which appeared to have been settled by their transfer from Plandon to him in the Fakenham manorial court on 27 March 1601 at the price of £1,450, payable by instalments. But a long undated letter in the *Papers* (Morgan et al *Nat Bacon V* 18–21) from Plandon to Alexander shows that their disputes were far from settled. It is an ill-organised series of complaints from a layman to a lawyer, beginning: 'Brother Alexander you were wont to set down, though untruly, what sums and when you paid them'. He insisted that, because Plandon had paid only £36 of the £800 due at Michaelmas 1601, he, Alexander, had 'forfeited his estate'. He must have previously argued that he had made payments to Plandon's creditors with his consent. Plandon had asked for details and he was keen to get things straight: 'Mr Bacon charged me that I should not intermingle the matter of the land with any of our other reckonings, therefore I am determined

9. Ancient of Furnival's Inn, CW Brooks *Pettifoggers and Vipers* 169 fn92, citing PRO IND 1356 m 1v. His son of the same name was disbarred for malpractice, exiled to Ireland, and became a notorious hanging judge there, knighted by Charles II.

to follow his direction'. He wanted a written detailed reply: 'It hath been made known to you and to Mr Bacon how I intend towards you but, if you still endeavour in this as in former things to make all good with words, you may be deceived'. And he ends his inexpert ramblings: 'I pray you when you have answered this send it to Mr Bacon or to me with the answer'. Despite the doubts of the editors of Volume V, a memorandum of 28 April 1603 must refer to the same dispute. Nathaniel's clerk Martin Man used 'Bland' for 'Plandon' except once, referring to a debt due to Thomas Plandon. But he mentioned the same debts as in Alexander's earlier letter, to Sheringham and Bullen. On 16 February 1604 Edward Coke wrote to Nathaniel (Morgan et al *Nat Bacon V* 74):

> I have received knowledge that there are very many suits betwixt this bearer my servant and one Plandon, his wife's brother. And that there are commissions awarded to you and others directed to examine witnesses and to end and determine the same suits. And forsomuch as I heartily wish a peace between them, lest the one should consume the estate of the other and in the end feel the sharpness of their own faults to their great hindrances, I heartily pray you in the behalf of both their goods to take the more pains at my request to reconcile all questions betwixt them; so shall you do a work of much piety betwixt them, and give me occasion to be heartily thankful to you for your travail therein to be taken....
> Edward Coke.

On 23 February 1604 Plandon wrote to Nathaniel, thanking him for his past efforts and asking him 'once again to take some further pains in that business' (Morgan et al *Nat Bacon V* 74–75). He asked Nathaniel to order the parties to state their cases fully in writing, thereby avoiding the need to call witnesses:

> I have therefore put down unto you in writing the true state of the cause as it standeth between us. I beseech you let my brother Alexander have a copy thereof and let him put down in writing wherein I have erred and I will answer thereunto and let us be at a perfect head before we trouble you to travail in the business....
> Robert Plandon.

On 27 February, presumably unaware of that letter, Alexander wrote to Nathaniel (Morgan et al *Nat Bacon V* 77):

> According to Your Worship's direction I sent my brother Plandon your letter unto whom I wrote wishing him to write his mind for answer, but he denied to write and to come, saying he was lame. But all his lameness was the want of Wolverstone, the only makebate [source of contention] betwixt us....
> PS Your Worship's letter was delivered him on Saturday morning by 8 o'clock.

And there all reference in the *Papers* ends, and we shall probably never know the outcome. But that was not the end of Alexander. His villainy knew no bounds. At the end of his life Nathaniel wrote:

Sir Nathaniel Bacon and other JPs in Norfolk to Sir James Lay LCJKB 1 August 1622.

Our duties remembered. Upon the petition of Edmund Bullock Esq it pleased your Lordship to refer unto us the examination of divers complaints made by several men dwelling near us for hard measure offered them by Jerome Alexander, one of the clerks of the King's Bench. And accordingly we called divers of those complainants before us, Mr Bullock & Alexander being also present, and heard what could be alleged by them against the said Alexander. And it appeared unto us that divers of them had heretofore made complaint of their griefs to Mr Bullock & by his advice some of them sought to one of us for relief. It appeared also that the carriage of Mr Alexander several ways hath not been justifiable both in the exercise of his place of stewardship in the Hundred courts and as an attorney above. Whereby many in this part of Norfolk where we dwell are earnest in their complaints against him....

Memoranda concerning complaints against Jerome Alexander 1 August 1622.
Remembrances upon hearing the matters informed against Mr Alexander.
1. Jackson's mare distrained for appearance of Pecell; as the beast of Pecell, Jackson's wife alleging in court the mare to be hers. Mr Alexander being steward received an oath of her and that done would not deliver the mare till she laid down 35s for Pecell's debt. After Mr Alexander being moved by the husband to restore the money, told him scoffingly that Pecell should lie with his wife for it. Not answered.
2. Robert Gray of Walsingham. That for a writ sued out by Mr Alexander, he took of him 20s, there being no proceeding against the defendant after the arrest. And refuseth to deliver a note of the charges, and yet promised Sir Hamon Strange to do it, upon his hearing the cause. Not answered.

A dozen other charges followed, any one of which, if proved, would have justified Alexander's dismissal and punishment; but that was Nathaniel's last preserved letter and the *Papers* end with his death just three months later.

A Tangential Insight   The nature and closeness of the relationship between Nathaniel and Coke is shown by a letter from Coke to Nathaniel (Morgan et al *Nat Bacon V* 257–258, reply 269–270) asking him to play the detective. Joan Cooke had been remanded in custody, charged with poisoning her husband Thomas, parish officer and overseer. Nathaniel had examined her. Coke commended his actions, particularly in not allowing bail, because poisoning one's husband was the most damnable crime and therefore petty treason. He made specific suggestions:

It were in mine opinion necessary to get that black stone that was supposed to be brought out of Iceland and to sift out that matter of the ratsbane... and to re-examine the widow, where and when she bought it.... The matter of unkindness between her and her husband would be thoroughly examined. Your true and loving friend. Edw Coke

Item Whether he chewed any tobacco that morning and whether he had any in the house.

Item Who were those that saw the body to know it after he was dead.

13. FRANCIS BACON

Francis Bacon is much better known as an arbitrator than Edward Coke, for all the wrong reasons, as Chapter 13 sets out. There is nowhere near the same evidence for the relations between Nathaniel and his half-brother as for those with Coke. It would be surprising if the puritan Nathaniel had got on well with the libertine Francis. The *Papers* throw a little light on their relationship. The first document is no more than a note from March or April 1604, with which Francis sent to Nathaniel 'copies of both the King's projects and of the Act of Recognition', signed 'Yors, Fr Bacon'. Francis was then a young lawyer seeking work and recognition by the new King.

On 25 July 1608 Francis, in reviewing the state of his finances, listed Nathaniel as someone he could call on as a surety,[10] but that may have been wishful thinking, part of Francis's fantasy of endless credit. The *Papers* hint that, as early as 1606, Nathaniel was suspicious of Francis's integrity as an arbitrator, when he intervened to remind Francis of his obligation to arbitrate impartially in a dispute in which he had acted as counsel for one of the parties (Morgan et al *Nat Bacon V* 256–260). The inhabitants of Southwold had petitioned the Council against Richard Gooch. The matter came by bill before the Star Chamber, which referred it to Francis for report. It was alleged that Gooch had maintained the unfounded complaints of Margaret Raphe, widow, against named persons and other inhabitants of Southwold, twenty persons in all, by bringing frivolous suits in Star Chamber and Chancery. The petitioners introduced what would today be objected to as irrelevant matter: a third of the town had been destroyed by fire, what was left had been ravaged by plague and Dunkirkers and 'hostile enemies of Spain'; and 'hard voyages in fisher fare and bad markets whereon the state of the town wholly dependeth' had taken their livelihoods away. They pointed out that Francis had been Gooch's counsel when bringing the bill in Chancery, and Gooch had worked for Francis and Nathaniel's brother Nicholas. He was hardly likely to be impartial. So they asked Nathaniel to write to Francis, asking him either to recuse himself or, if not, to act judicially rather than as an advocate. On 21 October 1606 two of the petitioners wrote a note to Nathaniel, asking for an answer to their request and setting out the details of their petition. For two years Gooch had wrongfully occupied town lands worth £50 a year in rent and cut and sold timber, with other wrongs, some of them 'continued by reason of

10. Lisa Jardine and Alan Stewart *Hostage to Fortune* 300.

an injunction grounded upon a report made by a doctor being one of the Masters of the Chancery'. On 25 October Nathaniel wrote to Francis:

> Good brother, I understand that there is a reference made unto you out of the Court of Star Chamber, of a bill there exhibited by the township of Southwold in Suffolk against R Gooch, my brother Bacon's servant and your client. And they of the town being not very rich, by reason of the great pestilence which hath been lately amongst them, and by other occasions of piracy and fire, are loth to hold on a chargeable contention, and therefore have entreated me to be a means unto you in their behalf, that some good course might be taken whereby there might be no continuance of the suits between them. The consideration hereof causeth me hereby to be a suitor unto you, that you will take knowledge of the grievances of both sides and, as a judge, advise and move such a proceeding as a peace may be concluded between them. And in so doing, as well Gooch as the townsmen of Southwold shall have great cause to hold themselves beholden unto you, and will be ready to do you any kindness or service for your travail so bestowed, and I also take it kindly at your hands. When I was at the last parliament I did hear some of them, and R Gooch also speak touching the differences between them, and I then thought Gooch in fault and did tell him that I would complain to his master for the unquiet carriage of himself.
>
> So I commend you to the grace and favour of God.

Hardly affectionate, but quite straightforward.[11] The tone became warmer when Nathaniel wanted something, writing on 10 November 1609, when Francis had become Solicitor General and was well in with James I:

> Good brother, let me be bold to entreat that your favour may be shewed in the report you are to make into the Court of Star Chamber touching G Southcott, a gent. of whom I think very well, and hope that his cause hanging in that court will prove such as shall not redound anything to his discredit.... when as a suitor to my daughter I did many ways enquire after him. I shall acknowledge myself beholden to you for any kindness you shall do him....
> Your very loving brother

Two years later, a letter of 3 November 1611 shows that such requests could be successful:

> Good brother, I am certified... what kindness and friendship you have shewed me for the quarrel made to Wissett lands in Suffolk, for which my wife and I do give you many thanks and will seek to requite your love herein... and entreat to be advised by you what course will be fittest in regard of the danger that may fall out hereafter... you can best direct me and thereupon I will rest.
> Your very loving brother.

The *Papers* then contain nothing until a letter of 19 September 1616, advising Francis, then Attorney General and Privy Councillor, that W

11. Adam Fox 'Custom, Memory' 100 gives an account of another matter, between Ellesmere LC and his copyhold tenants (for whom Francis, then Solicitor General, acted) citing Huntingdon Library, San Marino CA, Ellesmere MS 233.

Howsego, who was trying to establish his respectability, was the one who had slandered Nathaniel and their father and was the 'most disordered fellow that hath lived here these many years'.

Francis was promoted Lord Chancellor in January 1618 and at once Nathaniel wrote to him about his own claim which Francis as Lord Keeper had just decided in his favour. He addressed it formally 'Right Honorable' and signed 'Your Lordship's at commandment'. After acknowledging 'Your favour in hearing the cause between Sir Thomas Knyvett and myself', he reported that he had served the writ of execution but Knyvett had not complied. He was dealing with a man 'so addicted to his own mind that he will hardly be ruled by authority'. So 'I am bold to continue my former suit for your honour's help'.

Soon thereafter the *Papers* preserve a copy of Nathaniel's petition to Francis in Chancery for equitable relief, as 'the common law is without remedy'. He had bought the manors of Langham and Morston. Some of the land was leased 'at nothing like their true value'. The only income Nathaniel could expect was from fines, the payments due on renewals. But the tenants, particularly the crafty Katherine Grikes, had worked out a dodge, so that by fraudulent contracts they made 'secret transfers to one another... contrary to equity and good conscience'.

Others knew of Nathaniel's influence with Francis and sought to exploit it. On 12 October 1618 Edward Doyley wrote to him. He had an equity suit:

> Forasmuch as he is unacquainted with suits and feareth that he may be delayed, his humble suit unto you is that you would be pleased to afford him two or three lines to my Lord Chancellor, to entreat that his cause may be speedily dispatched.

On New Year's Eve 1618 Nathaniel thought it proper to ask Francis to appoint a young man 'of learning and good life' to 'a small living', the vicarage of Bramfield. It was not until 1621 that Francis's corruption as judge and arbitrator was proved against him and he fell from office. Nathaniel was still alive then and keeping his correspondence, but there is nothing there to show how he felt.

14. PRIVATE MEDIATIONS

Nathaniel's authority as a JP, his special skills as a mediator and no doubt his reputation for integrity and impartiality led not only to official commissions but to many private requests, such as that encouraged by Coke in the Cobbe dispute.

On 13 November 1601 Nathaniel mediated an end to a dispute over land and debts (Morgan et al *Nat Bacon IV* 219–220). Elizabeth, widow of Robert Earle, agreed to pay £100 in two instalments to John Earle, Robert's son, presumably by a previous marriage, who agreed to release her from all claims and convey to her all his father's lands, 'by release or any other assurance as shall be devised by learned counsel'. She also agreed to pay to Robert's married daughter, Margaret Slye, 'besides her legacy 20s after three years'. Richard Foster, rector of Burgh Parva, wrote to Nathaniel to ask him to 'make an end' of a dispute between his former servant, poor but honest, and a John Bacon – no relation – who was accusing him of trespass (Morgan et al *Nat Bacon V* 129–130). In September 1604 Nathaniel took detailed and rambling evidence in successfully mediating the settlement of a dispute between John Girdlestone and Ellen Howes, widow. On 25 September the neat and straightforward agreement is recorded (Morgan et al *Nat Bacon V* 126, 130). The parties were to exchange bonds, John and his brother were to make payments to Ellen, and she was to allow John to farm her copyhold land until her son was 14 – 'and all reckoning clear'.

Two settlements were recorded on one day, 25 August 1606 (Morgan et al *Nat Bacon V* 254). One was a simple exchange of a money payment for the release of a bond; the other of a dispute over Mundy's liberty to draw water from his neighbour King's well:

> King shall pay 10s unto Mundy towards the making of a well in his own ground. And Mundy to forbear to draw water at King's well hereafter. And the 10s is agreed to be left in Robert Walker's hand, and 5s thereof to be paid to Mundy so soon as he doth begin the well and the rest after it is finished. And each party releaseth the peace taken against one another and against the rest contained in the warrants made and granted by Sir Nathaniel Bacon and Mr Gwynne.

Nathaniel and Gwynne had referred to themselves and mediated a settlement of a matter which had come before them as JPs arising from mutual allegations of breaches of the peace. Has there ever been a legal system which could have produced a more refined resolution?

A letter of 17 July 1609 shows how Nathaniel dealt with a matrimonial dispute:

> Mrs Symonds, the causes of difference between your husband and you which I should reconcile by both your agreements if I can, I shall be content to hear between you either tomorrow in the forenoon or upon Wednesday here at my house... I mind only at this meeting to make some entrance into your causes... the causes are not like to be drawn to a conclusion upon the first nor second meeting. If your mother be with you, I desire that she may come also... nothing will be concluded before your brother do meet, and yet in the meantime I think it not amiss but rather a furtherance of peace to have this beginning made. Thus referring to your husband and yourself what to agree to...
> Your loving friend NB.

On 9 August and 9 December 1611 agreements are recorded as the results of Nathaniel's successful mediations. On 3 August 1618 Nathaniel's steward Matthew Clarke wrote to ask him to mediate a dispute between his bailiff and the principal debtor for whom he had stood surety, to avoid 'suits of higher nature on both sides, like to be of long continuance and large expense', and 'atone them as in conscience and equity shall stand best with your judgment'.

15. PRIVATE ARBITRATIONS

Sometimes the submission itself expressly showed that arbitration, not mediation, was required. As Christmas approached and 1602 came to an end, Nathaniel was as busy as ever. As sole arbitrator on 9 December he declared his award in a private arbitration between neighbours, Roger Bulwer (and his sons Edward and George) and John Athill (Morgan et al *Nat Bacon IV* 301). Athill must pay Roger 30s before 1 February, for a boar he had killed. 'All trespasses done in corn or grass at any time by either of them... shall be released of either side, because on the opening of them it appeared doubtful which of them had done the greater'. Disputes between Roger and Athill over rents and tithes 'by consent of both parties shall be determined by the judgment of Mr John Fountaine before the twelfth day next and, if he decide them not, referred to the judgment of Nathaniel Bacon Esq.' 'The demand of tithe hay from Mr George Bulwer by Mr Athill in the right of the vicar is referred to a trial at the Assizes in summer next'. And Nathaniel added: 'Memorandum: I have promised that no advantage shall be taken of bonds which have been formerly passed for abiding by this my order'. Athill's undated letter shows in detail how a submission worked and how arbitration was valued then (Morgan et al *Nat Bacon V* 113–114):

> Good Sir Nathaniel Bacon, mortal men should not have immortal suits, and suits commenced by fathers and continued by their children in an unchristian and uncharitable succession do often times ravel up and undermine the fathers' estates before they die, and in the end do utterly undo their heirs by descent, when they be dead, a cross and a curse, that contention by God's wrathful ordinance brings with it, which you in your wisdom and experience hath seen to fall upon divers families. Not far off – *sic obdurit cor Pharaonis* ['so he hardened Pharaoh's heart' *Exodus* 7.13 and 14] – through the which, by excessive fees disbursed upon exceeding lawyers, both Mr Bulwer's family and mine, shall hereafter fare the worse, for prevention whereof at the first, before any suit was set on foot between him and me, I for my part made an overture of peace unto him, above 10 years since, to submit all intended controversies to any men of worth and wisdom in all Norfolk to decide and censure the same.
>
> But Mr Bulwer then, before the walking spirit of the lands in question was any wise conjured, utterly refused that my peace offering, saying that he would not put his coat to dyeing, to never a man in England. But now of late (and somewhat too late for us both) he hath changed his mind and out of his own

voluntary, (the pleasingest motive that may be), it hath pleased him to come walking unto me in the pathway of peace, protesting to embrace that peace now which long since was offered unto him, before any money was spent, or rather spoiled, at law. Requesting at my hands a submission and a compromise of all matters in difference betwixt us, to some men of worship in the country (lawyers excepted, the minters of other men's coin, out of their true owners' purses into their own). Gladly I condescended to this his motion, as proceeding from God, and did put upon him first to choose one for himself and I would second it, suit and sort another of like quality and condition. He, for him, chose Sir Nathaniel Bacon, a knight in his opinion without exception. And I, purposing to choose one that was *omni exceptione major* [above all objection] and in all respects suitable and sortable that never would dissent in judgment, nor jar in the proceeding, chose for me your worship to be the judge, the justicer and *honorarius arbiter* [a technical term of classical Roman law for an arbitrator appointed informally by the parties] of all our controversies.

At which my seconding choice Mr Bulwer was so well pleased that presently off went our hats, on went our hands and hearts to a pacification, which was the first time that ever we two shook either hands or hearts together, making you by mutual and reciprocal consent our judge, if you please to assume that office upon you, *beati pacifici, exuenda est persona amici, et induenda judicis* [the blessed peacemaker must doff the character of friend and don that of judge] to end as in a moment ten years tedious and costly suits, thereby to give better satisfaction to Mr Bulwer, concerning his supposed right and title to the lands in question by delivering your opinion therein, than either the Lord Chancellor or the high court of the Chancery by decree, injunction and commission could do, or than I can do by paying 200 marks out of the said lands to his sister for her marriage portion, and by spending in suit or otherwise 400 marks more *in toto* paid and spent out of my poor purse, twice as much money as the recovered lands be worth. Thus stand I, *de damno vitando* [for avoidance of loss], a loser at the close, although I got somewhat at the crush. Thus contendeth he, *de irreparabili damno* [in relation to loss which cannot be recovered], for lawyers have irrevocably got his money. *Omnia vestigia antrorsum, nulla retrorsum, opera et impensa periit* [if every track leads forward, none back, then the toils and the costs have vanished]. Fearing tediousness I submit myself to your censure, and you and yours I do recommend to the protection of the Almighty, together with my duty remembered to the good Lady Bacon.

Both parties signed, though it was penned by Dr John Hunt, himself a civil lawyer and Master in Chancery (*c*1596–1615), a JP in Suffolk and an expert devotee of arbitration.[12]

Long before, in December 1594, the *Papers* had recorded another violent tithe dispute – with a vicious mastiff and heavies imported from Kent with long pikestaffs – which the parties had submitted to local mediation. Nathaniel's role was limited to fixing and allocating costs and acting as umpire if called on (Hassell Smith et al *Nat Bacon III* 285–287).

12. BP Levack *The Civil Lawyers* 241.

The matter arose again eight years later. On 27 December 1602 Nathaniel had signed a memorandum of evidence in disputes between Armiger and Franklin which spilled over into the new year (Morgan et al *Nat Bacon IV* 302–303). The land dispute was deferred until the following Whitsuntide, 'when a sight shall be had of the survey made in the meantime'. Certain trespasses were referred to the judgment of the arbitrators, Mr Holland and Mr Warde, 'on Monday next... and if they do not order it then it shall be decided by Nathaniel Bacon Esq'. Franklin's demands for tithes and wool and sheep were also 'referred to their examination and ordering'. 'Costs of suit and for battery with costs of suit, referred to Nathaniel Bacon when the other matters be brought to order'. On the same day Nathaniel signed an order for the hearing the following Monday. On time, an agreement between Armiger and Franklin was signed by Holland and Warde on 3 January (Morgan et al *Nat Bacon V* 1):

> First Mr Armiger is to pay unto Mr Franklin for the tithe hay 15s.
> Item Mr Armiger is to pay him for the tithe rakings five combes barley.
> Item Mr Armiger is to pay him for the tithe of tenscore couples of ewes and lambs sold to Mr Buggin 52s.
> Item for grasses occupied by Mr Armiger of the parsonage glebe for every acre 16d.
> The day of payment of the sums of money and barley to be set down by Mr Bacon.

'A remembrance of the proceeding and order of Nathaniel Bacon upon the hearing of the variance between Richard Neave and Edward Catton set down 17 May 1603' (Morgan et al *Nat Bacon V* 35) recorded Nathaniel's award in relation to 'certain lands in Wood Dalling'.

The realities of a married woman landowner's position are exemplified in a letter of 5 August 1612 from Sir Anthony Cope and his wife Anne, asking Nathaniel to act as arbitrator. Anne's father was Sir William Paston, grandfather of Coke's first wife Bridget, MP for Norfolk and about as much a Norfolk man as anyone could be. But:

> Sir, myself & my wife having a commission to be set up in Norfolk betwixt Sir John Heavingham & us, and although the same be my wife's native country, yet by reason of her long absence I know not whither she may be esteemed as a stranger amongst them, we have ever accounted of you as a good friend, & have made bold at this time to use your name as a commissioner for us, in a cause depending between Sir John Heavingham and my wife. I pray you, let us entreat your best observation in the carriage of the cause, for it seems very strange to my wife that so small an annuity given by her father, so long since, and confirmed by his approbation not long before his last breath, should now be denied. We have entreated a gentleman in this country to join with you in this commission, if your leisure might serve, we would request it might be presently after Stourbidge fair. The gentleman having occasions to [be in] Cambridge about that time, will be

ready to meet you at what time & place yourself shall nominate: not having other occasions to stay him there, the sooner the better. I pray you let us understand by this messenger when & where you will appoint this commission to be set on, near about for your own ease, that the parties themselves & the few witnesses might have sufficient warning of it. I have written to my brother Plumstead your neighbour to attend you, to know your present answer herein, whereby he may give warning to Sir John concerning the day & place by you nominated. So with our very loving salutations, hoping to entreat your pains herein, we commit you to God, and rest your assured loving friends.

Hanwell this 5 of August 1612.

[*Signed*] Anthony Cope   Anne Cope.

A cooperative effort to enlist Nathaniel's help in recovering on an obligation owed to the wife, written by the husband, signed by both.

Sometimes a dispute that started as a private arbitration might become the subject of a petition and be sent to commissioners. On 26 March 1615 John Greene wrote to Nathaniel suggesting how arrangements could best be made for the private resolution of his dispute with Allen Lampkin. If he was to be liable, he wanted the deed produced, rather than reliance be placed on 'the uncertain testimony of any man who will speak one thing today and another thing tomorrow, as I saw some did yesterday'. But early in 1616 Lampkin petitioned the King:

Humbly shewing unto your Majesty that whereas your poor petitioner with his wife and children, by the handiwork of God, were utterly undone by a storm of hail which fell 28 May 1613, wherein he lost to the value of £100. And being indebted to divers men and not able to give them full satisfaction, and having made over his lands and goods in trust to John Greene of King's Lynn in the county of Norfolk gent one of his creditors, to give him satisfaction: notwithstanding John Greene doth not cease to sue and molest your petitioner, contrary to our agreement, whereby I dare not stir out of my house to provide for my wife & children for fear of being imprisoned by him and one Edmund Sheringham... May it therefore please your Majesty to grant a commission to Sir Nathaniel Bacon, Sir Augustine Palgrave and Mr Thomas Athow, serjeant at law, or any two of them, to call before them both parties and to hear and determine of the matter according to law and equity, and as they shall then find it....

At the foot: From the Court at Newmarket 27 February 1615. His Majesty's pleasure is that the committees hereby desired, or any two of them, assisted with one or more of meet quality to be chosen by such of the adverse parties as shall be desirous to name any, shall call the parties before them and after hearing of the premisses mediate such a charitable agreement between the parties as shall be consonant to equity & justice: That so the petitioner if there be cause may be relieved and his Majesty no further troubled herein.

Signed: Roger Wilbraham.

On 25 April Sir Hamon Lestrange wrote to Nathaniel that Greene had asked him to join the panel but that he had apologised. Christopher Calthorpe was appointed in his place. A memorandum of 1 May records the details of the successful outcome, mediated by Nathaniel, Palgrave and Calthorpe.

16. NATHANIEL'S APPOINTMENTS

In his office as JP Nathaniel made his own appointments, as a letter to him from Robert Warren of 16 February 1614 shows. It relates in part to a quarrel over a game of cards:

> Sir according to your worship's appointment I have dealt in the difference between John Arnold of our town, and Edward Hobart of Great Snoring, both for the money in their disordered night play at cards as also about the business of buying the swine, and though I cannot with any comfort write in commendation of the parties of either side, yet the equity of the cause moveth me to inform your worship what I find in proof upon examination.... there being 2s 6d at stake, whereof one shilling was John Arnold's, the other Hobart's & 6d besides Richard Arnold's (who was half with his brother), the game being (as is affirmed) plain on Arnold's side & Hobart dispairing of his own, Hobart suddenly threw up his cards & snatched up all the money & went away therewith. And for the swine, it appeareth that it was in the custody & kept at the cost of John Arnold for 6 weeks & more.... Wheruppon I have been earnest in persuading Hobart to yield them back again of the play money 1s 6d at least, and... some thing towards the keeping of [the swine].... I cannot prevail with [Hobart] to part from one penny, but find him too stowre & stiff & too much obnixe: wherefore... I am enforced to return this information.

Failure; and no better outcome from Nathaniel's next appointment, reported on 5 May:

> Whereas there was a controversy between John Clipwell and Henry Gunthorpe, and your wourship ordered that it should be heard and determined by John Yates and me. Now these may be to let your good worship understand that Gunthorpe laboured both John Yates and me to take pains therein, and was so willing to have an end, that he entered bond in £10 to abide our award, to have the matter determined before Easter but it was almost not past a fortnight or three weeks before Easter ere Clipwell would enter bonds and, after the entering thereof very little or nothing did persuade us to meet or end the matter, until it grew so near Easter that the ships were ready to sail, that we could not have any leisure. Thereupon Gunthorpe desired that new bonds might be entered, for without that we would not deal in the business, and that we might have farther respite therein; unto which Clipwell did seem to be willing, but after Easter new bonds were newly made, and ready to seal, I myself told Clipwell that the bonds were newly made and ready to seal, wherewith he seemed to be offended, and said that he would enter no more bonds, but would still prosecute his suit against Gunthorpe. Thus I thought it my duty to inform your good worship of the truth thereof. Willm Halman.

Simple practical arrangements to resolve straightforward differences might have a better chance. On 22 July 1616 Nathaniel wrote to George Leeds that he had:

> heard Nicholas Allen & the widow Loveday speak together and by my persuasion they are both agreed that the wintercorn sown by her in the closes shall be laid into her barn, and the key kept thereof by yourself... to remain there till Mr Nicholas Thimblethorp shall be dealt with for the resolving of the question, whether upon his letting to Allen there was excepted and agreed to be reserved to the widow Loveday such corn as she had sown according to her covenant. And so, praying you to take upon you this trust, I commit you to God's keeping.

17.   COMPOSITIONS WITH CREDITORS

Arranging compositions with creditors was a frequent task, usually requiring Nathaniel to decide as arbitrator what debts were valid and their value, as well as the best arrangements for compounding them.[13] On 29 November 1602 Wilbraham, Master of Requests, had referred to Nathaniel and three others Ralph Dade's petition for 'some charitable moderation of the extremities of law' (Morgan et al *Nat Bacon IV* 296–297):

> After due examination of the cause, by your good inducements to persuade so with the creditors, as they may be charitably contented to give such days of payment and accept such satisfaction at the petitioner's hands, agreeable to his poor estate, as by you in conscience and equity shall be thought fit, if so you can, or else certify your opinions, and by whose default you could not end the same, to the end, if there be cause, Her Majesty may be eftsoons moved, for her further gracious pleasure towards the petitioner.

The full details of the mediated agreement are set out in a memorandum of 21 January 1603 (Morgan et al *Nat Bacon V* 2–3). John Deane, owed £10, accepted £9 at £1 a year, starting 'Michaelmas come twelvemonth', secured by a bond. Thomas Edimont was luckier: he was to be paid in full when due. John Catlock would accept £1 a year. Nathaniel's brother Nicholas, owed £8, would take £6 at £1 a year and the other £2 at 10s a year. More complicated arrangements were necessary for repayment of Robert Evered's debt, plus interest and charges. John Mottes' debt of £12 included contested sums for two cades of herrings and two warps of ling, and 5s lent to Dade's wife. Dade claimed he had paid 10s to Motte's wife. That was too difficult to be disposed of summarily, so it was agreed that John Deane and Richard Cooke should be deputed to look into the whole debt and what was found to be due would be payable by three annual instalments.

---

13. Too many for all to be quoted, e.g. Morgan et al *Nat Bacon V* 46–47, 50-52, 55, 57 all from the end of 1603; Chapter 7 above deals generally with compositions, protections and postponements on behalf of debtors.

Wilbraham referred the petition of old innkeeper Walter Sheltram to Nathaniel and Sir Henry Sidney on 12 November 1603 (Morgan et al *Nat Bacon V* 56). Sheltram claimed he needed time. Some creditors had agreed but others, 'being of an unconscionable mind', were seeking to recover their debts at law. The commission ordered the arbitrators to arrange a composition and, if that proved impossible, to certify the names of the obstinate creditors, for 'the King to be moved again for speedier relief'.

In August 1604 Wilbraham commissioned Nathaniel with Christopher Heydon and Henry Sydney to summon 'the creditors of Thomas Haylock, and treat and persuade with them to accept such reasonable satisfaction for their debts as his estate may be any ways able to perform'. A year later (Morgan et al *Nat Bacon V* 198–199) an unsigned memorandum reports to Nathaniel unsuccessful attempts to mediate, probably of Christopher Reve, bailiff and steward of the Duchy of Lancaster in Norfolk. 'Remembrances' follow, rough notes of evidence, which end with a note that the parties had agreed to meet again at Stiffkey on 13 August. Again in August 1609, Nathaniel reported only partial success in response to Wilbraham's:

> direction, signifying His Majesty's pleasure, that we should call before us the creditors of Thomas Hailock, and treat and persuade with them to accept such reasonable satisfaction for their debts as his estate may anyways be able to perform, and to certify if we found any obstinate in so charitable a course.

Alternatively, the petition might come from the creditors themselves, no less than 24 in the case of Edward Downes, who 'had become indebted to divers of them and divers others he hath procured to stand surety for him', some of whom had as a result been in prison for four years (Morgan et al *Nat Bacon V* 100–101). They petitioned Parliament. They had 'by course of law no remedy against him, for he standeth outlawed at many of their suits, and keepeth himself in a castle strong, accompanied by many desperate persons'. They asked that 'certain commissioners named in their bill may stand authorised by Act of Parliament to enquire out the certainty of the creditors' due debts or by them undertaken as sureties... to sell his lands and satisfy his debts and discharge his sureties'. Six commissioners were named, of whom two could act.

As late as 11 October 1619 Nathaniel joined Christopher Heydon in a response to the Master of Requests for a composition.

18. NATHANIEL AS A PARTY

It was inevitable that a man with so many interests should find himself a party to disputes. When that happened, Nathaniel showed his strong preference for mediation and arbitration. When Coke CJCP as assize judge referred a petition against Mrs Wood, which touched on Nathaniel's wife's dower, to John Wentworth, Nathaniel wrote to him, 12 April 1609, asking him 'to be content to take upon you the hearing... my servant will attend and inform you in particular with the state of it'. On 30 May he wrote again: 'Notwithstanding I am loth to continue the contention, if I may redeem my peace with some loss.... I will yet be content to give 5 marks more, and so end the strife'. Then on 19 October Wentworth's award is recorded. Nathaniel was to pay the Woods £5; they were to give up their claim to dower and 'do such acts as Sir Nathaniel at his own cost may devise for the extinguishment of their title'; and Nathaniel was to give up his claim on a bond made by Mrs Wood's former husband.

A few days later, Nathaniel was offering a friendly settlement of a potential dispute about trees on land he had leased from Edward Paston's father Thomas:

> Sir, there be in Barney Wood divers young trees more than I am tied to leave when my lease expireth and there be also much underwood whereof I can make some profit. And though there hath been unkind suits between your father and me yet I am willing that peace might be between you and me, and therefore do make offer unto you that if you will appoint a man to see these trees and underwood, I will appoint another to judge the value of them and, if they can agree... I shall forbear any more fell to be made.
> Your loving friend, N Bacon

Edward Paston's reply of 29 November was negative. Nathaniel had already done too much damage. He had better surrender the lease forthwith. Paston's father Thomas would accept it. Nathaniel replied by Edward's messenger that he would not surrender the lease prematurely but would do his best to make the necessary improvements, offering to appoint his man to join Edward Paston's in viewing the damage to the trees.

Some of Nathaniel's disputes were with men who had been his co-arbitrators. Early in 1611 Sir Christopher Heydon wrote to Nathaniel suggesting ways in which a difference between them might be settled. He addressed his letter to 'my especial good friend' and indeed they were close. Heydon had recently asked Nathaniel for a loan to help set up his son in London. Nathaniel's wife had lent plate to Heydon. Nevertheless there was some difference about copyhold land in Irmingland which Nathaniel said Thomas Catelyn had sold him as freehold. Nathaniel had suggested mediation and Heydon replied: 'I like well of your motion and, if it may please you to assign the day, I will entreat Mr Jervis to meet with him whom you shall appoint for you at Mr Fountain's'. There had been proceedings in Chancery, in which Nathaniel and Heydon had been ordered to make payments to Catelyn. On 11 January 1611 Nathaniel wrote to Catelyn:

> This charge growing upon me for land which you sold unto me as free land is, as I am advised, to be borne by you, and I pray you to consider of it, and let that be

yielded unto which is due, and no strife as I hope shall grow thereabout between us, for I will submit myself to them that can judge, if there be any question.

Catelyn had transferred the lands to Nathaniel and his wife Dorothy by indenture of 20 April 1605 and they were building Irmingland Hall on it. Some of the land was clearly freehold; the controversy arose about the tenure of other parts. On 16 July 1617 a Chancery order from Sir Julius Caesar required Christopher Calthorpe to produce 'all deeds and evidences concerning the land in question', but a note records that the parties had agreed to submit to the arbitration of their counsel.

19.   WOMEN

It is tempting to count the matters mentioned in this chapter and the number of women, parties in their own right; but sanguine statistics are the bane of social history and even a rough guess could mislead. Anyone who has read so far will have a fair impression that women were thoroughly and naturally involved. There was no bar against married women being parties to arbitration. Margaret Bosom had no need to involve her husband Adam in a complex claim on a bond involving her son by a previous marriage (Morgan et al *Nat Bacon V* 121–123). She gave evidence and signed her deposition herself.

Nathaniel took care to ensure that a deserted wife should not be cheated, however old her claim. A memorandum from some time in 1613 records:

One Ezeckiell Spacham above 30 years since purchased of Robert London a mesuage & certain grounds of the value of £8 a year in Foulsham & Norton and took a feoffment to himself & Anne his wife & their heirs. And afterwards intending to sell the same urged his wife to join in the sale, which she refusing he took a new feoffment from London to himself in fee and sold the same to Mr Tounshende and a fine was levied thereof. And Tounshende sold it to Holmes who sold it to John Athill. And this was about 20 years since. Holmes also sold 3 roods of the ground to John Erle and (as it is thought) 3 acres of meadow to William Hempstead. Spacham presently after the sale of the premises forsook his wife and went into Essex and married another woman and 14 years since went into Holland where he died.

Memorandum upon the repair of Athill & Hempstead to Sir Nathaniel Bacon & Mr Calthorp [another Norfolk JP] 29 December, Athill answered that he knew not but Spacham was alive, and so meant not to make any composition, and would submit the matter to the proceeding by law & not otherwise. This day the committee wrote to Houghton J in the poor woman's behalf certifying the case & her disability and praying allowance she might sue *in forma pauperis*.

Though this chapter is devoted to Nathaniel, the *Papers* show that concern for a woman was more widespread and that some of his reputation had

devolved on Martin Man, his clerk. On 6 June 1612 Thomas Daynes wrote
to him:

> I have written to my good friend Mistress Katherine Girton.... I pray ye by our
> mutual love to draw her to a reference and divert her from this expensive and
> exhausting course, which dries up estate and love, especially. Which, as it is to
> be wished among all, so chiefly among so near kindred as these litigants.... I
> pray, sir, fail not to be earnest with her that in no way she refuse a reference...
> and Mr Bagge will embrace it kindly... for them they must say the common
> saying: *viret lex si currit pecunia* [the law grows if the money flows].

But only four days later there is a record of Nathaniel and his brother
Sir Nicholas arranging the arbitration of another dispute, referred to them
from the prerogative court, between Katherine Girton and the Reverend
John Raphe and his unmarried sisters Rose and Abra. Raphe entered
into a bond of £3 to Katherine that he and his sisters would abide by the
award of Nicholas and Nathaniel on the division of the goods of the late
Mr Tasburgh between Katherine and the Raphes. The proceedings in the
prerogative court were stayed 'until the first court after Michaelmas, in
case the matter be not ended in the meantime by the arbitrators.... The
examinations taken by the commissioners at this time or hereafter shall
be shewed to the arbitrators privately for their information only'. An
inventory was attached, of apparel, a coverlet, wool and silver. On 17 July
Katherine wrote to Martin Man, about a matter:

> between Lewing and Hancock, I am desirous to know who are my
> commissioners... and how much money you have laid out for me, for it is too
> much to be indebted so many ways to you as I have been. Thus many thanks to
> you for this time a better requital hereafter, hoping that still you will have care
> of my business.

This was all part of the dispute over the Tasburgh estate. In a letter of 22
August Katherine wrote:

> Good Mr Man, You shall receive here enclosed Mr Blofeld's bill which I had
> of you, which I would entreat you to copy out and send him.... My lady by Sir
> Nicholas's appointment hath written unto Sir Nathaniel about my business and
> my cousin Raphes. Sir Nicholas is very ill... if he be perfectly recovered, I shall
> entreat him to appoint a time for the meeting.
>   Postscript.   Good Mr Man, let me entreat you to speak to Mr Blofeld to
> be very careful concerning my commission between Lewing and Hancock. I
> pray let me entreat you to be there and do me that kindness you can. Although
> I am not able to requite your kindness I hope I shall be one day. And further if
> I might entreat you to lay out the money for the charges for the commissioners,
> which you are better acquainted withal, better than any friend I shall have there,
> and you shall be sure to receive it of me again as soon as I come to Norwich. I

do hear by some that they do desire to have an end of the suit, which if it be so I
shall be very willing to accept of.

Katherine's letters end there but not the proceedings. As the editors of the
forthcoming *Bacon Papers VI*[14] explain in a footnote:

> Katherine Girton appears to have married Paul Cope of Bury within the next
> year or two, as Chancery documents show the couple in dispute with these two
> men in January 1615 over Edward Tasburgh's affairs. Gilbert Lewing claimed
> payment for land leased to Tasburgh... while Thomas Hancock (they claimed)
> had acted as his bailiff and sold corn and cattle to his own profit (TNA C2/Jas/
> C1/57, C19/7).

A much damaged document of 21 December 1621 records an agreement
which Nathaniel, with Sir Charles Cornwallis and John Richers, mediated
between Elizabeth Denny and her son John about various family lands, and:
'Whereas John Denny is charged to pay for the sustenance and education
of his brothers and sister at a rate fit for their degree and calling, he and
his mother agree to refer any differences on this score to the decision of
the mediators'.

20. CONCLUSIONS

Nathaniel was a busy man. No reliable numbers would be obtained by
counting references in the *Papers*. In a footnote (Morgan et al *Nat Bacon
V* 52 fn137) the editors reveal that he must have acted as mediator in many
more disputes than the *Papers* document:

> This is an example of mediation by a third party to avert or abort a formal
> process (in this case, in the Exchequer). Entries in Bacon's recognizance books
> [citations] suggest that this procedure was widely used but rarely figures in the
> formal records, beyond a note that the case was dropped.

But it is clear that he was rarely free for long from the burden of disputes,
perhaps averaging one of substance every month. A matter might require
him to ride for a day, stay at least two nights with the Pastons, spend a
day to inspect many acres of land and perhaps another to hear dozens
of witnesses' inexpert testimony. All that was a free service provided by
the State.

 This chapter has provided much detailed evidence of the work of one
man in a system which cannot realistically be faulted for its efficiency,
whether judged by the standards of its time or ours. That efficiency may
now seem to have come at a cost. Niceties of legal rights were sometimes

14. G Alan Metters, Victor Morgan, Elizabeth Rutledge and Barry Taylor eds *The Papers of
Nathaniel Bacon of Stiffkey VI* and *VII* (forthcoming) [Metters et al *Nat Bacon VI* and
VII].

overlooked. Many awards make orders which apply to non-parties. A good example is that of 28 June 1603 (Morgan et al *Nat Bacon V* 39), in a tithe dispute between Richard Boulter on the one hand and Gyles Mychell and Thomas Grene, referred to arbitrators from the Consistory Court. The calendar reads: 'Concerning covenants in a pair of indentures for land lately bargained and sold to Boulter by Mychell, Boulter may reasonably require Mychell's son Mardocheus, at his comng of age, to release to him all title and interest'.

By 1608, Nathaniel had gained such experience that he could take the initiative in a matter of great substance not just to individuals but to the whole community of Wells. A new quay must be made and the cutting be recut. The charges would have to fall on those who gained from them, but how were they to be apportioned? Nathaniel's own letter to the inhabitants of Wells says it all (Morgan et al *Nat Bacon VI* 22 January 1608):

Whereas somewhat before Christmas I came unto your town with purpose to try if I could persuade you and the rest of the townsmen to some indifferent course for the charge of making up the key [quay] where your ships lie before the town, and could not then bring the matter to any perfect agreement, and yet left it so as I was not without hope to have had it agreed upon between yourselves, and since not hearing that you be resolved of what course therein to be taken, I have thought good not thus to give over an action so fit to be performed but to entreat you for your best means that it may not be slacked any longer.... The difficulty & hindrance of your joint consents seemeth to grow, because the charge cannot be made equal to the ease & profit which each man shall take. To this I must give the answer. First the proportioning of the shipping, to two parts of the charge, & the land to the third, I think more indifferent than any other way that I can hear hitherto to be propounded, the rather because the shipping alone must maintain the key hereafter when it is once made. If a more equal way may be found out, which may please all parties, I shall be glad of it.... reasonable men will rather give way than suffer the work to come to nothing, whilst they strive how to make it equal in profit & charge. If question arise among you, how the key shall be maintained & governed when it is made, which is not so fit now to be debated upon, because it asketh good consideration & time to digest, what is best therein, I do advise that you will amongst yourselves hereafter agree upon so many articles for the government thereof as shall be within your general allowance and, wherein you differ & cannot agree, to submit your judgments to the judgment of my Lord of Northampton your lord, or some other whom yourselves shall think well of.... Therefore, for the benefit of them that come after you, I think it good to have this course taken, and let not this cause you to slack the present collection of the money, if you once agree. For my Lord's pleasure may be known & his consent got before the work be begun. If, through your slackness in making this key, it happen that my Lord of Northampton be sought unto, to grant it to private men, which I think he may do as in other places, if he will; then every man will be glad to get a part thereof, and so a private profit shall be made of that which may now easily be obtained at my

Lord's hands to be to the public good of the town, inasmuch as the town by a
public charge doth perform the same. Your neighbours by your entreaty may be
won hereunto and let no man stand too much upon his own judgment. I wish
well unto your town, & that alone causeth me to importune you thus much. So I
heartily commend you to God's keeping.

Your loving friend.

That was a draft which Nathaniel had corrected in his own hand. If nothing
else had survived to show his work, it would have been enough to prove so
much. He speaks plainly: 'It is almost impossible so to equal these things
but there will remain exceptions... and reasonable men will rather give
way'. And he has a thoroughly modern recognition of the proper place of
the mediator: 'If a more equal way may be found, which may please all
parties, I shall be glad.'

The *Papers* preserve a draft of Nathaniel's will which brings this chapter
to a poignant end. Its convolutions were bound to breed disputes, as indeed
they did for generations. At least he tried to provide for them. After a
general pious hope: 'God will bless them best who most desire peace':

I make my executors the Lady Anne Townshend the Lady Elizabeth Knyvett and
the Lady Wynefride Gawdye my three daughters, willing them to join together
in peace and not to do anything in the execution of this my will which shall be of
moment without the consent of two of them at the least and I entreat my brother
Edward Bacon to be supervisor of this my will and, if any question or doubt arise
upon the interpretation of any part of this my will, I do desire and entreat that
person or persons whom the cause shall concern to submit their judgments to
the judgment of my supervisor and if he by reason of his age or remote dwelling
cannot attend the deciding thereof then I entreat Mr Jarmye and Mr Gwynn the
lawyers to mediate & persuade that no suit or contention may arise.

12   EDWARD COKE

His works will last to be admired by the judicious posterity whilst Fame hath a trumpet left her, and any breath to blow therein.

Thomas Fuller[1]

Truly I never read weaker reasoning in any author of the law of England, than in Sir Edward Coke's *Institutes*, how well soever he could plead.

Thomas Hobbes[2]

Jus condere Cocus potuit, sed condere jure
Non potuit; potuit condere jura Coci.
Coke could cook up law but he could not cook up according to law; he could only cook up the laws of Coke.

Contemporary jingle[3]

Succedo arduus: Eduardus Cocus
I get there the hard way: Edward Coke

Coke's own anagram[4]

1.   INTRODUCTION

Edward Coke (1552–1634)[5] has had more influence on the development of the Common Law than anyone before or since. To cite him in support has been considered enough to win the argument. Since he fabricated the rule in *Vynior's Case*,[6] that an agreement to submit to arbitration is not binding, detractors of arbitration have recruited him as an ally. When in the 18th century English judges manufactured the doctrine that arbitration agreements were invalid because they 'ousted the jurisdiction' of the courts, and that doctrine crossed the Atlantic, Coke's authority was invoked. Some

---

1. Thomas Fuller *History of the Worthies* 452.
2. Thomas Hobbes *Dialogue Between a Philosopher* [Hobbes].
3. Cited and mistranslated by Catherine Drinker Bowen *The Lion and the Throne* [Bowen] 390. *Condere* means 'fabricate'– 'cook up', not 'cook', which is *coquere*; cf *ab urbe condita*, 'from when the city [Rome] was founded'.
4. Such anagrams were a common conceit, cf Thomas Egerton's, 'honors met age', does not quite work.
5. b February 1552; called to the Bar April 1578; Solicitor General June 1592; Attorney General June 1594; CJCP June 1606; CJKB October 1613; dismissed November 1616; d September 1634.
6. (1609) 8 Co Rep 80a; Chapter 19.

modern scholars have gone further, and suggested that Coke had, at least at the back of his mind, the need to construct a legal system for the use of an infant capitalism:[7] 'to translate the law of medieval England into doctrines adapted to a changing society and expanding economy'; 'to the marketplace of Adam Smith and Richard Posner, where enlightened self-interest is held to guide men's dealings with the grace of an invisible hand'. Some imaginative scholars portray Coke as a pioneer of 'economic liberalism', and of 'antiabsolutist constitutionalism'.[8]

Coke's published writings are voluminous. The strength of his voice in the *Reports* and *Institutes* drowns out those of his contemporaries. The multitude of his surviving manuscripts provides primary evidence from which much careful scholarship has produced exegesis and theory. It has led some to assume that Coke had a strategy of law reform, with a detailed agenda to achieve it:[9] 'Coke's interest in reform was programmatic.... Reform was the crucial influence on his legal thinking'; 'parliamentary records capture only a portion of his law reform agenda... a basically moralistic critique'.[10] A preference for the 'rule of law' through litigation, rather than resolution of disputes by informal means, has been assumed to be an essential element of that programme. No evidence supports such speculations.

The previous chapter provided plenty of evidence of Coke's use of arbitration, to dispose of his own disputes as well as those of others. There he was seen only in his relations with Nathaniel Bacon but there is plenty of other evidence of his interests, preferences and personal involvement. In this chapter they will be placed in a wider context. They can only be properly understood if the modern myths about Coke are seen for what they are.[11]

---

7. AD Boyer *Sir Edward Coke* [Boyer *Coke*] x and 134; AD Boyer 'Sir Edward Coke: Royal Servant, Royal Favorite' [Boyer *Royal*] is coloured by such assumptions.
8. TG Barnes 'A Cheshire Seductress' [Barnes *Seductress*] 20 and fnn 18–20, citing DO Wagner 'Coke and the Rise of Economic Liberalism'; Jean Beauté *Un Grand Juriste*; SD White *Sir Edward Coke* [White]. Barbara Malament 'The Economic Liberalism' gently mocks but trenchantly destroys the romantic anachronisms.
9. DC Smith *Sir Edward Coke* [Smith] 50, 176–177.
10. White 84.
11. There is an enormous body of work, ever expanding with new studies of primary sources and new things to say, including: Smith; Boyer *Coke*; AD Boyer ed *Law, Liberty and Parliament* [Boyer *Liberty*]. They provide ample citations of the other important work. My own list has over 100 items and a literature search would probably reveal something new and worthwhile every month, especially since the recent concentration on Coke's own huge mss library, on which modern scholarship began with JH Baker 'Coke's Notebooks' [Baker *Coke*], repr Boyer *Liberty* 357–386, breathtaking, now as then, for its originality and detailed mastery of the primary sources. With no attempt at comprehensiveness, the following have been essential reading on Coke as historian: George Garnett 'The Ould Fields'; Anthony Musson 'Myth, Mistake, Invention?'; Ian Williams 'The Tudor Genesis' and the enormous volume of works cited. JGA Pocock *The Ancient Constitution* [Pocock] uses Coke in a historiographical study.

2. COKE THE MAN

There can never have been two associated contemporaries more different in character than Coke (at first spelled Cooke and always so pronounced) and Francis Bacon, the subject of the next chapter. Coke was as brutally masculine as Bacon was effeminate. They were enemies from the start. Bacon was cleverer, the outstanding scientific thinker of his time, in some ways a better legal scholar and eventually as good an advocate at the highest level, slick where Coke was rough.[12] Bacon could think more ingeniously than perhaps anyone of his time. He was confident he could produce a digest of all of English law, no doubt on scientific principles. He offered to do one for James I. Coke was a man of action. He produced his *Institutes* and *Reports*, making up the law as he wanted it to be, laying the foundations of what is now known as the Common Law, and leaving its courts with as near to a general jurisdiction as they had until modern times.

Coke could be thoughtful and humane. He would have liked to see less hanging:[13]

> What a lamentable thing it is to see so many Christian men and women strangled on that cursed tree of the gallows, insomuch as if in a large field a man might see together all the Christians, that have but in one year, throughout England, come to that untimely and ignominious death, if there were any spark of grace or charity in him, it would make his heart to bleed for pity and compassion.

Coke was equally clear in asserting that torture was against the law of England:[14] 'There is no law to warrant tortures in this land.... And there is no one opinion in our books, or judicial record (that we have seen or remember), for the maintenance of tortures.' He knew that was just not true. He participated. Warrants for the use of torture were routinely issued under the royal prerogative. Coke and Bacon regularly signed them and they are neatly filed for our inspection in State Papers.[15] As assize judge Coke tried to check the 'extortion and oppression' of gaolers and local officers by drafting detailed directions for their fees and conduct'.[16] He was far ahead of his time in recognising the need for preventive justice, *justitia praeveniens*: 'it is better that the legal system be really preventative

---

12. As he showed in *Brereton's Case*, masterfully analysed in Barnes *Seductress* 359–382.
13. Coke *Third Institute* 244 Epilogue.
14. Coke *Third Institute* 35.
15. Bowen was prophetic; 60 years ago she wrote, 93: 'The truth is that government, unless prevented by the people at large, in all times and climes employs such methods as it finds convenient. "Cruel and unusual punishments", once used, will be used again, and, by a kind of tacit conspiracy, accepted.' One form, called in Coke's time 'Little Ease', is confinement in a box, as used in Guantanamo.
16. JS Cockburn *Western Assizes* 106 [Cockburn *Western*], though he dismisses 'as pious exaggeration the lament on executions with which Coke concludes the *Third Institute*' 131.

than that punishment be severe'. He may even have coined that phrase. He likened it to 'the rule of the physician for the safety of the body'. He thought it essential that children be educated to be law-abiding and prepared for work, which must be provided for them.

Coke had attributes that led, though only in the end, to his survival when Bacon fell. He lived within his ever-growing means. He could stick to the task, with determination and persistence: 'He was of wonderful painstaking', as John Aubrey wrote.[17]

3. COKE AND LADY HATTON

> He was a very handsome, proper man.... He married his second wife, the relict of Sir William Hatton [nephew and heir of Sir Christopher Hatton LC], who was with child when he married her: laying his hand on her belly (when he came to bed) and finding a child stir, 'What', said he, 'flesh in the pot?' 'Yes', quoth she, 'or else I would not have married a cook'.

That is Aubrey's gossip. The undisputed facts are that Elizabeth, Lady Hatton as she always insisted on being called, had preferred him to Bacon; that Coke proposed to her within a month of his beloved first wife's death and married her when she had been widowed for fifteen months, and he for only four. Moreover the ceremony, on 7 November 1598, was clandestine and illegal on three counts: no banns, not in their parish church, and at night. Everyone knew the rules. They had recently been re-established by statute. When threatened with excommunication, Coke, head bowed, told a direct lie: he did not know the law.

We may never know what was behind such an obvious stratagem. He got a young, lively, landed and noble wife, a friend of the Queen with influence at her court. What did she get? The story was she was pregnant by a servant. Coke was only 42 and tall, dark and handsome. Elizabeth was a Cecil. Her family would want to make sure she was properly looked after. They would want to avoid the slightest risk of scandal. If there was any possibility that she was pregnant, she must be married forthwith. Coke was a junior member of the Cecil party, loyal and grateful. Though not a social equal, he would just do.[18] Neither spouse ever enjoyed together the happiness they had had in their first marriages. When he broke open her bedroom drawer and stole a note for £4,000, Elizabeth left the matrimonial home and went to live with her father, the Earl of Exeter.[19] To the end of his life Coke never gave up his quest for his wife's land. Of course, by

17. Richard Barber ed *John Aubrey* [Barber *Aubrey*] 83–84.
18. Boyer *Coke* 216, citing AGR Smith *Servant of the Cecils* 74; FJ Fisher ed 'The State of England' 25.
19. *Calendar of State Papers Domestic* [*SPD*] *1634–1635* 405 'The Proceedings Betweene the Lady Hatton and Sir Edw Coke Attorney Generall to Queene Eliza': reprinted in Laura Norsworthy *The Lady of Bleeding Heart Yard* 275–278.

Coke's Common Law, a husband could not steal from his wife, though he could from her trustees. Later there were stories of domestic abuse, of both his wife and their fourteen-year-old daughter, Frances, whom he is said to have beaten until she agreed to marry Buckingham's older brother, who was in the euphemism of the time 'an amiable lunatic'.[20]

A woman with a mind of her own, neither prepared to hand over meekly what she knew was hers nor to wheedle for what she wanted, Lady Hatton was considered then, as some describe her still, as 'strong-willed, hot-tempered, emotive and articulate' or even 'a harridan... given to histrionics and vile temper tantrums'.[21] Would 'determined, passionate, clever and no pushover' do as well? Wife and daughter outlived Coke, mostly apart from him; he failed to spoil all their fun.

4. THE EARLY CAREER

In a private letter to Salisbury in 1608, Ellesmere LC, who knew him well but was rarely on his side, called Coke 'a foolish and frantic fellow... turbulently and idly broken-brained'.[22] He was notoriously violent in speech, though he suffered from the bully's weakness when threatened. He often wept,[23] and, in his own words, when the Queen took him to task in 1592:[24]

> My heart shaked within my body and all the parts of my body trembled so as I could neither mark the conclusion of her speech nor make any answer at all, nor until mine eyes gushed out with tears could be reduced to perfect memory.

Then she made him Solicitor General.[25]

Elizabeth preferred Coke, whom she trusted, to Bacon, whom she did not. Besides, Essex's persistent pleading for Bacon's advancement irritated her. So, when she had the chance, after playing with Essex for some months, she appointed Coke Attorney General on 10 April 1594. Bacon was petulant; his abject attempts to get second-best, Solicitor General, did not persuade the Queen, despite his gift of a jewel. She told

---

20. AD Boyer in the *ODNB* says: 'Little evidence supports the darker allegation that he tied Frances to the bedposts and whipped her until she agreed to the marriage'. So it would perhaps be safer to rely on what the Privy Council accepted as evidence of his violent behaviour, particularly in its letter to Coke of 11 July 1617 *APC* 35.297 below.
21. Boyer *Coke* 213; TG Barnes 'Introduction to Coke's Commentary on Littleton' [Barnes *Coke*] 9.
22. Boyer *Coke* citing BL Lansdowne MS 91.
23. He was overcome and burst into tears when prosecuting the poisoner Edward Squire, Boyer *Coke* 260.
24. JH Baker *The Legal Profession and the Common Law* 203.
25. Or perhaps he wept with gratitude, Baker *Coke* 384 and fn144, citing Coke's Notebooks MS C folios 86–87v.

the importunate Essex she would 'seek all England for a Solicitor before she would take Francis Bacon'. Coke did both jobs for more than a year.

Coke prosecuted in some famous political trials. From the first he showed his methods as a prosecutor and his amenability to political direction. Dr Rodrigo Lopez, the Queen's physician, was originally a Portuguese Jew but had converted to Christianity.[26] Coke, as Solicitor General, with Egerton leading him as Attorney General, reported that 'Lopez, a perjured murdering traitor, and Jewish doctor, worse than Judas himself, undertook to poison her'. He described in detail the physical realities of hanging, drawing and quartering. The Court might well ask why further torments could not be devised. Coke explained that such restraint was the King's own merciful wish.

Essex was one of the special commission at the Guildhall which made sure Lopez was convicted on 14 March 1594.[27] In Essex's own trial on 25 February 1602, on the other hand, Coke's prosecution, though comprehensive, was mostly measured.[28]

In November 1603, the new court moved to Winchester to avoid the plague. There Coke prosecuted Sir Walter Raleigh on a charge of treason, for plotting to kill the King, famously shouting: 'Thou art a monster! Thou hast an English face and a Spanish heart.... Thou viper.... There has never lived a viler viper on the face of the earth.' As Coke well knew, no man in England had proved himself a more determined enemy of Spain than Raleigh. Coke's bombast compared badly with Raleigh's composure and superiority in argument but all to no avail. This was a show trial. The jury quickly convicted. Raleigh was sentenced to be hanged but reprieved. All just before the end of 1603, the first year of the new king, in which about one in six Londoners had died of the plague.

The last great political trial in which Coke prosecuted was of those in the Gunpowder Plot and the Jesuits and other Catholics it implicated.[29] Coke had no need to convince jury or judges. Conviction was inevitable and could have been achieved by a fair prosecution. But Coke knew that his job was propaganda. There had been suggestions in Parliament that

---

26. The fullest record is 'narrative compiled by William Waad, Clerk to the Privy Council' BL Yelverton Mss, Additional Mss 48000–48196; entry no 48029 (Yelverton 33) 5 p117 f147; also *SPD* 12.247.102 and 166ff.

27. AG 10 April 1594 *SPD* 247.101. Coke's own rough notes, referring to 'Dr Roger Lopez, a Portuguese Jew' are at *SPD* 248.27. The phrase has also been attributed to Egerton [Boyer *Coke* 248 fn11]. There were few in England then whose attitude to Jews was not determined by the Church's preaching, that all Jews were children of the killers of Christ. Coke's slant is best shown in his ms notebook account, Harleian ms 6686 (MS C fol 82v–85v. *SPD* 12.248.26I. Boyer *Coke* 249 suggests that Essex did a deal with Cecil: his support for Coke as AG in return for Cecil agreeing to Lopez's conviction.

28. Bowen's description in her Chapter 12 is a masterpiece.

29. Bowen 257.

new and terrible punishments were needed. Coke explained that the King, 'with admirable clemency and moderation', would abide by the usual method of execution. He then described it at length in careful hideous detail, justifying each precise step.[30]

5. COKE THE HISTORIAN?

> That which I have written (as you know learned reader) in some of my former prefaces of the antiquity and excellency of our laws of England hath produced these two questions: first, whether historiographers do concur with that which there so constantly hath been affirmed? Secondly... what the body or text of the common law is? ... For the first... the books and records... are of that authority they need not the aid of any historian.[31]

Much of Coke's great archive of books and papers has survived. Recent exemplary scholarship has studied it exhaustively, not only in the family home at Holkham but dispersed in libraries in England and the United States. Some scholars have been concerned to show how bad a historian Coke was, others to rescue his reputation. But Coke was not a historian at all. He should not be judged as such. It is not that to do so would be anachronistic; there were plenty of historians then, John Selden was one, who applied recognisably modern standards to their work. Contemporaries did not account his scholarship highly. John Aubrey wrote that he was 'wonderful painstaking' but:[32] 'When the play called *Ignoramus* was acted with great applause before King James, they dressed Sir Ignoramus like Chief Justice Coke and cut his beard like him and feigned his voice'. Hobbes pointed out a specific, typical and devastating error. Coke had written that the book known as *Modus Tenendi Parliamentum* was written in the time of the Saxons, before the Conquest:[33]

> Mr Selden, a greater antiquary than Sir Edward Coke, in the last edition of his book of *Titles of Honour*, says that that book called *The Mode of Holding Parliaments* was not written till about the time of Richard II, and seems to me to prove it.

William Prynne, the Puritan zealot and Bencher of Lincoln's Inn, accused Coke of 'invisible misreported evidences', calling him: 'a better lawyer than antiquary, historian, or record man'.[34] But Coke's reputation among

---

30. There are historians who seek the comfort of relativism against the demands of morality and allow the public castration and disembowelment of political prisoners as no more than the custom of the times; even 'intellectual honesty' is relative for some: TFT Plucknett '*Bonham's Case*' [Plucknett] 150–185, 151: 'It is only by the standard of his own day that a true evaluation of his intellectual honesty can be formed'.
31. 8 Coke Rep 1.
32. Barber *Aubrey* 83–84.
33. Hobbes 167.
34. William Prynne *The First Part of a Brief Register* 554, 553.

lawyers has prevailed because he did not have to meet his critics on their terms. He relied on what he called authority, not historical evidence. In Coke's day it was a practice to quote maxims. For unthinking lawyers they encapsulated the law and substituted comfortable tradition for thought. The Latin gave them some standing. Coke just made them up as he required. His habit was, as Hobbes charged him:[35]

> to insinuate his own opinions among the people for the law of the land; for that also he endeavours by inserting Latin sentences, both in his text and in the margin, as if they were principles of the law of reason, without any authority of ancient lawyers, or any certainty of reason.

A modern scholar, eulogising Coke on his 500th birthday, at a dinner in Coke's own Inn, and trying to be kind, had to say:[36]

> As a rule of thumb it is well to remember that sentences beginning 'For it is an ancient maxim of the common law', followed by one of Coke's spurious Latin maxims... are apt to produce a new departure.... The longer the list of authorities reconciled, the greater the divergence from the cases cited.

Coke knew full well that what he said about the date of Domesday Book could not be true.[37] His dishonesty as a historian was matched by his deceitfulness as a lawyer. He must have known that a writ he cited could not have been of the date he relied on, so, finding a convenient gap in the text, he stuck in the date that suited his purpose.[38] That was more than ordinary chicanery. If he had been prosecuting himself, he would have made the capital charge of forgery stick.

Coke believed that the Common Law was what was best for everybody:[39] 'There is no knowledge of any laws (I speak of human) so necessary for all estates, and for all causes, concerning goods, land, or life, as the common laws of England.' But no new stuff:[40]

> *Quod novum judicium non dat jus novum, sed declarat antiquum, judicium est juris dictum, & per judicium jus est noviter revelatum quod diu fuit velatum* [That a new judgment does not give new law, but declares the old; a judgment is a statement of the law, and through a judgment law which had been hidden for a long time is newly revealed]. And it is true that the law sometimes sleeps and judgment wakens it.

35. Hobbes 96.
36. SE Thorne 'Sir Edward Coke' 7; Boyer *Royal* 5; and B Sharp and MC Fissel eds *Law and Authority* 64–76.
37. Boyer *Coke* 136–140 is enlightening on his shortcomings, though kind to Coke, calling his purposeful mendacity 'negligence' 139.
38. GO Sayles ed *Select Cases* lxiv–lxv.
39. 2 Co Rep vi.
40. 10 Co Rep 42a.

That really says it all. If you want to invent new law to produce the result you require in any case, pretend it has been the law all the time! If you can convince the court, you get away with it and your case becomes authority. What Coke wanted was to place the Common Law at the centre of an orderly legal system, with the Common Law courts in charge, courts of as general a jurisdiction as was practicable.[41]

Coke's first task was to confuse two meanings of 'common law'. Used here with capitals, the Common Law is what the Common Law courts administer. Coke had to spread that to comprehend the whole of the English legal system. Only then could he accomplish the takeover which was his single aim. Then he could make, or make up, all the rules. They could be found in his own *Reports*, or what he said the Druids had proclaimed in Greek. The simple fact is that Coke was working in the only way he knew, as a lawyer. He did what lawyers do, marshalling every bit of evidence and exploiting every argument which might support his case, with no thought of scholarly objectivity. But he went further, suppressing any evidence, argument or authority which was against him. I can find not one instance of him revealing an authority which went against him. What he wanted was authority, not historical evidence. Nothing could be a more satisfactory authority for the date of the Domesday Book than the aside of a judge reported in a 14th-century Year Book. Even the kindly Maitland wrote: 'it would be long to tell how much harm was thus done to the sober study of English legal history'.[42]

6.   CHIEF JUSTICE COKE

On 30 June 1606 Coke was appointed CJCP. At 52 he was physically and mentally strong. He could shout anyone down. Secure in the Cecil party, he was trusted by the King, who owed him much. Coke's transformation was noted later, in 1683:[43]

> It is a wonder that Sir Edward Coke, Lord Chief Justice, should differ from Mr Attorney Cook, for we know his thoughts in Sir Walter Raleigh's time and his speeches in Charles I's time; they are as different from each other as the times were, and in this particular that gentleman hath had more followers than precedents; but the query is: 'What is law?'

For Coke the answer was simple: 'law' meant the Common Law, the law dispensed in the Common Law courts, by a privileged and exclusive community of Common Lawyers. It encompassed the whole of the law

---

41. WJ Jones 'The Crown and the Courts' 286.
42. Introduction to WJ Whittaker ed *The Mirror of Justices* ix–x.
43. Bowen 293 quoting Sir Bartholomew Shower, Recorder of London, 1683 *State Trials* IX 273.

of old England. That was a novel notion, which Coke took great pains to pretend was old.

The great point at issue came to be whether the King was above the law, or, put another way, whether the law was what the King said it was. Coke knew what the English Common Law was. Only he could know, because he was making it up as he went along.[44] 'The King is under God and the law', in Coke's terms meant 'the law as I propound it'. As Hobbes wrote:[45]

> He did it on purpose to diminish the King's Authority, or to insinuate his own opinions among the People for the Law of the Land: for that he also endeavours by Inserting *Latin* Sentences, both in his Text, and in the Margin, as if they were Principles of the Law of Reason, without any Authoritie of Ancient Lawyers, or any certainty of Reason in themselves, to make Men believe they are the very grounds of the Law of *England*.

And he has got away with that, because what the times needed, and what has since been cherished, was: King under Parliament. But Coke wanted more than that: Parliament too under his Common Law. If it was the Common Law which gave the King divine power, accountable to none, it was just a matter of whose job it was to say what that law was.

Coke did not deny the royal prerogative when it suited him. He was clear that the King had prerogative power to imprison without trial, against which *habeas corpus* could not stand.[46] Nor was it Parliament's authority that Coke set up against the King's. Coke wrote to James I: 'Acts of Parliament are to be interpreted by the judges of the laws of England... this is expressly proved by many authorities and judgments reported in our books of law'. And then, in *Bonham's Case*, he made his claim even clearer:[47]

> In many cases the Common Law will control Acts of Parliament and sometimes adjudge them to be utterly void; for when an Act of Parliament is against common right and reason, or repugnant, or impossible to be performed, the Common Law will control it and adjudge such Act to be void.

That is from Coke's own report. Who could know better than he what was 'against common right and reason'? So controversies should be appeased if possible, by the application of the judges' artificial reason, with due regard to justice and expediency – consideration of the commonwealth.[48] Yet only Coke could have transformed those generalities into a weapon.

---

44. *Pace* Barnes *Coke* 23: 'The process in his mind was a matter of discovery, not fabrication'.
45. Hobbes 96.
46. *The Brewers' Case* (1615) 1 Rolle 134; 81 ER 382; *Salkingstowe's Case* (1615) 1 Rolle 219; 81 ER 444; Dawson *II* 641.
47. *Bonham's Case* Co Rep 8 107.
48. Co Litt 97b; Boyer *Coke* 88; Abraham Fraunce *The Lawiers Logike*.

First he had to establish that the law was what the judges said it was; then he had to fake it.

7. THE FIRST FALL

Coke fell on 26 June 1616. The King was present at the meeting of the Council:[49]

> The Lord Chief Justice, presenting himself on his knee at the Board, your Solicitor signified: that he was by your commandment to charge him for certain acts and speeches, wherein Your Majesty was much dissatisfied:
> 1. First an act done.
> 2. Secondly, speeches of high contempt uttered in a seat of justice.
> 3. Thirdly, uncomely and undutiful carriage in the presence of Your Majesty, your Privy Council, and your judges.

The act related to a debt of Sir Christopher Hatton, late Lord Chancellor, the uncle of Lady Hatton's first husband. Coke had told lies, denying his involvement in it, though the bond turned out to be partly in Coke's hand. The contempt arose from Coke as Chief Justice bullying a jury, threatening to commit them unless they found his way, and warning counsel that he would bar them from his court unless they did as he told them.[50] The third was most serious. In the King's presence, Coke had taken exception to 'your learned counsel in your presence for speaking by your commandment'; and in 1616 he had been the only judge to dissent from the otherwise unanimous opinion of his brethren in the *Case of Commendams* that the King might insist on being consulted before any court could pass judgment.

Coke dealt with the last point first, acknowledged 'for an error' the exception he took to the King's counsel, and said that he had insisted on delaying dealing with the *Commendams* point until it arose only because it had presented 'a multitude of questions, suddenly occurring to his mind'. As for the bond, it was twelve years ago and it had slipped his memory. After all, he had been much distracted by his services to the Crown in treason cases. And he had got nothing out of it – 'all the rest was his wife's'. He had indeed said there was a danger that the Common Law would be overthrown by Equity, 'and the light of the law be obscured', but he would not maintain the disagreement between the two courts, nor bring it into question, and, in any case, 'if it were an error', there was plenty of precedent. He said nothing to excuse his domineering of counsel and jurors.

---

49. *APC* 34.644; for Caesar's account Roland Usher, 'James I and Sir Edward Coke' 75.
50. JH Baker 'The Common Lawyers and the Chancery' [Baker *Chancery*] 266–268.

The report to the King ended: 'before us, as well in speech as in action, he behaved himself very modestly and submissively'. But Coke was brought back the following Sunday, on his knees, 'His Majesty was... in no way satisfied with his answers to any of the points':

> Nevertheless, such is His Majesty's clemency and goodness, as he is pleased not to proceed heavily against him, but rather to look upon the merit of his former services; and accordingly hath decreed:
>
> First: that he be sequestered from the Council Table, until His Majesty's pleasure be further known;
>
> Secondly: that he do forbear to ride this summer's circuit as Justice of Assize;
>
> Lastly: that during this vacation, while he hath time to live privately and dispose himself at home, he take into consideration and review his books of Reports, wherein (as His Majesty is informed) there be many exorbitant and extravagant opinions set down and published for good law.... Having corrected what in his discretion he found meet in those Reports, His Majesty's pleasure was that he should bring the same privately to himself, that he might consider thereof, as in his princely judgment should be found expedient.

'Expedient' – not 'accurate'. Two could play at making up the law, and the King would always win. Coke 'did in all humility prostrate himself to His Majesty's good pleasure, acknowledged the decree to be just and proceeded from His Majesty's exceeding mercy, than from his justice'. In March 1617 Bacon was made Lord Keeper and James I set off on his first return to Scotland, leaving Bacon effectively in charge and Coke in the doldrums.

8.　AMENDING THE REPORTS

JH Baker's assessment is based on a comprehensive and careful study of every available piece of evidence: 'It is unnecessary to sing the praises of Coke's *Reports* as sources of law and history. For all their quaint defects, they "will last while Fame hath a trumpet"'.[51] After more than forty years, that is still the prevailing view. Because mine is different, I must set out the evidence against, even though in a study of dispute resolution, and Coke as an arbitrator, any extended offering to the debate may well seem as irrelevant as it is presumptuous. As Hobbes said, Coke never reported the cases he lost:[52] 'Who can tell but there may have been given other judgments, in such cases, which have either been not preserved in the records, or else by Sir Edward Coke, because they were against his opinion, not alleged?' And, as even Plucknett conceded:[53] 'In at least one

---

51. Baker *Coke* 357; Baker's description of the discovery of Coke's own notebooks and other mss and how he has used them is fascinating.
52. His younger contemporary Croke did report some, a dozen cited in Boyer *Coke* 52 fn49.
53. Plucknett 168 fn57, citing JW Wallace *The Reporters* 174.

case Coke has been found guilty of reporting exactly the opposite of the actual decision'. He did report cases found nowhere else. Some of the fundamental rules of the Common Law were laid down by Coke himself, free of any judicial cooperation; for example the Rule in *Shelley's Case*, his earliest report:[54] the words 'to A for life, remainder to his heirs' give A a fee simple, with nothing to the heirs. That was not new, but became the sole and only necessary authority until modern times. Anderson's report, complaining that Coke had made it up, was ignored.[55]

What did James I want Coke to do to get rid of the errors in his *Reports*? He had reported more than 500 cases. They had been cited as law for years. On 2 October 1616 he handed his proposed amendments to a committee of Ellesmere, Bacon, Yelverton and Montague, a little list of but five trivial errors, with nothing about any of the fabrications on which he based his great political claims for the ascendancy of the Common Law. The King sought advice on how he should respond. Typically, Bacon preferred a crafty to a bold destruction:[56]

> To give every man his due, had it not been for Sir Edward Coke's *Reports* (which, though they may have errors and some peremptory and extrajudicial resolutions more than are warranted, yet they contain infinite good decisions and rulings over of cases) the law by this time had been almost like a ship without ballast.

But Bacon himself drafted the detailed charges and even the discharge by which Coke would be dismissed as Chief Justice, and the warrant appointing his successor with the name left blank.[57] On 16 November 1616 Coke was dismissed.

9. COKE AS A PARTY[58]

By the beginning of 1617 all had changed. The King had returned from Scotland. Bacon was no longer in charge. He had backed the wrong side in the wrangle about Frances Coke's marriage, putting too much trust in his friendship with Buckingham. When it suited him, Buckingham intended to take fourteen-year-old Frances and marry her to his simple-minded reprobate older brother, Sir John Villiers, against her wishes and those of

54. (1580) 1 Co Rep 93b.
55. (1580) 1 Anderson 81: '*rien de ceo fuit parle en le Court* [no such thing was said in Court]'; Baker *Coke* 370.
56. Bowen 382; from John Spedding ed *Letters* VI 65 and V 86 'too much *de proprio*'; V 399 'many exorbitant and extravagant opinions'; VI 87 'scattering and sowing his own conceits'. Baker *Coke* 369 and fn62.
57. Bowen 385–388.
58. Other examples are in Chapter 11 above, e.g. a letter of 2 March 1603 from Henry Warner, a friend of both sides, asked Sir Miles Corbett to arbitrate in a land dispute between Coke, then Attorney General, and Edward Paston (Morgan et al *Nat Bacon* V 11–12).

her mother and Bacon, who had been supporting her. Bacon soon saw he must capitulate, which he did with his usual self-abasement.

Coke was back in the Privy Council. His attempts to get his wife's land had got him into trouble with the Council, which did its best to reconcile them. On 25 June 1617 Lord Carew, Chancellor of the Exchequer Fulke Greville, Attorney General Yelverton and John Walter, attorney to Prince Charles, successfully mediated a settlement, set out in great detail.[59] And there was an arbitration clause:[60]

> In case any difference or question should yet in the meantime or hereafter arise betwixt Edward Coke and Lady Elizabeth concerning their private estate, which we hope shall never be, the Lord Keeper... hath assumed the same into his care, and will do that which belongeth unto him for accommodating all such differences, with the assistance of some one or two besides of this Table, such as his Lordship shall think good.

A week later, on 18 July 1617, the Council received a petition alleging that Coke had gone back on his undertaking to submit to arbitration the dispute about Hatton House and other property. It ordered him to convey the disputed properties forthwith or stand to Bacon's arbitration, 'with expedition'.[61] But on 13 August Coke was still prevaricating.[62] He was told to complete his examination of witnesses so that the matter could be disposed of within two months. On 17 October 1617 Coke complained to the Council that he had executed all the necessary conveyances to dispose of his differences with his wife but her trustees had failed to execute the counterparts.[63] Coke himself was one of the Council which ordered them to do so. But before this an even greater dispute had arisen and been settled. On 11 July 1617 the Council had written to Coke:[64]

> Whereas complaint hath been made unto us by your wife that her youngest daughter being gone a little into the country to take the air for a day or two, you followed after and with great violence brake open the doors, dragged out your daughter with such violence and fury she is fallen desperately sick. In regard whereof she humbly prayeth she may be presently brought to London, where she may have the help of physic for the recovery of her health.... This cause is appointed to be heard and examined by this Board on Tuesday next in the afternoon where we require you to be present.... deliver the person of your daughter to this bearer, the Clerk of the Council, to be kept in his house until the cause be heard.

59. *APC* 35.270 (wrongly dated 1716).
60. *APC* 35.274.
61. *APC* 35.309.
62. *APC* 35.322.
63. *APC* 35.348.
64. *APC* 35.296–297.

On Sunday 13 July the Council received another petition from Lady Hatton, 'complaining in somewhat a passionate and tragical manner'.[65] She repeated that Coke, with his son 'fighting Clem' and '10 or 11 servants weaponed in violent manner', had dragged off Frances, who was now so ill she could die. She must be brought to London at once, so that she could have the nursing and medicine she needed. The Council wrote to Coke, instructing him to hand Frances over to the Clerk of the Council. Coke simply refused. It was late and Frances was not 'in such extremity'. He would deliver her the next morning, which he did.

The Council heard the matter the following Tuesday. Coke's counsel alleged that Lady Hatton intended to smuggle Frances off to France. The Council unanimously considered Sir John a worthy match, but that it should be left to him to make the proper approaches, 'without any forced consent of the maid'. Coke must substantiate his allegation that Lady Hatton intended to carry Frances off to France; and he must answer the charge of riot. Coke had no evidence to support his allegation, nor any defence against the charge. Therefore:

> Order was given that the Attorney General should prefer an information into the court of Star Chamber against Sir Edward Coke for the force and riot.... And we enjoined Sir Edward Coke and his lady... to forbear all occasion of violence.

On 18 July 1617 the parties accepted the mediation of Sir Henry Yelverton, newly appointed Attorney General:[66]

> But now since this matter seemeth to have had a fairer conclusion, for that we find that the writings are perfected, and not only so but the parties Sir Edward Coke and his lady reconciled, and their daughter with both their good likings sent to live with her father and mother in Sir Edward Coke's house. Which good end hath been much furthered by the charitable endeavour of His Majesty's Attorney General. And the information and all other proceedings in the business is suspended and left wholly to His Majesty's pleasure.

Coke had managed to get Frances to write for him a letter, declaring that she was happy with the marriage, which was celebrated on 29 September 1617.

Coke was reappointed to the Privy Council the following Sunday. From then on he took his place as a judge in Star Chamber and 'showed himself more royalist than the king in the major state trials that took place in Star Chamber from 1617 to 1619. That the trials enabled him to settle some old scores with old adversaries added to the pleasure'.[67]

65. *APC* 35.315.
66. Daphne Du Maurier *Winding Stair* 107.
67. Barnes *Seductress* 380–381.

10.   COKE AS ARBITRATOR[68]

Every man of substance in his community (and occasionally a woman) could expect to be asked to help in the disputes of others. The judges and law officers were always in demand and Coke was often called on.[69] Sometimes he and Bacon were jointly appointed.[70] Chapter 11 provided ample evidence of his full involvement as arbitrator and party, as well regular appointer. During the period for which there are no Privy Council records, documents preserved in a manuscript in the British Library provide examples of Coke's work as arbitrator.[71]

From 12 May 1603 until June 1616 the Masters of Requests recorded actions they took in response to petitions. Many entries are brief notices of arbitrations, with no detail. Just one early example, folio 25 from 1603, can stand for hundreds. The petition of a widow, Joanne Moore, was sent to Attorney General Coke with instructions 'calling to himself one of quality and indifference to order or certify'. Many ask the arbitrators to supervise a composition with creditors.[72] The numbers are large: for one year May 1603 to May 1604 'of 416 cases of all types referred to arbitrators, 67 involved arbitrations with creditors'. For 1612–1614, of 282 references to arbitrators, 129 were for compositions with creditors. The words used for the process of mediation were: 'for toleration… a charitable composition'. The Masters of Requests commissioned Coke no less than ten times between 1603 and 1615.[73] When in June 1614 some of the creditors ignored the composition arranged by the arbitrators, James I instructed Coke CJKB to punish the offenders, if he found they had 'contemptuously disobeyed' the order.[74]

Chancery and King's Bench referred disputes to Coke not only for his opinion but also for him to dispose of by arbitration.[75] A badly damaged deed in the National Archives records Coke's award in a dispute about the lease of the manor of Nether Eatington.[76] Coke awarded that the lease was

---

68. As usual, the best entry is through JP Dawson 'The Privy Council and Private Law' [Dawson *I*] and [Dawson *II*]; also the many examples in Chapter 11.
69. *APC* 33.550 re a warren, to mediate or make order for peace until the trial; Coke had often been appointed in the time of Elizabeth I, e.g. Nat Arch C 78/103/14 (1602).
70. *APC* 33.563 on Sunday 25 September 1614. There are other examples of their joint appointment, e.g. in 1600 to advise on the problem of Common Law prohibitions against the Court of Admiralty, *APC* 30.43.
71. B Mus Lansdowne ms [Lansdowne] 266/1; Dawson *II* 630 fn127, 632 fn129, 633 fn135.
72. Dawson *II* 631 fn128.
73. Dawson *II* 633 fn135; Lansdowne folios 8a (1603), 25b (1603), 54b (1605), 80a (1607), 153a (1611) two cases, 211a (1612), 238a (1613), 252a (1614), 271b (1615).
74. Dawson *II* 634 fn138; Lansdowne fol 262b.
75. Smith 219 fnn37, 38, 39; *Sayre v Pomerye* (1611) C33/121 ff832v–833r; *Aikson? v Turner and Barwicke* C33/121 ff1,025r-1,026r; *Hendon v Godsall* (1611) C33/121 f1,045r.
76. Nat Arch WARD 2/62/241/138.

valid but raised the rent from 40 to 100 marks a year. He could hardly have done that if the matter had come before him as a Common Law judge. Coke expressed his preference for a mediated settlement 'that no spark or shadow of contention or unkindness may remain':[77] 'Coke intervened in a case between his servant and his servant's brother-in-law, warning that they would consume their estates, and urged them to arbitration'.

Chapter 7 gave examples of Coke's work as an arbitrator regularly appointed to handle commercial disputes, in 1614 between apothecaries, physicians and grocers in London; in 1616 and again in 1618 between the Pinmakers and Haberdashers Companies. On Sunday 2 June 1616 the Council asked Coke and others to hear what the clothiers had to say in response to complaints from woolgrowers from all parts of England and report by the end of the week. It seems from the evidence that there was no man in England more familiar with arbitration or happy to be a part of it. Nowhere in all this mass of evidence is there any indication that Coke's approach to mediation and arbitration was ever anything short of positive.

11. CONCLUSIONS

Coke had attributes that led, though only in the end, to his survival when Bacon fell. He lived within his ever-growing means. He could stick to the task, with determination and persistence. He lived to be eighty-two, in good health and disdaining medical attention. This prescription was found in his hand in the margin of his own copy of the *Reports*:

> If physic fail
> And naught avail
> Three doctors you should find:
> Doctor Good-Diet
> And Doctor Quiet
> And Doctor Merrymind.

Coke spent the later years of his career in Parliament. Charles I came to the throne in 1625 and thereafter Coke's struggle for Parliamentary sovereignty and his part in the Petition of Right have been well chronicled.[78] His last years he spent in Stoke Poges, working mainly on his *Institutes*. Charles I was suspicious of what he was up to. In April 1632 his papers were seized. Then his chambers in the Inner Temple were sealed. As he lay dying, after scarcely a day's illness in his life, he suffered the indignity and sadness of knowing his precious books and papers were being ransacked by the unsophisticated hands of the security forces.

77. Smith 24; fn 29 BL Add MS 12507 f67r.
78. Stephen Sedley has written best on this, e.g. his insights in *Lions Under the Throne* 183–189.

Whatever else can be said against Coke, he cannot be accused of ambivalence in his support of arbitration and mediation. *Berry v Perry*[79] will be considered in detail in Chapter 18; here it is enough to quote from his concluding encomium as CJKB, where he exhibited his weaknesses – for made-up maxims and faulty history – but his clear commitment to arbitration:

> The reason why awards are to be favoured: *Quia expedit reipublicæ, ut sit finis litium* [because it is for the country's good that there should be an end of litigation]... the day of an award is called the day of Love... *Ecce quam bonum et quam jucundum est habitare fratres in unum* [see how good and pleasing it is for brothers to live as one].

79. (1614) 3 Bulst 67; 81 ER 59.

13   FRANCIS BACON

Hail, happy genius of this ancient pile!
How comes it all things so about thee smile?
The fire, the wine, the men! And in the midst,
Thou stand'st as if some mystery thou did'st....
England's high Chancellor: the destined heir
In his soft cradle to his father's chair,
Whose even thread the Fates spin round and full,
Out of their choicest and their whitest wool.

Ben Jonson 1621[1]

A base spirit is ever most concomitant with the proudest mind, and surely never
so many parts, and so base and abject a spirit, tenanted together in any one
earthen cottage, as in this one man.

[Sir Anthony Weldon?] 1650[2]

All that were great and good loved him.

John Aubrey c1680[3]

1.   INTRODUCTION

Francis Bacon was no ordinary arbitrator. His work, and with it his
reputation, have been the subject of a literature even more voluminous
than his own writings. Much of it is partisan.[4] Yet nobody denies he was
the towering intellectual figure in the England of his time. He may well
have been the cleverest man ever to have been an arbitrator in England.
His own writings show his outstanding intellect: scholar, scientist,
philosopher, lawyer, judge and statesman.[5] He saw first and more clearly

1. Ben Jonson 'Ode on Lord Bacon's Birthday' in CH Herford et al eds *Ben Jonson* VIII
   436–438.
2. Sir AW *The Court and Character of King James*.
3. Richard Barber ed *John Aubrey* [Barber *Aubrey*] 35.
4. Too much to list here but Lisa Jardine and Alan Stewart *Hostage to Fortune* [Jardine
   Hostage] and DR Coquillette *Francis Bacon* [Coquillette] are fair, comprehensive and
   complementary. For the prosecution: the letters of his contemporary Simonds D'Ewes in
   John Halliwell ed *The Autobiography*; Lord Macaulay *Lord Bacon*; for the defence James
   Spedding *Evenings*; Nieves Mathews *Francis Bacon* [Mathews]; Daphne Du Maurier *The
   Winding Stair* [Du Maurier *Winding Stair*].
5. The standard edition has been James Spedding *The Works* [Spedding]. The Oxford Bacon
   project, with the School of Advanced Studies, University of London (1996 ongoing), will
   produce a new 15-volume edition to be published by OUP.

277

that, if knowledge is to be of any use, it must rest on untrammelled enquiry and experiment, rather than contemplation; *justificata est sapientia a filiis suis*, 'you must test knowledge by its results', was the slogan he adopted. And he put his ideas into practice. His insights are many, original and essential. How prophetic he was to recognise that responsibility dissipates when passed to a committee: 'which cannot possibly be done by a commission, where the care lies not principally upon one or two men'. And he argued the values of almond milk long before its present fad. Some of his sentences have caused many since to stop and think. Who could have better said: '"What is truth?", said jesting Pilate; and would not wait for an answer'. And 'hope is a good breakfast but an ill supper'. Or put more simply: 'Men fear death, as children fear to go in the dark.... It is as natural to die as to be born.' In a work on dispute resolution, every effort will be made to stick to the facts as found in the primary sources, but the arbitrator cannot be separated from the man.

2. BACON THE MAN

Throughout his life (1561–1626), Bacon was forever starting new projects without completing the ambitious ones his fecund brain had meticulously planned. When pressed, he sought refuge in ill health, which cannot have been helped by his appetite not only for purgatives but for opiates. He was always short of money, even when his income was enormous. His father died without providing for him and he was egregiously extravagant, especially on clothes for himself and his large retinue. He was never out of debt from youth to death. He spent much energy and time begging to pay his debts, repeatedly solemnly binding himself to loans which he knew he had no hope of repaying as they fell due. He was paid huge sums to bring about the downfall of his friends, and then to write up the results in propaganda pamphlets for royal use: £1,200 for that on his benefactor Essex. But it was never enough. He complained that 'The Queen hath done somewhat for me but not in the proportion I had hoped'.

He took advantage of arbitration to arrange the compromise of his own debts. In August 1600 he had mortgaged Twickenham Park to Nicholas Trott, a regular lender, for £950. When repayment fell due, he unusually had some cash, whatever was left of the £1,200 from the Queen, and some assets from his brother Anthony, who had just died.[6] The arbitrator, Lord Treasurer Buckhurst, employing his own auditor, fixed the amount and allowed time to pay.

All his life he fawned and flattered anyone, however despicable, whom he thought might help his advancement, offering, when a judge, to favour their causes. Buckingham in particular took full advantage of Bacon's

6. Jardine *Hostage* 258.

willingness as Chancery judge to find in favour of his friends.[7] Yet he was never short of contemporary and later supporters. John Aubrey sought to be fair: 'He was a paederast. His Ganymedes and favourites took bribes: but his lordship always gave judgement *secundum aequum et bonum* 'according to what was fair and good'.[8] But he was not above chicanery, for example suggesting to Egerton that by simply adding an intermediary he could disguise his own interest in a case in which he was judge.[9]

At the age of forty-two Bacon was still unmarried. He had tried once, but had lost Lady Hatton to his enemy Edward Coke. In 1603 he wrote to his cousin, then Sir Robert Cecil, later Lord Burghley, that he had cast his eye over the four daughters of the late Alderman Barnham, each of whom would receive on marriage £6,000 and £300 a year. He fancied Alice, 'an handsome maiden, to my liking'. She was just eleven. He married her when she was thirteen and they lived unhappily, mostly apart, until his death. They had no children. In his will he first provided for her and then changed his mind, grandiloquently leaving her nothing. He had nothing to leave, his executors not daring to prove his will and undertake the task of satisfying his great debts. Within days of his death she married their steward.[10]

3.   RISE TO POWER

Elizabeth I was wary of Bacon.[11] Though his father had been her Lord Keeper, as he often reminded her, and he had many influential relatives at court, including his cousin Burghley, whose support he often sought, she refused all his entreaties to secure any office.[12] Bacon was gay,[13] and she preferred the men about her to be straight. She would not even knight him, which must have been a snub which everyone recognised. Moreover, he committed the scarcely credible blunder of opposing her wishes in Parliament over the triple subsidy she was seeking.

7. Jardine *Hostage* 413–414 gives ample details.
8. Barber *Aubrey* 38. And a later anonymous attempt: A True-Born Englishman *Francis, Lord Bacon* 1721.
9. Jardine *Hostage* 191–194.
10. Bacon's supporters find little to admire in Alice. Nieves Mathews mentions her just once, 309: 'There is no evidence that Bacon was a practising homosexual.... But the portrait of Alice Bacon shows a hard face and she was said to have a sharp tongue'.
11. And of his 'pretty' brother Anthony, Essex's spymaster: Daphne Du Maurier *Golden Lads*.
12. His mother, Lady Anne Bacon, was a woman of piety and power. On 6 February 1567 Matthew Parker, Archbishop of Canterbury, asked her to mediate in his dispute with her husband, Jardine *Hostage* 32; John Bruce and TT Perowne *The Correspondence of Matthew Parker* 316.
13. The primary sources cited in Jardine *Hostage* are surprisingly full and frank, eg 162. There is no suggestion that all his young amanuenses were gay, e.g. Thomas Hobbes, Jardine *Hostage* 477.

Everything changed with the accession of James I: *La Reine Jacquette* for *Le Roi Elizabeth*. Bacon played up to the King's homosexual preferences, first paying court to Robert Carr, later Earl of Somerset, whom James I called his 'little wife', then particularly relying on the patronage of George Villiers, later Duke of Buckingham, whose relationship with the King the Queen condoned. Bacon won the King over by helping to destroy his own benefactors Somerset and Essex when they fell from favour. He was knighted (1603), appointed Solicitor General (1607), Attorney General (1613), Privy Councillor (1616), Lord Keeper (1617) and Lord Chancellor (1618). When begging for advancement, as soon as he heard of the death of Fleming CJKB on 7 August 1613, he was quick to remind James I 'how necessary it is for your Majesty to strengthen your service amongst the judges by a Chief Justice which is sure to your prerogative.' Nobody could accuse Bacon of being slow.[14] But he was then appointed Attorney General. He was a member of both the Virginia and Newfoundland companies but they seem to have produced no income for him.

4.   ARBITRATOR FOR THE COUNCIL

The Privy Council kept Bacon busy with appointments as arbitrator, mediator or adviser in disputes.[15] He reported on the activities of himself and five others in resolving a dispute about herrings in Yarmouth, and on one about French playing cards.[16] On 11 June 1613 the Council approved a report from Bacon, then Solicitor General, and Thomas Calvert, a Clerk of the Council, recommending the appointment of 'four indifferent arbitrators' to fix the amount of an annual payment in wheat. Even after he had been appointed Attorney General, the Council continued to refer matters to him for resolution. In 1614 Bacon and the Solicitor General Henry Yelverton were instructed to mediate between the Earl of Dorset and the City of London over Salisbury Court in Fleet Street 'some such course as shall be agreeable to equity and the contentment of both parties'.[17]

In the same year Bacon reported his successful mediation on the petition of Elizabeth, widow of Sir Jonathan Trelawney, with her new husband Sir Thomas Reynell, against Richard Connock. By letters patent Queen Elizabeth had granted Liskeard Park to Elizabeth, Jonathan Trelawney and another Trelawney now dead, for their lives, but the late Prince Henry had afterwards purported to lease it to his servant Connock for forty years. The Council had referred the petition to Bacon, who had 'industriously

---

14. Jardine *Hostage* 338.
15. eg *APC* 33.389; 33.399; 34.121 (buildings); 34.412 (Dutch immigrants); 34.553 (Eastland Co).
16. *APC* 34.319, 34.327; 34.325.
17. *APC* 33.399.

mediated an end between them'.[18] Elizabeth and her husband would give up their letters patent, bringing them to the Court of Chancery to be cancelled, and release to Connock all their title to the land, that is Elizabeth's life estate. Connock's counsel would devise the necessary instrument and Reynell would undertake that Elizabeth would execute it. Connock would pay Reynell (not Elizabeth) £250 in two instalments. And that would be recorded in the Council Books as an order.

Some matters seem perhaps too slight to warrant the attention of the senior Law Officer. He was Attorney General when in September 1614 the Council referred to him a complaint from the King's tailor and cutter that their monopoly had been usurped by others making clothes for Prince Henry and his servants. He was asked to consider 'the validity of the patents whereby the parties claimed the work, and to mediate some end or agreement between them'.[19] His clever solution was that Prince Henry would be allowed to choose his own tailor and cutter for his, but not his servants', clothes. The rights of the King's tailor and cutter were confirmed, with appropriate compensation.

In 1616 the Council referred to Bacon, Attorney General, and others the petition of the coastal members of the Eastland Company, who complained that the Governors of the Company were levying unjustified taxes on them. As he rose to higher offices, his use by the Council as an investigator and reporter diminished, though a document in the Gloucestershire Archives records an award he made in a matrimonial dispute in 1617.[20]

In the Ordinances in Chancery, which he issued as Chancellor in 1619, Bacon set out clearly and simply an intention to incorporate and exploit arbitration in a scheme for small claims:

15. All suits under the value of £10 are regularly to be dismissed.

98. Any man shall be admitted to defend *in forma pauperis* upon oath, but for plaintiffs they are ordinarily to be referred to the Court of Requests, or to the Provincial Councils, if the case arise in the jurisdictions, or to some gentlemen in the country, except it be in some special cases of commiseration, or potency of the adverse party.

Bacon was many years ahead of his time, not only in his thinking but in the clarity of his drafting.

5. THE DOWNFALL

Once he became Lord Chancellor, Bacon's self-importance knew no bounds. He assumed he would always be able to rely on his patrons,

18. *APC* 33.389.
19. *APC* 33.571.
20. Glos D547a/L12.

particularly Buckingham and Prince Charles. When James I made him Viscount St Alban (now always St Alban's), Bacon thanked him for 'the eighth rise, a diapason in music, a good number and accord for a close'. Ben Jonson's ode on his sixtieth birthday in 1621, one of the epigraphs that head this chapter, however clumsy, could have done little to reduce his self-esteem: 'Hail, happy genius of this ancient pile! How comes it all things so about thee smile?'

The self-satisfaction was short-lived. The fall started with a mediated settlement that went wrong.[21] John Wrenham (or Wraynham) had begun an action against Sir Edward Fisher in Chancery fifteen years before in 1606, when Egerton, Lord Ellesmere, was Chancellor. In 1608, Ellesmere followed what was so often the practice in Chancery and persuaded the parties to settle, leaving the annual value of the land to be set by the Master of the Rolls, Lord Bruce. Wrenham thought his assessment of £200 was too low and appealed to Ellesmere, who put it up to £340. Then Fisher pulled out of the settlement and the parties were still at odds when Bacon took over in 1617. Bacon decreed that the parties were bound by the earlier settlement and fixed the value at £200. By then there had been more than eighty hearings and Wrenham said he had spent £3,000. In 1616 James I had told the Star Chamber that he would not second-guess his judges. He would hear no complaints that their judgments were unjust, 'your accusing of an upright judge deserves double punishment... but if you find bribery or corruption, then come boldly'. So Wrenham had to decide what he would accuse Bacon of. The King himself heard Wrenham and asked him straight: 'Will you charge my Lord Chancellor with injustice or bribery?' Wrenham could only say Bacon had been unjust. Bacon replied by producing the report of the Master of the Rolls, on which he had properly relied. Wrenham prepared an elaborate reply, charging Bacon with 'cunning and rhetoric'. That brought him before the Star Chamber, charged with slander. His former counsel turned against him, saying that Bacon 'hath always despised riches and set honour and justice before his eyes'.

With everyone against him, Wrenham had to argue his own case. The Star Chamber would not let him go over all the details again. Silenced, he begged for mercy. He got none. The bishops chipped in with their merciless condemnations. Wrenham was guilty of blasphemy, no less: to speak against the Lord Chancellor was to speak 'not against God but those that are in the image of God'. All sixteen judges assembled in the Star Chamber agreed in the verdict and sentence. Poor Wrenham, penniless

21. This story is taken, with thanks and admiration, from JT Noonan Jr *Bribes* [Noonan], which first revealed Bacon's career as arbitrator to me and has provided most of the material for the rest of this chapter.

thanks to the shortcomings of the law, was fined £1,000, and sentenced to be put on a horse backwards, with 'his fault written on his head', from the Fleet to Westminster, where he would acknowledge his faults in each of the courts, then to stand in the pillory, have an ear cut off, paraded thence to Cheapside for his other ear to be removed, and then imprisoned for life. That was the example English justice then demanded. Bacon sat by then and said nothing but fourteen months later Wrenham was pardoned after Bacon's intervention.[22]

Bacon sat at the King's right hand at the opening of Parliament on 30 January 1621. Sir Lionel Cranfield, never Bacon's friend, asked why Sir Giles Mompesson had been granted a monopoly to license all inns and taverns in the kingdom, which he had abused. The King blamed his legal advisers. One was Bacon, though he was not named. Cranfield was chief judge of the Court of Wards. In a struggle for jurisdiction, each party had won in one court and had been imprisoned by the other for contempt. There were other complaints about corrupt practices in Chancery, particularly the unnecessary multiplication of fictitious orders and charges by clerks.

The complaints were getting closer to Bacon himself. Christopher Aubrey, a dissatisfied litigant, threatened him that, unless he found for him, he would tell the Commons he had already paid £100 for an order in his favour. Bacon summoned Sir George Hastings MP, Aubrey's counsel who had paid him that bribe, to his bedchamber and asked him to get Aubrey off his back. Bacon made Hastings no promises. No doubt, with the comfort of Wrenham's awful punishment to reassure him, and his accustomed self-assurance, in February 1621 he felt safe. His security, though, depended on the King's support, and that depended on Buckingham. But Bacon's constant meddling had irritated Buckingham. He had stumbled badly in 1617, when he tried to interfere in the intended marriage of Buckingham's brother to none other than Coke's ill-used daughter Frances, and found himself stranded on the wrong side.

Coke had recovered some influence with the King by 1621 and was confident that he could get at Bacon through his association with Mompesson in the monopolies scandal. Mompesson had escaped abroad before he could be tried by a meeting of Lords and Commons. But on the morning of 10 March 1621 James I unexpectedly appeared in the Lords. He was above the fray. Lord Chancellor Bacon and Lord Treasurer Cranfield would have to answer for themselves. He would not intervene, even if Buckingham himself were implicated. As for Coke, 'though he be very busy and called the father of the law... all is not law that they say, and I have told Sir Edward Coke that he would bring precedents of good kings' times'. As he had not, 'I hope you will punish him.... I think him

---

22. 16 July 1619 *Calendar of State Papers Domestic 1619–1623* 63.

an enemy to monarchy and a traitor to me'. Common Lawyers like Coke were 'wind instruments, their tongue being their pipe'. Buckingham threw himself on the King's good grace. Cranfield said that the licences were legal and he was not responsible for Mompesson's abuse of them. Bacon was not content with the same defence. He added an attack on Coke, while he thought he was down: 'I hope my acts and honesty shall well appear before his'.

Coke was nearly seventy. His only hope was to see off Bacon once and for all. And so he organised a devastating response to Bacon's challenge on which of them was the more honest. It is not clear how Coke managed to get so many witnesses to testify that they had themselves been guilty of bribery. On 14 March 1621, only four days after the King's intervention, Lord Treasurer Cranfield mounted the first attack before the Parliamentary Commission on the Courts, against Chancery's practice of interfering in actions of debt, the preserve of Common Pleas. But that, though public and general, was as nothing compared with Christopher Aubrey's petition to that Committee. He told the Committee of the £100 he had paid Bacon. Hastings told the Commons he had handed the money to Bacon in gold in a box. Then Sir Edward Egerton presented his petition and gave evidence that he had first given Bacon a silver basin worth £51 but that Bacon's steward Sharpleigh had demanded payment of another £1,000 to Bacon and £100 to himself. The best Egerton could do was £400 for Bacon and £100 for Sharpleigh, which his counsel, Sir Richard Young, testified he and Hastings had taken to Bacon. Bacon wrote forthwith to Buckingham: 'I know I have clean hands and a clean heart.... Greatness is the mark and accusation is the game. And if this be to be a Chancellor, I think if the great seal lay upon Hounslow Heath nobody would take it up.' If Buckingham and the King did not 'put an end to these miseries one way or another', he 'foresaw he would be sick'.

Coke persuaded the Commons that bribery was a crime, at Common Law though there was no statute, and they sent the matter to the Lords for judgment, setting 19 March as the date for a conference of the two houses. As he had threatened, Bacon was too ill to attend. Coke had the field to himself. The King, though, was still to be convinced. He proposed that a different committee of twelve MPs and six lords should examine the charges. Coke persuaded the Commons not to take that route. The next day the Commons heard the petition of Montagu Wood and his wife. They had a suit in Chancery against Lady Dorothy Wharton, who described how she had gone herself to bribe Bacon with £100 in a purse she had made herself and he had said: 'What lord could refuse a purse of so fair a lady's working?' And he wrote out the requested order with his own hand. But later his man Shute had told Lady Wharton that £200 more was needed to 'bring the order to life'. All this and more was presented to the Commons by Churchill, the Chancery registrar, responsible for the administration of Bacon's court and himself implicated in much of the corruption. The Commons assured him and the others who gave evidence that it would not be used to base prosecutions against them.

On 21 March the Lords set up three committees to hear groups of witnesses. They advised Bacon to attend. The evidence showed widespread and routine bribery, often by both sides. To be fair, if one of Bacon's decrees went against a party, it could usually, eventually, get its money back.

James I's behaviour may have been depraved. His idea of fun may have been no more refined than to have four black slaves stripped and made to dance in the snow until they dropped and later died of pneumonia.[23] But his religious beliefs were separate and firm. One was that when he sat on the throne he spoke for God. And when his judges sat, the 'seat of judgment is properly God's'. So, though he might bend in any other matter to the whims of his young sexual partners, his judges must be incorruptible. That was Bacon's problem. He wrote via Buckingham to the King on 25 March: 'I hope I shall not be found in a depraved habit of taking rewards to pervert justice, howsoever I be frail and partake of the abuses of the times', anticipating the moral relativism of his later apologists. But James I's resolve was firm. He told the Lords that he would protect no one, 'were he never so dear with me'. They were to 'proceed judicially and spare none'.

On 16 April Bacon met the King. He insisted he had never taken a bribe, never knowingly any gift before delivering judgment: 'I am still a virgin for matters that concern your person or your crown'. He was told that the Lords would decide. The next day the Lords heard 17 more witnesses. Bacon wrote again to the King: when he received the details of the charges, he would excuse or confess 'without fig leaves'. And he had a bad headache. Surely it would be enough if he were to lose his position as Lord Chancellor. With a touch of gallows humour, he suggested: 'because he that hath taken bribes is apt to give bribes, I will present Your Majesty with a bribe – a good history of England and a better digest of your laws'. Spedding's *Letters* include one of 22 April to the King:

> I do ingenuously confess and acknowledge that, having understood the particulars of the charge... I find matter sufficient and full, both to move me to desert the defence and to move your Lordships to condemn and censure me.

And, on 30 April to the Lords: 'I do plainly and ingenuously confess that I am guilty of corruption; and do renounce all defence'. He pleaded guilty to 28 charges and begged for mercy. First the letter was read out by the clerk. Then Coke read it out again, one can imagine with what emphasis and relish. The Attorney General read out the charges, the proofs, and

23. Du Maurier *Winding Stair* 21 but with no precise citation.

Bacon's confession for a third time. In the Commons, Coke provided precedents for hanging judges who took bribes. As Lord Chief Justice he had the satisfaction of declaring the judgment and sentence: fine and ransom £40,000; imprisonment in the Tower during the King's pleasure; permanently barred from all office, from Parliament and from Court. At least Bacon had escaped the death sentence and degradation.

As ever when in trouble, Bacon was ill. From his comfortable quarters in the Tower – it had one of the best libraries in England for the privileged – and despite his supposedly desperate illness, he wrote to Buckingham on 31 May. The sentence was just and 'fit for reformation' but he had always been a trusty friend and wise counsellor. He was out within a couple of days. The influence of Buckingham, Prince Charles and the King had prevailed over the sentence of the Lords and soon he was allowed home. There he fired off letters and devised chicaneries, the most bare-faced of which was to get his fine of £40,000 transferred to trustees, so that it could be set up as a bar against his creditors. As palpable a device as many a tax-dodging scheme today, like them it was effective because there was no practical and affordable means of breaking it. To get Buckingham's support for his restoration, Bacon had to give him his London home, York House, using a tricky collusive action, which attempted to ensure that his wife Alice would be cheated of her share.

6.   THE CROOKED ARBITRATOR

Only a handful of the bribery and corruption charges to which Bacon confessed related to his arbitrations. We shall never know their full extent. But they are enough to show how routine his venality had become. Judge Noonan must have the credit for an unbeatable summing up of Bacon's crooked arbitrations:[24]

> The 28 charges were based on 21 cases. Three related to a dispute where Bacon had acted as an arbiter between a society of grocers allied with apothecaries on the one side and a new society of grocers on the other. The Lords had heard witnesses in April who deposed that Bacon had £200 from the grocers, a taster of gold worth £400 to £500 from the apothecaries, and £100 from the new company of grocers. Bacon commented that this was 'no judicial business' but a composition between the parties, and he had thought 'all had received good', so he took from all. 'If I had taken it in the nature of a corrupt bribe, I knew it could not be concealed', because of the accounting the companies would make....
>
> In another commercial matter Sir Thomas Smith had approached Bacon on behalf of a company of French wine merchants who complained of

24. Noonan 354, based on 'Charges Against the Lord Chancellor' summarised by Bacon in 'The Confession and Humble Submission' art 24; Spedding VII 259–260; *Lords' Journal* III 79.

price-fixing by the London wine dealers. Smith offered Bacon £1,000 to help the French company. Bacon proceeded to negotiate on their behalf. But, when the negotiations faltered, the company filed a formal petition with the king, who then referred the matter to Bacon for action. Bacon admitted all this and further that, after the king's committing it to him, 'I dealt more earnestly and peremptorily in it and, I think, restrained in the messengers' hands for a day or two some that were the most forward'. The wine dealers, he insisted, 'still had a very competent gain'; but they had settled with the Chancellor's client after he had used his power to deprive their leaders of liberty. In this manner Bacon had been promised his money in advance of any official act, although he took pains to point out he received the £1,000 from the French company only when it was over.

The defence that in those cases he was acting as a private arbitrator or mediator would not wash. In the grocers' case one side's bribe was nine times that of the other's, who were unhappy with the award. He took into Chancery the wine merchants' dispute and there as judge imprisoned one party after accepting the other's retainer.

There were other arbitrations. Bacon had been paid £100 in Lady Wroth's inheritance matter. Sir Rowland Egerton had paid him £100 to get his award confirmed. Bacon put forward some extenuation against almost every charge, if only: 'it was a great fault of neglect in me that I looked no better to my servants'. So he was just negligent; it was his old friend Tobie Matthew, for example, who should bear the guilt. That was the confession of a lawyer, admitting only what the evidence prevented him denying.

7. THE END

From 1623 Bacon was back, regularly lecturing Buckingham and Prince Charles on whatever matter of the day caught his attention. With what mirth the wicked circle round James I and Prince Charles must have passed round the self-delusional missives. James I replaced Bacon as Chancellor with John Williams, Dean of Westminster, a forty-year-old non-lawyer, declaring he was: 'resolved to have no more lawyers (as men so bred and nuzzled in corruption that they could not leave it)'.

James I died on 27 March 1625, with Bacon still hoping for restoration, even appointment as ambassador, or perhaps Provost of Eton or even, at worst, the head of a Cambridge college. After all, a scientist who could then write that men with hairy chests died young, while if hair grew long below their waists they lived to a good age, was fit, at least in his own estimation, for any position of responsibility. It would be easy to pity Bacon, if he had not been so utterly self-centred and noisily hypocritical about it, and if he had not been so fiendishly clever. If James I deserves the soubriquet of the wisest fool in Christendom, surely Bacon was the most foolish savant. In Bacon's favour is that as Lord Chancellor he once showed concern for a widow with eight children; it would be churlish to ask how big a bribe she had paid.[25]

During the last twenty years of his life, and particularly from when he became Lord Chancellor at the start of 1618, Bacon made truly enormous sums of money. Yet at his death he was even more in debt than he had been in his youth. A rough reckoning reveals, for the seven years from January 1618 to February 1625:

From the office of Lord Chancellor, £3,000 p.a.	£21,000
From bribes (known)	£12,000
Other gifts @ £25,000 p.a.	£175,000

Say £200,000. Of course that is no more than a wild guess.[26] It is hardly likely that all those who had paid him bribes wanted to disclose them. It would be normal to show the true meaning of those sums by comparing them with the wage of a labourer or maid, perhaps a few pounds a year. A better comparison is with the £124,000 which Parliament granted to James I in 1606 as his first subsidy.

Even in death Bacon could not escape arbitration. A dispute between his widow Alice and his half-brother Nicholas, arising from the distribution of his estate, which in 1632 came before Lord Keeper Coventry, was referred to his arbitration by the parties' agreement.[27]

8. CONCLUSIONS

No one, not even Newton, not even Galileo, has had a greater or more beneficent influence on scientific thought than Bacon. He insisted that research should start with observation of phenomena. Only then had reason a role in discovering their causes. Contemplation was not enough. Deduction, reasoning *a priori*, from given arguments, must give way to induction, requiring first the *action* of observation before the application of reason. This insight has informed all science since. Its influence became accepted, then assumed, by serious thinkers, especially those in England who formed the Royal Society, as can be seen in the work of Robert Hooke, described in Chapter 15.

Bacon was caught out. A combination of determined victims and political changes brought him down from the eminence on which he felt free to exploit parties seeking his help. No evidence has yet been found to show that there were others, equally immoral but more obscure.

---

25. Coquillette 206–207 sets out Bacon's concern for women's rights; Holdsworth is disingenuous, *HEL* V xxxiii.
26. Noonan has a more moderate assessment 359–360.
27. Jardine *Hostage* 517; John Ritchie ed *Reports* xxvi.

14   GERARD MALYNES

To avoid some cunning delusions which might deceive the unskilful Reader of those books entitled *Lex Mercatoria* p409 and *The Maintenance of Free Trade* p16, wherein the author *Gerard Malynes* setteth down the admirable feats (as he termeth them) which are to be done by bankers and exchangers, with the use and power of the exchange: but how these wonders may be effected he altogether omitteth, leaving the Reader in a strange opinion of these dark mysteries, which I cannot think he did for want of knowledge, for I find him skilful in many things which he hath both written and collected concerning the affairs of merchants... as he hath taken great pains for the good of others, so do his works of this kind deserve much praise; but where he hath disguised his own knowledge with sophistry to further some private ends by hurting the public good, there ought he to be discoverred and prevented.

Thomas Mun *England's Treasure by Forraign Trade* 45[1]

1.   INTRODUCTION

Gerard (or Garrett or Gerald) Malynes (or Malines or de Malines) and Thomas Mun (1571–1641) were roughly contemporary, though we know the dates of neither Malynes's birth nor death.[2] In 1622 he claimed that he had fifty years' experience of trade. He was still alive and active in 1641. Perhaps he was born in the early 1550s. He said he was a Lancashire lad, and took his name from the town near Antwerp where he was born. But his father, a Dutch mint master, had the same name. Moreover, our Gerard remained a foreigner all his life.

Mun was a wealthy mercer, increasingly successful throughout his life in international trade. In 1622 he was appointed Director of the East India Company. Malynes was always embroiled in disputes and usually burdened with unpayable debts. Both were early economists. Mun's mercantilism became the accepted ideology. No one ever took Malynes's theories of coinage and exchange seriously, or, if they did, they usually lost their money.

1. Thomas Mun *England's Treasure* was written in the 1620s but not published till 1664 [Mun].
2. Much of this section is taken from Perry Gauci's biography in the *ODNB*. I dealt with Malynes as arbitrator in 'Gerard Malynes, Arbitrator' [Roebuck *Malynes*].

2.   MALYNES: THE MAN AND THE MERCHANT

Malynes was an established merchant in London by 1588, when he lent the Government £200. In the 1590s he was locked in a dispute with John Honger, an Amsterdam merchant who accused him of misappropriating £18,000 entrusted to him as his London agent. Malynes was in prison between 1590 and 1596, and was only released by the intervention of William Cecil.[3] Like so many other characters in this book, Malynes was one of Walsingham's spies, and exploited that relationship when he could.

The Government sought his advice on commercial matters. He was already a commissioner of trade in the Low Countries, and the Privy Council appointed him in 1600 a commissioner to establish the true par of exchange. In 1601 he gave evidence to Parliament on Francis Bacon's Assurances Bill, which established a standing commission of arbitrators.[4] It may well be that Malynes had long been involved in arbitration by then, though the first evidence comes later. What is clear is that he was busy in business of different kinds. He invested in mining – lead, silver (with Lord Eure) and the alum mines discussed in Chapter 7. When these ventures failed, or at least his participation took him into debt, in 1607 he secured a royal protection against arrest, perhaps through Cecil's influence. The Privy Council had to curb this privilege in 1615 when he tried to use it as a defence to a claim for rent, pleading a 'protection granted to him by His Majesty eleven years since'.[5] The King left it to the Board to make an order '(notwithstanding the protection) as shall be according to equity and justice', which in turn required the Attorney General to 'direct a course for the satisfaction of the petitioner according to justice without further trouble'. Malynes agreed to settle the debt but defaulted, so that a further order had to be made.[6]

Malynes's obsession was money and the coinage. He followed his father's occupation as a mint master and in 1609 the Government of James I appointed him a commissioner of mint affairs. In 1612 he put his theory into practice. There was a need for farthings. Malynes suggested a Government issue. Lord Harington was granted a patent which he assigned to Malynes. The venture was a disaster. Nobody wanted 'Haringtons'. Malynes was imprisoned for debt and wrote to the King on 16 February 1619 that he had been ruined by his creditors paying him in his own farthings. As ever, though, he bounced back and in 1622 he is found giving his expert evidence to the standing commission on trade.

3. *APC* 30.365.
4. Roebuck *Golden Age* 236–238 and Chapter 7 above.
5. *APC* 36.163.
6. *APC* 36.267.

Malynes wrote many tracts on exchange but his arguments convinced few others. As Mun argued, England's economic problems arose from importing more than was exported, from the balance of trade, not monetary policy:[7]

> In vain therefore hath *Gerard Malines* laboured so long, and in so many printed books, to make the world believe that the undervaluing of our money in exchange doth exhaust our treasure, which is a mere fallacy.... As vainly hath he propounded a remedy by keeping the price of exchange by bills at the *par pro pari* by public authority, which were a new-found office without example in any part of the world.... This exchange goes beyond conjuring; I think verily that neither Doctor Faustus nor Banks his horse could ever do such admirable feats, although it is sure they had a devil to help them.

3. *CONSUETUDO, VEL, LEX MERCATORIA*

Malynes wrote that he was already 'stricken in years' when he published *Consuetudo, vel, Lex Mercatoria* in 1622. Two further editions appeared in his lifetime, 1629 and 1636, and one after his death, 1686. Despite its Latin title, it is entirely in English. It has always been acknowledged to be the fullest and most authoritative treatment of the commercial law and practice of its time.[8] Fair-minded Mun was full of praise (p48):

> And before I begin, I cannot choose but laugh to think how a worthy lawyer might be dejected in his laudable studies, when he should see more cunning in *Lex Mercatoria* by a little part of the merchants' profession, than in all the law-cases of his learned authors.

It includes a chapter on arbitration which deserves to be quoted in full:[9]

CHAP XV
Of Arbitrators and their Awards

The second mean or rather ordinarie course to end the questions & controversies arising between Merchants, is by way of arbitrement, when both parties do make choise of honest men to end their causes, which is voluntarie and in their own power, and therefore called *Arbitrium*, or free will, whence the name Arbitrator is derived and these men (by some called good men) give their judgements by awards, according to equitie and conscience, observing the custome of Merchants, and ought to be void of all partialitie more or lesse to the one and to the other; having only care that Right may take place according to the truth, and that the difference may be ended with brevitie and expedition: insomuch that

---

7. Mun 42, 48.
8. Gerard Malynes *Consuetudo* [Malynes]. I have used and cited the 1636 edition, published after *Gibson v Ferrers* was heard but before it was reported.
9. An excerpt from the 1686 edition, 'Of Arbitrators and their Awards' was published with notes in (1993) 9 *Arbitration International* 323–338. Malynes's work on *lex mercatoria* was noted by Lord Mustill (1988) 4 *Arbitration International* 86.

he may not be called an arbitrator who to please his friend maketh delaies, and propagateth their differences, but hee is rather a disturber and an enemy to justice and truth; wherefore the maner to elect arbitrators is worthy the observation. Some are contented to name foure or six persons on either side in writing, and refer the naming or electing of foure out of them by reciprocal proceeding, when one named the first person, another the second, and then again the third, and the other the fourth person. Others putting severall names in a paper, are contented that a meere stranger shall upon the back side of the paper pricke their names with a pin, or that (as they are numbered) the dice shall be cast upon them, accordingly by the number. Others put their names in severall papers, and cause them to be mingled & drawne by way of lot, by an indifferent person; which course may be thought allowable, as we have noted in the chapter of dividing of commodities by lots. Others will do the same by nomination of them, and drawing the longest and shortest straw, or by any other extraordinarie means of pointing, numbring, or describing, al tending to one end, to have indifferencie, and that partialitie may by al means be avoided.

Consideration must be had also, whether two, three, or all foure shall have authority to determine the cause, if they can, to be done within a limited time, wherein their award is to be delivered up, and whether they may name an Umpire or not. All which must be declared in the Bond of Compromise, unlesse the question be onely upon one point to be determined, wherein no bond is needfull but by way of assumpsit, by delivering a piece of coin each to other, and thereby binding themselves reciprocally upon the penaltie of a sum of mony to stand to the iudgement, it is ended.

And the said penaltie or forfeiture by assumpsit may be recovered by law and the Merchants Courts, as well as the forfeitures upon Bonds, if the party do not performe the sentence or award, if the award be lawfully made: to which end Arbitrators are to take notice of the five points following, which by law do make void all awards.

1. That the award be given up in writing within the time limited, by the bonds of the Compromise made between the parties.

2. That there be limited or appointed by the Award some reciprocall act to bee done by each party to other, which law requireth to be *Quid pro quo*, albeit never so small.

3. That they make a finall end, and do determine upon all the points or differences produced before them by specification or otherwise, if they be required so to doe, and authorised thereunto.

4. That they do not award any of the parties to do or perform any unlawfull act, or thing prohibited and against the law.

5. That they do not award any thing whereby any matter already determined by decree in Chancerie, or judgement at the Common Law, or any sentence judicially given in the cause, be infringed or medled withall.

These points ought to be observed for the reasons following. For touching the first, if the award be not delivered up in writing under the arbitrators hands and seals, if the condition of the Bond doe so limit the same; then have they no authoritie to doe the same after the time limited unto them by consent of the parties.

For the second point, Reason requireth in all humane actions a reciprocall act from one man to another, by deed of performance, called *Quid pro quo*, although it were a mans salarie for his pains; which in some cases causeth men to award, that each party shall pay so much to the Scrivener or Notarie for writing the said award: but this is no collateral act between the parties, neither is it any matter compromitted to the arbitrators: it is therefore better to expresse and award, That each party shall seale and deliver either, generall acquittances each to other, or with some exceptions therein, as the award will leade them.

The third point is considerable, where the differences are by both parties, or either of them, delivered in writing to the Arbitrators; for herein it is not sufficient to say, That the said arbitrators shall have power and authoritie to determine all questions, differences, doubts, controveries, matters of accounts, reckonings, or any other usual or generall words, from the beginning of the World untill the date of the Bond: but they must give their award upon every particular article and upon them all.

The fourth point, That the Arbitrators do not award any thing which is unlawfull, is to be understood of all things which are evill in themselves, called *Malum in se*, and of things called evill, because they are upon some respects and considerations prohibited, and therefore termed *Malum prohibitum*; as wearing of hats at all times, transportation of corn, eating of flesh in Lent, and the like, wherein there is a further consideration which requireth a distincton. As for example, an arbitrator or many Arbitrators do award, that a sum of money shall be paid to such a man during all the time he is unmaried, is good in Law; but to bind the party by award that he shall not marry, because he should enjoy the mony still, is unlawful and void by the Law.

The fifth point is of very great consequence, to bind the actions of men to the obedience of the Law, whereunto such reverence is due, that decrees, judgements, and sentences of Judiciall Courts of Record are alwaies of an higher nature than Arbitrators awards. Neverthelesse in many doubtfull questions the Civilians themselves (after long and curious debates) do assigne them to be determined by arbitrators having skil and knowledge of the Customes of merchants, which alwaies doe intend expedition.

And that is the cause wherefore an Umpire chosen upon arbitrable matters, hath an absolute authoritie to himself given, to end the matter alone, without hearing the Arbitrators, if he will: for albeit this is not without some danger, and that the ending of Arbitrators is to be preferred; yet brevitie and the expedition of justice in merchants affairs is much regarded, that by all means the same ought to be furthered. Hence it proceeded that the Merchants Courts, governed by Priors and Consuls (whereof we intreat in the next Chapter) have authoritie to reforme or confirm the sentence of arbitrators, when Merchants will appeale their arbitrement before them, rather than to go to Law: and with this proviso, That the appellation of the sentence of the said Arbitrators shall not be received by the said Prior and Consuls, before the Arbitrement be performed by the party that doth appeale, conditionally that restitution shall bee made if there be cause, upon the end of the processe. And the said Prior and Consuls are to note, that no

Merchant nor other, beeing of their jurisdiction, can transport or make over their interest to any person priviledged, and not subject to the said jurisdiction, be it by gift, sale, or exchange or by any other means, to the end thereby to avoid their authoritie; upon paine that the same transports and possessings shall be of none effect, and the losse of their right and cause. And all Notaries who shal receive any such transports, shall be punished by the said Prior and Consuls in a penaltie arbitrable: and further shall be condemned to pay unto the adverse party all his Costs and charges which he hath sustained by means thereof.

And to the end this expedition may by all means bee furthered, the said Prior and Consuls may distribute and refer causes unto the most ancient and expert Merchants in the matters in question, to make a true report of the state of the cause, according to the allegations and proofe of the parties, without any sallarie to be given to the sayd Merchants; howbeit in Italy some reward is given upon the Ricourse of Merchants.

These Merchants are to take the advice of the Advocat, Counsell and Atturny of the said Prior and Consuls in matters difficult, the better to discerne the right of the cause, to make the report more compleat, for the sooner ending of it according to reason and right, by the true affirmations of the Merchants. And not by feined, subtill and crafty writings, which oftentimes do darken the truth, under the colour of fair phrases declared in them, causing protraction and delayes.

Marcus Tul. Cicero hath truly set down the difference which is betweene Judges of the Law, and Arbitrators, inclining to the most easie and less chargeable course, saying, That the one is servile, the other is noble; the one is bound to the Law, the other is not; the one doth consist in fact, the other in justice; the one is proper to the Magistrats, the other is reserved to the Law; the one is written in the Law, the other is without the Law, the one is within the power, and the other is without the power of Magistrats: howbeit it is not forbidden that all justices of the peace may compound differences, and their authoritie doth enable them better thereunto. And in this regard it is said, That an Umpire doth represent the Lord Chancellours authoritie, because that Commissioners report of the Masters and of others of the Chancerie, or of Merchants, is the ground worke whereupon the Lord Chancellor doth deliver his sentence and maketh up his decrees. And the said Commissioners have a further authoritie and power, than Arbitrators; for they may examine witnesses upon oath, upon any thing in question where there wanteth proofe, or they may minister the said oath to either party, upon pregnant occasion to bolt out the truth. The like authoritie have the Prior and Consuls of Merchants: and moreover, their authoritie doth far exceed the power of Commissioners; for as Arbitrators have a determinat power to make an end of Controversies in generall termes, without declaration of particulars, so hath the Prior and Consuls to do the like; whereas Commissioners are to give a reason and declaration of their proceedings to the Lord Chancellor. Finally the Arbitrators authoritie implyeth a voluntarie command proceeding from both parties, which the Commissioners have not, but the Merchants Court hath.

As a statement of contemporary practice, that has not been challenged; in Chapter 18 the law it contains will be compared with that found in the law reports of the time.

4. *GIBSON v FERRERS*

What Malynes wrote was based not only on wide learning but on his own experience as a practising arbitrator, as appears from the report of *Gibson v Ferrers*, heard by the Court of Common Pleas in 1627 but reported only in 1657.[10] It contains many insights not only into contemporary arbitration law but also into the judges' attitudes to arbitration and the use they made of mediation. It also provides copious examples of the difficulties facing those who try to understand the primary sources. It was argued by Serjeant Hendon for the plaintiff and Serjeant Orlando Bridgman[11] for the defence, presumably before Winch J and all or some of Hobart CJ, Hutton and Harvey JJ, then judges of the Court of Common Pleas. Reports of that time usually designate arbitrators by initials only.[12] Perhaps the reporter thought that the name 'Gerrard de Malines' would be of interest.

The report is quite short and merits reproduction here in full. I have translated the Latin, removed some typographical and other errors and oddities and generally tidied up the text. It recites: 'Whereas there were differences between the parties concerning some accounts, now for the final determination of them they had put themselves upon the award and arbitrement of Gerrard de Malines'. They had entered into the usual bonds. The matter came before the court because a party refused to comply with the award. The major issue was whether an arbitrator could award interest – on the debt, not the award. The defence to a claim on the bond for non-fulfilment of the condition to satisfy the award was that the award of interest was usurious and therefore illegal.

Anthony Gibson brought an action of debt of £1,000 upon an obligation made 11 December 1623 and the Defendant came and demanded Oyer of the condition, and the condition recited that, whereas there were differences between the said parties concerning some accounts, now for the final determination of them they had put themselves upon the award and arbitrement of Gerrard de Malines, to be made before the last day of December next: 'if therefore Edward Ferrers... shall... perform... and keep the arbitrement of Gerrard de Malines, that then etc.'[13] Having heard this read out, the said Edward said that the aforesaid Anthony ought not to have his action against him,[14] because, he said, Gerrard de Malines did not make an arbitrement. The plaintiff replied and showed an

---

10. (1624) Winch 114–115 and 120–121, 124 ER 95–96 and 101, reproduced in full below.
11. An experienced arbitrator and the outstanding legal draftsman of his time, inventor of the strict settlement, see Chapter 6.
12. Another example, which may be of the equally well-known merchant John Scott, is in *Duport v Wildgoose* (1614) 2 Bulst 260; 80 ER 1106.
13. If this 'etc' were expanded it would read: 'then the amount of the bond should not be forfeited to the plaintiff'.
14. In Latin: '*quibus lectis et auditis idem Edwardus dicit quod praedictus Antonius actionem suam versus eum habere non debet.*' This is Ferrers' plea in defence, the condition having been revealed.

arbitrement, by which Malines awarded to the plaintiff interest to be paid for money, among various other things. Upon that the defendant demurred in law.

Serjeant Bridgman for the defendant: The arbitrement is void, for it is for the payment of interest. And I hold that arbitrators, who are judges indifferently chosen, may not award interest to be paid. That is an unlawful thing, for all the statutes which have been made concerning usury have branded that to be unlawful. Those differences which are submitted [to arbitration] ought to be intended to be lawful differences. And he cited a case in the King's Bench, where an action *on the case* was brought, upon a promise made upon consideration, that if the defendant will forbear the principal together with the interest, the plaintiff will pay that on a certain day. And it was adjudged that the action lies, because there was no certain interest set down. For, he said: If the certainty of the interest had been set down, the consideration would not have been good. If it is so unlawful that a man may not bind himself by his promise to do it, then *a fortiori* arbitrators may not award it. And it is void for another reason: interest was awarded for the period *after* the submission was made. And so I pray that the plaintiff may be barred.

Serjeant Hendon to the contrary: I hold the award to be good. Though it may be void for the interest, it is good for the residue. The non-payment is a breach of the condition. Where an award is made for something which is against the law, and for something which is within the law, the award is good for the one and void for the other. And so it is here.

Secondly, this award is not for interest. It is for damages which result from the plaintiff standing out of his money. Even if it were directly for usury, it would not be void. My brother Bridgman has cited a case where an *assumpsit* for usury was void. I know well what that judgment was because I was counsel in that case. Much was said in it about usury. Glanville was cited (Bk 9 cap 14),[15] which said that a usurer forfeited his goods. But that means those who live by regularly oppressing the people. And in that case no precedent was found where a contract for usury had been declared void.

In Noy 26 Edward III 24 [1352][16] an action for debt was brought for money given for usury. The usury was admitted. The statutes of 13 Elizabeth and 37 Henry VIII which were made against usury would be frivolous if such a contract should be merely void. Because they only made void those contracts which were for above ten per cent interest. So I pray judgment for the plaintiff.

There the first part of the report ends. But it continues again on p120.

Now the case of *Gibson v Ferrers*, which see before, was argued again by Serjeant Bridgman. He said as before that the award was not good for the interest. But he now agreed that covenants, bonds and contracts for usury are

---

15. The reference should be to Book 7 Chapter 16: '*Usurarii vero res omnes, sive testatus sive intestatus decesserit, domini regis sunt.*' 'All the chattels of a usurer, however, whether he dies testate or intestate, go to the lord king.' GDG Hall ed *Tractatus...Called Glanvill* 89.
16. Presumably *Hollingworth v Parkehurst* Noy 2; 74 ER 974, citing (1571) 13 Eliz 8, which confirmed (1545) 37 Henry VIII 9 making lending at no more than 10 per cent lawful.

good in law: But the statute of 17 Edward IV [1477] 5[17] provided that, if a man submits his dispute to arbitrators, they may not award that he and his wife shall levy a fine,[18] but, if the party himself promises to levy a fine, that is good and will bind the wife to perform it. Here is an award made only to one side and nothing is allowed to Ferrers. So the award is not good, 9 Edward IV 29, and 29 Henry VI 22. I pray that the plaintiff may be barred.

Serjeant Hendon replied: If an award is good in part, then, even if it is not good in respect of that part in which a breach is alleged, it is still good against a plea like this of *nullum fecerit arbitrium* [he shall have made no award]. If the other side then puts in evidence an award and assigns the breach, then the breach is not traversable because it is of the form and not of the substance of the action.

To that the Court answered that the cause of action is the breach of the award. The plaintiff ought to make this apparent to the Court. Otherwise he has no right of action. Though the breach is not traversable, it is still of the substance of the action. Because, if such a plea is pleaded, the plaintiff needs not only to prove the award but also the breach. Otherwise he loses.

Serjeant Hendon then argued the other point, about the claim not being for direct usury but for damages sustained by standing out of the money. If it were for interest, the claim would be good: As to that which has now been agreed by my brother Bridgman, that contracts and obligations for usury are good, I say then, by the same argument, an award for the same thing is good. Whatever a man may contract for, the same may be the subject of an award, if the contract will bear it and the usury is not *malum in se* but merely *malum prohibitum*, and is good by our law. In this case, though the arbitrator got the amount wrong, it became clear what it was after the award had been made. And an implied recompense is sufficient in this case.

But the Court said that drawing up the accounts in itself did not make an award, because it was not a good calculation. It was the ending of the controversies that made an award. But the opinion of the Court in this case was that the award was good, because an arbitrement should not be taken absolutely, upon the bare words. And the court commanded the parties to come back the following day in the Treasury. And it seems that this was for mediation to make an agreement, for the opinion seemed to be for the Plaintiff.

The court stated simply that it was up to the plaintiff to prove both the award and its breach by the defendant. The defendant's first defence was that Malynes had never delivered an award at all. The plaintiff produced the award and that settled that. Then the defendant raised the main issue, whether Malynes was right to award interest on the debt, particularly after the date of the submission. The technical defence to the claim on the bond, for non-fulfilment of the condition to satisfy the award, was that the award of interest was usurious and therefore illegal and that therefore the whole award was invalidated. Serjeant Hendon claimed first that the award was

---

17. This is an error. There is no such statute. This reference and the next two are to Year Book cases.
18. A fine is a final concord, made by the parties with leave of the court, used to convey land.

not for interest at all, but for damages, that is, for the loss of the use of the money after it should have been paid. Next he argued that, even if part of the award were illegal, the rest was enforceable and that was a complete answer to the defendant's plea that there was no award at all. Another defence was that, for an award to be valid, it must give something to both sides. If the plaintiff recovered the whole amount claimed, there must be evidence of a release of the debt. The court seems to have held that such a release could be implied: 'an implied recompense is sufficient in this case.'

The report is not a model of clarity. The defence must have suggested that Malynes had got his sums wrong, because Hendon responded that, even so, the right amount was clear in the award:

> But the Court said that drawing up the accounts in itself did not make an award, because it was not a good calculation. It was the ending of the controversies that made an award. But the opinion of the Court in this case was that the award was good, because an arbitrement should not be taken absolutely, upon the bare words.

Presumably that meant that the award should not be construed strictly.

The report suggests that the plaintiff won on all counts but the court did not give judgment in his favour: 'The court commanded the parties to come back the following day in the Treasury. And it seems that this was for mediation to make an agreement, for the opinion seemed to be for the Plaintiff'. So, after all that time, trouble and expense, the court thought it best for the parties to come to terms – and was prepared to help them do so.

Perhaps not a model for law reporters to follow, but how it illuminates the development of arbitration and mediation and their relations with the litigation process in the last years of James I! The best evidence is a statement by a primary source who did not realise its significance. The reporter did not know how the court resolved the matter, so *assumed* that mediation was what the court had ordered. He is not likely to have done so unless to make such an order was commonplace.

What did Malynes make of that process before Common Pleas? His own text on arbitration gives some clues. The report shows no sign of the judges accepting Malynes's dictum that: 'the Law-Merchant is predominant and over-ruling, for all nations do frame and direct their judgments thereafter'.[19] The authorities cited to the court were judgments of the Common Law courts, with no mention of *lex mercatoria*.

Malynes should have obeyed his own commandment and been careful to express in his award the winner's discharge of the debtor:[20] 'Arbitrators are to take note of the five points following... 2. That there be limited or appointed by the award some reciprocal act to be done by each party to

19. Malynes 295.
20. Malynes 298.

other, which the law requireth to be *quid pro quo*, albeit never so small'. And there he recommends, just to be sure, that the parties seal and deliver general acquittances to one another.

5. CONCLUSIONS

The law reports examined in Chapters 17 and 18 provide limited evidence of what legal rules, if any, applied in the daily practice of arbitration but much enlightenment of that practice. *Gibson v Ferrers* is such a report. The happy survival of its evidence of how one commercial arbitrator worked in 17th-century London, together with his own scholarly treatment of the subject, is unlikely to be replicated in any archive which survives from today. Now the parties, their legal advisers, and perhaps even the arbitrators themselves, are more concerned with confidentiality than showing to any community how acceptable was the outcome, as a fair, reasonable and efficient resolution of a dispute.

15   THE DIARISTS

If you ask me why I deem it worth while to fill up a page such as this day by day – shall I not reply, 'Worth-whileness hasn't very much to do with it'? ...We are all sustained at times by the thought that whatever we may be we are certainly a solitary manifestation of creation; not a single other creature in all the history of the world has been just as our self – not another will be like this. Why not put on record something of the world as seen by this lonely 'ego': here and there perhaps a sentence may be born whose father is reality.

William Soutar *Diaries of a Dying Man* 26 August 1934

1.   INTRODUCTION

Most diarists write for themselves. Who else could they expect to share their obsessions with their bowels and sniffles, their prayers and petty payments? Why otherwise write in cypher? But, when they survive, such diaries may contain more than a sentence or two of reality about disputes in which the diarist was involved, sometimes as arbitrator, more often as a party. The 17th century has provided the five examples presented in this chapter in chronological order: Sir Richard Cholmeley, the recusant; Walter Powell the royalist JP; the republican soldier Adam Eyre; the civil servant Samuel Pepys; and the scientist Robert Hooke. Two others, Margaret Hoby and Anne Clifford, have been saved for the next chapter, 'Women'.

2.   RICHARD CHOLMELEY

Introduction   Sir Richard Cholmeley (*c*1550?–1623) inherited the family estates of Brandsby and Brafferton in Yorkshire in 1602 and for the next twenty years kept a memorandum book in which he recorded in detail all his activities, as landowner and hands-on farmer. His accounts include the heavy fines and occasional bribes for his recusancy. He had to pay dearly for keeping Catholic servants, being rated 'for 4 servants each 9 months £360', and: 'to the King's Attorney General... for £20 per month for the recusancy of Mary Cholmley [née Hungate] my wife for 25 months'. The many legal claims against him often kept him busy in London and he described his legal affairs in detail. He had good relations with his lawyers, especially his attorney Richard Lutwidge. On 16 May 1620 he recorded that he had helped to settle a dispute between Lutwidge and his nephew, himself paying the nephew 3s 4d 'to stop his claims and win love'. He was ever keen to promote peaceful settlement. Towards the end of his life, on 7 January 1622, sick of the stone and in pain from a leg broken in a fall from his horse, he took the trouble to record: 'Mr Brackenbury and Mr Thweing reconciled upon his message by Christopher Herbert, mediator, and Mr Thweing's recognising his fault'.

Cholmeley's open recusancy prevented his appointment as a JP but he exercised jurisdiction in his own leet court, twice a year at Brafferton and Brandsby, either himself or through his deputy, the steward William Leyfe. Feelings in his part of Yorkshire ran high between Catholics and Protestants. Even a game of football could end up with one player calling his opponent a seminary priest, and the subsequent fight leading to litigation, 9 April 1620. But there are also lighter moments: falconry and breeding of dogs and horses, all manner of rearing and trading in livestock and trying to grow exotic trees; jollity and feasting at weddings and Christmas, with musicians and actors and jugglers, a far cry from the prevailing Protestantism; and even Cholmeley's delight at winning a lottery, drawing scraps of parchment, the prize a battered silver bowl. And among all the insights into his colourful life, there are details of multifarious disputes, and the mediations and arbitrations some of them produced.[1]

Francis Taylor   Cholmeley first mentions arbitration on 12 December 1604: 'Francis Taylor's suit should have been ordered by Mr Topham at the sitting at Rippon, in the plague time at York'. Then on 1 May 1606: 'Francis Taylor's bill of complaint served on me'; on 4 March 1607: 'Francis Taylor's suit against me put to arbitrament'; and in May 1607: 'I gave him 10s'. But that did not end it. Taylor was an apothecary who supplied Cholmeley with medicines but their difference was over the sale of corn. On 26 September 1609: 'Francis Taylor and I have referred our suit for Smallwood corn to Mr Topham'. That was Henry Topham, who would later play the same role in Cholmeley's dispute with Roger Weddell.

Newclose   On 12 February 1605 Cholmeley records:

Newclose arbitrated by Thomas Meyness of Kilvington esquire and Mr Thomas Babthorpe gentleman, that Christofer Dayle, Jane Key, Elizabeth Sympson, Thomas Burnett and Christofer Johnson should have the Newclose at Brafferton three years longer to those they have already had it, the three years beginning at the Annunciation next following, in full payment and satisfaction of the £100 that my late brother Marmaduke Cholmley had on them, and they are to give me in his bonds or bills for the same.

1. *The Memorandum Book of Richard Cholmeley [Cholmeley].*

Thomas Marshall   On 31 January 1608 there is a record of more litigation:

Thomas Marshall suit about the administration in Sir John Bennet's name and Dr Goodwyn's. My answer to his bill. Counsellor fees and for drawing it. Attorney's fees for two sittings. My rejoinder to his replication, counsellor's fees and for drawing it.

Blank spaces were left for the amounts to be filled in. Then on 31 March 1608: 'Arbitrators met at Sutton between Marshall, Dr Bennet etc and me but did not agree'. On 7 and 24 May 1608:

> Sheriff Marshall I offered to see his book and to pay him all I owed him, which he took upon his conscience was 22s 6d and 22d for his charges in suit, which I offered him before Mr Lawrence Rawdon and Roger Garret, but his answer was he would not let me see his book or take anything but by order of law...
>
> Marshall suit is to be heard. My brother[-in-law] Hungate agreed to pay him all unpaid in his bill and that in his book also, if on his conscience it be yet unpaid. Also 24s 2d, all to be paid presently after Michaelmas. I gave my brother[-in-law] to pay him £10 which he had all and returned nothing again.

That is hardly satisfactory evidence but it seems to suggest a mediated settlement.

Roger Weddell   On 22 February 1609 there is a long description of the start of a dispute with a tenant, Roger Weddell, which was to cause concern to Cholmeley for years to come. Weddell, who was the Archbishop of York's bailiff, had no love for his landlord, whom he despised as a papist:

> I blamed Roger Weddell for great spoil of my timber trees in his farm... and many other great wrongs done me daily.... He answered that I had good tenants and was ever complaining of them without cause.... I hearing him affirm all those untruths to my face did bid him provide himself of another landlord.... He answered I had long desired that.

Weddell did more than outface his landlord; on 17 October 1609 he followed him home and twice threatened him with violence:

> if I would not let him continue my tenant as he had been.... If anything should happen to me but good... thank myself for it.... Divers urging untruths and quarrelling speeches further did he use, having a long thick crabtree cudgel with a long thick and very sharp pike of iron in it... as though he would have suddenly struck at me.

Things moved slowly but on 31 March and 1, 2 and 4 April 1611:

> Sir John Gibson's butler Clarke brought Mr Topham's letter... and left it with my wife. Mr Topham had writ it at the instance of Sir John Gibson, who persuaded him that I did malice him without cause. He never had wronged me nor never would.

Mr Henry Topham's promise to me to move the Chancery... that Weddell's suit against me and Matthew Cooke might be dismissed.... Weddell's meddling after caused Mr Topham to say he was a very knave.

Weddell did offer him at my gates that Sir Thomas Fairfax and Sir John Gibson should have hearing of all matters betwixt us and then, if they tendered to me any agreement to my liking, I would accept it. But I told him of many great injuries that he had done me, contrary to that which he had made them believe. So he presently took his journey to London without any speech to be had by them therein.

Sir John Gibson (1576–1639) and Sir Thomas Fairfax (1559/60–1639) were outstanding figures in the local government of North Yorkshire and also had a hand in central government. Gibson, the son of a civil lawyer and master in Chancery, was a JP 1605–1639; member of the Council in the North 1616–1639; MP for Thirsk 1621; and member of a commission in 1625 to investigate Sir Arthur Ingram's management of the alum mines, discussed in Chapter 7. Fairfax was a soldier, father of the famous 'Black Tom', commander of Cromwell's New Model Army. A JP from 1592, he was MP for various constituencies 1586–1625; member of the Council in the North 1599–1640. His father Thomas had inherited Steeton only after arbitration by Sir Thomas Gargrave and held it only after Burghley had negotiated a settlement with his half-brother Edward. His claims to inherited land continued throughout his life. He was one of those who defended the Eures against the Hobys' complaint, described in the next chapter. In the elections of 1625, Fairfax stood with Wentworth against Sir John Savile for Yorkshire. The sheriff, none other than Sir Richard Cholmeley, tried to take a poll but Savile disrupted it. Cholmeley then declared for Wentworth and Fairfax. The committee for privileges overturned the result but Wentworth and Fairfax were eventually declared elected.

There is nothing then until 30 March 1612, a simple but unexplained: 'Matthew Cooke paid me further, as aforesaid £5 10s, which he at the Annunciation last received of Roger Weddell'. On 27 April 1617 there is a note: 'Roger Weddell to be indicted at Lammas Assizes next saith Carmell and W Fisher.' And that is the last of Weddell until 25 July 1620:

William Bearman [parson of Brandsby] came to Brandsby upon an arbitrament betwixt him and Roger Weddell about dilapidations. I sent for him, moved him to seal. He promised to come and bring Sir Thomas with him and seal, but did not but sent a letter by one of Sir Thomas's servants, who went from hence excusing his not coming and appointing me and Sir William Hungate to meet Thomas and him at York on Wednesday in assize week to effect the business. By letter I answered I could not be there at that time, neither know I whether Sir William would be there or not, therefore wished him to come over as he might do with speed without Sir Thomas, his presence being needless. And Sir William having sent me word... that he would see me at Brandsby on Monday in assize week, I wrote as much to Mr Bearman entreating him to come hither to Sir William Hungate to effect it, but he wrote back he would do nothing without Sir Thomas present, and therefore on Wednesday he would be at York with Sir Thomas to effect the lease. Sir William Hungate came to Brandsby. I went to York Assizes with him and then as followeth: Bearman at York Assizes fled from all former agreement, took counsel... Danport and Carvell and in case of conscience Dr Hodgson. Sir Guy Palmes and Jordan Metham could not move Bearman to perform his promise to Sir Thomas and words of full assurances many times after to us and many others yet now stands upon law and conscience and his oath in simony, laying himself open as I conjecture purposely to frustrate Sir William Hungate and Sir Thomas Belassis' grant now and my right hereafter and entitle Cambridge, though they persuade him it is as great a sin to violate his promise to Sir Thomas his dearest friend and discredit himself and Sir Thomas with us and with all doing contrary to covenant and therefore Sir Thomas bound to make Sir William satisfaction.

That was one arbitration that did not run smoothly and there is no knowing the outcome, but the record is evidence of the difficulties parties and arbitrators could face.

Robert Carlell   Even more bothersome than Weddell was Robert Carlell, who Cholmeley's younger sister Elizabeth married as her second husband. His name first appears in the list of Cholmeley's tenants at the start of his records:

> Robert Carlell Francis Smallwood's farm, old rent £5. Though I debar all my tenants by covenant when I let, to let... or return it to me, yet did I suffer him to buy Roger Conyers out for £20, reserving the rent that Conyers paid, being £14, out of which I allow Carlell's wife annuity £6 13s 4d.

Then in May 1607 there is another entry about Conyers:

> Roger Conyer's rent £14 I had by Hebdon's arb[itration] his winter corn and waire [spring] corn growing for £8 10s teaster [canopy] and 3 curtains, if not sufficient I was to have his nag to make it up £14 rent behind then and unpaid but I let him have his nag though the other was far short.

A note on 13 October 1612 describes Carlell's poor behaviour. He did not wait for Cholmeley to pay Elizabeth's annuity but stopped it out of the rent. He owed £15 6s 8d. So Cholmeley distrained on six cattle, on Carlell's farm but belonging to others. Cholmeley settled: 'I was contented to allow 20 nobles for my sister's annuity and forgive Carlell the rest, being 6s 8d.' They were not always on bad terms. Cholmeley visited Carlell and bought him presents at Christmas 1614, 1616 and 1617. Carlell was foreman of the jury at a sitting of the leet court at Brandsby on 11 May 1617. On 30 July he gave evidence against a poacher on Cholmeley's land 'with his pocket stretched out of a great bigness' and on 7 October against a woman wrongfully taking 'winding watling and writhing wands'. On 17 September Cholmeley sent Carlell with 3s 6d 'to quit' a man cited before the archdeacon. But then on 8 December 1619 Cholmeley's bailiff Henry Watson distrained on a horse and cow in Carlell's close for non-payment of rent. They belonged not to Carlell but to Thomas Cowlson, who went after Watson with an iron fork. Luckily Watson turned as he was struck from behind, so that the tines went into his stagskin doublet. Cowlson was subdued, but 'did miscall Watson filthily… hanging was too good for him… would to God he had killed him'. Carlell was one of those who asked Cowlson to allow the distress and:

> The same night after did Robert Carlell come late at night to my house, make his submission to me, procure friends to speak for him, pay me then his rent, promise me ever hereafter to pay £7 each rent day, to bring my sister his wife with him that I may pay her annuity, he to use her always well, and not to brabble with my servants and officers.

So one matter on which Cholmeley insisted was that he should pay Elizabeth's annuity to her directly and Carlell could not just deduct it from the rent. Carlell's 'submission' was shortlived. Perhaps there is nothing like a family Christmas party to bring out the worst in some people. On Boxing Day 1619:

> Robert Carlell on St Stephen's Day at night earnestly entreated Sir Henry Browne to move me to show him my favourable countenance… protesting he never did wrong me, and that he would lay his head under my feet to do him good. I answered, he and they all being my Christmas guests, it was no time to reckon up wrongs or griefs, but to be merry. He was still so earnest and Sir Henry for him that I said to him: 'Why then will you not speak to my man Watson… but frown upon him for doing his office, being my bailiff, which he seeming to Sir Henry Browne to be sorry for, at supper presently after Sir Henry Browne called for a bowl of beer, caused it to be given to Robert Carlell, and moved him to drink to Henry Watson, being waiting behind their backs. Whereat he paused a little, and then in an exceeding scornful and filthy fashion, after a rhyming manner, with the bowl of beer in his hand, called Watson knave and 'kiss my arse, shitten Harry', though he of his own accord before that at supper had taken Watson by the hand, taken gingerbread off the table and bestowed part on Harry, called on him to bring him some beer, which he willingly brought and the other did drink. Then first I and presently Sir Henry Browne reprehended him for his unmannerly carriage before his betters and to one who was an honester man than himself and I did esteem him so and would prove himself so. That night in the house he said he was not drunk and would not be persuaded he had said amiss or done any wrong. The next day day he came to church with a long sword about him, and so into the hall, and desired to make his submission to Sir Henry Browne and to myself by my brother Thomas Cholmley. We accepted it conditionally that he should be loving and no way

wrong us or my servants and tenants hereafter, otherwise this also we would not pardon, all which he promised.

Sir Henry Browne of Kyddington was Cholmeley's close friend, standing by him when he swore the oath of allegiance and lending him the ready money he needed for his pardon for recusancy. Browne was married to another Mary Hungate, daughter of Robert Hungate of Lincoln's Inn, 'my uncle' as Cholmeley called him when he entertained him, Henry and their families for three days in January 1619. On 9 March, not long before Robert Hungate died, Cholmeley recorded:

> My wife went to York to my uncle Robert with Sir Henry Browne and his lady to make peace if they can betwixt their eldest brothers and to draw Sir William to pay me the £100 my father gave.

Two women mediators.

On 12 January 1619 Cholmeley tells an even longer and more involved story about Carlell's shortcomings. Robert Hungate JP had issued a warrant to arrest Cowlson. Cholmeley's blacksmith was looking after Cowlson's cow, and Carlell his mare. Carlell asked the smith to let Cowlson take his cow. He refused. But that night the cow was stolen and the mare disappeared from Carlell's care. Tracks led through Cholmeley's lands, where none other than Roger Weddell's wife told the sleuthing smith that she had bought the cow from those who had a right to sell it, 'calling us all papist bloodsuckers'; 'the next day Robert Carlell reviled the smith for seeking after his own cow' and Weddell reprimanded John Sawman for fining Cowlson 12d for not paying Cholmeley a customary levy at his mill dam.

On 27 February 1619 the record says: 'the suit inter Henry Watson and Thomas Cowlson is to be heard at the next sitting' and on 12 April:

> Robert Carlell tendered instead of his half year rent but £3 13s 4d contrary to right and his own promise. I refused to take it. He went bragging all through the town he would pay no more, get it as I could, and that he would have Henry Watson's blood for being the cause, who in truth did never speak or meddle at all therein, or was present then. At the court I warned the steward not to employ him as a tenant on the jury or otherwise. After which he came and rounded me in the ear, asked if I would be content to take my rent on Sunday next being £7, for then he would surely bring it. I bid him bring it and see he brought it and his wife with him. I paid her five marks for half year annuity. I promised her of good will fourth of it.

But mediation might resolve even the bitterest conflict. On 8 May:

> Suit between Henry Watson and Thomas Cowlson at Cowlson's earnest solicitation, following us from place to place, was taken up or compounded as also the suit between Sir Henry Browne and Thomas Cowlson in the county

court, the other before the council established in this north. For both suits Cowlson entered two bills with sureties to pay Watson [blank] at Lammas, [blank] at Michaelmas in full satisfaction.

The gaps were filled on 2 June: 5 marks and 5 marks 4d. Though he was not expressly named, the context makes it clear that Cholmeley had a hand in the 'taking up and compounding'.

Conclusions   Cholmeley seems to have made use of alternatives to litigation routinely, if not almost automatically, whatever the dispute. Not all differences were hostile or of great value. On 28 November 1611 he witnessed the settlement of a matter in which his father was a party:

> Witness I of my father and John Auckland's agreement. First, he shall sit in some part of the house until Candlemas next and have the eatage of the ground till then with his own goods or those that was lately passed to his sons-in-law and no other. My father presently to enter into the tillage land and all the manure and to have all his straw this year, which Auckland doth promise to lay by for him as he thresheth it. And they are to choose, either of them, an arbitrator to view and appraise what reparations Auckland must make in and upon the house. And if the straw and manure on the land do not amount to it, Auckland must make it as much worth. If it be more, my father is to pay the over-plus.

And on 30 March 1612:

> Henry Filliskirke paid me for rent, the taking away of my doors, windows, locks, chamberfloors etc and defacing that house he dwelt in in Stearsby, according to Sir Thomas Fairfax's arbitrament, £12. And I paid him for all his leadings with his draught for me 5s 6d. He paid me further his part of rent due last Lady Day for my broom hills, 23s 4d.

Could anything be clearer evidence of how ordinary was the use of arbitration in Yorkshire then?

3.   WALTER POWELL

Compared with the riches of Cholmeley's records, those of Walter Powell (1582–1656) are scant. He was a small landowner and JP in Monmouth with royalist sympathies, who managed to survive the strife, though not without imprisonment in Raglan Castle in 1646, from which he persuaded the besiegers to allow him to escape. He kept in a pocket book the briefest of records of baptisms, marriages and burials in the parish of Llantilio, where until 1612 he lived with his uncle the vicar.[2] He called it: 'A book of old remembrances collected by me Walter Powell of the ages of me and my friends and children and of other matters happening in my

2. JA Bradney ed *The Diary of Walter Powell.*

occasions, collected out of my old Almanacks... of all which this book is a short breviat to be carried about me'. It begins with a brief list of the most important occurrences between 1560 and 1643, including that on 8 December 1618 he was sworn Deputy Sheriff. He changed to an annual record in 1606.

The few records of arbitrations have no detail and are of interest only for their ordinariness. Presumably they arose from his authority as a JP. In 1613 (p6): 'Arbitrament with Charles Jones 1 September, he paid £1 6s 8d to Alice, mother of the butcher baughe [=*bach*, little]'. Then there are perhaps a dozen references to commissions, with no detail to show definitely which, if any, were to arbitrate, though three consecutive entries for 1628 –1629 (p15) seem to be connected:

> 8 Sept   Commission per John Wm Parry at Burg' ad s's Herbert for part of the Golden Lion p'lor.
> 16 Jan   hearing in the Duchy, all with me, yet the decree stayed the entry.
> 20 Feb   Sir Humphrey May made his arbitrable decree to the contrary, which is overthrown since.

And 15 January 1630: 'Arbitrament between me and Walter Morice'. On 26 January 1631 he recorded his mother's death and his appointment the next day as solicitor by the Earl of Worcester. On 1 April 1639: 'I ended the matter between Matthew Wms, clerk, and Evans Wms ap Wm of Lanovor, see the almanack for contents of it'. If only we could!

4.   ADAM EYRE

Office was not a prerequisite to appointment. It was enough that one was recognised as a worthy figure in the community. An example is Adam Eyre (1614–1661), a captain in Fairfax's army and small landholder who farmed in the south-west tip of the Yorkshire Pennines. He kept a diary from 1647 to 1649.[3] Intermittently throughout he mentions differences he had with his tenant Edward Mitchell, who lived in the same house. As early as 10 January 1647 he noted:

> I this day promised John Marsden to refer the business between Edward Mitchell and me for assessments till Candlemas to the assessors *viz* John Wordsworth of Rodmore yate, Nathaniel Greaves and Nicholas Thurleston....
> 11 January   The assessors met here this morning to determine the difference between Edw M and myself, who, upon hearing of the business, declared [gap] to speak with the sequestrators about the same, where I stayed all night, and spent in beer 6d.

Eyre also served as arbitrator. On 25 January 1647: 'Thence to Denby, where we should have been on an arbitration between Raph Townrow of

3. Adam Eyre 'A Dyurnall' [Eyre].

Swinden and one More of Hoyland, but did nothing'. And as mediator, 8 February 1647:

I went to Silkston at the request of Nicholas Greaves, when William Wordsworth of Fallthwaite [said to be an ancestor of the poet] and I made an end of a controversy between Nicholas and one Timothy Hutchinson, fuller, of Stainbrough, in the presence of Thomas Hanson and John Wainwright.

And on 29 April 1647: 'Thence to Flocton, with one John Turner, where, with Mr Broadley, Mr Thurgoland and Lieutenant Houldsworth, we made an agreement between Turner and one Dixon and others'. On 3 May: 'I met with two Lynleys who came to request me to be a commissioner for them, and I directed them to Mr Eyre of Bramley for another'.

The next day's entry gives the first sign of a dispute in the parish of Peniston:

I went to Peniston and sent for Dickinson; and his wife first came and then he, whom I advised to take his best course of compromise with his neighbours, that the business might be no further followed, which would forever disable him; and he told me he thought to be vicar at Peniston, when somebody should be turned out of their estates.

On 10 May 1647 a note shows more of tenant Edward Mitchell's character and his relationship with Eyre. Anne Swallow kept an alehouse where Eyre spent a lot of time and money.

I went on foot with Ed M to the Deynehead above Hepworth to have seen a horse and home again 4 miles. And after dinner I went with him to Bulhouse to Anne Swallow's, where Captain Rich and I should have made Cholmeley Marsden and him friends but could not; and at night there fell quipping words between Francis Marsden and him; and Francis Marsden struck him on the face with his fist, so that his nose bled; and then Ed M rushed upon Francis, and Capt Rich pulled him off and helped Francis up, who pulled his handful of hair from Edward's head, and so they were parted; and this was done in presence of Capt Rich, Cholmeley Marsden and Anne Swallow; then we went home.

On 24 May:

This morn Ed M and his wife, I and my wife went to Birchworth, where we left our wives... Then I went to Peniston, where the vicar failed in bringing his men, and the business was referred wholly to Mr Clark, who ordered him to have £40 and to tarry till Midsummer but to preach no more and we gave bonds on all sides for performance of covenants... and I to pay him £40 on 24 June.... This day Dickinson called me a cozener in presence of both the arbitrator and bondsmen.

Eyre was not a lawyer, but he knew some law. On 8 June 1647 he lent his copy of Dalton *Justice of Peace* to Raph Wordsworth and on 24 June his

Statute Book to Robert Ward. At the end of October 1648 he recorded that he drew 'a pair of indentures' for an apprenticeship.

Eyre's father-in-law had trouble with his apprentice, Jane Goodyer. Eyre's intervention made no attempt at reconciliation. On 16 August 1647:

> This morn my wife's father called me up by break of day to go with him to Sir John Savile, he being summoned by a warrant concerning his apprentice, Jane Goodyer; whither I went and stayed in the field with Sir John two hours before they came, and then got a warrant to bring in the other parties and the apprentice, and then met Genn and others; so went back again, and had some speech with Sir John, who commanded us to come again, either on Thursday or else on Friday sennit [a week on Friday].

On 26 August 'my wife's father took Jane with him to Holmfirth'. The next day:

> Fawcett and his wife and Jane's brother promised to refer themselves to the churchwardens and overseers, who should meet about it the next Tuesday. And, if they could not agree, then to go before some justice of peace the next week.
> 31 August   I went to Holmfirth with Jane, my wife's father's apprentice, where James Genn the constable, the churchwardens and overseers for the Liberty, was met about her; and, after some conference thereof, I offered 4s for a month for her keeping and cleansing from lice; and thereupon her brother Joshua brought Fisher's wife, who took her for a month, and took 1s in earnest on my wife's father; and so home again.

Eyre drank a lot, carefully recording how much he spent on ale and wine. He did not treat his wife well, getting up to wickedness he could only record in cypher. His pious confusion was noted on 9 October. He was pleased with his new bookshelves:

> This day I stayed at home all day... I furnished the shelves with books and called upon God, my merciful father, to be my assistance and to guide me with His Spirit and began to read part of the preface to Sir Walter Rawleigh's *History of the World*. This night I whipped Jane for her foolishness, as yesterday I had done for her slothfulness; and hence I am induced to bewail my sinful life, for my failings in the presence of God Almighty are questionless greater than hers are to me.
> 1 November   I sent Jane away to James Genn, to Longley, with a letter to provide for her, for reason she stole bread from Edw Mitchell this morn, which I had forbidden her to do yesternight.
> 2   Jane went away yesterday...
> 3   I writ a note to Joseph, Jane's brother, to take some care that she might not go to the house of correction.

There the story of Jane ends, but so little expressed can imply so much.

The differences with Edward Mitchell were not resolved:

22 October   They brought him [Mitchell] home in the wain, and he coming home late at night from drinking, said he should be undone by two thieves, *viz* his landlord [i.e. Eyre himself] and Francis Haigh, in presence of Mary Swallow, John Goddard and Sara Thornton; and said I should pay for him, and came into my chamber to chide me.

11 December   I went to Peniston.... Came home with Capt Rich and Edw Mitchell, who had some talk between Ed and me, but to no purpose.

14 December   Mitchell gave answer to my paper at night and I returned him another and he another to me.

16 December   I gave Edw a note to tell him I was willing to refer myself to my neighbours, if before Tuesday next.

19 December   I entreated Wm Rich of Hornthwaite to go with me to Peniston tomorrow; and Edward said he had appointed Ralph Wordsworth to meet tomorrow at Earnshaw's at 10 o'clock. My wife was very unquiet and uncharitable also. God forgive her.

20 December   This morn I went to Peniston and met Edward Mitchell at John Earnshaw's, where we referred ourselves for all controversies between us to the arbitrement of Ralph Wordsworth and Wm Rich, and became bound in either of us £100 to the other to abide their end, so they made it within 13 days; and after that we gave them particulars of our demands, and spent each of us 1s, and gave Mr Didsbury for the bonds making each of us 6d; and after that I came home.

30 December   I went to Hornthwaite where Ralph Wordsworth, Wm Rich and Reginald Appleyard were together.... We had some talk of the business between Edw and me, apart but not together, but I perceive I must be a foul loser by him.

1 January 1648 I went to Peniston... and Wm Rich told me no end was likely to be made between Ed and me, so unhappy am I; but God Almighty... remove this present trouble from me, that thereby I may be spiritually enlarged to serve thee.

3 January   This morn I went towards Shore hall and met Cholmeley Wainwright in the way, and gave him my writ to get it broken up by the sheriff against Ed Mitchell.

11 January   This morn I ris betime and went to Shore hall and brought from Richd Wainwright my process, and he took nothing for his pains but 8d, which it cost him.... This morn Mitchell locked the house door and refused to send me the key; and I broke it off; and in my absence he discharged my wife for fetching any more of his coals; so she sent for Wm Wainwright, who brought 2 load; and then I sent him with the process for Mitchell to Wm Pasley, which is returnable *crastino Purificationis* [the day after the feast of the Purification]. [Then Eyre noted that he had moved furniture away from where Mitchell could get at it 'in the open house' and put on new locks – and confessed]:

All vows ought to be kept, but such is the weakness of my perverse and frail nature, as I can never persist in any good purpose without manifold temptations and failings... I never made vow... but I have most shamefully broken... neither have I any power of myself to think one good thought... have mercy upon me for Christ Jesus my Mediator's sake.

13 January   When I was come home, Reginald Appleyard was here, and requested me from Ralph Wordsworth and Wm Rich to meet them and Edward again; so I appointed Peniston on Monday next at 10 o'clock. Thus far I am in some more hope of the mercies of God than formerly.

14 January   Mitchell continues as froward as ever but I threatening to kill his mastiff, he sent her home. He opened the wainhouse door, which I had mowed with turfs to keep the wind from my horse; and I threw open the house door as often as I went in or out; and at night Wm Wordsworth came and enquired many things of me, by Mitchell's sending, I suppose.

15 January   This day Mitchell threw open the stable door and I the house door.

16 January   Mitchell had been at the alehouse all night. He had been at Sara's the last night also.

17 January   I went to Peniston and met Mitchell and the two men, but to no purpose, for their demands were the same as the last time here.

20 January   Hearing that Mitchell had indicted me at the sessions, I went to Wm Wordsworth and he went with me to Franc Haigh, who told me it was for words.

21 January   I went to Barnsley to enquire for a copy of the indictment, but the sessions were ended and all gone.

24 January   Towards night I went to Anne Bray, who told me that Mitchell was full of trembling and fear and would fain have an end.

25 January   Anne Bray came and told me in the stable that George came home and told her that Mitchell would fain have an end of the business, and would bind himself in £1,000 to abide the end of honest men, and that there was nothing done by him but he could undo it again... and John Mills, the soldier, told me that Mitchell reported in the alehouse yesterday that he would not have indicted me but that I had begun with him in serving process on him... and he would make me spend all I had. He also told me that Mitchell confessed at the Floshouse that, when I gave him the note which he pretends to be his lease, that I said there was other things to be considered, which we should think on when we made our lease.

31 January   I willed Wm Rich of Hornthwaite to labour an end between Mitchell and me.

1 February   Mr Ramsden and Wm Rich of Hornthwaite came hither and I agreed with Mitchell and drew articles between us.

17 February   I shall owe to Edward Mitchell at his going away for lime and manure left £11.

But Mitchell had not left by 28 March: 'I had some words with Mitchell about opening the gaps into the left sike [ditch]'; and 31 March: 'I had some talk with Mitchell in the afternoon, who promised to desist from all violence whatsoever, and he opened a cripple [an opening in a wall] and put his sheep on to the Newfield'. And finally:

1 April   This morn Mitchell and his wife went to church, to receive the sacrament, and he was drunk when he came home, and at night I sat with him by

the fire and he called for beer and promised to perform covenant with me in the presence of his servants, James and Mary.

There is nothing more of this 'business' and Eyre had leisure to enjoy and record, 3 and 4 April, going to see 'youths playing at football' and 'to see a match played at the football between Peniston and Thurleston'. He still had trouble with his wife, who would not bow to his will in matters of property. In the end – as far as the diary goes – he just gave up:

> 11 October 1648   This day I rested at home all day and walked into the fields, and I told my wife, since she would not join with me in sale, she should keep the house as she would, neither would I meddle with her at all.

5.   SAMUEL PEPYS

> The father of the Civil Service.... still governed by the moral standards, integrity and tradition of inflexible service on which in his lifetime he insisted... a permanent watchdog against corruption.
> As great a masterpiece in its own way as *Don Quixote* or *The Iliad*.[4]

Introduction   Samuel Pepys (1633–1703), born in London the second son of John Pepys, tailor, and Margaret Kite, butcher's daughter, was educated at St Paul's School and Magdalene College, Cambridge. His family had land in Brampton, Huntingdonshire, which Pepys inherited. He also had connections: his great-aunt Paulina was the mother of Edward Mountagu, Earl of Sandwich, who became Pepys's patron. In 1655 he married a 15-year-old French girl, Elizabeth St Michel, whose family had no money. They lived, mostly together but rarely happily, until she died in 1669. They had no children.

There are those who find Pepys an engaging character and there is much of interest in the nine volumes of his diaries, regularly kept from 1 January 1660 to 31 May 1669, when his eyesight became too bad for him to continue.[5] Others will be repelled by his callous treatment of women, particularly his wife and his sister, and the many women he bought, in one way or another, for furtive fumblings which, carefully recorded, never rise above the sophistication of a smutty schoolboy.[6] There is little to be admired, either, in his corrupt professional life, never averse to taking

---

4. Arthur Bryant *Samuel Pepys: The Man in the Making* [Bryant].
5. Robert Latham and William Mathews eds *The Diary of Samuel Pepys* [Latham and Mathews *Pepys Diary*]. Mountagu had experience of mediation at the highest level, having been 'despatched with a fleet to the Baltic in March 1659 to mediate in the war between Sweden and Denmark', Latham and Mathews *Pepys Diary* I xxiv.
6. Bryant saw it differently 315–316: 'His vitality, his sensitive and varying emotions and his unquenchable zest for life were irresistible' and accepts that 'much of Pepys' incontinence was probably due to the injury done in his youth to his genito-urinary system by the removal of so large a stone from his bladder'.

bribes and kick-backs and occasionally stealing and counterfeiting. There is a large literature on every aspect of Pepys. The discussion here is limited to just the parts of his *Diary* in which he describes his involvement in dispute resolution, usually as a party but occasionally as a resolver. Although he was appointed a JP in 1660, that was a formality, like his rank of captain, and he never acted as a JP in a way which might have involved dispute resolution.

Pepys was only 27 when the *Diary* started and 36 when it ended. He lived to be 70. He survived plague and fire and revolution and a short imprisonment in 1679. He cannot easily be put into any faction in politics or religion. He watched the execution of Charles I with joy, admired Cromwell, rejoiced at the Restoration. He was careful not to allow his religious opinions to affect his well-being. Perhaps he had none of substance, though he often went to church, where he eyed up the ladies before setting off for a bit of debauchery. To be fair to Pepys, CS Knighton's assessment of the *Diary* in the *ODNB* is kinder: 'The result is properly acclaimed as an astonishingly vivid and disciplined exercise in self-analysis, a historical document of the first rank, and a literary classic'. Pepys knew John Evelyn well and often wrote to him as a friend.[7] With him and with Robert Hooke, Pepys was an active Fellow of the Royal Society from 1665, its President in 1684.

The Diaries   Whatever faults Pepys had, he was frank. The *Diary*'s revelations about contemporary arbitration are reliable and enlightening. There was no reason for him to fabricate or embellish them. The first relevant entry shows the flavour well:

> 1 September 1660   Mr Moore and I and several others being invited by Mr Goodman, a friend of his, we dined at the Bull-head, on the best venison pasty that I ever did eat of in my life.... Here rise in discourse at table a dispute between Mr Moore and Dr Clerke, the former affirming that it was essential to a tragedy to have the argument of it true, which the Doctor denied and left to me to judge – and the cause to be determined next Tuesday morning at the same place upon the eating of the remains of the pasty and the loser to spend 10s.
>
> 4 September   So to the Bull-head where we had the remains of our pasty, where I did give my verdict against Mr Moore on last Saturday's wager. Where Dr Fuller coming in doth confirm me in my verdict.

That was Thomas Fuller, author of *The History of the Worthies of England*. Pepys found for Clerke, that tragedies need not be true. Henry Moore

7. Guy De La Bédoyère *Particular Friends: The Correspondence of Samuel Pepys and John Evelyn* [Bédoyère *Pepys Letters*].

was Pepys's friend and often adviser, a lawyer, also in Lord Sandwich's service.[8]

Pepys was then 28 and had begun to work for Mountagu, Lord Sandwich. Sandwich had fallen out with the Duke of Buckingham over a card game and challenged him to a duel: 'but my lord St Albans and the Queen and Abbot Mountagu did waylay them at their lodgings till the difference was made up, much to my Lord's honour, who hath got great reputation thereby'. Not by challenging the Duke but by agreeing to settle.

Most of Pepys's involvement in disputes arose out of family differences, in which he usually showed a preference for reconciliation. On 1 April 1661 he tried unsuccessfully to help in the differences between his father and mother over a maid. He was fond of his father, though he found him feckless. Sadly he thought his mother a shrew, probably mentally ill. He could never reconcile them. He had more success with his wife and her maid. On 10 July 1662 he got up early: 'Up by 4 o'clock and, when my wife was up, did call her and Sarah and did make up a difference between them – for she is so good a servant I am loath to part with her'. But, when he could not get the better of his wife in argument, 'for not commanding her servants as she ought', he more than once used violence. On 19 December 1664: 'I did strike her over her left eye such a blow, as the poor wretch did cry out and was in great pain; but her spirit was such as to endeavour to bite and scratch me'. That left her with a black eye for Christmas.

He was not too proud to seek the help of his servant William Hewer to mediate in the dispute which arose when, in October 1668, in the year before she died, his wife caught him in the kitchen with his hand up the maid's skirt. Pepys records the anatomical details of his fumblings with his usual relish, but also his shame at his folly, and concern for the maid, whom he accepted he had probably ruined. Then, as now, there were occupations in which women were not expected to repel the mauling of those with economic power over them. He recorded on 26 October that he had promised his wife never again to visit the actress Mrs Knipp or the beautiful Mrs Pearce, wife of the famous naval surgeon, who was famed for still looking only 20 after the birth of her 19th child. Who knows why a young girl, just hired as a maid, deloused and dressed, ran off at the first opportunity? Pepys instructed his no-good brother Tom, 21 August 1663, 'to get my clothes again and get the girl whipped'.[9]

Uncle Robert's Will   In October 1661 there is the first mention of Pepys's involvement in the affairs of his late uncle Robert, of whose estate

8. Moore was a barrister, Clerke a solicitor, Chancery's equivalent to a Common Law attorney.
9. A more generous modern assessment, giving more weight to the excuse that Pepys was a man of his time, is Laura Gowing 'Women in the World of Pepys'.

he was executor. His father, John Pepys, was his co-executor but seems to have left all the work and trouble to him. Robert's heir was his brother Thomas but Robert had devised all his land, including the family home at Brampton, to father John for life, remainder to Samuel, leaving Thomas only half an acre and £20 a year. The land was charged with the payment of £25 in annuities and there were legacies amounting to £200. Robert left nothing to his widow, Anne.

Mrs Goldsborough   The first dispute arose on 15 October 1661 with Mrs Goldsborough, who owed Robert £20 and had mortgaged land to him to secure that debt. Pepys arranged to meet her in St Paul's churchyard 'to treat about the difference which remains between my uncle and her'. He ignored her wild language and persuaded her to accept arbitration: 'so I appoint Mr Moore and she another against Friday next, to look into our papers and to see what can be done to conclude the matter'; and 17 October: 'So home and to look over my papers that concern the difference between us and Mrs Goldsborough and us; which cost me much pain but contented me much after it was done'. The next day:

> Moore and I to Mrs Goldsborough, who sent for a friend to meet with us, and so we were talking about the difference between us till 10 at night. I find it very troublesome, and have brought it into some hopes of an agreement – I offering to forgive her £16 that is yet due, according to my uncle's accounts, to us. So we left her friend to advise about it; and I hope to hear of her – for I would not by any means go to law with a woman of so devilish a tongue as she is.

The matter dragged on. A year later, 21 October 1662: 'Thence to see Mr Moore... we read over and discoursed about Mrs Goldsborough's business, and her son coming by my appointment thither, I did tell him our resolution as to her having her estate reconveyed to her'. By 29 June 1663 her husband was involved:

> I to the Temple and thence with my cousin Roger and Mr Goldsbrough to Gray's Inn to his counsel, Mr Rawworth, a very fine man. Where, it being the Question whether I as executor should give a warrant to Goldsborough in reconveying her estate back again, the mortgage being performed against all acts of the testator but only my own – my cousin said he never heard it asked before, and the other that it was always asked and he never heard it denied or scrupled before – so great a difference was there in their opinions, enough to make a man forswear ever having to do with the law. So they agreed to refer it to Serjeant Maynard.

There is no record of any award.

The Trices   The next claimant was uncle Robert's widow, Anne. She claimed that Robert owed her £200 on a bond given her on her marriage a decade before, plus interest since then, another £200. She had two sons of a previous marriage. Thomas Trice was a notary public, Jasper a Common Lawyer of the Middle Temple. On the whole, Samuel got on well enough with Thomas, whom he even asked to deal with the probate of Robert's will. But, when Samuel refused to pay them anything, they brought an action against him. He probably had a good defence to the action for interest, claiming that the £200 fell due only on Robert's death; but he was too clever by half. He replied with a delaying ploy, a bill in Chancery.

On the last day of the year, it was Pepys's practice to sum up the state of his affairs. On this matter he wrote: 'by my uncle's death, the whole care and trouble of all and settling of all lies upon me; which is very great because of lawsuits, especially that with T Trice about the interest of £200 – which will I hope be ended soon'. That was not to be. On 10 January 1662: 'I met Mr Moore, who tells me an injunction is granted in Chancery against T Trice, at which I was very glad, being before in some trouble for it'. Then on 18 January: 'Dr Williams... told me how T Trice hath spoke to him about getting me to meet, that our difference might be made up between us by ourselves – which I am glad of, and have appointed Monday next to be the day'; but on 22 January: 'meeting by appointment with Thos Trice and Dr Williams, in order to a treating about the difference between us. But I find there is no hopes of ending it but by law; and so after a pint or two of wine we parted'. Pepys's attempts to settle continued; 11 May 1663:

> By water and called upon Tom Trice, by appointment with Dr Williams; but the Doctor did not come, it seems by T Trice's desire, he thinking he should not be at leisure. However, we talked of our business and I do not find he will come to any lower terms than £150; which I think I shall not give him but by law. And so we parted.

On 9 July: 'I find my bill against Tom Trice dismissed, which troubles me, it being through my neglect and will put me to charges'. On 23 October:

> Mr Clerke tells me my injunction against Trice is dismissed again, which troubles me much – so I am to look after it in the afternoon.... Thence by appointment to the Six Clerks Office to meet Mr Clerke, which I did; and there waited all afternoon for Wilkinson, my attorney, but he came not; and so, vexed and weary, we parted. I endeavoured, but in vain, to have found Dr Williams, of whom I shall have use in Trice's business, but I could not find him. So, weary, walked home.... to prepare myself against T Trice....
> 24 October ... to the Six Clerks Office and discoursed with my attorney and solicitor; and he and I to Mr Turner, who puts me in great fear that I shall not get my bill retained again against Tom Trice, which troubles me.
> 27 October ... to Dr Williams, with him to the Six Clerks Office and there, by advice of his acquaintance, I find my case, through my neglect and the neglect of my lawyers, is come to be very bad, so that it will be very hard to get my bill retained again. However I got him [Dr Williams] to sign and swear an affidavit that there was treaties between T Trice and me, with as much advantage as I

could for me; but I will say that for him, he was most exact, as ever I saw man in my life, word by word what it was that he swore to; and though, God forgive me, I could have been almost naturally willing to have let him ignorantly have sworn to something that was not of itself very certain, either aye or no, yet out of his own conscience and care he altered the words himself, so as to make them very safe for him to swear. This I carrying to my clerk Wilkinson and telling him how I heard matters to stand with me, he, like a conceited fellow, made nothing of it but advised me to offer Trice's clerks the costs of the dismission, *viz* 46s 8d; which I did but they would not take it without his client. Immediately thereupon we parted, and met T Trice coming into the room; and he came to me and served me with a subpoena for these very costs, so I paid it him; but Lord, to see his resolution, and indeed discretion, in the wording of his receipt, he would have it most express, to my greatest disadvantage that could be; yet so as I could not deny to give it him – that being paid by my clerk; and then his beginning to ask why we could not think, being friends, of referring it or stating it first ourselves, and then put it to some good lawyer to judge in it. From one word to more, we were resolved to try, and to that end to step to the Pope's Head tavern. And there he and his clerk and attorney and I and my clerk and sent for Mr Smallwood; and by and by comes Mr Clerke my solicitor; and, after I had privately discoursed with my men and seen how doubtfully they talked, and what future certain charge and trouble it would be, with a doubtful victory, I resolved to condescend very low. And after some talk together, Trice and I retired, and he came to £150 the lowest and I bid him £80. So broke off and then went to our company; and they, putting us to a second private discourse, at last I was contented to give him £100, he to spend 40s of it among this good company that was with us. So we went to our company, both seeming well pleased that we were come to an end; And so I am, in the respects abovesaid, though it be a great sum for us to part with.

I am to pay him by giving him leave to buy about £40 worth of Piggot's land, and to strike off so much of Piggot's debt; and the other to give him bond to pay in 12 months after, without interest. Only, giving him power to buy more land of Piggot and paying him that way, as he did for the other, which I am well enough contented with – or at least to take the land at that price and give him the money. This last I did not tell him but I shall order it so.

Having agreed upon tomorrow come sennit for the spending of the 40s at Mr Rawlinson's, we parted, and I set T Trice down in Paul's churchyard, and I by coach home and to my office and there set down the day's passages; and so home to supper and to bed.

There Pepys has given by far the fullest account of how a mediation worked in the middle of the 17th century. The parties and their advisors had still to complete the formal settlement. On 10 November Pepys spent all afternoon and evening with his friend Henry Moore:

drawing a bond and release against tomorrow, for T Trice and I to come to a conclusion; in which I proceed with great fear and jealousy, knowing him to be a rogue and one that I fear hath at this time got too great a hank over me by the neglect of my lawyers.

There is no evidence in the *Diary* of Trice's roguery, but plenty of Pepys's, including those failed attempts to get Dr Williams to swear a false oath – 'God forgive me, I could have been almost naturally willing to have let him ignorantly have sworn to something that was not of itself very certain'.

Trice must have had some idea of what Pepys was trying to do. The next day a meeting with Trice failed when he did not turn up, but a week later, on 17 November, Pepys recorded:

> At noon I to the Change, where Mr Moore came to me, and by and by T Trice and my uncle Wight [William Wight, Samuel's father's half-brother]; and so we off to a tavern… and thence to a scrivener to draw up a bond; and to another tavern (the King's Head) we went; and, calling on my cousin Angier at the India House there, we eat a bit of pork from a cook's together; and after dinner did seal the bond, and I did take up the old bond of my uncle's to my aunt. And here T Trice before them doth own all matters in difference between us is clear as to this business. And that he will in six days give me it, under the hand of his attorney, that there is no judgment against the bond which may give me any future trouble.

So ended a dispute which cost the estate dear, as a result of Pepys's ineffectual attempts to delay paying a debt he never doubted was due, at least in part. Trice seems to have acted reasonably throughout and remained affable. Indeed, throughout 1664 Pepys sought Trice's legal advice about the estate of Pepys's brother Tom. Just before Christmas:

> 23 December 1664 Up and to my office. Then came by appointment cousin Tom Trice to me, and I paid him the £20 remaining due to him, upon the bond of £100 given him by agreement, November 1663, to end the difference between us about my aunt's, his mother's, money. And here, being willing to know the worst, I told him: 'I hope now there is nothing remaining between you and I of future dispute'. 'No', says he, 'Nothing at all that I know of, but only a small matter of about 20 or 30s that my father Pepys [his step-father Robert Pepys] received for me, of rent due to me in the country – which I will in a day or two bring you an account of'; and so we parted.

Pepys's own words show that he belatedly realised that he would have done better to have followed his often expressed general preference for reconciliation with specific practical steps. He was stubborn, neglectful and indeed dishonest, and the estate of which he was executor and from which he stood to gain paid the price.

Uncle Thomas   The Trice dispute was just one element in the troubled administration of uncle Robert's estate.[10] The sharpest thorn in Pepys's side

---

10. There is a large literature on his troubles, expanded now by internet contributions. The background is most easily accessible in Latham and Mathews *Pepys Diary* X, under Pepys, Robert 320–322.

was a poor relation, his uncle Thomas, who had a straightforward claim to an annuity under Robert's will and more arguable rights as Robert's heir to copyhold land at Graveley. The *Diary*'s first record is on 13 August 1661:

> Then my father and I went forth to Mr Rawlinson's [tavern]; where afterwards comes my uncle Thomas and his two sons and then my uncle Wight, by appointment of us all, and there we read the Will and told them how things are and what our thoughts are of kindness to my uncle Thomas if he doth carry himself peaceably; but otherwise if he persist to keep his caveat up against us. So he promised to withdraw it and seemed to be very well contented with things as they are. After a while drinking we paid all and parted.

The caveat was a notice to the world that the executors had no right to transfer the property to which it attached – the Graveley copyholds – until their ownership was settled. Thomas as heir would inherit them unless someone else could prove a better title. Samuel claimed them for the estate but could not produce the necessary documents of title, the surrenders, when the manor court met on 20 September. That morning 'no unkind words passed' between Pepys and uncle Thomas and his son. Pepys feigned friendship and they all drank together before the court sat, which comprised the manorial steward, Sir Robert Bernard, and two fellows of Jesus College, which owned the freehold. 'Where the jury were sworn, and I producing no surrender (though I told them there is and must be one somewhere) they find my uncle Thomas heir-at-law'. Samuel tried to persuade his uncle not to ask to be admitted forthwith but 'these rogues did persuade them to be admitted now'. Samuel was apt to call anyone who opposed him a rogue. 'After all was done, I openly wished them joy in it' and 'parted fairly, without any words'.

On 6 February 1662: 'About noon comes my uncle Thomas to me to ask for his annuity. And I tell him my mind freely. We had some high words, but I was willing to end all in peace; and so I made him dine with me, and I have hopes to work my ends upon him.' On 6 March: 'Then home, where my uncle Thomas (by promise and his son Tom) was to come to give me his answer whether he would have me go to law or arbitration with him. But he is unprovided to answer me and desires two days more'. It was young Tom who replied:

> 19 March   This noon came a letter from T Pepys the Turner, in answer to one of mine the other day to him, wherein I did check him for not coming to me, as he had promised, with his and his father's resolution about the difference between us. But he writes to me in the very same slighting terms that I did to him, without the least respect at all, but word for word as I did him – which argues a high and noble spirit in him; though it troubles me a little that he should make no more of my anger, yet I cannot blame him for doing so, he being the elder brother's son and not depending upon me at all.

On 10 October cousin Roger called on Pepys at home and told him 'plainly that it is my best way to study a composition with my uncle Thomas, for the law will not help us and that it is but folly to flatter ourselves. With which, though much to my trouble, yet I was well satisfied, because it told me what I am to trust to'. Uncle Thomas was threatening to have the will invalidated. Moreover, as heir he could claim any property that the will did not dispose of. Cholmeley Pigott had mortgaged land to Robert, giving him legal title. That was not mentioned in the will. Therefore it should go to uncle Thomas as heir. Pepys thought he could get round that clear law by forging bonds which would show Pigott owed Robert the money lent. Pepys could then sue on the bonds, without the mortgage: 11 October 'my design is to supplant him by pretending bonds as well as a mortgage for the same money, and so as executor have the benefit of the bonds'. 'Pretend' could at that time mean merely 'present', but not here, because there were none in existence. Pepys's forgery and criminal conspiracy are put beyond doubt by the entry on 13 October 1662: 'in comes Pigott with a counterfeit bond, which by agreement between us (though it be very just in itself) he hath made, by which I shall lay claim to the interest of the mortgage money'. Could this be the Pepys whose 'moral standards' are still those which remain 'a permanent watchdog against corruption'?

To be on the safe side, Pepys thought it wise to suborn the judge. So he travelled to Huntingdon and won Sir Robert Bernard's support, with the backing of his Admiralty boss:

> for counsel having a letter from my Lord Sandwich to that end. He doth give it me with much kindness in appearance and upon my desire doth promise to put off my uncle's admittance if he can fairly.... But we are liable to much trouble and that it will be best to come to an agreement if possible.

Pepys thought all was going well until he bumped into uncle Thomas and his son. They were civil enough, drinking a cup of beer together, but they were busy telling the tenants of the Pepys land at Brampton to pay rent to them not Pepys.

When the manor court sat the next day, the jury found that uncle Thomas was the heir-at-law. Sir Robert Bernard, presiding, told the jury that he had seen how 'the estate was devised to my father by my uncle's will, according to the custom of the manor'. The jury were not convinced that was the custom at all; and they had the final word on that. Nor were they happy with what they were told of Pigott's mortgage; but 'the steward [Bernard], as he promised me, did find pretentions very kindly and readily to put off their admittance'. Pepys thought that the other side would 'now listen to a treaty and agreement with us'.

The two sides must have agreed on some moves towards compromise, because Pepys reported on 12 November 1662:

To the Temple by appointment to my cousin Roger Pepys's chamber, where my uncle Thomas and his son Thomas met us, I having hopes that they would have agreed with me to have ended by my cousin Roger; but they will have two strangers to be for them, against two others of mine; and so we parted, without doing anything till they two send me the names of their arbitraters.

18 November   To Mr Phillips's chamber... . Here meeting my uncle Thomas, he and I to my cousin Roger's chamber, and there I did give my uncle him and Mr Phillips to be my two arbiters against Mr Cole and Punt. But I expect no great good of the matter.

29 November   ...calling upon my cousin Turner and Mr Calthrop at the Temple for their consent to be my arbitrators, which they are willing to.

30 November   My mind much disordered about my uncle's law-business, being now in an order of being arbitrated between us, which I wish to God it were done.

4 December   looking over my Brampton papers against tomorrow, that we are to meet with our counsel on both sides toward an arbitration.

Pepys was on the best of terms at that time with his patron and superior Lord Sandwich. They discussed their legal problems together. There was a suggestion that Sir Robert Bernard be appointed umpire in Pepys's arbitration. Lord Sandwich advised against that, 'he did not think him a man to be trusted at all'. Indeed Sandwich had him removed from the recordership of Huntingdon, and himself appointed in his place. Of course, Pepys knew Bernard was not to be trusted – he and Sandwich had just succeeded in suborning him.

The new year 1663 started well, with Pepys having 'great content, much joy, excepting only the ending of our difference with my uncle Thomas'. On 16 January: 'troubled in my mind more and more about uncle's business'. Uncle Thomas had taken the initiative and was suing the tenants for rent, hoping thereby to establish his ownership of the disputed land. Some other aspect had brought the will before the ecclesiastical authorities, because on 4 February Pepys had to appear before the Court of Arches to take an oath to give true answers to his uncle's claims. There is no record of what the arbitrators did but the parties continued to meet. On 5 February:

To the Temple and there at my cousin Roger Pepys's chamber met by appointment with my uncle Thomas and his son Thomas; and there, I showing them a true state of my uncle's estate as he hath left it with the debts &c left upon it, we did come to some quiet talk and fair offers toward an agreement on both sides – though I do offer quite to the losing of the profit of the whole estate for eight or ten years together; yet if we can gain peace and set my mind at a little liberty, I shall be glad of it. I did give them a copy of this state and we are to meet tomorrow with their answer.

6 February   Thence after dinner to my cousin Roger Pepys, where met us my uncle Thomas and his son; and after many high demands, we at last came to a kind of agreement upon very hard terms, which are to be prepared in writing

against Tuesday next.... My cousin Roger was so sensible of our coming to agreement that he could not forbear weeping; and indeed, though it be very hard, yet I am glad to my heart that we are like to end our trouble.

Pepys was not happy with the terms of the compromise but relieved it was all over. He wrote to his father the next day 'about the endeavour to come to a composition with my uncle, though a very bad one, desiring him to be contented therewith'. The actual signing and sealing took place at cousin Roger's chambers on Valentine's Day. Pepys belatedly realised how much he had lost by prevarication in paying what he knew he would have to. For probate purposes the personal estate had originally been valued at £372, Pepys's own estimate. Uncle Thomas would have been happy with half of that, but now much more had been discovered and Pepys would have to agree to handing over half of the total. And so:

All being done I took the father and son home by coach, and did pay them £30, the arrears of the father's annuity, and with great seeming love parted – and I presently to bed, my head aching mightily with the hot dispute I did hold with my cousin Roger and them in that business.

'Seeming'! Perhaps it was the constant need to dissemble that made life so stressful for Pepys.

This dispute had caused a rift between Pepys and uncle Wight, his father's half-brother, who Pepys thought had sided against him. Wight had complained to uncle Thomas that Pepys never saw him. On 26 March Pepys went to the Exchange, hoping to see Wight but missed him. The next day:

At noon to the Exchange and there by appointment met my uncles Thomas and Wight, and thence with them to a tavern and there paid my uncle Wight three pieces of gold for himself, my aunt and their son that is dead, left by my uncle Robert, and read over our agreement with my uncle Thomas and the state of our debts and legacies. And so good friendship, I think, is made up between us all, only we have the worst of it in having so much money to pay.

So ends the tale. Whatever became of the arbitration? Still the estate troubled Pepys. On 28 July 1664: 'My greatest trouble is the settling of the Brampton estate, that I may know what to expect and how to be able to leave it when I die, so as to be just to my promise to my uncle Thomas and his son'.

Edward Field   Just as time consuming and even more personally threatening was Pepys's dispute with Edward Field. Field was a whistleblower, or perhaps an informer out for a reward. The purchase of timber for the fleet was institutionally corrupt. Pepys was up to his ears in it, raking off as much as he considered he safely could. His excuse would please the relativist historian – everybody then was at it and he was not as bad as the others, and the King would have lost more if Pepys had not kept the graft within decent limits. The first mention is on 4 February 1662:

> This afternoon, going into the office, one met me and did serve a subpoena upon me from one Field, whom we did commit to prison the other day for some ill words he did give the office. The like he hath for others, but we shall scour him for it.

Field was no doubt as uppity a trouble-maker as Pepys was a self-important bureaucrat. Field had told the Navy Board that Turpin had purloined timber; and he complained when the Board did nothing. Pepys believed Field was motivated by 'spleen... or hopes of a reward' and had him arrested for his impudent slander.[11] Field was no pushover, though, and sued Pepys for wrongful arrest. Pepys's formal appointment as a justice of the peace did not protect him. The Board assumed that that office gave them all powers of arrest within the City but they were wrong. Their powers extended only to Middlesex, to the docks. Pepys was vulnerable because he did not enjoy the privilege the other Board members had as MPs. He was ordered to pay Field £30 damages and later the whole Board were ordered to pay £20 and costs. Field then claimed further damages of £250. On 13 April Pepys received a copy of Field's '(with whom we have lately had a great deal of trouble at the office)' petition to the King 'against our office for not doing justice upon his complaint to us of embezzlement of the King's stores.... we did not much fear it, the King referring it to the Duke of York'. On 21 October Pepys consulted Mr Leechmore, counsel at the Temple, and 'he tells me plainly that, there being a verdict against me, there is no help for it but it must proceed to judgment'; but he was still hopeful that 'the King will make it good to us'. He returned to the Temple on 20 November to seek the advice this time of Mr Thurland of counsel, who took him to Sir Matthew Hale, Lord Chief Baron. Thurland advised that: 'Field will have the better of us and that we must study and make up the business as well as we can'. On 13 December Pepys sat with Sir William Coventry, the other available member of the Board, Sir George Carteret, having already left:

> Field and Stint [his solicitor] did come and received the £41 given him by the judgment against me and Kembe [the messenger who had arrested Field]; and we did also sign bonds in £500 to stand to the award of Mr Porter and Smith for the rest – which however I did not sign to till I got Mr Coventry to go up with me to Sir W Penn,[12] and he did promise me before him to bear his share in what should be awarded.

11. Latham and Mathews *Pepys Diary* III p23 fn2.
12. Father of the American colonist.

Pepys's account of what happened on 21 February 1663 shows Pepys the storyteller at his best and demands full quotation:

> Towards noon there comes a man in, as if upon ordinary business, and shows me a writ from the Exchequer, called a Commission of Rebellion, and tells me that I am his prisoner in Field's business; which methought did strike me to the heart, to think that we could not sit in the middle of the King's business. I told him how and where we were employed, and bid him have a care; and perceiving that we were busy, he said he would, and did withdraw for an hour: in which time Sir J Minnes took coach and to Court, to see what he could do from thence; and our solicitor against Field came by chance and told me that he would go and satisfy the fees of the Court, and would end the business. So he went away about that, and I stayed in my closet, till by and by the man and four more of his fellows came to know what I would do; I told them stay till I heard from the King or my Lord Chief Baron, to both whom I had now sent. With that they consulted, and told me that if I would promise to stay in the house they would go and refresh themselves, and come again, and know what answer I had: so they away, and I home to dinner, whither by chance comes Mr Hawley and dined with me.
>
> Before I had dined, the bailiffs come back again with the constable, and at the office knock for me, but found me not there; and I, hearing in what manner they were come, did forbear letting them know where I was; so they stood knocking and enquiring for me. By and by at my parlour-window comes Sir W Batten's Mungo [a black servant], to tell me that his master and lady would have me come to their house through Sir J Minnes's lodgings, which I could not do; but, however, by ladders, did get over the pale between our yards, and so to their house, where I found them (as they have reason) to be much concerned for me, my lady especially.
>
> The fellows stayed in the yard swearing with one or two constables, and some time we locked them into the yard, and by and by let them out again, and so kept them all the afternoon, not letting them see me, or know where I was. One time I went up to the top of Sir W Batten's house, and out of one of their windows spoke to my wife out of one of ours; which methought, though I did it in mirth, yet I was sad to think what a sad thing it would be for me to be really in that condition. By and by comes Sir J Minnes, who (like himself and all that he do) tells us that he can do no good, but that my Lord Chancellor wonders that we did not cause the seamen to fall about their ears: which we wished we could have done without our being seen in it; and Captain Grove being there, he did give them some affront, and would have got some seamen to have drubbed them, but he had not time, nor did we think it fit to have done it, they having executed their commission; but there was occasion given that he did draw upon one of them and he did complain that Grove had pricked him in the breast, but no hurt done; but I see that Grove would have done our business to them if we had bid him. By and by comes Mr Clerke, our solicitor, who brings us a release from our adverse attorney, we paying the fees of the commission, which comes to five marks, and pay the charges of these fellows, which are called the commissioners, but are the most rake-shamed rogues that ever I saw in my life; so he showed them this release, and they seemed satisfied, and went away with him to their attorney to

be paid by him. But before they went, Sir W Batten and my lady did begin to taunt them, but the rogues answered them as high as themselves, and swore they would come again, and called me rogue and rebel, and they would bring the sheriff and untile his house, before he should harbour a rebel in his house, and that they would be here again shortly.

Well, at last they went away, and I by advice took occasion to go abroad, and walked through the street to show myself among the neighbours, that they might not think worse than the business is. Being met by Captn Taylor and Bowry, whose ship we have hired for Tangier, they walked along with me to Cornhill talking about their business, and after some difference about their prices we agreed, and so they would have me to a tavern, and there I drank one glass of wine and discoursed of something about freight of a ship that may bring me a little money, and so broke up, and I home to Sir W Batten's again, where Sir J Lawson, Captain Allen, Spragg, and several others, and all our discourse about the disgrace done to our office to be liable to this trouble, which we must get removed. Hither comes Mr Clerke by and by, and tells me that he hath paid the fees of the Court for the commission; but the men are not contented with under £5 for their charges, which he will not give them, and therefore advises me not to stir abroad till Monday that he comes or sends to me again, whereby I shall not be able to go to White Hall to the Duke of York as I ought. Here I stayed vexing, and yet pleased to see everybody, man and woman, my Lady and Mrs Turner especially, for me, till 10 at night; and so home, where my people are mightily surprised to see this business, but it troubles me not very much, it being nothing touching my particular person or estate....

To my office and set down this day's journal, and so home with my mind out of order, though not very sad with it, but ashamed for myself something, and for the honour of the office much more. So home and to bed.

And shame he should have felt, not only for abusing court officers when carrying out their essential duties of serving papers on him, but for giving his word as a gentleman that he would not abscond and then scuttling off in the basest fashion.[13] All good fun for Pepys and a picaresque tale for his biographers, but not for the bailiffs, whom he calls 'the most rake-shamed rogues', who would have had to answer to the court for unwisely trusting the word of the Clerk of the Acts.

On 24 February Clerke the solicitor woke Pepys up 'to consult me about Field's business, which we did by calling him up to my bedside, and he says we shall trounce him'. On 17 March Pepys heard the good news that Turpin had been acquitted of embezzling the King's timber. On 22 June he heard a rumour that Field had a judgment against Pepys for £400 in the Exchequer but Clerke reassured him that was untrue. On 27 June he went to Lincoln's Inn to look at the new gardens and met Clerke and his Exchequer attorney Long, whom he 'directed to come to the best and speediest composition

---

13. Why would Bryant not have mentioned this 90–102, where he calls Field a scoundrel and his actions 'a legal outrage'?

he could, which he will do'. He sought advice wherever he could get it but Field would not compromise. On 24 November: 'This day our trial was with Field; and I hear they have given him £20 damage more which is strange, but yet not so much as formerly I was afeared of'. But things got worse, 11 December 1663:

> Mr Clerke met me to tell me that Field hath a writ against me in this last business of £30 10s; and that he believes he will get an execution against me this morning. And though he told me it could not be well before noon and that he would stop it at the Sheriff's, yet it is hard to believe with what fear I did walk, and how I did doubt at every man I saw, and do start at the hearing of one cough behind my neck.

There is nothing in the *Diary* to tell how this dispute ended. The editors (p23 fn2) say: 'none of the papers concerning Field have survived in the Pepys collections'. Field's name does not appear in their volume X *Companion* or even their index (Latham and Mathews *Pepys Diary* XI).

There was much more to Pepys than the *Diary* reveals. He lived on for thirty years and left a mass of correspondence and other papers.[14] He settled down with a new partner, Mrs Skinner, and became the pillar of the Navy for which he is renowned.

Pepys the Maritime Arbitrator   Pepys must have learned something from all his experience as a party to so many different kinds of dispute. Certainly his knowledge of shipping was recognised. On 25 November 1663 he noted: 'Mr Bland came to me and had good discourse, and he hath chose me a referee for him in a business'. Then:

> 2 December   called on by Mr Bland, and with him to the Ship, a neighbour tavern, and there met his antagonist, Mr Custos, and his referee Mr Clerke, a merchant also, and begun the dispute about the freight of a ship hired by Mr Bland to carry provisions to Tangier, and the freight is now demanded; whereas he says the goods were some spoiled, some not delivered; and upon the whole demands £1,300 of the other. And their minds are both so high, their demands so distant, and their words so many and hot against one another, that I fear we shall bring it to nothing. But however, I am glad to see myself so capable of understanding the business as I find I do, and shall endeavour to do Mr Bland all the just service I can therein. Here we were in a bad room, which vexed me most; but we meet at another house next.
> 16 December   Home to dinner and then to the Star tavern hard by to our arbitration of Mr Bland's business; and at it a great while, but I find no order like to be kept in our enquiry, and Mr Clerke, the other arbitrator, one so far from being fit (though able as to his trade of a merchant) to enquire and to take pains in searching out the truth on both sides that we parted without doing anything, nor do I believe we shall at all even attain to anything in it.

---

14. Bédoyère *Pepys Letters* is a well-edited selection.

19 December   Then with Mr Bland to another meeting upon his arbitration; and seeing we were likely to do no good, I even put them upon it and they chose Sir W Rider[15] alone to end the matter, and so I am rid of it.

3 February 1664   To meet Sir W Rider and Mr Clerke; and there after much ado made an end, giving Mr Custos £202 against Mr Bland; which I endeavoured to bring down but could not, and think it well enough ended for Mr Bland for all that.

Pepys the arbitrator, a happy ending and evidence of what one party-appointed arbitrator considered his proper function.

Conclusions   The substantial use of the *Diary* and the many quotations are justified by the colour their detail adds to the story of 17th-century dispute resolution. No other source approaches Pepys. No criticism of him as a man detracts from his historical importance.

6.   ROBERT HOOKE

Introduction   Pepys and his wife were friends of Robert Hooke, the inventor (1635–1703), who recorded in his *Diary*[16] on 28 August 1676: 'I was twice with Mr Pepys who was very civil and kind'; on 15 December 1676 that he gave Mrs Pepys the recipe for white varnish and four days later: 'Mr Pepys master of the Trinity House made a long speech to no great purpose'. Thirteen years later, on 4 October 1689, Hooke wrote: 'Mr Pepys called... I showed him several optical experiments'. Pepys had admired Hooke from the start. On 15 February 1665, the day he was admitted as a Fellow of the Royal Society, he wrote: 'Above all, Mr Boyle today was at the meeting, and above him Mr Hooke, who is the most, and promises the least, of any man in the world that I ever saw'.

For this chapter, attention will be focussed on Hooke's diaries, edited by Robinson and Adams, with gaps filled by Gunther and Henderson; but Hooke's work as professional arbitrator has been revealed in much greater depth and detail by the research of Michael Cooper in Hooke's unsorted papers in the Corporation of London Records Office, which has the advantage of being informed by his professional expertise in surveying.[17]

---

15. Sir William Rider was a prosperous Baltic merchant with a fine house in the country at Bethnal Green, where he looked after Pepys's diaries and other valuables during the Great Fire.

16. HW Robinson and Walter Adams eds *The Diary of Robert Hooke* [Robinson and Adams *Hooke Diary*]. Other Hooke diaries have been discovered and edited: Diary 1688–1693: RT Gunther *Early Science* [Gunther]; Diary March–July 1672 and January 1681–May 1683: Felicity Henderson 'Unpublished Material' [Henderson].

17. 'There are two boxes of Viewers' manuscript reports and three volumes of transcripts of Viewers' reports in the Corporation of London Records Office', MAR Cooper 'Robert Hooke's Work' [Cooper *Hooke's Work*] 207.

From 1665 Hooke was Professor of Geometry (as mathematics was then called) at Gresham College in London, at the top of Threadneedle Street, where he had an apartment an easy walk from the coffee houses in Mincing Lane and the many taverns where he spent much of his waking hours. He was required to give lectures, though often no one bothered to turn up. No one could have had a more impressive collection of associates: Isaac Newton, Christopher Wren, John Locke, John Evelyn, John Aubrey (to whom he often lent money and who left him all his papers in his will), Edmond Halley, Hans Sloane and Leibnitz.

Hooke knew a lot about how things worked and, if he didn't, he meant – at least some day – to find out. He was always busy, often with bursts of manual labour, for example grinding lenses, surprising in a gentleman of his time. But he spent more time in coffee houses, sometimes making three calls a day, where he discussed with his peers his brainfuls of ideas. Nobody has ever equalled their variety. His speciality, if he had one, was springs, the metal variety, their physics as well as their practical uses; but these are only some of his other concerns: the weather, the motions of the planets, flying machines (Sunday 9 January 1676 'discoursed with Harry about my undertaking to fly'), a one-wheeled chariot, two-keeled ships, watches and clocks, magnets, music theory, anagrams, witches, the North-West Passage, a universal language, tones in Chinese, Confucius and chopsticks. He was a compulsive buyer of books in half a dozen languages on all subjects, including law, and read many of them. Some of his schemes he turned into inventions. He was proprietorial about the ideas which others developed or, like Isaac Newton, explained or proved with a better command of mathematics. His reputation has been harmed by critics who have stressed his exaggerated claims and belittled his contributions to the architectural practice of Christopher Wren, for whom he worked. That has led to generous attempts to rescue his reputation.[18]

The Diary   No claim of literary merit can be made for the *Diary*, whose entries are as spare as Pepys's are ample. An entry relevant to dispute resolution may be no more than a name, with nothing to distinguish it from the hundreds of similar but irrelevant entries. They stand there mute, among the careful details of his diet and health, bowel movements and sniffles and the doses of concoctions which illustrate the credulity of the hypochondriac. They include opiates to get him going and cannabis to calm him down. And there are occasional references to a sad little sex life, often lonely but sometimes explicitly exploiting his young servants, Bette, Doll, Nell and eventually his niece Grace, whom he took into his

18. Lisa Jardine *The Curious Life* [Jardine *Curious*]; Michael Cooper *'A More Beautiful City'* [Cooper *Beautiful*].

household at thirteen to find her a husband and was using by the time she was sixteen.[19] He was obliged to remain celibate if he wanted to keep his Gresham emoluments, particularly the large apartment in the college, where he lived for the rest of his life.

Views and Arbitrations   The *Diary* often records Hooke making a view.[20] The *OED* records the first surviving use of that word at the beginning of the 15th century. 'View', both noun and verb, may be used at three levels of specificity: to have a look at something; to make a formal inspection or survey of a place, as a court may do of the scene of a crime or an arbitrator of disputed property; or quite technically, to mean the City of London's procedure for investigating allegations of irregular building. For 150 years before the Great Fire of 1666 the City had been appointing City Viewers to 'take a view', in response to a complaint of irregular building lodged with the Court of Aldermen.[21]

That is what Hooke did for more than twenty years as City Surveyor after the Fire, when he was appointed on 4 October 1666 with Peter Mills and John Oliver to begin the process of clearing up the mess and getting the city back to work as quickly as possible. He had to measure plots, set boundaries, ensure that party walls were perpendicular, get rid of overhangs, widen streets or wharves and fix compensation. His reputation for technical meticulousness and absolute integrity ensured that the parties accepted most of his reports. Where differences arose, often from 'intermixtures' of interests, he and his colleagues would mediate or, if necessary, arbitrate. Invariably he was the one who wrote the report. His awards were usually accepted. If a party was recalcitrant, Hooke's opinion to the Court of Aldermen was accepted.

The *Diary* reveals many such views. They are not always easy to detect, or to distinguish from other activities. The Robinson and Adams edition starts on 1 August 1672 and runs to the last day of 1680. Hooke's first mentions of views are irrelevant, of books on 14 August 1672, then through a telescope, of Venus and Jupiter on 25 April 1673, but soon thereafter he starts to record his technical surveys:

29 April   View in Fleet Street *inter* Dr Ball and – Armes, painter.
30 April   View at Weevers, Tower Street, and at Philips in Bush Lane.
9 May   View for Boorder and in Newgate Market, Butcher Hall Lane.

19. Jardine *Curious* 257 had a kindlier view: 'Hooke, with his customary compassion for those fallen on hard times, took her in as "ruined"', when she went back to him after a brief stay with her father in the Isle of Wight; and Cooper, in the teeth of the evidence, Cooper *Beautiful* 69–70: 'it is not too fanciful to say that the relationship developed into one of love'.

20. The Privy Council might instruct its arbitrators to 'take a view', i.e. 'an enquiry and inspection taken upon the place', Chapter 4 above.

21. JS Loengard *London Viewers*.

Hooke then wrote out a certificate, which the parties bought from him for a fee (which he does not always bother to record) commensurate with the complexity, mostly ranging from 5 shillings to a guinea. That was usually enough to dispose of the matter, but sometimes Hooke had to try to mediate surviving differences and, if necessary, to arbitrate. His diary notes are almost always brief, often cryptic, and interspersed with other matters. Garaways was Hooke's favourite coffee house at that time. He sometimes visited it three times in a day and often spent most of Sunday and even Christmas Day there with his coterie. But he spread his custom widely. He often dined at home, at about 1pm. Just a few examples of entries in the *Diary* give the flavour:

14 August 1672   Pare sealed bond of arbitration at Mr Tillotson's.

31 August   Gave in arbitration to Mr Tillotson.

1 September   I invented an easy way for a music cylinder with pewter tipes pinched within cylindric rings.

2 September   Made instrument for eclipse of the stars by the moon.

4 September   Purged 7 times... urine had a cloudy sediment.

16 July 1673   From 8 till 12 at Fleet Ditch. View in Bell Alley and at Mr – Chamber. Refused 20/- of Pemberton. Dined at Swan, Old Fish Street. Mr Fitch's covenants examined. Viewed Old Fish Street Church with Dr [Christopher] Wren.

17 July   At St Paul's churchyard. Set out Sir P Neil's ground. Dined at home. View of Captain Powell, London Bridge.

16 September   Coles certificate 6s 8d. Mr Jagger in Pudding Lane 20s.

3 October   To 3 views in Cheapside 1 guinea.

7 January 1674 Rosemary in the bottoms of one's feet is a present remedy against the cramp also snake skins.

13 March   Viewed Smith's house and Hilliard's 6s 8d. At Mark Lane, Collins, quaker. At Mr Mayers. At Scotland Yard arbitration about Dover Pier.

15 March   [Sunday] At home till Garaways. Measured Harris's party wall with Shortgrave.

16 March   From Mr Anis in Guildhall 20s. From Esq Warder £5. From Mrs Jacobs a guinea. In Lime Street at Mitre Tavern arbitration.

7 April   Signed award for Fenchurch Street 10s. With Sir Thos. Player in Moorfields and at the Windmills viewing lands at Cripplegate and Bunhill Fields.

5 July   [Sunday] Drew up umpirage about St Martin's and Mrs Ellis. Sealed and delivered it at Hawkins in Birchen Lane.

13 November 1675   Discoursed of flying and many other things as anagrams. Sir Chr Wren. Importunate woman about party church wall. Sir Christopher surly.... At Montacue's, Man's [coffee house] and Rose [tavern] in Leicester fields. Ate hen and duck. To Paul's churchyard several orders for views.

3 May 1676   To Child's coffee house... saw gilded buttons, Shoe Lane, 2s per doz. To Man's coffee house.... Dined at home. With Fitch to Garaways about Mr Haak [a friend with whom Hooke regularly played chess]. They agreed upon

a sum certain but to refer the rest to me.... Eat eggs, vinegar and stewed prunes. Slept well.

3 March 1667   Primat [a builder] engaged me [as] an arbitrator for Sir Phil Mathews.

24 May   Met Fitch, Scarborough, Davys, talked about Fitch and arbitrator.

4 October   Received from Mr Gifford 2 guineas, promised to procure them workmen for arbitration.

17 October   Nominated Whiting umpire between Smart and Holt.

20 October   Bates had ended arbitration for £380 unworthily.

5 June 1678   At Child's. Gave to Robert Calcut our awards about Jenner and Tomplers. Received from him 40s.

15 July   Received a letter from Mr Boyle about Arbitration.

28 October   St Simon and Jude view with Oliver at St Peter's Church. At Guildhall coffee house. Signed award for R Calent and Warren from Calent 40s for view at Temple.

3 November 1679   To Sir J More at Stocks, ended that controversy between the Parish and foremen.

23 July 1680   Doegood, plasterer would not agree.... At Dr Busby's [Hooke's old schoolmaster] he desired me to agree with a plasterer and he would stand to the agreement. At Sir Ch Wren's tobacco stopper.... Unfortunate view at Puddle Dock.

These have been snippets, as most entries were, but occasionally one day's entry is fuller and gives a better picture of Hooke's working day. Just one example will have to serve:

Wednesday 5 December 1677   Met Banks at Jonathan's coffee house, then Mr Oliver about coach. Called at Silver Street view. View of Dorset drain for Governors of Bridewell and reported the want of it a nuisance. For view 6s 8d. At Guildhall, no commissioners of sewers, Andrews, Cole etc at Garaways, Hill etc. Recd from Mr Th Crisp by Mr Willoughby 4 guineas and 4 half guineas. Took bond from Steel, signed and delivered by Mr Willoughby to me. Dined at home. To Committee of City Lands. At Guildhall, then viewed in Silver Street. Met Davys at Man's coffee house. Discoursed with Mr Montacue. He seemed well satisfied in all things. Ordered Mr Scowen to pay me £50 upon the old and £50 upon the new building. He also ordered him to pay Tompion 10 guineas for watch. He promised to send me the French books which I should give him the titles of. Desired him to send me the agreements, designs and estimates. To Sir Chr Wren at Dr Holder's. Saw Mr Hobbes' new book of philosophy and a sermon against him. And Rapin's about philosophy. To Jonathan's, Garaway's son.

Those are all the express references in the *Diary* to arbitration. Perhaps they can allow glimpses, scattered and distorted, into Hooke's practice. It would be quite impossible to compile statistics from such *Diary* entries. Taking into account ambiguities and possible duplications, to say nothing of omissions, there are well over 400 separate references to views, only perhaps 17 mentions of arbitration. That is, of course, just for the period the *Diary* covers. Hooke started work as City Surveyor on 4 October 1666, while the rubble was still smouldering. The last record is for work done on 6 May 1693.[22] The Robinson and Adams edition of the *Diary* left gaps for March to July 1672 and January 1681 to May 1683, which have been filled by Felicity Henderson. Most of the entries for those periods reflect Hooke's obsession with the weather, but there are perhaps another 40 views, some with Wren. Many entries clearly record a view, though the word does not appear. For example, on 7 March 1681: 'From Mr Cox for Sir R How for Red Bull Alley 10s'. Then two days later: 'Delivered How's certif.' There is just one express mention of arbitration: 'At Toothe's [coffee house] Arbitrated between Heath and Helden 20s.'

Michael Cooper deserves special thanks and praise for providing the sources for what follows.[23] He estimated that the Fire devastated more than 80 per cent of the area within the city walls. Only rough figures are possible but he suggests:[24] 'About 13,000 houses were destroyed, making at least 65,000 people homeless... 90 parish churches... 52 livery company halls, Guildhall, the Royal Exchange'. Yet at most a few hundred people perished. Tents were set up in Finsbury Fields. The City moved its administrative headquarters from the ruined Guildhall to Gresham College and at once acted to clear the rubble, to stop unregulated rebuilding, to mark out plots and to arrange for compensation. The aldermen and other officials, many of them homeless themselves, saw that the necessary legislation was passed, with the Fire Court authorised to hear claims. The Lord Mayor and Court of Aldermen were ordered:[25]

> To cause an exact survey to be made of the whole ruins... that it may appear to whom all the houses and around did in truth belong... [no] person's right and interest should be sacrificed to the public benefit... without such recompense as in justice he ought to receive.... We make no doubt but such an Act of Parliament will pass as shall secure all men in what they shall and ought to possess.

Hooke was in the middle of it all. He had friends in the City who knew his strengths. The City could call on the experienced builders they already used as surveyors, but they needed a bigger mind – like Hooke's. Similarly the King knew what Christopher Wren could do. Both Hooke and Wren drew plans for the reconstruction, but both were too ambitious. It was not a spacious grid-plan city that was needed now. Immediately there had to be rebuilt a city which could function and retain the advantages it had gained

22. Cooper *Beautiful* 163.
23. Cooper *Beautiful* is his last word, presenting his conclusions for the general reader; he had earlier published Cooper *Hooke's Work* and two earlier parts of 'Robert Hooke's Work as Surveyor'.
24. Cooper *Beautiful* 102–103.
25. Cooper *Beautiful* 108 citing W de G Birch *The Historical Charters*.

as a commercial centre. Cooper's research discovered the relevant order of 4 October 1666:[26]

> His Majesty's pleasure that for the better and more expedition of this work he hath pleased to appoint Dr Wren, Mr May and Mr Pratt to join with such surveyors and artificers as should be appointed by the City to take an exact and speedy survey of all streets, lanes, alleys, houses and places destroyed by the late dismal fire, that every particular interest may be ascertained and provided for and better judgment made of the whole affair this Court doth therefore order that Mr Hooke, Reader of the Mathematics in Gresham College, Mr Mills and Mr Edward Jermyn do join with Dr Wren, Mr May and Mr Pratt in taking the survey.

Jermyn or Jerman was always too busy with his own building business and Mills often too ailing to help, so Hooke did it nearly all himself, later with John Oliver. He certainly drafted and signed the reports. Moreover, he employed his other expertise to experiment on the strengths of various kinds of brick, stone and wood to be used in the rebuilding. John Evelyn had criticised London's pollution in his pre-Fire *Fumifugium* of 1661, which Charles II ordered to be published and which was celebrated in a popular song:[27]

> 'Tis the sea-coal smoke
> That always London does environ,
> Which does our lungs and spirits choke,
> Our hangings spoil, and rust our iron.
> Let none at *Fumifuge* be scoffing
> Who heard at Church our Sunday's coughing.

Parliament legislated first to set up the Fire Court and then passed the first Rebuilding Act on 8 February 1667. Under its provisions 'Mills and Hooke had to make many hundreds of such decisions in the next decade', though 'always subject to the City's formal agreement, which was almost always given'.[28]

The Fire Court had sole jurisdiction over claims arising from disputes. It could not have handled such a caseload, had it not been for the dispute resolution skills of the surveyors. The usual procedure was for those who wished to rebuild to pay first a fee of 6s 8d – half a mark – to the City. They would be given a receipt and the name of the surveyor. The builder and the surveyor then had to negotiate the appropriate fee for the survey. The builder and the surveyor would meet on the site and examine the ground to find the old foundations. They would inspect deeds and take the testimony

26. Cooper *Beautiful* 115–116 citing unpublished Corporation of London Records Office Journal 46 f123r.
27. [John Evelyn] *Fumifugium*.
28. Cooper *Beautiful* 128 and 236 fn 67.

of witnesses. The surveyor then staked out the building lines, party walls and piers, recording his findings in a survey book. From these entries he produced a certificate, which he sold to the builder for the agreed fee. Cooper imagined the scene:[29]

> With his satchel containing measuring rods, chalk, survey books and writing materials, Hooke must have been a familiar sight in the years after the fire, as he stood amid the ruins, surrounded by a small group of neighbours and passers-by, some interested in just watching and listening, others with evidence or opinions to offer. His surveying was performed on a public stage, his measurements and staking out determined by justice and fairness. Disagreements were settled by the surveyor there and then on the basis of evidence clear to all, subject always to the approval of the Court of Aldermen.

Mills died in 1670. Oliver, who had been appointed in 1668, replaced him and took a much greater share of the load. Oliver and Hooke worked together until 1693. On 6 May Hooke recorded in his diary:[30] 'At Hublon's view 1 golden guinea. I paid J Oliver for yesterday's view 10s. Viewed it again with JO. I drew report at Jonathan's. We both signed it'. Mills and Oliver handed in their survey books to the City, Hooke did not. Cooper convincingly estimates that, of the 4,000 surveys completed, Hooke was responsible for perhaps 3,000, for which he may have received more than £1,500 in fees, in addition to his salary of £50 a year. That made him rich.

The reports of the surveyors were always to the Court of Aldermen, who made the formal order, but the wording shows that the surveyors sometimes expected their order to be final, as in practice it usually was. There is no evidence at all that the surveyors ever felt a need to distinguish between an award, an opinion, or indeed the report of a mediated settlement. Just three examples taken from Cooper's *Beautiful City* must suffice. The first is of a failed attempt to mediate a settlement. Hooke's *Diary* entry on Saturday 14 July 1677 merely says: 'With Sir J More, Dep Sexton and Bell at Deane's coffee house', with no mention of any dispute. But the report of Alderman More and Deputy Alderman Sexton, which Hooke prepared and signed says:[31]

> We the alderman and deputy of the ward of Walbrook have met upon the place and have viewed a small wall built by Mr Bell next adjoining the interest of Captain Pierce and find the same to be made use of as a party wall for Captain Pierce for which Mr Bell affirmeth he hath not received satisfaction according to the direction of Act of Parliament for Rebulding the City, the measurement of which we have received from Mr Bell... computed to amount to £24 11s... interest for 9 years £14... We have endeavoured to compose the difference

29. Cooper *Beautiful* 137–138.
30. Cooper 215; Gunther 237.
31. Cooper *Beautiful* 161, citing Corporation of London Records Office Miscellaneous MS93.14.

between them but being not able to end the same we humbly submit it to the grave judgment of this honourable Court.

On paper, Hooke seems to have played a subordinate role, but it is fairly obvious that he did all the work.

Cooper gives many examples of Hooke's opinions returned to the Lord Mayor. On 14 June 1686, Hooke wrote, for himself and three other City Viewers: 'We whose names are underwritten have met upon the place and have viewed all the matters complained of'.[32] Linch had complained that Harford had pulled down a flight of stairs and made holes in his chimney. The Viewers reported their findings in these words: 'it is our opinion', 'we further find', 'we find', 'we find', 'it is our opinion that Finch ought to set up the post in the place where it was before and Harford do forthwith satisfy himself about the substantialness of the partition and pay Linch the money due'. It was left to the Court of Aldermen to act on that opinion. But it is clear that sometimes the Viewers disposed of the dispute themselves by arbitration; from 8 July 1671:[33]

> Whereas... the Lord Mayor... was pleased to summon the surveyors of the City of London to view an intermixture between the interests of Mr Edward Harvey, Mr John Jackson and Mr John Neave situate on the south side of Goldsmiths Hall and on the north of Kerry [Carey] Lane, to do [as the Additional Act provides], we have met upon the place and viewed the interests and understood from the parties their several intermixtures, we order and appoint that Mr Harvey shall build the remaining part of the ground that is left... making use of the walls built by Mr Neave and Mr Jackson as party walls, paying unto them the moiety... and carry the party wall... upright upon the same foundations.... Mr Jackson shall have liberty to come home to the wall with that part of his house where he hath now placed windows.... And further that all differences touching any former intermixtures between Harvey and Jackson shall cease. Moreover we do order that Mr Neave shall pay unto Mr Harvey... £3 and that all differences between the parties touching any former intermixtures or yards shall cease.

That was an award which was intended to dispose finally of all differences between the parties. Even earlier, on 13 June 1668, Hooke reported the results of a view made by himself with Mills and Oliver, who had just been sworn in.[34] The differences included disputed title to land, which they excluded from their award and left the parties to litigate:

> We find that the north house of Mr Hawkes is built upon the walls that were erected before the fire and according to the setting out thereof by Mr Hooke,

32. Cooper *Beautiful* 155–156, citing Corporation of London Records Office Miscellaneous MS93.108.
33. Cooper *Beautiful* 154–155, citing Corporation of London Records Office Miscellaneous MS92.73. Cooper *Hooke's Work* 212 has a photograph of this document, perfectly legible, signed 'Rob: Hooke Jo: Oliver'.
34. Cooper *Beautiful* 157–158, citing Corporation of London Records Office Viewers' Reports i 19.

And whereas there is some dispute about part of the ground, whether it were Mr Conyer's ground or Mr Hawkes's, it being a matter of title we leave it to the determination of the law. As to the encroachment... we find it to have proceeded from a mensuration by Mr Jones, bricklayer... which we find to have been made by guess before the clearing of the ground... as confirmed by Mr Jones, who doth affirm notwithstanding that it was pretty near the truth.

The *Calendar* of the Fire Court survives, and shows that on 30 May 1667 it instructed Hooke and Mills to measure a courtyard off Cheapside and give an opinion on the likely effects on rights to light of intended building.[35] More than twenty years later, Hooke was still assisting the Fire Court. On 6 November 1691 he reported:[36]

I have viewed the matters in difference between Mr Nicholas Clark and William Sheldon concerning a shed built upon a yard, which Mr Clark complaineth doth obscure and darken the house lights of his house next adjoining... and being built of timber is dangerous in case of fire and contrary to the Act....

Hooke found the complaints justified. So it is clear that, from just after the fire, for the next twenty-odd years, Hooke was disposing of disputes, efficiently and with unprecedented technical skill, without concerning himself with distinctions about whether he was mediating, arbitrating or merely giving an opinion. If the parties accepted his resolution, sometimes after adjourning to a tavern or coffee house but more often expounded in public, with those who thought they knew the facts watching, that was an end of the matter. If not, a party might challenge Hooke. It seems few did.

Conclusions   Francis Bacon was a scientific genius whose turpitude brought arbitration into disrepute and damaged all those it touched. Hooke's scientific insights may not have been as deep, but his contributions brought great benefits, not only to the parties but to all who lived in the cleaner, healthier London he was instrumental in creating. His own words allow us to share his never-flagging wonder and determination to understand. In his *Micrographia*, published in 1665, with illustrations such as had never been seen before, he wrote:[37]

By the means of Telescopes, there is nothing so far distant but may be represented to our view; and by the help of Microscopes, there is nothing so small as to escape our enquiry; hence there is a new visible World discovered to our understanding. By this means the heavens are opened, and a vast number of new stars, and new motions, and new productions appear in them, to which all the ancient astronomers were utterly strangers. By this the Earth itself, which lies so near us, under our feet, shews quite a new thing to us, and in every little

35. Cooper *Beautiful* 158; PE Jones *The Fire Court* I 42–44.
36. Cooper *Beautiful* 160, citing Corporation of London Records Office Miscellaneous MS93.129.
37. Robert Hooke *Micrographia, or Some Physiological Descriptions of Minute Bodies*.

particle of its matter, we now behold almost as great a variety of creatures as we were able before to reckon up in the whole Universe itself.

'His genius lay in his ability to bridge the worlds of the mechanic's workshop and the learned man's philosophical speculations' concluded Cooper, and what better attributes for a construction arbitrator! He deserves Cooper's encomium:[38]

> Hooke's contribution to rebuilding in the aftermath... reveals personal attributes such as efficiency, fair-mindedness and an ability to settle disputes, and good administrative powers that are often seen to have been lacking in his scientific work. He met the demands not only of the merchants, traders and financiers of the City, who were his employers, but also of several hundreds of citizens with whom he dealt face to face, standing amidst stones, bricks and rubble, seeking speedy, feasible and equitable settlements of their disputes.

7. CONCLUSIONS

None of the diarists set out to provide historians with sources, or even to tell a story of dispute resolution. They all wrote for themselves. They therefore provide the most reliable evidence. The one famous diarist who wrote much for others to read and carefully edited his diaries did not publish any of it in his lifetime and says almost nothing of relevance. John Evelyn's *Diary*[39] is full of detail of London life in the 17th century. On 9 October 1665, when Evelyn was a Commissioner of Sick and Wounded Seamen and Prisoners of War, Pepys asked his advice about how best to facilitate payment to destitute sailors.[40] But neither his correspondence nor his diary says anything about the sailors' or any other disputes, even after he was appointed in 1662 a Commissioner for London 'for reforming the buildings, ways, streets and incumbrances' – except this for 26 May 1671, which may provide sufficient explanation and end this chapter fittingly:

> Having brought an action against one Cocke, for money which he had received for me, it had been referred to arbitration by that excellent good man, the Chief-Justice Hales,[41] but, this not succeeding, I went to advise with that famous lawyer, Mr Jones,[42] of Gray's Inn, and, 27th May, had a trial before Lord Chief-Justice Hales; and, after the lawyers had wrangled sufficiently, it was referred to a new arbitration. This was the very first suit at law that I ever had with any creature, and oh, that it might be the last!

38. Cooper *Beautiful* 217.
39. William Bray ed *The Diary of John Evelyn* is easily accessible in the Everyman's Library.
40. Bédoyère *Pepys Letters* 44 no34.
41. Sir Matthew Hale CJKB as late as 1662 ruled that witches existed as a matter of law; two poor old women were convicted and killed.
42. Not Sir Thomas Jones, later JKB, then CJCP, because he was of Lincoln's Inn. Quite probably Sir William Jones (1631–1682), later Solicitor-General and Attorney-General, Dryden's 'bull-faced Jonas', whom Evelyn would have favoured as a fellow anti-Catholic activist.

16 WOMEN

> All persons, both male and female, may submit to arbitrement except they be prohibited, by nature or by law... as women covert, without their husbands.
>
> *Arbitrium Redivivum* (1694) p13

> In argument with men, a woman ever
> Goes by the worse, whatever be her cause.
>
> John Milton *Samson Agonistes* (1671) I 93

1. INTRODUCTION

Milton (1608–1674) must never have met the women of this chapter who were his contemporaries. In the 17th century women played a greater part in legal affairs than some historians would have us believe.[1] For example, single and married women owned, bought, sold and left land by will; they routinely executed and witnessed legal documents.[2] Most women in London said they maintained themselves, wholly or in part, by their own work: not only 85 per cent of widows and 81 per cent of spinsters, which may not be so surprising, but 60 per cent of married women.[3]

The story of two young single women in London in October 1615 should suffice to give the lie to any assumption that women had no legal rights then, nor determination to exercise them:[4]

> Elizabeth and Frances, maiden daughters of the late Sir Henry Brunkard, each with a marriage portion of £3,000, took a house in the parish of St Clement Danes in order to follow their law suits. On a summer's evening in 1615 they repelled two unwanted drunken callers – a young Bachelor of Arts from Oxford and his friend from the Middle Temple – by emptying a chamberpot of urine on their heads. The girls secured the indictment of the 'roaring boyes', and when they fled the justices' warrant filed a bill in Star Chamber in October charging defamation, conspiracy, unlawful assembly, and forcible entry and praying a *ne exeat regno* on the grounds they were likely to flee the country.

---

1. But not WR Prest 'Law and Women's Rights' [Prest], particularly Pt I 169–172 and fn 16; or DM Stenton *The English Woman in History*.
2. *The Memorandum Book of of Richard Cholmeley of Brandsby 1602–1623* North Yorks Record Office Pubns 44 1988 [*Cholmeley*] 122. Craig Muldrew 'A Mutual Assent' [Muldrew *Mutual*] 55.
3. Muldrew *Mutual* 49 citing Peter Earle 'The Female Labour Market' 336–337.
4. TG Barnes 'Star Chamber Litigants' 9–10.

Women were not denied access to litigation and some preferred it, like Lady Anne Clifford and Joan Thynne. Lady Anne Clifford is dealt with at length below. Joan Thynne's letters show her preference for litigation, though she once asked her husband to act as arbitrator: 'Let me entreat you to end the suit between Richard Lingen and Mr Beaumont his brother-in-law, for that he is contented that you shall have the hearing of the matter between them'.[5] Many documents in national and local archives reveal that some women preferred private arbitration.[6] Their preferences depended on their circumstances. The non-lawyer Christopher Hatton, who danced so nicely into Elizabeth's favour that she later made him Lord Chancellor, noted in 1563 Mary Egerton's 'unwillingness to conform herself to Her Majesty's proceedings from a certain preciseness of conscience incident to divers of her sex, without reason or measure oftentimes'.[7] That did not stop Mary from acting as arbitrator.

Two Yorkshire women have been chosen to represent the range of women's involvement. The lives of Margaret Hoby and Anne Clifford were full of dispute settlement. Though both were privileged with property and authority, and were not too distantly related, in many ways they could hardly have had more different personalities; but both were kind enough to keep diaries which provide ample evidence of their involvement in disputes.

2. MARGARET HOBY

The life of Margaret Hoby (1571–1633) is evidence of a married woman's involvement in mediation and arbitration, both as party and resolver in her own right. She was the third wife of Sir Thomas Posthumous Hoby and he her third husband. Her previous two were Walter, brother of Essex, Elizabeth I's favourite, and Thomas, brother of Sir Philip Sidney. Her father, landowner Arthur Dakins, was a JP, as were all her husbands. The Hobys' home was the manor of Hackness, North Yorkshire, which Margaret had inherited on her father's death and to which she had brought her previous husbands. She stayed close to her mother, Thomasine, co-executrix of Arthur Dakins' will, whom she often visited at her home nearby in Linton.

Hoby (1566–1640) was an MP for most of the years 1597 to 1628.[8] His father, also Sir Thomas, was ambassador to France, translated Castiglione *The Courtier* and died at thirty-six. His mother, Elizabeth Cooke, was an even better scholar. Her sister Mildred married William Cecil, Lord

---

5. AD Wall ed *Two Elizabethan Women* 2–23.
6. Nat Arch E 134/9JasI/Hil10 (lease); E 134/10ChasI/Mich 64; Norfolk GIL/4/194, 718x8. Laura Gowing 'Language, Power and the Law' 26–47.
7. Roebuck *Golden Age* 154.
8. The background is fuller in Felicity Heal 'Reputation and Honour' [Heal].

Burghley; her sister Anne married Lord Keeper Nicholas Bacon, father of Francis and Nathaniel. When Hoby wrote to Francis Bacon, congratulating him on his marriage, Bacon replied:[9] 'Your loving congratulations for my doubled life, as you call it, I thank you for. No man may better conceive the joys of a good wife than yourself with whom I dare not compare'. So Hoby had connections, though he was an outsider in North Yorkshire, representing central Government and the new religion in a part of the country that never relished control from London and clung to the old faith. In particular, their neighbours the recusant Cholmeleys and the Eures resented Hoby's interference in their previously unchallenged power.

At Hackness Margaret presided over not only a considerable household but an agricultural business, supervising sowing and reaping, planting and timber cutting. She took upon herself a wider range of responsibilities in the community: not only as nurse, dressing serious wounds, and as midwife, but even when necessary as surgeon. On 26 June 1601 she attempted a delicate operation:[10]

> This day in the afternoon I had a child brought to see... who had no fundament, and had no passage for excrement but at the mouth. I was earnestly entreated to cut the place to see if any passage could be made but, although I cut deep and searched, there was none to be found.

Among all the routine entries in her diaries of her regular devotions, many telling us no more than that she got up, prayed, had her breakfast, prayed again, went to church, came home, prayed again, did religious exercises, dined, prayed and went to bed – day after day – there are glimpses of disputes, some in her household which she settled, some in which she was a party.

She and Hoby worked together and were sometimes joined as parties to litigation, as at Christmas 1604: 'This morning did William Harrison serve a subpoena on Mr Hoby and myself to answer to I know not what'. But she also routinely took charge herself of legal matters. On 24 January 1601 she wrote:

> After prayers I went to work and, having read a little, I talked with some that came to dine with us, as Mr Betnam, Mr Stillington and Mr Smith: after dinner I talked with Mr Betnam, and after a while came in Mr Etherington, Mr Jenkins and Mr Bridges. After I concluded with Mr Betnam touching a recognisance, and so I went to private prayers.

9. James Spedding ed *The Works of Francis Bacon* 298–299 [Spedding].
10. DM Meads ed *Diary of Lady Margaret Hoby* [Meads]; Joanna Moody ed *Private Life* [Moody]; Craig Muldrew 'The Culture of Reconciliation' [Muldrew] 932 fnn73, 75.

Mr Betnam seems to have been an adviser, perhaps a lawyer. The Hobys went to stay at his house in Kent to escape the plague. Margaret dealt with the various men on her own, though Hoby was there for dinner.

On 24 September 1601 Margaret records: 'I sealed a lease of the Intake to Stephen Tubley'. This act of a married woman without her husband was not worthy of comment. She might settle a claim. The diary entry for 1 December 1600 records: 'After I was ready and had prayed and read, I walked, set my hand to a release to my cousin Strangeways of all the debts and suits that I might claim anything from him and so went to dinner'. Margaret was close to another cousin, Robert Dakins, who visited her often. They read together and discussed religion. In the summer of 1601 he was buying from her and her mother the family home at Linton. There were two other Dakins cousins, Sir Arthur the father and his son of the same name. 'My old cousin Arthur Dakins' visited on 18 June 1601. Two days later: 'I talked with my brother Dakins about his son and after dinner we walked abroad'. The entry for the next day, read on its own, might more easily refer to Cousin Robert, but in its context must show the continuation of a discussion with Sir Arthur: 'After private prayers I read abroad with my cousin Dakins. After I came home and had dined, I talked of good matters with him, and he read to me, and after we went forth and saw some sheep he was to buy'. And then the next day's entry is simply: 'This day, in the afternoon, came my young cousin, Arthur Dakins, and so his father and he were reconciled'.

Margaret must have been of help to her husband in his work as a JP, including conciliation. On 4 September 1601: 'Mr Hoby and I talked of some complaints made to him; then I dined and after dinner I copied out a letter which Mr Hoby had written to the Bishop of Limerick, touching his agreement to peace'. John Thornborough, Bishop of Limerick, and his wife were old friends and visitors to Hackness. Margaret always referred to her husband as 'Mr Hoby', though he had been knighted in 1594.

There were ten manservants at Hackness. One of them, John Wasse, seems to have been a source of trouble. At the North Riding Quarter Sessions in 1616 his name appears with Sir Arthur Dakins':[11]

Northallerton July 1616
That Will Haynes and Will Richeson, constables of Allerton, be fined 5s each for not executing a warrant from Sir Arthur Dakins for the apprehension of John Wasse.
That John Wasse of Allerton, on his submission, be fined 2s 6d etc.

Of course, that may be another John Wasse from the one in Margaret's diary for 5 and 6 September 1601:

11. Eleanor Trotter *Seventeenth Century Life* 94 fn2 citing North Riding Quarter Sessions Reports I p268.

After private prayers I had occasion to return to prayer again by a domestical injury; and after dinner I used my accustomed exercises about the house; and, after I had perused John Wasse's accusing letter, I went to private prayer.

Before I went to church Wasse asked me forgiveness....

After I had again been at the church, I dressed Hilary's finger, talked with Anne Mathew about some abuse, and at my time went to private prayer.

The first hint of the great dispute which occupied so much of Margaret's time later comes in entries for late August 1600. On 27 and 28 she wrote:

After I was ready I spake with Mr Ewrie, who was so drunk I soon made an end of that I had no reason to stay for.... Then, having talked with Mr Hoby about the abuse offered by Mr Ewere and his Company, I went to private prayer and so to bed....

The details are best described in Hoby's enclosure with his petition to the Privy Council of 5 September 1600, which, with Eure's reply and the other relevant documents is in an appendix to Joanna Moody's book.[12] In brief, Sir William Eure had land adjoining Hackness. He and Hoby were both Yorkshire JPs and vied for position, Hoby being a strong Puritan and scourge of recusants and others, like the Eures, whose beliefs did not constrain them to behave as Hoby thought God required. The Eures were old nobility, dating back to the Conquest. Hoby was a newcomer, in Hackness only in his wife's right. Sir William Eure, his son William and their retinue had descended on Hackness and quite deliberately dishonoured Hoby by abusing his hospitality, drinking, playing cards, blaspheming and mocking his religious service with his servants. They stayed all night carousing and would leave only when Margaret agreed next morning to admit Sir William to her bedchamber. Typically she tried to take the heat out of the dispute: 'she prayed him to depart the house in quietness'. But Eure was not yet finished. He told a Hoby servant: 'Tell thy master he hath sent me scurvy messages and the next time I meet him I will tell him so, if he be upon the bench, and will pull him by the beard'. Hardly a brave boast: Hoby was famously tiny. Eure then left but not before smashing a few windows. On Saturday and Sunday, 3 and 4 October 1601, Margaret wrote:

We came to York and was invited to supper to my lord of Limerick, where after supper I had much talk, little to my comfort.... The 5 day, 6, 7, 8, 9 and 10, both Mr Hoby and myself was solicited by my lord president [of the Council in the North] and my lord of Limerick and others, to take up [i.e. settle] our suit with my lord Eure in the Star Chamber, which in regard of Christian peace we were inclined unto; but, perceiving ourselves to be wronged, in regard that an end was sought which would have tended much to our discredits, and that the truth of our injuries would not be considered, we came away abruptly on Saturday the 10 of this month.

12. Moody 239–245 and in Heal.

Thomas Cecil, 2nd Lord Burghley, was then President of the Council in the North. He was Hoby's cousin, his father having married Hoby's aunt Mildred. His deputy was Lord Eure, who, as Hoby wrote in his petition, was 'father, brother and cousin to the offenders'. When the matter came before the Council, and was referred to the Star Chamber, it became political. Cecil had just presided over the downfall of Essex. Everything conspired to favour the Hobys:[13]

> Sir Thomas was of utility to the Privy Council in the North Riding, especially in the work of monitoring the arrival of Catholic priests on the coasts.... Cecil could scarcely undermine so useful a figure in this dark corner of the land. If this consideration was always relevant, the timing of the Star Chamber case was fortunate; for both Sir William Eure and Richard Cholmley [our Richard Cholmeley of Chapter 15] were caught in the fringes of the Essex rebellion. Eure was imprisoned for questionable conversations with James VI [of Scotland, James I of England], probably on Essex's behalf: Cholmley, who was in London at the time of the rising because of the Hoby dispute, took some minor part for the earl.

It is no surprise, then, to find Margaret as intransigent as Thomas in rejecting an out-of-court private settlement, however hard her friend the bishop might try to persuade her of her godly duty; and their steadfast defence of their honour paid off. On 17 February 1602 she recorded simply: 'Mr Hoby came from London having ended all his business there, I praise god'. And on 29 June, without triumph or even undue satisfaction, she wrote:

> This day came the Lord Eure and his men to Hackness to pay £100 which was appointed them and others to pay, by the lords of the Privy Council in the Star Chamber, for their riot committed and uncivil behaviour at Hackness; and so it fell out that, as it was done in the sight of our tenants, so many of the tenants were by when the money was brought, which I note, as seeing the justice and mercy of god to his servants in manifesting to the world, who little regards them, that he will bring down their enemies unto them.

And the Eures had to pay that fine every year until modern times.

3. ANNE CLIFFORD

Anne Clifford (1590–1676) was the only surviving child of the Earl of Cumberland and Margaret, daughter of the Earl of Bedford.[14] Her father died when she was fifteen, deeply in debt, leaving his estates to his brother Francis, with £15,000 to Anne as her portion. But most of his lands were not his to devise; he had only a life estate; they were entailed to his heir,

---

13. Heal 175.
14. RT Spence 'Clifford, Anne' *ODNB*; RT Spence *Lady Anne Clifford*; Martin Holmes *Proud Northern Lady* [Holmes].

and that was Anne, his only surviving child. Her mother sued to recover them and the dispute lasted forty years. On her mother's death in 1616 Anne took charge and it became her lifelong obsession.

Anne was small of stature but not of spirit or of self-worth. Her mother and aunt were invited to be pall bearers at the funeral of Elizabeth I. Anne was not. She was then only thirteen, and probably six inches or more too short, but she was not pleased:[15] 'My mother and my aunt Warwick being mourners, but I was not allowed to be one because I was not high enough, which did much trouble me then'. Anne married Richard Sackville, Earl of Dorset, when she was nineteen. He died in 1624. In 1630 she married Philip Herbert, Earl of Pembroke and Montgomery, but throughout both marriages she kept her own name and was always known as Lady Anne Clifford. She was scholarly and single-minded. Her diaries start in 1603 and run intermittently to her death. The first collection is the Knole Diary 1603–1619; then there is a gap, partly filled by other manuscript sources; then the Kendal Diary 1650–1675, with scraps she dictated in the last year 1676.

The Knole Diary   The first reference to 'this Business', as she calls her property battles, is on 17 February 1616, while her mother was still alive. 'Persuade' meant then no more than 'try to persuade':

> Upon the 16th my Lady Grantham and Mrs Newton came to see me. The next day she told me the Archbishop of Canterbury would come to see me, and she persuaded me very earnestly to agree to this business, which I took as a great argument of her love. My cousin Russell came to me the same day and chid me and told me of all my faults and errors in this business – he made me weep bitterly.... Upon the 17th my Lord Archbishop of Canterbury, my Lord William Howard, my Lord Roos, my cousin Russell, my brother Sackville and a great company of men of note were all in the gallery at Dorset House, where the Archbishop took me aside and talked with me privately one hour and a half and persuaded me both by divine and human means to set my hand to their arguments. But my answer to His Lordship was that I would do nothing till my Lady and I had conferred together. Much persuasion was made by him and all the company, sometimes terrifying me and sometimes flattering me, but at length it was concluded that I should leave and go to my mother and send an answer by 22 March next whether I will agree to the business or not, and to this prayer my Lord of Canterbury and the rest of the Lords have set their hands. Next day was a marvellous day to me through the mercy of God, for it was generally thought that I must either have sealed the Agreement or else have parted with my Lord.

Tiny twenty-six-year-old Anne and her mother on one side, her husband, family, the archbishop and half the Government on the other! The Court

15. DJH Clifford ed *The Diaries* [*Clifford Diaries*].

of Common Pleas had decided in 1615 that Anne could choose either the £15,000 or lands in Skipton and Westmoreland. The agreement being forced on her was that she should accept the terms of the will: her uncle Francis, now Earl of Cumberland, should have all the land and Anne the £15,000. Her husband was happy to go along with that, knowing he could then get his hands on that money. On 26 February Anne recorded their parting 'with a heavy heart considering how many things stood between my Lord and I'. Then on 20 March:

> Lord William Howard with his son, my cousin William Howard, and Mr John Dudley came hither to take the answer of my mother and myself which was a direct denial to stand to the judges' award. The same day came Sir Timothy Whittington hither, who did all he could to mitigate the anger between Lord William Howard and my mother, so at last we parted all good friends.

Anne spent 31 March and 1 April with her mother 'and had much talk about this Business', then 'a grievous and heavy parting'. She got 'a cold welcome' when next she met her husband and told him 'I had left those writings which the Judges and my Lord would have me sign and seal behind with my mother'. On 18 April she received 'a letter from my Lord to let me know this was the last time of asking me whether I would set my hand to this Award of the Judges. Upon the 19th I returned to my Lord for answer that I would not stand to the Award of the Judges what misery soever it cost me'. And misery came at once. Sackville declared that they would live apart and he would have their daughter, still not two years old. On 3 May: 'When I considered it would both make my Lord more angry with me and be worse for the child, I resolved to let her go'. On 11 May Sackville sent Anne back his wedding ring and she returned his. She got all the gossip from well-wishers: he had won £200 on a cockfight, and was having fun at the horse races, bowling alleys and plays, while she was 'condemned by most folks because I would not consent to the Agreement, so as I may truly say, I am like an owl in the desert'.

Anne was constantly pestered by friend and foe to sign the agreement to allow the dispute to be arbitrated. Not all, though; on 28 May: 'Lady Selby came hither to see me and told me that she had heard some folks say that I have done well in not consenting to the composition'. Then, on 29 May, she heard that her mother had died. In her will she provided that she should be buried at Alnwick, not Skipton, 'I took that as a sign that I should be dispossessed of the inheritance of my forefathers'. But then a codicil was found that said Anne should decide the place of burial, 'which was some contentment to my aggrieved soul'. But even Anne's friends who brought condolences took the opportunity to try to persuade her in her grief to sign the Agreement.

Sackville changed tack. On 8 June he 'desired to have me pass my rights of the lands of Westmoreland to him and my child'. On 17 June he sent her a conveyance, which she refused to sign. On 19: 'My Lord came down for me... and persuaded me to consent to his business and assured me how kind and good a husband he would be to me'. The next day they went up to London, where: 'I passed by fine (before my Lord Hubbard) the inheritance of Westmoreland to my Lord if I had no heirs of my own body'. But, of course, she had their daughter, so Sackville would only take if she died and young Anne died childless.

In London she met the Queen 'who used me exceedingly well' and on Sunday 30 June she went with Lady Robert Rich and others by barge to Greenwich, where she said farewell 'to the Queen and all my friends':

> About this time it was agreed between my Lord and me that Mrs Bathurst should go away from the child and that Willoughby should have charge of her until I should appoint it otherwise. He gave me his faithful promise that he would come after me into the North as soon as he could, and that the child should come out of hand, so that my Lord and I were never greater friends than at this time.

On 1 August she entertained Bromley B and Nichols J, assize judges on the Northern Circuit, and agreed to take from them and settle a dispute involving her tenants which had come before them at the assizes.

Relations with her husband improved. On 1 July she had signed over to him 'a great part of my Third in my Lord's land', on his promise to make her the appropriate jointure, and on her departure 'my Lord brought me down to the coach side, where we had a loving and kind parting'. This harmony continued. On 24 August they were sharing 'the green velvet bed' in her mother's old room and 'on 28 I wrought stitch work and my Lord sat and read by me'. But when he left for London, he would not let her join him. He had had a row with 'my cousin Clifford', heir to uncle Cumberland. To avoid a duel, the Privy Council summoned them both, and 'the King made them friends, giving my Lord marvellous good words, and willed him to send for me because he meant to make an Agreement himself between us'. And there begins the saga of royal attempts to mediate.[16]

Her husband had prepared well. He sent for her to London and met her in Islington with ten or eleven coaches, full of their friends. Their child was waiting for her at Dorset House, which was 'well dressed up' to greet her. That evening she and her husband and daughter were entertained by the Lord Treasurer. She wrote nothing of Christmas but on 27 December: 'I dined at my Lady Elizabeth Gray's lodgings at Somerset House, where I met Lady Compton and Lady Fielding and spoke to them about my coming

---

16. A footnote for 4 November records: 'My Lord Cork [Coke] was displaced and Montague made Lord Chief Justice in his stead'.

to the King'. After dinner, Sackville took her to Lady Arundel's to see the pictures and statues. She knew she was being prepared:

> All this time of my being at London I was much sent to and visited by many, being unexpected that ever matters should have gone so well with me and my Lord, everybody persuading me to hear and make an end since the King had taken the matter in hand.

On New Year's Day 1617 Anne went to Somerset House to meet the Queen and a host of fine ladies, with 'a great deal of company that came along with the King and the Prince'. Lady Arundel saw her chance and 'had much talk with me about the Business and persuaded me to yield to the King in all things'. Moreover, 'As the King passed by he kissed me. Afterwards the Queen... kissed me and used me very kindly'. On 8 January Anne and her husband went to Knowle, where they 'had a falling out about the land'. He sulked for a couple of days and then left for London without telling Anne. Then he sent for her to go 'to London the next day because I was to go before the King on Monday next.' Anne's own account of their meeting does little to support the assumption that every woman then was a helpless victim of legal and social oppression. Not Anne!

> Upon the 18th being Saturday I went presently after dinner to the Queen to the Drawing Chamber, where my Lady Derby told the Queen how my Business stood and that I was to go to the King; so she promised me she would do all the good in it she could. [Anne's footnote adds: 'The Queen gave me a warning not to trust my matters absolutely to the King lest he should deceive me'.] When I had stayed but a little while there I was sent for out, my Lord and I going through Lord Buckingham's chamber, who brought us into the King, being in the Drawing Chamber. He put out all that were there, and my Lord and I kneeled by his chair side, when he persuaded us both to peace, and to put the whole matter wholly into his hands. Which my Lord consented to, but I beseeched His Majesty to pardon me, for that I would never part with Westmoreland while I lived upon any condition whatsoever. Sometimes he used fair means and persuasions and sometimes foul means, but I was resolved before, so as nothing would move me.

At that stage Sackville was hoping he would get his way without a fight: 'At this time I was much bounden to my Lord, for he was far kinder to me in all these Businesses than I expected, and was very unwilling that the King should do me any public disgrace'. But it was not to last:

> Upon the 20th I and my Lord went presently after dinner to the Court. He went up the King's side... about 8 o'clock I was sent for up to the King in his Drawing Chamber, when the door was locked and nobody suffered to stay there but my Lord and I, my uncle Cumberland, my cousin Clifford, my lords Arundel, Pembroke, Montgomery [Anne's husband-to-be] and Sir John Digby. For lawyers there were my Lord Chief Justice Montague and Hobart, Yelverton

and the King's Solicitor Sir Randall Crewe, that was to speak for my Lord and I. The King asked us all if we would submit to his judgment in this case. My uncle Cumberland, my cousin Clifford and my Lord answered they would, but I would never agree to it without Westmoreland, at which the King grew in a great chaff, my lord of Pembroke and the King's Solicitor speaking much against me. At last, when they saw there was no remedy, my Lord, fearing the King would do me some public disgrace, desired Sir John Digby would open the door, who went out with me and persuaded me much to yield to the King. My lord Hay came to me, to whom I told in brief how this Business stood. Presently, after my Lord came from the King when it was resolved that, if I would not come to an Agreement, there should be an Agreement made without me. We went down... and so came home.

This day I may say I was led miraculously by God's Providence, and next to that I trust all my Good to the worth and nobleness of my Lord's disposition, for neither I nor anybody else thought I should have passed over this day so well as I have done.

All parties knew that there could be no arbitration unless both sides willingly submitted to it. Anne's agreement was a condition of the validity of any such agreement, whatever the King might do, but that did not stop James I from threatening to take the law into his own hands.

In the next few days Anne's concern was for her daughter who was having fits, but she found time on 22 January to write to Sackville to thank him 'for his noble usage towards me in London'.

Upon the 30th Mr Amherst the Preacher came hither to see me with whom I had much talk. He told me that now they began to think at London that I had done well in not referring this Business to the King, and that everybody said God had a hand in it. [Anne's footnote: All this time of my being in the country there was much ado in London about my Business, in so much that my Lord, my uncle Cumberland, my cousin Clifford, with the Chief Justice and counsel of both sides, on divers times with the King about it, and then the King, hearing it go so directly for me, he said there was a law in England to keep me from the land. There was at this time much cock-fighting at the Court, where my Lord's cocks did fight against the King's. Although this Business was somewhat chargeable to my Lord, yet it brought him into great grace and favour with the King, so as he useth him very kindly and speaketh very often and better of him than of any other man. My Lord grew very great with my Lord of Arundel.]

On 4 February: 'Thomas Woodyat came from London and brought a squirrel to the child, and my Lord wrote me a letter by which I perceived my Lord was clean out with me, and how much my enemies have wrought against me'. On 7: 'Mr Oberton and I had a great deal of talk, he telling me how much I was condemned in the world, and what strange censures most folks made of my courses'. On 12:

Rivers came from London and told me that the Judge had been with the King divers times about my Business, but as yet the Award is not published but it is thought that it will be much according to the Award that was formerly set down by the Judges. He told me that he had been with Lord William, who, as he thought, did not well like the Agreement, considering how he had heretofore shewn himself in the Business.

Upon the 16th my Lord came hither from London before dinner and told me how the whole state of my Business went and how things stood at Court....

Upon the 22nd Legge came down and brought me word that the King would make a composition and take a course to put me from my right to the lands, so as if I did not consider it speedily it would be too late, and how bitter the King stood against me....

Upon the 27th my Lord writ me word that the King had referred the drawing and perfecting the Business to the Solicitor.

On 14 March Anne heard that 'My Lord and my uncle were agreed and the writings sealed' and her footnote declares that Cumberland and Clifford and her husband 'signed and sealed the writings and made a final conclusion of my Business, and did what they could to cut me off from my right, but I referred my cause to God'. Sackville visited Anne on 27 March and they discussed the Business: 'he had acknowledged no statutes and the matter was not so fully finished, but there was a place for me to come in.... I found this time that he was nothing as much discontented with this agreement as I thought he would have been'. Then on 4 April:

My Lord told me he had as yet passed no fines and recoveries of my land, but that my uncle Cumberland had acknowledged statutes for payment of the money. And that all the writings were left with my Lord Keeper [Francis Bacon] and Lord Hobart till 21st next term, at which time they were fully to be concluded on. This was strange news to me for I thought all matters had been finished.

The 5th, my Lord went up to my closet and said how little money I had left contrary to all they had told him. Sometimes I had fair words from him and sometimes foul, but I took all patiently and did strive to give him as much content and assurance of my love as I could possibly, yet I told him I would never part with Westmoreland upon any condition whatever.

Upon the 7th, my Lord lay in my chamber. Upon the 8th, I sat by my Lord and my brother[-in-law] Sackville in the Drawing Chamber and heard much talk about my Businesses....

The 16th my Lord and I had much talk about these Businesses, he urging me still to go to London to sign and seal, but I told him that my promise was so far passed to my mother and to all the world that I would never do it, whatever became of me and mine. [17th] My Lord told me he was resolved never to move me more in these Businesses, because he saw how fully I was bent.

The 19th I signed 33 letters with my own hand which I sent to the tenants in Westmoreland. The same night my Lord and I had much talk and persuaded me to these Businesses, but I would not, yet I told him I was in perfect charity with all the world.

> The 20th, being Easter Day, my Lord and I received Communion... yet in the afternoon my Lord and I had a great falling out....
> The 23rd... my Lord should have lain with me but he and I fell out about matters.... The 24th... this night my Lord came to lie in my chamber.

On 7 May Anne notes that her husband was one of the great company which followed Francis Bacon on his triumphal procession to Westminster as Lord Keeper. She declared that she did not write to her husband because he did not write to her. He needed money. He was 'most discontented with me for not doing this Business, for he must be fain to buy land for the payment of the money which will much encumber his estate'. Then on 18 May: 'All in Westmoreland was surrendered to my uncle Cumberland'. On 25 May:

> My cousin Russell wrote to let me know how my Lord had cancelled my jointure he made upon me last June when I went into the North, and by these proceedings I may see how much my Lord is offended with me, and that my enemies have the upper hand of me.

She wrote and told him 'how ill I took his cancelling my jointure, but yet told him I was content to bear it with patience whatsoever he thought fit'. Cousin Clifford was already in Westmoreland but: 'all the tenants were very well affected towards me and very ill towards them' [31 May]. There was little progress in June, no 'Business or Agreement was fully concluded, in regard there was nothing had passed the Great Seal'. In July Anne was 'still working and sad' and unwell. She was told: 'My Lord was setting his land upon his brother, and that the value of the fines I released to my Lord was very great, which did much perplex me'. She wrote to Sackville 'desiring him to come hither because I found myself very ill'. Worse arrived with a copy of the King's Award on 9 March, 'being as ill for me as possible'. 'Presently my Lord came down hither, he being something kinder to me than he was, out of pity in regard he saw me so much troubled'.[17] Before he left on a prolonged hunting trip in early August, Sackville gave Anne back his grandmother's ring but she makes no mention of giving him the wedding ring she had taken back. He returned to Knowle on 29 September: 'At this Michaelmas did my Lord receive £4,000 of my uncle the Earl of Cumberland and which was the first penny that I received of my Portion'. On 4 November, after 'an extreme good feast':

> I went to the Court where the Queen sent for me into her own bedchamber and here I spoke to the King [Anne's footnote: King James kissed me when I was with him, and that was the first time that I ever was so near King James as

17. Anne's footnote here reads: 'About this time there was great stir about my Lady Hatton's daughter – my brother Sackville undertaking to carry her away with men and horses'. The story is told in Chapter 12.

to touch him. She seems to have forgotten the earlier kiss]. He used me very graciously and bid me go to His Attorney who would inform him more of my desires.... I carried Mr Davis to Gray's Inn to the Attorney, when I told him His Majesty's pleasure. From thence I went to Mr Walton's lodgings to entreat his advice and help in this Business.

There is little about 'the Business' in the diary in the early months of 1619. On Whitsunday Anne noted 'my Lord protesting that he would be a very good husband to me and that I should receive no prejudice by releasing my Thirds'. The Queen died and Anne spent nights watching by her body, as Sackville sat by the sick King's bed.

Westmoreland matters seemed to have been going well, but on 8 May 1619 the Lord Chancellor Francis Bacon summoned two of Anne's tenants and told them 'to be good tenants to my uncle Cumberland, whereat the poor men were much perplexed and troubled but I gave them the best comfort and encouragement I could'. She notes the next day that 'Mr Sherborne promised to speak to the Chancellor on behalf of the tenants' and two days later that Lord William Howard promised 'to do all the good he could in the Northern Business'. And in a footnote: 'About this time my Lord of Doncaster went to his Embassage into Germany being sent by the King both to the Emperor and the Pope to mediate between them'. Another footnote at the end of May reads:

After supper my Lord and I walked before the gate, where I told him how good he was to everybody else and how unkind to me. In conclusion he promised me in a manner that he would make me a jointure of £4,000 a year, whereof part should be of that land that he has assured to my uncle Cumberland.

The year ended with Anne thinking she might be pregnant and on 15 December: 'My Lord and I had a great falling out, he saying that if ever my land came to me I should assure it as he would have me'. There the *Knole Diary* ends.

Harleian MS 6177 Various manuscript sources are evidence for the next thirty years, in which Anne had three sons, who all died, and another daughter, Isabella, born in 1622, who survived. Sackville died in 1624, having managed to spend almost all of the vast fortune he had inherited:[18]

On 10 July 1623 my Lord, being then very sickly, did make over to me my jointure of those lands in Sussex, part whereof I now enjoy, and part thereof I have assigned and made over to my two daughters. My first Lord died 28 March 1624... but I was not with him when he died, being very sick myself.... In his own nature of a just mind, of a sweet disposition and very valiant in his own person.... Though I was happy in many respects being his wife, yet was

18. *Clifford Diaries* 91–92, 95 citing BL Harleian MS 6177.

I most unhappy in having the malicious hatred of his brother, then Sir Edward Sackville, towards me... till his own death in 1652....

In August 1628 were the first claims made by way of law and advice of counsel after the Awards to maintain my right in the lands of my inheritance in Craven and Westmoreland.

Then she surprised everyone by marrying again:

On 3 June [1630]... was I married to my second husband Philip Herbert, Earl of Pembroke and Montgomery, Lord Chamberlain of the King's Household and Knight of the Garter, he being then one of the greatest subjects in the kingdom.... This second marriage of mine was wonderfully brought to pass by the providence of God for the crossing and disappointing the envy, malice and sinister practices of my Enemies.

That seems clear enough and unsurprising, knowing Anne's obsession. She had married the most powerful man she could find to help her with her claims. Herbert, widowed for scarcely more than a year, was one of those men, then 'my Lord Montgomery', who was with James I when he browbeat her on 20 January 1617. Herbert knew Anne's Business well. Could he be relied on to support her in it?

From 1630 to 1634 Anne and Herbert lived together at his town house in Whitehall. She bore two sons, who died at birth. At the end of 1634 she left him there, 'by reason of some discontent', and settled at his house at Wilton in Wiltshire till his death in 1650. But long before then Anne had got what she wanted from him:[19]

Being still mindful to vindicate my right and interest in the lands and my inheritance in Westmoreland and Craven, in August and September 1632, by commission under my second Lord's and my hand and seal, procured legal claims to be made, as were formerly executed in the time of my widowhood; which claims are also entered in the records of the time when I was Countess of Pembroke. Also in August 1637 the second claims, while I was Countess of Pembroke in the lifetime of my second Lord, were made in like manner to all the lands in mine inheritance... the last claims made thereunto, for the Civil Wars broke out in the Northern parts, so that no more claims could be made there, during my uncle Cumberland and his son's lifetime.

5 June 1635 did my second Lord in Baynard's Castle make over to me my jointure in those lands of his in the Isle of Sheppey in Kent, which he had formerly made in jointure to his first wife ... and released his right to all my lands in Westmoreland, and £5,000 out of the lands in Craven for a part of my younger daughter's portion.

The discontent was probably the difference about Isabella's marriage. Herbert wanted her to marry one of his sons but she was determined to marry her own choice. Anne supported her and she got her way. But Anne's greatest satisfaction can be read into her report that on 21 January 1641 old Uncle Cumberland finally died, and only two years later his detested son and heir Henry Clifford.

Even the Civil War could not force Anne and Herbert to live together. They left Wilton together on 12 October 1642 but Herbert went to his lodgings in the Cockpit in St James's Park, while Anne and Isabella went to Baynard's Castle, where Anne stayed for six years and nine months, 'the Civil Wars being then very hot in England. So that I may say it was a place of refuge for me to hide myself in till these troubles were over-passed'. Her safety there was secured by another benefit she got from her second marriage: Herbert had gone over to Cromwell. And so it was on 3 June 1649 that Anne 'took my last leave of my second husband the Earl of Pembroke in his lodgings in the Cockpit'; and on 11 July she said goodbye to her two daughters and their families and left for Skipton Castle. She took a week to get there, and stayed until 7 July, when she left for Appleby Castle, where she stayed until the following February. Home at last in her ancestral estates!

At once she started to rebuild her castles, showing the same defiance of Cromwell as she had to James I: 'Let him destroy my castles if he will, as often as he levels them I will rebuild them, so long as he leaves me a shilling in my pocket'. Of course, that was for her diary; she had neither the intention nor the means of military or even political opposition to Cromwell. Her ambitions were quite different and no doubt Cromwell, the political pragmatist, had more pressing problems. Anne concentrated on the disputes of her tenants. Restoring her manorial courts and acting as 'sheriffess' as she called herself, she could lord it over them. Poor Murgatroyd should have known better than defy her. He refused to hand over the traditional annual 'boon hen'. Having secured an easy victory over him in her own court, she invited him to the castle for dinner and served him his hen. And she was content to quote: 'The 16th Psalm: The lot is fallen unto me in a pleasant place. I have a fair heritage'.[20]

The Kendal Diary From 1652 to 1675 Anne kept what is now known as the *Kendal Diary*. It says something of her concerns with differences between her and her tenants and between them. On 13 February 1651 she arrived in Skipton. She wrote that she enjoyed herself in 'those kind of country affairs about my estate', which included suits and differences in law, which:[21]

> began to grow hot between my tenants in Westmoreland and some of my tenants in Craven and me. Which suits with my tenants in Westmoreland are still depending and God knows how long they may last. But the differences

20. *Clifford Diaries* 107.
21. *Clifford Diaries* 113.

with my tenants in Craven were for the most part by compromise and agreement reconciled and taken up.

At this time cousin Elizabeth Clifford, Countess of Cork and heiress of the Earl of Cumberland, stayed at her house in Bolton in Craven, and she and Anne often dined together. Each had claims to land against the other, but 'we passed them by as Prov. 19. 1'.[22] That spirit of forbearance did not apply to her Westmoreland tenants, who were getting the better of her:

6 November 1652 was my cause in Chancery between me and my tenants in Westmoreland dismissed out of that court and I was left to my remedy at Common Law, to which Business God send me some good conclusion, for it hath been both chargeable and troublesome to me.... 1653 did I cause several courts to be kept in my name in divers of my manors within the county of Westmoreland. But the tenants being obstinate and no fractor [factor?], i.e. though they appeared, would not answer as they were called. And also many causes of the Enactment [presumably one of the Inclosure Acts] did I cause to be sealed in this county, in order to a trial with my tenants at Common Law. (God save them good signs).

The assize judges stayed with Anne at Appleby Castle when they held the assizes there, as they did each year thereafter, except in 1651, when there were no assizes on the Northern Circuit because of the Civil War. In 1653 they dismissed her action against her Westmoreland tenants, 'by reason of a general exception taken against most of the jury'. So it was transferred to London, into the Common Pleas, where on 9 November 1653 it: 'was given against me by the jury against evidence and direction of the court, and of the judgment of all that heard the case debated'.

But in matters of law there is nothing like perseverance, a bottomless purse and, perhaps, a cousin on the bench:[23]

16 May was the cause between me and my Westmoreland tenants heard at the Common Pleas bar in Westminster Hall, before four of the Chief Judges there: my cousin Oliver St John, LCJCP, Judge Atkyns, Judge Hugh Wyndham and Judge Matthew Hale.[24] Where a jury approval being sworn, and my cause was openly pleaded by Serjeant Maynard, Serjeant Newdigate and Serjeant Furnivall, who were of counsel for me; and Serjeant Earle and Serjeant Evers, counsel for my tenants. At which time they put me upon all manner of proofs, being plaintiffs in the cause. Though they were made forth by my witnesses very full to the satisfaction of the court. So that the jury gave me in a verdict for me

22. 'Better is the poor that walketh in his integrity, than he that is perverse in his lips, and is a fool.' Less apposite than Proverbs 22. 28, quoted when Anne had her Westmoreland boundaries ridden, for the first time since her mother died: 'Remove not the ancient landmark, which thy fathers have set'.
23. *Clifford Diaries* 133.
24. I have given the spellings by which they are now known; all were Parliamentary appointments, none reappointed at the Restoration.

against my tenants. And the next day 17th another jury appeared for the second trial, but the same went by default of the tenants, who only appeared but would not appeal at all. So that the jury did not go from the bar but immediately gave in another verdict on my behalf and the court thereupon awarded me costs in both the causes, value £250, and both verdicts exemplified under the seal of the court.

Oliver St John was a fine lawyer, counsel for John Hampden, cruel prosecutor of Strafford but, according to Campbell:[25] 'the first Englishman who ever seriously planned the establishment of a republican form of government'. He was related to Cromwell through his first two wives. He was a devious man, always ready to manipulate the truth and change sides to his own advantage. His parentage is obscure, the unreliable Clarendon saying he was a 'natural son of the house of Bullingbrook'. He presided on 12 November, sitting again with Atkyns [not Adams], Wyndham and Hale JJ, when:

> The case between me and my Westmoreland tenants heard in Westminster Hall... James Straker was defendant against me on the tenants' behalf.... Appeared not, nor any for him. So as he was nonsuited, £100 costs were against him, and the land decided to be mine and not the tenants'.

She lost no time: 'And since, I leased it out to another for 21 years'. A fourth trial before the same court on 23 April 1657 came to the same conclusion.

In February 1657 she ejected James Walker's family from the house he had rented from her, payment in arrears, and let it to John Salkeld for 21 years, payment in advance:

> By that means I altered the tenure of this land, which was the principal thing I was at in my suits in law with my Westmoreland tenants, as being a great benefit and advantage to me and my posterity, and not only to me but to all the landlords and tenants in that county.

Not all tenants would have seen it that way, especially those who had fought so hard and lost their traditional rights and were landed with huge bills for costs. Who knows what Captain Robert Atkinson felt? In 1664 Anne records that he, 'one of my tenants in Mallerstang, and that great enemy, was condemned to be hanged, drawn and quartered as a traitor to the King, for having had a hand in the late plot and conspiracy'. Twysden J and Turnor B, the assize judges who condemned him, were then staying at Appleby Castle. Her displeasure against Captain Atkinson, though, did not extend to his widow, Elizabeth. Anne records twelve years later on 14 January 1676: 'Mrs Elizabeth Atkinson... after dinner she came into my chamber and I kissed her and gave her 2s'. Moreover, Anne is said to

25. John Lord Campbell *The Lives of the Chief Justices* I 447.

have allowed Mrs Atkinson and her children to continue as her tenants at a nominal rent after her husband's execution.[26]

There must never have been a party more determined to reject arbitration. Martin Holmes quotes a manuscript biography of Lady Anne, now lost, which told of Cromwell's attempt to persuade her where James I had failed, appointing a commission of local gentry to attend her at Appleby to discuss the tenants' claims:[27]

> She used them with all kindness and courtesy, but told them plainly she would never refer any of her concerns in that kind to the Protector or any person living, but leave it wholly to the discretion of the law; adding further that she had refused to submit to King James on the like account, would never do it to the Protector, whatever hazard or danger she incurred thereby.

The Dictations   The last entry in the *Kendal Diary* is for 1 November 1675. The *Clifford Diaries* reproduce the notes taken at Anne's dictation by various clerks. They are as revealing as they are poignant, as Anne looked back on affairs of fifty or sixty years before, particularly the Business. She was then an old woman, confined to her bedroom but there she entertained nearly every day a throng of visitors. The women she kissed and took the men's hands. Often she gave them modest presents. And she could hear them as they dined in the next room. She was still in many ways the great Lady Anne Clifford, buying the wine and having bed linen made for her 'Family', as she called her many households, but making much of the obsessions of age: her loose stools and almost every night 'a very ill fit of the wind', and marking carefully when she cut her nails. Yet she still made promises to ensure that those who asked her nicely were elected to the next Parliament.[28] And on New Year's Day 1676:

> And this evening about 7 o'clock, after I was in bed, did Allan Strickland commit some disorders in my house, of which I was acquainted next morning by Mr Thomas Gabetis, my sheriff; but he, showing a great regret and compassion for those misdemeanours, I was moved upon his ingenious acknowledgment and confession to pardon him.

Her physical confinement and the passing years did nothing to confine her reminiscences, blessed with an undiminished grasp of detail which makes these last notes so valuable for an understanding of her Business. On 17 January 1676:

> I remembered how this day was 59 years since... I went out of Knowle House to Great Dorset House to my first Lord, the occasion being an Award that King James would have made concerning the lands of my ancient inheritance.... The

---

26. *Clifford Diaries* 245.
27. Holmes 152.
28. On 7 January and 22 February 1676, *Clifford Diaries* 242, 267.

18th day I remembered... I went with my first Lord before King James, into his Inner Drawing Chamber at Whitehall, where the King earnestly desired me to subscribe to an award which he intended to make betwixt me and my Lord on the one part, and my uncle of Cumberland and his son Henry Lord Clifford on the other part, concerning the lands of ancient inheritance in Craven and Westmoreland. But (by God's grace) I began to deny it, it being the first time I was ever before that King.... The 19th day I remembered how this day was 59 years and then Sunday in the afternoon in the withdrawing chamber of Queen Anne the Dane in the Court at Whitehall, did that Queen admonish me to persist in my denial of trusting my cause concerning my lands of inheritance to her husband King James' award, which admonition of hers and other of my friends did much to confirm me in my purpose, so as the next day I gave that King an absolute denial accordingly, which by God's Providence tended much to the good of me and mine.... The 20th day I remembered how... I went with my first Lord to the Court at Whitehall, where in the inner withdrawing chamber King James desired and urged me to submit to the Award which he would make concerning my lands of inheritance, but I absolutely denied to do so, wherein I was guided by a great Providence of God for the good of me and mine.

A month later on 17 February 1676:

And I remember how this day was 60 years when I and my first Lord, the Earl of Dorset, lay in Little Dorset House in London town and in the afternoon in the best gallery of Great Dorset House did George Abbot, Archbishop of Canterbury, and many others come to my first Lord and me, and did earnestly persuade me both by fair words and threatenings to stand to the Award the four chief Judges would then make betwixt my first Lord and me of the one part and my uncle of Cumberland and his son on the other part, concerning the lands of mine inheritance. [20 March] I remembered how this day was 60 years I and my blessed mother... give in our answer in writing that we would not stand to the Award the then four chief Judges meant to make concerning the lands of mine inheritance, which did spin out a great deal of trouble to us, yet God turned it for the best.

Anne usually ended each entry with a biblical reference. Her last was to Psalm 121: 'I will lift up mine eyes unto the hills, from whence cometh my help. My help cometh from the Lord'. She never wavered in her faith that she had won God over to her side. How could he have dared otherwise? As her faithful amanuensis Edward Hassell wrote two days later:

On Wednesday 22nd about 6 o'clock in the afternoon, after she had endured all her pains with a most Christian fortitude, always answering those who asked her how she did with – 'I thank God I am very well' – which were her last words directed to mortals, she with much cheerfulness, in her own chamber in Brougham Castle, wherein her noble father was born and her blessed mother died, yielded up her precious soul into the hands of her merciful Redeemer.

Even the prospect of death could not break her spirit.

4. WOMEN AS PARTIES

In practice, there seems to have been nothing to inhibit any woman from submitting a dispute to mediation or arbitration. The supposed incapacity of a feme covert to do so without her husband seems not to have been a bar. Certainly neither James I nor Oliver Cromwell saw any in Anne Clifford's case.

By arrangement with her opponent, a woman might arrange an arbitration of two JPs quite separately from the assizes.[29] The Western Circuit Assize Orders 1629–1648 contain exactly 200 orders relating to the settlement of disputes; in 55 of them one or more of the parties are women.[30] They include single women, whether unmarried or widowed, and married women with or without their husbands. Their status to sue and their right to be heard are never questioned. Equally with men they were required by the Poor Law to take poor children as apprentices.[31] They were equally expected to enter into bonds in their own names.[32]

The wide range of matters dispel any notion that women were always helpless bystanders. Helen Badcock was as ingenious as she was resourceful. Up before the Devon Assizes on 1 August 1631, one of a group charged with 'divers outrages and abuses' including battery, she 'cunningly had herself called while the prosecutor, Robert Yewe, was instructing counsel out of court'. Denham B discharged her and awarded a writ of good behaviour against Yewe, 'because he had bound her to appear and then produced no evidence against her'. When the truth came out, the court discharged that writ and issued one against Helen and her cronies, to appear at the next assizes.[33]

Widows sued one another and had their disputes mediated, and married women appeared with no sign of their husbands.[34] The records do not bother to distinguish women who had never been married. Their status to sue and be sued was never questioned.[35] They might have to be attached for breach of an award.[36] The JPs might determine their title to land.[37]

29. Cockburn *Western* 1069.
30. Cockburn *Western* 2, 28, 43, 49, 73, 79, 104, 192, 221, 251, 287, 364, 371, 372, 402, 403, 408, 435, 436, 510, 530, 636, 679, 696, 698, 721, 723, 748, 769, 779, 792, 797, 847, 850, 851, 856, 857, 892, 902, 926, 992, 1003, 1012, 1018, 1069, 1088, 1091, 1094, 1117, 1127, 1131, 1135, 113, 1137, 1197.
31. Cockburn *Western* 1003.
32. Cockburn *Western* 1117.
33. Cockburn *Western* 167.
34. Cockburn *Western* 73, 28, 408.
35. Cockburn *Western* 436; Thomasine Bennett seems to be such, and Easter Collins and Mary Poole in their 'dispute over a gold ring' 510.
36. Cockburn *Western* 43.
37. Cockburn *Western* 104, 221.

There is no clue in the record of the Wiltshire Assizes of 31 August 1648 to explain why it was Mary Archer who prosecuted three men for theft of a sword, a bow and 47s 6d from her cleric husband. On their acquittal, the accused claimed that Mary's prosecution was malicious. A JP was appointed to negotiate a settlement. If the parties would not be reconciled and he found that the prosecution was malicious, he was told to bind Mary over to the next assizes.

A woman might prefer to arrange a private arbitration. On 25 January 1638 Elizabeth Corbett wrote to Captain Davies, via Thomas Tyler at the sign of the Green Man on Ludgate Hill.[38] She asked him to mediate 'with my lord of Bridgwater' as arbitrator in her claim for certain grounds called 'Haremoor', which her late husband, Sir Andrew Corbett, had inherited from his father.

Women often appeared in their own right as parties before the Privy Council, both petitioning and defending. The Council, though impliedly, sometimes recognised their rights to trade on their own account, as it did by granting the widow Margaret Greenslade a licence to trade in biscuit.[39] Elizabeth I's Council had consistently shown a special concern for women petitioning in their own right.[40] Many were widows.[41] That concern continued under James I, his Council regularly sending their petitions to be mediated or arbitrated, for example that about Charity Williams's dowry, to two Bristol aldermen, to 'endeavour to make a friendly end by the best means you can'.[42] An example of this general concern was the Council's instructions for the care of 'poor, mad Katherine Markham', with a messenger to accompany her to her place of asylum; and orders for payment of her maintenance, when it fell into arrears.[43] But any poor widow could expect the Council to send her petition to arbitrators, especially if she complained against oppression by some overweening authority.[44]

The Council was ever ready to force reluctant husbands to pay the maintenance they owed. When Sir John Molyneux was threatening to escape abroad it told the Lord Chancellor to issue a writ *ne exeat regno*, 'lest he leave the realm', and ordered the Archbishop of Canterbury to hear 'the differences between the petitioner and her husband and order some course as shall be just and reasonable for the relief of the petitioner'.[45]

Widows, like everyone else, should normally use the usual course of litigation to establish their rights, in Jersey as in England. The Council

38. Shropshire 5422/1–2.
39. *APC* 46.141.
40. Roebuck *Golden Age* 146–149; *APC* 34.92.
41. *APC* 34.295.
42. *APC* 38.340.
43. *APC* 34.150; 34.338.
44. *APC* 37.401; 37.402.
45. *APC* 35.39.

wrote to the Bailiff and Jurats of Jersey, on behalf of 'the poor widow of that Isle, Mary le Dentu':[46]

> Although we can give no further credit to this complaint than to a bare information, and doubt not that the way to justice in that Isle lies open as well to the poor as to others of ability [i.e. property] and strength for the righting of all wrongs according to equity, yet, because there is some show of hard usage and oppression to the widow and fatherless, we require you... to take an indifferent hearing and... order some course to provide for the relief of the poor orphans, agreeable to equity and good reason.

That shows that the policies and sensitivities which inspired the work of Elizabeth I's Council had survived and were still potent ten years after her death. They continued into later reigns, however much the Council protested that litigation was the appropriate course for the resolution of the disputes of widows, as for everybody else. For example, in 1629 the Council referred the petition of Dorothy Gardner, 'whose distressed condition we greatly commiserate', to the Council in the North 'to settle a final order consonant to equity and justice'.[47] Two consecutive entries for a busy New Year's Eve 1622 illustrate the differences between the Council's stated policy and practice.[48] Two Kent JPs were sent the petitions of two widows, Elizabeth Jewler and Anne Wright:

> Although it is not usual for this Board to take knowledge of such causes as are properly determined at the law, nevertheless in regard of the great age and poverty of the petitioners (as they inform) we have been moved to recommend their complaint to your examination... to mediate some equitable agreement and end.

There is no hint of the nature of the dispute there; nor is it clear whether it was between the two widows or by them against others. But the next record is of a letter to three Somerset JPs (including John Paulet, a party elsewhere), requiring them to arbitrate a claim for a debt of £40 and tithes against the widow of William Godden. There is no suggestion of poverty on either side there, nor any other reason for not sending the parties to the appropriate court. A letter in 1626 to four Lincolnshire JPs (or any two) asked them to mediate 'some friendly and charitable end' between the unnamed bearer, 'a poor decayed widow', and Sir Anthony Irby, a young Lincolnshire landowner, later MP for Boston and four times married, who was alleged to be refusing to hand over her dower:[49]

> though we are not apt to give way to such informations but rather leave them to be righted in a legal course of justice yet the misery of this poor woman... will not allow a long and tedious suit in respect of her years and necessity.

46. *APC* 33.453.
47. *APC* 45.98.
48. *APC* 38.384.
49. *APC* 41.98.

A later letter reveals that Irby had refused mediation with the widow, Mrs Chapman, and her son:[50] 'none of them that are complained of will be drawn by fair means (without suit of laws which the petitioners are unable to undergo) to give any reasonable satisfaction to these poor people'. And so the mediators were told:

> to deal effectually with them to extend some charitable relief to the poor woman and her son, as in conscience and equity you think reasonable; which if they refuse to do then set down the reasons of their refusal under their hands and send them unto us, whereupon some further course shall be taken in behalf of the poor petitioners, as to equity shall appertain.

But there was another side to the story. On Mrs Chapman's death, Irby petitioned the Council, claiming that he, not her son, was the rightful heir of her husband.[51] He was prepared to give 'all just satisfaction' to the complainants but would make no grant that might put in question his rightful title to the land. He asked the Council either to 'take a view of the evidences' itself, or to 'refer him to a legal course'. It decided to 'leave the same to the ordinary course of law which is most fit and proper for the full and final determining thereof'.

In 1622 six Chester JPs were asked to deal with the petition of two poor widows called Foster, presumably sisters-in-law.[52] They complained that two men had 'taken privily over their heads a lease of a tenement wherein the petitioners and their ancestors have lived time out of mind'. They and their eight poor children would be forced to beg their bread and become a burden on the country. The Council declared that they deserved compassion, and 'in these times of scarcity and dearth it is rather expedient to provide for the relief and satisfaction of the poor, especially those that are industrious and by their own labours maintain themselves'. So 'in respect of your near abode to the place, take this complaint into your consideration and mediate effectually with the defendants on the poor petitioners' behalf'. And the Council wrote to the Bishop of London, Gaudie J and four others, asking them to 'use your best endeavours for the mediating some good end', on the petition of Elizabeth Sutherton of Norwich, a poor widow, 'forasmuch as her case seemeth such as deserveth pity and compassion'.[53]

If compassion required a composition with creditors, the first task was to ensure what debts were genuine. Those commissioned by the Council would have to 'mediate' them, as they did for Ellen Smyth, as described in Chapter 7.

50. *APC* 43.441.
51. *APC* 44.221.
52. *APC* 38.470.
53. *APC* 33.654.

The Council's sympathies were aroused when a widow alleged that her 'extreme poverty' was the result of 'much wrong and oppression done' by an attorney-at-law and the vicar, who had conspired to rob her of her husband's estate by forging a will.[54] Because she was 'wanting means to recover her right by the circular and accustomed course of law', the Council instructed six local gentlemen, or any three, 'to use your best means for the mediating some final end' or report so that 'further order may be given as shall agree with justice and equity and the distressed state of this poor woman'. So the criteria were to be not only the merits of the dispute but the poor widow's needs.

Similarly, Caesar MR was commissioned to deal with the petition of the widow Lady Tarbuck, in a land dispute with the man to whom her husband had improperly sold land over which she had a claim.[55]

> Although herein she might have her ordinary remedy by law, yet because it seems her estate is weak, and she not able to contend in suit, treat and mediate between them as you in your discretion shall think fit, procuring the lady such satisfaction as you shall find her case to deserve.

Not all widows were equal. In 1616 the Dowager Lady Effingham was riding through her park in Bletchingley with some servants, when they were attacked by the servants of the defendants, the Lord High Admiral, Lord Howard of Effingham and first Earl of Nottingham, hero of the defeat of the Armada, Privy Councillor, and his son, also Lord Howard of Effingham.[56] Lady Effingham, presumably the widow of Nottingham's eldest son, who had recently died, claimed the park as part of her jointure. The record for 7 July 1616 states:

> Forasmuch as the question doth not seem to be of so great difficulty, but may easily be determined without tedious suit in law, a course not beseeming persons so near allied, and of so eminent quality as you be: we have therefore thought it fit to refer the examination and consideration of the claims on both sides to our very good lord, the Lord Chancellor, and His Majesty's Attorney General [Francis Bacon], to make an end of this unkind controversy.... Whereunto we do not doubt but you, being persons of honour, will willingly submit yourselves... as her Ladyship hath done... according to justice and equity; wherein you may assure yourselves there shall be no delay. And so, expecting your lordships' answers by this bearer, we bid &c.

There the Council had thought it best to have the matter resolved by the arbitration of a committee of two of its own members. That would be by the parties' consent, Lady Effingham having already submitted and the defendants hardly likely to refuse. Then followed a letter to two Surrey JPs

54. *APC* 33.479.
55. *APC* 35.272.
56. *APC* 34.659.

instructing them to take special care to ensure that the peace be kept and its breakers punished, 'until the matter in controversy may be quietly and peaceably determined, which we hope will ere long be performed'. Only ten days later the arbitrators reported. Lady Effingham owned the park. The defendants' claim was based on a purported grant of her late husband to one of his keepers, the deed itself 'justly suspected for some erasure'. In any case her husband had no right to interfere with her jointure, which gave her the park for life. The right to the reversion, claimed both by 'the now Lord of Effingham and the daughter of the late Lord of Effingham by the Lady Dowager, being now in her minority, is thought fit to be left to a legal trial in the Court of Wards'. The Council approved the report 'in every point, whereunto Lord Effingham did willingly condescend and submit himself.' He agreed to keep the suspect deed safe for further examination.

The Mosleys held the manor of Manchester and only sold their right to hold court to the city in 1835. There had been an Oswald Mosley since at least the time of King John. On 24 June 1624 the Council dealt with the petition of Elizabeth, widow of Oswald Mosley, son of Oswald Mosley, writing to the Lord Keeper:[57]

> We call to mind that her cause hath been heard before your Lordship and us in the Court of Star Chamber, where the Court found not sufficient cause to convict the defendants of forgery of a will, yet it was conceived by the Court... that there was great cause that the petitioner and her son should be relieved in equity; we refer the further consideration of her cause to your Lordship to hear and determine with as much expedition (according to equity) as may be afforded to the poor gentlewoman, being not able to endure any long suit in law.

The Council never made it clear how poor widows had to be to qualify for the adjective and the Council's special concern. Perhaps it just meant the condition of any who were looking at litigation.

There was no problem in a married woman petitioning in her own name and right. In 1621 the Council commissioned the Bishop of Bath and Wells and four local JPs (or any three of them of whom the bishop must be one) to arbitrate in an unspecified dispute on the petition of Marjorie, wife of Simon Court, gentleman, 'forasmuch as the truth cannot be more conveniently examined than in the country where the parties live'.[58] They were charged to 'set down some such course for the relief of the petitioner as shall be agreeable to justice and equity'.

When women banded together, they presented a formidable force. The Council was sympathetic to the wage claims of the weavers and spinsters of Sudbury. On 16 February 1631:[59]

57. *APC* 39.251.
58. *APC* 37.411.
59. *APC* 46.230.

A petition was this day presented to the Board by Sylva Harbert, widow, on behalf of herself and divers others, showing that the poor spinsters, weavers and combers of wool in Sudbury and places near adjoining in the counties of Suffolk and Essex are of late by the Clothiers there (who are now grown rich by the labours of the said poor people), so much abridged of their former and usual wages that they (who in times past maintained their families in good sort) are now in such distress by the abatement of their wages, in these times of scarcity and dearth, that they are constrained to sell their beds, wheels and working tools for want of bread.

The Council 'recommended' the petition to seven JPs and two Sudbury aldermen, 'or any four, whereof one JP of each county and one alderman to be three':

to settle such a course for the relief of the Petitioners, by causing just and orderly payment to be made to them of their due and accustomed wages, as that they may have no further cause to complain, nor the Board be further troubled. And in case any particular person shall be found (either out of the hardness of his heart towards the poor or out of private ends or humour) refractory to such courses as the Commissioners shall think reasonable and just, that then they bind over every such person to answer the same before the Board.

The Government of Charles I had made clear where its sympathies lay in this dispute between the new capitalist clothiers and the traditional women workers. Counsel for the clothiers might expect to find it hard to persuade the panel that their clients' case was the more 'reasonable and just'.

There were effective pressures on women to agree to mediation, which men were spared:[60]

Neighbours – whether men or women – sometimes made determined efforts to resolve the situation by recourse to the various formal and informal mechanisms of mediation and arbitration that were so widely used in early modern English society, but these could only work if the culprit was amenable. A number of witnesses against Catherine Barnaby claimed that 'the parishioners would be willing to remit all suits and to be quiet if she... would consent thereto, but... she refused it'. Such women became liable to the cucking-stool when the patience of neighbours finally snapped. The exasperated John Dickenson told Catherine Barnaby that 'if she did not mend her manners, he would have her ducked' – and eventually he did just that.

There seems to have been no similar sanction on ill-mannered male litigants.

5. WOMEN AS MEDIATORS AND ARBITRATORS

Women were rarely appointed arbitrators, though there was nothing in English law to prevent it.[61] Frances, Duchess of Lennox and Richmond

60. Martin Ingram 'Scolding Women' 72.
61. Roebuck *Golden Age* 153–154.

was no ordinary woman. The daughter of Thomas, 1st Viscount Howard, youngest son of the Duke of Norfolk, she was first married to the son of a London vintner, who left her a wealthy widow of twenty. Two years later she married Edward Seymour, Earl of Hertford, forty years older than her. He died in 1621 and within two months she had married the Duke of Lennox, cousin of James I and a Privy Councillor, created Duke of Richmond in 1623. He died in February 1624. She retained both titles, Lennox and Richmond, and was popularly known as the 'Double Duchess'. She died in 1629. Craig Muldrew concludes, after considering a range of primary sources:[62]

> There is evidence that they were involved in settling disputes within a familial context and between each other. Oliver Heywood, when writing about his mother's character, claimed that, 'she was very useful in reconciling differences and making up breaches, taking much pains yet great delight in that work'. The Countess of Warwick also recorded reconciling Sir Richard Everard and his son, and on other occasions made peace between various female neighbours.

The Coventry clothiers had a licence to dress cloth. Its extent was challenged by the drapers. On 24 March 1627 the Council took upon itself the determination of their respective rights but one point was delegated to 'the Duchess of Lennox to decide on Hopkins's successor as alnager, since she is administratrix of the Duke who appointed him'.

Letters in the East Sussex Record Office preserve evidence of the attempts by Elizabeth, Countess of Monmouth, to mediate in the differences between her sister Margaret Trevor and Margaret's son Sir John.[63] The Warwickshire County Record Office contains a letter dated 16 April 1642, in which the mediators in a matter between Henry Seward and William Chance delegate to 'Mistress Throckmorton' to decide which of their children should have money left by Edward Seward.[64] Mary (Boyle) Rich, Countess of Warwick (1625–1678), kept a diary most of which records her spiritual thoughts as she converted from Catholic to Protestant. She did not welcome but accepted as her Christian duty the peaceful settlement of disputes, her own and others':[65]

> ... I met in the trust my dear Lord had imposed upon me as his executrix, in the sale of lands for raising portions and payment of debts, by reason of Mr Jesop's death, who was one of the trustees, with a great many stops and troubles in my business, which, having not been formerly versed in things of law, I found very uneasy and troublesome to me; but yet the great desire I had to see my

62. Muldrew 932 fn76; Turner *Heywood* I 50; and Croker *Warwick* fn77.
63. GLY/562.
64. ?Mary, wife of Sir Robert Throckmorton, Warwickshire landowner, Warwick CR 1998/ Box 63/ Folder 1/36.
65. YC Croker ed *Some Specialities* 37.

Lord's will fulfilled, made me go through my disturbing business with some patience and diligence; and God was so merciful unto me, as He did, beyond my expectation, raise my some faithful, knowing, and affectionate friends, to let me see my dear Lord's will fulfilled; and though there was a great many several persons I had to deal with, yet I satisfied them all so well, as I never had anything between them and me passed what was determined by going to law, but all that was in dispute between us, was always agreed on between ourselves in a kind and friendly way; for which O Lord, I bless thee.

In particular, she reconciled Sir Richard Everard and his son.[66]

Lady Anne Bacon, Francis Bacon's mother, was an influential Protestant theologian, with a command of Latin, French, Italian and Greek and probably some Hebrew. She tried hard to get her son to follow her example of a godly life, quite without success, but at least her reputation as a mediator was unsullied, so much so that on 6 February 1567 Matthew Parker, Archbishop of Canterbury, asked her to mediate in his dispute with her husband, Sir Nicholas, then Elizabeth I's Lord Keeper.[67]

6. CONCLUSIONS

Centuries before, the judges of the King's Bench had taken for granted the authority of a queen to mediate:[68] 'Stephen was king *de facto*, and by the mediation of Maud the Empress, his mother, the dukedom of Normandy was granted to him'. But that was exceptional. One product of the primary sources of the 17th century is the evidence which rebuts the assumption that women were socially, let alone legally, excluded from a man's world of disputes. What is surprising is that so much testimony survives of the activities of women of all kinds. As claimants and defendants they have a bigger part in the records than often supposed. They sometimes acted as resolvers, too. Oliver Heywood may not have been the only man to have learned how to mediate from his mother. Many others might have said with him:[69] 'She was very useful in reconciling differences and making up breaches, taking much pains, yet great delight in that work'.

66. BL Add MSS 27351–6, 1 March, 30 May, 8 and 14 June 1677 (from Muldrew 932).
67. John Bruce and TT Perowne *The Correspondence of Matthew Parker* 316.
68. *R v William Levet* (1612) 1 Bulst 194; 80 ER 882.
69. Heywood *Turner* I p50 quoted by Muldrew 932.

PART FOUR

ARBITRATION AND THE LAW

17   THE LAW: THE SUBMISSION

> When the poor and oppressed want right, they meet with law, which (as 'tis managed) is their greatest wrong.
>
> John Warr[1]

> Only those historians unwilling to master the lawyer's approach to problems have written off principles and issues of law as entirely irrelevant to the settlement of disputes.
>
> RH Helmholz[2]

> Arbitrement is much esteemed and greatly favoured in our Common Law; the end thereof being privately to compose differences between parties by the judgment of honest men; and to prevent the great trouble and frequent expense of law-suits: This therefore, being rightly understood and practised, may undoubtedly save our purses and produce much peace and tranquillity amongst us.... A general good should be generally known and enjoyed. To this end therefore this treatise is compiled, that the people in general may have benefit thereby which is the chief end of the publisher, who is a hearty well-wisher to peace and the public interest.
>
> Preface to *Arbitrium Redivivum*[3]

1.   INTRODUCTION

What might have been expected to be the central study of this book has been deferred until now because the law and legal system can only be understood in context. All the previous chapters have described the reality, setting the scene for the next four. They will deal with the creation of the dispute resolution process, the parties' submission to others; the award or settlement; the difficult *Vynior's Case*; and efforts to reform the law, culminating in the Arbitration Act 1698. The authorities are dealt with in detail, often with copious quotations. Non-lawyers should feel no guilt if they skip over them.

Even at the end of the 16th century the tradition was still as Bracton had declared it 350 years before:[4]

---

1. John Warr *The Corruption and Deficiency of the Laws*.
2. RH Helmholz book review of Arnold 733.
3. *Arbitrium Redivivum*... By the Author of *Regula Placitandi* [*Arbitrium Redivivum*]. The identity of the author of *Regula Placitandi* is equally unknown.
4. SE Thorne *Bracton* II 19 (in Thorne's translation).

> Though in almost all lands use is made of the *leges* and the *ius scriptum*, England alone uses unwritten law and custom. There law derives from nothing written but from what usage has approved.... The English have many things by custom which they do not have by law, as in the various counties, cities, boroughs and vills.

The royal courts, applying what was to become known as the Common Law, were not courts of general jurisdiction. To start litigation there, a party needed to buy a licence to sue from the sovereign, represented by the Lord Chancellor: a writ in a Common Law court or a bill in Chancery. So it was, as earlier chapters have shown, that subjects with grievances might take their petitions to the King in person or to some other manifestation of royal government.

To understand any community and how it deals now or has dealt with disputes, it is essential to avoid the Positivist ideology which restricts the definition of law to rules laid down by a sovereign and assigns an inferior status to what it insists on calling custom rather than customary law. Customs were recognised to be part of the law throughout the 17th century. The most popular legal dictionary is good evidence. The 1708 edition of *Cowell* retains the entry from the first in 1607:[5]

> **Custome**, *Consuetudo*, is all one significatation [*sic*] with our Common Lawyers and Civilians, being by both accounted a part of the Law [quotes Thorne *Bracton*]. It may not unaptly be thus defined, *Custom* is a Law or Right not written, which being established by long use, and the consent of our Ancestors, hath been, and is daily practised.

'Not unaptly' indeed, as he is there quoting the very words of Edward Coke's own definition.[6] Social historians have recognised the true significance of customary law:[7]

> In thousands of manors, parishes and boroughs, throughout the country at this time, the legal, economic and social relationships between landlords and tenants, clergymen and their flocks, or a corporation and its citizens were governed by sets of customary rules and regulations which determined the rights and obligations of all parties.... They comprised a set of rules and a body of lore which structured the practices and rhythms of daily life.

It was that customary law which the local courts applied, not the Common Law of the royal courts.

Of course, as soon as there is a state, with a sovereign claiming jurisdiction over all its inhabitants, then expressly or impliedly it is royal authority which legitimates all law, with some exceptions allowed, such

---

5. [John Cowell] *A Law Dictionary*.
6. Edward Coke 'The Complete Copyholder' 59.
7. Adam Fox 'Custom, Memory' [Fox] 93 and the sources in 112 fn9.

as the dictates of religion. By the beginning of the 17th century, it was accepted, by those who thought about such things, that all law sprang from the Crown in one way or another. Custom, though still law, could not be set up against royal authority, though the Crown would not normally override the customary rights of its tenants. The Court of Exchequer insisted in 1609 that it was the King's 'disposition not to interrupt the ancient and settled customs and privileges of any of his tenants but to suffer them to enjoy the same according to justice and equity'.[8]

There was no opposing power in the state. Elizabeth I and her successor had a duty to ensure the rule of law; and they were the only ones who could say what that was. That was thought of as the monarch's obligation rather than the royal prerogative. It was an integral part of the ruler's job to dispense justice. The preservation of the King's Peace throughout the kingdom was as vital as the defence against external enemies.

The Common Law was as much a function of the royal prerogative as equity was, in whatever shape. The Common Law was not the basic norm, with equity an extension or relaxation. It was inconceivable that anyone then should argue the superiority of rules over merits. Moreover, from the highest to the lowest, antipathy against the Common Law was general. Its practitioners were not popular:[9]

> There are in number of Sergents about 30, Counsellers about 2,000, and as many atturneys, besides soliciters and pettifoggers an infinite number, there being no province citty towne nor scarce village free from them, unless the Isle of Anglesey, which boast they never had lawyers nor foxes.

It is, therefore, essential for an understanding of later developments to avoid the anachronisms which have beset so much legal history,[10] and to remember that everything changed with Coke. Roebuck *Golden Age*[11] described the way the law worked in Elizabeth I's England. At his accession James I, a Scot unfamiliar with any English law, had at least to pretend to accept it.

There was still in the 17th century a faint colouring introduced into educated thinking from the theological controversies about free will, *arbitrium liberum*. Arbitration was there for any parties who wanted it, to do with as they liked, unconstrained by the language, the technicalities or the precedents of the law. It necessarily followed that the parties could set the terms of their agreement to arbitrate, as to content, persons, time, manner and anything else, so long as it did not cross the lines of legality

---

8. National Archives E126/1 fols129v, 130r, 133–136 cited by *Fox* 114 fn28.
9. FJ Fisher ed 'The State of England' 25. Wilson was an envious civil lawyer.
10. As Dawson always does, JP Dawson 'The Privy Council' I and II [Dawson *I* and *II*] eg *I* 427.
11. Roebuck *Golden Age* ch.16.

or countervailing public policies. Arbitration's primary purpose was to restore harmony within a community by resolving a difference between individuals. Litigation had a poorer chance, because one party won and the other lost. Losing parties were unlikely to accept decisions gladly. From the beginning of recorded time all those involved understood the psychology of avoiding the 'all or nothing' result. As long as winners got the best they could reasonably expect, they would not usually mind some allowance to the other side. Losing parties would not be happy, but they were more likely to accept the award without further fuss if it gave them some sop, even a mere formal token. That would allow them at least to make-believe that they had not lost respect. And their community wanted peace. But lawyers could not leave well alone. As the cases cited in the next chapter amply confirm, they made 'mutuality' a legal requirement of a valid award, insisting upon it over and over again as a legal rule, when it was already a social reality; and when, once it became a matter of law, it was available to be exploited by chicanery, until equally specious exceptions were invented and accepted by judges who favoured arbitration.

2.   LAW REPORTS AND ABRIDGMENTS

Any attempt to show how the law relating to arbitration developed between 1603 and 1702 requires a study of all the reported cases, but cannot rely on them. Not all of them were cited, let alone adopted in practice and, even of those, some were given little weight. The scorn with which contemporaries dismissed them as authorities was shown in Chapter 2, where they were considered as historical sources. With such warnings in our ears, reflecting 'the unanimous opinion of those 17th century lawyers who knew good from bad', we shall tread warily among the reports. Of course, their poor reputation provided opportunities for judges to dismiss them, not on their legal weight but just the name of the reporter:[12] 'Pressed by an authority, it is found safer to discredit a reporter than to depart from precedent. Lord Mansfield was quite unscrupulous in this way; and the influence may be detected in minds more dispassionate than his'.

But there was a body of law in practice, which compilers of abridgments and the earliest writers of texts tried to capture. It is there that the history of the law is to be found. The law might reside in the bosom of the judges, or in the corporate wisdom of the Inns of Court, but parties had to rely on those from whom they sought advice and assistance; and they, then as now, would go to their books. There they would find the same few authorities, repeated again and again, interspersed with advice about the best way to go about resolving disputes without litigation, rarely rising above the unnecessary padding: 'do not appoint an infant, an idiot or an outlaw' –

12. Wallace xxvii.

as if anyone would! Sometimes the lawyers would clumsily attempt to convert customary best practice into a legal prerequisite and then make it an opportunity for chicanery, as they did with the requirement that something must be given to the loser, if only a token. Best practice certainly, but hardly an excuse for a court to strike down a perfectly sound award.

Judges did not consider abridgments of any authority. On New Year's Day 1609 in *Fraunce's Case*, King's Bench had to deal with the regularly recurring problem of notice of an award.[13] As Coke reported:

> When a man binds himself to perform the award of a stranger, it is not necessary to give him notice that the stranger has made his award.... But if a man binds himself in a bond to perform the award of JS and JS makes an award, the obligor ought to take notice thereof at his peril; and there Brian, Vavasor, and Catesby JJ agreed, that in the case of arbitrament, the obligor ought to take notice at his peril, and so they said it was adjudged in the same King's time in the King's Bench; and so is the law without question, against a sudden opinion in Fitz Arbit 13, Br Arb 37, Mar Arb 190, 4 Co 82 b 8 E 4 1 a, Ace *Juxon v Thornhill*... So *nota* a good difference, when a man binds himself to do or perform any thing to be awarded by a stranger, he thereby takes upon himself to take notice at his peril of all things.

An attempt has been made to ensure that no relevant authority has been overlooked by searching every case reported in the *English Reports* between 1603 and 1703 for any mention of arbitration or mediation. Nearly 3,000 were revealed by searches for 'arbit-', 'mediat-' and 'award', but far fewer contain anything of importance. Most of the references to awards were irrelevant – of awards of damages or writs – though some arbitrations would not otherwise have been discovered. All those which contain anything apposite are considered as authorities in the appropriate places in the following statements of the law. They must be read carefully. Sometimes they clearly say the opposite of what they meant. In a leading authority on construction:[14]

> *Arbitrimentum est boni viri arbitrium.* As to the words here, they are to have such an exposition which may lawfully stand with the act done... First, four are elected, the obligation to stand to their award; afterwards there comes a modification... by four or three of them; and so the sense of these words are so as the same award of the things comprimitted be made by four or by three of them.
> *The reason of this is, because an award is to make an end of differences and contentions, and to settle peace between the parties. And for this cause we ought* [not] *to uphold such awards made, if by any means we can by the rules of law....*
> [A] more strict and perfect view there is none, and in this it is like unto an optick glass. This arbitrement here is good, well made, and pursuing the

13. (1609) 8 Co Rep 89; 77 ER 609.
14. *Anonymous* (1614) 3 Bulstr 66; 81 ER 57.

submission.... And here the intent is very apparent, that four or three were to make this award; so that this intent is plain and perspicuous.

The reason why arbitriments ought to have so great favour is this, when after a submission between me and another, and I have made him satisfaction according to the award, if after this so done, he will trouble me, and urge me to plead to him, for this vexation, there is a special writ in the Register fol 111, called *breve de arbitratione facta*. In which damages are to be recovered for the vexation, and it were good, that some one would bring this writ.

The [not] in the second paragraph is clearly an error. Nothing could be clearer than the King's Bench's intention to confirm its policy to uphold awards.

3.   VALIDITY OF SUBMISSION AND ARBITRABILITY

This chapter examines the authorities which purport to state the law governing the creation of arbitration: the submission. The next deals with awards. The requirements for a valid arbitration had been stated in the middle of the 16th century in *Browne v Meverell*:[15] 'To every award are five things incident, *scilicet* matter of controversy, submission, parties to the submission, arbitrators, and the delivering up of the award. And of this opinion were Dyer CJ and Browne J'. Typically there was no decision in that case, let alone a rule stated by the judges in the form of a *ratio decidendi*. None should ever be expected at that time. Reports often fail to say what the decision was. In that case it was expressed that the parties settled without waiting for one: 'but the judgment is not entered, for the parties agreed; and the matter was well debated by the Serjeants and Judges'. Yet, though no rule of law can be found there, that is how the books begin.[16]

Consent   That the consent of the parties was essential was acknowledged both in law and practice. Nothing could be plainer than the case of Lady Anne Clifford in Chapter 16. All manner of threats might be employed, even by the King, but no arbitration could be imposed without consent. In *Bendick v Thatcher*,[17]

T petitions the King to refer the matter to three justices. They make an award. B will not stand to it. T sues him in the Court of Requests, for performance of an award. B confesses the reference, but denies his consent to it, or assent of the award. And yet for not standing to that award, he was committed to the Fleet by the Court of Requests, and now B brought an *habeas corpus*. And by the Court

15. (1561) 2 Dyer 216b (debt on bond).
16. *Arbitrium Redivivum* 2–3; John March *Actions for Slander* [March] 151–152; William Sheppard *Grand Abridgment* [Sheppard *Abridgment*] 1 repeated 6.
17. (1606) Noy 141; 74 ER 104.

this difference was agreed, when the party submits himself to an arbitrament, by an extrajudicial course, as by consent, there he cannot be sued in equity, or imprisoned for non-performance of the award; unless he hath any time agreed or assented to it. But when by any Court the matter is referred... and the party will not stand to it, the Court may commit him.

From the requirement of consent it followed that neither a submission nor an award could bind anyone other than a party unless they agreed.[18]

Subject Matter　　　Those who wished to submit their disputes to arbitration neither knew nor cared what restrictions the Common Law might hope to place on their powers, but when a successful party wished to enforce an award, the other's lawyer might try his luck with a defence that the matter was not arbitrable. Clever lawyers build bricks from the slightest wisps of straw. *Arbitrium Redivivum* 3–7 is a list of limitations:

1. Things and actions merely personal and uncertain are arbitrable, as trespass etc, though the submission be not by deed.
Arbitrement ought to be of a duty uncertain.
2. But things certain are not arbitrable (but when the submission is by specialty) if they be not joined with others uncertain, as debt with trespass.
3. Controversy of debt alone cannot be put into arbitrement; but contract of debt with another thing may well be put in arbitrement....
4. Also an annuity is not arbitrable if the submission be not by specialty, that is by deed or bond wherein the parties covenant or are bound to stand to the award.
5. Nor a freehold....
6. Nor debt upon arrearages of account before auditors, because such debt is due by record.
7. And, it seems, such things as were not *in rerum natura* at the time of the submission... [e.g. lambs born later].
8. Matters concerning criminal offences, as treasons, felonies etc... for it is for the benefit of the kingdom and commonwealth that such offenders be made known and punished.
9. Also causes matrimonial seem not arbitrable, lest men should separate those whom God hath joined together.
To conclude generally, no chattels real or mixed, no debts by deed or record, no annuities, or freeholds are of themselves arbitrable. Yet in such cases, though the things themselves be not arbitrable, yet if a man will bind himself to stand to an award, such bond is good. And for the non-performance of the award the bond will be forfeited.

And that is just the point. No party well advised would submit a dispute to arbitration without insisting that the other party enter into a bond. The amount to be forfeited on failure to abide by the award would be fixed high enough to ensure compliance. If the matter in dispute were £100, then the

18. *Chalke v Peter* (1610) Godb 167; 78 ER 102; 2 Brownl 322; 123 ER 966.

bond could be for £500. The court might be persuaded that the matter was
not arbitrable but that would not mean the bond would not be enforceable
on default of submitting to arbitration or obeying the award. Then the court
was faced with the problem of the unfairness of making a party pay £500
in relation to a debt which even the creditor never claimed to be more
than £100. And so to *Vynior's Case*. It is too easy for us to see the courts
struggling with what seem to be artificial legal quibbles. Judges – then as
now – could usually be relied on to feel more comfortable if they believed
they had come to a fair judgment. But they did not always say so.

The parties decided what they wanted to submit to arbitration. I have
found no evidence of parties ever considering whether their dispute was
of a kind which the law allowed them to submit. The question would
arise only when lawyers for the party against whom the award had gone
were trying to avoid its enforcement. Only then would they try their luck
with a defence that the subject matter was not arbitrable. Earlier chapters
provide evidence that every kind of matter in *Arbitrium Redivivum*'s list
of prohibitions was made the subject of successful arbitrations, whatever
the law said.

Debt　　A distinction was drawn between a dispute over something
which needed to be ascertained, which was arbitrable, and a fixed sum,
like a debt, which was not. No parties would ever have seen that distinction
for themselves. No sum is more fixed than that in a claim in debt for £120
for goods sold and delivered. But lawyers today know what happens when
they are asked to provide a defence, to allow their clients to escape or
postpone payment of their debts. Then for the first time the purchaser,
whose only excuse had been that he had not got the money, remembers
that delivery was late, not at the place provided for in the contract, and the
goods did not meet the contract description; moreover, there was a flaw in
the bundle of documents that accompanied the bill by which payment was
to be made. That should be enough to transform a simple debt into a whole
range of issues and at least buy time. So, if the debtor wanted the award to
stand, and act as a stay to an action of debt, counsel must show that it did
more than dispose of a simple debt claim.

Arbitrium Redivivum's garbled attempt to state the law could hardly
have been less helpful. It would have its reader believe that there was
a rule: controversy of debt alone cannot be put into arbitrement; and an
exception where the submission was by deed. It was repeatedly stated that
no valid award could be made in a dispute over a simple debt. A party's
counsel would raise that point and the court would accept the rule. But,
knowing where the merits lay and recognising a trick when it saw one,

the court would find that there was some other element in dispute, which would suffice to exclude the rule's operation:[19]

> No concord or arbitrament can be pleaded to a recognizance or to an action of debt by specialty because debt is a thing certain, and a thing never [*sic*] certain is not to be arbitrated as a thing uncertain, as an account or such, but a debt with other uncertain things can be arbitrated. *Topcliff v Fitzherbert.*

Sheppard's account[20] is far from clear or convincing:

> If one sue for a debt upon a record, or especialty; and it be put to arbitrement, and an award is that he shall pay all or part of it, it is void, for it is not arbitrable. 10 H.7.4. Some think debt on a contract alone may be arbitrable, but it is clear it is arbitrable amongst other things.... Nor debts due by bond, bill or covenant, or on a simple contract alone; nor debts upon arrearages of account before auditors... and yet so as upon special engagements to perform such awards, they must do so, or bear the penalty, *Samonds case*. But debts due for expence about business or for travail; and so also (as some think) are debts on a contract or damage certain, being joined with trespass or other things incertain, that all these are arbitrable before, or after any suit begun; yea some think a debt on a contract alone is arbitrable, Co 8 *Baspole's Case* 97.... If a man demand £5 for businesses he hath done for another; this is arbitrable, *Sower and Bradford.*

Quite a challenge for a lawyer trying to make sense of that before advising a client! Whatever the law was declared to be, the sources in Chapter 7 reveal many arbitrations in disputes about no more than simply whether a debt was owed by one party to the other, ending in awards which were enforced, often by instalments, and sometimes proportionately with debts to other creditors.

Certainty   Every authority repeats that an award must be certain, a requirement dealt with in the next chapter, and Sheppard extends that requirement to the submission:[21] 'A submission also must be certain for it may be void for incertainty as an arbitrement may be.' That is rather a statement of the obvious than a rule of law.[22] How would one go about enforcing an uncertain obligation? If the subject matter was not quantified because it had still to come into existence, the uncertainty made the award void, *Arbitrium Redivivum*:[23] '7. And, it seems, such things as were not *in rerum natura* at the time of the submission...' The cases support the obvious.[24]

---

19. WH Bryson *Cases Concerning Equity* I 201 no169.
20. Sheppard *Abridgment* 6.
21. Sheppard *Abridgment* 4.
22. March 192–198.
23. *Arbitrium Redivivum* 6.
24. *Thinne v Rigby* (1611) Cro Jac 314; 79 ER 269.

Land   *Arbitrium Redivivum* states,[25] citing Year Book authority of Edward III and Henry IV:

> 5. Nor a freehold. Yet some hold that a freehold may be awarded by deed where the submission be by specialty. But 21 E 3.26 saith, an arbitrement that one party shall have the land out of the possession of the other doth not give a freehold.

As early as 1310 a plaintiff had pleaded a submission to arbitration.[26] Hervey de Stanton J insisted:[27] 'The simple point in issue here is the recovery of freehold land. That cannot be by the order of anyone without the King's writ.' That law was clear enough: an award could not itself transfer title. In 1384, in a dispute about an advowson,[28] Belknap CJ had insisted: 'Land cannot pass without livery'. The transfer of ownership of land required livery of seisin, formal, overt and express symbolic transfer. That was good theory but was it good law? How did it work in practice? Already in 1338 Shardelow J had said that:[29] 'Where two people have a dispute about land and... they submit it to arbitration, and the arbitrators award that they should hold it in common, if B brings an assize against A, A can properly plead the arbitration as a bar.' By the 17th century, as Chapter 5 has shown, the prevailing practice was for arbitrators to make an award which decided who owned the land and to order the parties to execute the necessary conveyances. In that way a land dispute could be disposed of by arbitration, even if the submission was by simple contract. *Sheppard* put it this way:

> [p4]   The award of a personal chattle, as that IS one of the parties shall have a horse (in question between them) doth alter the property of it, and give it so to IS that he may have a detinue for it. And so also of a chattle real, as in the case before of a lease for years. But in matter of freehold arbitrement can neither give a title, nor bind a right. Dyer 183. Lean 2.130. Croo 2.223. *Trustor v Yewre*. 21 H7 29. 14 H4 19.
>
> [p5]   But differences about land, and the estates therein, chattles real, and personal things in action, accompts, and most things may be referred to arbitrement. Dyer 183. Co 5.78. And for chattles, they may dispose of them and give the property or interest thereof as they please; but a freehold is not arbitrable. Nor can they dispose of land as the Chancery, and Common-Law courts may do; yet they may award that one of the parties shall enjoy the land, and the other not disturb him; or that the one of them shall give the other a bond for the quiet enjoying of it, or the like: and if the parties be bound by any especialty, or *assumpsit* to perform the award, and do not, he may sue upon it....

25. *Arbitrium Redivivum* 6.
26. The old law was stated in Roebuck *Middle Ages* 106–135.
27. DJ Seipp Year Books database [Seipp] 1310.101 YBB 3 Trin Ed II; (1905) 20 SS 182.
28. Seipp 1384.037am YBB Mich 8 Ric II 8 Ames 51–56.
29. Seipp 1338.273ass YBB 12 Ed III Lib Ass 36.25.

[p8] If the submission be of the right, title and possession of land, and the award is made of the possession onely and nothing said of the right, yet it is good for so much as it reacheth unto.

And also:[30]

If the award be, That one of the parties shall have the land in question between them, and it is in another's possession, this is void. For an award cannot order a freehold, and yet if there be any bond or *assumpsit* to perform the award, and it be not performed, the party may be sued upon it.

March,[31] in full and in Latin, provides the necessary precedent:

In debt upon a bond with condition for performance of an arbitrement, after oyer of the condition the defendant pleads the arbitrement in these words, in which the defendant covenants to assure such freehold lands, and surrender such copyhold lands (amongst other things) to the plaintiff and his heirs.

Elsewhere *Arbitrium Redivivum*[32] simply assumes that land disputes are arbitrable: 'The award may be made of a thing incident or accessory, as if it be of title and possession of land, the award may be made also of the evidences and charters concerning the land'.

And March spells out the issue:[33]

There was a case which was betwixt Robert Tiderby the father and Robert Tiderby the son, which was thus: they bound themselves to stand to the award of IS concerning all controversies, quarrels and debates, right, title and possession of or concerning the manor of Dale. IS awarded a conveyance... to certain uses....

Where arbitrators have power over the principal, they have power over the accessory; and therefore the right and title of the land, being put to the award of IS which is the principal, he hath power to make an award of the charters, which are the accessory.

Chattels Real   Chattels are all property other than freehold land. Chattels real are property which on the owner's death intestate passes not to the heir like the freehold but to the personal representatives. They include leaseholds and tenancies at will.

Chattels Personal   Here there was no problem, *Arbitrium Redivivum*:[34] 'In chattels personal arbitrement transfers the property'.

30. Sheppard *Abridgment* 12.
31. March 281–296.
32. *Arbitrium Redivivum* p45.
33. March 175.
34. *Arbitrium Redivivum* 4.

Chattels Mixed   There are no such things as chattels mixed; they are a figment of unclear thinking. There was an action for chattels real, an action for chattels personal, and a mixed action, which was for chattels real plus damages.

The Common Law was clear: transfer of title to freehold land required livery of seisin. No award of itself could transfer title; but it might validly order parties to do whatever was legally required to transfer any kind of ownership of land or chattels real. A party who disobeyed an award of title to freehold land forfeited the bond, provided that the award was made by deed. March:[35]

> But I take this as a general rule, that no chattles real or mixed, no debts by deed, or record, no annuities nor freeholds are of themselves arbitrable, though that the submission be by deed, and I shall prove it thus. If they were arbitrable of themselves then upon an action brought in any of these cases, an arbitrement were a good plea in bar.... But for further proof of this ground that I have laid down; it is taken as a general rule in *Blakes Case*, in my L. *Coke*'s 6 Book.... So I say in this case, though the thing itself be not arbitrable, yet if a man in such case will bind himself to stand to an award, the bond is good.

So the best efforts to state the law said that arbitrators could not transfer title to freehold land. They could, though, tell parties to do what was necessary, and punish them with forfeiture of the bond, their own chosen punishment, if they refused. Chapter 5 has many examples of awards ordering the parties to execute the necessary conveyances, and, while they were at it, doing what no court could do in resolving ancillary problems.[36]

Illegality and Public Policy   On the arbitrability of disputes involving crimes *Arbitrium Redivivum* states:[37]

> 8. Matters concerning criminal offences, as treasons, felonies etc, touching the crime, seem not to be arbitrable, for it is for the benefit of a kingdom and commonwealth that such offenders be made known and punished.

Seem? Again *Arbitrium Redivivum* states no firm rule.

The 17th century was blighted by great upheavals, not only natural disasters like plague and fire but political, including civil wars. Violence was sometimes the process which contending parties chose or could not avoid. But some of the most deadly disputes were successfully settled privately, whatever the legal authorities might say about felonies being non-arbitrable. Lesser crimes and other wrongs were commonly subsumed

---

35. March 154–156.
36. Private Shropshire 3890/2/3/8–9; Sheffield OD/845; public 34.521 (Council); Cockburn *Western* 43 (assizes).
37. *Arbitrium Redivivum* 7 quoted March 156.

into civil claims and disposed of privately, with or without the State's intervention.

Even quarrels which disturbed the public peace could be disposed of privately. Perhaps counter-intuitively, or so it might seem to a modern reader, the Privy Council could separate the public from the private, sending to the courts the private dispute over the title to a warren, but requiring mediation of the riotous conduct of the parties.[38] It asked Coke CJKB to 'order some course between the parties', who were 'not far dwellers from your Lordship', for 'a friendly agreement or some directions for preservation of the peace until it may be ended by due course of law'. After an unsuccessful night-time attack, one party was threatening 'a new assault with greater fierceness and strength... tumult, riot and bloodshed'. Mediation should put an end to that. But the Council was careful 'not to meddle with the right which either party may pretend but to leave the same to the ordinary course of justice'.

At the start of the century, Margaret Hoby tried to calm the riotous behaviour of Lord Eure and his men, as described in Chapter 16, and later insisted not on their criminal prosecution but civil recompense.

In the strife between King and Parliament, both sides seem to have accepted the relevance and the possibility of arbitration, according to one 18th-century newspaper account:[39]

> The King harkened to some secret propositions from the Presbyterian party, and designed to make an absolute breach between the parliament and the army, which occasioned Ireton to say to him: 'Sir, you have an intention to be arbitrator between the parliament and us, and we mean to be so between you and the parliament'.

What is perhaps more surprising is that Lady Brilliana Harley, daughter of the Lady Conway who figured so prominently in Roebuck *Golden Age*,[40] should attempt to mediate the lifting of a siege, as she is shown to have done in letters dated 26 July to 6 September 1643, asking Sir John Scudamore to mediate with the King.[41]

Arbitrium Redivivum and other authorities made a distinction between more serious crimes, 'treasons, felonies &c', which could not be disposed of by arbitration, and the rest, which could. What exactly '&c' meant was never settled. In any case, it did not matter because nobody took any notice of the authorities if the parties were determined to settle; and the State usually left them to it.

---

38. *APC* 33.550.
39. *Read's Weekly Journal or British Gazetteer* 3 February 1759.
40. 273–276.
41. Longleat PO/VOLXXIII; 'The manuscripts of His Grace the Duke of Portland, preserved at Welbeck Abbey'. On openlibrary.org.

The authorities are far from consistent, between one another or even within themselves. In *Horton v Benson*:[42]

> An indictment for a battery cannot be referred to arbitration. Resolved, Where the submission is general and conditional to end all controversies, that an indictment for a battery was a controversy between the parties within the meaning of the submission; for that is the King's suit, and if the arbitrators did award the ceasing of such a prosecution, it would be void, because it would be to obstruct justice. That causes criminal are not arbitrable, see West's *Symbol* Pt 2 § 33, cited Bacon *Abr* Arbitrament (A). Noy's *Maxims* ch50 p108. Unless the reference be by the recommendation of the Court, *Baker v Townsend* also Domat's *Civil Law* I 225; II 623, 1st ed by Strahan.

But there are many examples of the courts allowing a dispute arising from physical violence to be arbitrated. In *Bilfoord v Flint*:[43]

> In an action brought for non-performance of an award made, the case appeared to be this; the defendant shewed how that he & the plaintiff had submitted themselves unto the award of IF concerning a battery by the plaintiff upon him, who did award the defendant to release the action, and the plaintiff to pay unto him 10s in satisfaction for the battery.

In *Dimmock v Hanson*,[44] even an action for treasonable words was submitted to arbitrators:

> Whereas the defendant had spoken treasonable words of the plaintiff to Oliver Protector, there was in 1661 a submission to arbitrators, who awarded the defendant to pay money... demurred to the replication, that the matter is pardoned by the Act of Oblivion, and so no ground for the award; but *Curia contrà*, for the defendant may be one of the persons excepted. Judgment for the plaintiff.

The fact that a dispute involved an allegation of a crime did not inhibit the Privy Council from referring it to arbitration. Laurence Barroughs complained that Captain Tourney had committed 'grievous oppressions and violences upon him'.[45] Sir Francis Willoughby and Sir William Beecher were required to 'take some such course for the satisfaction of the complainant as they shall in discretion find to be most agreeable to reason and equity'. They reported a week later on 13 March.[46] There was some evidence of money owing to Barroughs but rather than take time to ascertain it, 'in regard of the miserable condition of Barroughs and according to his own request', they had ordered Tourney to pay him £15

42. (1675) Freem KB 204; 89 ER 145.
43. (1612) 2 Bulst 117; 80 ER 997.
44. (1662) 1 Keb 661; 83 ER 1171.
45. *APC* 44.356.
46. *APC* 44.361.

out of the pay he was due and a further £15 out of his next pay due in June. That would be full satisfaction. The Council ratified the report.

The Star Chamber under James I would send a dispute to be arbitrated, even though it involved the 'felonies &c' of assault, forcible entry, forgery, conspiracy, or even perjury or unlawful assembly.[47] The assize judges, too, referred disputes with a criminal element to be mediated and arbitrated: battery, barratry, riot, trespass, assault and battery, deceit, forcible entry and malicious prosecution.[48]

MJ Ingram has ransacked the Wiltshire records and found: 'One of the best sources of information about arbitration procedures are church court deposition books; they do not refer only to the settlement of ecclesiastical causes'.[49] His sources include mediations of batteries and other crimes.

There was no inhibition against submitting differences arising from torts, civil wrongs such as fraud, defamation, and trespass, though the facts revealed the elements of a criminal offence.[50]

In 1623 the Council commissioned six London merchants (or any three) to 'mediate an indifferent end and agreement, such as shall be equal and just' for the petitioner, Robert Whitgrave, a 'young man who might suffer much in his estate unless he find some more speedy relief than can be obtained by a legal course'.[51] His complaint 'containeth matter of much deceit and unconscionable dealing' in an agreement to ship goods to Italy and back, the defendants fraudulently detaining goods of his worth 12,000 ducats. Only if the mediation failed would the Council take a further interest and make an order.

Thomas Gobbons, clothier of Taunton, had earlier petitioned the Council, though there is no record of it, and came back to insist that he had suffered from the defendants' fraud.[52] 'In regard of the great poverty by him pretended and the interest of his wife and twelve children', two Somerset JPs were required to 'mediate some equitable agreement and end between them'.

Slander was rife in 17th-century England and a ready cause of strife which could upset a community where social standing mattered. There was plenty of litigation,[53] but the most common way to deal with a dispute arising from slander was to refer it to mediation,[54] privately arranged by

---

47. Nat Arch STAC 870/8; STAC 8/102/8; STAC 8/79/18; STAC 8/53/17; STAC 8/153/12; STAC 8/54/19; STAC 8/53/17.
48. Cockburn *Western* 28, 366, 565, 1005, 1110, 1197.
49. Ingram 326 fn103 with many references.
50. *Putt v Rawstern* (1691) 3 Mod 1; 87 ER 1.
51. *APC* 38.52.
52. *APC* 38.383.
53. *Linch v Dacy* (1663) 1 Keb 848; 83 ER 1278 is just an example: 'action on the case for calling the plaintiff traitor. Defendant pleads a submission and award made'.
54. JA Sharpe 'Such Disagreement Betwix Neighbours' [Sharpe] 176.

mutual friends. One example from 1625 represents many. Two women had insulted each other's appearance:[55]

> Jane Orton and Jane Hutchinson by both their mutual consents referred all actions suits and controversies... concerning the words to the arbitrement of friends by whose mediation they were made lovers and friends and thereupon drank and ate together.

On 22 June 1621 the Council commissioned two Norfolk JPs to deal with Scarlett Neve's complaint of unspecified slander of him by the townsmen of Shipdam, requiring them 'to take such course for the ending of the business as shall be agreeable to law and justice'.[56]

The parties to disputes arising from slander were often persuaded to have them resolved within their parish. Ecclesiastical authorities accepted the injunctions of the scriptures and other texts to bring the parties back to amity in Christian charity. As John Godolphin put it in 1678:[57]

> Yet, were it not for the sweetness of revenge, and the encouragement of the Law, such actions might be better spared than what it costs to maintain them; and such ill-scented suits do favour worse being kept alive in a tribunal, than they would by being buried in oblivion, specially if the defamed considered, that to forget injuries is the best use we can make of a bad memory.

There are many examples of both private and public arbitrations in matters involving trespass, in which it was just a matter of form to plead the defendant's violence;[58] but many of the trespasses settled by arbitrators were substantial wrongs. In the interstices of a dispute about an enclosure, the arbitrators might dispose of a claim of cattle trespass which rested on contested ownership.[59]

Matrimonial Disputes   On disputes between husband and wife March simply says: 'causes matrimonial are not arbitrable'.[60] *Arbitrium Redivivum* is less clear: '9. Also causes matrimonial seem not arbitrable, lest men should separate those whom God hath joined together.'[61] Again, *Arbitrium Redivivum*'s use of 'seem' reveals uncertainty at best. How far those exclusions were from the reality of practice has been shown in Chapter 6, with its examples of assize judges, the Privy Council and even the House of Lords arranging for the arbitration of disputes relating to

---

55. Borthwick Institute of Historical Research CP 1625/2 cited Sharpe 176.
56. *APC* 37.404.
57. John Godolphin *Repertorium Canonicum*; I have used the 3rd edn (1687) 62.
58. William Rastell *A Collection of Entries* [Rastell] 607.
59. Norfolk EVL 184, 454x7.
60. March 158.
61. *Arbitrium Redivivum* 7.

maintenance of deserted wives, wife-beating and marriage settlements, which were often the subject of private arbitration.

4. THE REQUIREMENT OF A SPECIALTY

Arbitrium Redivivum required some submissions to be by deed, if they were to be arbitrable, and made general conclusions. Specifically it declared that the submission of a dispute about an annuity had to be by deed: '4. Also an annuity is not arbitrable if the submission be not by specialty, that is by deed or bond wherein the parties covenant or are bound to stand to the award.'[62] All the authorities cited are pre-1600. Yet examples have been given in Chapters 6 and 7 of the submission to arbitrators of both family and commercial disputes about annuities. Some at least were not made by deed, but were nevertheless effective.

5. BONDS[63]

Deeds were effective legal tools. One way to circumvent restrictions on arbitrability was to enter into a bond, a deed incorporating a promise to pay a penalty for failure to cooperate in the arbitration or perform the award. All parties, if wise or well advised, would bind each other in that way. The liability to the penalty would pass on death to the makers' representatives, against their estates, which the obligation on an *assumpsit* created by mutual promises would not. *Arbitrium Redivivum*:[64]

> To conclude, generally, no chattels real or mixt, no debts by deed or record, no annuities, or freeholds are of themselves arbitrable. Yet in such cases, though the things themselves be not arbitrable, yet if a man will bind himself to stand to an award, such bond is good. And for the non-performance of the award the bond will be forfeited.... And 'tis the usual course to sue the bond on non-performance of the award.

The amount would be set high enough to ensure compliance. Bonds had been used routinely for over a century, whether the arbitration was arranged by the Council, or courts, or the parties privately. One survives from a private arbitration in York in 1484, which clearly was based on a standard precedent.[65] They were in general use throughout the 17th century, and by its end printers were selling forms. The researches of Horwitz and Oldham have found:[66]

---

62. *Arbitrium Redivivum* 5.
63. The classic treatment remains AWB Simpson 'The Penal Bond' [Simpson], on which much of this section is based. March 164–165.
64. *Arbitrium Redivivum* 7, 77.
65. Roebuck *Middle Ages* 3–4.
66. Henry Horwitz and James Oldham 'John Locke' citing PRO Chancery 109/20 pt1 (unsorted box).

So conventional was the use of the bond... that some printers produced forms with blanks for this purpose. Thus, in the year Locke penned his thoughts on trade [1696] and the multiplicity of lawyers, Thomas Tooke and Thomas Atwood, two London traders, agreed to submit their differences to arbitration; Tooke's agreement under bond of £500 to perform 'the award, order, arbitrament, final end and determination' of two other London citizens – drawn up using such a blank form – survives among Atwood's papers.

The National Archives contain many bonds to submit to arbitration.[67] Family and local archives retained the original bonds long after a successful award had made them otiose.[68] They are the most prevalent documents, of which hundreds have survived,[69] but they follow the simple pattern of the ones in the Shakespeare Centre from 1609, by which Jane, John and Edmund Gregory were bound to submit to arbitration their differences about a rent increase, or that in the Lincoln archives from 1653 which bound William Priest to Sibilla Holbech to abide by the arbitration of William Purefoy.[70] A bond in the National Archives dated 19 February 1607 arose in a matter before the Privy Council. It bound Oswald Durant, clothworker, in the sum of £500 to abide by the arbitration of Thomas Caesar, Sir Julius's brother. Durant had become indebted to a goldsmith, Daniel Raymon, and an agate cutter, John Loy, and his wife Sara. Another bond of the same date for £200 joins Edward Parnell, founder, in Durant's obligation.[71]

If, for whatever reason, the parties preferred not to enter into bonds, they could rely on the contract concluded by their mutual promises to submit to the arbitration. Then on breach the injured party sued in *assumpsit*, Latin for 'he undertook', the name of the writ, technically a form of trespass upon the case, for damages for breach of contract.

The parties could, of course, revoke the bond by mutual consent, in the same manner in which they created it. But, as long as the bond stood, any failure to perform the condition activated the penalty. Unilateral revocation of the submission was such a failure. As Sheppard put it, with typical lack of clarity:[72]

That let the submission be how it will by word or writing, and be naked, or clothed with an engagement by obligation or *assumpsit*, yet before the award is made it may be countermanded, and the arbitrators discharged of the work;

67. e.g. Nat Arch C2/Jas1/B1/50; PL 6/1/31; WARD 2/56/199/51; WARD 2/59/221/24; WARD 2/54A/184/17; WARD 254A/184/18.
68. e.g. Norfolk KL/C50/102 and 104; York Archae MD335/3/7/23 (Lady Savile).
69. e.g. Met ACC/0249/0426 and 0427; P92/SAV/820 and 821; Shropshire 1514/428.
70. Shakes DR10/1625, 1626, 1710 and 1238; Lincoln JARVIS I/C/34.
71. Nat Arch WARD 2/54A/184/17 and 18; bonds were entered into by persons other than parties, adding their guarantee to the undertaking to abide by the arbitration, West York WYL230/3142.
72. Sheppard *Abridgment* 4–5.

yet with these differences: (1) That where there is a naked submission by word, there the revocation may be by word; but if it be in writing, the countermand must be in writing also, for it must be *eodem modo* as the submission is. (2) If the submission be naked, and either of the parties countermand it, and discharge the arbitrators, the other hath no remedy against him: but if he undertake by especialty, or *assumpsit* to abide the award of IS, and after revoke it, the revocation is not good [here the contrary must be meant]; but he may be sued on the especialty or promise, for he hath broken that. (3) That in all these cases, where the party shall revoke his submission he must do it by giving notice of his mind therein to the arbitrators: but where there be two or more on the side of the parties that submit to the award, one or some of them may not revoke without the rest, and then especially when the submission is by deed. Co 8.81.5.78. Fitz Arbitrement 21.21.

In *Noble v Harris*,[73] the plaintiff's action on a conditional bond succeeded against the defendant's plea that he had revoked the submission before the award was made and that the plaintiff had later accepted that revocation. The court held: 'The revocation being a breach, it is not aided by consent or agreement after but, if it had been said to have been revoked by consent of the plaintiff, the penalty had been saved'.

Judgment on the bond barred any action on the debt or other obligation. The judgment was, in the eyes of the Common Lawyers, of a higher nature than the bond, which became 'transformed and metamorphosed into a matter of record'.[74]

In an arbitration under the auspices of the Privy Council, it would ensure that the bonds were fair and practicable, often suggesting that the arbitrators should be allowed to extend the time prescribed by the bond, if they thought that appropriate. Those bonds were kept in the council chest and returned on performance. A mediated settlement would be a sufficient discharge.

By the end of the century Equity might grant an injunction to relieve an obligor who could not pay because of some unforeseen disaster,[75] and the Common Law courts had to some degree followed.[76]

This development involves a recognition of the notion that a contracting party should only be permitted to receive *compensation* for loss actually suffered... with a view to putting the innocent party into the position he would have been in if the contract had been performed.... the courts asking in each case whether *this* penalty ought to be forfeit if the general aim of the law was to compensate rather than to punish.

73. (1688) 3 Keble 745; JH Cohen *Commercial Arbitration* 145.
74. *Higgens's Case* (1605) 6 Co Rep 44b.
75. Nat Arch C6/402/74 (1699).
76. *Friend v Burgh* Rep T F 437; Simpson 417–420.

A court which had referred a matter to arbitration might be faced with a problem of enforcement, when a party was dissatisfied with the award and refused to take the amount awarded and hand up the bond.[77]

Recognisances   Recognisances were orders of the Privy Council. Dawson's description cannot be bettered:[78]

> The recognizance, like the bond, consisted of an acknowledgment of indebtedness for a specified sum of money, conditioned to be void if the obligor complied with the requirement laid upon him, and specified in the obligation.... used most frequently as a means of ensuring attendance before the Council.

Conditions   If the parties made it a condition of the bond that the award should dispose of all their controversies, that condition had to be fulfilled for the award to be valid.[79] A condition was usually introduced in Latin by the words *ita quod*, invariably translated literally as 'so that'. That was not natural English then nor since but it stuck. A better translation would be 'provided that'.

Eventually, under the Statute of Fines and Penalties 1696,[80] a claim on a bond was limited to the provable loss. But what loss could a party to a bond prove when the other party failed to perform the condition to submit to arbitration? What was the financial equivalent of being forced to litigate rather than arbitrate? That problem had been considered in *Vynior's Case* in 1609. It became of no practical importance once the Arbitration Act 1698 had given statutory authority to the rule of court procedure described in the next chapter.

6. CAPACITY OF PARTIES

March put the matter in simple legal terms:[81] 'I take this to be regularly true, that no person, which is not of ability in judgment of Law to make a grant &c, can submit himself to an arbitrement'; which *Arbitrium Redivivum* expands:[82] 'All persons both male and female may submit to arbitrement, except they be prohibited by nature or by law, as infants, madmen... dumb, deaf or blind but if... they can write and read'.

Infants   At Common Law, an infant was any person, male or female, under the age of twenty-one. Infants could not make a deed, and so could neither submit by deed nor enter into a bond,[83] but:

77. Nat Arch E134/23and 24Chas2/Hil16.
78. Dawson *II* 636.
79. *Young v Taylor* (1591) 4 Leonard 94 (debt on bond).
80. (1696) 8 & 9 Wm III.
81. March 152.
82. *Arbitrium Redivivum* 13.
83. *Arbitrium Redivivum* 14.

otherwise 'tis said if an infant submit himself to an award, he shall be bound to perform it as well as a man of full age. But this hath since been adjudged to the contrary, *Rudson v Yates*, 15 *Car BR*.[84] That the submission of an infant to an arbitrement was absolutely void.

In *Roberts v Newbold*,[85] in King's Bench:

it was objected, that one of the parties to the submission was an infant, who cannot by law submit; and if no submission no award, and Shower cited March 141, *Rudston v Yates*, but the Court held, that though an infant cannot submit, yet his guardian may submit for him and bind himself, that the infant shall perform the award, as was done in this case.

Rudston v Yates merits quotation:[86]

Rudston brought an action of debt upon an obligation against Yates for not performance of an award according to the condition of the bond: the defendant pleaded that the arbitrators *non fecerunt arbitrium*, upon which they were at issue, and found for the plaintiff; and it was now moved in arrest of judgment... for other matters, or contracts of other nature which are of his own provision, those he cannot do. Secondly, an arbitrator is a Judge; and if an infant should be permitted to make an arbitrator, he should make a Judge, who by the law is not permitted to make an attorny, which were against reason... counsel for the plaintiff said, that the case was not that the infant submitted himself to the award, but that a man of full age bound himself that the infant should perform the award, which was said by the Court quite to alter the case. To that Trevor said, that the case is all one; for there cannot be an award if there be not first a submission: and then the submission being void, the award will be void, and so by consequence the bond: and to prove it, he cited 10 Rep 171b [*Vynior's Case*], where it was adjudged that the non-performance of a void award did not forfeit the bond, and many other cases to that purpose. And the Court agreed, that if the condition of a bond recite, that where an infant hath submitted himself to an award, that the defendant doth bind himself that the infant shall perform it, that the same makes the bond void....

Further, it was agreed, that if it appear afterwards to be to his prejudice, that that shall make the award void; but the principal point was not adjudged, because that the parties agreed.... if no submission, no award; and therefore he gave judgment against the plaintiff. Heath J also against the plaintiff: true it is, that in this case a stranger is bound that the infant shall perform the award, but that recites the submission by the infant; and the issue is, whether they made any award or not, so as the ground is, whether there be any submission or not; for no submission, no award, that so by consequence judgment ought to be given against the plaintiff: and he held clearly that the submission is void, that an

---

84. '*BR*' is *Arbitrium Redivivum*'s abbreviation of *Banco Regis* KB; March cites the case as *Rudston v Yates*; it is further considered below.
85. (1699) Comb 318; 90 ER 501.
86. (1639) March NC 111, 141; 82 ER 434, 448.

infant cannot submit himself to an arbitrament.... the submission is void, and not voidable only.

In *Knight v Stone*,[87] an infant, who had assaulted Margerie, agreed, jointly with his father, to submit to arbitration of her claim in trespass. The case is variously reported, but it is clear that there was an award to her of 20s by instalments and that: 'The main question was whether an infant could submit to arbitration or not, and the Court unanimously said he could; and when the infant came of age, or while still an infant, he could agree to a release'. This was followed in *Young v Fowler*:[88] 'An infant was bound by arbitrament.... for his schooling', citing *Stone v Knight*.

In *Grange v Tiving*,[89]

> In *Stone and Newman's Case* it was adjudged that an infant may submit to an arbitrament; it is but voidable.... In March p144, Bramston CJ is stated to have said, 'That whereas by *Stone v Knight* Latch 207, it appeared that the award should be voidable at the election of the infant, he held that the submission ought to be either absolutely good or absolutely void, the aim of an award being to compose controversies.' But *Gill v Russel* Freeman 62, 139, is cited as an authority, that 'an infant may be a party to a submission'.

In *Gill v Russell*:[90]

> An infant and one of full age A, join in a bond to perform an award, and it is awarded that they or either of them shall pay £10, and that the plaintiff shall release to them after they have released to him. The bond is valid as to A, although voidable as to the infant, and the award good and mutual, although the infant cannot make a good release. If an infant and man of full age seal an obligation, it is voidable as to the infant, and valid as to the other. An award that one of the parties and a stranger shall do an act, is binding on the party, and void as to the stranger. Debt upon an obligation to perform an award. Russell Junior pleads *deins age*. Russell Senior pleads *nullum fecerunt arbitrium*. The plaintiff replies, and sets forth the award, and... defendant rejoins, that his co-obligor was within age at the time of submission, and at the time when the award was to be performed. The plaintiff demurs.... Marsh, 111. Popham, 16, where an infant submitted himself, a third person was bound that he should perform the award; and it was adjudged that the submission was void, and consequently the arbitrament and the obligation. But the Court seemed to deny that case;... voidable only and not void, see Sir W. Jo. 164. Comb. 318. 2 Lev. 17. Bac. Abr. Arbitrament (C). 3 Viner, 110. But the bond of an infant with a penalty

87. (1627) W Jones 164; 82 ER 88; also *Stone v Withipool* (1625) Lat 21, 207; 82 ER 254, 348; *Stone v Knight* (1626) Noy 93; 74 ER 1059. Other less helpful reports are *Coles v Surye* (1626) Benl 182; 73 ER 1041.
88. (1639) March NC 38; 82 ER 401.
89. (1665) O Bridg 107; 124 ER 494.
90. (1672) Freem KB 62, 139; 89 ER 48, 101. Also *Cavendish* (1676) 1 Ch Cas 279; 22 ER 800.

is said to be void.... if the infant could not give such a release as was ordered, the obligation was forfeited; however, being it was awarded that the plaintiffs should give a release, (though it were after such releases given by the defendants *ut supra*, which was impossible by reason of the infancy), yet it was an award of both parties. And so judgment was given for the plaintiff.

After such a welter of conflicting and confused authorities, it can only be tentatively suggested that an infant's submission gave rise to challenges.

Women[91]   There has never been in England any legal inhibition on women acting as arbitrators. Few records have survived of working women arbitrating and none would be expected. Women at the very top of society presided over feudal courts and were occasionally appointed to arbitrate. Of women in between, social expectations would limit their appointment, but it was not unknown, even in the 16th century.[92]

But at Common Law their marriage annulled any agreement to submit, as it did all their existing contracts.[93] In *Harcourt v Sherrard and Dame Anderson*,[94]

Defendant having by answer consented that an award made by her father might be confirmed, prayed she might amend her answer, she having made oath, that she never read the award and that her answer was prepared by her father, who had wronged her in the award. Motion denied *per Cur*. The defendant the Lady Anderson having by her answer consented that an award made by her father might be confirmed, desired leave to amend her answer in that particular, having made oath, that she never read the award; and that such answer was prepared for her by her father, who had wronged her in the award; but the court refused to give her leave to amend her answer.... one reason why the Court denied this motion was because the father 'was an arbitrator of the defendant's (ie Lady Anderson's) own chusing,' but this circumstance does not appear in any part of the statement.

In *Anonymous*:[95]

A and B were bound to stand to the arbitrament of JS concerning a matter which did arise on the part of the wife of B before coverture.... awarded, that A should pay to B and his wife £10 at a place out of the jurisdiction and for that cause the judgment was not well given. Secondly, because that the award was that

91. Prest *Women* 169–187, particularly Pt I pp169–172 and fn16; DM Stenton *The English Woman in History*, 1957.
92. e.g. mediation by Mary Egerton and Jane Mapples in Roebuck *Golden Age* 19, 154, 319; and others in Chapter 16 above.
93. *Anonymus* (1636) W Jones 388; 82 ER 203; *Saccum et Uxor v Norton et Uxor* (1670) 2 Keb 865; 84 ER 547.
94. (1702) 2 Vern in Ch 434; 23 ER 878; also *Samin v Norton & Uxor* (1671) 3 Keb 9; 84 ER 565; *Parsons v Pierce* (1670) 2 Keb 872; 84 ER 551; *Temperance Kirby, Spinster, Executrix of Dame Jane Ormsby v Gilbert Ormsby* (1701) Colles 134; 1 ER 217.
95. (1640) March NC 77; 82 Er 419.

payment should be made to B and his wife, which was out of the submission....
As to the second, the controversie did arise by reason of the wife: and therefore
the award was within the submission, being made that the payment should be
to both.

That did not apply to his submission when a male party got married.[96] If
the single woman had entered into a bond, her marriage would not only
revoke the submission but forfeit the bond, so that she – and her husband
– would be subject to the penalty.

It was said that no 'women covert without their husbands' could make a
valid submission, but:[97]

> a man may submit for himself and his wife, and bind himself that she shall stand
> to the award, but she is not bound. An infant also may submit, and yet he is not
> bound by the award but at his choice, or perhaps may make it good at his age,
> as she when she is discovert: others may enter into bond for them, or they for
> themselves, but the bonds to stand to award will be void, save only in the case
> of a man for his wife.

How far all that represented reality was made clear in Chapter 16, which
described the many submissions which women, single, widowed and
married, made in practice, to say nothing of Lady Anne Clifford's successful
refusal join her husband's submission of their dispute to James I. As Prest
put it:[98] 'How English women were treated as objects of or under the law
can and should be separated from the question of how far English women
as subjects managed to use that same law to their own ends'.

Religious and Criminals   Capacity to submit to arbitration was also
denied to 'persons civilly dead; as monks, friars, canons, professed nuns
&c', and those 'attainted of felony or treason and persons outlawed or
waved[99] in personal actions, for they have no goods'.[100]

7. ARBITRATORS

Qualification   The law allowed the parties to choose whomever they
wished to arbitrate. That liberty even extended to the appointment of one
of the parties themselves: 'If a defendant agree to refer the matter to the
plaintiff, he cannot object to the award that the plaintiff was a judge in
his own cause'.[101] Though an award that A should pay B £50 and beg B's

---

96. *Arbitrium Redivivum* 12.
97. Sheppard *Abridgment* 6.
98. Prest *Women* 183.
99. To wave (more usually waive) was to deprive a person, usually a woman, of the
    protection of the law.
100. *Arbitrium Redivivum* 14–15.
101. *Matthew v Ollerton* (1693) 4 Mod 226; 87 ER 362; (1693) Comb 218; 90 ER 438.

pardon in whatever manner B determined was good for the debt but void for the rest:[102] 'for the arbitrator was to determine, and not to make B his own judge in his own cause'.

The practice was described in Chapter 10. *Arbitrium Redivivum* prescribes the minimum qualifications:[103]

> That they have sufficient skill of the matter submitted to them and have neither legal nor natural impediments. That they be not infants, who by reason of their few years may want discretion and knowledge. That they be neither mad nor idiots, for such are void of understanding. That they be neither deaf, dumb or blind, for thereby their principal senses necessary for the apprehension of the matter may be impaired... not notorious by outlawry etc... void of malice and favour to either of the parties.

But the text is careful to state: 'These are thought to be fit qualities, though the law prescribes no rules herein'. And March is clear:[104]

> I do not find in our law that either legal or natural disabilities do hinder any man from being an arbitrator, or avoid his sentence, and certainly they do not.... Besides they are chosen by the parties themselves, and, if they be not competent judges, the fault is theirs that chose them.

There were practical restrictions: it would be hard for a blind person to act, impossible for someone who was deaf without the help of sign language then. No one has ever wanted to appoint someone suffering from such a degree of mental illness that they cannot understand, or be trusted to act rationally. There was no legal bar against appointing an infant, but there are no records of anyone trying to do so. Any statements in the books on wise choices are of policy, not law.

Number   There is no trace of any law attempting to determine the number of arbitrators,[105] except perhaps for the customary law of merchants, as set out for example in the *Black Book of the Admiralty*,[106] where any future dispute about loading was required to be submitted to two 'good men of the art of the sea'. The very nature of the process and the expectations of the parties usually determined that each should appoint one or two, resulting in an even number, as discussed in Chapter 10.

Criminal Liability   Sheppard gives authority, for criminal sanctions against corruption: [107] 'Corruption in arbitrators to make them partial may be punished by indictment'.

---

102. *Glover v Barrie* (1698) 1 Salk 71; 91 ER 67.
103. *Arbitrium Redivivum* 19.
104. March 159.
105. Unlike in Scotland, where there had been legislation since the time of their James I.
106. Travers Twiss ed *The Black Book of the Admiralty* III 116.
107. Sheppard *Abridgment* Yelverton 62.

Umpires   An umpire is one (rarely more) appointed to make an award if the arbitrators fail or refuse to make one. Sheppard[108] describes the role:

> An umpire is the same in effect with an arbitrator, for he is one chosen by the arbitrators finally to order and determine the matter in difference between them, if the arbitrators cannot, or do not order by the day agreed upon between them.

Sheppard was sloppy there. In most cases it was the parties who named the umpire, though it is true that they sometimes left the choice to the arbitrators. He noted the distinction between umpires, who take upon themselves alone to decide when arbitrators fail, and a third arbitrator added to make an odd number:[109]

> The submission was to 4 persons and the umpirage of another, and the mutual promises were to stand to the order of them five, and they all made their award together; and it was held good. But had the submission been to them 4, and if they could not agree, then to the umpirage of the 5th, Bulstr 1 184 it had been better.

8.   CONCLUSIONS

Arbitrium Redivivum sets out the powers of an arbitrator:[110] 'His power is larger than the power of any ordinary or other extraordinary judge; for an arbitrator hath power to judge according to the compromise or submission after his own mind, as well of the fact as of the law'; and the duties:[111] 'First, to hear the grief of the party. Secondly to judge according to equity. Thirdly to give notice of his award'.

Those who have disputes ask others to help them only if both sides want to. They must agree on what they require the third parties to do, on the submission. They need no laws to help them. Practice reflected that. It was only when a disagreement arose during the arbitral process, or the award or mediated settlement was challenged, that a party would resort to the courts. The Courts of Common Law and Equity did not seek opportunities to interfere. The initiatives came from lawyers for disappointed arbitrants.

The next chapter will explain how the courts responded to such challenges to the effectiveness of awards.

---

108. Sheppard *Abridgment* 1.
109. Sheppard *Abridgment* 7.
110. *Arbitrium Redivivum* 18.
111. *Arbitrium Redivivum* 20.

18   THE LAW: THE AWARD

It would appear from these volumes, that it has been in the law as in some other sciences; and that while, in the fondness of self-glorification, our age has thought that with *it* was born all knowledge, we are in truth, left in the rear by times which we regard as buried in superstition and darkness.

JW Wallace[1]

In this the law is so at this day, that the wisest man in the country cannot make an award that a hole cannot be picked in it to make it void.

William Sheppard *England's Balme*[2]

1.   INTRODUCTION

The last chapter was concerned to show how the law enforced the practical reality and the intentions of the parties that arbitrators should have only such powers as the parties give them. It follows that anything they attempt to deal with in their award cannot be valid if it exceeds the powers given them expressly or impliedly by the submission. This chapter addresses the problems faced by a party whose attempts to enforce an award are challenged in court. The most usual defences were that the award exceeded the arbitrator's powers; that it was uncertain; that it lacked the necessary mutuality, failing to give something to both sides; and the many other quibbles of pleading. It concludes with an account of the development of the procedure by which parties could involve the courts in enforcement of their award by making it a 'rule of court'.

Arbitrium Redivivum states the requirements of a valid award:[3]

In the form of every arbitrement six things are specially to be regarded:
1. That it be made according to the very submission touching the things submitted, or necessarily depending thereupon...
2. That it ought to be certain.
3. That it ought to be equal, and appoint either party to give or do unto the other something beneficial in the appearance at the least.

1. JW Wallace *The Reporters* [Wallace].
2. William Sheppard *England's Balme* [Sheppard *Balme*], address to the reader, see Chapter 20.
3. *Arbitrium Redivivum* 40–41.

4. That the performance thereof be possible and lawful, and within the power of the parties.

5. That there be a means how either party may by law attain unto that which is thereby awarded unto him.

6. That it be a final end of the controversies submitted and, if it fail in any of these points, then it is said the whole arbitrement shall be void.

This chapter will show how accurately that statement reflects the law as the courts applied it.

2. SCOPE

Many of the reported cases describe lawyers' efforts to escape from an award by pleading that it exceeded the submission.[4] 'If it do not pursue and be made according to the power given them by the submission, it will not be good... It may not be larger nor narrower than the authority given thereby' as Sheppard put it.[5] The way in which the judges approached their task of determining the scope and meaning of an award may best be illustrated by a substantial quotation from a leading case, reported under various names. In *Perry v Berry*,[6] which was reported four times under different names, the submission was to four arbitrators: '*Ita quod* [provided that] the said arbitriment be so made, and delivered in writing, under the hands and seals of these four, or of any three of them'. Three of the arbitrators made the award and delivered it under their hands and seals. The case was much argued and the judges changed their minds. The clearest report is *Berry v Penring*:

> A submission to the arbitration of four persons, so as the award be made at such a time by the four, or by any three of them, creates a divided authority; and an award by any three of them is good.... The condition was, to stand, to the arbitrament and order of four persons, naming their names, of all actions &c, so as the same award be made and delivered up in writing under the hands and seals of the four, or any three of them. The defendant pleaded, *nullum fecerunt arbitrium* [they made no award]. The plaintiff shews, that three of them made an arbitrament under their hands and seals; and shews what; and assigns for breach the not paying of a certain sum of money, which they arbitrated to be paid. The defendant thereupon demurred, pretending this arbitrament to be void, because it was not made by all the four arbitrators; for the arbitrative authority is given to them all four, and not to three of them: and the words, 'so as the same...' first inclined to that opinion; but, after several arguments at the Bar, they all *seriatim* delivered their opinions, that the arbitrament was good; for every part of the

---

4. *Goffe v Browne* (1607) Hob 190; 80 ER 337; e.g. an arbitrator had no power to require a party to provide security, *Duport v Wildegoose* (1614) 2 Bulst 260; 80 ER 1106.

5. Sheppard *Abridgment* 2.

6. *Perry v Berry* (1615) 3 Bulst 69; 81 ER 60; *Berrie v Perrie* (1615) 1 Rolle 223; 81 ER 447; (1616) 3 Bulst 62; 81 ER 54; *Berrie v Penring* (1616) Cro Jac 399; 79 ER 341.

condition being weighed, the intent appears, that it should be sufficient if three...
But all the justices and Barons agreed that the arbitrament was good enough; for
the 'so as' explains sufficiently the submission to all or to three of them, and that
disjoins all the authority.

Coke CJ: Yet there is a repugnancy here: it is clear, that four ought to make
the award, yet his meaning peradventure was, that three might make the award
as well as four, but we are not now to judge upon his meaning, so as the same
award be made by four, and put in writing by three: the one may be a plow-man...
This matter was moved again, and long argued.... an arbitriment ought always
to have a benign and a favorable construction, the same being according to its
definition, *judicium boni viri, secundum æquum & bonum*, and therefore to be
construed favorably....

Doddridge J: Without all question, the meaning of the parties here was, that
this award might be made by them four, to whom the submission was, or to any
three of them: it is one thing to make an award, and another thing to make this
in writing, and to deliver this up.

Haughton J: The meaning here was of the parties, that these four, or any three
of them might make the award.

Coke CJ: I do as yet somewhat doubt of this case, because here is but an
authority.... this award thus made by three of the arbitrators is a good award.
And to prove this, it resteth upon the construction of the bond. The first part
of the condition is for the performance of the award of four; if he had stayed
there, and said no more, then they all four were to have made the award, but he
proceeds further with an *ita quod* the award by them, or by any three of them be
made, and... this *ita quod*.... hath here explained three things. First, who ought
to be the arbitrators. Secondly, in what manner their arbitrament is to be made.
Thirdly, the time before which the award ought to be made. And all this stands
well together, and may well be made parcel of the first part....

Hussey, Fairfax and Catesby JJ in the Exchequer Chamber:.... And to make
this more evident, it appears Coke 5 pars, fol 103 in *Hungate's Case*, that an
arbitriment is to be taken according to the true meaning of the parties, notwithstanding the words of this do enforce it otherwise; and so it shall be here in this
case, where the award made by three is a good award pursuing the submission,
and so ought to have been performed by the defendant....

Doddridge J:.... judgment ought to be given for the plaintiff. By the condition
of the bond, he is to stand to the award of four *ita quod* the same award of the
arbitrators or any three of them be made and given in writing before such a day...
the difficulty is not great, if you will consider the context of these words.... the
same ought to have a favourable exposition.

The issue there may seem to have been a lawyer's quibble, but there was
something of substance. A submission to four arbitrators, for them to make
an award, which any three may deliver, requires all four to make the award.
What were the words in this case? They were not ambiguous: 'provided
that the award be made and delivered up in writing under the hands and
seals of the four, or any three of them'. The various reports do, however,
allow an understanding of how lawyers and judges approached their tasks

then, and the eventual determination of the judges to support arbitration. They also show the variable quality of the reporting.

If the award exceeded the scope of the arbitrator's authority, must it wholly fail, or was it valid for what was within the submission? Sheppard stated that it would still be valid insofar as it was within, but invalid for the part without. He cited no authority and contradicted himself with this obscurity:[7]

> Yet in some cases where it may seem larger than the submission it may be good by a restriction of *de & super praemissis*, or by defect of the pleading of his adversary, Hob. 190. And generally, where an arbitrement is void in part it is void in all as to things though not to persons, especially where one part of it depends upon another. Croo.2.l49.

But the cases are clearer. The reference there to Hobart's Reports is to *Goffe v Browne*,[8] where the submission was of all matters in dispute at the date of the bond but the award was of all matters up to the date of the award. The plaintiff recovered as if the award had been restricted to the matters submitted:

> which must be either because *de et super praemissis* may report a restraint to the things submitted, or else that no new causes shall be supposed, except they were alleged, or else that the award of all causes may be reasonably understood all causes submitted.

In *Barnes v Greenwel*,[9] the submission was of all disputes up to the date of the bond, 4 September. The award declared that it dealt with disputes up to 3 September. The court held that that was good enough: any other disputes arising on that one day would have had to be proved.

And *Webb v Ingram*:[10]

> This award is now confessed by this demurrer to be made of more than was submitted; and being entire in this point, all which is awarded on Ingram's part (being one entire clause) is void; and then nothing is awarded on the other part, and therefore void: But all the justices and barons held, that it was a good arbitrament... when the award comprehends that which is submitted and more, it is good for that which is submitted, and void for the residue...

Conversely, arbitrators could not be expected to deal with disputes which were not part of the submission. In *Middleton v Weeks*:[11]

> If a submission be so that the award &c it is sufficient if it contain all matters notified, though there are other matters between the parties not noticed... The

7. Sheppard *Abridgment* 2.
8. *Goffe v Browne* (1607) Hob 190; 80 ER 337 cited above.
9. (1601) Cro Eliz 858 (debt on bond).
10. (1622) Cro Jac 663; 79 ER 574.
11. (1607) Cro Jac 200; 79 ER 175; also (1608) 1 Brownl 62; 123 ER 666.

plaintiff shews an award. The defendant saith that such other things were in controversy, whereof they had not made any award. It was thereupon demurred, because it was not shewn that the arbitrators had notice of such things in controversy; for it sufficeth if the arbitrators make an award of such matters whereof they are informed. Coke.

Umpires   *Arbitrium Redivivum* states the obvious, that an umpire cannot make an award unless arbitrators have failed to do so within their allotted time and deals with an umpire's partial award:[12]

> If the parties submit themselves to the award of certain persons, and if they cannot agree, then to the ordinance of another, as umpire: if the arbitrators make their award of parcels, the umpire shall not make his award of the other remaining part. But if the submission be such that the umpire shall make his award of the whole or of part, then it is said he may make award of such part with which the arbitrators have not meddled.

Hardly a distinction which could be said to follow the presumed intention of the parties.

3. CERTAINTY

The terms of the award must be certain.[13] They must deal with all the matters submitted, unless the submission allowed, expressly or impliedly, a partial award.

Sheppard insists that awards be construed strictly:[14] 'It shall not have a favourable construction, as a deed or will shall have to bring it to the intention of the parties, for it is in nature of a judgment, and must be plain and compleat'. For example:[15] 'If the submission be of all actions, causes of actions are not included in this. Co. on Lit. 285.' That is plain wrong. March got it right: 'an award shall be construed according to the intent or meaning of the arbitrators and not according to the words only' as cases cited later will show.

That is certain which can be rendered certain, is a maxim of the law for example:[16]

> 6. In an Action upon the Case on promise to perform an award on submission to A and B when their occasion will permit, *Keeling* conceived that only a convenient time was to be given, at least after request, which *Twisden* and *Moreton* agreed, but *Windham* was contrary, and that they have time during

12. *Arbitrium Redivivum* 66.
13. *Arbitrium Redivivum* 49–52; March 163–164; *Samon v Pitt* (1595) Cro Eliz 432; 5 Coke's Rep 77b (*assumpsit*); *Wilmer v Oldfield* (1587) 1 Leonard 304; Savile 120; *Thinne v Rigby* (1612) Jenk 340; 145 ER 247.
14. Sheppard *Abridgment* 1.
15. Sheppard *Abridgment* 4.
16. *Arbitrium Redivivum* 11–12.

their lives, as if it had been to be made at their wills and pleasure. But, if it be to be made generally without any time limited, the law implieth it must be done in convenient time. And it hath been agreed by the Court, that though the submission be when their conveniences permit, yet after request or convenient notice the party may revoke on neglect by the arbitrators.

If part of the award did not make sense, that would not be enough to make it void, for 'any words, by which the intention of the parties can appear, are sufficient;[17] 'Awards are now considered with great latitude and less strictness than they were formerly, and it is right that they should be so construed, because they are made by judges of the parties' own choosing'.[18]

4. MUTUALITY

The requirement that the award give something to each party is a good example of the courts inventing an artificial legal requirement, which no parties ever would have intended, and then devising the means of avoiding it. If the award was that the claimant should recover on a claim for debt of £150, there would be two defences. The first, that there could be no arbitration of a fixed sum, was dealt with in the last chapter. The second, that the award merely gave £150 to the claimant, without giving anything to the defendant, was circumvented by the court inferring an implied discharge by the plaintiff, and finding that that was a sufficient *quid pro quo. Arbitrium Redivivum*'s requirement '3. That it ought to be equal'[19] is absurd. It would mean that the only valid award was one which split the difference. The continuation 'give something beneficial in the appearance at the least' to each side makes better sense, though no authority is cited to support it.

There is evidence from as early as 1382 that lawyers were drafting awards to ensure that they provided for at least a token payment from each side.[20] It was enough that the award should order that one party should receive payment and the other a release from the debt in return. And the judges were quick to infer such a discharge if one were not expressed. Sheppard was in no doubt:[21]

> An arbitrement made onely for the one side, and nothing for the other, is void in law. As that one shall pay money, or give bond for money to the other, and the other do nothing for it. But if it be that one shall give bond to pay, or pay a debt, and that the other shall be discharged of the debt, Co.8.72. or that one shall pay such a debt to the other he owes him, for the payment is a discharge, there

17. *Butler v Wigge* (1666) 1 Saunders 61; 85 ER 72.
18. *Robinet v Cobb* 83 ER 641, 643; (1683) 3 Lev 183, 188.
19. *Arbitrium Redivivum* 3.
20. Roebuck *Middle Ages* 368–369.
21. Sheppard *Abridgment* 10.

must be somewhat express or implied given to either party. *Idem*. That one shall pay money to the other, and say not for what, is not good. Hob.50.218. So an award, that the one party shall pay to the other in satisfaction of all trespasses and injuries done to him by the other party before the day of the submission, so much, is good. The award is a discharge, and may be pleaded in barre for a discharge. Brownl. 310, 311.

Perhaps it was because Sheppard felt uncomfortable with the artificiality of the mutuality requirement that he repeated it six times in much the same form.[22] But March was more careful:[23] 'a small or seeming satisfaction, only so the award be on both sides, may be good enough'. And judges would readily imply a *quid pro quo*. He gives many examples in his full treatment of this lawyers' paradise of artificialities. And yet courts could not always be relied on to produce a sensible result. In *Tilford v French*:[24]

> A parol submission to an award, does not imply a promise to perform it…. Debt for £50 and declares, that the plaintiff and defendant mutually submitted to the award of JS who awarded, that the defendant should pay to the plaintiff £50 and that the plaintiff on payment thereof should [deliver writings] and make to him a release: after verdict for the plaintiff judgment was stayed and given for the defendant, because the award is void; for that the defendant had no remedy for the writings and the release upon this parol submission; for it did not imply any promise to perform it, and so it is an award of one part only.

By 1693 it was clear:[25] 'Two submit to an award, and nothing was awarded as to one, but only that all actions should cease: yet the Court held it to be a good award'.

Holt CJ still demanded mutuality when all others had abandoned it, so a wise plaintiff waited until he was absent:[26]

> An award directing the release of a duty without giving a satisfaction for it is not valid before the release is executed…. For an award is no plea in bar, unless something be awarded in satisfaction of the plaintiff's demand; and nothing being awarded for the goods sold and delivered, it is ill. For though there is a general release awarded, yet of itself that will be no bar, according to the case of *Freeman v Barnard*, though the suing of an action in such case may be a breach of the award, upon which the defendant might bring his action….
>
> Afterwards at another day (*absente* Holt CJ)… per Gould J, it is without doubt, that if nothing be awarded but the general releases, the plea will be null….

22. And (1646) *Capell v Allen* Sty 44; 82 ER 517; Al 10; 82 ER 887; *Baspole's Case* discussed below was cited as authority for the requirement that an award must give something to both sides, expressly or by implication, and approved (though not necessarily followed), *Nichols v Grunnion* (1614) Hob 49; 80 ER 199 (KB); (1614) 1 Brownl 58; 123 ER 663 (CP): 'There was no judgment in this case'.
23. March 211.
24. (1662) 1 Lev 113; 83 ER 324; 1 Keb 599; 83 ER 1135.
25. *Edwards v Pierce* (1693) Comb 212; 90 ER 435.
26. *Clapcott v Davy* (1700) 1 Ld Raym 611; 91 ER 1309.

for an award cannot be made good by implication. If the defendant would not have delivered the bill of sale, the plaintiff could not have assigned a breach of the award by implication. [However] judgment was given for the plaintiff, *absente* Holt CJ.

5. VALIDITY

If the arbitrators make a void award, they may not correct their error. The void award terminates their powers, Sheppard:[27]

> 13. That if an obligation be to stand to an Award, and a void Arbitrement is made, which is as none at all, the obligation is void also, for it is become impossible by the Act of the Arbitrator. Fitz. Obligation 17. Jenk. Cent.3. case 31.

Arbitrium Redivivum makes much of a rule that arbitrators may not delegate their powers,[28] citing *Samon's Case*,[29] though in practice that was often done, but with the parties' consent, easily implied if not expressed. Sheppard adds:[30] 'An award that one of the parties shall make such a release to the other as councell shall advise is good, for this is but a ministeriall act: but if they had appointed a judiciall act to be done so by another, it had been void. Styles 217.'

No appeal lay from a valid award, Sheppard:[31] '16. The sentence... is definitive and absolute, from which there is no appeal to any court either of law or equity, and... no writ of error lieth to reverse their judgment. Dyer 356. Co.5.78'.

Chancery was ever ready to enforce an award,[32] by subpoena if necessary.[33] There was nothing to stop an arbitrator imposing a penalty for failure to perform an award. In *Holland v Heale*:[34]

> they had submitted and obliged themselves to stand to the arbitrament of A who awards that the defendant should pay to the plaintiff 10s before Easter, and that if the defendant did not perform the said arbitrament, that then he should pay £5 to the plaintiff, that the 10s is not paid, and now the plaintiff brought an action for the £5 and adjudged, that debt well lies for that penalty.

The courts would not allow an award to stand if it was tainted by fraud, *Norgate v Ponder*,[35] where the Court of Chancery required: 'That the

---

27. Sheppard *Abridgment* 2, repeated 4 and 6.
28. *Arbitrium Redivivum* 42.
29. Sheppard *Abridgment* 2; March 164.
30. Sheppard *Abridgment* 7.
31. Sheppard *Abridgment* 3.
32. *Kenner v Horner* (1606) Ch Cas 158; 21 ER 92.
33. *Lovet v Chamberlen* (1606) Ch Cas 164; 21 ER 95.
34. (1603) Noy 108; 74 ER 1073.
35. (1627) Nels 6; 21 ER 775.

Bond to stand to the Award, and the Arbitration itself, and the Releases and the other Bond executed by the Parties, should be brought into Court and cancelled'. If a bankrupt made a submission without disclosing the bankruptcy to the other party, the subsequent award was valid if made without knowledge of the bankruptcy.[36]

The requirement of mutuality did not apply if the submission was made a rule of court:[37]

A submission to award was of all matters in controversy by rule of Court; and an award was made, that so much money should be paid of one side, and nothing was awarded of the other side; and it was moved to set it aside.... Holt CJ: 'The common exceptions against an award will not hold here, it being an award upon submission by rule of Court'.

6. PLEADINGS AND QUIBBLES

To an action to enforce an award it was common form for the defendant first to plead no award had been made, *nullum fecit arbitrium*, to which the plaintiff then submitted the award and the defendant demurred on some technicality.

A good and sufficient example of how the pleadings worked is *Freeman v Baspoule*, heard by Common Pleas on New Year's Day 1609.[38] The parties were the representatives of a debtor and creditor, both dead. They agreed:

to stand to the award accordingly, so that the said arbitrator makes his award of all the matters and controversies between them before such a day... the arbitrator before the day recited the assumpsit, and the debt as aforesaid, and agreed that the heir should pay the administrator so much money, and that published according to their submission: and in action upon the case, *nullum fecit arbitrium* was pleaded, and upon demurrer, it was objected that the award was void. First, for that it was for one party only, and nothing was arbitrated of the other, and to prove this the book of 7 H. 6, 6, was cited, and 39 H. 6, 9. See 2 R. 3, 18 b. And this also appears by the pleading of an award, for he which pleads it; that he hath performed all things which are to be performed of his part: and... of his part, by which it appears that there ought to be performance of both parts, and by consequence one award to both parties, according to 22 H. 6, 52. Secondly, that the award was void, for that, that the submission was of all controversies &c so that the arbitrator delivered his award of all controversies &c. And there was no award of the said suit between the parties, and for that

36. *Whitacre v Pawlin* (1691) 2 Vern 229; 23 ER 748 followed *Peters v Soame* (1701) 2 Vern 428; 23 ER 874.
37. *Anonymous v Palmer* (1703) 12 Mod 234; 88 ER 1285.
38. (1609) 2 Brownl 309; 123 ER 959, followed in *Maw v Samuel* (1617) 2 Rolle 1; 81 ER 619; *May v Samuel's Case* (1617) Pop 134; 79 ER 1236; *Lumley v Hutton* (1617) Cro Jac 447; 79 ER 383; and *Burnell v Wood* (1618) 2 Rolle 22; 81 ER 633.

he hath not made an arbitrement of all controversies, and by that the award was void; and to prove that, the books in 4 Eliz. Dyer, 216, Pumfreie's award, and 19 Eliz. Dyer, 356, 39, and 39 H. 6, 9, where it is said, that if the submission were of all things, and the arbitrement of one only, that is a void abitrement. Thirdly, for that it was not limited within the award, at what day, nor at what place the money should be paid by the heir to the administrator, and it is uncertain, and for that shall be void, as it is in Samon's case, 5 Coke, 77 b. where the arbitrator awards, that one party shall enter into bond to another for enjoying of certain lands, and doth not say in what... for the uncertainty, and so in this case. But it was answered and resolved, that the arbitrement was good.

And to the first objection it was resolved, and agreed, that every award ought to have respect to both parties, if it be not a matter which concerns one party only, and neither recompence nor acquittal due to the other party, in which case the award shall be good: and it was resolved in the principal case, that the award was made of both parties, for one was to have money, and the other, though there was no express mention, should be discharged of his assumpsit, yet the award was a good discharge in law, and may be pleaded in bar upon an action brought upon the assumpsit, and to the second objection, it was agreed, that where submission is, with ita quod, &c. as above, that there the arbitrators ought to make arbitrement, of all the variances and controversies, referred to their arbitrement, and if they do make no arbitrement, of all the matters of which the submission is made, the award is void, but if the submission be general, as of all matters in variance or controversie between them: there if the arbitrator makes his award of all matters which are known to him, the award shall be good: as my Lord Coke conceived, though that there are other matters in variance, of which the arbitrator hath no notice.... And to the third objection it was answered and resolved, that the award was good, notwithstanding that no place be expressed where the money shall be paid... but Foster conceived that it is not good, for it seemed to him, that if the award shall be good, that the obligation of submission shall be immediately forfeited, for that there was neither time nor place... this was answered with the books of 3 H. 7, 16 Ed. 4, where it is said that if an arbitrator award that one party shall pay such a sum of money at such a day, and keeps the award in his pocket till such a day be past, that yet the obligation shall not be forfeited: and so it was resolved and adjudged by all the other justices, that the award was good, and judgement was entered accordingly.

And, a litle later in 1609 King's Bench heard *Barret v Fletcher*, thrice reported.[39]

Debt, upon an obligation of £500 conditioned to stand to the award of JS and TD so that &c. The defendant pleaded that the arbitrators did not make any award. The plaintiff replies and shews the award but assigns no breach. The defendant rejoins that the award pleaded is not the arbitrators' award; whereupon issue being joined, a verdict was given for the plaintiff.

39. (1609) Cro Jac 22; 79 ER 192; 1 Brownl 105; 123 ER 694; Yel 152; 80 ER 102. There are many cases on the technicalities of pleadings: *James Osborn's Case* (1613) 10 Co Rep 130; 77 ER 1123.

Every arbitrement ought to be expounded and intended according to the intent of the arbitrators, and not literally, 10 *Co. f.* 57. *b*. But if the intent of the arbitrators will not stand with the law, then the parties shall perform it according to those words, in such sense as agrees with the law. And note, it hath been held, that an averment shall not be allowed to shew the intent of the arbitrators, if it be not expressed in the award, either directly or by circumstance, *Dyer* 242. *Redivivum* pp73–74.

Notice   A matter of much judicial controversy was the requirement of notice of an award having been made:[40]

> *Whether the Compromittors which have bound themselves to stand to an award, are bound to take notice of it at their own peril, or not?* This very point is as much controverted and debated in 8 *Ed* 4, *The Duchess of Suffolk's Case* by all the judges in the Exchequer Chamber, as it is possible for a case to be.

But the answer had been decided. No notice was necessary: 'the compromittor must take notice of it at his own peril'. The bond in common use provided that the award should be made in writing and 'ready to be delivered to the parties or such of them as shall require the same'.[41] Then the parties 'are obliged to take notice of the award at their peril'.

Signing and Sealing   *Sallows v Girling* provides a good example of an unsuccessful quibble and a successful plea.[42] A matter had been submitted to four arbitrators, any three or two to make an award under their hands and seals. Two had made the award but not sealed it. Yelverton's first argument for the defence was that, although the submission allowed two to sign and seal, all four had to make the award. The court gave short shrift to that. But his second argument prevailed: that sealing the award, incorporating it into a deed, was expressly necessary.[43]

If the submission required the award to be 'signed, sealed and delivered', it was held to be void if not signed, though even a cross would have done.[44] But other attempts to plead that no award had been made because it was required to be signed, sealed and delivered, but had not been signed, were dismissed by all the judges of King's Bench: 'sealing is signing enough'.[45]

That did not mean that the judges would not revel in the nuances of the technical Latin vocabulary, discussing alternatives which had nothing to

---

40. March 190–191.
41. *Arbitrium Redivivum* 39–40.
42. (1612) Cro Jac 277; 79 ER 238.
43. And delivery as a deed was required, *Dr Leyfield's Case* (1610) Co Rep 88; 77 ER 1057.
44. *Scott v Scott* (1611) 1 Bulst 110; 80 ER 806.
45. *Bradshaw v Walker* (1619) Palm 97; 81 ER 996; *Anonymous* (1619) Palm 109; 81 ER 1002.

do with the merits and which the lawyers would have difficulty in getting the parties to understand.[46]

Two long and detailed reports of *Kynaston v Jones* show the lengths to which counsel in King's Bench went in fabricating unsubstantial arguments, ending in a desperate and unsuccessful plea that a bond had to be in Latin.[47] But on the whole all courts tended to allow commonsense constructions of the parties' words. In Coke's report of *Baspole's Case*,[48] he followed the sensible words of counsel:

> Serjeant Williams observes in *Berks v Trippet* 1 Saund 32 a: 'These nice distinctions are now disregarded, Courts of Justice being at present more liberal in the construction of awards than formerly. And, therefore, an award may be good, though made of less than is contained in the submission; as if the submission be of all actions, trespasses, demands, and controversies, and the award be made of some only, the award is good; for no more shall be presumed to have been made known to the arbitrator: but if in fact other causes of action were made known to the arbitrator, then such award would be bad.

There is plenty of evidence from as early as the last years of Elizabeth I's reign that most judges gave short shrift to lawyers' quibbles;[49] but there was nothing to stop counsel from raising any point they thought they could get away with. They risked the judges' scorn but the more preposterous the argument, the more likely it was to catch the attention of a reporter. Much of the 'case law' in the abridgments is of that kind up to the end of the century. *Arbitrium Redivivum* quotes Style *Practical Register*.[50] *Style* was obsessed with an issue that never arose in practice, only in the mind of a lawyer desperate to avoid the dispute being decided on the merits. Such was the suggestion that provision for the award to be made somewhere other than at a party's or an arbitrator's house made not only a submission void, but even an award that payment should be made there.[51] Why? Because the owner of that property might have refused permission for the hearing to be held there.

---

46. *Freeman v Sheen* (1612) 2 Bulst 93; 80 ER 986; *Judith Hanson v Liversedge* (1690) 2 Vent 239, 242; 86 ER 416, 417; Carth 156; 90 ER 695.
47. (1647) Al 85; 82 ER 928; Sty 97; 82 ER 559.
48. (1609) 8 Co Rep 97; 77 ER 624, also reported (1610) Cro Jac 285; 9 ER 244; 1 Bulst 144; 80 ER 837. *Baspole's Case* was cited in a case full of quibbles: *Lindsey v Astey or Aston* (1612) 2 Bulst 38; 80 ER 941.
49. Roebuck *Golden Age* 321–322; *Sharley v Richardson* (1593) Cro Eliz 291; but see Popham J's own report *Sherry v Richardson* (1593) Poph 15; *Withers v Drew* (1599) Cro Eliz 676; *Roof v Lighte Baker Dyer* II 359 (1578?); *Fuller v Spackman* (1587) Cro Eliz 66; *Vanvivee v Vanvivee* (1590) Cro Eliz 177; *Wenman v Handford Baker Dyer* I 169–171; *Hungate's Case* (1601) 3 Coke's Rep 210; *Parker v Parker* (1595) Cro Eliz 448; *Block v Palgrave* (1600) Cro Eliz 797; *Alford v Lee* (1587) Cro Eliz 54; 2 Leon 110.
50. *Arbitrium Redivivum* 68–72.
51. Both *Arbitrium Redivivum* and Style cite the recent case law: *Mich. 22 Car. BR* 1 *Keble* 753. 16 *Car* 2 *BR Pract Regist* 27. *Keble* 1 13 *Car* 2 *Mich*.

What is found in *Arbitrium Redivivum* is mirrored in the work of Continental scholars of just that time, however different their legal culture may have been, as represented by Nicholas of the Sparrows:[52]

> Quaestio VII
> *An conveniri per litigantes possit, ut arbiter certam ferat sententiam?*
> Can the parties in their submission tell the arbiter what award to make?

After minute consideration, not of the cases of course but a dozen learned writers, the conclusion was:

> *Veram solutionem esse, quod non licet convenire ut certam in individuo sententiam vel arbiter, vel judex ferat. Tunc enim judicium esset de nihilo, & deficeret judicandi cardo…. Et hunc sensum & nos sequendum opinamur.*
>
> The right answer is that one cannot make an agreement that someone, whether arbiter or judge, should make a certain decision; for that would then be a nothing judgment and leave no way open for a decision to be made…. And in our opinion this is the meaning we should follow.

Just as it seems inconceivable that such a question could arise in practice in Frankfurt in 1685, so many of the statements of law which fill our abridgments purport to dispose of disputes which are just as unlikely ever to have arisen. If the parties wanted to agree on the award which their arbitrators were to make, there would be nothing to stop them – then as now – covertly colluding in the choice of evidence and argument to produce the required award.

7. PERFORMANCE AND ENFORCEMENT

The ordinary method of enforcing a promise to submit to a private arbitration was an action on the bond. If there was no bond, then the injured party could sue for breach of contract, if one could be proved, though it would be difficult to quantify the damages. If a party failed to abide by an award, again an action on the bond would usually be enough; without a bond there was an action to enforce both submission and award, but with all the expense, delay and chicanery of a Common Law action. *Arbitrium Redivivum* states:[53] 'Note, upon submission by word only there is no remedy to enforce the party to perform the award; but an action on the case for reciprocal promises will lie'. There was another advantage in making the award by deed: no action could otherwise be brought if the party against whom the award had been made had died.[54]

The courts would not enforce that part of an award which awarded costs or made provision for payment for engrossing the award.[55]

---

52. Nicolas de Passeribus *Conciliatio Cunctarum Legum* 107–110.
53. *Arbitrium Redivivum* 8.
54. *Hampton v Boyer* (1597) Cro Eliz 557 (debt).
55. *Perry v Barry* (1615) Bridg 90; *Bussfield v Bussfield* (1619) Cro Jac 578.

The Privy Council had its own powerful weapon. There were a few recalcitrants who were prepared to go to prison rather than do as the council told them, but the threat of arrest and imprisonment usually sufficed.[56] Similarly the assize judges enforced their orders by threats of binding over to the next assizes,[57] sometimes with imprisonment.[58] But by the latter part of the century a practice had been established, a routine even, which was streamlined rather than created by the Arbitration Act 1698.

8. STAY AND BAR

Awards and indeed submissions were successfully pleaded as bars to litigation on the same claims, whether the arbitration was public or private. A problem might have arisen from the indiscriminate use of the word *arbitrement* for both submission and award. It did not, however, because either could be pleaded as a stay to litigation. Statham's *Abridgment* had stated *c*1490:[59] 'It is a good plea to say that they submitted to arbitration, which is not a deed and this is in trespass', i.e. in contract, *assumpsit*. So not only an award but the mere submission would be enough to prevent parties going back on their promise to accept arbitration as a substitute for litigation. *Arbitrium Redivivum* states:[60] 'By arbitrement the controversy passes into a matter judged of and, therefore, where the party brings his action for the wrong done him, it is a good plea that he submitted himself to the arbitrement'. Expressly, therefore, not only an award but a submission would suffice.

Sheppard is typically verbose:[61]

> Arbitrement, if it be good and well made, and any thing awarded for a wrong done, that the party hath or can tell how to recover, or amends for it being not performed, as where there is an obligation or assumpsit to perform it, there it puts an end to the matter referred: so that if there were a cause of suit before *transeunt in rem judicatam*, so that if either party sue upon any thing that is arbitrated, the award may be pleaded in bar to the suit; as to say, That they submitted the matter in difference to the award of IS for that matter alone or for that with others, and that he awarded him to pay so much money such a day, and the day is not yet come.... but if it be not performed, then the party is free to take his remedy for the first wrong, and hath his election to sue upon the award, or upon the cause he had before the award.

56. Dawson *II* 639; Julian Critchlow [Critchlow] 296.
57. Cockburn *Western* has too many examples to cite but e.g. 577, 686.
58. Cockburn *Western* 196, 215 (expressly for contempt), 401, 623, 687, 834.
59. 'Est bon pladir quil sot mis en arbitrem, q nest unc fait &c, & ceo en trns &c'; *Seipp* 1390.003am YBB Hil 13 Rich II Ames 104–105; Statham 123; Fitzherbert 26; Roebuck *Middle Ages* 371.
60. *Arbitrium Redivivum* 75.
61. Sheppard *Abridgment* 3.

Rastell's *Entries* has examples. Under the heading 'Barre per Arbitrement', the defendant, in an action of trespass 'by force of arms', pleaded an award, the plaintiff replied that there had been none, and the issue went to a jury. There are similar entries when not an award but a mere submission was held to be sufficient bar. Under the heading 'Barres en Quare Impedit' an award of a privately arranged arbitration was successfully pleaded as a bar, where a prioress and a bishop had submitted their dispute to the Chief Justice of the King's Bench.[62]

If parties could bind themselves by contract to submit a particular dispute or future disputes in general to arbitration, that would reduce litigation. That was accepted as a good thing, as much by judges and lawyers as by potential parties.

So an agreement to submit to arbitration could be pleaded as a bar to a later action on the same claim. An award should have been an even firmer bar. Yet, as the last chapter showed, the Common Law intermittently insisted that an award was no defence to a claim in debt for a fixed sum.[63] That was such an artificial rule that even the Common Law judges sought ways to circumvent it, and invented exceptions which usually worked if the defendant's lawyers knew the ropes, for example by persuading the court that the claim was not for a fixed sum but damages,[64] or was for a fixed sum plus something else.[65] The sum awarded need not have been handed over, if the award created a new action in debt.[66] By 1682 Chancery would grant an injunction to stop proceedings in King's Bench in breach of an award.[67]

In Jones' Case,[68] the King's Bench (Montagu CJ, Croke, Doddridge and Houghton JJ) refused to set aside an award when the plaintiff alleged that he had later found new documentary evidence: 'An arbitrament is res judicata... the settlement of controversies and, if prohibition were allowed here, any award could be called in question'. But, following the authority of Coke, *Arbitrium Redivivum* insists:[69]

> In personal duty grounded upon a specialty, plea of arbitrement is not available... and the Lord Cook in his Reports *Li. 4. F.43. b. 44. a.* says, that an arbitrement is no plea when an action is founded upon a deed, when it is in the realty, except in such cases where damages alone are to be recovered.

62. Rastell 156, 607.
63. Brooke 25 citing YB 4 Henry VI 17 (1426); *Waberley v Cockerel* (1541) 1 Dyer 51a.
64. *Sower v Bradfield* (1595) Cro Eliz 422.
65. *Bret v JS* (1600) Cro Eliz 756, *Morris v Creech* (1670) 1 Levinz 292, *Fane v Prior of Tonbridge* (1524) 91 Selden Society 19, *Farrer v Bates* (1646) Aleyn 4.
66. The law is dealt with within the Common Law of accord and satisfaction in MC McGaw 'Travels in Alsatia' [McGaw] 131–187.
67. Nat Arch C 6/386/79.
68. (1617) I Rolle 380; JH Cohen *Commercial Arbitration and the Law* [Cohen] 145.
69. *Arbitrium Redivivum* 4–5.

Arbitrium Redivivum sets out the pleading rules:[70]

> As to pleading an award in bar of an action in these cases, observe
>
> 1. That where an award is for payment of money, for which there is remedy, and the day of payment not past, in such case an award pleaded will be a good bar to an action.
>
> 2. Where the day of payment is past, it will be no bar to plead an award, without pleading of payment by the party.
>
> 3. Where the day of payment is past, and though it appear that the arbitrement is not executed, yet if there be no default in the defendant, it may be a good bar to plead an award.
>
> 4. Where an award is for doing a thing for which the party hath no remedy (though the day be not come in which the thing ought to be done) in such case it will be no bar of an action to plead the award.

All that was old law from the 16th century. What was new was the Statute of Limitation 1624,[71] which provided that 'Debt upon an award by word of mouth... must be sued for within six years after the cause of action'.[72] There was no such limitation period for an action on a deed.

One case reported five times arose from a referral by rule of court:[73]

> Arbitrement. In debt upon an award the defendant pleads the Statute of Limitations... ruled this was not within the statute for that is grounded on the judgment; and this award is said to be made in writing, so the debt is in a manner grounded on a specialty, and so... debts inferior to lending or contract are within the statute, and so would this be, were it debt on an award by paroll, but *per Curiam* this award being pleaded to be under hand and seal, it's *quasi* a specialty; and so out of the statute.

Horwitz and Oldham discovered an important bit of evidence of practice in 1694:[74]

> The agreement of two partners in a Lambeth distillery is worth noting. Along with the conventional provisions for settlement of disputes by arbitration (in this instance backed up with mutual penal bonds of £500), the parties covenanted that, should the arbitration fail, nothing given in by either side as evidence in the arbitration should 'be made use of... or produced in evidence or testimony by the other' in any subsequent litigation.

9. RULE OF COURT

Chapter 4 described how all kinds of court referred matters to arbitration. From the middle of the 15th century, a court might refer to arbitration an

---

70. *Arbitrium Redivivum* 63–64.
71. (1624) 21 Jac 16.
72. *Arbitrium Redivivum* 77.
73. *Hosden v Harris* (1667) 2 Keb 462, 497; 84 ER 290, 312; *Hodgson v Harris* (1668) 1 Lev 273; 83 ER 403; *Hodsden v Harridge* (1668) 2 Saund 61, 64; 85 ER 672, 693; *Hodson v Harwich* (1668) 2 Keb 5333; 84 ER 334.
74. Henry Horwitz and James Oldham 'John Locke' [Horwitz and Oldham] 141 fn19 citing PRO C103/189 *Mason v Markes* 1694.

action started before it at *nisi prius*. It would order, by a rule of court, that the parties' agreement to submit, made before the court, must be obeyed. From about the middle of the 17th century, that occasional practice began to be standard procedure. Parties to a dispute would commence an action, intending from the start to ask the court to submit it to arbitration. The court automatically agreed and the submission became what was known as a rule of court.[75] Any refusal by either party to facilitate the arbitration or perform the award was then a contempt of court, subjecting the recalcitrant party to attachment, imprisonment until submission to the rule. In law a party might have the right to resile from the submission, but was unlikely to enjoy exercising it in prison.[76] The court appointed the arbitrators, with the parties' approval: sometimes one judge, sometimes members of the jury there at *nisi prius*, occasionally merchants to deal with disputed accounts.[77] When they had declared their award, the plaintiff would enter judgment with the defendant's automatic consent. The award would expressly declare that it was final, not subject to appeal, and that no relief against it would be allowed in equity. Common Law judges refused to hear argument that such an award had been made in error. A Chancery court might consider the merits of an award made under its own rule of court but would then enforce it by decree. There is some suggestion in the cases that some judges did not favour attachment of recalcitrant parties, but the preamble to the Arbitration Act 1698 expressly authorised it.[78]

As early as 1635:[79]

> The Bill was to be relieved against an Award submitted to by the Parties, and Bonds given to perform it. Court declared, They would neither confirm nor overthrow such Awards, unless Circumvention or Corruption were proved. But otherwise if the Award was made by Order of Court.

In 1665:[80]

> Glyn prayed an attachment against the defendant for nonperformance of an award submitted to by rule of the Court made by consent, as is used in Common Bench, which the Court refused, because hereby all awards would be affirmed as good how void soever.

---

75. McGaw 33–35; in *Styles v Trist* (1661) 1 Keble 130 Twisden J said that the practice was then not more than seven years old, Critchlow 295 fn710.

76. *Hide v Petit* (1670) 1 Ch Cas 185.

77. Hale CB in *Tremenhere v Tresillian* (1670) 1 Siderfin 452; jurymen in *Hall v Mister* (1699) 1 Salkeld 84.

78. McGaw fnn147, 150, 152, 153. It will be for research into 18th-century practice to show the use of bonds even after they had lost their *in terrorem* effect, as it came to be called.

79. *Greenhill v Church* (1635) Rep Ch 88; 21 ER 737.

80. *Kene v Fleming* (1665) 2 Keb 22; 84 ER 14 and *Approved Men of Guildford v Mills* (1665) 2 Keb 1; 84 ER 1.

And in 1698:[81]

> What shall be good cause to set aside an award made by rule of Court, and what not…. Where an award is made by rule of Court, it shall not be set aside, unless there was practice with the arbitrators, or some irregularity; as want of notice of the meeting. Also you shall not take exceptions to the formality.

Common Pleas would routinely attach, that is imprison, a recalcitrant party. King's Bench seems to have been less willing:[82] 'While thirteen orders were entered in Common Pleas between 1656 and 1660 to compel performance of awards made under *nisi prius* references, the Rule Books of King's Bench during these years are devoid of any parallels'. The liberty of the subject was at stake, if by mere affidavit a party to an award could have an alleged defaulter imprisoned without trial. Better, it was thought, to 'leave the party to his action, the rule being evidence of his submission'.[83] Later, though, both King's Bench and Common Pleas allowed, as a matter of course, defaulting parties to be attached unless they could show cause. The application must be on an arbitration agreement made a rule of court, but that became routine by the 1690s. In 1697, '26 such rules were entered in Common Pleas and another 22 in King's Bench'.[84]

The law reports of the second half of the 17th century are full of cases in which attempts to disturb a rule of court were unsuccessful.[85] *Squib v Bradshaw* is one in Chancery:[86]

> Whether Exceptions are to be admitted to an Award on a Reference by Consent. The Question was, If upon a Submission by Order of Court by Consent to Arbitrators, and the Award to be final and stand decreed, any Exceptions lie to such an Award as to a Report. And whether, if it were an unjust Award, the Court ought to decree it; and whether the Court should examine the Justice of the Award, and the Merits of it; which the Master of the Rolls had taken upon him to do in this Cause, by ordering the Arbitrators to certify the Court whether they had considered of certain Particulars, which the Party disliking the Award said they had not, which were in Issue in the Cause.
>
> And upon an Appeal… the Court examined the Justice of the Award, which in this Cause, and the next Precedent, the Court did think upon Circumstances

81. *Anonymous* (1698) 1 Salk 71; 91 ER 66.
82. Horwitz and Oldham 142.
83. DEC Yale *Lord Nottingham's 'Manual'* 309; Horwitz and Oldham 142 fnn21 and 22.
84. Horwitz and Oldham 143.
85. *Turbill's Case* (1666) 1 Saund 67; 85 ER 76 (foreign attachment); *Morgatroyd v Morgatroyd* (1668) 2 Keb 585; 84 ER 368 (KB grants attachment on rule from Assizes); *Derbishire v Canon* (1668) 2 Keb 575, 579; 64 ER 362, 364; (1669) 1 Mod 221; 86 ER 700 (when the party comes in upon the attachment, he may allege, that the award is void); followed *Tremenhere v Tresilim* (1669) 2 Keb 664; 84 ER 416 as *Clemenhere v Pasco Tresilian* (1669) 2 Keb 645; 84 ER 400; *Miller v Clapshaw* (1670) 2 Keb 812; 84 ER 513.
86. (1670) 1 Ch Cas 186; 22 ER 754.

might be done; and that if an unjust Award was desired to be confirmed by Decree, and the Court informed of it, the Court ought not to decree it. Note: An Award made in Pursuance of an Order of Court, must be confirmed as in case of a Master's Report.

But in *Hide v Petit* in Chancery:[87]

A Submission to an Award by Consent of Parties by Order of this Court is revokable. The Parties in Court signed an Order by Consent to refer their Matters to Arbitrators finally to determine, and their Award to be final, and stand ratified by Decree without any Appeal.... the Judges were both of Opinion, that there could be no Submission to an Award in Law or Equity, but what was revokable, and that nothing under a Legislative Power can make such a Submission.... for which the Court might justly lay the Party by the Heels. And so in this Cause an Attachment was awarded against him *nisi causa*. In this Case it was observed, that whereas formerly the Course was upon Submission to award an Attachment against the Party failing, yet of late the Courts of Law do refuse to grant Attachments... but leave the Party to his Action, the Rule being Evidence of his Submission. In the principal Case the Arbitrators had determined some Matters, and had left others undetermined, and submitted those other Matters to the Court: And whether this was therefore such an Award (being but Part of the Matters referred) as was fit for the Court to decree, was the Question. And though at Law an Award may be good, though but for Part of the Matters referred, unless the Submission be conditional to make an Award on the Premisses; yet Equity, as it was insisted, ought not to decree such an Award, unless it be of all Matters referred. And so were both the Judges of that Opinion; for it is not a Determination pursuant to the Reference, and so the Award was set aside. Note: Equity will rarely set aside an Award, except for manifest Partiality, Corruption or Injustice in the Arbitrators. 1 Vern 157; 2 Vern 251, 485, 514 &c, or except there be apparent Error in the Body of the Award, 1 Vern 158, &c, as where it appears to be made on a plain Mistake of Law or Fact.

Holt v Berry confirmed 'this being a settled course now'.[88] Even if the award 'be bad in law':[89] 'If an award made a rule of Court by consent of parties be bad in point of law, yet the Court will compel...'. At the same time in 1694, in *Forster v Brunetti*:[90]

Attachment lies for not performing award, though not strictly good in law, if not impossible. But personal demand is necessary. Attachment lies not for not performing an award, made upon a rule of Court, without a personal demand. Holt CJ remembered the first attachment of this kind was a case in Kelynge's time; in which, and ever since, a personal demand has been thought necessary. In such cases of awards, though they be not legally good, attachment lies for

---

87. (1670) 1 Ch Cas 185; 22 ER 754 before the Lord Keeper, Master of the Rolls, Rainsford and Windham JJ.
88. (1676) 3 Keb 844; 84 ER 1045.
89. *Skip v Chamberleyn* (1694) Comb 303; 90 492.
90. (1696) 1 Salk 83; 93 ER 78. This report contains later commentary.

non-performance. *Aliter* if impossible.... The course of proceeding to obtain an attachment is this: the award must be tendered to the party against whom it is intended to move for the attachment, and, if he refuse to accept it, affidavit of the due execution of the award, and of such tender and refusal, must be made, and, on that, an application made to the Court for a rule of Court; then a copy of this rule must be served on the party refusing to accept the award; if he still refuse to accept it, an affidavit must be made of personal service of the rule... then on application, grounded on that affidavit, an attachment will be ordered of course... When the award is accepted, but the money being demanded is not paid, an affidavit must be made of the due execution of the award, and of the demand and refusal of the money; and an unstamped indorsement of an award is a sufficient authority to a third person to demand the money awarded.

In *Hall v Mister*:[91]

> Attachment upon an award of the three foremen, a verdict being given for security.... If a rule be... to the three foremen of the jury, and that the plaintiff shall have a verdict for his security; after the award made the plaintiff may either enter up judgment on the verdict, or have an attachment for not obeying the rule of Court, it being in his election which way he will execute the award; and this was affirmed by Mr Northey, and at the Bar, to be the constant practice.... To obtain leave, it is necessary to produce an affidavit of the due execution of the award, and the demand of the money awarded, as it is to obtain an attachment.

By the end of our period the policy of the King's Bench was clear: the parties had chosen their own arbitrators and could not be heard to complain against their award except for fraud or exceeding the authority given by the submission. In *Morris v Reynolds*,[92] the defendant alleged that the arbitrators, three foremen of the jury, had not given him time enough to be heard or to produce a witness. Holt CJ: 'The arbitrators being judges of the party's own choosing, he shall not come and say, they have not done him justice, and put the Court to examine it. *Aliter* where they exceed their authority' and 'to all practice, that he had known in his experience... in such case the integrity of the arbitrators (whom the parties by consent have chosen to be their Judges) shall never be arraigned'. 'Powell J said, that seeing they could not give the party any costs, he should never be for examining into awards again'.

If a party to a rule of court had been attached for contempt but died, or was declared a lunatic, the attachment ended automatically.[93]

10. CONCLUSIONS

This chapter has shown how, by the end of the 17th century, the legal system had settled down to accommodate the practice of arbitration. It

91. (1699) 1 Salk 84; 91 ER 79; and *Freeman v Bernard* (1697) 1 Ld Raym 247; 91 ER 1061.
92. (1703) Holt KB 81; 90 ER 943; 1 Salk 73; 91 ER 69; 2 Ld Raym 857; 92 ER 73.
93. *Webster v Bishop* (1703) Prec Ch 223; 24 ER 108; 2 Vern 444; 23 ER 884.

may well have been that, as in earlier centuries, most parties who called on others to help in their differences arranged private arbitrations. Litigation, even of the formal kind involved in the rule of court, was expensive, and the royal courts inaccessible to many when travel was not easy. But, for those who could afford it, the rule of court procedure was efficient and the evidence shows it was attractive. For them it could replace the reliance on bonds. But bonds were the legal machinery for making arbitration work, whether private or official, throughout the century. The next chapter deals with *Vynior's Case*, which confirmed, at its start, the effectiveness of the penalty when the terms of a bond were broken.

19   VYNIOR'S CASE

The process of reviewing in 'reverse order' the ways of thinking of Coke...
gave me a time of enjoyment comparable somewhat with the pleasures of the
Museum staff when tearing down and reconstructing Perneb's tomb.

JH Cohen[1]

They are not reports at all in the strict sense of the term... to a large extent ...
they contain his own statement of the law.... In connection with his habit of
editing the conclusions of the courts in accordance with his own views of the
law... Coke is not always accurate.

Van Vechten Veeder[2]

Hereout have sprung many absurd and strange opinions, which being carried
about in a common charm, and fathered on grave and reverend judges, many
times with the multitude and sometimes with the learned, receive such allowance,
as either beguile or bedazzle their conceits and judgments.

Sir Edward Coke CJCP[3]

1.   INTRODUCTION

Sir Edward Coke's character and contribution to English law were subjects
of Chapter 12, which dealt with the peculiarities of his law reporting. In
1612, as Chief Justice of the Common Pleas, he reported *Vynior's Case*,[4]
over which he had presided three years before. That report has determined
the assumptions of later generations of lawyers and judges in England,
and more particularly in the United States, about judicial attitudes to
arbitration.[5]

The way in which bonds were used to support submissions was dealt
with in the last chapter and, for the previous century, in Roebuck *Golden
Age*. *Arbitrium Redivivum* tells us what the usual practice was:[6] 'And 'tis

---

1. JH Cohen *Commercial Arbitration* [Cohen] xiii.
2. VV Veeder 'The English Reports 1537–1865' 133.
3. 1 Co Rep xxvii; I have used the 'new edition' in 6 vols, JH Thomas and JF Fraser eds
   1826.
4. *Vynior's Case* (1609) 8 Co Rep 80a to 83a [*Vynior*].
5. There are many studies of Coke's reports but TFT Plucknett 'The Genesis of Coke's
   Reports' [Plucknett] is still helpful. Part 1 of Coke's Reports had appeared in 1600. The
   first seven parts were based on Coke's own manuscripts and included cases from as early
   as 1572 but most of Part 8 was made up of recent cases.
6. *Arbitrium Redivivum* 77.

the usual course to sue the Bond on Non-performance of the Award'. As *Arbitrium Redivivum* understood it:[7]

> 4. But if the Submission be by Bond (as most commonly it is), though by some not thought so convenient, for that thereby the Parties may hazard the Penalty of the Bond (for a Trifle or small matter) though afterwards countermanded, yet the Bond seemeth to be forfeited. And so says *Brook. tit. Arbit.* 35.
> 5. And so it is adjudged 8 *Co. fol.* 82. That though a Man be bound to stand to an Arbitrement, yet he may countermand the Arbitrators; but in this Case it was further resolved that by the Countermand or Revocation of the power the Bond is forfeited, because he was bound to stand to the Award which he does not do when he discharges the Arbitrator.

The arbitrators must be given notice of the countermand, though that may be implied.[8]

March elicits this from Coke's report:[9]

> But that which is the last and best authority is *Vinyor's Case*; where it is resolved that, though a man be bound to stand to the arbitrement &c yet he may countermand the arbitrators; the reason that is given is, because a man cannot by his own act make such an authority, power, or warrant not countermandable, which by the Law and its own proper nature is countermandable.

But the bond was forfeited; and where the submission was by deed, the countermand was ineffectual unless it was by deed.[10] Whether by deed or not, notice must be given.

2. THE FACTS

The facts are straightforward and undisputed. Robert Vynior brought an action of debt against William Wilde on a bond of £20, dated 15 July 1608, to secure performance of a promise to submit to the arbitration and award of William Rugge.[11] The dispute was over only 22 pence, for parish tax. Wilde refused to submit to the arbitration.

Vynior did not at first claim the full £20 of the bond. He claimed only £10, which he said was the damage he had suffered from the breach. Wilde asked that the bond be read, which it was, showing that its purpose was to secure the arbitration. Wilde argued that he had revoked the submission to the arbitrator, so that the bond was avoided. Vynior then claimed the full £20 on the bond and the court awarded him that sum.

---

7. *Arbitrium Redivivum* 10–11.
8. *Arbitrium Redivivum* 12 citing *Vynior*.
9. John March *Actions for Slander* [March] 165.
10. March 166.
11. A William Wilde is mentioned in the Nathaniel Bacon Papers as holder of a bond on 25 August 1606 Morgan et al *Nat Bacon V* 254 and a Vynior in 1604 Morgan et al *Nat Bacon V* 96.

3. COKE'S REPORT

But Coke's report did not stop there; it went on to fabricate new rules which have beset the law of arbitration until modern times: the law, though not necessarily the practice. The temptation must be resisted to find in *Vynior* the moment when lawyers took over arbitration in England. It cannot be assumed from what some legal authorities have written that *Vynior* had[12] 'such extraordinary vitality that its doctrine alone has limited the development of arbitration in commercial disputes in all common law countries'. That may be true about the law; about the practice more evidence is needed.

Later studies will have to show the effects on practice of the judges' creation of the notion that arbitration agreements could 'oust the jurisdiction of the courts', but neither the idea nor the phrase was known before *Kill v Hollister* in 1746.[13] This book is concerned with the 17th century. There is little evidence that *Vynior* inhibited the practice or indeed the development of either private or public arbitration then, whatever Coke might have intended.

Because so much depends on a close scrutiny of everything that Coke reported about Vynior, it must be quoted at length:[14]

And in this case three points were resolved:
1. That although W Wilde the defendant was bound in a bond to stand, abide, observe &c the rule, &c arbitrament, &c yet he might countermand it; for a man cannot by his act make such authority, power, or warrant not countermandable; as if I make a letter of attorney to make livery, or to sue an action &c in my name; or if I assign auditors to take an account; or if I make one my factor; or if I submit myself to an arbitrament; although these are made by express words irrevocable, or just that I grant or am bound that all these shall stand irrevocably, yet they may be revoked: so if I make my testament and last will irrevocable, yet I may revoke it, for my act or my words cannot alter the judgment of the law, to make that irrevocable which is of its own nature revocable.

And therefore (where it is said in 5 Ed 4 3b if I am bound to stand to the award which IS shall make, I could not discharge that arbitrament, because I am bound to stand to his award, but if it be without obligation it is otherwise), it was there resolved, that in both cases the authority of the arbitrator may be revoked; but then in the one case he shall forfeit his bond, and in the other he shall lose nothing; for, *ex nuda submissione non oritur actio* [no action arises from a bare submission]; and therewith agrees *Brooke* in abridging the said book of 5 Ed 4 3b and so the book of 5 Ed 4 is well explained. *Vide* 21 H 6 30a 28 29; H 6 6b; 49 E 3 9a; 18 E 4 9; 8 Ed 4 10.

---

12. PL Sayre 'Development of Commercial Arbitration Law' 597.
13. *Kill v Hollister* (1746) 1 Wilson 129, Roebuck *Short History* lxi–lxiii.
14. 8 Co Rep 81b–83a.

2. It was resolved that the plaintiff need not aver, that Willian Rugge had notice of the countermand, for that is implied in these words *revocavit* [he revoked] &c, for without notice it is no revocation or abrogation of the authority; and therefore if there was no notice then the defendant might take issue *quod non revocavit* [which he did not revoke], and if there was no notice it should be found for the defendant, as if a man pleads *quod feoffavit, dedit*, or *demisit pro termino vitae* [that he made a feoffment, or granted, or gave a life tenancy], it implies livery, for without livery it is no feoffment, gift, or demise; but there is a difference when two things are requisite to the performance of an act, and both things are to be done by one and the same party, as in the case of feoffment, gift, demise, revocation, countermand &c. And when two things are requisite to be performed by several persons, as of a grant of a reversion, attornment is not implied in it, and yet without attornment the grant hath not perfection, but forasmuch as the grant is made by one, and the attornment is to be made by another, it is not implied in the pleading of the grant of one; but in the other case both things are to be done by one and the same person and that makes the difference.

And therewith agrees 21 H 6 30a, where W Bridges brought an action of debt for £200 on an arbitrament against William Bentley; the defendant pleaded that, before any judgment or award made by the arbitrators, William Bentley discharged the arbitrators at Coventry; and it was held a good bar, and yet he did not aver any notice to be given. So it is adjudged in 28 H 6 6b; 6 H 7 10 &c.

3. It was resolved that by this countermand or revocation of the power of the arbitrator, the obligee shall take benefit of the bond, for two reasons: 1. Because he has broken the words of the condition... 'stand to &c' and he who countermands doth not 'stand to', which words were put in such conditions to the intent that there should be no countermand, but that an end should be made by the arbitrator of the controversy, and that the power of the arbitrator should continue till he had made an award, and, when the award is made, then there are words to compel the parties to perform it... and this form was invented by prudent antiquity; and it is good to follow in such cases the ancient forms and precedents, which are full of knowledge and wisdom, and with this resolution agrees 5 Ed 4 3b which is to be intended *ut supra* that the obligor cannot discharge the arbitrament but that he shall forfeit his bond; and the book gives the reason, which is the cause of this resolution, *scilicet* because I am bound 'to stand to his award', which I do not when I discharge the arbitrator. The other reason is, because now the obligor has by his own act made the condition of the bond (which was endorsed for the benefit of the obligor, to save him from the penalty of the bond) impossible to be performed, and by consequence his bond is become single, and without the benefit of or help of any condition, because he has disabled himself to perform the condition.... And afterwards judgment was given for the plaintiff.

That is, Vynior recovered the full £20 Wilde owed him on the bond.

Everything else said and reported by Coke must be obiter. It did not decide the case. It bound no judge to follow it. It might well be persuasive, coming from such an authority as Coke. Let us look at the arguments.

4. THE ARGUMENTS

The defendant had argued: 'a man may not make such authority not countermandable, which is by the law and of its own nature countermandable'.
That has since been accepted by most as settled law.[15]

Coke supported his opinion by examples: a grant of power of attorney to
make livery of seisin or to bring or defend an action; authority to auditors
to take an account; appointment of a factor; appointment of an arbitrator;
making a will.

It is still true that all wills are revocable until the testator's death; but
promises to make provision may be binding and damages recoverable for
their breach. Mutual wills imply such promises; indeed equity will enforce
them.

The other examples rest on a simple howler, or a lawyer's despairing
trick, which before and consistently since Coke's time has been exposed
as such and rejected. Simply, arbitrators are not agents. Evidence from all
times and places reveals a clear distinction between the role of an agent,
who acts entirely as an extension of the principal, and that of one or more
appointed to settle or adjudicate a dispute. True it was that in Coke's time
each side often appointed one or more, and an even number acted. But they
were assumed, and required by law, to be free from the control of the party
who appointed them.

There is no English authority which holds that an arbitrator is an agent.[16]
Therefore, the analogies with attorneys, factors and auditors are no more
than facile and obvious stratagems. And Coke must have known that, even
if arbitrators were agents, their principals could not countermand their
authority if it were 'coupled with an interest'.

So Coke was simply dishonest. Lawyers are not allowed to argue what
they know to be false law. Coke certainly cannot be accused of being so
ignorant of the law that he could honestly suggest that arbitrators were
agents. He was also unprofessional in other ways. He was selective in his
citation of earlier cases. He suppressed those which were against him as he
had become accustomed to doing when he was an advocate.[17]

5. OTHER REPORTS

By far the best analysis and appraisal of *Vynior* is still that published
nearly a century ago by JH Cohen of the New York Bar [Cohen]. The New

---

15. e.g. March 164; Matthew Bacon *The Compleat Arbitrator* sIII; Stewart Kyd *A Treatise
    on the Law of Awards* 31–32 [Kyd *Treatise*].
16. Thurlow LC in *Calcraft v Roebuck* (1790) 1 Vesey Jr 221, 226; Loughborough LC in
    Lonsdale v Littledale (1794) 2 Vesey Jr 451, 452; Eldon LC in *Fetherstone v Cooper*
    (1803) 9 Vesey Jr 67, 67a.
17. A practice not unknown of one recent judge: Roebuck 'The Diplock Report'.

York Chamber of Commerce had briefed him 'to dig under the mound of debris covering the ancient doctrine'. With little Latin or Law French, but with great application and ingenuity, he overcame the lack of resources easily to hand. Today's scholars may be impatient with the slow pace at which the primary sources are edited and published. We should honour Cohen's labours and willingness to test every bit of evidence then and there available to him. With no sign of the usual deference to authority, he used that evidence, not only to find Coke quite unreliable at best, but also to assess the work of almost all the judges who followed him, in England and the United States, as third rate. Nor is he uncritical of March, the only generally accepted textbook on arbitration in 1648, or of the abridgments, particularly Brooke.[18] Much of what follows in this chapter has been made easier by Cohen's pioneering work.

Cohen discovered two other reports of *Vynior's Case*. He also found the relevant reference to the Plea Rolls, though he mistook it for a Year Book citation and had no means of access to it.

Under the name *Wilde v Vinor*, Brownlow and Goldesborough report:[19]

Debt upon an obligation to perform an award. The defendant pleads that the arbitrators made no award; the plaintiff replies that the defendant in writing did revoke and null the authority of the arbitrators. Foster held the bond was forfeited, though he might revoke. The plea was that he did discharge the arbitrators against the form of the condition. My Lord Coke held that the power was countermandable; if the submission be by writing, the countermand must be by writing; if by word, I may countermand by word. If two bind themselves, one cannot countermand alone. If obligor or obligee disable by their own act to make the condition void, the bond is single, 14 H 7. If I am bound to enfeoff A, and I marry her before the day, the bond is forfeited, 18 E 4 18.20; the great doubt was because no express notice, but notice was implied. And the bond forfeited, because he did not stand to it. Judgment for the plaintiff.

It would seem, perhaps, that Foster, for the plaintiff, did not even argue that the submission was not countermandable. The plaintiff had tried to be fair, asking first for damages only for what he had suffered. When faced with a technical defence, he no doubt saw no reason against suing for the whole penalty. Wilde may not have been satisfied that he had paid so heavily for bad advice and an enduring, if malevolent, impact on the Common Law.

Inexplicably, under a different name, *Vivion v Wilde*, the case is reported again in the next part of the same reports, but rather differently, and on a different point.[20]

A man was bound in an obligation to another with condition to stand to, abide and perform the award of two arbitrators and, before award, by his writing the

18. Robert Brooke *La Graunde Abridgement* [Brooke].
19. (1609) 1 Brownl. 62; 123 ER 666.
20. (1609) 2 Brownl. 290; 123 ER 948.

obligor revoked the authority of one of the arbitrators: and it was agreed by
all that this obligation is become single without condition. And yet it was not
pleaded that the arbitrator had notice of the revocation before the award made.
And yet, for that it was pleaded that *revocavit*, it was agreed that that implies
notice, for without notice it is no revocation. But it was agreed that, if a man
submit himself to the award of another, and after he revokes his authority, but
before the arbitrator had notice of that he makes the award, the award is good
and shall be performed.

So, if a man make a feoffment, and letter of attorney to make livery, and
before livery made he revokes the power of the attorney; but before notice the
attorney makes livery, this is good; but if the feoffor makes release or feoffment
to another before the livery made by the other, this is a countermand in law
and shall be good without notice, for *fortior est dispositio legis quam hominis*
[the authority of the law is stronger than that of a person]. But, where a man
makes actual revocation of the authority, and before notice the other executes
his authority, and in pleading the other pleads *quod revocavit*, the other party
may reply *quod non revocavit*, and give in evidence that he hath no notice of that
before the execution of his authority, and that is good, for without notice it is no
revocation, where revocation is the act of the party.

The case is entred Trinity 7 Jacobi rotulo 2629. *Vivion* against *Wilde*.

Brownlow and Goldesborough were both prothonotaries, officials whose
duties included the recording of civil actions. They had ready access to the
Plea Rolls, which they noted at the end of that passage.[21]

Vynior was often followed throughout the rest of the century and
thereafter.[22] Coke knew or should have known what was written there, but
not all the fault for what followed can be attributed to him. It would be
unscholarly to excuse, worse to attempt to disguise, the slovenly and even
obsequious misuse of Coke's report by judges since his time. He said quite
plainly what he was doing:[23]

> Now that I have taken upon me to make a report of their arguments, I ought to
> do the same as truly, fully, and sincerely as possibly I can. Howbeit, seeing that
> almost every judge had in the course of his argument a peculiar method, and I
> must only hold myself to one, I shall give no just offence to any if I challenge
> that which of right is due to every reporter, that is, to reduce the sum and effect of
> all to such a method as, upon consideration had of all the arguments, the reporter
> himself thinkest to be fittest and clearest for the right understanding of the true
> reasons and causes of the judgment and resolution of the case in question.

When the reporter was Coke, at least, what he 'thinketh to be fittest' was
the law. And that was his justification for the leeway he allowed himself.

21. 7 Jac 1 rot 2629.
22. *Wilson v Barton* (1672) Nels 148; 21 ER 812.
23. *Calvin's Case* 7 Co Rep 4a.

6. THE EXTENSIONS OF *VYNIOR*

The courts were prepared to extend the *Vynior* rule to remarkable lengths. In a matter which had been through the courts for years, the parties eventually agreed to arbitration and got an order in Chancery confirming the submission. When counsel for one party realised the two merchants appointed to arbitrate were going to find against him, in the middle of the hearing, he revoked the appointment. In *Hide v Petit* Bridgman LC, sitting with Rainsford J of King's Bench and Wilde J of Common Pleas, held:[24]

> Though it were an abuse of the court in the defendant to retract his consent, after he had attended the reference, having first subscribed the reference under his hand; yet such a consent, giving a bare authority only, was revocable.... An authority in its nature is revocable by law, though referred by order of court.

If there was no bond, so deep-seated was *Vynior* by 1670 that such chicanery was accepted even in the highest court of Equity.

It was left to a monster, perhaps the most inhuman judge ever to have sat in an English court, to try to knock some sense into this perversion of legal principle. In 1685 Sir George Jeffreys had just been elevated at the age of 40 from CJKB to Lord Chancellor, having satisfied the King by his unprecedented inhumanity in presiding at the Bloody Assizes. Well over a thousand of those found to have been on the wrong side in the Monmouth Rebellion were tried, if they did not die first of gaol fever. Convicted on little or no evidence, often despite the jury's reservations, they were hanged, drawn and quartered, women burned, or transported in their hundreds to the West Indies where they were employed as little more than slaves.

Before his imprisonment in the Tower after James II fled in 1688, and his death there in 1689 at the age of only 45, Jeffreys just had time to preside in *Norton v Mascall*.[25] Arbitrators had delivered an award. The successful party sued in Chancery to enforce it. The defendant pleaded that the award was void, 'it being a voluntary submission of the parties, and the reference not directed by this court'. At first instance, Guildford MR called for precedents, read the award, and declared he would not enforce it. Jeffreys LC on appeal declared that he saw no reason not to enforce the award, 'being in part executed and assented unto', and ordered the defendant to perform it.

'Sir Edward Coke's *obiter dicta* have cast a long shadow down the centuries', as a leading Australian judge said recently:[26]

---

24. (1670) Freeman Ch 133; (1670) 1 Ch Cas 185; 22 ER 754.
25. *Norton v Mascall* (1685) 2 Chan Cas 304.
26. Patrick Keane CJ Federal Court (now J of the High Ct) 'Meeting the Challenge of Regional Forum Competition or Our House Rules' (2012) *Fed J Schol* 9.

It was not unusual for Sir Edward Coke, when making a lofty pronouncement, to be a little less than disciplined in his language. Sometimes, his pronouncements had little to do with the actual decision at all. *Vynior's Case* is an example of such a case. In that case, the Court did not permit the award debtor to countermand the arbitration agreement. Indeed, it ordered the judgment debtor to pay the amount due under the award plus damages for the breach of the arbitration agreement.

Such a shadow, indeed, that so eminent a judge could get it so wrong today. Whatever *Vynior* decided, it did allow the award debtor to countermand the arbitration agreement. All the reports agree that it did not order 'the judgment debtor to pay the amount plus damages due under the award'. It simply made him pay the amount he had promised by his bond. Vynior's claim for damages for breach of the submission was rejected specifically because Wilde had successfully countermanded his promise.

7.   COKE AFTER *VYNIOR*

A superficial comprehension of *Vynior's Case* has led some to find that Coke was jealous of, if not opposed to, any means of resolving disputes other than through the Common Law courts. There is nothing to support that conclusion and overwhelming evidence in the primary sources to negate it. Those found in Nathaniel Bacon's archives were set out in Chapter 11. In 1609, when he decided *Vynior*, Coke had been CJCP for three years. Already, as Attorney General and assize judge, he had appointed Nathaniel many times to help clear his case load. One may perhaps presume that Nathaniel was not the only arbitrator Coke appointed.

Moreover, Chapter 12 has shown that Coke submitted himself to the mediation and arbitration of his own disputes, with his wife over her property and over Coke's abuse of his daughter, with an arbitration clause in the settlement. In that chapter, too, is the evidence of Coke's own activities as an arbitrator.

8.   CONCLUSIONS[27]

Of course, the whole basis of the rule in *Vynior's Case* is chicanery: lawyer-induced immorality. A lawyer must always have explained to a client how to avoid a straightforward ethical duty, one which in other circumstances all lawyers would trumpet as fundamental, indeed sacred: *pacta sunt servanda*, the sanctity of contracts, the foundation of commerce – but not if you can wriggle out by a legal trick.

Fortunately for commerce, the practice of arbitration was not seriously affected by the unsatisfactory legal system. Commercial people knew how

---

27. Cohen 146–147 'recapitulates the elements which furnish the explanation for this arrested development', forcefully and usually convincingly.

to ensure performance. Throughout the 17th century they got on with their business, submitting their inevitable disputes to mediation and arbitration, confident that other sanctions, most commonly goodwill and reputation, would be enough to safeguard their interests. The law reports show only the aberrant, not the normal and routine. It is doubtful whether a merchant who once relied on *Vynior's Case* would retain sufficient credit to continue to trade.

Later evidence from North America reveals a different reality, but there is little to suggest that the rule in *Vynior's Case* affected the development of the practice of arbitration in England at all. As Edmond Wingate wrote in 1658, half a century after *Vynior's Case*:[28]

> *Vinyor's* A being bound to stand to the award of B countermands the authority of the arbitrator. In this case the bond is forfeit; because the condition is that A the obligor should stand to and abide &c, which form was invented by prudent antiquity, to the end he should not revoke the submission. And it is good always to pursue (in such cases) the ancient forms and presidents, which are full of knowledge and wisdom.

Indeed, *Vynior's Case* is paradoxical. Usually presented as a blow to arbitration, even as evidence of judicial animosity, it is nothing of the kind. By ensuring that bonds to submit and accept the award were enforceable for breach of condition, by a judgment in favour of the plaintiff for the full amount of the bond, *Vynior* ensured that arbitration flourished. The later tendency to reduce the amount recoverable to something more like compensation developed only after the Arbitration Act 1698, the subject of the next chapter, had provided a statutory procedure of enforcement.

---

28. Edmond Wingate *Maximes of Reason* 749.

20 LAW REFORM AND THE ARBITRATION ACT 1698

> When you are writing laws you are testing words to find their utmost power. Like spells, they have to make things happen in the real world, and like spells, they only work if people believe in them.
>
> Hilary Mantel *Wolf Hall*

> The knowledge of the Common Law doth in no way conduct to the making of a statesman.... it were no wisdom to choose mercenary lawyers to make laws; because they are the first men to invent subtleties to evade them.... The reformation of the Courts of Justice ... if you have many lawyers, they will never suffer any effectual law to pass for this purpose. Because they get more by the corruption and delays of the law, than by the law itself.
>
> Anonymous pamphlet 20 November 1646[1]

1. INTRODUCTION

The legislation which is always rightly credited with laying at least one or two of the foundation stones of the modern law and practice of arbitration in England is the Arbitration Act 1698, but it was by no means the first attempt at statutory law reform. In December 1601 Francis Bacon had probably drafted and successfully introduced to Parliament the Merchants Assurances Act 1601,[2] which set up a standing arbitration commission 'for the hearing and determining of causes arising, and policies of assurances'. His disgraceful end stultified his repeated schemes to reform the law but there were others who saw the need for legislation, including the unsuccessful William Sheppard, 'Cromwell's Law Reformer',[3] and then the political philosopher John Locke.

2. LAW REFORM IN THE INTERREGNUM

In 1646 the Parliament set up two law reform commissions, with no result. Then in January 1652 its Law Committee commissioned 21 men, none of

---

1. *A Looking Glass for all Proud, Ambitious, Covetous and Corrupt Lawyers* cited by Donald Veall *The Popular Movement* [Veall] 205.
2. (1601) 43 Eliz 12, Roebuck *Golden Age* 236–238.
3. NL Matthews *William Sheppard* [Matthews].

them MPs, with Sir Matthew Hale presiding, to advise it on law reform. It took its duties seriously and in six months produced no less than 16 bills. They covered criminal, matrimonial, probate and mercantile law; criminal and civil procedure; county and small claims courts; deeds registries; and the legal professions. A year later the Nominated Parliament passed many of the bills and set up new permanent law commissions. The next month the Barebones Parliament tried to abolish the abuses of Chancery but it was stymied by the lawyers. The impetus was lost, Cromwell became Lord Protector and made Hale CJCP. On 15 December 1653 a Council of Officers adopted the Instrument of Government, which provided for a Lord Protector as head of state and appointed Cromwell. In many ways it foreshadowed the Bill of Rights.

3.   WILLIAM SHEPPARD

Cromwell at once appointed William Sheppard, a Puritan country lawyer from Gloucester, to set to work on a programme of law reform.[4] His salary was £300 a year, substantial though much less than he could earn in private practice, which he had to give up. By any standard he was a prolific author. He wrote twenty-seven books, including his posthumous *Grand Abridgment*, discussed in Chapter 2. He was given ample resources and two years. Unlike the law reform commissions of the Commonwealth, he had to compromise with no other committee members or pressure groups. By the end of 1655, Sheppard had published two reports to the Council of State, on registration of deeds and on reform of the county courts.

His *Epitome*, published in May 1656, was an attempt at an encyclopaedic dictionary.[5] Under the heading *Arbitrement* it collected hundreds of entries, set out with no more order than that of a lawyer's commonplace book of the period. It is the best representative of its kind and a serious attempt to include all the relevant sources of law. For that reason it is reproduced here as Appendix 2.

In October 1656, less than five months later, he published his law reform tract *England's Balme*.[6] In his address to the reader he wrote:

> Dear Countrymen,
> It hath been to me (as in all ages to good men) a grief to see, that of all nations the English should live like wolves and tigers in matters of *meum* and *tuum*: I have cast in my dose for the cure, and wish wiser heads and stronger hands would take up the work.

4. WB Willcox 'Lawyers and Litigants' [Willcox] describes the realities of life as country lawyer in Gloucester in Sheppard's time, with examples of arbitration.
5. William Sheppard *An Epitome* [Sheppard *Epitome*].
6. William Sheppard *England's Balme* [Sheppard *Balme*].

Sheppard's remedies included a wider and compulsory provision for arbitration. He presented his suggestions in an unusually helpful way, making it easy for the reader to comprehend and to criticise, accept or reject. First he stated what he called the grievance, then his proposed remedy, as when he discussed dispute resolution:[7]

> *Grievance*   It is objected, That suits of Law, (especially in the Great Courts at *Westminster*) are exceeding troublesome and tedious, that the Cure is worse than the Disease; insomuch that most wise Men will rather lose their Right, and suffer much Wrong, than seek their Remedy by a Suit in Law. And a Man can hardly there come to obtain the end and fruit of his Suit in less time than in a whole year at the soonest. The Causes hereof are conceived to be especially in these things.
>
> *Grievance*   That the Courts at Westminster are overburthened with business.
>
> *Remedy*   It is offered, as to the cure hereof, to consider of these things:
>
>   *Arbitrators*   1. To provide all that may be to prevent suits; as countenance arbitrements; to let arbitrators have power to give an oath to witnesses; and when they have made an award, to let it be performed: for in this the law is so at this day, that the wisest man in the country cannot make an award that a hole cannot be picked in it to make it void.
>
>   *References*   2. That daysmen be appointed in every hundred, High Constables and some others for the ending (if possible) of all differences about slanders of men's persons: and that no suit be brought for these things, till it hath been before them, or arbitrators of their own choice; and that they, and the arbitrators, do always certify to the judge that shall hear the cause, what they found and their opinion in it.
>
>   *Demand of the Debt Before Suit*   3. That if the defendant live within ten miles of the plaintiff, he shall before he sue, send or speak to him, and demand satisfaction.
>
>   *Difference about Ways or Boundaries*   4. That if any difference be or is like to be, about a tree, or way, or boundary, where it should go; either of the parties shall sue out a commission to gentlemen chosen by the Lords Commissioners to end it by order without a suit.
>
>   *Penal Contracts*   5. That no penal bond or mortgage exceeding ten pounds in the hundred be admitted good.
>
>   But if suits must be brought, then to present their bringing (as much as may be) in the Great Courts. And for this, to consider hereof, that in all those courts, and all others, but the County, Hundred Courts and Court Baron, these rules be observed.

Sheppard was then advanced to the rank of serjeant-at-law. His proposals were put before Parliament but conservative forces there ensured none of the bills passed. Cromwell was offered and refused the Crown and in the political turmoil his cautious bent prevailed:[8]

7. Sheppard *Balme* 58–60.
8. Matthews 266.

Realizing that the success of his government depended on the support of the propertied classes, Cromwell had chosen Sheppard to devise a reform that would ensure security of property while it sought to institute legal equality. But the propertied classes of the nation remained apprehensive and this reluctance to sanction further changes partly explains both the failure of constitutional ratification and the lack of interest in the enactment of specific reforms.

The lawyers in the Commons provided the technical expertise to see off the reforms. Sheppard was paid off and went home to the country, pleading for a pension. He got £100 a year, plenty to live on modestly but probably never paid.[9] Sheppard's practice took a while to recover and he spent his time in writing, on theology as well as throwing together more of his apparently endless stream of legal volumes.

There were plenty of other voices raised and pens employed to no greater effect. John March, the author of the first major treatise devoted to the law of arbitration, was one, though he did not recommend arbitration as a cure.[10] Others did. Hugh Peters, for example, suggested that every parish and hundred should choose three men every year to acts as 'peacemakers' or 'friendmakers'.[11] The Levellers also recommended arbitration, Winstanley recommending peacemakers, who would first try to settle all civil disputes through mediation.[12] Henry Robinson would have abolished the whole judicial system forthwith.[13] Instead JPs would sit everywhere, every day, delivering their judgments within two days but always trying first to mediate a settlement.

At that time there were still many men who, like Sheppard, believed in the possibility under Cromwell of transforming English society into a godly commonwealth, where there would be no 'wolves and tigers', or, if any remained, they would be constrained by their god-fearing community. Such dreams were never realised; they faded with the rest of the law reforms which Cromwell pretended to accept but which were never taken further.

Veall's monograph is full and fair. He is perhaps a little kind to Cromwell:[14]

> What was wanted was a New Model Judiciary of lawyers who had clear ideas about law reform and felt strongly about them. Cromwell, cautious and empirical as he was, never dismissed law reform as impractical. He kept emphasizing the

9. Matthews 186–230.
10. John March *Amicus Reipublicae* 19 May 1652 E 1360 (1).
11. Veall 119; Hugh Peters *A Word for the Army* 11 October 1647 and *Good Work for a Good Magistrate* 17 June 3–11.
12. Gerard Winstanley *Law of Freedom*.
13. Henry Robinson *Certain Considerations in Order to Obtain a More Speedy Cheap and Equal System of Justice Throughout the Nation* 14 November 1650 E 616 (2) and *Certain Proposals in Order to a New Modelling of the Laws and Law Proceedings* 1653 5–11, 17, 18, 22, 23; Veall 176.
14. Veall 239.

need for it, but said its achievement was difficult because of the opposition of property owners and the corrupt interest of lawyers.

Cromwell was a property owner before all else. Whatever his religious beliefs, he assumed the rights of landed wealth. If lawyers sought their own advantage, that could be called corrupt, but Cromwell's god's hand was there to protect the rich man in his country house and keep the poor man at his gate. He was so successful as a politician because he knew well the difference between words and deeds. He could play the old soldier:[15]

> I remember well, in the old Parliament, that we were more than three months and could not get over the word 'incumbrances'.... I think verily at the least, the delays in suits, and the excessiveness in fees... and those various things I do not know the names they bear – I have heard talk of 'demurrers' and such like things as I scarce know – but I say certainly that the people are greatly suffering in this respect.

Artifice worthy of Odysseus! He knew that, as long as he kept talking, his opponents might be content to respond with words. They would not act unless he did. So he died in power with next to none of his promises of law reform fulfilled,

4. JOHN LOCKE

The names of two great English philosophers of the 17th century have appeared in earlier chapters: Francis Bacon and Thomas Hobbes. At its end perhaps the greatest political thinker of his age, John Locke, was most instrumental in the development of arbitration. He drafted the Arbitration Act 1698. In 1993 Henry Horwitz and James Oldham published an article whose many qualities have never been surpassed by any scholar who has written on the history of arbitration.[16] The temptation to rehash what they found in the primary sources is easily overcome by the conviction that they have said it best and that the reader has a right to direct access to their results. They have generously agreed that I should quote them often and at length.

On 19 August 1696 the Board of Trade, newly created by William III's Government, sat to deal with a full and miscellaneous agenda. They 'inspected a model of a spinning wheel which would make it easy for a girl 10 years old to spin 800 yards of flax for a penny, and to earn 10 pence a day'. They discussed workhouses and beggars, and 'the better establishment of credit by paper' and 'a-la-modes made by the lustring company'. Then they came to dispute resolution:[17]

---

15. Cited by Sir Stephen Sedley in his searching Sir Henry Hodge Memorial Lecture 2013 'Cromwell's Constitution: Public Law in the Interregnum' 7.
16. Henry Horwitz and James Oldham 'John Locke' [Horwitz and Oldham].
17. HR Fox Bourne *The Life of John Locke* [Fox Bourne] 355–358.

They examined Gilbert Heathcote, one of the leading merchants of London and a friend of Locke's, and several other merchants trading with Sweden and the Baltic, about the condition of English commerce with those parts, and made similar enquiries of Paul Daranda and other merchants about trade with Holland, and the value of a consulate at Rotterdam, as a result of which Mr Locke was desired to draw up a scheme of some method of determining differences between merchants by referees that might be decisive without appeal.

Locke's was a scholarly response. He appreciated the value of comparative research. He sought the help of his friend Benjamin Furly, an English merchant in Rotterdam. Furly wrote a long and helpful letter on Friday 7 September 1696, which included:[18]

As to the other matter about Arbitration, and the Condemnation of the Court of Justice or Hoogen Raad in Holland, herewith I send you the Translation of a Compromisse or bond of Award, at present in my hands, and under my direction, together with the Double condemnation of the said High Court.

The first is the Condemnation upon the Bond itself, which commonly one of the parties that is most earnest for an end, obtains, sending the compromisse to his Attorney to demand Condemnation upon it. He speaks to one of the Attorneys, whichever he will, to assist in it. These two exhibit the Compromisse to the Court, by which they are authorised the one to demand, the other to consent to the condemnation, which they doing accordingly, the court condemns the parties to stand to their agreement, inserting from word to word the Compromisse in their condemnation – which being once done they cannot fly from it, but must suffer the Arbitrators to go forward to a final sentence.

The last condemnation is commonly taken out by the Arbitrators themselves, before the parties know how the sentence lies, by sending it to one of the Attorneys, and upon it the court condemns them in the sentence, as before they had done in the Compromisse, Bond, or Agreement. And that done there remains no remedy, be the sentence what it will, there is no appeal, being confirmed by the highest Court in the Nation. But if any of the Arbitrators should privately give notice to either party how things are gone, so that he can time enough get to The Hague to revoke the Letter of Attorney, and seek Reduction, as they call it here, the Court will hearken to the plaintiff.

You will find in the compromisse words sublined, which are by me added to the copy I translated, because I found it defective. And I am perhaps like to fall into a suit at Law for want of those or such like words, for, by my marrying my wife, I am become uncapable of remaining an Arbitrator, and though, in the reason of the thing, I being *civiliter mortuus*, my wife ought to have the same faculty of choosing one in my place, as she has in case I had died; yet compromisses being, as the lawyers call it, *stricti juris*, and not binding beyond the letter – my brother-in-law, they say, needs not consent to it, and so, notwith-

18. Furly had experience as a party. He wrote to Locke on 1 May 1699: 'our differences being not alone submitted to arbitration, but mediation of two able men our friends and neighbours.... And they tell me that they are persuaded that my brother is in earnest to have an end, so is my dearest and I, though it should be with the loss of £1000'.

standing all the precaution used to prevent its being disannulled, yet, for want of adding that clause, 'Or become any other way incapacitated to remain an Arbitrator' it may by him be disannulled.

In the compromisse commonly each party states his case, as briefly as he can, that it may appear whereunto the Commission extends, Except where they had been at Law, and then reference (as in this copy) is made to the declaration of the Plaintiff and answer of the Defendant in the Registers.

I know nothing more needfull to give you a full and distinct notion of this affair. If I be mistaken, pray inform me and I shall endeavour to explain myself better if I can; for I would be glad to see so good and serviceable a thing introduced in my native Country.

Onely one caution I must give you, from experience, That the Compromisse must impower the last court of Appeal to pass this Condemnation, for if any inferior court should do it, a superior might give relief, to either party complaining. For I once was in a case, wherein the Notary, whether by mistake or order, had put in the Court (or Hof) of Holland, instead of the High Council or Hogen Raad. When we had passed Sentence, and the Plaintiff went about to Execute, the Lawyers found that flaw, and appealed to the Hogen Raad; But they labouring with both parties very hard, till they brought them to submit a second time, to other Arbitrators, under their condemnation, which other Arbitrators, hearing all *de novo*, confirmed our sentence and there was an end.

Locke reported back to the Board of Trade in November 1696:

Mr Locke acquainted the board that, in order to draw up a scheme of some method for determining differences between merchants by referees, he had enquired into the methods practised in Holland for that purpose but found them too intricate and too different from our methods to be put in practice here, whereupon he had consulted with others experienced in our laws, who had drawn up a draft of an Act of Parliament for that purpose, which he delivered unto the board.

Locke's early biographer described what happened next:[19]

A few days after doing that, Locke had to go down to Gates for the winter. His draft bill was considered in his absence, and a statement of certain alterations suggested in it by Brathwayte was sent down to him. These he returned in due time with his own corrections, and those corrections being adopted by the other commissioners, a fair copy of the document was forwarded to King William for his approval and in due time became law.

Locke shared with his lay contemporaries a poor opinion of lawyers, and the 'intricacy of law' which he thought hindered trade.[20] This bill would do the trick:[21]

In forwarding the measure to the Privy Council, the board reiterated that its aim was to remedy the 'great obstructions in trade arising from the tedious

19. Fox Bourne II 358, citing Board of Trade Papers, Journal A 200–229, 288, 288; 854, 85a.
20. Horwitz and Oldham 139.
21. Horwitz and Oldham 143–144.

determination of controversies between merchants and traders in matters of accompt or trade in our ordinary methods'. The new procedures would be accessible to others than men of trade and business but it was on the grounds of the 'very great advantage to the trade of this kingdom' that Locke and his colleagues urged its adoption.

The King took his time and sought advice, and added a clause expressly permitting challenges to awards for arbitrators' misconduct, before the Bill was introduced in the Lords late in February. It received the royal assent on 16 May 1698.[22]

5.   THE 1698 ACT

An Act for Determining Differences by Arbitration
9th of William III cap xv

Whereas it hath been found by Experience That References made by Rule of Court have contributed much to the Ease of the Subject in the determining of Controversies because the Parties become thereby obliged to submitt to the Award of the Arbitrators under the Penalty of Imprisonment for their Contempt in case they refuse Submission Now for promoting Trade and rendring the Awards of Arbitrators the more effectual in all Cases for the final Determination of Controversies referred to them by Merchants and Traders or others concerning Matters of Account or Trade or other Matters

Be it enacted by the King's most Excellent Majesty by and with the Advice and Consent of the Lords Spiritual and Temporal and Commons in Parliament assembled and by Authority of the same That from & after the Eleventh Day of May which shall be in the yeare of our Lord One thousand six hundred ninety eight It shall and may be lawfull for all Merchants and Traders & others desiring to end any Controversie Suit or Quarrel Controversies Suits or Quarrels (for which there is no other Remedy but by Personal Action or Suit in Equity) by Arbitration to agree that their Submission of their Suit to the Award or Umpirage of any person or persons should be made a Rule of any of His Majesties Courts of Record which the Parties shall choose and to insert such their Agreement in their Submission or the Condition of the Bond or Promise whereby they oblidge themselves respectively to submitt to the Award or Umpirage of any Person or Persons which Agreement being so made and inserted in their Submission or Promise or Condition of their respective Bonds shall or may upon producing an Affidavit thereof made by the Witnesses thereunto or any one of them in the Court of which the same is agreed to be made a Rule & reading and filing the said Affidavitt in Court be entred of Record in such Court and a Rule shall thereupon be made by the said Court that the Parties shall submitt to & finally be concluded by the Arbitration or Umpirage which shall be made concerning them by the Arbitrators or Umpire pursuant to such Submission And in case of Disobedience to such Arbitration or Umpirage the Party neglecting or refusing to performe and execute the same or any part thereof shall be subject to all the

22.   William III 1697–8 Cap XV Rot Parl 9 Gul III 3 n5.

Penalties of contemning a Rule of Court when hee is a Suitor or Defendant in such Court and the Court on Motion shall issue Processe accordingly which Processe shall not be stopt or delayed in its Execution by any Order Rule Command or Processe of any other Court either of Law or Equity unlesse it shall be made appeare on Oath to such Court that the Arbitrators or Umpire misbehaved themselves and that such Award Arbitration or Umpirage was procured by Corruption or other undue Means.

II. Arbitration unduly procured, void.
And be it further enacted by the Authority aforesaid That any Arbitration or Umpirage procured by Corruption or undue Means shall be judged and esteemed void and of none Effect and accordingly be sett aside by any Court of Law or Equity so as Complaint of such Corruption or undue Practise be made in the Court where the Rule is made for Submission to such Arbitration or Umpirage before the last Day of the next Terme after such Arbitration or Umpirage made and published to the Parties Any thing in this Act contained to the contrary notwithstanding.

Nothing could be clearer: the Act was based on the rule of court procedure, which had 'contributed much to the ease of the subject in the determining of controversies'.

6. THE EFFECTS OF THE ACT

The 1698 Act seems to have had just the effect it sought. As a later commentator on *Veale v Warner* explained:[23]

the Court of KB in the reign of Charles II, when Kelynge was CJ, began to compel a performance of the award by attachment, as for a contempt of a rule of Court. 1 Salk 83, *Forster v Brunetti* 1 Sid 54, *Stiles v Triste*. It afterwards became the common practice to issue out an attachment for not performing an award. And it was found by experience, as the preamble of the above-mentioned statute recites, that the enforcing of the performance of awards by attachment had contributed much to the ease of the subject. Therefore the first section of the statute enables parties to make a submission to arbitration by bond, or other writing, a rule of Court.

Horwitz and Oldham's careful counting shows a decline in litigation after the Act and fewer rules of court entered. They see: 'the volume of litigation transacted by the central courts at a low ebb as a decline which began in the 1680s plumbed new depths'.[24] But less litigation is – at least prima facie – a cause for general rejoicing. And, if merchants were not bothering to enter rules of court, was not that because their preference for arbitration was producing a practical alternative to what lawyers had to offer? As Horwitz

23. *Veale v Warner* (1668) 1, 323, 326; 85 ER 463, 468.
24. Horwitz and Oldham 145.

and Oldham say:[25] 'there is suggestive, if not conclusive, evidence of frequent and expanding provision for arbitration in business contracts during the 1700s'. What more could Locke have asked for? Soon after the Act, arbitration clauses, which had been in use in England for centuries, became routine in insurance, construction, partnership and many other standard form contracts.[26]

Figures from the latter part of the 18th century show that 'in both courts the initial step of feeing counsel and paying court charges to have a rule entered was more often than not enough to bring the other party into compliance with the terms of the award'.[27] It is probably safe to assume that even that initial step was unnecessary in most matters. Most unsuccessful parties, at all times and places it seems, prefer to perform the awards against them, if they can. And, as Horwitz and Oldham conclude:[28] 'As our analysis reveals, the provisions of the Act did work. For many of the parties who entered their arbitration as rules of court... no further action appears to have been necessary to secure enforcement of the awards.'

For many more it must have been enough to know that such enforcement procedures were available. That would have been sufficient to ensure performance. Moreover:[29] 'Undue reliance on either contemporary legal writers such as Bacon or Kyd or the printed reports of leading cases... can provide clues; they are not a substitute for investigation of the judicial records'. True enough, and how much more could be learned if it were possible to exhaust the information to be found in the masses of primary sources recording evidence of completely private arbitrations, which never entered the legal system?

6.   CONCLUSIONS

By the end of the 17th century there was just beginning to be evidence of an embryonic profession of arbitrator. Robert Hooke and his colleagues working as City Surveyors made a lot of money from their surveys and perhaps substantial fees from arbitrations. It will be for others to find the evidence and tell the tale of developments in the 18th century.

---

25. Horwitz and Oldham 147.
26. They had been in use in England for centuries, Roebuck *Golden Age* 303–305.
27. Horwitz and Oldham 152.
28. Horwitz and Oldham 155.
29. Horwitz and Oldham 156–157.

PART FIVE

CONCLUSIONS

21   CONCLUSIONS

To destroy a sufficiently deep-seated delusion it is necessary to show not only its absurdity but also its origins.

Sir Lewis Namier[1]

On this point, legal and economic theory is greatly at fault. Imbued with modern ideas, current theory tends towards *a priori* notions of evolution, and claims to follow a so-called necessary logic; in fact, however, it remains based on old traditions. Nothing could be more dangerous than... this 'unconscious sociology'.

Marcel Mauss *The Gift* p54.[2]

Western society has chosen for itself the organization best suited to its purposes and one I might call legalistic. The limits of human rights and rightness are determined by a system of laws; such limits are very broad. People in the West have acquired considerable skill in using, interpreting, and manipulating law (though laws tend to be too complicated for an average person to understand without the help of an expert). Every conflict is solved according to the letter of the law and this is considered to be the ultimate solution. If one is right from a legal point of view, nothing more is required, nobody may mention that one could still not be right, and urge self-restraint or a renunciation of these rights, call for sacrifice and selfless risk: this would simply sound absurd. Voluntary self-restraint is almost unheard of: everybody strives toward further expansion to the extreme limit of the legal frames.... I have spent all my life under a communist regime and I will tell you that a society without any objective legal scale is a terrible one indeed. But a society with no other scale but the legal one is not quite worthy of man either. A society which is based on the letter of the law and never reaches any higher is taking very scarce advantage of the high level of human possibilities. The letter of the law is too cold and formal to have a beneficial influence on society. Whenever the tissue of life is woven of legalistic relations, there is an atmosphere of moral mediocrity, paralyzing man's noblest impulses.

Alexander Solzhenitsyn[3]

---

1. LB Namier *Avenues of History* 120, quoted as epigraph by Ivo Mosley *In the Name of the People*.
2. Marcel Mauss *The Gift* 54.
3. Alexander Solzhenitsyn, 'A World Split Apart'.

1.   INTRODUCTION

Everybody knows what gin is. It is easy to describe, even to define. Similarly tonic. But, when you are actually drinking a gin and tonic, you would rarely think of them separately. They have lost their separateness. Their value lies in them being mingled. That is how it was with mediation and arbitration. Both were naturally subsumed in the routine processes of resolving disputes.

The 17th century saw great changes in English life, yet few in the ways in which parties managed their disputes, and those few only towards its end. Parties of all kinds still submitted them to be resolved, usually by an even number of third parties, first by them trying to find an agreed settlement and, if that failed, by their determination. Those were the usual processes, whether the arbitration was arranged privately or under government auspices.

In 1641 the Privy Council lost almost all its judicial powers and ceased to be the Government. Yet at local levels, through all the civil strife, the assizes and the JPs continued the administration, including arranging arbitrations, as their records have shown. One example of the kind of settlement the Government expected its mediators to achieve will have to suffice. It comes from 1621 and contains most of the elements.[4] In the middle of a busy day on 31 January 1625, as James I lay dying, quite out of action in the agonies of gout and arthritis and kidney stones, his Council wrote three letters, to the Lord Keeper, the Chancellor of the Duchy and the JPs of Middlesex, telling them to look after the interests of the enterprising Italian they called Sadley, who had opened a delicatessen in the Strand, as related in Chapter 1.[5]

With such evidence of a proper sense of priorities, who would dare to suggest that the Privy Council of that time was less refined in the discharge of its responsibilities than any Cabinet of our own day?

2.   THE ECONOMY

At the beginning of the century England was still a land of local communities. The central government of the royal court left the cities and bigger towns room for some independence and the rest of the country to local gentry, formally as JPs or otherwise. By the end of the century economic changes were affecting that distribution. As economic relations came to be governed by the new capitalism, so social relations changed. Capitalism requires that risks be allocated with certainty. Contracts must be performed even though circumstances change. There is no room for 'fair

4. *APC* 37.397–399.
5. *APC* 39.449.

solutions'. The law must require debts to be paid in full, and when they fall due. Any exceptions must be restricted and determined by predictable law, not discretion. Community interest was no longer dominant. Individual rights had to be paramount and they were legal rights, determined by the Common Law.

None of the sources suggests that confidentiality was a prime concern of those who submitted their disputes to others. Property then depended on public acceptance. When land was transferred, custom required an outward show, a performance of a ritual called livery of seisin.

3. THE LAW

One of the many insights for which JH Cohen deserves thanks is:[6]

> If arbitration was so early and so much a part of the 'known and uncontroverted law' to be found in 'the most ancient repositories of the decisions of our courts', how came it to be so arrested in its development as part of the English Common Law?

How indeed? Edward Coke CJCP has been held responsible in *Vynior's Case* for arresting the development of the Common Law, English but even more American. But did that arrest the development of arbitration? Not the practice, as has been shown by the primary sources which survive. Nor in the other venues in which disputes involving arbitration were heard, outside the Common Law courts. Did not *Vynior*'s insistence on the enforceability of the penalty provide the solid foundation for the development of arbitration thereafter?

Oliver Wendell Holmes called his book *The Common Law*. That allowed him to write:[7] 'the contracts enforced by the civil courts were few and simple'. What could he have meant by 'civil courts'? His statement is true only if, with staggering anachronism, he is suggesting that there were no courts enforcing contracts other than the Common Law courts, when in fact the great majority of contract cases were being decided by other tribunals: of borough, fair, Mayor of London, shire, hundred and leet, to say nothing of the Church. Few of their records survive, fewer still have been edited into a readily available form. But that lack does not justify exclusive concentration on the Common Law courts. Holmes never meant that, though his limited scope persists. He and many of his successors have not concerned themselves with the law by which most people were then bound and bound themselves.

6. JH Cohen *Commercial Arbitration* [Cohen] 106.
7. OW Holmes *The Common Law* 259.

It is understandable that a 17th-century Common Law judge like Matthew Hale should have written:[8] 'The Common Law is not only a very just and excellent law in itself, but is singularly accommodated to the English Government, and to the disposition of the English nation… incorporated into their very temperament'. It is easy to show that self-satisfaction to be false. It confuses the common law as the whole of the law which had slowly evolved in many different forms and jurisdictions from time immemorial, on the one hand, and the Common Law on the other, the rules laid down by the King's judges in the royal courts of King's Bench and Common Pleas, Assizes, perhaps extending to Chancery and Exchequer and JPs. The latter was lawyers' law, and just what the newly powerful merchants wanted, where a contract was binding and had to be performed, whether that was fair or not. Changed circumstances? Too bad! How else could risk be quantified and reliably distributed? Perhaps that was why Hale advised Samuel Pepys to choose arbitration and avoid litigation if he could.[9]

There is no similar excuse for a modern sociological historian to write of the Common Law:[10] 'It was thought of in much the same way as religion, as an almost mystical intellectual system which was a central part of the ideology of the political nation.' Leaving aside the problem that there were at that time so many cults contending over what that 'mystical intellectual system' was, from which confusion the common law never suffered, the primary sources are all against such a contention, none more so than the Essex working man Sharpe quotes:[11] 'By God I do not care a turd neither for the King or his laws'.

It was not so much that the lawyers took over work formerly done by others as that the practice of arbitration came increasingly within the legal system. Craig Muldrew, writing of the period 1560 to 1640, detected signs of this change from the 16th century:[12] 'as the market grew more complex and disputes became more difficult to resolve, increasingly the authority of the law had to be invoked'. He collected data from many courts and, extrapolating from estimates, concluded there were every year in the 1580s '400,000 suits being initiated in urban courts' and 'well over 500,000 private suits in the thousands of small rural courts'. Add to them litigation in the higher courts and that would mean a million private matters being brought to litigation every year. Muldrew then adds: 'This represents over one suit initiated for every household in the country'. Of course it does nothing of the sort unless 'represents' is given an unusual meaning. Only

8. Matthew Hale *The History of the Common Law* 30.
9. Chapter 15 above.
10. James Sharpe 'The People and the Law' 244.
11. ERO D/B3/3/149; PRO ASSI 35/45/1/54.
12. Muldrew 915.

a tiny minority of households in any year were ever involved in litigation, then as now. But a little shift is obvious by the end of the 17th century and the passing of the Arbitration Act 1698.

What happened can be detected from examination of the primary sources, which show how the practice changed. Parties had relied on bonds to ensure each other's performance of the submission and award. The invariable practice was to make sure that the amount promised in the bond was more than the amount of the claim. It was a penalty rather than an attempt to quantify what a party might lose if the other did not comply with the condition, which was to submit to the arranged arbitration and perform the award. Of course, plaintiffs who had recovered the penalty could forgo the excess, as in *Vynior's Case*. But they could hardly be trusted to do so; and the courts were uncomfortable in enforcing payment of the full amount on failure of the condition. And so, more and more as the century drew to its close, lawyers found ways of persuading judges not to enforce the bond in full. Being no longer able to rely on a bond, lawyers advised their clients to take advantage of an offer which the courts were showing a greater willingness to make. At the parties' request, the court would accept a claim and refer it automatically to arbitration, arranged by the court with arbitrators appointed by the court, with the parties' consent. That process came to be called a rule of court. It became routine and was firmly established by the Arbitration Act 1698.[13]

From then on, well-advised parties took advantage of the rule of court. It was quite cheap and the courts' control made it effective. The lawyers had made ordinary arbitration their own and never looked back. Yet research already begun into the primary sources may well produce evidence that privately arranged processes of settling disputes by mediation and arbitration continued in no less volume in later years. Not until the 18th century do the most careful historians detect what they call 'an osmotic process of legalization'.[14] Even then they were not able to rely on a comparison of court-sponsored arbitration with the great mass of private arbitration records, whose size and nature are only now being discovered.

4. THE PROFESSIONAL ARBITRATOR

Moreover, the merchants in that new world needed new skills. It was no longer enough to know more than others about grain, or timber, or sheep, or shipping. The new financial knowhow that capitalism needed was not easily acquired. The old world of dispute resolution had to change, too. Whereas it had been enough to find arbitrators who were respected in the community and had the experience to resolve problems

---

13. Critchlow 297; McGaw 158.
14. Horwitz and Oldham 154–155.

in the community's best interest, now there was a demand for expertise, particularly in accounts. By the beginning of the 18th century, there were those who offered their expert services as accountants. Francis Boorman has found newspaper sources showing that some of them advertised their special skills in resolving disputes. Some still felt so uncomfortable at the transition from respected amateur to hired professional that they also advertised that they had given their fees to charity.[15] The example of Robert Hooke in Chapter 15 showed that, when necessity demanded, the Government as early as 1666 could quickly and efficiently make use of professional arbitration.

5.   THE END?

The end crowns all;
And that old common arbitrator, Time,
Will one day end it.
        William Shakespeare *Troilus and Cressida* Act IV scene 1 lines 25–27

John Baker's words more than forty years ago are still as apposite as they were then prophetic:[16]

It is a pleasure reserved for the present generation to set out on explorations of the records, assisted by plans constructed by painful scholarship, but never knowing whether the plan will point them in the right direction. The prospect, though challenging, is not entirely hopeful. There are far more questions than answers, and many more questions than we have yet learned to ask. There are few volunteers coming forward who can add some feeling for the common law to their expertise in history. The sources remain in an appalling state of intellectual, if not physical, neglect.... For anyone who will contribute to this work, there is a lifetime of rewarding study ahead.

Whenever the temptation to theorise about arbitration cannot be resisted, it is essential to keep in mind that litigation is not now and never has been the norm. Until comparatively recently in human history, there were no courts in which litigation was possible. They are creatures of a state, a government of a territory, which must protect it from outside attack and internal strife. But, long after organisation into states became almost universal, most parties resolved their differences by argument, what we call negotiation. Of course there were always those who preferred violence but communities have usually been able to limit and handle that.

When negotiation failed, the parties might seek the help of others. What did they expect them to do? In England, from the earliest times to the end of the 17th century, at least, each side would appoint one or two, who

15. FC Boorman 'Advertising Arbitration' 118–121.
16. JH Baker 'Introduction' in JH Baker ed *Legal Records* 2; Baker *Dark Age* 23.

would be expected to present their arguments for them, but with greater objectivity than they could themselves, and therefore with a greater chance of finding a compromise. If either party rejected their suggestion, they would expect in most cases to be asked to make a decision, an award which the parties would have to accept. That was the norm.

Of course, everybody knew the difference between mediation and arbitration. Those very words were in constant use in the sources, sometimes expressly to limit the third parties' roles to one process or the other. But, in the whole process of resolving the dispute, there was no advantage seen in keeping mediation and arbitration distinct. There are many records of the final solution being mediated after the formal award had been declared. It happens today.

Throughout recorded history, it had been common in some circumstances to appoint only one arbitrator. That required someone in whom both parties had equal confidence. At some stage in the 18th century, in England at least, it became more usual to have an odd number. The arbitrators were no longer expected to be the parties' advocates. By then the whole process was being transformed into what we know today. More of the elements and attributes of litigation were adopted. When we discuss any aspect of the theory of dispute resolution, it is essential not to assume that what is familiar now is integral.

The anonymous author of *Arbitrium Redivivum* concluded his preface 'To the Reader':

> A general Good should be generally known and enjoyed. To this End therefore this Treatise is compiled, that the People in general may have Benefit thereby which is the chief end of the Publisher, who is a hearty Well-wisher to Peace and the Public Interest. *Vale*.

What better way to end this volume, too, the last of mine devoted to answering those moral imperatives, peace and the common good. And it will be well to remember the epigraph with which my first effort began:[17]

> It is hard to tell at the outset whether your contribution, when it is finished, is going to be worthy of your hypothesis. There are many things, written in prose as well as verse, which aroused great expectations as long as they stayed in the minds of their authors. But when they were completed and shown to others, they got a reputation far inferior to what had been expected. And yet – just the undertaking itself is so worthwhile, the search for what others have neglected....
> Isocrates *To Nicocles* 7–8

17. Roebuck *Ancient Greek* 3 and 194–199. Isocrates was a friend of Socrates. He died in 338BC at the age of 98.

APPENDIX 1

Arbitrium Redivivum 1694

Arbitrium Redivivum: or the Law of Arbitration; collected from the Law-Books both Ancient and Modern, and deduced to these Times: Wherein the whole Learning of Awards or Arbitrements is methodically treated with Several Forms of Submissions by way of Covenants and Bond; As also several Forms of Arbitrements or Awards

By the Author of *Regula Placitandi*

TO THE READER

Arbitrement is much esteemed and greatly favoured in our Common Law; the end thereof being privately to compose Differences between Parties by the Judgment of honest Men; and to prevent the great Trouble and frequent Expense of Law-Suits: This therefore being rightly understood and practised, may undoubtedly save our Purses and procure much Peace and Tranquility amongst us; but on the other hand through Ignorance and Defect of good Arbitrators we may rune our selves into far greater dangers, than we thereby thought to avoid, and so make that our Ruine which is intended for our Happiness. For though it be said, That the Power of Arbitrators is such, that they may judge according to their Will and Pleasure, and therefore greater than that of any publick Judge; yet they must keep themselves within their Jurisdiction, and their Awards must be measured by the Rules of the Law. 'Tis true they are not so tied up to Formalities as our Lawyers; notwithstanding there are many things must be observed to make their Arbitrements good and effectual. All which are methodically laid down in this small Treatise; and though much may be said concerning Arbitrements in the Law-Books, yet it is mostly mixt with other Matters, or else lies so privately under the Shadow of some other Title, that it hath not been so much as heard of by those who are most concerned to make use of it; and therefore answers not the End for which it was intended. A general Good should be generally known and enjoyed. To this End therefore this Treatise is compiled, that the People in general may have Benefit thereby which is the chief end of the Publisher, who is a hearty Well-wisher to Peace and the Publick Interest. *Vale.*

THE LAW OF ARBITREMENT

Arbitrement what   Arbitrement in Latin *arbitrium*, is an Award, Determination or Judgment made, or given between persons in Controversie, by the Arbitrators or Umpire, being such person or persons as are thereunto elected, by the Parties controverting, for the ending and pacifying the said Controversie according to the Submission or Compromise of the said Parties, and agreeable to Reason and good Conscience. It is said to be called an Arbitrement, either because the Judges elected therein, may determine the Controversie not according the Law, but according to their Opinion and Judgment as honest Men: Or else because the Parties to the Controversie, have submitted themselves to the Judgment of the Arbitrators, not by Compulsion or Coercion of the Law, but of their own accord. It is also called an Award, of the French Word *Agarder*, which signifies to *decide* or *judge*, and sometimes in the Saxon or Old English, it was called a *Love-Day*, because of the Quiet and Tranquility that should follow the ending of the Controversie.

Incidents to Arbitrement   There are five things incident to every Award or Arbitrement.

1. Matter of Controversie.
2. Submission to the Arbitrators.
3. The Parties to the Submission.
4. The Arbitrators or Umpire.
5. The Manner of the Award or yielding up their Judgment.

CHAP. I

First therefore we must see what Matters in Controversie may be submitted to Arbitrement, and what not.

1. Things and Actions merely personal and incertain are arbitrable, as Trespass &c though the Submission be not by Deed. Arbitrement ought to be of a Duty incertain.
2. But things certain are not arbitrable (but when the Submission is by Specialty) if they be not joined with others incertain, as Debt with Trespass. Controversie of Debt alone cannot be put into Arbitrement; but Contract of Debt with another thing may well be put in Arbitrement. Debt upon Contract without Specialty by the Resolution of some Books may be put in Arbitrement.
3. Chattels real or mixt, as Charters of Lands, are not arbitrable by themselves, if the Submission be not by Specialty. In Real Actions Arbitrement is no plea. In Mixt Actions, Arbitrement is no Plea, if the Submission be not by Deed. In Personal Actions on personal Wrongs,

Arbitrement is a Plea, although the Submission be not by Deed. In a Controversie concerning the Property in Real Chattels an Arbitrement transfers the Property of them according to the Award. In Chattels personal Arbitrement transfers the Property. In personal Duty grounded upon a Specialty, Plea of Arbitrement is not available. And the Lord Cook in his Reports *Li* 4 f43b 44a says That an Arbitrement is no Plea when an Action is founded upon a Deed, when it is in the Realty, except in such Cases where Damages alone are to be recovered.

a. Note, Action Real claimeth Title of Freehold in Land. Personal claimeth Debt, Goods or Damages. Mixt claimeth not only a real thing, but Damages for the Wrong. Chattels Real are such as belong not immediately to the person of a Man, but to some other thing by way of dependency, as a Box with Charters of Land, Apples on a Tree, or a Tree it self growing on the ground, or issuing out of some moveable things, as a Lease or Rent. Chattels personal belong immediately to the person of a Man, as a Bow, Horse &c.

4. Also an Annuity is not arbitrable if the Submission be not by Specialty, that is, by Deed or Bond, wherein the Parties covenant or are bound to stand to the Award.

5. Nor a Freehold. Yet some hold that a Freehold may be awarded by Deed where the Submission is by Specialty. But 21 E 3 26 saith, an Arbitrement that the one Party shall have the Land out of the possession of the other, doth not give a Freehold.

6. Nor Debt upon Arrerages of Account before Auditors, because such Debt is due by Record. In a Controversie grounded upon a Matter of Record, Arbitrement shall not be regarded.

7. And it seems that such things as were not *in Rerum Natura* at the time of the Submission, (though they happen to be before the Award made) are not arbitrable as if the Submission be of Ewes with Lamb, which after the Submission and before the Award made, have Lambs: It seemeth the Arbitrators have no power to make any Award touching the Lambs.

8. Matters concerning Criminal Offences, as Treasons, Felonies &c touching the Crime, seem not to be arbitrable, for it is for the Benefit of a Kingdom and Commonwealth that such Offenders be made known and punished.

9. Also Causes Matrimonial seem not arbitrable, lest Men should separate those whom God hath joyned together.

To conclude, generally, No Chattels real or mixt, no Debts by Deed or Record, no Annuities, nor Freeholds are of themselves arbitrable. Yet in such cases though the things themselves be not arbitrable, yet if a Man will bind himself to stand to an Award, such Bond is good: And for the Non-performance of the Award the Bond will be forfeited.

CHAP. II

Concerning the Submission, and the Circumstances to be regarded therein

The Submission or Compromise is the Faculty or power of pronouncing Sentence (between Persons at Controversie) given to Arbitrators by the Parties mutual private Consent without publick Authority. And every Submission is either General, or Special. General, as of all Quarrels, Actions, Executions, Demands &c. Special, as when 'tis only of certain Matters, Facts and Things, as of a Trespass, or all Actions of Trespass, or of Debt or Detinue &c.

Submissions are in two manners, either by Writing or by Word. [Note, upon Submission by Word only there is no remedy to enforce the Party to perform the Award; but an Action on the Case for reciprocal promises will lie; and if Mony be awarded an Action of Debt will lie.] Those that are by Writing are either by Obligation or by Covenant. Which Obligation is either of Record, as a Recognizance, or by Deed between the Parties. And this Submission by Writing or by Word is either absolute or conditional, as *so that*, or *provided that*, the Award be delivered by a certain day or time, sealed or unsealed, indented, and the like; and in such Cases, the Time, Manner and Matter must be exactly observed, or the Arbitrement will be void. But it is necessary that every Compromise or Submission be made by Writing [and convenient time and place therein limited for the yielding up of their Award to the Parties &c] (with the Parties Covenants or Bonds to perform the Award that shall thereupon be made) That thereby the Arbitrators may know their powers and the Parties how far they are subject to their Sentence. And also lest their Labour and Judgment therein should be frustrate for want of means to compel the same to be executed.

1. For it seems, That if the Submission be without Deed, either of the Parties may countermand, and discharge the Arbitrators without Deed, and shall lose nothing upon notice to the Arbitrators of such discharge; except there be divers persons concerned.
2. And if divers of one part and divers of the other part submit themselves to Arbitrement without Deed, one of them of the one part cannot discharge the Arbitrators without the other his Companions of the same party; for they were chosen by joynt Authority.
3. And if the Submission be by Deed, the Discharge must likewise be by Deed. And 'tis said, that in such case, one of the Parties alone cannot countermand the Arbitrators.
4. But if the Submission be by Bond (as most commonly it is, though by some not thought so convenient, for that thereby the Parties may hazard the Penalty of the Bond for a Trifle or small matter) though afterwards countermanded, yet the Bond seemeth to be forfeited. And so says *Brook tit Arbit* 35.

5. And so it is adjudged 8 *Co fol* 82. That though a Man be bound to stand to an Arbitrement, yet he may countermand the Arbitrators; but in this Case it was further resolved that by the Countermand and Revocation of the power the Bond is forfeited, because he was bound to stand to the Award which he does not do when he discharges the Arbitrator.

6. In an Action upon the Case on promise to perform an Award on Submission to *A* and *B* when their occasion will permit, *Keeling* conceived that only a convenient time was to be given, at least after Request, which *Twisden* and *Moreton* agreed, but *Windham* was contrary, and that they have time during their Lives, as if it had been to be made at their Wills and Pleasure. But if it be to be made generally without any time limited the Law implieth it must be done in convenient time. And it hath been agreed by the Court, That though the Submission be when their Conveniences permit, yet after Request or convenient notice the Party may revoke on neglect by the Arbitrators.

And it was said, that where a Woman sole submits by Bond to stand to Award, and before the Award marries, this is a Revocation of the Submission and Forfeiture of the Bond; but the Parties agreeing to enter into new Bond, it was adjourned, 2 *Keb* 865, 877. 3 *Leon* p9.

But upon a Countermand there must be Notice given to the Arbitrators, for in pleading the Defendant may take Issue upon it, That he did not revoke or countermand it. And if there were no Notice it shall be found for the Defendant; but the Plaintiff need not aver an express Notice so he shew an implied one.

CHAP. III

Concerning the Parties to the Submission or Compromise; Persons chiefly regarded in Submission, are the striving Persons and the Arbitrators

The Persons striving be they between whom the Controversie dependeth, and which submit or compromit the same. And they must be two at the least, the Plaintiff and the Defendant, of which sometime there be two or more of a side or Party.

What Persons may submit to Arbitrement, and what not All Persons, both Male and Female may submit to Arbitrement, except they be prohibited by Nature or by Law, as Infants, Madmen, Lunaticks and Ideots, also such as are Dumb, Deaf or Blind by Nature, but if it be by Chance, and they can write and read, 'tis said they may well by writing compromit or submit to Arbitrement. And 'tis said that Infants are hindred to submit, but it seemeth to be meant by Deed, because their Covenants and Bonds are void; but otherwise 'tis said if an Infant submit himself to an Award, he shall be bound to perform it as well as a Man of full age, 13 H 4 12a, 10 H 6 14a. But this hath been adjudged since to the contrary, betwixt *Rudson* and *Yates*, 15 *Car BR*. That the Submission of an Infant to an Arbitrement was absolutely void. As Women Covert without their Husbands, and Persons civilly dead; as Monks, Fryers, Canons, professed Nuns &c. So such as are compelled thereto by threats and imprisonment, for in submission, the consent ought to be free. Also such as are attainted of Felony or Treason, and persons Outlawed or waved in personal Actions, for they have no Goods. So they that have joynt power with others, cannot singly submit in relation to such power, without their fellows. As, a Dean without a Chapter, a Mayor without his Commonalty, the Master of a College or Hospital without his Fellows; and so of other Societies and Guilds. And generally it seemeth, that in Award such persons may only of themselves submit, as may of themselves make good Grants.

If one of the Parties submit himself to an Arbitrement on the one part, and a Deputy on the other part in the name of the other party, the Arbitrement thereupon made betwixt them seems to be good.

The Husband may submit himself to an Award for himself and his Wife, for the Chattels of which he had disposition in Right, and by reason of his Wife, and it shall bind his Wife, and upon such a submission, mony awarded to be paid to him and his Wife is good.

If divers on the one part have done a Wrong or Trespass to another, and he to whom the wrong is done and one of the others submit themselves to an Award, upon the Award made, the others not being Parties to the submission, shall have advantage in extinguishment of the Trespass. If divers of the one part submit themselves to the Award of certain persons, and divers of the other part, the Arbitrators have power to make an Award for matters between them joyntly, and so for matters between them severally. If divers of the one part and of the other part submit themselves to the Award of one, who makes an Award betwixt some of the one party and some of the other party, and not betwixt them all, and say not any thing in his Award concerning the others, yet such an Award is good. An Award between one of the one side and one of other is sufficient, on a submission by several. Note, if the submission be, that they will stand to the Award of the Arbitrators for the whole matters submitted or any parcel thereof.

CHAP. IV

Concerning the Arbitrators and Umpire, and their Power, with several Presidents of Submission

Arbiter signifies an Arbitrator or an Umpire. They are properly called Arbitrators who (having no power from the Law) are made choice of for Judges, by the consent of the Parties in Controversie to whom it is submitted, that their Sentence shall stand. *Johannes Paulus Lancellotus* in his Institutes of the Canon Law.

And by our Law Books an Arbitrator is described to be a private or extraordinary Judge, chosen by the Parties, to appease the debates between them, and to arbitrate and adjudge according to their good intent.

Who because the Controversie is committed to his pleasure and Arbitrement is term'd an Arbitrator; and for that it is done by the mutual promise or compromise of the Parties, he is called *Compromissarius Judex*.

His power is larger than the power of any ordinary or other extraordinary Judge; for an Arbitrator hath power to judge according to the compromise or submission, after his own mind, as well of the Fact as of the Law, but the other Judges are tyed to a prescript form, limited to them by the Law or Magistrate. And since his power is so great and incontrovertible, Men ought to be cautious how they make choice of Arbitrators; therefore it is thought fit that such persons be Elected as are sufficient and indifferent.

That they have sufficient skill of the matter submitted to them and have neither legal nor natural impediments.

That they be not Infants, who by reason of their few years may want discretion and knowledge.

That they be neither Mad, nor Ideots, for such are void of Understanding.

That they be neither Deaf, Dumb or Blind, for thereby their principal Senses necessary for the apprehension of the Matter may be impaired.

As for indifferency, That they may be void of Malice and Favour to either of the parties, that they be not notorious by Outlawry, Excommunicated, Irreligious, nor Covetous, for though he hath absolute power, yet his Judgment or Sentence ought to be sincere and incorrupt, according to right and equity, without malice, flattery and every other vicious affection or perturbation, which may in any sort lead him awry from the right Path of Justice and Equity. *West Symb. Part* 2 *Sect.* 27. These are thought to be fit Qualities, though the Law prescribes no rules herein.

Having shewn what persons are most fit to be Elected Arbitrators, we will proceed, respecting in the Arbitrator these three things.

1. His Ordinance, from whom it is.
2. His Authority, what it is.
3. His Duty, wherein it consists.

Touching his Ordinance, he is Ordained, by these two things, *viz.* by the Election of the Parties, and by his own undertaking of the charge. Touching his Authority, what it is; it is derived from the submission, and extendeth no farther, and thereby he is Judge between the Parties, and therefore he cannot transfer his Authority over to any other. Touching his duty, it consisteth in three things. First, to hear the grief of the Party. Secondly, to judge according to Equity. Thirdly, to give notice of his Award.

Of the two first Branches enough hath been said before, only it remaineth to set down some Forms and Precedents of Election and Submission in Writing, which are the best and most in use.

[Here follow precedents for the submission, and for the bond (in Latin and English), with practice notes]

CHAP. V

The Duty of the Parties after submission, and concerning publishing the Award, Notice and Delivery.

The Election and Submission being thus made. In the next place it is the Duty of the Parties to come before the Arbitrators, and to shew their Grievances, and the Arbitrators ought to hear them, and to judge accordingly, or otherwise they are no good Judges. The Arbitrators having heard their Grievances and Matters, and agreed upon their Award, the third part of the Duty of an Arbitrator is the publishing or notifying of his Award. And it is to be considered, That the publishing or notifying of an Award is either provided for and ordained by the submission it self, Or else it is left and permitted to the discretion of the Arbitrator. If it be provided for by the submission, as sometimes it is and may be, that the same Award made be notified by the Arbitrators to the parties or some of them, &c. and that either by a certain day or time, or else without limitation of any time. Then in such case its said Arbitrement is no Arbitrement before it be pronounced. Also, where by the submission it is appointed or conditionally provided, that the Award shall be delivered to the Parties, &c. it is then no Arbitrement in Law before it be delivered in Deed. But, if the submission be, That the Award shall be delivered to the Parties (&c.) before such a day, requiring the same, and no certain day limited when it ought to be delivered, then the Parties are obliged to take notice of the Award at their peril.

If divers of the one party, and divers of the other part submit themselves to Arbitrement of another, provided that he shall deliver to the Parties or one of them, the Arbitrator is not obliged to deliver it to two of one Party. Or to one of each Party, but 'tis sufficient to deliver it to any of the said Parties. If the submission be, That the Arbitrement shall be delivered before such a day, it may as well be delivered by Word as by Deed; if the submission be not, that it shall be delivered by Deed or Writing. If the submission be that the Arbitrement be delivered, it may be made in one County and delivered in another County. If the submission be by Deed, and the time past in which the Arbitrement ought to be made, the parties cannot prorogue the time over to make the Award, without a new submission to that purpose; and whatsoever the Arbitrators do award after the time appointed, is void. But if the submission be without Deed, the Parties may prorogue the time which was given to make the Award. If the Arbitrators make their Award between the Parties one day, and give their judgment therein, they cannot make another Award between the Parties another day, albeit the time given by the submission is not expired.

An Arbitrement cannot be made part at one time and part at another, albeit it be within the time of submission. Note, this is meant where it is declared or pronounced to the Parties by pieces or parcels. But the Arbitrators may discourse betwixt themselves, and agree upon one thing one day, and of another thing another day, and in the end make one intire Award of the whole, and it is good. If the Arbitrators Award one thing on one part, and before they can agree of their Award for the remainder, the time given by the submission expire, their whole Award is void.

Lastly, where by the submission there is no order taken for the delivery or publication of the Award, then in honesty and conscience the Arbitrator is obliged to make notice to the Parties of it. But in rigour of Law the Arbitrement it self is intended to be a thing known. And therefore the Parties to the Arbitrement are bound to take notice of it at their Peril, especially if they be bound to stand to the Award &c. Although the Parties are not to have notice given them of the Arbitrement, yet if the Arbitrators award that one of the Parties shall do an act which depends on another first to be done of the other Party, he shall have notice of it. But now all submissions are usually by Bond, conditionally, so as the Award be made in Writing, and ready to be delivered to the Parties or such of them as shall require the same, &c. and in this case it is clearly resolved and agreed, That the Parties having so bound themselves are obliged to take notice of the Award at their peril.

CHAP. VI

What things are chiefly to be regarded in Arbitrements or Awards; and first that it must be according to the submission

Having now received the Award from the Arbitrators, Next we come to examine the Arbitrements themselves, and to see what things are chiefly to be regarded in them. In the form of every Arbitrement six things are specially to be regarded,

1. That it be made according to the very submission touching the things submitted, or necessarily depending thereupon, and every other circumstance, as aforesaid.
2. That it ought to be certain.
3. That it ought to be equal, and appoint either Party to give or do unto the other something beneficial in the appearance at the least.

4. That the performance thereof be possible and lawful, and within the power of the Parties.
5. That there be a means how either Party may by Law attain unto that which is thereby awarded unto him.
6. That it be a final end of the Controversies submitted: And if it fail in any of these points, then it is said the whole Arbitrement shall be void.

First, that it be made according to the submission. An Arbitrement which is made of a matter not contained in the submission is void, as followeth, It may be void as to the submission in three respects,

1. Of the Persons submitting &c.
2. Of the things or matter submitted.
3. Of the circumstances of the submission.

First, as to the Persons.

If the Arbitrators award that one of the Parties shall do an act to a Stranger, as make a feoffment or the like, such Arbitrement is said to be void, but see after Chapter 13 where 'tis said otherwise. So if it Award a thing to be done by a Stranger, it is also void as to the Stranger, *Moor and Bedel's Case*. See the General Rules after.

If the Arbitrement be that the Parties shall stand to the Award of the Stranger, it is void, for power cannot be assigned, 5 Coke *Samon's Case*. But if a Stranger had made an Arbitrement before between the said Parties, an Award to stand to such an Arbitrement of the Stranger, its said is good. And this may be, because the former Arbitrement is a thing already done and certain. If the Arbitrement be, That the Parties shall perform the Award of another formerly made between the said Parties; whereas in truth there is no such Award, yet the Arbitrement is good (*prima facie*) at first sight, until it be known that there be no such Award. If an Arbitrement be that an act limited by the Award shall be done by the advice and counsel of another, such an Award hath been thought to be good, but by others ill, because not final, and incertain whether the Counsel will advise. But if the act be to be done by the advice of the Arbitrator himself, this is to make two Awards, and so void. See after *Chap* 13. Concerning Payment in the House of a Stranger: Concerning Payment at the House of a Stranger: Concerning Payment at or in the House of a Stranger.

2dly. As to the things.
If one be chosen to make an Award on one thing, and he makes it upon another, the Arbitrement is void: As if the submission be of all things in variance betwixt the Parties; and the Award is of things not in variance. *Pl. Com.* 396a. So if the submission be of the Right and Interest of Land, and the Award is concerning the Profits only of the Land, *Dyer* f242. So if the

submission be of the Manor of *D* and the Award is of the Manor of *S*. So if the submission be of all Causes till that time, and the Award is of a Release of all Causes to the time of the Award, especially if any new Causes be shewn. But if the Award be made of and concerning the Premises, and that such a day to come, the one party shall pay the other £10 and that the party shall make general Release; this Release shall be supposed only of the Causes submitted. But if the submission be of a Thing, the Award may be made of a thing incident or accessory, as if it be of Title and Possession of Land, the Award may be made also of the Evidence and Charters concerning the Land. *Mich 9 Jac Tiderby and Tiderby*.

Note also that it is said, That if the submission is of things personal, the Arbitrators may award, That one of the Parties shall do an act which is of a thing real in satisfaction of a personal Wrong. Also If the submission be of a thing real, the Arbitrator may award satisfaction to be made of a thing personal.

General Rules

Where an award is made for more than is submitted, it is good for that part which is submitted, and void for the residue. So where the Award is, That the Parties shall do such Acts, and a Stranger such Acts, the Award may be good as to the Parties, tho' void as to the Stranger. And in some Cases where the Award is of less things than were submitted it will be void, as where two or three things are put in Arbitrement joyntly, and an Award is made of part and not of the whole. But if the Submission be of all Actions real and personal, and an Award is made of all Actions personal only, this hath been adjudged to be good. And it hath also been adjudged that though there are many matters in Controversie, yet if one only be shewn to the Arbitrator, he may make an Award of this, for the Arbitrator is a Stranger to the particulars, and the Parties who are Privy, ought to shew the Causes of their Controversie to him or otherwise most Arbitrements might be avoided by the Parties concealment. 8 *Co*. f98.

Where the Submission is without Deed, an Award may be made of part of the things only, and good so it be with Deed, and the Submission either general or special, and not conditional. But where the Submission is either general or special by Deed conditional, with the Words *Provided that*, or *So as the said Award concerning the Premises be made in Writing &c. and delivered by such a time &c*. In such Case the Award must be made of all the Matters submitted. 8 *Co*. f98. *Dyer* 216, 242.

And note, That where a Man in pleading an Award made upon a general Submission conditional, says the same was made of and concerning the Premises, and shews only one Matter (among many) to be awarded, this shall be good and intended an Award of all Causes submitted, until the contrary be shewn, and he is not obliged to aver that is all. But it is otherwise in pleading an Award made upon a special Conditional Submission, for then the Award must be expressly alledged to be made of all things or otherwise it is naught, because in a special Submission conditional the causes are apparently set forth. So upon the general Submission Conditional, when other Causes are shewn than were pleaded, the Award will be void, because that it was conditional.

3ly. Circumstances.

An Award may be void in respect of the Circumstances of the Submission, as where the Submission is, That the Award be delivered in Writing under their Hands and Seals; and the party pleads a Delivery, but says not under their Hands and Seals, it shall be supposed to be no Arbitrement according to the Submission, and therefore no Cause of Action. For upon these Submissions conditional, as to writing, sealing and delivery, &c all the Circumstances must be observed, and awarded of, at or before the day appointed, otherwise all is void, *Dyer* 243, 4 *Co.* 103.

General Rules

Again observe, that where an Award is of one single Matter only, or of many, and all out of the Submission, such Award is totally void. So where the Award is of one single Matter only, or of many, and all within the Submission; yet if it be not of all Matters submitted, or not agreeing in Circumstances: Where the Submission is by Specialty conditional, in such Case also the Award will be totally void. But where an Award, is of one thing only, or of several things, part within the Submission and part out, there the Award is void only as to that which is out, and good for the Remainder. Yet though it may be void in part and good in part, it cannot be totally void only as to one of the Parties and good against the other, for if it be void against one it is void against both: an Arbitrement ought to be of both sides, and equally binding. 5 *Co.* 77. 8 *Co.* 98. 10 *Co.* 31. And the Law is held the same as to these things where the Parties are tyed by Promise only.

Now where an Award is totally void, there a Bond can never be forfeited for the Non-performance of it; for such an Award is as if no Award, and the Law requires not the Observation of that which is void. 10 *Co.* 31. *Keil.* 175. Again, where the Award is void in part only, there the Bond may be forfeited for not observing the Award, especially for that which is contained in the Submission, though not for that which is out; and therefore if the Breach be assigned in that part which is void the Action will not lie. But a Breach may be assigned for that which is within the Submission, and the Bond will be forfeited for the Non-performance of it. 7 *Jac. in B.R. Lawrence* versus *Carr* 10 *Co*. 131.

CHAP. VII

That an Award ought to be certain.

If the Arbitrators award that one of the Parties shall enter into a Bond to the other, and doth not award in what time, such Award is void for the Uncertainty, 5 *Co*. 77, 78. And where the Award is of things within the Submission, and is uncertain in any part that concerns a Party to the Submission, it is void in the whole. *Hill*. 15 *Car. In B.R.* Yet a small Variation is not material; as if the Award be that one of the Parties shall discharge the other of the Bond of the Penalty of £100 or thereabouts, this was held a sufficient Certainty, *Pach*. 15 *Car. in B.R.* Also an Award that is seemingly uncertain, and yet may be reduced to Certainty is good enough, as that the Defendant shall pay so much during the continuance of such a Lease, naming it &c. Here the payment of the Mony is referred to the Continuance of the Lease, which is certain, and therefore the Award good, *Pasch* 5 *Jac in B.R. Girling* versus *Gosnold*, *Hob*. 68. *Dyer* 242.

CHAP. VIII

That an Award must be equal, and appoint either Party something beneficial.

An Award ought to be equal, that is, mutually satisfactory, and appoint either Party to give or do unto the other something beneficial in the appearance at the least. An Arbitrement is no Plea in Trespass, if nothing be awarded to the Plaintiff for amends. In Trespass of Goods taken, it is not good Pleading an Award, that the Defendant should retain part of the Goods and the Plaintiff have the rest. So in Debt, to plead an Award that the Plaintiff should have one Moiety, and the Defendant the other, or should pay part and keep part, this is no Plea. *Fitz. Arb*. 19. And therefore such an Award is void, and without good reason. For In Trespass for taking away of Goods, the Defendant pleaded an Award, that because the Defendant had taken away the Plaintiff's Goods, he should therefore carry and redeliver them to the Plaintiff, which he had done, this was held naught; for redelivery of the Plaintiffs own Goods could be no satisfaction, much less the redelivery of part of them. But if upon the Delivery of Goods, he for whom they are to be delivered may have any benefit by such Delivery in satisfaction of the Wrong, then the Arbitrement is good. As if the Defendant had been awarded to have carried the Goods to such a place for the Plaintiffs benefit.

If two submit themselves to Arbitrement of all Trespasses &c. between them, and it is awarded that the one shall make amends to the other, and nothing is awarded for the other's Benefit, this Award is void being but on one side. So if it were that the one only shall go quit against the other. *Hob*. 68. For such Arbitrements are only on one side. But where there is an Acquittance or express Satisfaction on both sides, or on one side only with an implied discharge on the other, the Award may in such case be good. An Award that the one shall give to the other a Quart of Wine, or some such small Recompense in satisfaction of the Wrong, is good. So, for that the one has done more Trespass to the other than the other to him, he shall pay the other a Peny in satisfaction, and that he shall be quit against him. An Award for that the Wrongs done by the Parties each to other are equal, they shall therefore be quit each against the other is said to be good. Yet 'tis said to be otherwise, if the Submission was by Word of Mouth. *Quaere*.

Where divers of the one Party and the other submit themselves to Award, and the Arbitrement is, That one of one of the Parties shall pay to one other of the other Party so much, without saying any thing of the others, it is said to be a good Award, for that the others, it may be, have no Cause to have any thing.

If the Arbitrement be, that one of the Parties shall pay a greater Sum in value than the Wrong which he has done requires, as £10 where but 5s damage and the like; yet the Award is said to be good, for that it lies in the discretion of the Arbitrators, who are judges, especially of things uncertain, as Trespass, and the like; but of things certain, as Debt, &c. (as before) it may be otherwise.

Again as to an implied Discharge, If it be awarded, That the Defendant shall pay £10 for a Trespass, it is good. So that the Defendant shall pay a Peny to the Plaintiff in Satisfaction of all manner of Actions, if the Defendant shew that he hath paid it, it is a good Bar. Because these imply a Discharge to the Defendant. But if the Award be that he that is bound in a Bond shall pay the Debt, this does not imply a Discharge; for payment in such Case without Acquittance is no Discharge to him. *Hob*. 68. and therefore the Award void, unless there be provision for a Discharge, See 8 *Co*. 98. An Award that in satisfaction of the Wrong the Parties shall intermarry, is no good Award, for it is no satisfaction. That one of the Parties is in arrear in Accompt, shall account with the other, is held no Satisfaction, *Fitz. Abr*. 27.

CHAP. IX

That the Performance of an Award must be possible, lawful, and within the Parties Power, without the Aid of others.

If an Award be to do a thing impossible, as to turn the River of *Thames* to run over the Cellar of *Westminster* within a day, or to pay a Sum of Mony at a day already past, or to release all Right in such a Manor, where in truth there is no such, and the like; such an Award is void, and the Bond not forfeited.

But if the Thing seem feasable and possible though very hard and difficult, yet the Award may be good, and the Party ought to perform it. As, That I shall at such a time go to such a place, and bring from thence, such a thing as is not there; in this case I ought to buy the thing and convey it to the place, and bring it from thence &c. If the Award be that I should pay £1000 within an hour &c. I am bound to do it though perhaps I have not £10 and so of the like.

Again, an Award ought to be lawful, therefore that which is unlawful is void. Many things in general acceptation are against Law because they do not agree with Law, but in this place it is meant of things which are expressly forbidden by the Law, as if it be awarded that the Defendant shall kill, rob, steal, forge a Deed, or the like. *Co.* on *Lit.* 206b.

Again the performance ought to be within the Parties power, without the Aid of others. If the Award be that I shall make a Stranger pay £20 to the Plaintiff, it is void, for I cannot force him to do it. So if it be that I shall pay £40 thus, 10 in hand, and three several persons to be bound every one for £10 apiece; this hath been held void. For this lies at the Will of Stranger, whether he will be bound or not. But where I may do the things awarded my self, or force it to be done, the Award is good. If the Award be that one of the Parties shall pay a Sum to the other, and that the other in consideration shall discharge him of a Bond, in which they two were bound to another person: In this Case it was held that the thing was feasible by the Party himself; for if the day of payment was not come, the payment of the Mony at the day would be a good Discharge of the Bond, and so a good Acquittal of the other Party; and if the day of payment was past, it was held he might pay the Mony, and force the Obligee in Chancery to deliver up the Bond though forfeited, or else the Party might suffer an Action to be brought against him upon the Bond, and then discharge and pay it. It was also held that where any are seized, &c. to my use, and that I have an Interest and Power to compel them to do the thing awarded upon my part, that in such Case the Award is good, and I ought to compel them. And this is a general Rule, That where I may do the thing awarded my self without the Aid of another, or it lies in my power to enforce the doing thereof by others; in such Case the Award is good, and I am obliged to perform it.

CHAP. X

That there be a means by Law to attain unto the thing awarded.

This is chiefly meant where the Submission is without Specialty, As, If in Trespass an Award be pleaded, that one Party should pay a Sum of Mony, and release to the other all Actions of Trespass &c, and that after the other should release to him, this is not good, because if the one pays the Mony and releases, he cannot after force the other to release to him. Yet it may be a good Plea if the Party pleading shews that he has performed his part, as appears after.

If the Defendant in an Action of Trespass pleads an Award, that he should be bound to the other by a day not yet come, this will be no Bar, for if he should, the other would be without Remedy to compel him to make the Bond. But if the submission were by Bond, though such a Plea as above will be no Bar to the Action, because there is no means to enforce the making of a Bond, Release, or other Collateral Matter, yet if the party do not make it, he will thereby forfeit the Penalty of his Bond.

Where the submission is without Bond, if the Award be for payment of Mony at a day to come, it is good, because an Action of Debt will lye for the Mony upon such Award, if it be not paid, the Party, if he please, may resort to his force Action.

Also if an Award be to do a Collateral thing, as make a Release &c for which there is no remedy, yet if it appear to be executed, the Award will be held a good Plea. And if the Collateral thing appear not to be executed, yet if the submission be by Bond, the Bond will be forfeited for non-performance of the thing awarded.

As to pleading an Award in Bar of an Action, in these Cases, observe

1. That where an Award is for payment of Mony, for which there is Remedy, and the day of payment not past, in such case an Award pleaded will be a good Bar to an Action.
2. Where the day of payment is past, it will be no Bar to plead an Award, without pleading of payment by the Party.
3. Where the day of payment is past, and though it appear that the Arbitrement is not executed, yet if there be no default in the Defendant, it may be a good Bar to plead an Award.
4. Where an Award is for doing a thing for which the Party hath no remedy (though the day be not come in which the thing ought to be done) in such case it will be no Bar of an Action to plead an Award.

CHAP. XI

That an Award must be final.

That it be a final end of the Controversies submitted. This is to be understood with respect to what is said before, That though an Award may be good of part of the things only submitted, yet it must be final as to that part, or else it will be void. As if an Award be, That the Parties shall be non-suit one against the other, in Actions depending betwixt them; this Award is void being not final, for after non-suits the Parties may begin again, and thus there is no end of the Controversie. And so it is where the Award is of one side only, because it does not determine the Controversie between the Parties. And so where it is incertain, for such an Award cannot decide the Controversie, 5 *Co.* 78. And 'tis a general Rule, That the Law doth reject all Arbitrements, which leave the matter in Controversie in suspence or unconcluded, for it is the proper Office of an Arbitrement to put an end to Controversie. *In Com. Banco, Emery* cont. *Emery.*

Note, The Arbitrators may ordain in their Award, an Act to be done for the better performance of their Award as to enter into Bond &c.

CHAP. XII

Concerning an Umpire

If the Parties submit themselves to the Award of certain Persons, and if they cannot agree, then to the Ordinance of another, as Umpire: If the Arbitrators make their Award of Parcels, The Umpire shall not make his Award of the other remaining part. But if the submission be such, That the Umpire shall make his Award of the whole or of part, then its said he may make Award of such part with which the Arbitrators have not medled.

In Debt upon a Bond Conditional to perform an Award, to be made by two, by such a day, and if they cannot agree, then to the Umpirage of *A.B.* so he awarded by the same time; and there said, that where the Arbitrators and Umpire have the same time, if either make an Award its sufficient; but then all agreed, That an absolute refusal of the Arbitrators should be alledged, as to say, That they did not, nor could not make the Award, 2 *Keb.* 562, 619. *Syderf.* 428. *Mod. Rep.* 15.

If the Arbitrators did wholly desert it, the umpire may Award; for if the Arbitrators desert only one while, they may take it up within the time, *Syderf.* 455. But where the Arbitrators are left to chuse the Umpire in the same time, and do so, they thereupon relinquish their power, especially where the Submission to an Umpire, is upon their disagreement, otherwise an Award by the Umpire within their time is void, 1 *Keble* 6. 848. 2 *Keble* 714. *Mod. Rep.* 274.

In debt upon a Bond to perform an Award of Arbitrators, so as it be made by the second of *March*, and if it not agreed then, to the umpirage of whom *A.* and *B.* elect, so as he Award by the fifth of *March*. It was objected, That the Umpire was elected but the third of *March*, but the Court said, if he were elected on the fourth, it was sufficient, 3 *Keble* 387.

Note, That the usual course is now by Bond, with a time over for the Umpire, in case the Arbitrators make no Award.

CHAP. XIII

Some things of Note concerning Arbitrement, Registred by Mr. Stiles *in his* Practical Register, *as followeth.*

An Award that is made, That one of the Parties who submitted themselves to the Award, shall pay mony in the House of a Stranger, is not good, for this is to Award him to do a thing which will make him a Trespasser, and so lyable to an Action, which is unreasonable, *Mich*. 22 *Car. B.R*. But if the Award be to pay the Mony in the House of one of the Parties that submitted to the Award, such an Award is good, for it implies a Licence from the Party for him to pay it there, *Pract. Regist*. 27.

Award to pay Mony in or at the House of *J.S*. The Plaintiff saith it was not paid at the House which the Court held to be well enough, and if it were paid in the House, it may be given in Evidence on issue, That it was paid at the House, 1 *Keble* 753. 16 *Car*. 2 *B.R*. An Award to pay Mony at the House of a Stranger may be good, for he may come to the House in many cases and be no Trespasser; but if he cannot come to the Strangers House, without being a Trespasser to him, there such an Award is not thought good, *Pract. Reg*. 27. And by *Keble 1.13 Car*. 2 Where payment is to be in the House of a Stranger, he shall not be presumed to be able to perform it, but otherwise where the Payment is to be at the House of a Stranger.

A Conditional Award is not good because it is not final to determine the Matters in difference submitted to the Arbitration, *Mich*. 22 *Car. B.R*.

If all the Matters submitted to the Arbitrators be not awarded upon, the Award is not good, *Pasch* 23 *Car. B.R. Pract. Reg*.27. That is, when the Submission is by Deed Conditional, see before *Chap*. 6.

An uncertain and doubtful Award is not good, because it makes not an end of all the Matters submitted unto by both Parties, but leaves them at large, to sue and trouble each other, as they were before the Award made, *Trin*. 23 *Car. B.R*.

An Award may be void in some part, and yet good in another, *viz*. if the Award do make an end of all the Differences submitted unto the Arbitrators by the Parties, *Trin*. 23 *Car. B.R. Mich* 24 *Car. B.R*.

An Award ought to be final and certain, else it is not good, *Mich*. 23 *Car. B.R. Pract. Reg*. 28.

If each Party submitting to the Award hath power by the Award to compel the other Party either by Law or Equity to perform the Award, the Award is good enough although the Party be thereby put to his Action, *Mich*. 24 *Car. B.R. Pract. Reg*. 28.

An Award, that a thing shall be done to a Stranger is a good Award, if it appear that the Parties who submitted to the Award have benefit by the doing it, *Pract. Reg*. 28. See before *Chap*. 6.

If an Award be good in any part of it to all the Parties that did submit to it, if the Award be broken in that part, an Action will lie for that Breach, *Pract. Reg*. 28.

An Arbitrator cannot delegate or transfer the Power given him by the Parties that submitted to the Arbitration; for it is contrary to the Submission;

but an Arbitrator may refer a ministerial act touching the Arbitration to another, *Pract. Reg.* 28. As that the Parties shall enter into Bond (for such a Sum awarded) as Counsel shall advise.

Note, it was held a good Award, that an Action should be commenced betwixt the Parties by advice of *W.* and *P.*

The Court will not suppose any thing to be awarded in an Award, which is not submitted unto, except the contrary be made to appear, *Pract. Reg.* 28.

Thus you see most of the former Cases confirmed by this Register, And farther, That a thing may be awarded, to be done to a Stranger, See before.

CHAP. XIV

How an Arbitrement shall be expounded and intended.

Every Arbitrement is a Judgment. And there is Diversity where a Man is judged by Authority of the Law, and by Election of the Party himself; for a Judge of Record does not give Judgment against the Parties if so be they are not called before him by Process of Law; but otherwise it is of an Arbitrator, who is Judge between the Parties. And whereas every Judgment of Record shall be executed literally according to the Warrant issuing out of the Record, upon and for the executing the said Judgment. Yet nevertheless, Every Arbitrement ought to be expounded and intended according to the intent of the Arbitrators, and not literally, 10 *Co. f.57.b.* But if the intent of the Arbitrators will not stand with the Law, then the Parties shall perform it according to those Words, in such Sense as agrees with the Law.

And note, it hath been held, That an Averment shall not be allowed to shew the intent of the Arbitrators, if it be not expressed in the Award, either directly or by Circumstance, *Dyer* 242.

CHAP. XV

The Effect of an Arbitrement or Award.

The Effect of an Arbitrement or Award is as follows: By Arbitrement the Controversie passes into a Matter judged of. And therefore where a Party brings his Action for the Wrong done him, 'tis a good Plea That he submitted himself to the Arbitrement of such and such, who awarded that he should pay so much &c, but the day of payment of it is not yet come. But if the day of Payment be passed, he ought to shew that he tendred the Mony at the Day and that he is yet ready to pay it &c. See before Chap. 10.

For Arbitrement by which the Arbitrators award, that one of the Parties shall pay Mony, does give an Action. And it is now held by the Court That Debt upon an Award by Word of Mouth is within the Statute of Limitation, 21 *Jac* 16. That it must be sued for within six years after the Cause of

Action: But Debt upon an Award under Hand and Seal, is as if it were a Specialty, and so out of the Statute. This is the same if the Submission be without Deed.

And if the Parties do not perform the Arbitrement, the Party is restored to his first Action. But yet it is at his Election to have a Writ of Debt, upon the Award, or the first Action. But if the Payment be made, the first Wrong is altogether determined by the Award. And if the Arbitrators award, that one of the Parties shall pay so much Mony, and either of them is bound to the other to stand to the Award, the Party may have an Action on the Award, and also the Deed if the Award be not performed. *Quaere*.

If the Submission be by Word, and the Award is, That one of the Parties shall do a Collateral Act, other than payment of Mony, it gives no Action; and if it be not indeed executed and satisfied, the Arbitrement hath no Effect, and such Arbitrement does not determine the first Wrong. Yet if the Subnission be by Bond, if a Collateral Act be awarded to be done, if it be not performed, the Bond shall be forfeit. And 'tis the usual course to sue the Bond on Non-performance of the Award.

CHAP. XVI

Concerning the Performance of an Award with several Presidents of Awards, Umpirage and Release

Lastly we are to consider the Performance of the Award, whereof it is said, That The Parties ought to do all that in them is to perform it. See before *Chap*. 9.

If by the Arbitrement it is awarded, That an Act shall be done which a Man may perform in two manners, the one way by himself, and by the other way he must have the Aid of another person, the Party ought to perform it by such means as he himself can do, without the Aid of another.

Arbitrement ought not to be performed in part, and in part not. But though an Arbitrement cannot be made by the Arbitrators, part at one time and part at another time, yet it may be performed part at one time and part at another time. But this must be before the Day limited.

The Parties shall have reasonable time allowed them for the Performance of an Award if no time be limited.

If the Act that the Arbitrators shall award that one of the Parties shall perform, cannot be performed before another Act first done by the other Party, if the Party does not do the first Act, the other is excused.

Arbitrement, that one Party shall pay Mony, and the other shall make a Release, it shall be done at one and the same time, if there be no Bond to perform the award. But if there be an Obligation to perform the Award, then either ought to perform his part under the peril of the Obligation. If a Bond be made to stand to an Arbitrement, though the Arbitrement is void in Law, yet it is said it ought to be performed, otherwise the Bond shall be forfeited. This must be meant when the Award is only void in part, See before *Chap.* 6. But if an Action be brought upon such void Award, the Action shall not be maintained.

If the Matter contained in the Award, and the Matter contained in the Submission, of which the Arbitrators ought to award, differ in Words or in Circumstance. The Parties to the Arbitrement shall not in a Suit thereupon be allowed to aver, that it is all one. See before *Chap.* 14.

Thus have I shown you the whole Law of Arbitrement by Method and Rule; wherein if you find some things twice, it is not without some Reason, either relating to the Method or the Matter of an Award. There may be many other things said of Arbitrement in later Books, as in the three Books of *Keble*'s Reports; but these things being no more then what is already said, and especially belonging to Pleading, I shall omit them.

[here follow *Some Several Forms of Awards, Arbitrements and Umpirage*]

APPENDIX 2

Arbitration in Sheppard's *Abridgment* 1675

William Sheppard *A Grand Abridgment of the Common and Statute Law of England*[1]

ARBITREMENT AND ARBITRATORS

Arbitrement is an Award or Judgment made by one or more at the Request of some parties for the ending of some difference between them. An Arbitrator is he, or one of them so chosen, said to be an extraordinary Judge in matter of difference between party and party by their mutual consent, and their authority is given to them by the parties litigant to hear and determine the matter in difference between them to whose judgement they bind themselves to stand: It is called an Arbitrement, either because these Judges may determine it *ex boni viri arbitrio*, not being bound to the strict Rules of Law, or because they have submitted to them, not by compulsory means but *ex libero arbitrio*. Terms ley, West Symb, 2 part. Sect 21.

Arbitrement some say is General, when it is an Award of all Actions, demands and differences between the parties upon such a Reference thereof unto them: or Special, where the Reference and Award upon it is only of one or more matters of difference mentioned between them, but whichever it is it is called a Judgment.

The Award also may be made and rendred, either in writing or by word of mouth.

An Umpire is the same in effect with an Arbitrator, for he is one chosen by the Arbitrators finally to order, and determine the matter in difference between them, if the Arbitrators cannot, or do not order by the day agreed upon between them.

For this take these things in general:

1. That there are five things incident to an Arbitrement: (1) Matter of Controversie; (2) Submission to the award of the persons chosen; (3) Parties to the Submission; (4) Arbitrators; (5) The making of an award by word or writing. Co.10.137. Dyer 2t7.

1. Repetitions of the number of arbitrators are shown in **bold**.

2. That the Submission is the agreement of both parties to abide and submit to the order made by the Arbitrators: this is sometimes made between the parties reciprocally, and sometimes to the Arbitrator. It is made between the parties sometimes by Bond, sometimes by Covenant, sometimes by Promise, and it may be good either way. And so it may be without any of these by a bare Submission and agreement only to refer it to them: and an Obligation or Assumpsit to stand to the award of IS and ID hath in it an Implicite Submission to their award. This is also sometimes absolute without reference to any time: and sometimes Conditional, as a Submission to their award if it be made by such a day, Co.10.13 1.5.78.20.H.6. 1 8. Trin. 18 Jac.*Cyprian Salters case.*

3. That if the award be Repugnant, insensible, incertain, against Law, not definitive, or on the one side only, it may be void, Yelverton 98. for it shall not have a favourable construction as a Deed or Will shall have to bring it to the intent of parties, for it is in nature of a Judgment, and must be plain and compleat. Yelverton 98. Croo. 1.3,4. Co.5.77.

4. That if it do not pursue, and be made according to the power given them by the Submission, it will not be good. Bendloes 38. It may not be larger nor narrower than the authority given thereby. Jenk, Cent. 3. case 6.

5. Arbitrators may not refer their Arbitrement to others, or to an Umpire, unless the Submission be so made to them, nor may they make their arbitrement in their own Names, and the Name of a third person to whom no submission was made; nor may they alter their Award being once made. Jenk. Cent. 3. Case 61, Co.71.

6. The Arbitrement must be always pursuing the Submission, so as if it be so said by Bond, or Assumpsit, so as it be delivered under Hand and Seal, or at such a day, or in such a place, so it must be. Croo.2.577.

7. That an Arbitrement may be made Conditional, that if such a thing be not done by one of the parties, the Award shall be void, Croo.2.423.525.

8. That where the Award comprehends that which is submitted and more, it is good for that submitted, and void for the rest.

9. That the Arbitrators may not award the one Party to procure a Stranger to do a thing. More case 11. Nor may they award all of the one part and none of the other part. More case 885. Hob.49. They may not make it larger, nor straiter or narrower than the Submission. Hob.190. And yet in some Cases where it may seem larger than the Submission, it may be good by a restriction of *de & super praemissis*, or by defect of the pleading of his Adversary, Hob.190. And generally, where an Arbitrement is void in part it is void in all as to things though not to persons, especially where one part of it depends upon another. Croo.2.149.

10. That Corruption in Arbitrators to make them partial may be punished by Indictment, Yelverton 62.

11. The Submission and reference to the Arbitrators for the making of an Award must be made clearly and plainly before the Award can be made; and this they may make upon what terms they please (as afterwards it will appear) and then the Award is to be made accordingly.

12. For the Award itself it must be looked unto that there be persons submitting, they be able, and therefore that they do not make an Award upon strangers that never submitted to award, for it must be between privies and parties, and the parties able, not Infants or Feme Coverts, &c. And that they pursue the authority by the Submission, and therein make a plain, honest and just Award, that may at least have a shew of respect to both sides, and of some satisfaction for the wrong done referred to them: and that they award that to the party, that he may know how to come by, and that the Award made be possible, reasonable, sensible, lawful and final and definitive, for if it be defective in either of these it may be naught, and void, as in the examples following.

13. That if an obligation be to stand to an Award, and a void Arbitrement is made, which is as none at all, the obligation is void also, for it is become impossible by the Act of the Arbitrator. Fitz. Obligation 17. Jenk. Cent.3. case 31.

14. So that now upon the whole it may be observed, That an Award sometimes becomes invalid and void for something that goes before the making of it, and sometimes for what is in the manner or matter of the Award itself: and sometimes for what comes after the Award itself, or is *ex post facto*. Before, when the Persons submitting are not able to submit, or have not submitted, as when it is to oblige Strangers, not parties nor Privies: or when the matters referred to the Arbitrators are not things that lie in Arbitrement, and there is no collateral security to bind the parties to perform it, or when the Submission is not legal, or being so it is determined by Revocation of it before it be made. In the Award, where it pursues not the Submission, or is incertain, unreasonable, imperfect, insensible, against Law, of the one side only, without appearance of satisfaction for wrong, and not final or definitive. After the Award, when some due Circumstance is not observed, as publication or Notice after the Award according to the Submission: For all or any of these causes an Award may become void. Co.4.1. Kelw.99. Co.5.78.8.98.10.13 1. 17 E.4.5; 12 H3 .5; 19 H.8.36; 13 H.4.12; 8 E.4.10. Co.8.92.

15. There is a difference between Arbitrement and Concord; for that it may be pleaded though the time of performance of it be not yet come; But a Concord must be executed and satisfied before it can be pleaded,

for there is no means to force the doing of it, as there is in case of Arbitrement. Dyer 75. Kelw.121. Plow.11. 19 H.6.37.

16. The sentence of these Arbitrators is definitive and absolute, from which there is no Appeal to any Court either of Law or Equity, and if they are, no writ of Errour lieth to reverse their Judgment. Dyer 356. Co.5.78.

17. Arbitrement, if it be good and well made, and any thing awarded for a wrong done, that the party hath or can tell how to recover, or amends for it being not performed, as where there is an Obligation or Assumpsit to perform it, there it puts an end to the matter referred: so that if there were a cause of Suit before *transeunt in rem judicatam*, so that if either party sue upon any thing that is arbitrated, the award may be pleaded in Bar to the Suit; as to say, That they submitted the matter in difference to the award of IS for that matter alone or for that with others, and that he awarded him to pay so much money such a day, and the day is not yet come. For an Arbitrement that one of the parties shall pay money to the other doth give the other an Action for this money: and if the time be past for payment, he may say, he paid it at the time, or tendred it, and it was refused; but if it be not performed, then the party is free to take his Remedy for the first wrong, and hath his Election to sue upon the Award, or upon the cause he had before the Award. 6 H.7. 1.11. Plow. 6.20 H.6.41.

18. Where the Submission is, *Ita quod promulgat. utriq parti*, this must be to every one that doth submit to the Award. More case 885. Co.5.103.

If a Submission be to 4, so as any 3, or all 4 make it; this is good if made by 3 of them. More case 1154. The Condition was to stand to the Award of 4, so it be made by them, or any two of them before such a day, and it was held well made by two of them. Yelverton 203. So if two on the one side, and one on the other side put themselves to the Arbitrement of IS by this he may as well arbitrate any thing between the two on the one side, as between them and him on the other side. Idem. 2 R.3.18.

An Award is in the middle of a Term that A should surcease his Suit, yet he proceeded to Judgment this Term (which relates to the first day) and it was held void, for the Suit by the Judgement did cease before. Yelverton 35.

If the Award of Recompense for a wrong done be performed, that wrong is altogether determined. And where the Submission is by Statute Obligation, or Assumpsit, and either party refuse to perform it, the party to whom the thing is to be done may have his Action either on the Statute, Bond or Assumpsit, or upon the Judgment of the Arbitrators which he will. 21 E.4.41. But if there be a Submission, and no Award, or a void Award which is all one with no Award, or there be only a bare Submission without Bond or Assumpsit, and the Award be to do such a thing for which the party can have no Remedy, being a Collateral thing, as to make a Feoffment, ac[count] or any'thing else but payment of money. In these cases the party shall not be barred in any Suit upon the matter put into compromise, neither will Action lie for not performance of that Award. *Ex nuda submissione non oritur Actio*. But if there be an Obligation or Assumpsit to perform the Award, and a collateral thing be awarded, and it be not done, the Obligation, or Assumpsit may be sued. 20 H.6.9. 5 E.4.7. 9 E.4.44. 16 E.4.9. 20 H.6.12. Co.5. *Samons case*.

Debt on an Obligation to perform an Award: and the Award was, That the Defendant should enjoy a house of which the Plaintiff was Lessee for years during the Term, paying to the Plaintiff yearly 20s and for not payment of this, Debt was brought, and it was held to lie, for it was part of the Award. Croo. 1.211. *Persons alias Strowd v Parsons*.

An Action it is thought by some may lie for non-performance of an Award upon a bare Submission in some Cases where it is to perform a collateral thing, as to make a Release, or the like, and he shall declare upon a mutual Promise to perform the Award. 20 H.6.20. Co.8.98. Trin.18 Jac. B.R. *Broom & Doning*.

The Award of a personal Chattle, as that IS one of the parties shall have a horse (in question between them) doth alter the property of it, and give it so to IS that he may have a Detinue for it. And so also of a Chattle Real, as in the case before of a Lease for years. But in matter of Freehold Arbitrement can neither give a Title, nor bind a Right. Dyer 183. Lean 2.130. Croo.2.223. *Trustor v Yewre*. 21H.7.29. 14H.4.19. If the Award be naught and defective, no Action will lie upon it, nor upon the Obligation or Assumpsit to perform it. Co.10.131. M.4 Jac. *Hains and Honnywood*. When two at the same time enter into several Bonds to stand to an award, this is but one Submission. Croo.3.433.

That the Husband may submit himself to an Award for himself and his Wife for her Goods and Chattles to bind her. 27 H.7.29.

A Condition was to stand to the Award of 4 that were named, so the same be made and delivered up in writing under the hands and Seals of the 4 or any 3 of them; and it was held good upon this Submission though made by 3 of them. Croo.2.399.

An Infant may not submit to an Award, or any body for him; and if he by Bond tie himself, or another for him to stand to an Award, it will be void. March 111. Pl.139.141. Pl.215.

A Submission may be as they agree, so as the Award be delivered such a day at such a place in certain, and then it must be pursued accordingly. Croo.3.216.226.263.3.3.

Where divers do a wrong to one, and one of these and he to whom the wrong is done submit to an Award, if any be made, the other parties, no parties to the Submission may take advantage of it to extinguish the wrong. 7 H.4.31. 20 H.6.12.

A submission to an Award by a Deputy; as where one party for himself, and a Deputy for and in the name of another submit to an Award; this is good, and the award made upon it good. Dyer 270.

It may be by several Bonds, or by one Bond made at one and the same time, and it must be to make a Reference or submission by agreement of the parties on both sides, and this may be by Statute, or Recognisance with a Defeasance, or by Obligation with a Condition, or by Covenant, or by an Assumpsit, or Promise, or without all this by a bare agreement to refer the matter to such a person or persons: and the Condition, or Assumpsit to abide an Award doth imply a submission to stand to their Award. Co. 10131.5.78. 20 H.6.18.

If the Submission be of all Actions, causes of Actions are not included in this. Co. on Lit. 285.

If divers be parties to the Submission, and one submit at one time, and another at another time; it seems this is not good, but the sure way is to submit all at one time. By Justice Bridgman.

If the Submission be of one thing, within this may be included any thing incident to that thing, and thereof an Arbitrement may be made upon this Submission. 8 H.6.18. 19 E.4.1. 5 H7.22.

That if the submission be by obligation with Condition to perform an Award, so as it be delivered *utrique eorum* before such a day, this must be delivered to each of the parties, or it is not sufficient. Broo. Condition 46.

A Submission also must be certain for it may be void for incertainty as an Arbitrement may be. Croo. 1.432.

Where the Submission is to 4 Arbitrators, and the arbitrement is made by 3 of them only; yet it seemeth good. Bridgman 91.

That let the Submission be how it will by word or writing, and be naked, or clothed with an engagement by Obligation or Assumpsit, yet before the Award is made it may be countermanded, and the Arbitrators discharged of the work; yet with these differences: (1) That where there is a naked Submission by word, there the Revocation may be by word; but if it be in writing, the Countermand must be in writing also, for it must be *eodem modo* as the submission is. (2) If the submission be naked, and either of the parties countermand it, and discharge the Arbitrators, the other hath no remedy against him: But if he undertake by Especialty, or Assumpsit to abide the Award of IS, and after revoke it, the Revocation is not good; But he may be sued on the Especialty or Promise, for he hath broken that. (3) That in all these cases, where the party shall revoke his Submission he must do it by giving notice of his mind therein to the Arbitrators: But where there be two or more on the side of the parties that submit to the Award, one or some of them may not revoke without the rest, and then especially when the Submission is by Deed. Co. 8.81.5.78. Fitz. Arbitrement 21.21 H.6.20.3 E.4.3.8 E.4.10.12 28.H.66 21H.6.30.

The Submission was that A B and C should make the Arbitrement in writing or by word, and one of them pronounced it and declared the substance of it, and the others agreed to it; and it was held not good, and that it should have been in writing. Lawsons case, by Davenport Chief Baron at the Assises.

Abritrators may not assign their power, or leave any part of it to be performed by another as a Deputy. Co.5.77. But after the Submission, they may either take it upon them, or refuse to meddle with it as they please; and if they do undertake it, they are then to appoint time and place for it: and then and there the parties are to wait upon them to notifie their Controversies to them, and otherwise they are not to take notice of it; and after they have understood the cause by the hearing of the parties, and their matters of difference at large, then they are to make their award *secundum allegata & probata*; But they may not enjoyn any Oath to the Witnesses, and yet they may take any evidence from any man upon Oath if he will voluntarily give it: and this they must do themselves, and not by any other by their appointment, for that will not be good; and after the Award made, then they must notifie it to the parties: And herein they must observe that order that the parties have given in their Submission precisely; as where in the Submission it is said, That it shall be published and notified, then it must be done, and so done as they have agreed and declared that it shall be done: and if it be, That it shall be notified in writing, then so it must be; and if to all the parties, then so it must be: and if it be that it be at such a time and place, then so it must be. Co. 4.82. Co.5. *Samons case* 8.98. 8 E.4.10.21. 20 E.4.8.

The Condition of a Bond was, To stand to the Award of A chosen by the parties to arbitrate of, for, in and upon the Dilapidations of the Parsonage of S and also of, in and upon all and singular Actions, Suits, Quarrels, debates had and depending in variance betwixt the parties, so as the same award be made, had, sealed and delivered in writing under the Seal of the Arbitrator before, etc. A made an Award thus, (*viz*) The award made by me A on the parties, &c. and the Award was only of the dilapidations with a Protestation, That he would not meddle with the rest; and it was held a good Award between the parties: But that the Arbitrator had disabled himself because he did not arbitrate all. And that if a Submission be of two things only, and the Award but of one, if they have not further notice of the other, it is good. Croo. 2130. Godb.164.16. The Award until it be published and made known by the Arbitrators to the parties is no award to bind them: But if it be left to the discretion of the Arbitrators and no order be taken in the Submission for the publication of it, in that case the Arbitrators are not bound (in Law but in honesty only) to notifie it, and the parties are bound at their perill to take notice of it: and yet where one of them is to do any thing that depends upon another thing to be done before it, there he must have notice of that other thing, when done by the other party. See for all this 8 E.4.10. 47 E.3.21. Co.4. *Samons case*. 8.98. 8 E.4.10.21. 1H.7.5. Plow. 218. Co.4.825.103. 20 E.4.8.

If divers on the one side, and divers on the other side submit themselves to the Award of divers, the Arbitrators may make an Award for matters that are between them jointly and severally: and they may make their award between some of the one part and some of the other, and not meddle with the rest, unless the Submission be so as they must meddle with all or none: for if the Submission will warrant it, the Arbitrator may protest against the medling with some parcel and make an award of the rest; and an award made of that which is within the Submission, is good. Plow.289. 22 E.4.22. 19 H.6.6. 21 H.7.29.

If the Submission be so, That the Award shall be delivered to the party, or before such a day if he desire it; If he desire it not, they need not deliver, but he must take notice of it whatever it be at his peril. 8 E.4.18.21. But one is not bound to perform till he can know what the Award is. Brownl. 31 1.

For Matters arbitrable it is to be known, That the most apt and proper matters to be ended by Arbitrements are personal wrongs, and uncertain duties, as Trespasses and the like: But differences about Land, and the Estates therein, Chattles real, and personal things in Action, Accompts, and most things may be referred to Arbitrement. Dyer 183. Co.5.78.

And for Chattles, they may dispose of them and give the property or Interest thereof as they please; But a Freehold is not arbitrable. Nor can they dispose of Land as the Chancery, and Common-law Courts may do; yet they may award that one of the parties shall enjoy the Land, and the other not disturb him; or that the one of them shall give the other a Bond for the quiet enjoying of it, or the like: and if the parties be bound by any Especialty, or Assumpsit to perform the Award, and do not, he may sue upon it, 9 H.6.60. Kelw. 99. 21 E.3.26. 14 H.4.18,19,24. Broo.Abridgm. 5.30. Co.8.137. 14 H.4.19.12 Ass. pl. 25.

The damages recovered in an Action of Wast after Judgment entred for it, is Arbitrable. M. 29 Eliz. B.R. More.

The Office of a Steward of Courts, and an Annuity for his fees for keeping of the Courts may be arbitrable. See Croo I. case 796.

Arbitrators may make an arbitrement of Actions joint and several, where one of them and two others submit themselves to their Arbitrement. 2 R.3. 13.

If one sue for a Debt upon a Record, or Especialty; and it be put to arbitrement, and an Award is That he shall pay all or part of it, it is void, for it is not Arbitrable. 10 H.7.4.

Some think Debt on a Contract alone may be arbitrable, but it is clear it is arbitrable amongst other things.45 E.3.36. 6 H.4.6. 4 H.6.l7. 10 H.7.4. Fitz Arbitrement 23.

Matters of Common-wealth, and Marriage it seems are not arbitrable at all. West. Symb. p146. Nor Debts due by Bond, Bill or Covenant, or on a Simple Contract alone; Nor debts upon Arrearages of Account before Auditors, nor things that are not *in rerum natura* at the time of the Submission, though they after happen to be; Nor Annuities, Wast or detainment of Charters: and yet so as upon special engagements to perform such awards, they must do so, or bear the Penalty. 4 E.3.16. Dyer 51. 6 H.4.6. 4 H.6.17. 10 H.7.4. 9 H.6.60. 14 H.4.18. Co.5 *Samonds case*. But Debts due for expence about business or for travail; and so also (as some think) are Debts on a Contract or damage certain, being joined with Trespass or other things incertain, that all these are arbitrable before, or after any Suit begun; yea some think a Debt on a Contract alone is arbitrable. Co. 8. *Baspoles case* 97. Finches ley 181. If a man demand £5 for Businesses he hath done for another; this is arbitrable. Adjudged 37 Eliz. C.B. *Sower and Bradford*.

Any persons may submit to an Award: a man may submit for himself and his Wife, and bind himself That she shall stand to the Award, but she is not bound. An Infant also may submit, and yet he is not bound by the Award but at his choice, or perhaps may make it good at his age, as she when she is discovert: Others may enter into Bond for them, or they for themselves, but the Bonds to stand to award will be void, save only in the case of a man for his Wife. Latch. 207. Marsh 111.141 .

In every good Award there must be these five things as incident: (1) Matter of Controversie, and that must be such a matter as is arbitrable: (2) There must be a good Submission of the parties to the Award: (3) Parties to the Submission: (4) Arbitrators: (5) An Award; and if either of these be wanting, the Award is not good, 10 H.7.4. Co.10.137. Dyer 2l7. 19 E.4.1. and good Notice of the Award.

The Condition of the Obligation was to stand to an Award made in writing under Hand and Seal indented and delivered before such a day, and it was sealed, but not under the hand of the Arbitrator; and it was held void, and in such a case if the Arbitrator cannot write, he must set his mark to it. Bulstr. 1.1 10.

If the Submission be, as usually it is, to stand to an award so it be made by a day certain, or be in writing, or under Seal, and be delivered by a day, and the Arbitrators make it after the day, or do not make it in that manner and order as is set down, the Award is void. 7 H.6.40. yet see Styles 110.

That an Exception to an Award is, that it was not well set forth, for he did not shew that the Award was delivered up by the Arbitrators according to the Submission; And it was said by Rolls who then gave the Rule that it was well enough, See it there.

The Condition was to perform the Award of 4 chosen by them, so that the said Award be made and delivered in writing; And this to be of all Causes between them, and the same to be made by them 4, 3, or 2 of them. And it was held in this case, That if the Award were made by 2 of them it is well enough. And that it shall be intended to be made of all matters unless the contrary be shewed in their pleading. Bulstr. 1.123.

If a Stranger have drawn an Award before, and the Award made by the arbitrators is, that the parties shall perform that Award; this will be as good as if they had drawn it themselves. 8 E.4 10.39 H.6.10.

The Arbitrator may make his Award the same day that the Bond doth bear Date that is made to stand to the award. Latch.l4.

The Submission was to 4 persons and the umpirage of another, and the mutual Promises were to stand to the order of them five, and they all made their Award together; and it was held good. But had the Submission been to them 4, and if they could not agree, then to the umpirage of the 5th, Bulstr.1.184. it had been better.

If the Arbitrators meet and agree one day of all matters, at another day within the time meet again and perfect the Award, this may be well enough. But if the Submission be by deed, and a time set to make the Arbitrement, and the Arbitrators meet, and prorogue it to a time after the day, and then do it; this is not good. But if the Submission were by word onely it might be good. And if they make an Award one day, and after in the time limited make another Award; Or make part of the Award one day, and part at another day, and both within the time set; or make part of it before, and part of it after the day set for it within which to be done; in these Cases without a new Submission these Awards cannot be good. 49 E.3.9. 22 H.6.52. 33 H.6.28. 39 H.6.12. 8 E.4.10. 19 E.4.1 nor may they make 2 Awards one after another. 22 H.652.

An Award that one of the parties shall make such a Release to the other as Councell shall advise is good, for this is but a ministeriall Act: but if they had appointed a Judiciall Act to be done so by another, it had been void. Styles 217.

If an Award be that one of the parties shall levy a Fine, make a Feoffment, enter a Retraxit by Nonsuit, or Discontinue his Action, or make defaults in a *praecipe quod reddat*, or the like, where the Concurrence of others with him is necessary to the doing of the Act; yet it seems the Award is good. 5H.7.22. So that the party shall do any Judiciall Act, the award is good, albeit it cannot be done without the help of a stranger. 19 H.6.38. 19 E.4.5.

The Award was upon a Reference of the Dammages recovered in Wast, that the one party should pay to the other so much money at severall dayes, and that JD (a stranger) should do other things not within the Submission, and for this to be done by the Stranger void. M 29 Eliz. BR. Moor and Bedell.

An Award that either of the parties shall do a thing against law; As that one of them shall rob, or beat the other, or disseise him of his Freehold, must needs be naught, at the least for so much of it. And where the Award is out of the Submission or against Law, the obligation to perform the Award is void also. Godb.12.13.

An Award to pay more than the Interest allowed by the Statute for forbearance of money is not good if it be *eo nomine*, but by way of dammage it may be good. And to order the payment of the legall Interest is good. Winch.114.

The Arbitrement that is made of a thing not within the Submission is void. **Submission to 4, so as they 4, or any 3 of them make the Award; this may be made by three of them, More case 1154. but if the Submission be to 4 onely, it seems not good made by 3 of them.**

The Arbitrement must be pursuing the submission, or it will not be good, Bendl.3g. Croo.3.433. If that say it must be under hand and Seal, or in writing, or delivered at such a time in such a place etc, so it must be done. Croo.Abridg. case 2256.

The Submission was to stand to the Award of, etc, of all Suits etc. stirred and depending till the day of the date of the bond [4th September 42 Eliz.] so as the award be made of the Premises before such a day, they made an award of all matters until 3rd of September; And it was held good, though not till 4th of September. For if a Suit now depending it must be in Suit before the 4th day. Croo.1.358. Barnes etc. If the Submission be for all the land discended, and the Award is of White-acre, and Black-acre onely; this by an Averment, that this was of all the land discended, may be good enough, by Just. Barckley [Berkeley JKB], 11 Car.B.R.

Where the Submission is in writing by obligation of all causes, demands etc. or of divers things specially named, without the proviso in the Condition, So that, etc. and the award is of part of the things: Or if the Submission be by divers persons, and they make an award between some of them onely, this is good. But if the Submission be of certain things in speciall with a proviso in the Condition. That the award be made of all of the premises. etc. by such a day or the like; there the award must be made of all, or it will be void. Co.8.79. Yet it must end all controversies notified to the Arbitrators. Hob.49.190.

If the Award exceed the Submission it is void for all, with this Difference between a thing severable and a thing entire, As where the Submission is of all Suits, and the award that the one shall release to the other all Suits, Debts, etc. So if Divers Suits be about Tithe, and other matters between the parties, and they submit etc. the Arbitrators award that all Suits between them shall cease and all controversies end, the one shall pay to the other

£20 in recompence of all wrongs; this is adjudged a good award for the Tithe. Trin.18 Jac.B.R. *Ingrams case*.

The Submission was the 29th of December of all matters, And the Award was of so much in satisfaction of causes and matters untill the 28th of December, and so excluded one day before the Submission, yet it was held good, For it is said they made an Award *de praemissis* and nothing else is shewed to be arisen upon the 28th day, it shall be intended of all. Co.8.99.

If A and B the 1 of May submit to JS for all matters from the beginning of the world to the Date of the Submission, in June following they make an Award that A shall pay to B £10 etc. and that B shall make him a generall Release, and this be an end of all matters between them from the beginning of the world to the Date of the Award; this is good: and yet if other matters be shewed to be between the parties between the Date of the Submission and the Date of the Award, Contra. 9 E.4.44. 8 H.6.18. 9 H.7.15.7 H.6.40. 36 H.6.11. Co.8.98. Dyer 216. If the Submission be of the Right, Title and possession of land, and the award is made of the possession onely and nothing said of the Right, yet it is good for so much as it reacheth unto. 19 H.6.6. 36 H.6.8. Hetley 4.

The Submission was by Bond in generall for all Actions, Suits and demands whatsoever; and part of the award was That the one of them should deliver to the other certain cloths by such a day, and it was held good, and within the Submission. More 948.

If an Award be made in one but delivered in another County, it is good enough. Dyer 218. If the Submission be by divers on both sides, so that the Award be delivered to the parties or one of them; if in this case it be delivered to both, or all of one side, or to one of either side, it is good enough. Dyer 218.

If the Submission be of all Suits and Controversies then depending, and the Award is made of a Difference not then in Suit, yet this is good. M. 10 Car.B.R. per Curiam. But if the Submission be of all Actions personall, and the Award is of Actions reall, this is not good. 7 H.6.40. Plow.306. So if it be of all Actions reall and the Award be of Actions personall, 7 H.6.40. 19 H.6.36. Co.10.132. So if the Submission be for all matters between them until the 10th of May, and they Award, that a Release shall be given of all Actions till the 20th of May; this is a void Award. 7 H.6.40. l9 H.63 Dyer 242. If the Submission be of all causes depending between them *ab initio mundi* etc. and the award be of all causes *a principio* omitting depending; this is not good. B.R. Adjudg. Haines, &c.

A and B 12 Febr. 12 Jac. bind themselves by the Condition of an obligation to stand to the Award of JS for all matters before 20th of March next. And the 18th of March JS makes his Award, That A shall pay to B £20 in April and £20 in June, and then that each of the parties shall make general Acquittances of all demands to the day of the making of the Acquittances. And it was held, That the Award was good for all that was submitted unto, and void for the rest; and therefore if the breach be assigned in that which was submitted unto, the Action will lie. Bridgman 58. Co.10.131.

If the Submission be of things personall, and the Award is, that one of the parties shall do an Act of a thing reall, in satisfaction of a personall wrong, *Et sic e contra*, or the Submission be of one thing, and the Award is made of somewhat incident to it or necessarily depending upon it. So if the Submission be of all Actions reall and personall, and the Award is onely of matters personall, or matters reall, it is good in these cases for this, if nothing else be notified to them. 9 E .4.44. 8 H.6. 1 8. 9 H.7. 15. 7 H.6.40. Dyer 216.

If A on the one side and 3 others on the other side submit to Arbitrement for all Actions and Demands between them; And the Award is made of some matters between them 3 on the one side onely, this is not good. Dyer 242. Co.8.92.

But in all cases where the words or manner of the Submission be Conditional, That the Award must be of all matters or none, there perhaps it will not be a good Award unless it be made of all. See Paschae 9 Jac. *Sallows case*. Hill. 14 Jac. *Lee and Pain*. C.B. 43 Eliz.C.B. *Barnes case*. Co.8.98. Dyer 216.

Where the Condition of the obligation is, to stand to an Award for divers matters named, there it must be made of all or none. But if it be for all matters, or between divers persons, and some matters onely, or all between some of the persons onely are notified; there an Award of them alone may be good. And if it be of particulars, without such a Conditionall Restraint or Conclusion, there an Award of any part of it may be good. 7 H.6.40 19 H6.36 36 H.6.11. Dyer 242. Bulstr.1.123.184.

In Debt upon an Arbitrement, The Plaintiff declared, That the Defendant and he *posuerunt se in Arbitrium, ordinationem et Judicium* JC &c. chosen *de jure, titulo, et interesse in quibusdam Messuagiis, &c.* And the award was, That the Defendant should pay to the Plaintiff, £16 *in plenum satisfactionem,* And it was held good, though not shewed that any thing was awarded to the Defendant; for the Plaintiff is not to shew in his declaration all the Award, but that onely which doth entitle him to the thing etc. And if the Defendant will impeach the Award, it must come on his part. And it was adjudged for the Plaintiff. Lean 1.72. Croo 2.354. *Ormelade v Cook*.

If the Submission be generall of all Actions and demands, etc. and there is but one cause or matter between them; and an Award is made in this, it is good. And so if there be many matters between them, and one of them onely is made known to them, this will be good for that one thing. But where the Condition is in speciall, and with a proviso that the Award shall be made of the premises, or words to the like effect, there the Arbitrators

must make an Arbitrement of all, or it will not be good. Co.8.78. And
therefore where a Reference was of 9 Articles, and the Award made onely
for 6 of them, some have held it void. Goldsb.l25. pl.14. yet see Bridgman
93. The Submission was of all matters so as it were made by such a day.
And the Arbitrators had notice of some matters only, and made an Award
of them. But where the Submission is as before, they must make an Award
of all matters notified to them. But where the Submission is without any
such *Ita quod*, there they may make their award of some of the matters
only made known unto them, and not of the rest. But if it be of 3 things,
or some Particulars, with a general clause of all other matters, in that case
they must make the Award for that which is particularly named without
any other notice given to them. 7 H.6.40. Croo.2.200. 19 H.6.6. Dyer 216.
39 H.6.10. Dyer 356. It is said if the Submission be of all things, and
the Award onely of one, this is void. 39 H.6.9. But how this is is shewed
before. And this is agreed That where the Submission is with Condition,
So that the same Award be notifyed to the parties or some of them by a day,
and it be well made but is not after delivered according to the Condition,
then it is a void Award let it be made never so well. But if the Condition run
thus, That it be delivered to the parties before a day *petentibus hoc*, There
they are not bound to deliver it till it be desired. And if the Submission be
by divers on both sides, provided it be delivered to the parties or one of
them, he must deliver it to some or one of them, or the Award will be void.
Broo. Condition 46. 1 H3.5. Dyer 218. **If it be to stand to the Award of
4, etc. so it be delivered by the Arbitrators or one of them, or any 3, or
2 of them, delivery by one 2, or 3 of them is good.** And if it be, So it be
delivered by such, there delivery by word of mouth will be good enough.
But if it say, If it be delivered in writing, Contra. 5 H.7.5. Dyer 218. See
more of this, Dyer 216.39.356. 39 H.6.9.

An Arbitrement made onely for the one side, and nothing for the other,
is void in law. As that one shall pay money, or give bond for money to the
other, and the other do nothing for it. But if it be that one shall give bond
to pay, or pay a debt, and that the other shall be discharged of the Debt,
Co.8.72. or that one shall pay such a debt to the other he owes him, for the
payment is a discharge, there must be somewhat express or implied given
to either party. *Idem.* That one shall pay money to the other, and say not
for what, is not good. Hob.50.218. So an Award, That the one party shall
pay to the other in satisfaction of all Trespasses and Injuries done to him
by the other party before the day of the Submission, so much, is good.
The Award is a discharge, ind may be pleaded in Barre for a Discharge.
Brownl. 310, 311.

An Award was upon a Reference of a Controverfie between them for the
Tithes of corn and hay in S and an award that the Defendant should pay
the Plaint. mony before such a day; And for this all Suits to cease between

them; It was objected That the Award being entire, and nothing given to the Defendant and void in part, was so in all; But it was held good for the Tithes and void for any thing else, although other Controversies were between them; for when the Award comprehends that which is submitted and more, it is good for that submitted and void for the rest. Croo.2.663. *Web v Ingram.*

An Arbitrement made, That one party shall pay money to the other party, and then the other shall release all Actions to him, is good. And if a man demand £5 of B for business done for him, and this is referred to Arbitrement, and the Arbitrator award that B shall pay to A £4 in full satisfaction of the same Debt and no more, this is a good Award. *Sower and Bradfield* Adjudg. Trin. 31 Eliz.B.R. 7 H.6.40. Co.8.98. But if a Suit be put in Arbitrement and the Award is that the Plaintiff shall not proceed or shall be nonsuited, or the like; it seems these are not good Awards. 19 H.6.36. Plow. 11. 5 H.7.2. 21H.7.28. 36 H.6.15. 7 H.6.40. Co.8.98.

If all matters be referred between two, and the Award is, That one party shall go quit of all Actions that the other hath against him, & say nothing of the Actions he hath against the other, this is not a good Award. So if between the Garnisher and the Plaintiff in a detinue the Award be, that the Garnisher shall go quit of all Suits had by the Plaintiff against him, and nothing is said of the quarrels of the Garnisher had against the Plaintiff. 7 H.6.40. Co.8.98.

If a Difference in a Debt of £10 due by Contract, and the Award is, That he shall pay 40s Costs, this is good, for hereby he is discharged of the Debt that paies it. And if the Reference be for divers Trespasses done by the one of the parties to the other, and the Award is, that he that hath done the Trespaises shall pay £10 for the Trespasses, & order nothing to be done by the other, yet this is good, for hereby the other is discharged of any Action that may be brought against him for those Trespasses. So if the award be, That where one of them hath received 20s of the other, and they have done divers Trespasses one to another, that the one shall pay to the other his 20s and they shall go quit one against another. So where divers matters be of both sides, and the Award is that they shall be Friends, all controversies and matters shall cease, and the one shall pay the other 12d. Co.9.98.22. E4.25.20 H.6.19.7 H.4.31.20 H.6.18. 19 H.6.6. 10 H.6.4.

A Submission was of all Trespasses, Duties and Demands; and the same day the Arbitrators awarded That the Defendant should pay to the Plaintiff in satisfaction of all Trespasses and Injuries done to the Plaintiff by the Defendant before the Date of the Submission, so much, etc. And it was held good, For by payment of the money he was quit of all Trespasses, and it shall not be intended that they had notice of more, but that the Trespasses were done onely by the Defendant; and if otherwise, the Defendant is to shew it. And where a Submission is of all Actions and not with a Condition so that it be made of the premises, if they make an Award of part it is good for that part whereof they made their Award. But if the Submission be Conditionall, it is otherwise. Croo.2.354. *Ormlade v Cook*. Debt was on an obligation to perform an Award of all Suits and Demands between the parties so as it be made of and upon the premises ready to be delivered to the parties before such a day, etc. and that they made such an Award *de et super premissis* (viz) that the Plaintiff should have and enjoy a horse in controversie between them, and that the Defendant should pay him £3 before Michaelmas towards his charges, and they should release one to the other all matters whatsoever betwixt that and Michaelmas, and the breach laid for not payment of the £3. And on a Demurrer it was held good for the Plaintiff; for though it were pleaded that the Arbitrement was made *de et super praemissis*, yet these generall words will not help the Plaintiff unless the Plaintiff averre that there were no more causes between them, and then the Release appointed being void, there is nothing ordered for the Defendants Benefit. Croo.2.352. *Stayne v Wild*. See more of this, 7 H.6.6. 39 H.6.9. 2 R.3.18. 22 H.6.52.

If the Arbitrators award one party to enter into an obligation, and say not in what sum it is void. More case 489. So if it be that one of the parties shall become bound to the other in the summe of.... with a Blank; it is naught. Yelverton 98. Co.5.77.

Two are bound to stand to the award of JS *Ita quod* the award be made before 15 Michaelmas, and that the obligor have notice of it 14 dayes before 15 Michaelmas, to attend the Arbitrement, and 15 Michaelmas was 14 dayes before the Date of the obligation, and so the notice impossible to be performed, the obligation was held good, and the Condition void. Fitz obligation 17. Jenk. Cent. 116.

The difference was about trees, and it was awarded, that one of them should have the Trees and the other pay to him £10 for them at such a time, or give him good Security, not saying what, nor for what; And it was held naught. Jenk. Cent.8. case. 96.

An Award to pay money though no time be set, (and then it must be paid in convenient time) is good. An Award that one party should enter into Bond to the other that he and his wife should have, and enjoy such lands in controversie, not saying in what Summe, and for his wife a Stranger, held naught. Jenk. Cent.3. case. 80.

If divers Trespasses be referred to Arbitrement, and the award is, That the one of the parties shall make the other party amends, and say not what amends; this is a void Award. 18 E.4.11. 39 H.6.9. So that one of them shall enter into an obligation with a Condition to do any thing, and say not what the Summe in the obligation should be. So that one of them shall give a Release to the other, and say not what Release. Co.5. *Samons case* March 18.pl.42.

Debt was on a Bond to perform an Award which was, That each party should give to the other within 4 dayes after the award, a generall Release of all Demands till the day of the obligation; provided, That if either of them dislike the award within 20 days after it is made, and within that time 10s. the Arbitrement to be void; That the first part of the award was good, and the proviso being repugnant void, and the Bond forfeit by not giving a Release. Croo.1.688.

On a Bond with Condition to perform an Award, which was thus, Whereas there was a Controversie between the parties concerning the Lease of a house in C which one of the parties claimed by Lease from BC one of the Plaintiffs for 6 years rendring £15 paid quarterly which was behind for a year, That he should for this Rent pay to F the other Plaintiff £13. 6s. 8d. and that he should enjoy it for 3 years and a half, and pay yearly for it to F £15 at Mich. and the Annunciation, etc or within 40 days after, and if he failed, then the award for enjoying it should be void, and it was held a good Award though Conditionall, for it is absolute if the other pay the Rent. Croo.2.423.

If the Award be, That one of the parties shall have the land in question between them, and it is in anothers possession, this is void. For an Award cannot order a Freehold, And yet if there be any Bond or Assumpsit to perform the award, and it be not performed, the party may be sued upon it. Plow. 11. 20 H.6.52. 5 E.4.7. 19 H.6.36.

A was indebted to B and they both died, the heir of A for good consideration assumed to the administrator of B. that he would pay to the Administrator of the Debt, and for not payment according to the Assumpsit the Administrator brought an Action, and then they submitted to the Award of C and became bound the one to the other to stand to the award accordingly, so that the Arbitrator make it of all matters between them before such a day. The Arbitrator made his award of all matters and Controversies between them before such a day, C the Arbitrator before the day recited the Assumpsit, and the Debt as aforesaid, and ordered that the heir should pay the Administrator so much money, and that published according to their Submission. And it was in question by an Action on the case brought by the Administrator, and *nullum fecit Arbitrium* pleaded, and adjudged for the plaintiff. Brownl. 309. *Freeman and Bespowle.* And there agreed that every award must respect both parties if it be not a matter which concerns one party only, and neither Recompence, nor Acquitall due to the other party, and there it is good. And that where the Submission is as there *Ita quod* &c. that there the Arbitrators must make their award of all the variances referred to them, else void. But if the Submission be generall, and but part is made known to them, and they make an Award of that, it is good enough. And it was held good albeit no place was set where the money should be paid, that shall have a reasonable Construction, and the party shall have a reasonable time for payment of the money also. 3 H.7.16 E .4.

The Award was that the one party should pay upon the 21th of May then following £20 to the other, and that the other *super predictum primum diem Maii* should release, etc. And it was held naught, for the Release was to be made upon the said first of May, and there was no such day, it was held void, and no payment need to be, but void in part it is void in all. Croo. Abridg. Case 2056.

If the Award be That one of the parties shall release the Surety of the Peace to W and in truth there is none such to be released. 21 E.4.40. 9 E.4.44,49. So if it be That one of them shall release to the other the Suit that he hath against him, and in truth there is no such Suit in being. 20 E.4.38.

An award was That one of the parties should pay unto the other £20 per Annum during the Continuance of 2 leases for years in being of the Parsonage of Y etc. Not shewing for what time the leases were, and the continuance of them, but it was set forth by the Plaintiff; and it was held certain enough, for the payment is referred to the Continuance of the leases which is certain. *Id certum quod certum reddi potest*, 3 Jac. B.R. *Girling and Gosnold*.

GLOSSARY

Abridgment, a collection of notes of cases (sometimes statutes) in some sort of order, usually alphabetical, following the form of a lawyer's commonplace book.

Acquittance, release or discharge from a debt or other obligation.

Adjudication, in this work used for any form of decision of a dispute.

Advowson, the right to recommend a member of the clergy to a benefice.

Alnager, the royal official who (until 1699) tested cloth and collected the duty on it.

Annuity, a scheme by which a financer takes a lump sum from the annuitant in return for periodical payments, for life or a term of years.

Arbitration, the processes (other than litigation) by which parties to a dispute submit it to a third party to resolve and by which that resolution is reached and enforced.

Arbitration agreement, a contract by which the parties agree to submit to arbitration all or some of the disputes which have arisen or may arise between them and provide who is to arbitrate.

Arbitration clause, a clause in a contract by which the parties agree to submit to arbitration all or some of the disputes which may arise in the future between them and provide who is to arbitrate.

Arbitrement, arbiterment, arbitriment, arbitrament are alternative spellings. All are used for both the arbitration and the award.

Assize is a word of multiple meanings. It first meant a sitting or session. It became used for the legislation passed there. Other procedures took the name, e.g. the assize of novel disseisin. Then the annual sessions of itinerant judges became known as assizes.

Assumpsit, Latin for 'he undertook'; an action (technically on a writ of trespass) for breach of contract in which the plaintiff alleged the defendant undertook an obligation.

Attachment, arrest of a person for contempt of an order; or of debts or property to secure payment.

Attainder, forfeiture of land and rights on conviction of treason or felony.

Attorney, a person appointed to act in one's place, in particular in legal matters.

Attornment, an acknowledgment that one holds land as another's tenant.

Averment, an affirmation made with an offer of proof as a fact before a jury.

Cartulary, a collection of charters or other records or the place where they are kept.

Charter, a written document granting rights, particularly in land.

Chattel, any property other than freehold land.

Chattel real, leasehold land.

Chattels mixt, mixed, a figment of lawyers' sloppy thinking. There was a mixed action, for both chattels real (freehold land) and chattels personal (other property).

Compromissum, an agreement to submit disputes to arbitration, enforceable by a penalty.

Concord, a settlement approved and made enforceable by a court.

Conveyance, a deed transferring ownership of land.

Court Leet, the customary court of a manor.

Covenant, a promise made in a deed.

Covert see **Feme**.

Defeasance, the making void of a condition.

Demurrer, a pleading that, even if the other party's pleading were accepted, it would not prevail in law.

Detainer, Detainment, unlawful possession of another's goods.

Detinue, an action for the recovery of personal property, which the defendant is alleged to have wrongful possession of.

Disseisin, see **Seisin**.

Distrain, distress, the taking of chattels from a wrongdoer without a judgment as a pledge to redress the wrong.

Dower, the share in a man's estate which went to his widow on his death; often arranged at the church door before witnesses at the wedding.

Enfeoff, see **Feoffment**

Entries, Books of, collections of precedents of pleadings.

Fee, an inheritable estate in land.

Feme Covert, a married woman.

Feme Sole, a single woman.

Feoffment, the formal transfer by a feoffor to a feoffee of ownership and possession of land and other hereditaments by livery of seisin.

Fine, the final settlement of litigation and its record.

Freehold, the tenure by which land is held in fee simple, fee tail or life estate.

Gage, something deposited as security.

Garnishment, attachment of a debt.

Gavelkind, a tenure by which land descended to all sons equally.

Hereditament, property that may be inherited.

Hundred, subdivision of a shire, with its own court.

Indifferent, unbiased.

Infant, any person, male or female, under the age of twenty-one.

Interim award, a temporary award, disposing of the dispute for the time being; it may be total or partial.

Interlocutory, interim, provisional, not yet final.

Ita quod, 'provided that'; the formal introduction to a condition of a bond or other submission to arbitration.

Law Officers, the Attorney General and Solicitor General.

Livery, see **Seisin**.

Loveday, a day allowed for the settlement of a dispute.

Mark, a coin or reckoning figure of the value of thirteen shillings and four pence, two-thirds of a pound.

Mediation, a process by which a third party helps the parties to settle a dispute.

Messuage, a house with the outbuildings and land associated with it.

Mortgage, a conveyance of land by a debtor to a creditor as security for a loan, redeemable when the loan is repaid.

Nisi Prius, 'unless before'; the writ to the sheriff required him to arrange a jury trial at Westminster unless the matter would have already been dealt with by itinerant judges in the shire assembly.

Palatinate, the counties of Cheshire, Durham and Lancashire.

Panel, a tribunal of arbitrators sitting together, analogous to a bench of judges.

Partial award, an award which deals with only part of a dispute; it may be interim or final.

Quitclaim, (verb) to renounce a claim; (noun) the renunciation; a method of transferring the whole of one's interest in property.

Seisin, originally the Anglo-Norman equivalent of possession in a general sense, seisin became a technical term for the freehold possession of land or chattels.

Sheriff, the chief royal officer in a shire.

Shire, an administrative district comprised of hundreds (called wapentakes in some parts) under the supervision of a sheriff.

Sole see **Feme.**

Specialty, a deed.

States General, (1) 1579–1795 the provinces of the Dutch Republic; (2) Assembly of the three estates (nobles, clergy, commoners) in France before the Revolution.

Stranger, foreigner.

Tenement, landholding.

Tithe, a tax imposed by the church of one-tenth of annual produce.

Umpire, a person appointed by the parties to make an award if arbitrators cannot agree.

Wardship, the custody and guardianship of heirs and their property until they came of age.

CHRONOLOGY

1566   James I b 19 June s of Mary, Queen of Scots and Henry Stewart, Lord Darnley.
1567   Darnley murdered February. Mary flees. James VI of Scotland July.
1589   James VI of Scotland m Anne of Denmark.
1603   James VI crowned **James I** of England. Tokugawa Shogunate in Japan. Shakespeare *Hamlet*. Plot to impose cousin Arabella Stuart. Raleigh imprisoned. Plague. First English bank. Ellesmere LC.
1604   First Parliament. Peace treaty with Spain.
1605   Guy Fawkes Gunpowder Plot. Death of Mughal Emperor Akhbar. Shakespeare *King Lear*.
1606   Plymouth Co to Maine and New England; London Co to Virginia. Shakespeare *Macbeth*. Coke CJCP.
1607   Protestants from Scotland and England settle in Ulster. Parliament rejects union with Scotland. All English and Scots born after James I's accession automatically citizens of both countries. Virginia Co founds Jamestown. *Vynior's Case*.
1608   French establish Quebec. Mughal Emperor grants East India Co first concession. Lands confiscated from Irish clans given to English and Scottish settlers.
1609   Shakespeare *Sonnets*.
1610   Parliament prorogued, then reassembled. Louis XIII King of France. Dutch bring tea to Europe.
1611   Parliament dissolved. King James Authorised Version of the Bible. Shakespeare *The Tempest*.
1612   d Henry, Prince of Wales. Tobacco grown in Virginia.
1613   Virginia colonists destroy French settlement. Galileo supports Copernicus. Coke CJKB.
1614   Second 'Addled' Parliament; dissolved.
1615   *Earl of Oxford's Case*.
1616   d Shakespeare. Raleigh sent to Guiana for El Dorado gold. Coke dismissed. *Ignoramus*. *Case of Commendams*.
1617   Villiers Duke of Buckingham and PC. Bacon LK.
1618   Raleigh executed for treason. Bacon LC.
1619   First slaves to Virginia. First colonial assembly under Governor Yeardley.
1620   *Mayflower*. Pilgrim Fathers found New Plymouth.
1621   Francis Bacon impeached. Wyatt Governor of Virginia. Rubens and Van Dyck fl.
1622   Parliament dissolved. Last of Year Books. Overbury Trials. Malynes *Consuetudo*.
1624   War with Spain. James I's last Parliament. Virginia Co dissolved; Crown Colony.

1625   d James I. Accession **Charles I**, m Henrietta Maria of France. Colonial Office. Plague. Grotius *De Jure Belli et Pacis*. Rembrandt fl.

1627   War with France.

1628   Petition of Right. 1st Duke of Buckingham murdered. Coke *Institutes I*. Harvey discovers blood circulation.

1629   Peace of Susa ends war with France. Parliament dissolved, rule without 1629–1640. Ferdinando Gorges and John Mason establish New Hampshire. Grand Remonstrance.

1630   England and France Treaty of Madrid. Massachusetts Bay Colony.

1631   Royal Commission to enquire into differences between courts. Doddridge *English Lawyer*.

1632   Maryland Charter. London's first coffee house.

1633   Lancashire Witches trial.

1634   Ship money levied.

1636   Rhode Island founded.

1637   Ferdinando Gorges given Massachusetts. East India Co sets up factories in Canton.

1638   Torture formally abolished in England. *Ship Money Case*.

1640   Short and Long Parliaments. Van Diemen takes Malacca.

1641   Star Chamber and all prerogative courts abolished. Council loses most judicial powers. Grand Remonstrance.

1642   Outbreak of Civil War. Battle of Edgehill. Tasman discovers Tasmania and New Zealand; later Tonga, Fiji, New Guinea and Australian mainland. First income and property taxes.

1643   Battle of Newbury. Last Ming emperor hangs himself. Milton *Areopagitica*.

1644   New Model Army. Battle of Marston Moor.

1645   Battle of Naseby. End of Civil War. John Milton fl.

1646   Charles I surrenders. Feudal tenures and Court of Wards abolished.

1647   Charles I escapes. March *Actions for Slander*. Putney Agreement of the People.

1648   Battle of Preston. Pride's Purge. Charles I captured and put on trial.

1649   Charles I executed. Monarchy abolished. Commonwealth. **Cromwell** Lord Protector. House of Lords abolished. Council of State. House of Commons supreme authority. Levellers arrested, Burford executions. Many Royalists flee to Virginia.

1650   Montrose executed. Scots defeated at Battle of Dunbar. New High Court. Act prohibiting trade with the Royalist colonies Virginia, Bermuda, Barbados and Antigua. Tea first drunk in England and first coffee house, in Oxford. English compulsory in law.

1651   Charles II crowned king of Scots, invades. Battle of Worcester, Royalist defeat. Charles II escapes to France. Hobbes *Leviathan*. Navigation Act.

1652   Barbados, Virginia and Maryland submit to Commonwealth; Parliament appoints Hale commission to investigate reform of the legal system. Parliament decrees judges to be paid fixed salary, not fees and perquisites. Bill for union of England and Scotland. Act of Pardon and Oblivion. Dutch settle Cape of Good Hope. First Anglo-Dutch War. France recognises Commonwealth.

1653   Oliver Cromwell dissolves Long Parliament. Nominated Assembly (Barebones Parliament). John Lilburne tried, acquitted, imprisoned. Parliament surrenders powers to Cromwell 'Lord Protector'. Commercial treaty with Portugal. Instrument of Government.

1654   Peace with Holland. First Protectorate Parliament.
1655   Parliament dissolved. Eleven military districts. Buccaneers rule in Jamaica.
1656   Second Protectorate Parliament. Sheppard *England's Balme*. Major Generals.
1657   Humble Petition and Advice. Cromwell refuses title of king, appoints new House of Lords. Treaty of Paris. East India first modern joint stock company. General Post Office. Style *Practical Register*. Wingate *Maximes*.
1658   Parliament summoned and dissolved. d Cromwell. Richard Cromwell Protector.
1659   Parliament summoned and dissolved. Army restores Rump Parliament. *Lambert v Monk*.
1660   Monk enters London. Convention Parliament invites **Charles II**. Restoration. Pepys starts diary. Military tenures and feudal dues abolished. Navigation Acts renewed restricting carriage of goods to Americas to British ships.
1661   Cavalier Parliament. Lambert executed.
1662   Charles m Catherine of Braganza. Act of Uniformity. Molière *L'Ecole des Femmes*. Royal Society charter. Boyle's Law.
1663   Turnpike Act. North Carolina founded. Hearth tax.
1664   Second Anglo-Dutch War. English seize New Amsterdam. First sprung coaches.
1665   Great Plague of London. Newton on gravity, binomial theorem etc.
1666   France declares war. Louis XIV Edict against Huguenots. Bunyan *Grace Abounding*. Great Fire of London. Stradivarius fl.
1667   Treaty of Breda, peace with Dutch. Clarendon dismissed. Cabal appointed. Milton *Paradise Lost*. Racine *Andromaque*.
1668   Triple Alliance: England, United Provinces, Sweden. Treaty of Lisbon: Portugal's independence. East India Co in Bombay. Rolle *Abridgment*.
1669   James, Duke of York declares Roman Catholic. Last meeting of 9 (of former 166 members) of Hanseatic League. Mogul emperor Aurangzeb destroys all non-Muslim churches and schools.
1670   Treaty of Dover with France. Pascal *Pensées*. South Carolina and Bahamas founded. Hudson Bay Co.
1671   Royal Exchange. Pirate Henry Morgan deputy governor of Jamaica.
1672   Third Anglo-Dutch War. Second Declaration of Indulgence.
1673   Charles forced to withdraw Declaration of Indulgence. End of Cabal.
1674   Treaty of Westminster ends Dutch War.
1675   Louis XIV gives Charles II 500,000 crowns, secret deal, Parliament prorogued. Spinoza *Ethics*.
1677   Parliament. 2nd Duke of Buckingham and Shaftesbury to Tower. Mary, daughter of James, Duke of York, m William of Orange. Aphra Behn *The Rover*.
1678   Murder of Edmund Godfrey. Titus Oates' Popish Plot. Danby impeached. Charles II switches alliance to United Provinces against French. Bunyan *Pilgrim's Progress*.
1679   Cavalier Parliament dissolved. Third Parliament. Habeas Corpus Act. Fourth Parliament. Petition for elected Parliament (Whigs) opposed by Tories.
1680   Exclusion Bill
1681   Charles II refuses to sign Exclusion Bill. Commons withholds supply. Third Exclusion Bill. New Parliament, Oxford. France claims Louisiana.

1682 Shaftesbury flees. Halley's comet.

1683 Rye House plot. Russell and Sydney executed. Dutch merchants in Canton.

1685 d Charles II. **James II**. Battle of Sedgmoor. Monmouth beheaded. Jeffreys CJ's Bloody Assize. Parliament dissolved for refusing to repeal Test Act. East India Co new charter, war against Aurangzeb. Chinese ports open to foreigners. French settle in Texas.

1686 James II claims power to dispense with statutes. *Godden v Hales* challenges Test Act. Court of High Commission. William of Orange's League of Augsburg (Empire, Sweden, Spain, United Provinces) against France. Appointments of Roman Catholics to army, church.

1687 Declaration of Indulgence. Newton *Philosophiae Naturalis Principia Mathematica*.

1688 Second Declaration of Indulgence. William of Orange invited, James II flees. William summons Parliament. Dampier explores Australia. Aphra Behn *Oroonoko*.

1689 Convention Parliament. Declaration of Rights. **William and Mary** proclaimed king and queen. Toleration Act. Louis XIV declares war on England and Spain. Peter the Great Tsar. John Locke *On Civil Government*. Purcell *Dido and Aeneas*. Bill of Rights.

1690 Convention Parliament dissolved. Battle of Beachy Head, French defeat English and Dutch fleets and burn Teignmouth. Battle of the Boyne. Land Tax. John Locke *Essay Concerning Human Understanding*.

1692 Marlborough suspected of treason and dismissed. Massacre of Glencoe. French attempted invasion, fleet destroyed. Lloyd's Coffee House centre of London's marine insurance.

1693 National Debt. New East India Co charter. Kingston, Jamaica, founded. Purcell *The Fairy Queen*.

1694 Marlborough restored but blamed for failure of attack on Brest. d Mary. Triennial Act. Bank of England. *Arbitrium Redivivum*.

1695 William III recaptures Namur. Licensing Act lapses, freedom of press.

1696 Barclay Plot. Treason Act. William III accepts Sweden's mediation in War of Grand Alliance. Board of Trade. Window tax.

1697 Fenwick executed for treason.

1698 Arbitration Act.

1700 Second Partition Treaty.

1701 Act of Settlement. d James II. Detroit settled. War of Spanish Succession.

1702 William III dismisses Tory Government. d William III. **Anne**. French settle Alabama.

BIBLIOGRAPHY

Official Sources
Acts and Ordinances of the Interregnum
Acts of the Privy Council see Dasent
Calendar of State Papers Domestic 1619–1623
History of Parliament
Lords Journal
National Archives
Parliamentary Archives
Statutes of the Realm 7 1695–1701 London, Record Commission 1820

Newspapers
Daily Courant issue 1691 London 1707
English Post with News Forieign and Domestick issue 47 London 1701
London Gazette issue 3681 London 1701
London Post with Intelligence Foreign and Domestick issue 136 London 1701
Read's Weekly Journal or British Gazetteer issue 4016 London 1759

Pamphlets
Hugh Peters *A Word for the Army* 11 October 1647 E 410 (16)
— *Good Work for a Good Magistrate* 17 June 1651 E 1364 (2) 3–11
Henry Robinson *Certain Considerations in Order to Obtain a More Speedy Cheap and Equal System of Justice Throughout the Nation* 14 November 1650 E 616 (2)
— *Certain Proposals in Order to a New Modelling of the Laws and Law Proceedings* 1653
Gerard Winstanley *Law of Freedom* Sabine 545

Anonymous
Anon (by the Author of *Regula Placitandi*) *Arbitrium Redivivum: or the Law of Arbitration; collected from the Law-Books both Ancient and Modern, and deduced to these Times: Wherein the whole Learning of Awards or Arbitrements is methodically treated with Several Forms of Submissions by way of Covenants and Bond; As also several Forms of Arbitrements or Awards* London, Isaac Cleeve 1694
IL (ed TE) *Lawes Resolutions of Women's Rights: or Lawes Provision for Woemen* London, Assigns of John More 1632
'By an Impartial Hand' *The Lives of All the Lords Chancellors* II 135–145 London, Printed for R Burrough and J Baker, 1708
The Memorandum Book of Richard Cholmeley of Brandsby, 1602-1623 North Yorks Record Office 44 1968

A True-Born Englishman *Francis, Lord Bacon: or the Case of National Corruption and Bribery* London, J Roberts 1721

A

LW Abbott *Law Reporting in England 1485–1585* London, Athlone Press 1973
ER Adair *The Sources for the History of the Council in the Sixteenth and Seventeenth Centuries* London, SPCK 1924, reprinted Port Washington NY, Kennikat Press 1971
Norma Adams 'The Judicial Conflict over Tithes' (1937) 52 *English Historical R* 1–22
IW Archer *The Pursuit of Stability in Elizabethan London* Cambridge, Cambridge University Press 2003

B

Francis Bacon *De Augmentis Scientiarum* Amsterdam, Ravestein 1662
— *Novum Organum Scientiarum* London, Wyngaerden 1620
Francis Bacon *Letters and Life* see Spedding; *Reports* see Ritchie; *Works* see Spedding
[Matthew Bacon] *The Compleat Arbitrator* By a Gentleman of the Middle Temple, London, Nutt and Gosling 1731 reprinted with a New Introduction by Derek Roebuck, Law Book Exchange, Clark NJ 2009
Nathaniel Bacon see Hassell Smith et al; Morgan et al; Saunders
JJ Bagley and F Tyrer eds *The Great Diurnal of Nicholas Blundell of Little Crosby, Lancashire* Record Society of Lancashire and Cheshire, Liverpool 1968–1972
JH Baker 'Coke's Notebooks and the Sources of His Reports' (1972) 30 *Cambridge Law Journal* 59–86
— 'The Common Lawyers and the Chancery: 1616' (1969) 9 *Irish Jurist* 368–392
— 'The Dark Age of English Legal History, 1500–1700' in Dafydd Jenkins ed *Legal History Studies 1972* Cardiff, University of Wales Press 1975 1–27
— ed *English Legal Manuscripts* microfiche IDC
— *An Introduction to English Legal History* London, Butterworths 3rd edn 1990
— *The Legal Profession and the Common Law: Historical Essays* London, Hambledon Press 1986
— ed *Legal Records and the Historian* London, Royal Historical Society 1975
— *The Oxford History of the Laws of England* VI 1483–1558 Oxford, Oxford University Press 2003
— ed *Reports from the Lost Notebooks of Sir James Dyer* 2 vols (1994) 109 and (1995) 110 London, Selden Society
Richard Baker *Theatrum Redivivum: or the Theatre Vindicated* London, Eaglesfield 1662
Richard Barber ed *John Aubrey: Brief Lives* London, Folio Society 1975
TG Barnes 'A Cheshire Seductress, Precedent and a "Sore Blow" to Star Chamber' in MS Arnold et al eds *On the Laws and Customs of England* Chapel Hill, University of North Carolina Press 1981
— 'Introduction to Coke's Commentary on Littleton' in AD Boyer ed *Law, Liberty and Parliament: Selected Essays on the Writings of Sir Edward Coke* Indianapolis, Liberty Fund 2004
— ed *Somerset Assize Orders 1629–1640* Frome, Somerset Record Society 1959 and *Somerset Assize Orders 1640–1649* 1971
— 'Star Chamber Litigants and Their Counsel, 1596–1641' in JH Baker ed *Legal Records and the Historian* London, Royal Historical Society 1978 7–28

JL Barton 'Equity in the Medieval Common Law' in RA Newman ed *Equity in the World's Legal Systems* Brussels, Bruylant 1973 39–155

Jonathan Bate and Eric Rasmussen eds *The RSC Shakespeare: William Shakespeare Complete Works* London, Macmillan 2007

EH Bates-Harbin ed *Somerset Quarter Sessions Records 1625–1639* London, Somerset Record Society 1908

— *Somerset Quarter Sessions Records 1646–1660* London, Somerset Record Society 1912

Jean Beauté *Un Grand Juriste Anglais: Sir Edward Coke 1552–1634* Paris, Presses Universitaires de France 1975

Guy De La Bédoyère see De La Bédoyère

James Behrens 'The History of Mediation of Probate Disputes' (2002) 68 *Arbitration* 138–143

Thomas Birch *Memoirs of the Reign of Queen Elizabeth from 1581 Until Her Death* London, Millar 2 vols 1754

W de G Birch *The Historical Charters and Constitutional Documents of the City of London* London, Whiting revised ed 1887

William Blackstone *Commentaries on the Laws of England* Oxford, Clarendon Press 1765

FC Boorman 'Advertising Arbitration: The Origins of the Profession' (2016) 82 *Arbitration* 118–121

John Bossy ed *Disputes and Settlements: Law and Human Relations in the West* Cambridge, Cambridge University Press 1983

Catherine Drinker Bowen *The Lion and the Throne: The Life and Times of Sir Edward Coke (1552–1634)* Boston, Little Brown 1956

AD Boyer ed *Law, Liberty and Parliament: Selected Essays on the Writings of Sir Edward Coke* Indianapolis, Liberty Fund 2004

— *Sir Edward Coke and the Elizabethan Age* Stanford, Stanford University Press 2003

— 'Sir Edward Coke: Royal Servant, Royal Favorite' http://www.law.harvard.edu/ programs/ames_foundation/BLHC07/Boyer%20Sir%20Edward%20Coke%20 -%20Royal%20Servant%20and%20Royal%20Favorite.pdf [Accessed 9 July 2016]

JA Bradney ed *The Diary of Walter Powell of Llantilio Crosseny in the County of Monmouth, Gentleman, 1603–1654* Bristol, John Wright 1907

William Bray ed *The Diary of John Evelyn* London, Dent 2 vols 1907

JS Brewer and W Bullen eds *Calendar of the Carew Manuscripts Preserved in the Archiepiscopal Palace at Lambeth* London, Public Record Office 6 vols 1867–1873

Asa Briggs *A Social History of England* Harmondsworth, Penguin 1991

Robert Brooke *La Graunde Abridgement* London, Richard Tottell 1573

CW Brooks *Pettifoggers and Vipers of the Commonwealth* Cambridge, Cambridge University Press 1986

Christopher Brooks and Michael Lobban eds *Communities and Courts in Britain 1150–1900* London, Hambledon Press 1997

FW Brooks ed *Supplementary Stiffkey Papers* London, Royal Historical Society, Camden Miscellany XVI 1936

John Bruce and TT Perowne *The Correspondence of Matthew Parker* Cambridge, Cambridge University Press (Parker Society) 1853

Arthur Bryant *Samuel Pepys: The Man in the Making* London, Collins new edn 1967

WH Bryson *Cases Concerning Equity and the Courts of Equity 1550–1660* 2 vols (2000) 117 and (2001) 118 London, Selden Society

— 'The Equity Jurisdiction of the Exchequer' in Dafydd Jenkins ed *Legal History Studies 1972* Cardiff, University of Wales Press 1975

— 'Law Reports in England from 1603 to 1660' in Chantal Stebbings ed *Law Reporting in England* London, Hambledon Press 1995 113–122

C

John Lord Campbell *The Lives of the Chief Justices of England* London, Murray 2nd edn, 3 vols 1858

Bernard Capp 'Life, Love and Litigation' (2004) 182 *Past and Present* 55–83

Edward Chamberlain *Angliae Notitia or the Present State of England* London, Sawbridge and Wells 1684

WA Champion 'Recourse to the Law and the Meaning of the Great Litigation Decline, 1650–1755: Some Clues from the Shrewsbury Local Courts' in CW Brooks and Michael Lobban eds *Communities and Courts in Britain 1150–1900* London, Hambledon Press 1997 179–198

ML Cioni *Women and Law in Elizabethan England with Particular Reference to the Court of Chancery* New York, Garland Publishing 1985

Kenneth Charlton *Women, Religion and Education in Early Modern England* London, Routledge 1999

DJH Clifford ed *The Diaries of Lady Anne Clifford* Stroud, Sutton revised pbk 1992, 1998

JS Cockburn *A History of English Assizes 1558–1714* Cambridge, Cambridge University Press 1972

— *Western Circuit Assize Orders 1629–1648* London, Royal Historical Society 1976 (Camden Socy 4th series XVII)

HAL Cockerell and Edwin Green *The British Insurance Business: A Guide to its History and Records* Sheffield, Sheffield Academic Press 2nd edn 1994

JH Cohen *Commercial Arbitration and the Law* New York, Appleton 1918

Edward Coke 'The Complete Copyholder' in William Hawkins ed *Three Law Tracts* London, Worrall 1764

— *The Institutes of the Lawes of England* in 4 parts, various dates and edns, now reprinted Clark NJ, Law Book Exchange 2002

MAR Cooper 'Robert Hooke's Work as a Surveyor for the City of London in the Aftermath of the Great Fire' *Notes and Records of the Royal Society* Pt 1 (1997) 51 161–174; Pt 2 (1998) 52 25–38; Pt 3 'Settlement of Disputes and Complaints Arising from Rebuilding' (1998) 52 205–220

Michael Cooper *'A More Beautiful City': Robert Hooke and the Rebuilding of London After the Great Fire* Stroud, Sutton 2003

DR Coquillette *The Civilian Writers of Doctors' Commons, London: Three Centuries of Juristic Innovation in Comparative, Commercial and International Law* Berlin, Duncker and Humblot 1988

— *Francis Bacon* Edinburgh, Edinburgh University Press 1992

John Cowell *Institutiones Juris Anglicani* Cambridge, Legat 1605

[John Cowell] *A Law Dictionary: or, the Interpreter of Words and Terms Used either in the Common or Statute Laws of that Part of Great Britain call'd England; and in Tenures and Jocular Customs* London, D Browne and others 1708

JD Cowley *A Bibliography of Abridgments, Digests, Dictionaries and Indexes of English Law to the Year 1800* London, Quaritch for the Selden Society 1932

Thomas Craig *Ius Feudale* Edinburgh, Ruddiman 1732

GHJ Critchlow 'The Concept of Arbitration' PhD thesis, King's College London 2001

YC Croker ed *Some Specialities in the Life of M Warwick* London, Percy Society 1848

TC Curtis 'Quarter Sessions Appearances and Their Background: a Seventeenth-Century Regional Study' in JS Cockburn ed *Crime in England: 1550–1800* London, Methuen 1977 135–154

Richard Cust and PG Lake 'Sir Richard Grosvenor and the Rhetoric of Magistracy' (1981) 52 *Historical Research* 40–53

D

JR Dasent ed *Acts of the Privy Council of England* New Series London, HMSO 32 vols 1890–1964

JP Dawson 'The Privy Council and Private Law in the Tudor and Stuart Periods: I and II' (1950) 48 *Michigan Law Review* 393–428 and 627–656

— *A History of Lay Judges* Cambridge, Mass, Harvard University Press 1960

James Daybell, '"Suche newes as on the Quenes hye wayes we have mett": the News and Intelligence Networks of Elizabeth Talbot, Countess of Shrewsbury (c1527–1608)' in James Daybell ed *Women and Politics in Early Modern England, 1450–1700* Aldershot, Ashgate 2004 114–131

Guy De La Bédoyère *Particular Friends: The Correspondence of Samuel Pepys and John Evelyn* Woodbridge, Boydell 2nd edn 2005

Nicolas de Passeribus see Passeribus

Denzil, Lord Hollis *The Grand Question Concerning the Judicature of the House of Peers* London, Janeway 1669

AV Dicey *The Privy Council* London, Macmillan 1887

Charles Dickens *Oliver Twist* London, Richard Bentley 1838

John Doddridge *The English Lawyer* London, More 1631

— *The Lawyers Light: or, A Due Direction for the Study of the Law... written by the Reverend and Learned Professor thereof, JD To which is Annexed for the Affinitie of the subject, another Treatise, called The Use of the Law* London, Benjamin Fisher 1628

Philippe Dollinger *The German Hansa* Stanford, Stanford University Press 1970

Charles Du Fresne, Sieur Ducange *Glossarium Manuale ad Scriptores Mediae et Infimae Latinitatis, ex Magnis Glossariis Caroli du Fresne, Domini du Cange, et Carpentarii in Compendium Redactum, Multisque Verbis et Dicendi Formulis Auctum*, Halle, Widow Gebauer and Son 1772

Daphne Du Maurier *Golden Lads: a Study of Anthony Bacon, Francis and their Friends* London, Gollancz 1975

— *The Winding Stair: Francis Bacon, His Rise and Fall* New York, Doubleday 1977

Wilbur Dunkel *William Lambarde, Elizabethan Jurist 1536–1601* New Brunswick, Rutgers University Press 1965

DN Durant *Bess of Hardwick: Portrait of an Elizabethan Dynast* London, Peter Owen 1999

E

Peter Earle 'The Female Labour Market in London in the Late 17th and Early 18th Centuries' (1989) 42 *Economic History R* 2nd series 328–353

Henry Elsynge *The Manner of Holding Parliaments in England* Shannon, Irish University Press 1971

GR Elton 'The Rule of Law in Sixteenth-Century England' in AJ Slavin ed *Tudor Men and Institutions: Studies in English Law and Government* Baton Rouge, Louisiana State University Press 1972 265–294

FG Emmison *Elizabethan Life: Wills of the Essex Gentry and Merchants* Chelmsford, Essex Record Office 1978

John Evelyn *The Diaries of John Evelyn* London, Boydell Press 2003

[John Evelyn] *Fumifugium, or, The Inconveniencie of the Aer and Smoak of London Dissipated Together With Some Remedies Humbly Proposed by JE Esq to His Sacred Majestie and to the Parliament Now Assembled* London, Bedel and Collins 1661

Adam Eyre 'A Dyurnall, or Catalogue of All my Accions and Expences from the 1st of January 1647' in *Yorkshire Diaries and Autobiographies in the Seventeenth and Eighteenth Centuries* London, Surtees Society LXV 1875

F

FJ Fisher ed 'The State of England by Sir Thomas Wilson, AD 1600' XVI *Camden Miscellany* London, Royal Historical Society 1936

Anthony Fitzherbert *La Graunde Abridgement* London, John Rastell 3 vols 1514–1516

Adam Fox 'Custom, Memory and the Authority of Writing' in Paul Griffiths, Adam Fox and Steve Hindle eds *The Experience of Authority in Early Modern England* London, Macmillan 1996 89–116

HR Fox Bourne *The Life of John Locke* London, King 2 vols 1876

Antonia Fraser *The Weaker Vessel: Women's Lot in Seventeenth Century England* London, Phoenix Press 2002

Abraham Fraunce *The Lawiers Logike* London, How 1588 reprinted Clark NJ, Law Book Exchange 2013

Thomas Fuller *History of the Worthies of England* London, TG, WL and WG 1662

G

George Garnett '"The Ould Fields": Law and History in the Prefaces to Sir Edward Coke's Reports' (2013) 34 *Journal of Legal History* 245–284

JH Gleason *The Justices of the Peace in England 1558–1640* Oxford, Clarendon Press 1969

John Godolphin *Repertorium Canonicum: or, an Abridgment of the Ecclesiastical Laws of this Realm, Consistent with the Temporal* London, Atkins 3rd edn 1687

Laura Gowing 'Language, Power and the Law: Women's Slander Litigation in Early Modern London' in Jenny Kermode and Garthine Walker eds *Women, Crime and the Courts in Early Modern England* London, University College of London Press 1994 26–47

— 'Women in the World of Pepys' in Margarette Lincoln ed *Samuel Pepys: Plague, Fire, Revolution* London, Thames and Hudson 2015 72–79

Charles Gross 'The Court of Piepowder' (1906) 20 *Quarterly Journal of Economics* 231–249 (revised, reprinted)

— ed *Select Cases Concerning the Law Merchant* I London (1908) 23 Selden Society

RT Gunther *Early Science in Oxford: Part X The Life and Work of Robert Hooke Pt IV* Oxford, printed for the author 1935

John Guy and Hugh Beale *Law and Social Change in British History* London, Royal Historical Society 1984

H
Matthew Hale *The History of the Common Law of England* Chicago, Chicago University Press 1971

GDG Hall ed *Tractatus de Legibus et Consuetudinibus Regni Anglie Qui Glanvilla Vocatur: The Treatise on the Laws and Customs of the Realm of England Commonly Called Glanvill* London, Nelson for the Selden Society 1965

Hubert Hall ed *Select Cases Concerning the Law Merchant* II London, (1929) 46 Selden Society

John Halliwell ed *The Autobiography and Correspondence of Sir Simonds D'Ewes Bart During the Reigns of James I and Charles I* London, Richard Bentley 2 vols 1845

TD Hardy *Syllabus of Documents in Rymer's Foedera* London, Rolls Ser 3 vols 1869–1885

Christopher Harrison 'Manor Courts and the Governance of Tudor England' in Christopher Brooks and Michael Lobban *Communities and Courts in Britain 1150–1900* London, Hambledon Press 1997 43–59

George Harrison *Substance of a Report on the Laws and Jurisdiction of the Stannaries in Cornwall* London, Longman et al 1835

William Harrison *An Historical Description of the Iland of Britaine* London, New Shakespere Society 1877

JS Hart *Justice Upon Petition: the House of Lords and the Reformation of Justice 1621–1675* London, Harper Collins 1991

A Hassell Smith, GM Baker and RW Kenny eds *The Papers of Nathaniel Bacon of Stiffkey* Norwich, Norfolk Record Society I 1556–1577, XLVI 1978/1979

— and GM Baker eds *The Papers of Nathaniel Bacon of Stiffkey* Norwich, Norfolk Record Society II 1578–1585, XLIX 1983

—, — *The Papers of Nathaniel Bacon of Stiffkey* Norwich, Norfolk Record Society III 1586–1595 LIII 1990

Felicity Heal 'Reputation and Honour in Court and Country: Lady Elizabeth Russell and Sir Thomas Hoby' (1996) 6 *Transactions of the Royal Historical Society* 161–178

H Hearder and HR Loyn eds *British Government and Administration: Studies Presented to SB Chrimes* Cardiff, University of Wales Press 1974

RH Helmholz 'Canon Law and English Common Law' Selden Society Lecture 1983 now in *The Selden Society Lectures* Buffalo NY, Hein 2003 513–534

— *Marriage Litigation in Medieval England* Cambridge, Cambridge University Press 1974

— *Select Cases on Defamation to 1600* London, 101 Selden Society [1985] 66–67

— book review of MS Arnold et al eds *On the Laws and Customs of England: Essays in Honor of Samuel E Thorne* Chapel Hill, University of North Carolina Press 1981 in (1982) 95 *Harvard Law Review* 723–734

Felicity Henderson 'Unpublished Material from the Memorandum Book of Robert Hooke, Guildhall Library MS 1758' (2007) 61 *Notes and Records of the Royal Society* 129–175

George Herbert *A Priest to the Temple or the Country Parson* London, Tooke 1652

CH Herford, Percy Simpson and Evelyn Simpson eds *Ben Jonson* Oxford, Clarendon Press 11 vols 1925–1952

Christopher Hill *God's Englishman: Oliver Cromwell and the English Revolution* Harmondsworth, Penguin 1970

LM Hill ed *The Ancient State Authoritie, and Proceedings of the Court of Requests by Sir Julius Caesar* London, Cambridge University Press 1975

Steve Hindle 'The Keeping of the Public Peace' in Paul Griffiths, Adam Fox and Steve Hindle eds *The Experience of Authority in Early Modern England* London, Macmillan 1996 213–248

Thomas Hobbes *Dialogue Between a Philosopher and a Student of the Common Laws of England* (?1673) Chicago, University of Chicago Press 1971

Pearl Hogrefe 'Legal Rights of Tudor Women and their Circumvention by Men and Women' (1972) 33 *Sixteenth Century Journal* 97–105.

WS Holdsworth *A History of English Law* London, Methuen 17 vols 1903–1972

Martin Holmes *Proud Northern Lady: Lady Anne Clifford 1590–1676* Chichester, Phillimore corrected, reprinted 1984

OW Holmes *The Common Law* Boston, Little Brown 1881

Robert Hooke *Micrographia, or Some Physiological Descriptions of Minute Bodies Made by Magnifying Glasses with Observations and Enquiries Thereupon* New York, Dover, reprinted 1961. See also Henderson; Gunther; and Robinson and Adams

— *Diary* see Robinson and Adams; see also Gunther; Henderson

Richard Hooker *Laws of Ecclesiastical Polity* in *The Works of That Learned and Judicious Divine, Mr Richard Hooker: with an Account of His Life and Death. Arranged by John Keble* Oxford, Clarendon Press 1876

Henry Horwitz and James Oldham 'John Locke, Lord Mansfield and Arbitration During the Eighteenth Century' (1993) 36 *The Historical Journal* 137–159

Hostiensis [Henricus de Segusio] *Lectura in Quinque Libros Decretalium* Paris 1512

Ralph Houlbrooke *Church Courts and the People during the English Reformation 1520–1570* Oxford, Oxford University Press 1979

B Howell et al ed *A Complete Collection of State Trials* London, Longman 21 vols 1816

Kate Hubbard *A Material Girl: Bess of Hardwick, 1527–1608* London, Short Books 2001

William Hudson *A Treatise of the Court of Star Chamber* first printed in *Collectanea Juridica II* London, Brooke 1792, reprinted Birmingham, Al, Legal Classics Library 1986 with an Introduction by TG Barnes

I

David Ibbetson 'Common Law and *Ius Commune*' Selden Society Lecture 2001 now in *The Selden Society Lectures* Buffalo NY, Hein 2003 673–705

— 'Law and Custom: Insurance in Sixteenth-Century England' (2008) 29 *Journal of Legal History* 291–308

— and Matthew Dyson eds *Law and Legal Process: Substantive Law and Procedure in English Legal History* Cambridge, Cambridge University Press 2013

Martin Ingram '"Scolding Women Cucked or Washed": a Crisis in Gender Relations in Early Modern England?' in Jennifer Kermode and Garthine Walker eds, *Women, Crime and the Courts in Early Modern England* London, UCL Press 1999 48–80

MJ Ingram *Church Courts, Sex and Marriage in England, 1570-1640* Cambridge, Cambridge University Press 1988

— 'Communities and Courts: Law and Disorder in Early 17th Century Wiltshire' in JS Cockburn ed *Crime in England 1550–1800* London, Methuen 1977 110–134

J

Charles Jackson ed *The Autobiography of Mrs Alice Thornton, of East Newton, Co. York* Cambridge, Cambridge University Press 2010

Lisa Jardine *The Curious Life of Robert Hooke: the Man Who Measured London* London, Harper Collins 2003

— and Alan Stewart *Hostage to Fortune: The Troubled Life of Francis Bacon 1561–1626* London, Gollancz 1998

Dafydd Jenkins ed *Legal History Studies 1972* Cardiff, University of Wales Press 1975

PE Jones *The Fire Court, Calendar to the Judgments and Decrees* London, Corporation of London 2 vols 1966

WJ Jones 'The Crown and the Courts in England, 1603–1625' in AD Boyer ed *Law, Liberty and Parliament* Indianapolis, Liberty Fund 2004

— 'Elizabethan Marine Insurance: the Judicial Undergrowth' (1960) 2 *Business History* 53–66

— 'The Exchequer of Chester in the Last Years of Elizabeth I' in AJ Slavin ed *Tudor Men and Institutions* Baton Rouge, Louisiana State UP University Press 1972 123–170

K

Patrick Keane 'Meeting the Challenge of Regional Forum Competition or Our House Rules' (2012) *Federal Judicial Scholarship* 9

JL Kermode and Garthine Walker (eds), *Women, Crime and the Courts in Early Modern England* London, UCL Press 1999

JM Keynes *The End of Laissez-Faire* London, Hogarth Press 1926

AKR Kirafly *Potter's Historical Introduction to English Law and its Institutions* London, Sweet & Maxwell 4th edn 1962

MC Klingelsmith (tr) *Statham's Abridgment of the Law* Clark NJ, Lawbook Exchange (reprinted) 2 vols 2007

LA Knafla *Law and Politics in Jacobean England* Cambridge, Cambridge University Press 1977

Stewart Kyd *A Treatise on the Law of Awards* London, Johnson and others 2nd edn 1799; reprinted with a new Introduction by Derek Roebuck, Clark NJ, Law Book Exchange 2009

L

William Lambarde *Archeion, or, A Discourse upon the High Courts of Justice in England* London, Seile 1635 and see McIlwain

— *Eirenarcha, or of the Office of the Justices of the Peace* London, Assigns Tottell 1588

Norma Landau *Justices of the Peace 1679–1760* Berkeley, University of California Press 1984

Lansdowne MS British Museum MS BL 266

William Langland *Piers Plowman* see Skeat

Agnes Latham and Joyce Youngs eds *The Letters of Sir Walter Ralegh* Exeter, University of Exeter Press 1999

Robert Latham and William Mathews eds *The Diary of Samuel Pepys* London, Bell 10 vols 1970–1983; XI Index London, Harper Collins 1995

IS Leadam ed *Select Cases in the Court of Requests AD 1497–1569* (1898) 12 Selden Society

MD Legge 'Anglo-Norman and the Historian' (1941) 26 *History* 163–175

BP Levack *The Civil Lawyers in England 1603–1641: a Political Study* Oxford, Clarendon Press 1973

J Lilburne *The Just Man's Justification* London 1647

TH Lloyd *England and the German Hanse, 1157–1611: a Study of Their Trade and Commercial Diplomacy* Cambridge, Cambridge University Press 2002

Edmund Lodge *Illustrations of British History* 5 vols London, Nicol 1791

JS Loengard *London Viewers and Their Certificates 1508–1558* London, London Record Society 1989

John Loftis ed *The Memoirs of Anne, Lady Halkett, and Ann, Lady Fanshawe* Oxford, Clarendon Press 1979

MS Lovell *Bess of Hardwick: First Lady of Chatsworth* London, Abacus 2006

William Lyndwood *Provinciale, seu Constitutiones Anglie* Antwerp, Brickman 1525

M

Lord Macaulay *Lord Bacon* London, Longman 1873

Alan Macfarlane ed *The Diary of Ralph Josselin, 1616–1683* Oxford, Oxford University Press new edn 1991

— *The Family Life of Ralph Josselin: a 17th Century Clergyman* Cambridge, Cambridge University Press 1977

MC McGaw 'Travels in Alsatia: "Judges of the Parties' Own Chusing", "Monstrous Powers", and the Role of the Courts' in Anthony Thornton and William Godwin eds *Construction Law: Themes and Practice* London, Sweet & Maxwell 1998 131–187

CH McIlwain and PL Ward ed *Archeion, or a Discourse on the High Courts of Justice in England* Cambridge, Mass, Harvard University Press 1957

Michael Macnair 'The Nature and Function of the Early Chancery Reports' in Chantal Stebbings ed *Law Reporting in England* London, Hambledon Press 1995 123–132

Michael Maier *Jocus Severus, hoc est, Tribunal Aequum* Frankfurt am Main, Theodore de Brij 1617

FW Maitland *Equity also the Forms of Action at Common Law* Cambridge, Cambridge University Press 1909

— 'Introduction' to WJ Whittaker *The Mirror of Justices* (1893) 7 London Selden Society

Barbara Malament 'The "Economic Liberalism" of Sir Edward Coke' (1967) 76 *Yale Law Journal* 1321–1358 reprinted in AD Boyer ed *Law, Liberty and Parliament* Indianapolis, Liberty Fund 2004 186–223

Gerard Malynes *Consuetudo, vel, Lex Mercatoria, or The Antient Law-Merchant, Divided into Three Parts: According to the Essentiall Parts of Trafficke* London, Islip 1622, 2nd edn R Young for Nicolas Bourne 1636

John March *Actions for Slander... to which is added Awards or Arbitrements Methodised under several Grounds and Heads collected out of our Year-Books and other Private Authentic Authorities, wherein is principally showed what Arbitrements are good in Law and what not* London, Walbank 1648

— 2nd edition 1648 added *The Second Part of Actions for Slanders, with a Second Part of Arbitrements, together with Directions and Presidents to them very usefull to all Men. To which is added Libels &c* London, printed for Mathew Walbancke, at Grayes Inne Gate 1649

— 3rd enlarged edn WB [William Brown] London, Elizabeth Walbanck 1674

— *Amicus Reipublicae, the Commonwealth's Friend, or an Exact and Speedie Course to Justice and Right, and for Preventing and Determining of tedious Law Suits...* London, Eaglesfield 1651

RG Marsden *Select Pleas in the Court of Admiralty I* (1894) 6 Selden Society and *II* (1897) 11 Selden Society

Karl Marx and Friedrich Engels *The German Ideology* Amherst NY, Prometheus Books 1998

Nieves Mathews *Francis Bacon: the History of a Character Assassination* New Haven, Yale University Press 1996

NL Matthews *William Sheppard, Cromwell's Law Reformer* Cambridge, Cambridge University Press 1984

Marcel Mauss *The Gift* London, Routledge 1970

DM Meads ed *The Diary of Lady Margaret Hoby, 1599–1605* London, Routledge & Sons 1930

TC Mendenhall *The Shrewsbury Drapers and the Welsh Wool Trade in the XVI and XVII Centuries* Oxford, Oxford University Press 1953

Charlotte Merton 'The Women who Served Queen Mary and Queen Elizabeth: Ladies, Gentlewomen and Maids of the Privy Chamber 1553–1603' Cambridge University PhD thesis 1992

G Alan Metters 'The Rulers and Merchants of King's Lynn in the Early 17th Century' University of East Anglia PhD thesis 1982

— Victor Morgan, Elizabeth Rutledge and Barry Taylor eds *The Papers of Nathaniel Bacon of Stiffkey* VI (1608–1613) and VII (1614–1622. Forthcoming.

DE Mingay *Enclosure and the Small Farmer in the Age of the Industrial Revolution* London, Macmillan 1968

Louis Moland *Oeuvres Complètes de Voltaire* Paris, Garnier 1877–1885

Cecil Monro *Acta Cancellariae, or Selections from the Records of the Court of Chancery Remaining in the Office of Reports and Entries* London, Benning 1847

Joanna Moody ed *The Private Life of an Elizabethan Lady: the Diary of Lady Margaret Hoby 1599–1605* Thrupp, Sutton 1998

HJ Morehouse ed 'The Diurnall of Adam Eyre' in *Yorkshire Diaries and Autobiographies in the 17th and 18th Centuries* London, Surtees Society LXV 1875

Victor Morgan, Jane Key and Barry Taylor eds *The Papers of Nathaniel Bacon of Stiffkey* Norwich, Norfolk Record Society IV 1596–1602, LXIV 2000

— Elizabeth Rutledge and Barry Taylor eds *The Papers of Nathaniel Bacon of Stiffkey* Norwich, Norfolk Record Society V 1603–1607, LXXIV 2010

John Morrill 'The Stuarts' in KO Morgan ed *The Oxford History of Britain* Oxford, Oxford University Press 1988 327–398

Ivo Mosley *In the Name of the People* Exeter, Societas 2013

Craig Muldrew 'The Culture of Reconciliation: Community and the Settlement of Economic Disputes in Early Modern England' (1996) 39 *The Historical Journal* 915–942

— '"A Mutual Assent of Her Mind"? Women, Debt, Litigation and Contract in Early Modern England (2003) *History Workshop Journal* (Spring) 55(1) 47–71

Thomas Mun *England's Treasure by Forraign Trade or The Balance of Our Forraign Trade is The Rule of our Treasure* London, Thomas Clark 1664, reprinted Oxford, Basil Blackwell 1928

Anthony Musson 'Arbitration and the Legal Profession in Late Medieval England', in David Ibbetson and Matthew Dyson eds *Law and Legal Process: Substantive Law and Procedure in English Legal History*, Cambridge, Cambridge University Press 2013 56–76

— 'Myth, Mistake, Invention? Excavating the Foundations of the English Legal Tradition' in Andrew Lewis and Michael Lobban eds *Law and History: Current Legal Issues 2003* Oxford, Oxford University Press 2004 63–81

MJ Mustill and SC Boyd *The Law and Practice of Commercial Arbitration in England* London, Butterworths 1st edn 1982, 2nd edn 1989

N

LB Namier *Avenues of History* London, Hamish Hamilton 1952

JE Neale *Queen Elizabeth I* London, Jonathan Cape 1934, Penguin reprinted, revised 1971

RA Newman ed *Equity in the World's Legal Systems* Brussels, Bruylant 1973

JT Noonan Jr *Bribes* Berkeley, University of California Press 1984

Laura Norsworthy *The Lady of Bleeding Heart Yard* London, John Murray 1935

Roger North *Discourses on the Study of the Laws* London, Baldwin 1824

O

James Oldham and Su Jin Kim 'Arbitration in America: The Early History' (2013) 31 *Law and History R* 241–266

P

Nicolas de Passeribus *Conciliatio Cunctarum Legum etc* (3rd edn JG Simon) August Boetius, Frankfurt and Leipzig 1685

RR Pennington *Stannary Law: A History of the Mining Law of Cornwall and Devon* Newton Abbot, David and Charles 1973

Samuel Pepys *Correspondence* see De La Bédoyère; *Diary* see Latham and Mathews

TFT Plucknett '*Bonham's Case* and Judicial Review' (1926) 40 *Harvard Law Review* 30–70 reprinted in AD Boyer ed *Law, Liberty and Parliament: Selected Essays on the Writings of Sir Edward Coke* Indianapolis, Liberty Fund 2004 150–185

— *A Concise History of the Common Law* London, Butterworths 2nd edn 1936

— 'The Genesis of Coke's Reports' (1942) 27 *Cornell Law Quarterly* 190–213 reprinted in TFT Plucknett *Studies in Legal History* London, Hambledon Press 1983

JGA Pocock *The Ancient Constitution and the Feudal Law: A Study of English Historical Thought in the Seventeenth Century: A Reissue with a Retrospect* Cambridge, Cambridge University Press 1987

Karl Polanyi *The Great Transformation* Boston, Beacon Press 1944

Linda A Pollock 'Honor, Gender, and Reconciliation in Elite Culture, 1570–1700' (2007) 46 *Journal of British Studies* 3–29

Vincent Ponko Jr 'The Privy Council and the Spirit of Elizabethan Economic Management, 1558–1603' (1968) 58 *Transactions of the American Philosophical Society (New Series)* 1–63

Eric Poole 'West's *Symboleography*: An Elizabethan Formulary' in John Guy and Hugh Beale eds *Law and Social Change in British History* London, Royal Historical Society 1984 96–106

Linda Porter *Katherine the Queen* London, Pan 2010

WR Prest 'Counsellors' Fees and Earnings in the Age of Sir Edward Coke' in JH Baker ed *Legal Records and the Historian* London, Royal Historical Society 1978 165–184

— 'Law and Women's Rights in Early Modern England' (1991) 6 *The Seventeenth Century* 169–187

William Prynne *The First Part of a Brief Register, Kalendar and Survey of the Several Kinds, Forms of all Parliamentary Writs* London, printed for the author 1664

MB Pulman *The Elizabethan Privy Council in the Fifteen-Seventies* Berkeley, University of California Press 1971

R

Steve Rappaport *Worlds Within Worlds: Structures of Life in Sixteenth-Century London* Cambridge, Cambridge University Press revised edn 2002

William Rastell *A Colleccion of Entries of Declarations, Barres...* London, Atkins 1670

Carole Rawcliffe and Susan Flower 'English Noblemen and Their Advisers: Consultation and Collaboration in the Later Middle Ages' (1986) 25 *J British Studies* 157–177

Conyers Read ed *William Lambarde and Local Government, His 'Ephemeris' and Twenty-Nine Charges to Juries and Commissions* Ithaca NY, Folger 1962

Thomas Ridley *A View of the Civile and Ecclesiasticall Law: and Wherein the Practice of Them is Streitned and may be Relieved Within This Land* Oxford, Davis 3rd edn 1662

John Ritchie ed *Reports of Cases Decided by Francis Bacon, Baron Verulam, Viscount St Albans, Lord Chancellor of England, in the High Court of Chancery (1617–1621)* London, Sweet & Maxwell 1932

HW Robinson and Walter Adams *The Diary of Robert Hooke MA MD FRS 1672–1680* London, Taylor and Francis 1935

Derek Roebuck *Ancient Greek Arbitration* Oxford, HOLO Books 2001

— 'L'Arbitrage en Droit Anglais avant 1558' (2002) 3 *Revue de l'Arbitrage* 535–577

— *The Background of the Common Law* Oxford, Oxford University Press 2nd edn 1990

— '"Best to Reconcile": Mediation and Arbitration in the Ancient Greek World' (2000) 66 *Arbitration* 275–287

— *The Charitable Arbitrator: How to Mediate and Arbitrate in Louis XIV's France* Oxford, HOLO Books 2002

— 'The Corporeity of a Cobweb: French in England before AD1204' in *Disputes and Differences* 215–232

— 'The Diplock Report on Mercenaries' *New Statesman* 13 August 1976, reprinted in *Disputes and Differences* 79–83

— *Disputes and Differences: Comparisons in Law, Language and History* Oxford, HOLO Books 2010

— *Early English Arbitration* Oxford, HOLO Books 2008

— 'Gerard Malynes, Arbitrator' (1996) 62 *Arbitration* 12–15, reprinted in Derek Roebuck *Disputes and Differences* 312–317

— *The Golden Age of Arbitration: Dispute Resolution under Elizabeth I* Oxford HOLO Books 2015
— 'Insights into Equity' (2003) 15 *Bond Law Review* 74–85 reprinted in *Disputes and Differences* 262–272
— 'The Life and Death of the *Compromissum*' (2011) 1 *Revista Română de Arbitraj* 29–39
— 'The London Centre for International Mediation and Arbitration in the Reign of Elizabeth I (2014) 30 *Arbitration International* 577–588
— *Mediation and Arbitration in the Middle Ages: England 1154 to 1558* Oxford HOLO Books 2013
— *A Miscellany of Disputes* Oxford, HOLO Books 2000
— 'The Myth of Modern Mediation' (2007) 73 *Arbitration* 105–116
— 'Odds or Evens: How Many Arbitrators?' (2014) 80 *Arbitration* 8–15
— 'A Short History of Arbitration' in Neil Kaplan, Jill Spruce and Michael Moser *Hong Kong and China Arbitration: Cases and Materials* Hong Kong, Butterworths 1994
— 'Sources for the History of Arbitration: a Bibliographical Introduction' (1998) 14 *Arbitration International* 236–343
— 'Time to Think: Understanding Dispute Management' (2011) 72 *Arbitration* 342–350
— and Bruno de Loynes de Fumichon *Roman Arbitration* Oxford, HOLO Books 2004
HE Rollins ed *Old English Ballads 1553–1625* Cambridge, Cambridge University Press 1920
Ian Rowney 'Arbitration in Gentry Disputes of the Later Middle Ages' (1982) 67 *History* 367–376
Thomas Rymer *Foedera, Conventiones, Literæ etc* The Hague, Neaulme 1739

S

WL Sachse ed *The Diary of Roger Lowe of Ashton-in-Makerfield, Lancashire 1663–1674* New Haven, Yale University Press 1938
FR Sanborn *Origins of the Early English Maritime and Commercial Law* New York, American Historical Association 1930
HW Saunders ed *The Official Papers of Sir Nathaniel Bacon of Stiffkey, Norfolk, as Justice of the Peace 1580–1620* London, Royal Historical Society (Camden 3rd series XXVI) 1915
GO Sayles ed *Select Cases in the Court of King's Bench under Edward III V* (1957) 76 Selden Society
PL Sayre 'Development of Commercial Arbitration Law' (1928) 37 *Yale Law Journal* 595
RJ Schoeck 'The Libraries of Common Lawyers in Renaissance England' (1962) 6 *Manuscripta* 155
Stephen Sedley 'Cromwell's Constitution: Public Law in the Interregnum' Sir Henry Hodge Memorial Lecture 2013
— 'The Law as History' All Souls Neill Lecture March 2016
— *Lions Under the Throne: Essays on the History of English Public Law* Cambridge, Cambridge University Press 2015
— and Laurence Kaplan *A Spark in the Ashes: The Pamphlets of John Warr* London, Verso 1992
DJ Seipp Year Books database http://www.bu.edu/law/faculty-scholarship/legal-history-the-year-books/ [accessed 9 July 2016]

B Sharp and MC Fissel eds *Law and Authority in Early Modern England: Essays Presented to Thomas Garden Barnes* Newark, University of Delaware Press 2007

JA Sharpe '"Such Disagreement Betwyx Neighbours": Litigation and Human Relations in Early Modern England' in John Bossy ed *Disputes and Settlements: Law and Human Relations in the West* Cambridge, Cambridge University Press 1983 167–187

James Sharpe 'The People and the Law' in Barry Reay ed *Popular Culture in 17th Century England* London, Croom Helm 1985 244–270

William Sheppard *England's Balme: or, Proposals by Way of Grievance and Remedy; Humbly Presented to His Highness and the Parliament: Towards the Regulation of the Law, and Better Administration of Justice, Tending to the Great Ease and Benefit of the Good People of the Nation* London, Henry Fletcher 1657 (rite 1656)

— *An Epitome of all the Common & Statute Laws of this Nation, Now in Force* London, Lee, Pakeman 1656

— *Grand Abridgment of the Common and Statute Law of England* London, Vaughan 1675

AWB Simpson 'The Penal Bond with Conditional Defeasance' (1966) 82 *Law Quarterly Review* 392–422

WW Skeat ed *The Vision of William Concerning Piers the Plowman* Oxford, Clarendon Press 1886

AJ Slavin ed *Tudor Men and Institutions: Studies in English Law and Government* Baton Rouge, Louisiana State University Press 1972

Adam Smith *The Wealth of Nations* Edinburgh, Strahan 1776

AGR Smith *Servant of the Cecils: The Life of Sir Michael Hickes 1543–1612* London, Cape 1977

DC Smith *Sir Edward Coke and the Reformation of the Laws: Religion, Politics and Jurisprudence, 1578–1616* Cambridge, Cambridge University Press 2014

Peter Smith 'Petitionary Negotiation in a Community in Conflict: King's Lynn and West Norfolk c1575 to 1662' University of East Anglia PhD thesis 2012 https://ueaeprints.uea.ac.uk/40587/1/2012SmithPPhD.pdf [accessed 9 July 2016]

Alexander Solzhenitsyn, 'A World Split Apart' – Commencement Address delivered at Harvard University, 8 June 1978 http://www.americanrhetoric.com/speeches/alexandersolzhenitsynharvard.htm [accessed 9 July 2016]

William Soutar *Diaries of a Dying Man* London, Canongate Classics 1988

James Spedding *Evenings with a Reviewer or Macaulay and Bacon* London, Kegan Paul 2 vols 1881

— ed *Letters and Life of Bacon* VI London 1869 reprinted Nabu Press on demand

— *The Works of Francis Bacon* London, Hurd and Houghton 1864 now Cambridge, Cambridge University Press 2011

RT Spence *Lady Anne Clifford: Countess of Pembroke, Dorset and Montgomery, 1590–1676* Stroud, Sutton 1997

GD Squibb *Doctors' Commons: a History of the College of Advocates and Doctors of Law* Oxford, Clarendon Press 1977

Statham's Abridgment see Klingelsmith

DM Stenton *The English Woman in History* London, Allen and Unwin 1957

Lawrence Stone *Elizabethan: Sir Horatio Palavicino* Oxford, Clarendon Press 1956

Tim Stretton *Women Waging Law in Elizabethan England* Cambridge, Cambridge University Press 1998

William Style *Regestrum Practicale: Or the Practical Register, Consisting of Rules, Orders, and Observations Concerning the Common-Laws, and the Practice Thereof...* London, Adams 1657

DS Sutton, Judith Gill and Matthew Gearing eds *Russell on Arbitration* London, Thomson Sweet & Maxwell 23rd edn 2007

T

RH Tawney, Foreword to Max Weber *The Protestant Ethic and the Spirit of Capitalism* London, Unwin 1930

Courtney Thomas '"The Honour & Credite of the Whole House", Family Unity and Honour in Early Modern England' (2013) 10 *Cultural and Social History* 329–345

Keith Thomas *Religion and Magic* Harmondsworth, Penguin 1973

SE Thorne translated and revised ed *Bracton on the Laws and Customs of England* Cambridge Mass, Belknap Press of Harvard University Press for Selden Society 4 vols 1968

— 'Sir Edward Coke: 1552–1952', in [Victor Tunkel ed] *The Selden Society Lectures 1952–2001* Buffalo, Hein 2003 1–18

Anthony Thornton and William Godwin eds *Construction Law: Themes and Practice* London, Sweet & Maxwell 1998

Heywood Townshend *Historical Collections: Or, An Exact Account of the Proceedings of the Four Last Parliaments of Q. Elizabeth* pp 218–310 London, T Basset, W Crooke and W Cademan 1680, *British History Online* http://www.british-history.ac.uk/no-series/parliament-proceedings-eliz1 [accessed 9 July 2016]

Israel Treiman 'Majority Control in Compositions: Its Historical Origins and Development' (1938) 24 *Virginia Law Review* 507–527

Eleanor Trotter *Seventeenth Century Life in the Country Parish* Cambridge, Cambridge University Press 1919

J Horsfall Turner ed *The Rev Oliver Heywood BA, 1630–1702: His Autobiography, Diaries, Anecdotes and Event Books* 4 vols Bayes, Bingley and Brighouse, various printers for the editor, 1882–1885

Travers Twiss ed *The Black Book of the Admiralty with an Appendix* London, Longman (Rolls Series) 4 vols 1871–1876

U

Roland Usher, 'James I and Sir Edward Coke' (1903) 18 *English Historical Review* 664–673

V

WR Vance 'The Early History of Insurance Law' in *Select Essays in Anglo-American Legal History* London, Wildy reprinted 1968 III 98–116

JP Van Niekirk *The Development of the Principles of Insurance Law in the Netherlands: From 1500 to 1800* Cape Town, Juta 1999

Donald Veall *The Popular Movement for Law Reform 1640–1660* Oxford, Clarendon Press 1970

VV Veeder 'The English Reports 1537–1865' in *Select Essays in Anglo-American Legal History* II London, Wildy reprinted 1968 123–168

W

DO Wagner 'Coke and the Rise of Economic Liberalism' (1935) 6 *Economic History Review* 30–44 and (1937) 7 *Economic History Review* 217–220

DM Walker ed *The Oxford Companion to Law* Oxford, Clarendon Press 1980

AD Wall ed *Two Elizabethan Women: Correspondence of Joan and Maria Thynne: 1575–1611* Devizes, Wiltshire Record Society 1983

JW Wallace *The Reporters, Chronologically Arranged: With Occasional Remarks Upon Their Respective Merits* Philadelphia, Johnson 2nd edn 1845

Izaak Walton *The Lives of John Donne etc* London, Methuen 1895

John Warr *The Corruption and Deficiency of the Laws of England* in Stephen Sedley and Laurence Kaplan *A Spark in the Ashes: The Pamphlets of John Warr* London, Verso 1992

Peter Webster 'Beyond the Letter of the Law' 2012, http://www.thea.ltd.uk/construction-law-files/Beyond-the-Letter-of-the-Law.pdf [accessed 9 July 2016]

Sir AW [Anthony Welson?] *The Court and Character of King James* London, John Wright 1650

William West *The First Part of Symboleographie: Which may be Termed the Art, or Description, of Instruments and Presidents* London, Miles Flesher, last edition 1647

— *The Second Part of Symboleography, Newly Corrected and Amended, and Very Much Enlarged in All the Foure Severall Treatises… of Compromises and Arbitrements…* London, Miles Flesher and Robert Young, last edition 1641, reprinted Clark NJ, Lawbook Exchange 2008

SD White *Sir Edward Coke and the 'Grievances of the Commonwealth' 1621–1628* Chapel Hill, University of North Carolina Press 1979

WJ Whittaker ed *The Mirror of Justices* (1893) London 7 Selden Society

Alison Wiggins, Alan Bryson, DS Smith, Anke Timmermann and Graham Williams eds *Bess of Hardwick's Letters: The Complete Correspondence, c1550–1608*, Glasgow, University of Glasgow, web development Katherine Rogers, University of Sheffield Humanities Research Institute (April 2013) http://www.bessofhardwick.org/letter.jsp?letter=149 [accessed 9 July 2016]

Henry Wilkinson *The Debt Book: Or, A Treatise Upon Romans 13.8…* London, Robert Bird 1625

WB Willcox 'Lawyers and Litigants in Stuart England: a County Sample' (1939) 24 *Cornell Law Review* 533–556

Ian Williams 'The Tudor Genesis of Edward Coke's Immemorial Common Law' (2012) 43 *Sixteenth Century Journal* 103–123

Lionel Williams 'The Crown and the Provincial Immigrant Communities in Elizabethan England' in H Hearder and HR Loyn eds *British Government and Administration: Studies Presented to SB Chrimes* Cardiff, University of Wales Press 1974 117–131

Edmond Wingate *Maximes of Reason* London, Lee &c 1658

Andy Wood 'Custom, Identity and Resistance: English Free Miners and Their Law c1550–1800' in Paul Griffiths, Adam Fox and Steve Hindle eds *The Experience of Authority in Early Modern England* London, Macmillan 1996 249–285

GE Woodbine 'The Language of English Law' (1943) 18 *Speculum* 395–436

DM Woodward *Port Books*, Short Guides to Records No 22, London, Historical Association 2011

Keith Wrightson *English Society 1580–1680* London, Harper Collins 1993

— 'The Politics of the Parish in Early Modern England' in Paul Griffiths, Adam Fox and Steve Hindle eds *The Experience of Authority in Early Modern England* London, Macmillan 1996 10–46

Y

DEC Yale *Lord Nottingham's 'Manual of Chancery Practice' and 'Prolegomena of Chancery and Equity'* Cambridge, Cambridge University Press 1965

Z

Richard Zouch *The Jurisdiction of the Admiralty of England Asserted* London, Basset 1686

INDEX

There are no entries for 'arbitration', 'mediation', 'settlement' or 'award', which are on nearly every page. Nor are there entries for the many mentions of courts or judicial offices, e.g. 'Chancery', or 'Master of the Rolls', or 'Council' or 'Privy Council'. Personal names appear only if they are of significance. Those who recorded names were rarely concerned with consistency, let alone accuracy. Kings and queens appear too often to be included. The full citations in the footnotes make a Table of Cases unnecessary; only the most important merit entries, e.g. *Vynior's Case*, *Case of Commendams*.

Abridgments 21–3, 81, 374–5, 408–9, 420, 423, 429, 473–89

Accounts 103, 107, 114, 119, 121, 124, 126–31, 134, 142, 145–6, 166, 293, 295–8, 300, 316, 413, 420, 422, 435, 446, 453, 464, 480

Administration of Estates 102–3, 135, 199, 319

Admiralty see Ships

Advowsons 9, 82, 196–7, 380

Agency 74, 114, 134–5, 203, 290, 422

Alehouses see Taverns

Aliens see Foreigners

America, United States and see the individual colonies 5, 24, 34, 182, 265, 324, 418, 423, 427, 443

Amsterdam 130, 183, 290

Anne, Queen 11, 190

Annuities 48, 102, 103, 106, 121, 142, 173, 196, 211, 228, 298, 304–6, 316, 320, 323, 377, 382, 387, 453, 479, 480

Appeals 39, 48, 72, 128, 143, 152, 157, 199–200, 207, 221, 282, 293, 356, 404, 413–15, 426, 433–4, 475

Apprentices 67, 135, 139, 145, 148–9, 185, 189, 217, 310, 359

Arbitration Act 1698 26, 371, 390, 410, 413, 427–37, 445

Arbitration Clauses 6, 12, 41–2, 111, 135, 141, 171, 220, 258, 272, 426, 437

Arbitrium Redivivum 3, 22, 25–6, 339, 371, 377–83, 386–7, 390, 395, 396, 401, 402, 404, 408–13, 418–19, 449, Appendix 1

Architects see Survey, Surveyors

Archives 5, 11, 14–19, 30–1, 44–7, 64, 65, 75, 82, 89, 99, 103, 114, 132, 135, 141, 151, 153, 173, 181, 190–1, 196–7, 203, 210, 265, 274, 281, 299, 340, 388, 426

Aristotle 24

Assault, Battery 235, 248, 359, 383–5, 392

Assumpsit 119, 292, 296, 380, 381, 387–9, 405–6, 410, 473–9, 488

Attorneys, Solicitors 22, 28, 59, 106, 200, 235, 239, 241, 300, 302, 308, 317–19, 324–6, 352, 363, 422, 433

Aubrey, John 262, 265, 277, 279, 283–4, 329

Auditors 130, 278, 377–9, 420, 422, 453, 480

Bacon, Anthony 211, 278, 279
  Francis xiv, 3, 17, 44, 48, 72, 75, 95, 121, 132, 144, 173, 180, 187, 196, 203, 215, 242–4, 261, 264, 277–88, 290, 337, 341, 350, 363, 367, 428, 432
  Nathaniel 66, 70, 74, 81, 82, 196, 202, 210–58, 260, 341, 426
  Nicholas, father of Francis 341
  Nicholas, brother of Francis 51, 74, 211, 217

Baker, JH 9, 14, 20, 27, 270, 446

Bankruptcy 118, 120, 141, 405
Bar, arbitration agreement and ward as
    410–12
Barristers 121, 127, 193, 208
Battery see Assault
Berry v Perry 276, 398
Bess of Hardwick 41–2, 152, 198
Bill of Rights 429
Binding Over 16, 70, 73–4, 87, 148,
    160, 234, 360, 365, 410
Blackstone, William 62–3, 125
Bonds 387–9 *et passim*
Bonham's Case 268
Bordeaux 115–16
Boundaries 61, 92–5, 190, 330, 430
Bracton 371–2
Bribery see Corruption
Bridgman, Orlando 33, 111, 295–7,
    425, 475
Bristol 19, 34, 39, 116, 122, 131, 159,
    360
Brooke's *Abridgment* 22, 420, 423
Brunkard, Elizabeth and Frances 339
Buckingham, George Villiers, Duke of
    271, 278, 280–7, 315, 348
Building see Construction
Bureaucracy 35, 324
Burghley, Lord, (Robert, Thomas and
    William Cecil) 279, 303, 340–1,
    344
Business see Commerce

Caesar, Julius 11, 49, 51, 57, 90, 108,
    111, 125, 127, 137, 139, 143–5,
    184, 186, 204, 215, 254, 363,
    388
Cambridge, Cambridgeshire 117, 140,
    163, 171, 193, 211, 248, 287, 304,
    313
Canon Law see Church
Canterbury and Archbishop of 5, 29,
    46, 76, 99, 100, 103, 107, 143,
    157, 173, 182, 184, 345, 358, 360,
    367
Capacity 149, 359, 390–3
Capitalism 7, 9, 260, 442, 445
Card Game, Playing Cards 250, 280,
    315, 343
Categories and Definitions 28–42, 43,
    58, 67

Catholics, Recusants 4, 6–7, 29, 185,
    237, 264, 300–1, 341–4, 366
Cecil see Burghley
Certainty 119, 252, 296, 379, 401–2,
    406, 461, 475
Chance, Lot 43, 154, 195, 292
Channel Islands xiii, 3, 48, 54, 107,
    128, 184, 206–7, 360–1
Charges see Fees
Charity 46, 90, 122, 130, 172–3, 179,
    185, 362, 446
Chester, Cheshire 11, 19, 39, 40, 50,
    72–4, 84, 111, 120–3, 137–8, 157,
    177, 183, 194, 202–4, 362
Chicanery 173, 177, 266, 279, 374–5,
    409, 425, 426
Cholmeley, Richard 300–11, 344
Christmas 36, 54, 55, 129–30, 164,
    168, 220, 223, 246, 257, 301,
    304–5, 315, 319, 335, 341, 347
Church, Canon Law, Ecclesiastical
    Disputes 5, 31, 44, 102, 151–69,
    173, 443, 455
Cinque Ports 54, 184, 193–4, 455
Civil Law, Civil Lawyers 24, 28, 44,
    49, 65, 115, 133, 156, 170, 247,
    303
Clifford, Lady Anne 83, 100, 177, 300,
    340, 344–59, 376, 394
Cloth, Clothworkers 18, 47, 127,
    138–40, 145, 167, 187, 197, 275,
    365–6, 385, 388, 481
Coal, Collieries 21, 31, 36–7, 54, 104,
    154, 311, 334
Coffee Houses see Taverns
Coke, Edward 259–76 *et passim*
Coke, Frances 263, 271, 273, 283
Colchester 170, 187–8
Collusive Concords 237, 286
Commendams, Case of 269
Commerce, Trade 7, 10, 72, 93,
    114–50, 185–9, 195, 275, 286,
    289–92, 299, 327, 334, 360, 387,
    420, 423, 426, 427, 432–5
Commission for Causes for Assurances
    290, 428
Community 10, 12, 34, 64, 72, 89, 98,
    111, 121, 153, 158, 173–4, 185,
    192–3, 211, 257, 267, 274, 299,
    308, 341, 372, 374, 385, 431,
    442–6

Competition see Monopolies

Compositions with Creditors 17, 69, 75, 121–5, 251–2, 274, 362

Confidentiality 89, 299, 443

Conservators of Commerce 115

Conspiracy 321, 339, 385

Construction, Building 91, 92–7, 254, 330–8, 354, 437

Conway, Lady 383

Corbett, Miles 81–2, 193, 214, 223, 238, 271

Corn see Wheat

Cornwall 16, 69, 83, 177

Cornwallis, Charles 95, 215–17, 221, 256

Corruption, Bribery 66, 141, 173, 192, 231, 244, 279, 282–8, 300, 313–14, 321, 323, 395, 413, 415, 428, 432, 436, 455, 472

Costs 12, 32, 36, 39, 56, 69, 71, 94, 116, 135, 172, 173, 179, 200–1, 223, 225, 247–8, 294, 318, 324, 356, 409, 416, 484

Coventry 36, 366, 421

Crime 66, 67, 81, 109, 235, 241, 377, 382–5, 394–5, 451

Cumberland, Earl of 83, 344–58

Custom, Customary Law 10, 29, 44, 60, 75, 83, 84, 89–91, 96, 135–42, 177, 208, 291–3, 306, 321, 372–5, 395, 413

Damages 36–7, 42, 69, 71, 296–8

Daysman 209

Debt 119–21 *et passim*

Defamation see Slander

Definitions see Categories

Delay, Speed 12, 38, 39, 42, 48, 56, 60–3, 76, 90, 94, 97, 112. 115–16, 130, 132, 140, 143, 146, 151, 170, 172–3, 179–82, 201–2, 218, 220, 227, 234, 236–7, 244, 252, 294, 303, 317, 319, 326, 334, 338, 363, 385, 409, 428, 432, 436, 446

Deputy Lieutenants 55, 181, 183, 203, 212

Derby, Earl of 39, 48, 55, 84, 120, 177, 180

Devon 16, 35, 38, 69, 71, 87, 191, 152, 156, 159, 179, 183, 359

Diaries 300–38 *et passim*

Dicey, AV 76

Disease see Health

Doctors' Commons 200

Documents Only Arbitration 170–1, 196

Doddridge, (or Doddridge) John 22, 24, 29, 155, 229, 394, 411

Dorset and Earl of, Richard Sackville 7, 16, 54–5, 69, 83, 107, 110, 131, 332, 345, 358

Dover 6, 116, 181, 184, 189, 331

Dower 57, 87–8, 163, 201, 252–3, 361

Drapers 138–9, 143, 187, 366

Duels 213, 315, 347

Dunkirk, Dunkirkers 116, 242

Durham 159, 242

Dutch see Low Countries

East India Company 7, 93, 116, 143–4, 289

Eastland Company 131, 144–5, 281

Ecclesiastical Disputes see Church

Egerton, Lord see Ellesmere LC

Egerton, Mary 340

Ellesmere LC 82, 111, 197, 213, 219, 224–6, 231, 238, 243, 263–4, 271, 279, 282, 284

Enclosures 88–90, 96, 386

Engrossing, Forestalling and Regrating 9

Essex 73, 117, 140, 161–2, 187–8, 216, 254, 344, 444

Essex, Earl of 263–4, 278, 280, 340

Estates General see States General

Eure Family 290, 343–4, 383

Evelyn, John 314, 329, 334, 338

Expediency 38–41, 52, 117, 121, 128, 144, 187, 192, 195, 201, 268, 270, 362

Experts 103, 127–8, 139, 141, 148, 193, 201–2, 218, 290, 294, 328, 334, 441, 446

Eyre, Adam 35, 300, 308–13

Fairfax, Thomas 5, 25, 90, 162, 225, 229, 303, 307–8, 399

Fees, Charges 12, 72, 183, 208, 246, 251, 255, 257, 261, 271, 283–6, 294, 302, 317, 325–6, 331–5, 432, 437, 446, 477, 485

Felony 149, 167, 377, 382–3, 385, 394, 451, 454
Field, Edward 323–7
Fire, Great Fire of London 1666 xiii, 3, 17, 38, 77, 95, 124, 208, 242–3, 330, 333–7, 382
Flanders, Flemish see Low Countries
Flexibility 35, 42, 82, 88, 205
Football 301, 313
Foreigners, Foreign Trade, Foreign Policy 48, 49, 114–15, 131, 136, 177, 183–91, 228, 289
Forgery 130, 234, 266, 321, 364, 385, 463
Forms, Formulas see Precedents
France, French 4, 6, 28, 110, 115–16, 124, 127, 133, 143, 149, 185–6, 191, 194, 286–7
Fraud 52, 85, 118, 120, 130, 179, 224, 385, 404, 416
French Language, Law French 21, 28–30, 33, 88, 367, 423, 450
Fuller, Thomas 259, 314

Gaudie, Gawdy, Cawdye, 51, 234, 235, 258, 362
Germany, Germans 124, 153, 184, 185, 190, 352
Gibson v Ferrers 26, 295–9
Gin and Tonic 442
Goldsmiths 40, 143, 148, 336, 388
Gorges, Ferdinando 34, 127, 194
Gregory Family 100, 197–8, 388
Gresham College 329–34
Greville, Fulke 85, 143, 186, 272
Grotius, Hugo 62–3
Guilds and Companies 143–9, 454
Gunpowder Plot 4, 264

Habeas Corpus 124, 268, 376
Haberdashers 93, 136–7, 275
Hale, Matthew 21, 202, 324, 355, 356, 413, 429, 444
Hatton, Lady 47, 262–3, 269, 273, 279
Health, Disease, Illness, Physicians, Surgeons, Medicine 8, 25, 54, 109, 136, 162–3, 177, 182, 189, 262, 264, 272–5, 278, 286, 301, 315, 329, 337, 341, 395
Heydon, Cristopher 214–15, 231, 238, 252–3

Heywood, Oliver 153, 160–1, 366–7
Hide v Petit 415, 425
Hobart, Henry 23. 143, 186, 215, 220, 295, 350, 400
Hobbes, Thomas 43, 259, 265–8, 270, 332, 432
Hoby, Margaret 15, 300, 303, 340–4, 383
Holland see Low Countries
Holt, John 14, 21, 45, 205–6, 403–5, 415, 416
Honour 45, 47, 157, 224, 282, 315, 326, 344, 363
Hooke, Robert 3, 38, 77, 95, 196, 208, 288, 300, 314, 328=38, 437, 446
Hunt, John 231, 247
Hutton, Richard 92, 96–7, 156, 201, 295

Illegality 295, 297, 298, 382–6
Illness see Health
Immigrants, Refugees 89, 185–9
Imprisonment see Prisons
Infancy 177, 374, 390–5, 453–5, 472, 474, 478
Inns see Taverns
Inspection see View
Insurance 132–4, 437
Interest see Usury
Intermixture 330, 336
Interstate, International 189–91
Ireland, Irish xiii, 3, 46, 54, 57–8, 95, 128, 184, 194, 204
Iron, Ironmonger 104, 137, 143, 334
Italy, Italians 8, 124, 294, 367, 385, 442

Jeffreys, George 198, 200, 425
Jointures 87–8, 100, 126, 347, 351–3, 363–4
Josselin, Ralph 153, 161–70, 208

Lambarde, William 72
Lambert, Lady 56–8
Lancashire, Duchy of Lancaster 19, 64, 75, 143, 160, 172, 212, 231, 252, 289
Latin 4, 22, 25, 28, 29, 63, 154, 213, 223, 266, 268, 295, 367, 381, 388, 390, 407, 408, 423, 450, 456
Laud, Archbishop 5, 153

Law French see French language
Law Merchant, *Lex Mercatoria* 26,
     114, 291–5, 298
Leigh, Urien 72, 202
Lennox and Richmond, Frances,
     Duchess of 365–6
Levant Company 93, 146, 147
Lex Mercatoria see Law Merchant
Livery Companies see Guilds
Locke, John 329, 388, 428, 432–5, 437
London, Lord Mayor of 49, 54, 93,
     108, 117, 125, 132, 136, 143, 186,
     333, 336
Lopez, Rodrigo 189, 264
Lot see Chance
Low Countries 5, 6, 25, 89, 92–6, 115,
     116, 121, 135, 183–90, 289

Maintenance, Wife's 54, 99–101, 104,
     108–10, 360, 387
Malynes, Gerard (Senior and Junior)
     22, 26, 124, 195, 196, 289–99
Man, Isle of 3, 103
Man, Martin 210, 213, 240, 255
Mansfield, Lord 374
March, John 22, 25, 431
Marine, Mariners, Maritime Law see
     Ships
Marriage. Matrimonial Disputes
     108–11, 339–70 *et passim*
Medical, Medicine see Health
Mercers 138–9, 177, 289
Merchant Adventurers 144
Merchants see Commerce
Merchants' Assurances Act 1601 428
Mines, Mining 140–2, 198, 290
Mint, The 124, 143
Moneylenders 40
Monopolies, Patents, Competition 135,
     142, 148, 182–6, 194, 290
Moots 26–7
More Family 196–7
Mountagu, Edward see Sandwich
Mun, Thomas 289–91
Murder 67, 109
Muscovy Company 93, 146
Mutuality 374, 397, 402–5

Neighbours 157–8, 167, 169, 174, 185,
     194, 210, 213, 229, 234–7, 245,
     246, 249, 258, 309, 311, 326–7,
     335, 341, 365–6
Netherlands see Low Countries
New England 82, 111, 182
Newton, Isaac 329
Nisi Prius 16, 35, 67–71, 413–14
Norfolk, Duke of 84, 366
North, Roger 22, 29

Oates, Titus 198–201
Oaths 69, 74, 118, 128–9, 231, 238,
     241, 281, 294, 304, 306, 315, 319,
     322, 393, 430, 436, 476
Order see Public Order
Orphans 103, 148, 164, 206, 361
Oxford, 38, 91, 100, 156, 160, 170,
     189, 193, 196, 203, 339

Partners, Partnership 97, 114, 130,
     134–5, 412, 437
Pastons 81, 236–9, 248, 253, 256
Patents see Monopolies
Peacemakers 169, 177, 247, 431
Penning Family 215–22, 233
Pepys, Samuel 3, 195, 300, 313–29,
     338, 344
Perjury 385
Pews 31, 153–5, 227, 231
Physicians see Health
Pins 136–7
Piracy 122, 148, 183, 184, 189, 243
Plague 3, 47, 124, 169, 217, 264, 301,
     342, 382
Pleading 22, 25, 26, 28, 133, 137, 154,
     290, 397, 398, 400, 405–12, 421,
     424, 431, 453, 459–61, 464, 469,
     471, 479
Plucknett, TFT 270
Plymouth 34, 127, 194
Policy see Public Policy
Poor, Poverty 50, 64, 65, 76, 85, 181,
     201, 217, 227, 233, 361, 363, 385
     et passim
Popham, John 213–14, 228–9
Portions 32, 82, 99–101, 105, 108, 111,
     134, 165, 218, 233, 247, 339, 344,
     349–53, 366
Portugal, Portuguese 6, 116, 185, 264
Powell, Walter 300, 307

Precedents, Formulas, Forms 22, 25, 35, 41, 42, 63, 75, 194, 195, 283, 387–8, 421, 427, 449, 456, 469

Prerogative, Prerogative Courts 44, 123, 173, 255, 261, 268, 280, 373

Prisons, Imprisonment, Gaol 16, 50, 57, 70, 85, 95, 101, 104–5, 121, 124–5, 129, 164, 178, 198, 231, 249, 252, 261, 268, 283, 286, 287, 290, 307, 314, 324, 344, 377, 410, 413–14, 425, 435, 454

Prize 132

Probate 103, 199, 271, 317, 323, 429

Professional Arbitrators see Fees

Prohibitions 134, 155–6, 411

Protestants 4, 190, 217, 238, 301, 366, 367

Public Order 11, 81

Public Policy 126, 136, 187, 382–6

Raleigh, Walter 18, 264, 267

Rastell, William 22. 23. 411

Recognisance 73, 341, 390, 475

Reform, Law Reform 7, 9, 124, 260, 371, 428–40

Refugees see Immigrants

Relativism 285, 324

Revocation 388–9, 419–24, 453, 472, 475

Rights of Way 82, 91

Riot 96, 151, 273, 344, 383, 385

Robinson, Henry 92–5, 431

Roman law 24, 29, 63, 81, 217

Rule of Court 206, 390, 397, 405, 412–17, 435–6, 445

Sackville see Dorset

Sadley, Jeromio 8, 442

Sailors see Ships

Salt 126

Sandwich, Earl of, Edward Mountagu 313, 315, 322

Schools 91, 161, 172, 203, 313, 392

Scotland, Scots 3–6, 10, 44, 47, 95, 270

Sedley, Stephen 8, 442

Shakespeare, William xiii, 185–6, 197, 217, 388, 446

Sheppard, William 22, 81, 379, 380, 388, 395–400, 404, 410, 428–32, 470–487

Ships, Shipping, Admiralty, Sailors, Marine, Maitime Law 5, 44, 49, 55, 58, 62, 74, 92, 116, 117, 127, 131–4, 183–5, 193, 224, 232, 257, 271, 321, 326–7, 338, 385, 395, 445

Shrewsbury, Earl of 41–2, 74–5, 138–9, 198, 203

Silk, Silkworkers 117, 142

Slander, Defamation 148, 179, 244, 282, 324, 339, 385–6, 430

Slaves 285, 425

Soap, Soapmakers 118, 127, 131

Soldiers 54–5, 130, 142, 167, 225, 300, 303, 312

Solicitors see Attorneys

Somerset 16, 18, 39, 61, 67, 69, 87, 106, 108, 141, 149, 280, 361, 385

Southampton 105, 178

Spain, Spanish 4, 55, 95, 115, 124, 184, 185, 189–90, 217, 242, 264

Speed see Delay

Spelman, Henry 82, 223–4, 228, 229

Staplers 138, 144

States General, Estates General 5, 33, 116, 137, 190

Statute of Limitations 1624 412, 416, 467

Stay 410–12

Strangers see Foreigners

Style, William 20, 22, 23, 25, 108

Sunday 54, 95, 126, 135, 138, 143, 160, 184, 187, 203, 270, 273–5, 306, 329, 331, 343, 347, 352, 358

Surety 106, 118, 122, 223, 234, 242, 246, 252, 487

Surgeons see Health

Survey, Surveyors 36–8, 84, 89, 95, 97, 208, 218–19, 226, 230, 248, 328, 330, 333–6, 437

Taverns, Inns, Coffee Houses, Alehouses 67, 126, 173, 217, 283, 309, 312, 318–20, 323, 326–35, 337

Tawney, RH 7

Textbooks 21, 23, 26, 423

Theft 360

Theory 4, 60, 152, 260, 290, 380, 441, 446–7

Thynne, Joan 340

Tithes 9, 11, 32, 42, 82, 99, 141,
   155–7, 172, 246–8, 257, 261,
   480–4
Tithingman 67
Torts see Wrongs
Torture 124, 261
Translation 4, 8, 22, 26, 63, 133, 154,
   177, 187, 260, 340, 390, 433
Treason 5, 6, 54, 241, 264, 269, 377,
   382–4, 394, 451, 454
Treaties 6, 25, 115–16, 149, 190, 214
Trespass 24, 37, 152, 224, 227, 229,
   245–8, 377, 379, 385–8, 392, 403,
   408, 410, 411, 450–4, 461–6, 477,
   478, 483–5
Trinity House 54, 127, 131, 144, 183,
   328
Trust, Breach of 39, 111. 134, 214

Umpires 70, 74, 76, 83, 103, 107, 130,
   142, 151–4, 203, 204–8, 216, 218,
   222. 232, 247, 292–4, 396, 401,
   435, 436, 450, 454, 465, 470, 471
United States see America
Universities and Colleges 170–1 and
   see Oxford and Cambridge
Usury 296–7

Validity 122–3, 349, 376–86, 404–5
Valuation see View
Venice 8, 190
Vermuyden, Cornelius 96–7
View, Inspection, Valuation 36–8, 51,
   92–7, 136, 145, 172, 187, 196,
   208, 215, 218, 220, 227, 237–8,
   242, 252, 307–38
Villiers see Buckingham
Vintners see Wine

Virginia 93, 122, 196, 197, 280
Vynior's Case 23, 259, 371, 378,
   390–1, 417, 418–27, 443, 445

Wages 102, 127, 148, 217, 365
Wales, Welsh xiii, 3, 36, 44, 56, 74, 82,
   83, 111, 138, 139, 151, 154, 203,
   209
Walsingham, Francis 290
Water 37–8, 91, 96, 245, 317
Wheat, Corn 9, 42, 48, 82, 87, 104,
   144, 149, 225, 228–30, 246, 251,
   256, 280, 293, 301, 304, 483
Whitelock, Bulstrode 29
Williams, John LC 227, 287
Wills 102–3, 402, 422, 453
Winchester 70, 84, 92–4, 156, 172, 264
Wine, Vintners 8, 31, 136, 142, 174,
   277, 286–7, 310, 317, 326, 357,
   366, 462
Wingate, Edmond 23, 427
Women 254, 339–70, and see by name
   as Parties 359–65
   as Mediators and Arbitrators 365–7
Wren, Christopher 329, 331–4
Wrenham, John 282–3
Wool 138, 248, 255, 275, 365
Wrongs, Torts 56, 107, 116, 178, 181,
   242, 303, 305, 361, 382, 385, 386,
   450, 462, 477, 481

Yarmouth 54, 280
Year Books 22, 24, 267, 380, 423
Yelverton, Henry 25, 95, 144, 188,
   271–3, 280, 348, 407
York 35, 42, 68, 90, 97, 104, 106, 109,
   119, 141, 151, 156, 159, 160, 178,
   179, 182, 300–8, 340–3, 387